George IV

George IV

Inspiration of the Regency

STEVEN PARISSIEN

St. Martin's Press ⚇ New York

www.stmartins.com

Library of Congress Cataloging-in-Publication Data

Parissien, Steven.
    George IV : inspiration of the Regency / Steven Parissien—
1st U.S. ed.
        p. cm.
    Originally published: London : John Murray, 2001.
    Includes bibliographical references and index.
    ISBN 0-312-28402-0
    1. George IV, King of Great Britain, 1762–1830. 2. Great
Britain—History— George IV, 1820–1830. 3. Great Britain—Kings
and rulers—Biography. 4. Regency—Great Britain. I. Title.

DA538.A1 P37 2002
941.07'4'092—dc21
[B]   2001048993

First published in Great Britain by John Murray (Publishers) Ltd as
George IV: The Grand Entertainment

First U.S. Edition: April 2002

10 9 8 7 6 5 4 3 2 1

For Leslie Mitchell

Contents

Contents

Illustrations

The author and publishers would like to thank the following for permission to reproduce illustrations: p. 1, p. 3 above and p. 10, Private Collection; p. 2 above, p. 3 below and p. 9 above, The Yale Centre for British Art, Paul Mellon Collection; p. 2 below, His Grace the Bishop of Worcester and the Church Commissioners; p. 4 above and p. 12, National Portrait Gallery, London; p. 5, p. 8 below, p. 13 above and p. 15, British Museum; p. 8 above, Bristol City Museum and Art Gallery; p. 14 above, Mark Fiernes, Royal Collection © 2000 Her Majesty Queen Elizabeth II; p. 14 below, Royal Collection © 2000 Her Majesty Queen Elizabeth II; p. 16, V & A Picture Library.

Preface

While I sincerely hope that *The Grand Entertainment* will surprise, inform and amuse, it is worth stating at the outset that it contains no startling revelations concerning George IV's relationships with women. The tale of his legion of rotund mistresses and his disastrous marriage has often been told, and I make no claim to provide new evidence of further sexual improprieties or alleged offspring. Nor is my purpose to castigate George for his sexual immorality – as a recent historian has rightly pointed out, by the aristocratic standards of the day, in this he was actually no worse than many of his wealthy contemporaries.[1] *The Grand Entertainment* seeks instead to examine how George's behaviour affected the contemporary view of the monarch and the monarchy, and to place him in a broader cultural context, to look at his achievements in the light of what genuinely excited and motivated him, and at how his considerable ambitions were translated into the artistic, architectural and social settings with which he is generally associated.

At the same time, I have used an unashamedly old-fashioned framework. Studying for history A-level in the dim and distant past, one book that made a particularly deep impression on me was Lacey Baldwin Smith's stunningly vivid description of Henry VIII's last years.[2] I still consider *Henry VIII, The Mask of Royalty* a splendid example of how to construct an entertaining, informative and well-researched biography, and have accordingly borrowed both the concept, and the title of Smith's first chapter.

For thirty years there has been nothing to rival Christopher Hibbert's exemplary *George IV* of 1971–2 (published in one volume in 1976). This was the first biography to look beyond the familiar image of George IV as unparalleled royal connoisseur and to analyse, and where necessary criticise, the man himself. It has consequently long remained the standard work on this intriguing sovereign. Nevertheless, like the proverbial London bus, two new biographies of George IV appeared at the end of the last decade: Saul David's *Prince of Pleasure* of 1998 (which, rather confusingly, has the same title as J. B. Priestley's 1969 study and Andrew Barlow's 1998 edition of Brighton-related prints), and E. A. Smith's volume (1999) for the Yale Monarchs series. The late 1990s also saw the publication of a number of major studies on key figures in George IV's circle, most notably Flora Fraser's *The Unruly Queen* (1996), Amanda Foreman's *Georgiana, Duchess of Devonshire* (1998) and Christopher Hibbert's *George III* (1998). Saul David's entertaining study of the Prince's earlier years revealed interesting new material about his private life. The late E. A. Smith's *George IV* was a far more ambitious attempt to rehabilitate a monarch whom even the royal scholar Arthur Aspinall, to Smith's disappointment, had censured for 'his weakness of character, his self-indulgence and neglect of his duties of his position, and his supposed incompetence in affairs of state', and his traditionally-planned biography, completed shortly before his death, bravely sought to emphasise George's 'good points'. Smith's claims that the Prince's conduct during the Napoleonic Wars originated 'from a sense of patriotic duty' and that he was 'often kind and generous to his friends and towards those who served him well' raised a few critics' eyebrows. He blamed Caroline of Brunswick as much as George for the failure of their marriage – 'her later history showed what an unsuitable partner she was for such a fastidious husband' – and, even more controversially, excused George's countless affairs with the claim that 'he was seeking companionship which his marriage could not give him' – an age-old male excuse for serial infidelity.[3] Most astonishingly, Smith cast George IV as 'an important figure in the preservation of the status and constitutional importance of the Crown in British politics':

> What George IV did achieve was to preserve for the crown a role in the political governance of the nation at a time when that role could easily have been reduced to a cipher. Victoria and Albert may well have accepted the diminution of the royal function to a purely advisory one...: George IV however deserves credit for its survival, and for its enduring relevance to British politics.[4]

In view of the perennial casting of George IV as a Bad Man but a Good Patron, E. A. Smith's revisionism was to be expected. Neither Smith nor his predecessors, however, attempted to revisit the traditional image of him 'as a knowledgeable and discriminating patron of the arts'. Since Hibbert's magnificent book appeared, considerable work on the relationship between George and his physical environment has been done by leading scholars – most notably John Martin Robinson, Andrew Saint, Sean Sawyer and David Watkin in the field of architectural history; art historians Christopher Lloyd, Stephen Lloyd, Oliver Millar and Martin Postle; print historians David Alexander, Andrew Barlow, Ellen D'Oench and Diana Donald; landscape historian Jane Roberts; fashion historians Valerie Cumming and Aileen Ribeiro; furniture historians Geoffrey de Bellaigue and Hugh Roberts; and political historians such as David Cannadine, Linda Colley and Leslie Mitchell. I am hugely in debt to these and other experts, without whose work this book would never have been contemplated.

What is most remarkable about George's Regency and reign is not, as E. A. Smith claimed, his role in preserving the status and respect accorded the monarchy, but that it survived his appalling neglect of his office and its responsibilities. During the nineteenth century the monarchy suffered successively from George III's insanity, George IV's self-obsession, William IV's cavalier attitude to Parliament and, after 1861, Victoria's refusal to fulfil her constitutional role. Yet by the beginning of the twentieth century it was once again in rude health. The explanation for this lies in part in the events and circumstances of George's adulthood, when what Linda Colley and others have defined as a growing sense of national identity, of a genuine 'Britishness', encompassed the basic concept of constitutional monarchy while relegating the actual incumbent of the throne to a marginal role: celebrated in abstract as head of state, the sovereign in effect had limited powers and, crucially, was answerable to Parliament, an apparently successful constitutional balance which was one of the key factors that helped many Britons to define their own sense of place and worth. Prince Albert must surely be credited with enabling the monarchy to weather the changing circumstances of the middle years of the century, ensuring that by 1901 the ancient institution, repackaged and reformed, was able once again to play a significant part in the life of everyday Britons.

George IV was, by the time of his death, largely an irrelevance in the constitutional equation. Although, ironically, many of the pageants and settings he devised for his own pleasure and amusement were subsequently adapted as key symbols in the iconography of British monarchy, for most of his subjects he remained, as George Cruikshank defined him in 1814, *The Grand Entertainment*.[5]

NOTE ON STYLE

Contemporary quotations have been only lightly modified, for readability, and spelling of proper names generally follows modern/anglicised usage (for example, 'Cologne' for 'Köln').

Acknowledgements

I would like to thank the staff of the Paul Mellon Centre for their support, generosity and patience. I must also thank my former PMC colleague Evelyn Newby for her sterling work in producing *The Farington Index* (published by Yale University Press for the Paul Mellon Centre in 1998), a book which has made my task, and that of anyone working in this area, immensely easier.

Profuse thanks must also go to Shelley Bennett of the Huntington Library in San Marino, California; Melissa Gold and her colleagues at the Yale Center for British Art, New Haven, Connecticut; Sheila O'Connell of the British Museum's Prints and Drawings Department; Jo Wallace of the Victoria and Albert Museum; Miss Pamela Clark and the staff of the Royal Archives, Windsor; Andrew Holt; John Ingamells; and Christine and Jacqueline Riding. And I would particularly like to acknowledge the invaluable assistance of Brian Allen, Leslie Mitchell, Timothy Mowl and Martin Postle in commenting in detail on the text.

Most importantly, I would like to thank Kit Wedd for her wise counsel and my agent, Sara Menguc, for her support and skill.

Without all of these people, the book would never have become a reality.

Steven Parissien
Acton, 1999

PART I

Introduction

I

The Face of Death

No – ask it not, ask it not, dear Doctor H–lf–rd –
If nought but a Peerage can gladden thy life ...
              Thomas Moore, *New Creation of Peers* ...

B Y THE BEGINNING of 1830, it was clear that King George IV was
sinking fast. His Private Secretary and former physician, Sir
William Knighton, found in February that his health 'seem'd to . . .
depend on drink', that there was 'great irritability in his frame' and that
on occasion he 'did not seem in a very clear state of understanding'.
In Knighton's judgement the King's heart was 'much loaded with fat';
accordingly, he opined, 'His Majesty's death will be sudden'. George
had become, in addition, completely blind in one eye, while a cataract
seriously restricted the vision of the other. By March 1830 he was
describing himself as 'blind as a beetle', and by May was forced to
approve government legislation by using an ink stamp of his signature
in the presence of three witnesses. He was also almost constantly in
bed, surfacing in May only to take 'some exercise in a wheel-chair in
the picture gallery' at Windsor.[1]

However, George's alarming condition did not appear to affect his
appetite. In March 1830 the Prime Minister, the Duke of Wellington,
wrote incredulously to his confidante Harriet Arbuthnot that one
night, after going to bed, the King had consumed 'two glasses of hot
ale and toast, three glasses of claret, some strawberries!! and a glass of
brandy'. On 10 April he wrote:

> What do you think of his breakfast yesterday for an Invalid? A Pidgeon
> and Beef Steak Pye of which he eat two Pigeons and three Beefsteaks,
> Three parts of a bottle of Mozelle, a Glass of Dry Champagne, two
> Glasses of Port [and] a Glass of Brandy.

3

This gargantuan meal was, Wellington observed, followed by a substantial dose of laudanum – extract of opium in solution. George's reliance on laudanum was intensifying. By the end of 1829 he was regularly taking a hundred drops or more before important state occasions. His metabolism was growing so used to it that by the spring of 1830 'he could take over 250 drops in a period of thirty-six hours' and still remain capable of conversation.[2] The side-effects of this dependency – bouts of over-excitement followed by depression, severe lethargy and confusion of mind – were hardly improved by the amount of alcohol that he habitually drank shortly before or immediately after (or on occasion at the same time as) taking this fashionable drug.

At the end of April 1830 George's principal physician, Sir Henry Halford, diagnosed 'water in [the] membrane of heart, chest and belly' and observed that the King's legs (never of elfin proportions) were now excessively swollen; accordingly, legs and belly were tapped throughout the next month, producing numerous pints of fluid. On 1 May the Duke of Sussex offered his brother the use of a invalid chair contrived for him when he himself had had difficulty breathing, a gesture which, together with the Bishop of Chichester's exhortations in Sussex's favour, prompted George in his decay to dismiss the enmity which had existed between him and his more liberal brother for over two decades. Two weeks later it was reported that 'for two or three days the King has rarely recognised anybody', and on 15 May the Poet Laureate, Robert Southey, wrote that 'it was thought on Monday that he could not live four-and-twenty hours'.[3]

The King was in the care of Henry Halford, the 'eel-backed baronet' whose years of service with the royal family and determined social sycophancy had earned him many enemies. Born plain Henry Vaughan and educated at Rugby, Christ Church, Oxford and Edinburgh, where he studied medicine, he had in 1806 attended the last illnesses of the Duchess of Devonshire and Charles James Fox. The fame that his care of these illustrious Whigs engendered fuelled his social ambition and helped to win him clients more prominent still: after 1810 he attended George III, Queen Charlotte and their daughters. He also took care to cultivate the dukes of Wellington and Cumberland and, most importantly, the new Regent. At the same time, he was careful to maintain his reputation for a soothing bedside manner by evading as many medical decisions as possible. By 1813 he had secured the confidence of the Prince Regent's daughter, Princess Charlotte, and had metamorphosed into a clandestine royal marriage-

broker. In the following years he was charged by the Prince 'to negotiate a marriage between the Duke of Brunswick and Princess Mary
[George's sister] of which it was to be understood the latter knew
nothing', and subsequently to smooth the path for Charlotte's union
with the Prince of Orange.[4]

A contemporary colleague attributed to Halford 'all the advantages
of address and manners', qualities which had enabled him to 'give
importance, plausibility, and fascination, even to the long-winded
detail of nothing'; conducting himself with 'delicacy, prudence and
good sense', the doctor had 'shewed himself equally adroit as a courtier ... and as a physician'. If the two professions ever clashed, it was
the role of courtier that Halford took more seriously. In 1810, not
wishing to be the bearer of bad tidings or to upset George III, Halford
assured a dying Princess Amelia that her terminal disease was actually
'more of the mind than the body'. Amelia perceptively observed that
the doctor would rather risk her life than her parents' anger.[5]

Halford was duly rewarded not only with the presidency of the
Royal College of Physicians, which he held until his death in 1844, but,
in 1825, with a knighthood – George IV dubbed him Knight
Commander of the Hanoverian Guelphic Order – and subsequently
with a baronetcy. In January 1822 George declared to Halford that
henceforward the President of the Royal College 'should always hold
the title of Physician in Ordinary to the King'. Halford's position at
Court was thus cemented. Nevertheless, his ambition was clearly not
satisfied, for he later complained that honours for medics went no
higher than a baronetcy.[6]

As early as 1814 Halford had gleefully observed to his wife that the
Prince Regent's numerous illnesses meant he had 'employment in
abundance', which he could exploit to make himself invaluable at
Court. That June he proudly boasted that George III's 'sole
confidence is in me, and my communications are the only ones with
ministers'. His rivals in the medical profession, however, were rightly
suspicious of the uses to which Halford put his privileged position.
The Lancet dismissed Halford's bulletins on George IV's deteriorating
health of 1830 as 'vague, unsatisfactory and mysterious' and, as the
King's condition worsened, as 'utterly and entirely destitute of information', suggesting that Halford and his assistants were hopelessly
unaware 'of the precarious situation of their royal patient'. Two weeks
before the King's death, the journal's criticisms became more incisive.
Not only were Halford's bulletins now deemed 'scandalous' and

'ambiguously framed', but Halford himself appeared to have little idea of how to proceed, preferring only to administer ether and opium (neat, or in the form of laudanum) as sedatives. 'The integuments have been again punctured', *The Lancet* warned, 'but his body and his extremities, from the immense collection of water, are still enormously swollen.'[7]

By May 1830 even George's prodigious appetite had disappeared, and to be horizontal on his bed was a trial. On 3 May the politician John Croker recorded in his diary:

> The King is aware of his own situation, and contemplates it, as I learn, boldly. He sits bolstered up in bed, or in a chair, incapable of lying down; his head, they say, falls on his breast; his appetite is gone, and though neither speechless nor senseless, he is very torpid, and evidently fading rapidly away.[8]

On 14 May Wellington reported that the King 'looked wasted and wasting'. On 3 June Halford told Maria Fitzherbert, the Catholic divorcée whom George had illegally married in 1785, that he was much worse:

> The King has been, and continues to be, excessively ill, with embarrassment and difficulty of breathing. The worst circumstances under which I ever witnessed the Dukes of Clarence and Sussex, under their attacks of spasmodic asthma, hardly come up to his Majesty's distress at times. What is to be the result I can hardly venture to say with confidence. His Majesty's constitution is a gigantic one, and his elasticity under the most severe pressure exceeds what I have ever witnessed in thirty-eight years' experience.

Mrs Fitzherbert wrote to her former lover immediately. George did not answer – or perhaps was not able to – but after reading her letter placed it under his pillow.[9] On 4 June Halford announced to the world that 'The King has lost his irritability, and is all patience and resignation'. On 14 June, in the presence only of Halford, a clergyman, and Lady Conyngham, his last and ubiquitous mistress, 'His Majesty prepared himself to receive the Sacrament about three o'clock and went through this religious office with great piety and devotion'. Four days later he was quite unable lie down. Halford confidently reported to his wife that 'it will all be over in a week', and three days later wrote that, since his lungs and heart were so 'diseased', the King surely would die soon. On 24 June Halford cheerfully announced to his wife that

'Things are coming to a conclusion' and 'I shall be released about Monday'. All he told the government ministers, however, was that 'The King's cough continues with considerable expectoration'. The next day Sir Walter Scott, who had much to thank George for, wrote to Maria Edgeworth that 'The term of the King's illness is considered as inevitable, and is expected with great apprehension and anxiety.'[10]

Halford, it seems, could not wait for his royal patron to expire. On 23 June 1830 his coachman, Tom, was fined £60 for carrying furniture away from Windsor Castle in his master's carriage, having been apprehended trying to make a quiet getaway at five o'clock in the morning, before the Court awoke. It is unlikely that Tom was acting without his employer's approbation. Halford had indeed already admitted to his wife that he had begun collecting souvenirs, having 'taken some of the gilding of the King's sick-room', including 'a swallow nest from China' on which he had had his eye for some time, for 'Mr Kebbel's collection of curios'. Nor was Halford the only royal confidant to take advantage of George's predicament. Before leaving his death-bed Lady Conyngham purloined as much booty as possible, and her subsequent hurried journey from Windsor to Ireland, in a coach laden with baggage full of her paramour's costly presents and other extravagant items of a provenance at best dubious, was a gift to the satirists. William Heath depicted her piling royal plate into a chest and pushing a wheelbarrow full of clothes and kitchenware out of Windsor Castle, assuring her husband, 'I've taken care of myself depend on it'. Another contemporary print (possibly also by Heath) showed Lord and Lady Conyngham, laden with royal plunder, being accosted by William IV with the words: 'Come come be off, you got the length of your Old Master's foot to a fine purpose, but you don't stay here any longer, nor any of yr Crew, & I think your Boxes ought to be searched, for they are much fuller than when you first came to the Inn.'[11]

George IV finally died at 3.15 a.m. on the morning of Sunday 26 June 1830.[12] He had passed 'a large evacuation mix'd with blood' at 3 a.m. and Halford had been duly summoned. Allegedly George cried out to his servants 'Sir Henry, Sir Henry! Fetch him – This is death!', an exclamation which, according to the doctor, proved his last. Shortly after Halford's arrival – together with Knighton – the King's 'lips grew livid, and he dropped his head on the page's shoulder' and closed his eyes for the last time. Croker later quoted other supposed witnesses to conjure a more poetic and fitting death-bed scene: 'His last words were, putting his hands on the pit of his stomach, as if he felt a peculiar sensation there, "Surely this must be death", and it was so.' Halford himself, however, dispassionately recorded only that 'I was up the stairs in five minutes, and he died but eight minutes afterwards.'[13]

Halford's post-mortem examination revealed a tumour on the King's bladder 'the size of an orange' and a grossly enlarged heart, which was surrounded by fat. He made no attempt to explain the bland unconcern of his earlier public pronouncements, however, and his final report was as annoyingly vague as his previous bulletins. It merely stated that the King's death had been caused by 'fat at the heart', which was no surprise to anyone.[14] George's immediate and acerbic biographer Robert Huish suggested that the King had had 'an extensively diseased organisation of the heart', an observation which this savage critic then enlarged into a graphic display of *schadenfreude:* 'The torture which the King suffered during the paroxysm of his disaster must have been excruciating, since it was said that his moans were at times even heard by the sentinels on duty in the quadrangles.' More recent medical pronouncements consider porphyria, his father's great ailment, to have been the principal cause of George IV's recurring illnesses, and of his death.[15]

The immediate reaction to the King's demise was predictably mixed. Halford wrote happily to his wife: 'Congratulate me on being released at last.' However, adroit politican as always, he made sure that he was the first to inform the Duke of Clarence, now King William IV, of the death of his brother, and thus of his own succession. Wellington's official eulogy in the House of Lords was predictably generous and diplomatic. The victor of Waterloo and now former Prime Minister extolled the late King's polished manners, his 'degree of cultivation', his learning and his 'condescension, affability and kindness of disposition', all of which 'made him far surpass in accomplishments all his subjects, and made him one of the most remarkable Sovereigns of our time'.[16]

Many in the arts who had profited from George's keen interest and support regretted the loss of their royal patron. The painter Benjamin Haydon found much to admire in him:

Thus died as thorougbred an Englishman as ever existed in the country. He admired her sports, gloried in her prejudices, had confidence in her bottom and spirit, and to him, and him alone, is the destruction of Napoleon owing. I have lost in him my sincere admirer; and had not his wishes been perpetually thwarted he would have given me ample and adequate employment'.[17]

Another painter whose career had definitely prospered as a result of George's generous patronage, David Wilkie, appeared to be equally sincere when he wrote: 'I have lost the greatest friend I have ever met with ... whose gracious generosity has done much more for me than I deserved.' In similar vein, Wilkie's countryman Sir Walter Scott wrote to Knighton on 14 July to 'express my deep sorrow for the loss of a sovereign whose gentle and generous disposition, and singular manner and captivating conversation, rendered him as much the darling of private society, as his heartfelt interest in the general welfare of the country, and the constant and steady course of wise measures by which he raised his reign to such a state of triumphal prosperity, made him justly delighted in by his subjects.'[18]

Few, however, would have recognised in Scott's encomium the Britain of 1830. While artists, architects and writers acknowledged that his successors were unlikely to support their professions so lavishly, while educational and children's charities bemoaned the loss of an unfailingly generous source of financial aid,[19] George IV died largely unlamented by the majority of his subjects, to whom he had become a distant irrelevance hidden behind the tall thickets of Windsor Great Park. In sharp contrast to the many public displays of grief which had so passionately marked the tragic death of his daughter Charlotte thirteen years before, the death of George IV was generally greeted with stolid indifference or even faint amusement. On 28 June 1830 *The Times* launched a barrage of invective against the late monarch, and must have assumed that its opinions were shared by the majority of its readers. Almost before George's body was cold, *The Times* obituarist was lambasting his 'unceasing and unbounded prodigality', his 'indifference to the feelings of others' and 'the tawdry childishness of Carlton House and the mountebank Pavilion, or cluster of pagodas at Brighton', and labelling his conspicuous over-consumption of food, wine and women 'little higher than that of animal indulgence'.

In the same way that many of the great ceremonials of his Regency and reign had been rendered unintentionally comical or ludicrous, so George IV's funeral at Windsor Castle on 15 July quickly degenerated into farce. Far more spectators had turned out for Nelson's funeral in 1805, and for that of George III in 1820. The funeral car was as bulky and vulgar as its occupant. The new King, William IV, behaved as if he were at a garden party, talking animatedly and excitedly to all and sundry ('so that the most frivolous things were overheard', declared one onlooker) and walking out early. In St George's Chapel, *The Times* observed 'not a single mark of sympathy' amongst the congregation, which largely comprised 'the servants of the household, the friends of the carpenters and upholsterers, the petty tradesmen of the town', rather than those of 'public character or official situation'. The wounding of Sir Astley Cooper by a piece of woodwork falling from the choir stalls appeared more interesting to the *Times*'s correspondent than the actual funeral proceedings. The anonymous journalist's judgement on the occasion was that 'We never saw so motley, so rude, so ill-managed a body of persons.'[20] Robert Huish, too, gleefully recorded the apparent absence of grief or pity during the Windsor ceremony. The gathering locals reminded him rather of 'a crowd hastening to some raree-show, than to the chamber of death', while 'there seemed to be a predominant feeling not to mourn at all, and it was only in the immediate presence of the body that [many] put on a lugubrious show'. As for the congregation within the chapel, he snorted, 'the assemblage might have been considered one collected together upon some joyous festival'. After the service, he added, 'we did not hear any one word of praise of his late Majesty, nor one syllable of regret' at his passing.[21]

Away from Windsor, few of the population seemed to care deeply about the King's death; if anything, the day assigned for its commemoration was devoted instead to a celebration. William Cobbett – admittedly a far from unbiased commentator – noted that on the day of the funeral 'the whole of the immense population [of London] seemed, with one accord, as if by positive compact, to be resolved on a *day of pleasure*.' The scene which Cobbett described was not one of popular grief, or even melancholy, at the loss of a much-loved sovereign:

> The Thames was almost literally *covered* with water-vehicles of every description. More than ten thousand people went by water to Richmond, and, it was said that fourteen thousand went to Gravesend; while all the villages, short of those distances, exhibited scenes like those of a Whit Monday, rows of men on benches, out of doors, drinking and smoking; dances on the green-sward; fiddling, singing, and all those other demonstrations of a resolution to cast away care for the moment.[22]

From 14 July George IV's body had lain in state in the newly-completed Great Drawing Room at Windsor Castle,[23] beneath his own monogram and the badge of the Order of the Garter, of which he had been so inordinately proud during his lifetime. The decorative context – Wyatville's vivid crimson walls, Siena marble chimney-piece, 'Tudorbethan' bay windows and richly-gilded ceiling – nicely epitomised the late King's gaudily eclectic taste.

George's excesses and enthusiasms were even reflected in the manner of his burial. Both the ceremony and the coffin itself were predictably expensive. Modern commentators have pointed out the marked contrast between the cost of this funeral and that of the modest interment of his brother, the Duke of Sussex, in the public cemetery at Kensal Green in 1843.[24] By his will of 1796 George had directed that his coffin be specially constructed so that a side panel could be subsequently removed; his intention was that on Maria Fitzherbert's death her coffin should be placed alongside his and the adjoining panels be whisked away, enabling their remains to intermingle forever more, a romantic notion devised by George III for himself and his wife Queen Charlotte. However, since George IV had never been legally married to Maria Fitzherbert, and since both William IV and his government preferred that the whole affair be quietly forgotten, this melodramatic instruction from beyond the grave was quietly ignored by his executors. (When she died in 1837, Maria Fitzherbert was buried in the churchyard of St John the Baptist in Brighton.) However, one request of the 1796 will was executed: as the Duke of Wellington discovered on closely inspecting the body, George was buried wearing a chain around his neck which carried a locket in which nestled Cosway's diamond-encrusted miniature of Maria Fitzherbert. To bolster this romantic if juvenile gesture with pecuniary proof of his enduring attachment, George had also dictated a last-minute alteration to his will, increasing Mrs Fitzherbert's pension, already a healthy £6,000 a year, to a more-than-substantial £10,000.

Maria Fitzherbert and those in the world of the visual arts may have genuinely mourned George IV, but contemporary accounts place them in a minority. The caustic pen of Princess Lieven, wife of the Russian Ambassador, recorded some months after the funeral that 'As for the late King he is completely forgotten, and, if remembered, it is only to criticise his morals. It is in the middle and lower classes especially that he left a very unfavourable impression.'[25] Robert Southey could not forget that George IV, supposedly a staunch defender of Protestantism, had allowed his government to pass the Catholic Emancipation Act of 1829, granting Catholics freedom of worship and full civil rights. Even before the King's death Southey judged that 'He failed most woefully in his solemn and sworn duty on one great occasion, and we are feeling the effects of that moral cowardice on his part.'[26] Even the local Windsor newspaper was surprisingly vehement in its denunciation of its former royal resident, castigating 'the anti-social manner in which George IV eked out the later years of his existence'. Politician and diarist Charles Greville preferred to remember him not only as 'capricious' and 'luxurious, liking nothing but the society of listeners and flatterers', but also as 'a plain, vulgar gentleman opening his doors to all the world'. To the satirist Robert Seymour, George was merely 'the tipsy King', holding aloft a brimming goblet.[27]

Much of what George IV left was demolished or dispersed. His cooks and his French servants were immediately dismissed by William IV, who would 'have none but English', and with scant regard for technological innovation and an innate suspicion of any of his brother's 'improvements', William also ripped out all the gas-lights and gas pipes so recently and laboriously installed at Windsor Castle.[28] The Great Park's menagerie was closed and its animals despatched to the new London Zoo, while the German band was dismissed and replaced with a locally-recruited orchestra. The lavish redecoration of the new interiors at Windsor was also brought to a sudden halt. Just before George's death, the Treasury had stubbornly refused to pay more than the £143,000 originally budgeted for furniture and interiors – by June 1830 the suppliers Morel and Seddon exceeded this by almost fifty per cent – until a Parliamentary Select Committee had investigated the cost and quality of the work. In the event, Windsor Castle fared far better than most of George's other royal residences, for the 1831 Select Committee found little fault with the work commissioned or costs incurred by the architect Sir Jeffry Wyatville (who, unlike Nash at Buckingham Palace, emerged from the inquiry with his reputation virtually intact), and found itself unable to establish criteria by which to judge the value of the furniture made by Morel and Seddon. Work on the castle began again, and even Morel and Seddon's bill was largely paid. However, this did not mean the enormously expensive remodelling was universally judged to be in the nation's interest. *The Times*, seeking ways to excoriate the late King, his architect and his suppliers in public, seized on an English-made sideboard at Windsor as typical of George's poor judgement and outrageous extravagance: not only was it 'massive, gaudy and tasteless', but it had 'been charged at £8,000' by Morel and Seddon. Later, in a shamefaced retraction, the newspaper admitted that the actual cost of the piece was only 'one-eighth of the sum' previously quoted. In George IV's Britain, a thousand pounds was nevertheless a lot to pay for one item of furniture.[29]

William IV also opened all the avenues in Windsor Great Park to the public – a gesture of considerable symbolic significance. As George grew increasingly reclusive, so the Park's thoroughfares had been closed, to ensure that he should not be glimpsed by any of his curious subjects; similarly, the curtilage of his retreat at the Royal Lodge had been planted with thick hedges to screen him from prying eyes. William's reversal of this policy publicly demonstrated that he did not intend to mimic his brother's antisocial tendencies and, more importantly, that he at least had nothing to hide. Even the terrace and flower garden at Windsor Castle were thrown open to visitors. The politician and diarist Thomas Creevey was by no means the only commentator to record the popularity of the announcement ('We could hear the people saying perpetually "This is something like. What a change!"'). On 10 August 1830 Charles Greville and some of his friends drove their carriage along what only weeks before had been a private road bisecting the Great Park, and merrily imagined that the ghost of George IV 'must have been indignant at seeing us scampering all about his most secret recesses'.[30] In 1832, the *Windsor and Eton Express* gleefully published excerpts from the Prussian envoy Prince Pückler-Muskau's account of his posting to Britain in 1826–28 which included scathing criticisms of the elaborate security measures which had been ordered by the late King.

Nor did, George's extensive new London residence escape parliamentary censure. John Nash was removed from all further responsibility for Buckingham Palace, the new wings he had added to the building having for the most part already been demolished. He lived to see his grand palace entrance disfigured but, perhaps happily for him, died before the architect chosen by Parliament as his successor, the capable but uninspired Edward Blore, had closed his great courtyard and altered the decoration and even the function of many of his interiors.

Even with Nash gone, Buckingham Palace still failed to win approval from its new owner. In 1831 William seriously suggested that the site be converted into barracks for 1,500 Foot Guards, a scheme successfully blocked by the then Prime Minister, Lord Grey, on grounds of cost. Two years later the King proposed that the two Houses of Parliament be moved into it from the Palace of Westminster, which in turn should be 'converted into a Residence for the Lord Chancellor, and into Courts of Law'. To William IV, the calamitous fire which razed much of the old Palace of Westminster in October 1834 seemed a heavenly intervention. Cheerfully surveying the charred ruins, he bellowed across to the Speaker, Charles Manners-Sutton, 'Mind, I mean Buckingham Palace as a permanent gift!' Only Blore's indication of the considerable additional cost involved in converting it for parliamentary use prevented the King's ambitious scheme being executed. William subsequently went into a sulk, but found his spluttered protestations that it was *his* prerogative to choose where Parliament met skilfully countered by the Prime Minister, Lord Melbourne, who cannily suggested that, if the King *were* in his generosity to offer a royal residence for conversion to parliamentary use, both Houses would undoubtedly find the Palace of St James's more conveniently situated. The following month William summarily dismissed Melbourne's majority Whig government, precipitating a constitutional crisis on a scale not seen for fifty years.[31]

Edward Blore was entrusted not merely with crisis management at Buckingham Palace but with bringing to completion, as cheaply and as quickly as possible, Nash's great gateway to the site. By July 1831 the sculptors working on what is now known as the Marble Arch, the internationally renowned Richard Westmacott, John Rossi, Francis Chantrey and Edward Baily, had not been paid for three years. Blore brusquely solved the dilemma by adding a crude, unadorned attic storey to the arch and redirecting most of the sculptors' reliefs and statues to the interiors of Buckingham Palace or to William Wilkins's nearby National Gallery. The equestrian bronze of George IV destined for the Arch's summit still languished in Sir Francis Chantrey's studio at the sculptor's death in 1841, and was hastily found a plinth in Charles Barry's new development of Trafalgar Square.[32] It is perhaps appropriate that Chantrey's statue should have come to rest in a site named, in contravention of George IV's own practice, not after himself or any member of his family but in memory of the naval hero whose achievement was one of the many he long aspired to equal.

In perhaps the most symbolic act of all, William resolved that the bizarre, rustic-Gothic Windsor Great Park retreat on which his late brother had spent £200,000 since 1824, and in which he had lived for most of his last four years, should be largely demolished. As early as 10

July 1830, the *Windsor and Eton Express* announced confidently that William IV would 'certainly never make the Royal Lodge a permanent abode' and that 'a great part of the Cottage is to be pulled down', adding on 2 October that 'the adjacent buildings will now also be speedily brought under the hammer'. To add insult to injury, furniture from the Royal Lodge and nearby Cumberland Lodge was not redirected to either Windsor Castle or other royal residences, but sold at auction.[33]

Not all George IV's creations in the Great Park were obliterated. The Royal Lodge's Chapel was to be retained 'for the benefit of the servants of the Park Establishment' – again, possibly a joke at the late King's expense – and the brand-new dining room was given a stay of execution. Some of the Royal Lodge's building materials were recycled for Queen Adelaide's Lodge, a simple, quaintly domestic building on which work began in December 1830. The rest of the Royal Lodge, however, was pulled down as quickly as possible; all that was allowed to remain was a plain, stuccoed remnant. At the south end of Windsor Great Park the bizarre Chinese Fishing Temple George had caused to be built at Virginia Water was left intact, but was rarely used by William or the rest of the royal family. When Prince Albert visited it in February 1840 he found it derelict, and on the point of being razed. The Prince, perhaps more sympathetic to the memory of George IV than were his wife or her relatives, halted the demolition work. However, George's niece had the last word: after Albert's death Queen Victoria ordered the demolition of the Temple in 1867.[34]

In 1965 the royal historian Sir Owen Morshead observed that 'George IV had melted like a snowman: only the clothes remained – and their dispersal at public auction created a nine days' wonder'.[35] The clothes sale, no doubt prompted by William's intense embarrassment at the wardrobes full of vivid costumes he had inherited from his brother, lasted for three days and ran to 438 lots, but the amount raised was disappointing. The late King's coronation costume, including the gold-embroidered, fur-lined crimson cape and silver doublet and hose, fetched only 127 guineas (something over £130) – far less than had been anticipated. Britain, observed Princess Lieven, 'is quite a new world'; in her estimation, the inevitable contrasts being drawn between the present and former reigns was 'altogether favourable to the present'.[36]

Over the next two decades most Britons – including the royal family – did their best to forget the excesses and embarrassments of

George's Regency and reign. When Barry and Pugin's new Palace of Westminster eventually arose on the ashes of the old, its iconography contained numerous references to great British monarchs of the past, as well as to Victoria; George IV, however, was noticeable by his absence. As far as most Victorians were concerned, the old reprobate had indeed melted like a snowman. As *The Times* had declared on his death, 'Nothing remains to be said about George IV but to pay, as pay we must, for his profusion.'[37]

Never in modern times has a sovereign died so unlamented, nor has the person of the monarch – rather than the institution – attracted so little respect after death. Robert Huish's venomous biography of 1830-1 declared of the late King that, with a personal income 'exceeding the national revenue of a third-rate power, there appeared to be no limit to his desires, nor any restraint to his profusion'. Rejecting the argument that 'his example was too secluded to operate dangerously on the manners of the people', Huish claimed instead that George IV had contributed more 'to the demoralisation of society than any prince recorded in the pages of history'. This is surely, however, to overrate his importance. His relevance to British society and British politics had by 1830 become peripheral. He had clearly not, as J. B. Trotter had piously hoped in 1811, metamorphosed from Prince Regent into 'a great king – the lover of his people – the protector of liberty and defender of the laws – as bright, if not brighter, than any of his predecessors'. Nor, on the other hand, was he popularly regarded as a menace to the nation's constitutional equanimity – as was, for example, his former friend Charles X of France. Rather, by the time of his death George IV was generally viewed by his subjects as little more than an entertaining sideshow – if a somewhat expensive and reclusive one. Far from representing, as E. A. Smith alleged, 'a vital stage in the transition from the personal rule of the king to the rule of the Cabinet and Parliament', in his obsessive self-interest George IV marginalised the figure of the monarch to the extent that by 1830 he was almost irrelevant to the governance of the kingdom. His grandiose gestures did not provide ominous templates for his successors but became bywords for senseless extravagance, to be avoided at all costs. As David Cannadine has remarked, 'George IV's flirtation with grandeur was so unsuccessful that it was not repeated for the next half century'.[38]

As Prince, Regent and King, George strove to fashion an idealised image of himself. His glittering collections and ambitious building programmes, the colourful pageants devised for his Coronation and his visit to Edinburgh, his fascination with soldiering and with the trappings and symbols of military success – all testified to his seemingly inexhaustible desire to promote himself to a place in the nation's heart which his conduct alone signally did not win him. Depressed by his evident failure to merge ideal with reality, in his later years the ailing King simply withdrew into a fantasy world of laudanum and chinoiserie.

This book seeks to examine the steps by which George IV's life reached the ignominious nadir of 1830 – how his charm, his wit, his innate aesthetic sense, his enthusiasm and his imagination left him insufficiently equipped to rise to the challenge of a nation daily growing in self-confidence and wealth. It is among the conundrums of history that one of the most gifted of British monarchs was by the time of his death also one of the most despised. The following chapters attempt to discover what went wrong, and why such a fascinating and intelligent monarch should so patently have failed to play the part he had written for himself.

2

Family and Friends

Said a Sovereign to a Note,
In the pocket of my coat,
Where they met, in a neat purse of leather,
'How happens it, I prithee,
That though I'm wedded *with* thee,
Fair Pound, we can never live together?'
Thomas Moore, *Dialogue Between a*
Sovereign and a One Pound Note

GEORGE IV'S TALENTS and insecurities can, unsurprisingly, be traced directly to his relationship with his parents. Much of his aesthetic sense appears to have been inherited from his father, who was in many ways an equally accomplished connoisseur. However, George's collecting policy and building programmes were guided by an overwhelming desire to shock his parents and to reject his father's values. This reaction to the stifling morality of George III's Court was perhaps inevitable. It was certainly in the family tradition: both George II and Prince Frederick had loathed their fathers. In George IV's case, he had good reason to feel aggrieved at an upbringing that was notably deficient in terms of both academic achievement and emotional support.

George Augustus Frederick, twenty-first Prince of Wales, was born on 12 August 1762 – and promptly pronounced by the Earl of Huntingdon to be a girl. Honours came early: born Prince of Wales, Duke of Cornwall, Duke of Rothesay, Earl of Chester, Earl of Carrick and Baron of Renfrew, at the age of three he was made a Knight of the Garter. For the rest of his life he was to cherish and display the title and badge of this medieval order, founded by Edward III in 1348.

The Prince spent his early years not at the royal stronghold of Windsor Castle, home of the Order of the Garter, but in the modest villas his father seemed to prefer to the many castles and palaces at his disposal, and particularly in the small, seventeenth-century lodge in Richmond Park extended in 1761–2 by William Chambers. (It is instructive that George III refused Chambers permission to rebuild the lodge on a larger scale.[1]) In 1772 the growing royal family was moved to the White House at Kew, adjacent to Chambers' surreal fantasy-park, Kew Gardens, where George III had spent much of his lonely and secluded childhood. The White House, a modest structure originally built for Frederick, Prince of Wales by William Kent in 1731–5, was now extended by Chambers to receive the family of George III.[2] Yet its inflexible plan soon proved inadequate for the accommodation of the growing number of royal children, and in 1773 the two eldest Princes, George and Frederick, were provided with their own establishment at the nearby Dutch House, an unassuming, old-fashioned red brick building of 1631 on the edge of Kew Gardens, subsequently given the inappropriately grandiose title of 'Kew Palace'. Three years later the four younger Princes were moved into two small cottages on the south side of Kew Green – one of which had been previously occupied by George III's influential tutor, the Earl of Bute.[3] The Prince of Wales's adult preference for rambling and elaborately-decorated new homes must surely have been a direct reaction to the relatively cramped and sober environment of those undersized and unpretentious homes of his youth.

George was the first of fifteen children, all but two of whom survived into adulthood. George III's second child, Frederick (later Duke of York), was born in 1763; William – created Duke of Clarence in 1789, and destined to succeed his eldest brother as King William IV in 1830 – followed in 1765. Thereafter Queen Charlotte, fulfilling her dynastic role by being almost perpetually pregnant, gave birth with efficient regularity: to Charlotte (later Queen of Württemberg) in 1766; to Edward (later Duke of Kent, and father of Queen Victoria) in 1767; to Augusta in 1768; to Elizabeth (later Landgravine of Hesse-Homburg) in 1770; to Ernest (who was created Duke of Cumberland in 1799, and became King of Hanover on William's death in 1837) in 1771; to Augustus (later Duke of Sussex) in 1773; to Adolphus (later Duke of Cambridge) in 1774; and to Mary in 1776, Sophia in 1777, Octavius in 1779, Alfred in 1780 and Amelia in 1783. The last two sons were decidedly sickly, and died in infancy. George saw little of

Octavius (their father's favourite) and Alfred before their premature deaths, aged four and two respectively; nor indeed was he particularly close to their elder sisters, who preferred the company of the bluff and jovial William or the kindly Adolphus. He was, however, to prove a surprisingly steadfast friend to Amelia.

The royal children's lives were generally simple, even spartan. For the most part they were confined to Kew, and only exhibited at their parents' dull Court at St James's Palace on occasional Thursdays. Even within these decidedly modest confines, however, young George began early to demonstrate his innate intelligence and precocity. For example, when he was inoculated against smallpox in March 1766 (a precaution exemplifying the enthusiasm with which his parents espoused the latest scientific advances), a lady-in-waiting asked whether he minded being confined to bed after this procedure, to which he laconically replied, 'I lie and make reflections'[4] – an unwitting prophecy of how he was to spend much of his later life.

The Hanoverians did not believe in fostering academic achievement through the employment of gifted tutors. As had been the case in earlier generations, the principal quality sought in potential instructors for the Prince of Wales was respectability rather than inspiration. His first English teacher, Miss Margaret Planta, was 'quiet, patient, plodding [and] persevering'. In 1771, when he was nine years old, a governor and an ecclesiastical 'preceptor' were appointed to supervise the education of both George and Frederick, and to ensure that there was no moral laxity in their upbringing. The governor was the Earl of Holdernesse, a 'formal piece of dullness' in Horace Walpole's opinion, whose principal claim to the post was having served with little distinction in the Whig administrations of the 1750s. Holdernesse spent most of his time lecturing his young charges on truth and morality, and appears to have been poorly regarded by the Prince. However, the preceptor – Dr William Markham, Dean of Christ Church, Oxford, and Bishop of Chester – seems to have won his affection. 'Your good instruction, your kindness, your good nature will never be effaced from my heart,' he wrote to Markham in 1774. Even more to his liking was his sub-governor, Leonard Smelt, a talented former army officer and amateur artist who, Saul David suggests, may have inculcated in the developing youth a love both of art and of things military.[5]

Frustrated and ill, Holdernesse resigned his post in 1776. Inexplicably, Markham and Smelt were then abruptly dismissed, the former on the tenuous grounds that he had undermined the Earl's authority. George was most upset at Markham's departure, but his attempts to intervene on the Bishop's behalf failed to persuade his father, who remained adamant. (And George did not learn anything from this episode; thirty years later he treated his own daughter's favourite tutors in much the same offhand manner.) Holdernesse was replaced by the Earl of Ailesbury, whom Walpole thought even duller than his predecessor and 'totally unfit to educate the Prince of Wales', while Dr Richard Hurd, Bishop of Lichfield, was appointed in Markham's stead. Although Hurd was notoriously strict – the King and Queen always held that more discipline was required in their sons' education – he devised a relatively imaginative curriculum which included history, government, law, mathematics, philosophy and literature in addition to the customary disciplines of religion, morals and Greek. George was also encouraged both to appreciate the fine arts and to unravel the mysteries of bread-making, a liberal attitude which surely had some bearing on his subsequent love of pictures and fondness for food. Hurd was rarely deluded where the character and abilities of his royal pupil were concerned, however; asked in 1777, to comment on George's progress, he allegedly made the now celebrated observation that 'He will either be the most polished gentleman or the most accomplished blackguard in Europe'. The prescient addendum that George might be 'possibly an admixture of both' neatly anticipated the judgement of most obituarists of 1830.[6]

Despite the evident failings of his formal education, George became remarkably accomplished. By 1783 he spoke and wrote French well, and corresponded with his mother in that language – rather than in her native German – for the rest of her life. The American envoy Richard Rush later lauded him as an 'excellent linguist' who spoke not only many European languages but also Hebrew. He could play the piano moderately, and the cello well. He also inherited an interest in architecture from his father, who before his accession had learned much from William Chambers – rewarded in 1782 with the Surveyor-Generalship of the reformed King's Works.[7] This interest became a passion which was to mould and define his whole life.

In his pitiless account of George IV's life, Robert Huish was quick to blame both his subject's poor education and the vices he had managed to master even before he came of age on his parents, and was neither the first nor the last to depict George III's Court as one of Teutonic tediousness, infected with the lurking bacillus of continental absolutism. The young Prince was 'confined within a very limited circle' in his early years, and his subsequent education, specifically designed 'to ingraft the free and independent spirit of the British constitution on the despotic and absolute principles of German aristocracy', was 'ill calculated to make him either a prudent prince or a great monarch'. Instead, Huish argued, the austerity of his formative years ensured that 'the moment of his Royal Highness's emancipation [was] that of a prisoner released from confinement', and in consequence, on his twenty-first birthday in 1783, 'he plunged at once into the joys of Society with all the avidity of the fainting traveller who hastens to the gushing spring to allay the torments of his thirst'.[8] Maria Fitzherbert's biographer W. H. Wilkins, writing shortly after the 1914–18 war, displayed a similarly xenophobic tendency in criticising not only the 'harsh and despotic' parental regime laid down by George III but, in particular, the parsimony and small-mindedness of his Mecklenburg queen, who was 'imbued with the spirit of the little German Court from whence she came'. Wilkins came to see Queen Charlotte as the figure primarily responsible for the dysfunctional nature of the late Georgian royal family: 'She inflamed the King's mind against the Prince of Wales and the Duke of York, with stories of their misconduct during the struggle for the Regency. She put the worst construction on their actions and motives, and did all in her power to prevent them from having free access to their father.' In his view the enmity between the Queen and her eldest sons reached a climax in the duel early in 1789 between the Queen's creature Colonel Lennox (who 'had gone about everywhere publicly abusing the Prince of Wales and the Duke of York') and the Duke of York himself. The Queen then prevented the royal brothers from informing the King, convalescing from his first serious attack of 'insanity', about the whole shabby incident.[9]

George's relationship with his parents was awkward from the outset. He could apparently do no right as far as they were concerned, and consequently became the recipient of countless moral strictures and homilies. His mother sent him, at the tender age of eight, a pocketbook full of the most pompous ethical guidelines, including exhortations to 'Abhor all vice' and 'Disdain all flattery' ('it will corrupt your manners and render you contemptible before the world'), and ordaining that his principal goal should be to offer 'the highest love, affection and duty towards the King'. On his sixteenth birthday George received a letter from his father which omitted good wishes for the day in favour of complaints about his 'debauched behaviour'. The King's and Queen's reaction to their eldest son's evident wish to escape from the stifling strait-jacket of home life was to restrict his social parameters still further. 'I shall not permit the going to balls or assemblies at private houses,' the King informed the Prince in 1780. 'As to masquerades you already know my disapprobation of them in this country, and I cannot by any means agree to any of my children going to them.' The strict guidelines he drew up for his eighteen-year-old son included directions on when to go to church, how to travel, and with whom he should consort. Small wonder that the young Prince rebelled against such pious guardians of royal virtue.

George's relations with his mean-spirited and puritanical mother were always strained. Her lack of warmth may indeed explain his increasing reliance on older, motherly mistresses after 1785. She took years to forgive him for his behaviour at the time of the Regency Crisis of 1788–9, but had good reason to complain about his evident impatience and want of respect the next time the King was seriously ill, in 1801. While she denounced the staging of inappropriate 'singing and dancing' at Carlton House during what was supposed to be a time of national anxiety, George was entertaining a host of politicians, in ill-disguised preparation for a Regency government. In May 1804 George refused to attend the celebration of her birthday, smarting like a schoolboy over his father's refusal to grant him military promotion. By 1812, however, his daughter Princess Charlotte was observing with '*how much marked deference*' he was treating the Queen, 'and upon *what a good understanding* they appeared to be together'. Although Princess Charlotte was no fool – she noted, for example, that any *rapprochement* with his parents was 'not a *good sign* with regard to his measures in Government and politics' – she concluded that her father was now '*quite governed* by his mother and the Manchester Square folks'.[10] Yet six years later, George could barely wait for his mother's death before beginning to remodel her former home, Buckingham House.

With his father, George's relationship was even more distant. In contrast to many Continental monarchs, George III never involved himself in the day-to-day detail of his son's education – except to administer a beating when he was deemed to have transgressed, which was often. More serious was his failure to make any attempt to verse his eldest son in matters of parliamentary practice, statesmanship or foreign policy, subjects it was likely the Prince would have to master one day. Instead, he sent him a torrent of advice 'on the propriety of your conduct'. In particular, the King urged his son to remember that he had been placed in his privileged position by God, and to 'place ever your chief care on obeying the commands of your Creator ... Every hour will shew you that no comfort can be obtained without that', constantly reminding him 'that you are ... accountable to him for your conduct'.[11] When this paragon of virtue was struck down with what appeared to be insanity in the autumn of 1788, the Prince of Wales's eagerness to supplant his father was undisguised, and seriously weakened the already frayed bonds between father and son.

The outbreak of the French Revolution in July 1789, and in particular the regicidal turn which events in Paris took early in 1793, encouraged George to re-evaluate his relationship with his father. An understandable instinct for self-preservation led him to admit that the news of Louis XVI's execution on 24 January 1793 had filled him 'with a species of sentiment towards my father which surpasses all description'. Yet in the face of George III's persistent refusal to provide him with a serious military role in the ensuing war with revolutionary France, relations rapidly cooled once more. By 1805, as the MP and inveterate gossip Thomas Creevey noted, the Prince was being 'very indiscreet about the King's infirmities'. Significantly, almost the last lucid action of the ailing King in the autumn of 1810 was to contradict his eldest son's wishes, assuring Lord Liverpool that he would personally recall the Prime Minister, Spencer Perceval, should his son sack Perceval on attaining the Regency.[12] Only when the old King lapsed into senile dotage and was effectively imprisoned did the Prince of Wales feel able to laud the homely morality and simple certainties which his father had preached. After 1811, when his father was unable to contradict him, the Prince began to recast his upbringing, fabricating a father–son relationship which had never actually existed and astounding listeners with increasingly fictional accounts of his steadfast support for George III's uncompromising principles.

One of the old King's most settled convictions – which must surely have secretly irked George – was that his second son, Frederick (created Duke of York in 1784), could do no wrong. Frederick was openly referred to by George III as his 'dearest son', and while the Prince of Wales was excoriated for his conduct during the King's illness of 1788–9, Frederick – who had been as impatient as his brother to see a Regency established – was quickly forgiven by his doting father. Publicly denouncing the Prince of Wales's mounting debts, George III secretly asked Pitt's government (in vain, as it turned out) to relieve his brother's. York was provided with a series of glittering military commands such as were refused his older brother, culminating in the inexperienced Prince being given command of the British army contingent sent to Flanders in 1795. Frederick's subsequent failure there was readily excused by his adoring parents, who preferred to blame the incompetence of his Austrian allies. Three years later the Duke was appointed Commander-in-Chief of the British army, and his lacklustre and unproductive leadership of the abortive Dutch campaign of 1799, during which he notoriously spent much of his time marching his men to the top of the hill and down again, was similarly glossed over.

Despite George III's blatant favouritism, however, the Prince of Wales remained far closer to his brother Frederick than to either of his parents or to any other member of his family. It was to terminate this unhealthy influence that in 1781 Frederick was sent by his father to join the army in Hanover. Nevertheless, soon after his return from Germany in 1787 Frederick became a regular visitor to Brighton Pavilion – much to George III's disgust – and cheerfully began to adopt his brother's more debauched habits. Thomas Grenville described the young Duke of York as being 'totally guided' by his brother, and 'thoroughly initiated into all the extravagances and debaucheries of this most *virtuous* metropolis'. General James Grant, himself no puritan, later noted that the Prince had taught Frederick to 'drink in the most liberal and copious way', adding that 'the Duke in return has been equally successful in teaching his brother to lose his money at all sorts of play ... to the amount, as we are told, of very large sums'.[13] A century and a half later Arthur Aspinall described the Duke as 'an excellent Commander-in-Chief with a practically insane wife and a private ménage that was as ludicrous as it was degrading' who 'abandoned himself in his declining years to the lowest creatures'.[14]

While George and Frederick briefly fell out in 1792 over the French Revolution – George initially adopted the approved Foxite stance, but subsequently concurred with his father's and brother's denunciation of the revolutionaries – and, more revealingly, over the funding of their respective debts, during the early 1790s they still found time to discuss equine and military matters. The Duke of York's subsequent service abroad continued to rankle with his brother, at least until the Prince's assumption of Regency powers in 1811 enabled him to promote himself overnight. In May 1795, for example, the artist and diarist Joseph Farington reported that the Duke and the Prince were 'at this time in a state of animosity' over York's foreign service, and 'do not speak'.[15] Such tensions surfaced again in 1809, when George failed to denounce his brother's dismissal as Commander-in-Chief of the British army. York's mistress, Mary Anne Clarke, was accused in the House of Commons of having sold army commissions, a traffic from which the Duke was widely rumoured to have benefited personally. (While he was disgraced, Mary Anne proved nobody's fool: having printed 20,000 copies of her memoirs, she only agreed to release the love-letters she had received from the Duke in return for £10,000 in cash and a government pension of £400 a year.) George's initial support wilted as evidence mounted against the pair, and though the King and Queen demanded that he publicly announce his unequivocal faith in the Duke's probity, George eventually yielded to advice from Whig leaders and ostentatiously stood aside from the case – an attitude which one observer labelled as 'only another proof of his great weakness and indecision'. The Duke of York was acquitted by the House of having been involved in the sale; yet because he had been injudicious enough to discuss matters of army patronage with his mistress, he was summarily sacked as commander-in-chief. His parents were horrified, and naturally blamed George for his lack of fraternal devotion. Two years later George belatedly attempted to make amends. Virtually his first act as Regent, on 25 May 1811, was to restore the Duke to the supreme command of the army. But the damage had been done. Once again George had appeared faithless, negligent of the interests even of his close relatives. In the opinion of one commentator, 'he had emerged from the sad affair with his reputation more tarnished than ever'.[16]

Even the grief George felt at the Duke of York's death took second place to his personal diversions. After a visit to the Royal Lodge at Windsor on 16 March 1827, Charles Greville reported that the King had expressed his sorrow at his brother's recent demise by declaring that he 'was a loss to him such as no one could conceive, and that he felt it every instant'; however, this touching if typically self-centered sentiment was set incongruously in the midst of a passionate diatribe about his horses.[17] Thereafter, while he was ostensibly keen to have a memorial to his brother erected on the site of the now-demolished Carlton House, serious work only began on Benjamin Dean Wyatt's column after George's own death. He had, meanwhile, evinced no interest whatsoever in helping to defray the Duke of York's vast debts of £700,000, leaving it to Parliament to pay off the Duke's servants, and to the Duke of Wellington to suggest quixotically that an army subscription might cover the remainder.

George's relations with his other brothers were even less edifying. He was always happy to gossip about them behind their backs; on one occasion in 1811 he made startlingly tasteless remarks about 'the huge size of the penis of one of his Royal brothers' in a mixed company which included the Duke and Duchess of York and their attendants. He was especially irreverent about his brother William, Duke of Clarence – a boisterous, honest, unintellectual boy who in 1779, at the age of fourteen, was sent into the Navy and subsequently added pre-dilections for intemperate violence and alcohol abuse to his existing qualities. At times, however, the two could be almost affectionate. When in January 1788 William, having returned from Canada in defiance of naval and parental orders, was commanded by George III to remain at Plymouth in disgrace, he was ostentatiously fêted there by the Prince of Wales and the Duke of York. (While Frederick had been made a duke at twenty-one, William had had to blackmail his father with the threat of standing as a Whig MP to win the dukedom of Clarence in 1789.) At a public dinner in 1804 – following 'a long harangue in favour of the Catholics' which he later disowned – the Prince of Wales, according to Thomas Creevey, 'took occasion to tell us that his brother, William, and himself were the only two of his family who were not Germans'.[18] Yet Clarence quickly grew bored with the cultural milieu of Carlton House, and from 1791 spent much of his time at Petersham with his mistress, the actress Dorothy Jordan. Here his tendency to open his mouth without engaging his brain soon earned him enmity and derision. In 1791 George told York that their brother William 'has been saying some very foolish things to the King respecting us', while in 1796 Farington reported the common gossip that the Prince had 'little opinion of the Duke [of Clarence]' – yet in 1805 William was confidently announcing himself to be George's favourite brother.[19] William's relationship with his fellow-officer Admiral Nelson, whom he could genuinely claim as a friend, was par-ticularly galling to George – who in later life was always ready to appropriate the Admiral's memory and deeds for himself. Nevertheless, the new Regent did create his brother Admiral of the Fleet in 1811 (and, sixteen years later, for a brief period, he was the first Lord High Admiral of the Royal Navy since 1708). In 1814, more-over, William was entrusted with the redolently symbolic task of escorting the restored Bourbon Louis XVIII back to his French homeland, and subsequently helped fund William's odyssey of 1817, when he scoured Europe for a suitable heiress. Dorothy Jordan, mother of his ten illegitimate children, was abruptly pensioned off when George ordered his brother to marry and beget a legitimate heir. At the same time, George dissuaded William from his more eccentric choices, which included the Dowager Lady Downshire and the Oxfordshire heiress Miss Wyckham.[20] Even after his marriage to Princess Adelaide in 1818, however, William preferred to live far from his elder brother – first in relative obscurity in Hanover, later at Bushey Park in Middlesex. Only the death of the Duke of York in 1827, which made his own succession likely, thrust him back into the limelight.

Irascible and argumentative, Edward, Duke of Kent, was never popular with any of his brothers. Banished abroad to serve in the army for much of his early life, he proved a disappointment in the West Indies and Canada and a resounding failure in Gibraltar, from where he was sent home in disgrace in 1803. Thereafter he lived in semi-retirement, largely ignored by George. Forced, like his brother William, to conclude a respectable marriage when Princess Charlotte's death in 1817 left only a string of ageing royal dukes in the line of succession, he hastily wed the formidable Princess Mary Louise Victoria of Saxe-Coburg-Saalfeld, sister of Charlotte's widower Prince Leopold and herself a widow with two children. The announcement on 24 May 1819 that the new Duchess had given birth to a child (and, more importantly, an heir), Princess Victoria, forced George to take more notice of his widely-despised brother. However, he refused to contemplate the likelihood of any of Edward's progeny ever ascending the throne, and after Kent's death on 22 January 1820 urged the Duke of York – whose own wife had died in August 1820 – to remarry as soon as possible. In the event, of course, it was Kent's only child, a little girl barely seven months old when her father died (and to whom George IV, to his credit, subsequently showed every kindness), who inherited the throne on the death of her Uncle William in 1837.

If George generally treated Kent with disdain, he appeared – particularly after his appointment as Regent in 1811 – to rely heavily on the advice of his brother Ernest, Duke of Cumberland. Tall and thin, gruff and taciturn (Creevey was amazed to meet a member of the royal family who actually spoke very little[21]), Cumberland was the temperamental and physical opposite of the Prince of Wales. His political utterances, whether made in private or in the House of Lords, were markedly reactionary, and in sharp contrast to the fashionable Whig sentiments which George affected in his early years. When the news broke on 31 May 1810 that Cumberland's valet, Joseph Sellis, had attempted to assassinate his royal master, and had nearly succeeded, the Duke's unpopular reputation as an ultra-conservative together with his scarred and sinister appearance ensured that the story rapidly metamorphosed into rumours that he had murdered Sellis (who in truth committed suicide immediately after the attempt), that Sellis had been his homosexual lover, or, alternatively, that Mrs Sellis had been his mistress.

The apparently odd closeness between George and his brother Cumberland may have had its roots in their early shared resentment at the slowness of their military preferment: the King had refused to elevate George beyond the rank of honorary regimental colonel-in-chief, while Ernest's early career had abounded with slights suffered at his father's hands. Transferred in November 1793 from his adored Light Dragoons to the Heavy Cavalry which he hated – an illogical reassignment which George III refused to explain – Ernest was badly wounded in May 1794, but for several weeks was prevented by the King from returning home to convalesce. Perpetually frustrated by his lack of high command, particularly after his brother Frederick was appointed to command the Flanders expedition, in 1798 he finally won promotion to the rank of lieutenant-general – but only in the Hanoverian army. His father obstinately refused to award Cumberland the equivalent British rank until July 1799.

When the Duke of Cumberland was critically ill after Sellis's attempted assassination, George had him moved to safety in Carlton House. Princess Charlotte regarded 'Prince Whiskerandos', as she called her dour uncle, as her father's 'right hand', while Lady Holland remarked that she never saw the Regent without the brooding and sullen presence of brother Ernest. In June 1813 Cumberland himself wrote from Germany that George was the only brother 'with whom I have been in the habits of talking freely'.[22]

However, not all was sweetness and light between the two men. All his life George was subject to periodic, slightly mysterious bouts of illness – possibly porphyritic, like his father's. Following a severe recurrence of his symptoms in 1811, Cumberland, with whom he was supposedly 'such very good friends', was reported by Princess Charlotte to be spreading 'a most *villainous* ... lye' that the Regent '*was mad*'.[23] And when Cumberland proposed in May 1815 to return to

England with his new Duchess – already decidedly unpopular with the rest of the royal family for having formerly been tactless enough to marry the Prince of Solms-Braunfels while there was some question that the Duke of Cambridge was interested in her – George insisted that, upon his arrival in the country, Cumberland must arrange 'the immediate re-celebration of your marriage with the Duchess'. This humiliation was necessary, George asserted, in order to avoid 'the most serious and most disastrous disturbances and dissensions here, as well as perhaps abroad'. In truth, it was forced on Cumberland by his family, though the Queen simply refused to acknowledge the union at all. Princess Charlotte was piously removed by her father to Weymouth, far from the 'contagion' of Cumberland's *mésalliance*. Parliament refused the customary vote of additional funds on the occasion of a royal marriage – the Whigs seized the opportunity to hurl repeated personal insults at the reactionary Duke. In the end, on 23 September 1815, George's Private Secretary Benjamin Bloomfield was deputed to tell Cumberland that both he and his Duchess must immediately leave the country, and remain in Hanover until such time as the Regent and the Queen 'might yet heal their distresses' and feel able ' to receive [them] in the manner all must wish'. The Duchess was not finally received at Court until 1829, eleven years after the vexatious old Queen's death.[24]

Cumberland was undeniably useful to George in providing an alternative focus for public attention. In 1829, by which time George's own sexual athleticism clearly belonged in the past, it was widely rumoured not only that Cumberland had fathered a child on their sister, Princess Sophia ('the most atrocious scandal that has ever been spread about the reigning family of a civilised country', thundered Roger Fulford in 1933), but also that he had attempted to rape the Lord Chancellor's wife, Lady Lyndhurst. There was probably little truth in either of these accusations; but Lord Graves, husband of one of Cumberland's former mistresses, did cut his own throat in February 1830.[25] Predictably, Cumberland was soon being privately accused of Graves's murder, as he had been suspected in the case of his valet's 'suicide' two decades earlier. Besides such alleged enormities as these, George's own foibles looked positively endearing.

Suspicions of Cumberland's intentions, and indeed the recurrent discord among those of the royal brothers who were still alive, came to a head in the debates over Catholic Emancipation of 1828–9. The Duke of Clarence spoke in favour of the cause in the House of Lords, advocating the Bill as 'a measure of justice' while publicly rebuking his brother Cumberland (who was also present in the House) for having 'unjustly and infamously attacked the Duke of Wellington's government'. Cumberland protested fiercely against this personal assault, to which Clarence – in a riposte that was to make him for many months the toast of both Government and Opposition, as well as of the mob – replied that 'My illustrious relative has been so long abroad that he has almost forgotten what is due to the freedom of debate in this country'. The Duke of Sussex then joined in the attack on Cumberland, who later recorded his justifiable mortification at the 'most unpleasant scene' of 'three brothers of the highest rank ... disputing publicly in the eyes of the whole country'.[26] In these circumstances, a few adverse remarks by Lady Conyngham were enough to persuade George, ever malleable, to send Cumberland back across the Channel to Hanover early in 1830.

Relations between the Prince of Wales and the Duke of Sussex were always uncertain. Augustus, like his brother William, had been earmarked for a career in the Navy, but his precarious health put an end to these ambitions. Having travelled widely about Europe, and briefly contemplated joining the Church (the only member of the family to do so), in 1793 he scandalised his parents by marrying Lady Augusta Murray in Rome, in contravention of the Royal Marriage Act. Eight years passed before Sussex finally submitted to his father's will and separated from his illegal wife. In the meantime, George had sympathised with Augustus's predicament – no doubt recognising the obvious parallel between Lady Augusta and Maria Fitzherbert – to the extent of offering him a pension while he remained in Lisbon.

Shared experiences of secret marriages should perhaps have drawn Augustus and his eldest brother closer; but in the event, Sussex's Whig politics became increasingly distasteful to George, who after Fox's death in 1806 began to exhibit markedly reactionary tendencies. Sussex championed the cause of his niece Princess Charlotte's personal freedom in the House of Lords in July 1814, boldly declaring 'that retirement, coercion and seclusion were not the means calculated to instruct and give Princess Charlotte of Wales the most favourable idea of the beauty and advantages of the glorious constitution of this country'. After this, the Regent was barely civil to him.[27] In 1818 he kept Sussex waiting for four hours while their mother's will was read privately to him alone, then merely told the Duke he had better return the next day. Unsurprisingly, Sussex gave ostentatious support to

Queen Caroline during George IV's attempt to divorce her in 1820, and even made personal visits to her at Blackheath and Hammersmith when her trial was at its height. As we have seen, the two brothers were partially reconciled only in George's last weeks when, predictably, Sussex (not George) proffered an olive branch, in the shape of a specially-designed invalid chair.

George, twelve years old at the time of his birth, knew relatively little of his brother Adolphus, created Duke of Cambridge in 1801. Although young Adolphus became his father's favourite after the deaths of little Octavius and Alfred in 1782–23, in 1790 in company with his brothers Ernest and Augustus he was unceremoniously packed off to Germany – first to the University of Göttingen and then, on the outbreak of war in 1793, to the Hanoverian Army. Thereafter he divided his time between military service in Hanover, of which he was appointed Governor-General by the Prince Regent in 1814, and quiet retirement at St James's Palace and Windsor.

His tolerance, happy demeanour and suitably military bearing (though not his evident inability to keep quiet) impressed many of his countrymen. He apparently bore no grudge when in 1801 George III vetoed his proposed marriage to Princess Frederica of Mecklenburg-Strelitz (the woman whose marriage to the Duke of Cumberland fourteen years later was to be the cause of so much family strife), and in 1806 Farington remarked that 'The Duke of Cambridge is a very amiable man; very decent in his conduct and by his moderation keeps well with all his family.' Farington was not the only observer to contrast the Duke's relatively virtuous and debt-free life and his continuing good looks with the dissipation and physical disintegration of the Prince of Wales. Cambridge was lucky not to be blamed by George for the latter's disastrous marriage – having initially reported to him that Caroline of Brunswick's character was exactly like that of their sister Mary, whom he adored – and his own marriage was a marked contrast to those of his siblings. Propelled towards the altar, like his older brothers, after Princess Charlotte's death in 1817, his wedding to the glamorous Princess Augusta of Hesse-Cassell on 1 June 1818 earned rare public applause. Even the fact that his political views were scarcely more liberal than Cumberland's – Wellington regarded him as 'mad as Bedlam' – did not appear to affect the high reputation he enjoyed in the press.[28]

George's relationship with his sisters was more distant, but more consistently cordial. George III's daughters were kept in comparative poverty and relative seclusion, and allowed to see few men outside their family circle. In 1791 Charlotte, the Princess Royal, complained to George of 'the manner in which she was treated on all occasions, particularly by her mother, the constant restraint she was kept under, just like an infant, [and] the perpetual tiresome and confined life she was obliged to lead', and begged her brother to try to find her a husband, in order to effect her escape. Having fallen into what was described by one observer in 1794 as 'a kind of quiet, desperate state, without hope', two years later she leapt at an offer of marriage from the Prince of Württemberg, despite her father's reluctance to endorse the match, her suitor's enormous girth, and ominous tales concerning the demise of his first wife.[29]

George saw little of Augusta, Elizabeth, Mary and Sophia, but corresponded regularly with them all. During their youth they were rarely allowed to stray much beyond Kew or Windsor, which was soon popularly labelled the 'Windsor Nunnery'. Mary's and Elizabeth's relations with their eldest brother, and indeed their reputations generally, were not helped by the loveless marriages they contracted in their forties – Mary to the legendarily dim Duke of Gloucester (popularly known as 'Silly Billy') and Elizabeth to the enormously fat and malodorous Landgrave of Hesse-Homburg. Augusta died unmarried, having conceived unrequited passions for the royal doctor, Sir Henry Halford, and for the King's equerry, General Sir Brent Spencer – neither of which, she recognised, George III would ever sanction. Sophia bore that illegitimate child rumoured to have been fathered by her brother Ernest (a tale her brother Edward repeated with malicious glee whenever possible) but in reality probably the son of General Thomas Garth, a dull, elderly and notoriously unappealing equerry. After the birth, Sophia led the life of a semi-invalid, possibly another victim of porphyria; even so, she outlived most of her siblings, and died only in 1848.

George was closer to the gentle and unassuming Princess Amelia. Increasingly incapacitated with tuberculosis, in 1800 Amelia fell in love with Charles Fitzroy – yet another of the King's aristocratic equerries to become the focus of an unrequited royal passion. Inevitably, the proposed match was firmly rejected by Queen Charlotte, who did not even tell her husband about the embryonic affair. Amelia vented her subsequent frustration not to her father but to her brother George, echoing her sisters in vehemently denouncing their mother's lack of affection and the stifling social regime she had imposed upon her daughters. Amelia died in November 1810, and her will, while explicitly noting her father's and eldest brother's kindness to her during what turned out to be her last illness, significantly made no mention whatsoever of her mother. The inference was plain: Charlotte was a cold and unemotional soul who cared more for the correctness of Court protocol than for the sufferings of her children. A year and a half after Amelia's death George asked for his sister's death-mask. His somewhat belated desire for such a sentimental keepsake of his favourite sister was an implied rebuke to his callous mother; characteristically, however, the Prince never followed up his appeal, and in a few weeks had apparently forgotten all about the matter.[30]

The sheer size of his family presented considerable financial problems for George III. None of his children could be provided for from the Civil List, and were therefore dependent on Parliament for their (limited) income. Parliament in turn was reluctant to vote money to royal progeny who set the rest of the country such a bad moral and fiscal example. As John Brooke has pointed out, in 1800 – forty years after George III's accession – 'only two of [George III's] sons were married (one living apart from his wife) and he had only one legitimate grandchild'.[31]

If the conduct of his sons was disappointing and often notorious, the King was far from blameless. He himself, for example, did not always practise what he preached. He constantly reiterated to his sons in general, and to the Prince of Wales in particular, the importance of their duty to their nation. Yet when one of the men he most despised, Charles James Fox, entered into an unholy governmental alliance with the discredited former Prime Minister Lord North in 1783, George III's reaction was both irresponsible and juvenile: he informed the Prince of Wales that he was seriously considering abdicating the throne of Great Britain and retiring to his kingdom of Hanover. This aside must surely have set his previous comments regarding his monarchical mandate in a different light as far as the young Prince was concerned, and may indeed have prompted the near-identical refrain which later, as George IV, he was apt to fall back on whenever events seemed to be conspiring against him.

George III and Queen Charlotte never went out of their way to appease or mollify their children. In retaliation for his support of Fox and the Whigs in the 1784 election, for example, the royal parents meanly refused to observe George's birthday that year.[32] Eleven years later they refused to allow their sons Ernest and Adolphus leave from their German regiments to attend the Prince of Wales's wedding. More seriously, when the irascible but undoubtedly brave Ernest lost the sight of one eye fighting with the Allied armies against the French, neither parent wrote to offer condolences, nor was any attempt made to bring Ernest back to Britain.[33]

The King undoubtedly tried to be a loving father while his children were small, but once they reached puberty he and the Queen appear to have regarded their offspring as liabilities. It is perhaps significant that the death in infancy of his son Octavius – to which he constantly referred during his semi-conscious ravings of 1788–9 – was the episode in his children's lives which most seemed to affect George III. Similar displays of emotion were never expended on his eldest son. Throughout George's teens it was made abundantly clear that Frederick, not he, was his father's favourite child. It was Frederick, not George, who was allowed to join the army and to serve abroad. George was expected to sit quietly at home. When in 1793 the King reproved his eldest son for consistently rising late, George responded: 'I find, Sir, however late I rise, that the day is long enough for doing nothing' – a reference to his frustration at being prevented by the King from fighting for his country.[34]

George's upbringing was unnecessarily harsh, even for the late eighteenth century. He was explicitly denied the companionship of other children his own age – an exclusion clearly aimed at replicating his father's own lonely childhood at Kew, and which may help to explain George's subsequent facility for self-delusion and play-acting. By March 1782 Farmer George was already complaining that his eldest son's behaviour was 'so different to the plan I chalked out'.[35] Yet neither he nor his wife appears to have made much effort to understand their son. In July 1795, for example, the King ordered that nothing but brown bread was to be served in the Royal Household, to set an example of belt-tightening in time of war. Displaying either a keen sense of irony or, what is more likely, a complete indifference to her son's character, Queen Charlotte thereupon sent George a recipe for potato bread.

It is not difficult to deduce that George's later excesses originated in reaction to his parents' spartan regime. While the King 'drank but little wine', preferring to make 'Exercise, air and light … the grand fundamentals' of his daily regime, his eldest son sought to do exactly the opposite, and George III could not understand why.[36] Where his parents preferred plain brown bread, the Prince of Wales pointedly developed epicurean tastes. While his father insisted that the royal residences be maintained at a 'healthy' chill, as an adult George liked to swelter in overheated rooms. When he began to redecorate Buckingham House for his own use, it was pointed out to George that the luxurious carpet in Nash's new Blue Velvet Room would 'not accord with the views of the King, who thought such sources of warmth bad for health' – an observation guaranteed to encourage the installation of yet more sybaritic comforts.[37]

Bereft of a close relationship with his father, throughout his life George looked to other older men for guidance. Inevitably, the companions he chose were wholly out of place in his parents' stodgy and moralistic Court. The mentors with whom he liked to associate – Charles James Fox, Richard Cosway, Richard Brinsley Sheridan, George Brummell, Jack Payne, George Hanger – were not only mostly older, but were all figures viewed with distaste and even loathing by the King. Most were unlikely ever to be admitted within the sedate precincts of St James's Palace; few cared. As the artist Benjamin Haydon observed after George IV's death: 'The people the King liked had all a spice of vice in their nature.'[38]

To George III, his own brother Henry, Duke of Cumberland and Strathearn, was one of the most suspicious of his eldest son's intimates. The old Duke's disreputable *curriculum vitae* included running off with the wife of the Earl Grosvenor, marrying a commoner, and seducing a woman whose daughter thereafter insisted on being addressed as 'Princess Olive of Cumberland'. He scorned his brother's dull Court and sought his pleasures elsewhere; 'unbounded freedom reigns at Cumberland House', declared Horace Walpole, and its master, according to him, spoke 'nothing but the dialect of footmen and grooms'. It was Cumberland who introduced his nephew to the game of faro, and who encouraged him to establish an alternative court on the Sussex coast, far removed from the stiff and unyielding mores of St James's. In historian Sir Edward Parry's stentorian judgement, it was Cumberland who 'enabled [George] to discover and practise most of the vices of the rich and corrupt few'.[39]

Both Leonard Smelt and Dr Hurd had helped to interest young George in aesthetic matters, but his principal guide at the time of his coming of age was the extrovert and eccentric miniaturist Richard Cosway. By 1784 the Prince and his set were frequent visitors to the Sunday-evening musical soirées held by Richard and his wife Maria at their Berkeley Street home and at John Astley's salon at Schomberg

House.[40] The following year Cosway was appointed Principal Painter to His Royal Highness the Prince of Wales. This high-sounding title must be viewed, however, in the context of George's tendency, which became more marked as he grew older, to dole out real or imagined official posts in haphazard fashion to the various artists he encountered.

In his early years George also turned for advice to his First Equerry, Colonel Gerard Lake. So notoriously fickle was George's temperament that seldom did his friendships last more than a few years; Lake, however, remained close to him until his death. To separate his son from what he considered a deleterious influence, George III had Lake posted to America in 1781; on his return two years later the friendship recommenced, prompting the King to resort to more imaginative postings. During an eventful career Lake, appointed lieutenant-general in 1797, became notorious for his savage suppression of the United Irishmen in 1797–8, for which he earned a public rebuke for flagrant 'irregularities' from his commander-in-chief in Ireland, General Abercromby. Yet owing to George's influence he was subsequently appointed Commander-in-Chief of the Army in India and, on his return to Britain, created Viscount Lake of Delhi and Leswarree. A brief rupture occurred in 1804 – Lake had expected to be offered the Receivership of the Revenues of the Duchy of Cornwall (his brother had apparently 'lent him money on that security'), which George bestowed instead on Sheridan – but the general's pride was soothed with an accommodation by which the post would revert to him once he returned from India, which he did in 1807. George seems to have been genuinely distressed by Lake's death in February 1808: on hearing of it, he apparently fainted dead away – as he was prone to do on occasions he felt demanded a suitably dramatic reaction. He later commissioned a bust of the late Viscount from Nollekens, which on its delivery in 1814 was displayed at Windsor Castle.[41]

Lake's companionship was soon supplemented by that of three other serving officers: Captain (later Admiral) John Payne, Sir John Lade, and Captain John MacMahon, soon to become a lieutenant-colonel and the Prince's Private Secretary. George, always very impressionable, admired Lade for both his drinking exploits and his expertise in driving a coach-and-four. Lady Lade, née Letitia Smith, held even more appeal for a prince who sought to shock his parents: formerly a high-class courtesan and companion of the highwayman 'Sixteen-String Jack', she was now notorious for swearing in public. George was struck by her beauty, her spirit and her horsemanship, and it was soon rumoured that she had been a conquest of his prior to her marriage to Sir John in 1787. George provided the Lades with an annual pension of £300, and in 1793 commissioned Stubbs to paint Lady Lade on horseback (Stubbs's picture was still hanging at Carlton House at the time of the 1816 inventory).[42] Lady Lade – who in Huish's opinion represented 'all that was vile and despicable in woman' – was also rumoured to have procured for the Prince. Huish supported this hearsay with the story of the beautiful Elizabeth Harrington, to whom George allegedly took a fancy on the Richmond road and was subsequently formally introduced through the prompt and efficient offices of Letty Lade. In Huish's tragic tale, Miss Harrington thereby fell another 'victim to [the Prince's] libidinous desires'.[43]

Jack Payne, as far as the King and Queen were concerned, was another highly questionable confidant. Although a naval officer of proven worth, and MP for Huntingdon, he was also a notorious gambler and drinker. His appointment as Comptroller of the Prince's Household was spectacularly inappropriate, since he was known all over London to be financially untrustworthy. (He had been black-balled by Brooks's Club for his fiscal irregularities, even though the Prince himself had put him up for membership.) Such notoriety appears merely to have recommended him even more to George, however. By 1802 Payne, retired from the Navy as a rear-admiral, was known as an 'established Companion' of the Prince's, with his own apartments at Brighton Pavilion. The following year he was appointed to the lucrative sinecure of Treasurer of Greenwich Hospital.[44]

Equally suspect, in the King's eyes, were his son's debonair companions Charles Wyndham, Anthony St Leger and George Pitt, aristocrats' sons who spent much of their time drinking, assaulting watchmen, smashing up rooms and seducing women. Worst of all, however, was the Whig politician Charles James Fox. In 1784 George III had turned him out of office, in what Fox considered an ominously unconstitutional manner redolent of the practices of Continental absolutism. George's youthful devotion to Fox appears to have originated largely with his persistent desire to disturb and irritate his father. In the year of Fox's ejection from government, the Prince was widely depicted in popular prints helping his Whig friend to win the election at Westminster. In these caricatures, Fox was inevitably portrayed as the knowing corrupter of innocent royal youth: in one post-election pro-Pitt print of 1784 he is shown tempting George to 'Abjure thy Country and thy parents'; in another, of November 1784, he sings to his royal patron; 'You will one day be k——g, sir, and I at the helm.'[45]

By 1785 George was being routinely depicted in cartoons as Fox's willing pupil in debauchery, frequently shown gambling with his Whig friends Hanger, Sheridan, the Duchess of Devonshire and Fox himself. During Fox's denunciation of Warren Hastings in the House of Commons in 1786, Tories observed with alarm that the Prince appeared to be taking notes; by then the casting of Fox as Falstaff and George as Prince Hal had become a stock-in-trade of political cartoonists (Sheridan also appeared sometimes in a supporting role – appropriately, as Shakespeare's drunken Bardolph). By the time of the Regency Crisis of 1788–9, when it looked briefly as if the Prince of Wales might be called upon to deputise for his incapacitated father, such images had become commonplace. In one print a drunken Prince was shown bursting into his father's bedroom while his friends decided the office-holders of state by a game of cards. (Almost alone among contemporary caricaturists, James Gillray refused the Pitt government's shilling, and portrayed the Prince of Wales, flatteringly slender, celebrating 'The Triumph of Liberty'.) Before the onset of his illness, George III had made it plain to all who wished to hear that he considered Fox largely responsible for his eldest son's numerous failings – his womanising, his gambling, and his perennial debts – so that his addled declaration in December 1788 in favour of 'Mr Fox his friend' convinced all within earshot that the King had indeed gone mad. [46]

George's close friendship with the anglophile duc d'Orléans, cousin of Louis XVI of France and a notorious gambler and spendthrift – though reputedly the richest man in France – was regarded with almost as much distaste by George III as his adherence to Fox. In 1785 the Prince commissioned Joshua Reynolds to paint Orléans in Hussar uniform, a portrait which he later had engraved by J. R. Smith (like the uniforms so often donned by George himself, however, Orléans's sumptuous outfit was never worn anywhere near a battlefield), and in 1788 asked his mentor Richard Cosway to paint a miniature of the duke. A disturbing print of the same year depicted the pair in a sado-masochistic pose, a whip-wielding prince lying prostrate at the duke's feet. By the time of the outbreak of the French Revolution in July 1789, George and Orléans appeared to be inseparable. That October the Duchess of Devonshire noted that he 'now lives a good deal with the Duke of Orléans', and in 1790 Orléans generously agreed to lend George, impecunious as always, the considerable sum of £75,000.[47]

By 1793, however, Orléans had fallen dramatically out of favour, and Reynolds's canvas had been put into store. Having ingratiated himself with the moderate revolutionaries by styling himself 'Philippe-Égalité' on his return to France, Orléans went so far as to vote in favour of the execution of his cousin Louis XVI – an act which, as far as all Hanoverians were concerned, put him wholly beyond the pale. His excommunication was particularly convenient for George, since he felt himself absolved thereby from any further repayments of that massive loan of 1790. Nevertheless, Reynolds's picture was back on the walls of Carlton House following the conclusion of the Treaty of Vienna in 1815; by then Orléans was long dead, having been guillotined by the radicals a few months after Louis XVI's execution. Orléans's equally anglophile son – who was best remembered at Carlton House for having fallen asleep while seated between two of the most beautiful Whig hostesses of the day, Lady Jersey and Mrs Crewe – proved more acceptable than his father to the French people, and within weeks of George's own death was raised to the throne of France as King Louis-Philippe following the forcible ejection of the last of the Bourbons.

While Orléans's proximity to the French throne inevitably ensured that he retained a degree of social respectability, George's friend Richard Barry, seventh Earl of Barrymore, emphatically did not. Buttressed by the income from his extensive estates, Barrymore could afford to indulge in every kind of practical joke – on one occasion, at the instigation of his royal companion, he rode on horseback to the top of the staircase in Maria Fitzherbert's modest Brighton house. Barrymore spent extravagantly on entertainments for the Prince: during the Ascot Races in the summer of 1791 he laid out £1,785 on two banquets for George – who in the event attended neither.[48] His debauches earned Barrymore the nickname of 'Hellgate', a label which prompted wags to dub his clerical brother 'Newgate' (the Honourable and Reverend Augustus Barry was constantly in danger of imprisonment for debt), his club-footed brother 'Cripplegate', and his foul-mouthed sister 'Billingsgate'.

As worrying for his parents as his enthusiasm for the company of the duc d'Orléans and the Earl of Barrymore was the Prince's intimacy with George Hanger. It alarmed his biographers, too: Sir Edward Parry described with evident distaste his subject's 'pursuit of the wives and daughters of common citizens in company with such foul boon companions as Colonel Hanger and Colonel MacMahon'. When Charles Pigott's pamphlet *The Jockey Club* appeared in 1792, excoriating the behaviour and expenditure of the Prince's racing and drinking fraternity, Hanger was specifically labelled the worst perpetrator of their excesses (alongside Lade and Barrymore) and described as 'an egregious coxcomb' who never spoke unless 'to entertain the company with some instance ... of his own folly'. In 1803 Farington cited a typical instance of Hanger's influence on George's public manners:

> At one of the entertainments given by the Prince, His Royal Highness filled a glass with wine and wantonly threw it in Hanger's face. George [Hanger] without being disconcerted immediately filled his glass and throwing the wine in the face of the person who sat next to him bid him pass it round – an admirable instance of presence of mind and Judgement upon an occasion of coarse rudeness.[49]

Hanger was a constant feature of those cartoons of the late 1780s which focused on the domestic life of the Prince and Mrs Fitzherbert, invariably depicted alongside George's other gambling companions Charles James Fox and the celebrated playwright–politician Richard Brinsley Sheridan.

George's subsequent treatment of Sheridan illustrates one of the least savoury aspects of his character: his propensity to discard and forget friends as circumstances changed. Reminiscing decades after George's death, William Thackeray encapsulated the way the late King was 'fond and familiar' with his friends one day, then 'passed them on the next without recognition':

> On Monday he kissed and fondled poor Perdita, and on Tuesday he met her and did not know her. On Wednesday he was very affectionate with that wretched Brummell, and on Thursday forgot him.[50]

Farington made much of a particularly revealing episode of 1795, when Cliveden House in Buckinghamshire, the property of the Earl and Countess of Inchiquin, was destroyed by fire 'in less than four hours ... owing to a maid servant having carried a basket of Linnen upstairs with a Candle in her hand':

> The Prince of Wales saw the fire from the Terrace of Windsor and said it must either be Taplow Court or Cliefden, and they would have no water. – His reg[imen]t of light Horse were there, no part of which did He send or any message or further enquiry. This, considering the personal regard He has pretended to have for Lord Inchiquin, is a strong trait of his Character, Want of feeling. – Lord Inchiquin the next morning sent to the Col[onel] for some assistance and the Prince sent Comp[limen]ts.

Farington contrasted this shabby treatment of an established friend with George III's reaction on arriving at Windsor the following day – the King, with predictable courtesy, sent 'a most handsome letter to Lord Inchiquin on [his] misfortune'.[51]

To Sheridan, too, George was similarly far from a steadfast ally or reliable friend. At the beginning of the Regency Crisis in November 1788, while Fox was in Italy, Sheridan's ready wit and adept political management proved invaluable to the Prince, and even after Fox's return he remained the principal figure behind the campaign to pass a Regency Bill. One of his most successful coups in George's service was to ask 'the Conductors of the Public Prints not to mention the illness of the King' – a request which, while ostensibly in the King's interest, helped, as Sheridan had hoped, to spread 'Consternation and strange Reports' around the capital. He exerted all his considerable oratorical and diplomatic skills on George's behalf. He orchestrated the Opposition press, earning a rebuke from the pro-government *Times* for 'the false and scurrilous paragraphs with which the Opposition prints are daily furnished by Mr Surface and his would-be witty associates'. He recommended, for example, that George let Pitt and his cabinet decide whether to move the 'mad' King to Kew Gardens, leaving 'responsibility where it ought to rest' and thus distancing the Prince from the decision. He also secured the covert support of Pitt's wily Lord Chancellor, Lord Thurlow, in return for the promise of a post in the planned Regency government. By early December he was effectively the Prince's spokesman. It was Fox, not Sheridan, who gave Pitt the ammunition he sought, by demanding in the House of Commons that the Prince's royal powers be unfettered rather than restricted, and Sheridan who managed to limit the damage this demand caused. While Pittite MPs derided Fox – the people's champion, now seemingly metamorphosed into the defender of monarchical privilege – it was widely anticipated that Sheridan (despite the notorious disarray of his personal finances) would secure the key job of Chancellor of the Exchequer in a post-Pitt Regency ministry. It was Sheridan who encouraged the Irish Parliament to offer George the Regency of Ireland – somewhat prematurely, as it turned out – in December 1788, and who later canvassed support for his appointment as Ireland's Lord Lieutenant.

In the event, Pitt's delaying tactics worked, and Sheridan's efforts were in vain. By the time the Regency Bill passed the House of Commons, on 12 February 1789, the King was clearly recovering, and the Bill was never introduced into the Lords. Yet even after this setback, Sheridan appeared to remain indispensable. When George heard a rumour that, in view of his recent conduct and his mother's consequent coldness towards him, his parents planned to shift the succession to the Duke of York, it was to Sheridan that he turned in panic to negotiate with his brother.[52]

If George was reliant on Sheridan's diplomatic skills, he toyed remarkably negligently with the playwright–politician's evident loyalty. He argued bitterly with Sheridan in the summer of 1792, then refused to speak to him again for weeks, though that September he did try to heal the breach. In a surprisingly tender manner, he invited Sheridan to spend some time either in Brighton or at Carlton House:

> It is so long since I have either heard of you, or from you, yet I wish to know whether you are among the living. But to be serious, I wish extremely to see you … when there are events in this life which teas[e] a man's feelings for a time, I think the best way is to leave them to themselves, and not to pester or plague them with officious attentions, and then perhaps when they have had a sufficient phase of time to vent their feelings, they will with more pleasure meet the cordiality of their sincere friends; Such my dear Sheridan have been my ideas respecting you, and thus have I regulated my conduct towards you.[53]

The Prince's refusal four years later, under the pernicious influence of his mother, to grant him an audience should have warned Sheridan what to expect. George proudly told his father: 'I thought it right civilly to decline his visit, which I flatter myself will meet with your Majesty's approval.'[54] Clearly friendship took second place to George's more immediate personal aims – in this case, enlisting his father's support against Princess Caroline and for parliamentary repayment of his mounting debts. Once again, all was settled amicably between the two; but George had made his over-riding fixation on his own priorities abundantly clear.

When the King became severely ill again in 1801, Sheridan's name was once more talked of in connection with government office – the Chancellorship. Pitt had resigned in protest at George III's obstruction of Catholic relief, while Sheridan had found favour with the King. During a visit to the theatre in May 1800 the King was fired at as he entered the royal box: Sheridan instantly conducted the Queen and her daughters to safety with the excuse that there was a pickpocket in the building. On his recovery the King heaped praise on Sheridan, 'who he verily thought had a respect and regard for him[,] particularly dwelling on his conduct at Drury Lane Theatre when the attempt was made on his Majesty's life by the madman.'[55] When the King succumbed to another bout of 'madness' in February 1804, Sheridan once again acted as George's intermediary with the government. That month the Prince appointed Sheridan to the Receivership of the Revenues of the Duchy of Cornwall, a sinecure guaranteeing him an annual income estimated at upwards of £1,200, in order to relieve his personal debts. Not only had Sheridan stopped writing plays: he was growing ever more unreliable as a parliamentary performer as a result of his excessive drinking, and a recent bitter quarrel with Fox made it unlikely he would achieve high office in any future Fox ministry. The Receivership gave him a place on the Prince's Council, and its income was very welcome. Not surprisingly, Sheridan wrote to his royal benefactor that 'to the end of my Life I will strenuously employ every Faculty of my Mind in your service'; and he told the Prime Minister, Addington, that the offer had been 'wholly unsolicited'. Four years later George loaned Sheridan, now bankrupt, some money, and helped him win a minor office in Portland's government.[56]

Perhaps inevitably, the relationship fractured once George finally attained the long-awaited Regency in 1811 and no longer had any specific use for his wayward friend. Sheridan, though a physical wreck and a shadow of the political force he had once been, clearly hoped for great things. Much to his horror, however, he was directed by his royal patron to write to inform Perceval, now Prime Minister, that the Prince Regent proposed to continue with his Tory administration. Disillusioned by George's refusal to contemplate a Whig government, and by his increasingly frequent anti-Catholic pronouncements, Sheridan found himself in an impossible position. His drunken assertions at a St Patrick's Day banquet in 1812 that he 'knew well the principles of the Prince Regent' and was 'well satisfied … that they were all that Ireland could wish', and moreover that 'the Prince Regent remained unchangeably true to those principles', were very poorly received at Carlton House.[57] (In response to Sheridan's comments, the *Morning Post* printed a panegyric of the Regent, which in turn prompted the notoriously damning *Examiner* article, fiercely critical of him, which earned its author Leigh Hunt two years in prison.) The Prince now sought to muzzle Sheridan, and sent Lord Wellesley to offer him a junior position in the new government being formed by Liverpool following Perceval's assassination – an insulting offer which Sheridan proudly refused. Bereft of princely patronage or government help, he failed abysmally in his attempt to find himself an independent parliamentary seat in the 1812 election, coming bottom of the poll in Stafford. Without a seat, he lost the MP's immunity from arrest for debt, and George offered him 'an appartment in his own palace' as an asylum. He also volunteered a contribution of £3,000 towards the purchase of one of the parliamentary seats belonging to the rotten borough of Wootton Bassett; then MacMahon, suddenly and without explanation, withdrew the loan, on George's instructions. This left Sheridan without a seat, and firmly outside the Prince's charmed circle.[58]

As Sheridan's most recent biographer has written, 'The brutal truth was that now that he was in power the prince regent had no further use for Sheridan'. George's charitable instincts had not completely evaporated, however, and when a rumour reached Colonel MacMahon that Sheridan and his wife were living 'in a state of filth and stench that was quite intolerable' George offered a sum – variously reported as between £200 and £500 – to pay off the poor man's debts. According to the *New Times*, which supported George, Sheridan's friends turned the offer down, refusing to let him 'lay himself under obligations to the Prince Regent'. (The tale of this alleged financial assistance does not quite end there. Sheridan's biographer Thomas Moore was rebuked for not mentioning the Prince Regent's offer in his *Life of Sheridan*, published in 1825: Moore had been unable to credit the story.)

The account of George's celebrated last glimpse of his old friend Sheridan conjures a pitiful vignette. On 17 August 1815 the Prince, travelling by carriage to Brighton from the Duke of York's Surrey estate, passed through Leatherhead:

As he drove through the area the regent saw Sheridan about thirty yards ahead, walking along the pathway, wearing black stockings and a blue coat with metal buttons. He turned to his companion and said, 'There is

Sheridan'. As he spoke, Sheridan turned off into a lane, and never looked behind at the royal coach. It was the nearest the ruler of England would ever come again to the man on whom he had depended so much for nearly 40 years.[59]

Over the ensuing decades George has been persistently and perhaps rightly censured for not having halted his coach, or even called out. His vituperative obituarist of 1831 castigated him for his desertion of one of 'his former connexions', now 'cast off and totally forgotten':

[Sheridan] had been the private as well as the public friend of the Prince: he had laboured for him in his most intimate concerns; he had been intrusted in the most delicate and difficult private negotiations, and had proved himself a steady, and, to the Prince, an honest adherent. Yet this man, thus tried, was discarded without a pang, without a scruple, when no longer needed by the Prince, who 'never forgot old friends'.[60]

Sheridan died in June 1816, allegedly calling down 'Shame on the Regent for abandoning me'.

Faithlessness was indeed second nature to George. Even his closest servants and advisors, as well as friends like Sheridan, suffered from his callous inconstancy. His Household Treasurer, Colonel George Hotham, was forced to resign in 1787 in the wake of George's clumsy attempt to blame his mounting debts on Hotham's incompetence. Captain John Payne, Comptroller of the Household and purportedly a close friend, and Thomas Tyrwhitt, his Private Secretary, were both dismissed in 1796 because of their antipathy to Lady Jersey and support for Princess Caroline; insult was piled on injury when the Jerseys were given Payne's residence, next door to Carlton House. (Both men subsequently re-entered George's service, however. In his bizarre secret will made later that year he was already recalling Payne 'with truest affection', while Tyrwhitt was reinstated as Private Secretary the following year.)[61] Even the cleric who foolishly risked his reputation by conducting the marriage ceremony with Maria Fitzherbert in 1785 was shabbily treated, though at the very least he was owed something for his silence. The Reverend Robert Burt had naïvely agreed to officiate in return for £500 and a promise of preferment, but his subsequent requests to be appointed Dean of Peterborough, then later Prebend of Rochester, were ignored: George was terrified that any such appointment would lead to a public revelation of his illegal wedding and thus preclude the payment of his mounting debts. Fortunately Burt then settled for the modest living of Hoo St Mary's in Kent, and obligingly died in October 1791, before he could make any further nuisance of himself.[62]

Colonel MacMahon's treatment was equally brusque and heartless. On 29 July 1811 the Duke of Devonshire died, and on 1 August the Prince Regent told Spencer Perceval he wished to raise his Private Secretary to the Lord-Lieutenantcy of Derbyshire – a dizzy height customarily earmarked for the head of the county's greatest family. MacMahon's elevation in the sixth Duke's stead was, argued the Prime Minister, quite out of the question, at which point George not only lamely gave way but instantly abandoned the whole scheme. He was even duplicitous enough to write to the new Duke that he had appointed him Lord-Lieutenant on his father's death 'as token and as a proof' of his 'unqualified regard and affection' for the late Duke.[63] By the time of his death in 1817 MacMahon, then living in enforced retirement near Blackheath, had become unhinged with drink, bitterness, and grief at his wife's death. George despatched his physician, Sir William Knighton, to retrieve from MacMahon's house any royal correspondence his former servant might have retained (particularly letters to and from Maria Fitzherbert) and any other documents with the potential to prove embarrassing. Having accomplished this detestable task, Knighton rose hugely in his master's estimation (George was always at least momentarily grateful to anyone who could extricate him from his own mistakes or indiscretions). MacMahon was replaced as Private Secretary by another of the Prince's hard-drinking army cronies – a man who was, significantly, a close friend of his latest mistress, Lady Hertford: Lieutenant-Colonel Benjamin Bloomfield (from 1815, Sir Benjamin, from 1825 Baron Bloomfield).

While hard drinking was not the sole qualification for membership of George's inner circle, it certainly helped. George's aristocratic quaffing partners the dukes of Norfolk, Queensberry and Rutland may have been more socially respectable than the Bloomfields and MacMahons, but they were still deemed by St James's Palace to constitute unhelpful influences on the young Prince's character. The eleventh Duke of Norfolk was a particularly heavy drinker who shared George's passions for women and horse-racing; 'Jockey' Norfolk was also notorious for falling into a drunken sleep half-way through the evening. The fourth Duke of Queensberry spent most of his money on prostitutes and champagne – he was dismissed from his post as Lord of the Bedchamber by George III in 1789 because of his intemperate drinking. Both dukes were said to have fathered numerous illegimate children; Sir Osbert Sitwell once fantasised about the Duke of Norfolk watching from a back room while women carrying infants 'with unmistakable Howard features' arrived simultaneously at the bank to collect his payoffs.[64]

By no means all George's intimate friends were aristocrats. From his coming-of-age he had exhibited a propensity to include his personal servants among his friends, and even as late as December 1828 it was being reported that 'he talks to his pages with more openness and familiarity than to anybody'. To the liberal-minded this was encouraging, but to those of a more reactionary disposition it simply demonstrated the degradation of his sense of social respectability. An early friend and advisor was the cook Louis Weltje, co-owner with his brother of a cake shop in St James's Street (conveniently opposite Brooks's, a club the Prince often frequented, and close to St James's Palace). Two weeks after his twenty-first birthday George took Weltje into his service; he was described as 'steward and maitre d'hotel' in the Prince's accounts. By 1784 Weltje was widely regarded as one of his closest associates; a pro-Fox cartoon of March of that year, for example, is deliberately set outside the Weltjes' shop. In the summer of 1784 Weltje was sent to Brighton to look for suitable accommodation and initially rented Grove House for his royal master. Thereafter he was constantly featured in caricatures satirising George's life with Maria Fitzherbert. After 1786 – the year in which his brother Christopher was appointed steward to George's brother York – Weltje was depicted driving the pair's coach (pulled by horses named 'Whim' and 'Caprice') from Carlton House to Brighton; directing a picture auction at Carlton House to raise money for the debt-ridden princely household; posing, along with Fox and Hanger, as 'The Brighton Stud'; about to slice the 'Regency cake'; and, most bitingly, receiving with equanimity (again with Fox and Hanger) news of George III's assassination.[65] In the majority of these prints Fox evidently represents dangerous political radicalism and Hanger provides an eloquent symbol of upper-class degeneracy, while Weltje is included largely on account of his humble origins – an implied rebuke of George's readiness to consort with the lower social orders.

Weltje shared some of the young Prince's most abiding passions: horse-breeding, hunting, carriage-driving, and horse-racing. At the age of nineteen George boasted that he had driven a phaeton-and-four 'twenty-two miles in the two hours at a trot', and Thackeray relates how he once drove a carriage non-stop from Carlton House to Brighton in four and a half hours.[66] He was often to be seen during the 1780s and 90s driving his barouche, pulled by four or even six horses, along the Brighton seafront under the expert eye of his friend Sir John Lade. (On 15 July 1785 passengers on the London-to-Brighton public coach were startled to see the heir to the throne travelling as an outside passenger, seated behind the driver.) And much of George's youthful leisure time was taken up with stag- or fox-hunting, generally in Windsor Forest, Bagshot Heath or along the Hampshire–Surrey border, and often in company with his father and his brother Frederick. In the early 1790s he frequently hunted from Kempshott Park near Basingstoke, with his own pack of staghounds. After 1795 the hounds were transferred to The Grange, newly established as his Hampshire hunting and shooting base. At the same time, George leased Crichel House in Dorset – where, alleges Huish, he conducted not only hunting expeditions but also a clandestine affair. Critical as he was of his late sovereign, Huish felt obliged to acknowledge that he had been 'a most elegant and accomplished horseman' and 'fond of shooting'; he even suggested that those days in Hampshire represented 'the happiest period perhaps of his life'.[67]

Increasing girth put an end to George's hunting. However, if animals were corralled, following the practice of the day, he would still attempt to shoot as many as he could. During his brief stay in Hanover in 1821 he accounted for 2,326 head of game in this manner. As Huish sardonically relates: 'it was determined that a day should be set apart, when his Majesty was to be inducted into the art of slaughtering a few hundred of rabbits, hares, deer and wild-boars.'[68]

Throughout his life George was also an enthusiastic patron of the turf – an enthusiasm which mirrored that of Charles II a hundred or so years earlier and is still prevalent in the royal family today. Though his incapacity to stick with any one interest for long, allied to his multiplying debts, encouraged George to sell his stud as early as 1786, this did not prevent him from winning the Derby in 1788 with a horse called Sir Thomas. His complete withdrawal from racing in 1791 may well have been prompted as much by growing boredom with the racing fraternity and his embarrassing racing debts as by the scandal surrounding his horse Escape. The circumstances were that Escape, ridden by Sam Chifney at Newmarket on 20 October, fared poorly – only to come home by a large margin the next day, when the odds against were inevitably far longer and a win thus more profitable. Such in-and-out running naturally generated unsavoury rumours, and Sheridan was sent to Newmarket to prove that all had been fair and above-board. As a known confidant of the Prince, however, his word was insufficient to remove the taint of cheating. The affair was certainly clumsily managed: sending Sheridan to placate the racing fraternity was rather like pouring oil on a fire, while the notoriously debt-ridden Prince's betting windfall made the suggestion of foul play all too believable.[69] Even if George was an innocent party in this instance, his inability to manage his affairs in such a way as to protect his public reputation was once more glaringly evident. He vowed never to race his horses again – but his image as the 'first gentleman of Europe' had taken another severe knock.

George now withdrew to his toy soldiers and glittering uniforms, and rather than race them he embarked on a programme of having his favourite horses painted. He established a stud at Hampton Court in 1812, but rarely visited it, and it was sold in 1827. Yet he did not avoid the racecourse altogether: by the time of his accession in 1820 he was regularly to be seen at the Ascot meetings, conveniently near Windsor, and was still attending them as late as the summer of 1829.

In his youth George also exhibited a love of pugilism – bare-knuckle or prize fighting, the forerunner of today's boxing. To the horror of many at his parents' Court, he even attended a number of fights – a proceeding which, one biographer has suggested, 'must have naturally depreciated him in the estimation of the virtuous and good'. In 1787 he was personally involved in the arrangements for a match to be held at Shepherd's Bush between his own chair-man, a Mr Tring, and Sam Martin of Bath. The fight never took place, however, because fearful local magistrates ordered soldiers (ironically enough, from the Prince's own 10th Dragoons) to destroy the stage and disperse the crowd. The grimmer realities of the ring proved too much for George in the end. In 1788 he was present at a fight in Brighton in which one of the boxers was killed, and never afterwards saw another contest.[70]

Gentlemen of rank and fashion also indulged in gentler sports and pastimes, and George played cricket at Brighton, where he also bathed in the sea under the tutelage of Martha Gunn and 'Smoaker' John Miles. More ominously, however, he rapidly became addicted to gambling under the influence of such racy Whig friends as Charles James Fox, George Hanger, the duc d'Orléans and the Duchess of Devonshire, cronies whom Huish collectively dismissed as 'a set of titled cardsharpers'.[71] He was never remarkable for his powers of concentration, however, and his lack of attention at the table cost him dear; by the late 1780s his gambling debts were immense.

George's predilection for spending extravagantly beyond his means evinced itself very early, and throughout his life he lavished money not only on women (and their post-affair pensions) but on his clothes, on gambling, on horses, on paintings, and on his homes, which were constantly rebuilt, remodelled and redecorated at vast expense. Not all the blame for his rapidly-accumulating debts should be laid at his own feet, however: the seed of later troubles was sown when he came of age. In 1783 George III, in a characteristic gesture of misplaced parsimony, granted his eldest son an annual income from the Civil List of only £50,000 – half what his grandfather, his father, and he himself had enjoyed at the same age, with no allowance made for inflation. At the very beginning of his adult life, then, the Prince of Wales was seriously handicapped by the limited resources available to him.

This does not of course excuse his subsequent prodigality. His debts were a subject for satire as early as 1784, when caricaturists began to portray him in the company of moneylenders. As early as June 1783 Parliament was being approached to relieve his debts; by October 1784 his Treasurer, Colonel Hotham, noted: 'It is with grief and vexation that I now see your Royal Highness ... totally in the hands, and at the mercy of your builder, your upholsterer, your jeweller and your tailor.'[72] Less than three years later, Pitt felt obliged to introduce into the House of Commons a motion authorising the public payment of the Prince of Wales's debts, which now stood at a staggering £210,000.

George's initial reaction to this embarrassment was one to which he frequently resorted in later years: an expressed desire to run away from the consequences of his own actions, and if possible to leave the country. In 1786, in reply to his father's justifiable accusation that he had 'deranged his affairs', the Prince proposed living abroad – a singularly impractical suggestion that would probably have entailed an even greater expenditure on home and household. His father was distinctly unimpressed by this proposed course of action, and insisted he stay at home and face the music.[73] Instead of flight, George was forced to retrench. Typically, this involved others making real sacrifices, rather than any on his own part. Briefly – but ostentatiously – he shut down much of Carlton House and suspended the new building work being executed there; much of his household was dismissed, and he raised £7,000 through the sale of some horses and carriages; but other areas of expenditure, such as presents for Maria Fitzherbert or new fittings for his homes, barely diminished. He also proposed living in the country, rather than at Carlton House, and did indeed spend much of the next two years at Kempshott and his newly-built Brighton Pavilion – where the real attractions were not any reduction in expenditure but, respectively, hunting and Mrs Fitzherbert. However, such gestures were mere window-dressing. Carlton House was run down, not shut down; Holland's ambitious programme of works was not abandoned, merely postponed. Meanwhile, George spent £54,000 on jewellery for Maria Fitzherbert.

These early debts were finally paid off in June 1787, and his Civil List allowance was slightly increased. Cobbett, writing in 1830, denounced this timely relief as 'perfectly monstrous', and reminded his readers that the Prince's new annual income of £60,000 a year represented 'money enough to maintain 3,000 labourers' families'. Within a year, however, George had managed to amass a fresh set of financial obligations. Unsurprisingly, his father was again not impressed, rightly guessing that in the negotiations over his debts his son had deliberately concealed details of his personal expenditure; and he did not believe George's assurances in May 1787 that he would 'reorder his finances'.[74] How right the King was: in 1790 the Prince's principal creditors felt they had no option but to call in £300,000-worth of debts. George and his two equally impecunious brothers were only saved from spectacular financial ruin by taking advantage of the duc d'Orléans's generous offer of substantial loans – which, as we have seen, remained largely outstanding at the duke's execution three years later. (One of George's first actions on succeeding in 1820 was a formal liquidation of the late duke's embarrassingly large loan.) The disreputable royal trio were pummelled accordingly by the print-sellers, appropriately cast by one cartoonist as *The Insolvent Brothers*. Lord Lonsdale tried to salvage some dignity from the wreck by suggesting development of the Crown land to the north of Marylebone to pay the Prince's debts, a prescient idea not taken seriously at the time but evidently remembered sixteen years later, when the lease of what was to become Regent's Park reverted to the Crown. For some, however, George's profligacy was beyond a joke. In June 1788 a civil servant, George Hesse, shot himself over gambling debts incurred in the Prince's company.[75]

On 22 October 1794 Pitt noted that the Prince of Wales's debts stood at £552,000, and that if all his revenue from the Duchy of

Cornwall was used to that end, repayment would take twenty-five years. Carlton House, he hoped with naïve optimism, could be finished for a sum 'not to exceed £20,000'. This clearly lukewarm support ensured that the motion to have the Prince's debts once again paid by the nation failed by 148 votes to 93 when introduced into the House of Commons on 6 June 1795. An ill-timed motion to increase the Prince's Civil List allowance, brought forward by Sheridan, lost even more heavily, by 153 votes to 29. In the event, however, the Prince's marriage in April of that year to Caroline of Brunswick, and the prospect of a Protestant heir to the throne, secured from Parliament a vote of £100,000 a year over and above the Duchy revenues. George had no choice but to agree to his father's stipulation to concur with 'any reasonable restrictions as Mr Pitt may propose'.[76] Only the desperate need to pay off his debts had driven him to the expedient of a legal marriage, and in the years before his Regency he was forced to make additional concessions. In August 1799, for example, the Attorney-General 'decreed that the Prince of Wales's Income is to be charged with Income tax', while the January 1803 write-off of £650,000 (which did not, incidentally, include the considerable sums still owed to French furniture-makers for items supplied to Carlton House) was only steered through the Commons after the Prime Minister, Henry Addington, had promised to introduce an Annuity Bill to provide an alternative and more closely-supervised source of funds for the Prince to spend on his palaces and paintings.[77]

Not everyone saw George as the guilty party. In 1787 James Gillray depicted the King and Queen as 'Monstrous Crows' in hard-heartedly refusing to indulge their eldest son, while George Cruikshank later portrayed the Prince and his equally debt-ridden brothers York and Clarence as beggars outside a church being studiously ignored by their hypocritical parents. In other prints, however, Cruikshank began insidiously to link increased taxes not with the cost of the war with France but explicitly with the Prince of Wales's spiralling personal expenditure.[78]

The size and nature of George's extravagances ensured that there was always a scandal waiting to erupt. In 1801 a jeweller, Nathaniel Jefferys, publicly advertised his outstanding debt – a sizeable £16,808 1s. 6d – in the hope that this would shame the Prince into payment. Reimbursement was not forthcoming, so Jefferys then tried another, more audacious tack, in April 1802 requesting the Prince's help to become MP for Coventry, since he had been forced 'to withdraw from my present line of business'. Constant entreaties to George and his Household falling on deaf ears, in 1806 Jefferys resorted to publishing a small book outlining his grievances. His case was a strong one, but no doubt equally convincing indictments could have been framed by numerous other creditors. Jefferys claimed that in 1790 he had lent the Prince, who had been a frequent customer, £1,585 11s. 7d. to pay off Mrs Fitzherbert's debts; that, nevertheless, 'the moment misfortune overtook me, the Prince of Wales totally deserted me', and that 'The only return made by Mrs Fitzherbert ... was the purchase at different times' of goods worth £120. Jefferys was never paid for jewellery made for George's marriage to Caroline of Brunswick (£54,000), nor for that commissioned as presents for his mother and sisters. In 1791 the Prince had borrowed a further £420, 'saying it would be returned within ten days'; he was lucky to be repaid after a year. His business crippled by sums owed but as yet unpaid by the Prince of Wales, Jefferys took the matter to Pitt, who reduced the amount owed by thirty per cent, but agreed to forward the case. By August 1797, however, Jefferys had still received nothing, 'and does not know when He shall'. Ignored by both the Prince and Pitt, he went bankrupt in 1799.[79] If his subsequent publication did him little good, it served to alert others to the dangers of over-exposing themselves to George's financial irresponsibility. As late as 1829 his Private Secretary, Sir William Knighton, thought it prudent to disclaim responsibility for outstanding debts to royal jewellers Rundell, Bridge and Rundell, in an attempt to ensure that his own reputation would be safeguarded in the event of bankruptcy or scandal. George's standing was such that even his closest advisors found it advisable to distance themselves from his actions.

PART II

Governing Passions

3

The 'Amorous and Inconstant Sexagenarian'

For though you've bright eyes and twelve thousand a year,
It is still but too true you're a Papist, my dear ...
Thomas Moore, *The Twopenny Post-bag,* Letter I

GEORGE III's ROYAL Marriage Act of 1772 has caused countless problems to Britain's royal family in the two centuries or so since it was passed. Rushed through Parliament in response to his brother Henry, Duke of Cumberland's elopement and Calais marriage to Anne Horton (née Luttrel) the previous year – a morganatic marriage of which the King wholeheartedly disapproved – the Act required the Sovereign's consent for marriages involving members of the royal family. Even its instigator, however, could not have guessed how quickly its provisions would be flouted. (One recent biographer has suggested that George III himself had secretly married a commoner and thus was 'not only a bigamist but also a hypocrite'.[1]) The whole edifice of royal respectability and family values which George III worked so hard to create was, in the years following his eldest son's coming-of-age, rapidly demolished brick by brick.

Some indication of the young Prince's future predilections was given in 1779, when he fell in love with Mary Hamilton, one of his sisters' sub-governesses. Remarkably self-aware at the age of only seventeen, he admitted to Mary that he was 'rather too fond of wine and women'. The affair appears to have gone little further than the despatch of a lock of his hair, since Mary sensibly rejected his advances even though George threatened suicide to ensure her submission. Threatened or 'attempted' suicide was a tactic to which

George reverted with wearying frequency throughout his life; in June 1796, for example, according to Farington, 'a report prevailed generally that he had shot himself'. Only Miss Hamilton's threat to resign her Court office if he persisted persuaded George to agree, reluctantly, to address her 'by the endearing names of *friend and Sister*, and no longer with the impetuous passion of a Lover urging his Suit'.[2]

Mary Hamilton was the first of many. Before his twenty-first birthday George had allegedly had an affair with the 'flirt, Mrs Hodges' and enjoyed a possibly innocent relationship with Lady Sarah Campbell – to whom he wrote, after their meeting at his father's birthday celebrations, that she had 'open'd the wound of my heart'.[3] His first serious lover, however, was the actress Mary Robinson. Mary, one of the great beauties of the age, was painted by all the leading artists of the day: Reynolds, Cosway, Romney, Hoppner, Stroehling, Zoffany and Gainsborough. Born Mary Darby, daughter of the captain of a Bristol whaler, she married Thomas Robinson, a Harrow-educated articled legal clerk, in 1774 when she was only sixteen. Mr Robinson turned out to be illegitimate, and a spendthrift, and in 1775 was sentenced to fifteen months in the Fleet Prison for debt – a sentence his wife was obliged to serve with him. In desperation she turned to two well-placed patrons to help her establish herself in society: the Duchess of Devonshire, to whom she sent a volume of the poems she had penned in prison, and the playwright Richard Brinsley Sheridan. He auditioned Mary on her release from the Fleet and, impressed by her talent and her good looks, recommended her to the actor–manager David Garrick. She first appeared on stage as Juliet on 10 December 1776, and thereafter was regularly cast by both Garrick and Sheridan.

On 3 December 1779 the Prince of Wales saw Mary Robinson in a Garrick production of *A Winter's Tale*, in which she played Perdita. Not for the first and certainly not for the last time, he was instantly smitten. Sending her a love-note by Lord Malden (who in the next few months was to play the parts of both chaperon and pander), he subsequently bombarded her with letters – signing himself 'Florizel', Perdita's lover in *A Winter's Tale*. Soon 'Perdita' was being smuggled into the Prince's apartments at Carlton House and Windsor. Sometimes these assignations were arranged to enable her to sit for Cosway, or for Stroehling (George, naturally, had himself painted by Cosway in the guise of Florizel). Usually, though, their purpose was more carnal. Having engineered Mary a clandestine sitting at Kew Palace with the miniaturist Jeremiah Meyer, George put the resultant portrait in a locket containing a paper heart on which were written the optimistic sentiments 'Je ne change qu'en mourant' and 'Unalterable to my Perdita thro' life'. Encouraged by his promises of eternal love and, more pertinently, of financial support, 'Perdita' Robinson left the stage in May 1780 and was subsequently maintained by George – who, by the signed contract she so wisely demanded, agreed to pay her £20,000 when he came of age.

Newspaper stories of the romance – which some journalists good-naturedly likened to Charles II's pursuit of Nell Gwyn – infuriated the King, who warned his son that 'your love of dissipation has for some months been through ill nature trumpeted in the public papers'. Citing the need for the royal family to set an example to their subjects, a theme to which he was to return constantly over the next thirty years, he declared that 'every one in this world has his peculiar duties to perform' and that 'the good or bad example set by those in the higher stations must have some effect on the general conduct of those in inferior ones'.[4] George III's solution was to transfer the Prince and his small household from Kew to his parents' newly-converted residence, Buckingham House, where his conduct could be more properly supervised.

In the event, his father's strictures proved unnecessary. George's attention soon wandered; early in 1782, for example, he was being seen publicly with the beautiful courtesan and wit Elizabeth Armistead. Lord George Cavendish, whose mistress Armistead ostensibly was at this time, discovered the couple in his own house – the Prince hiding behind a door. (Cavendish, summoning more gallantry than his rival, merely bowed and left.) Mrs Robinson had the embarrassment of bumping into Elizabeth Armistead on Hounslow Heath, returning from a meeting with the Prince. Simultaneously, George was wooing one of the Maids of Honour, Harriet Vernon, aged seventeen, and later the 'illiterate and ignorant' though voluptuous Charlotte Fortescue, whose alleged submission – 'lightly clothed' – to her royal master on the beach at Brighton provided the inspiration for Rex Whistler's splendidly mischievous painting of 1944, now in the Brighton Pavilion. It appears that in reality Charlotte may have successfully resisted the Prince's charms, only to fall victim to the even more dubious attractions of George Hanger.

Meanwhile, the Prince found time to break off the affair with Mary Robinson brusquely, by letter. Following its despatch, he initially refused even to speak to her. 'When he saw me in Hyde Park [the day after],' declared the injured Mrs Robinson later, 'he turned his head away to avoid seeing me, and affected not to know me.' A few years afterwards, writing to the Duchess of Devonshire on the subject of his abandonment of Perdita, George, complacent and untroubled, had the effrontery to boast that 'Out of sight out of mind, I know, is an old proverb, and but too often the case with many people, but it is not the least, my dearest Duchess, applicable to me.'[5]

Perdita Robinson was by no means the last woman to discover exactly what George's assurances of lifelong fealty really meant. She did, however, manage to convert his comparatively worthless bond for £20,000 into an annual pension of £500 for herself (and her daughter from a previous liaison) by threatening to expose the existence of the bond, knowledge of which the Prince had always kept from his parents, as well as his candid and potentially highly embarrassing love-letters of 1780. Even forty-eight years later, Huish saw fit to censure George's conduct towards Mrs Robinson as unjustifiable 'on any principle of honour, feeling or humanity', and several of the King's obituarists rehearsed her grievances against a prince

who when the fit was over insulted his poor mistress – who concentrating his considerations wholly on himself forgot her and her wants – who without a thought, without a pang, let her fall from affluence to poverty – who when his own purpose was obtained, without explanation, with brutal abruptness left her at once and for ever.'[6]

Mrs Armistead, too, soon found herself dumped; she left for Paris and later enjoyed an infinitely more rewarding position as the devoted companion of Charles James Fox – himself rumoured to have had an earlier affair with Perdita. Mary Robinson's own subsequent life, however, was not one of great happiness. She became the mistress of Colonel Sir Banastre Tarleton, famed soldier of the American War, whom visitors to the Royal Academy exhibition of 1782 saw so forcefully immortalised on canvas by Sir Joshua Reynolds. In October 1783 she was paralysed from the waist down as a result of a horrific miscarriage. Further crippled by arthritis, she died in 1800.[7]

The gorgeous Mrs Robinson apparently captured the public imagination, and long after the affair was over caricaturists were still associating her with the Prince. She was depicted as his companion in satirical commentaries of 1783 and 1784 which featured the failure of Fox's India Bill, George III's dismissal of his Whig government, the subsequent General Election, and the King's appointment of the twenty-four-year-old William Pitt as Prime Minister. In September 1784 she was portrayed in one print clothed in rags, begging from the heedless Prince of Wales; as late as 1788 a contemporary artist less aware of the machinations of Carlton House illustrated the Prince and Tarleton vying for Perdita's hand; and George Cruikshank was still resurrecting the memory of the affair when George married Caroline of Brunswick in 1795. From the mid 1780s, though, satirists were also beginning to link the Prince with a far more socially respectable figure: Georgiana, Duchess of Devonshire, the pipe-smoking Whig who happily sold kisses for votes to aid her friend Fox in his Westminster election campaign of 1784. George gave Georgiana a key to Carlton House in 1787, and magnanimously paid off her gambling debts – by then almost £20,000 – when she was pregnant in 1789. Yet the Duchess's most recent biographer, Amanda Foreman, has found no concrete evidence of any sexual aspect to this undoubtedly close friendship.[8]

Other caricaturists sought more obvious targets. In 1784 and again in 1785 Rowlandson pictured the Prince of Wales in the company of prostitutes; a year later a rival had him demanding 'a brisk wench in clean straw'. It was also widely rumoured that he was having an affair with Maria, the vivacious and highly talented wife of his friend Richard Cosway, and in 1786, in his play *The Royal Academicians*, Anthony Pasquin spelt out details of the putative affair in the most unsubtle language. (Maria Cosway was a friend, incidentally, of Mary Robinson.) The story persisted for decades, and though no real proof of it was ever uncovered, the satirists labelled the Cosways' Schomberg House 'a first rate house of assignation'. By 1786, the *Morning Post* was turning its attention to the alleged relationship between Maria Cosway and the duc d'Orléans.[9]

George's documented affair with Perdita Robinson was followed by numerous other liaisons – with women of the Court, such as Lady Augusta Campbell and Lady Melbourne; with the wives of members of the diplomatic corps, such as the Countess von Hardenburg; with friends' wives, such as Elizabeth Billington (who was also the mistress of George's companion-in-drink the Duke of Rutland); or simply with chance acquaintances, such as Grace Eliot and Elizabeth Harrington. Most were brief affairs – George soon tired of even the most beautiful and intelligent women – and their termination was generally followed by undignified scrambles for unwisely-promised pensions. A brief liaison with the Franco-Welsh singer Anna Maria Crouch was typical in many ways. Though rumoured to have been little more than a one-night stand (the Prince, asserted Farington, 'was only with Her once'), it nevertheless seems to have required George's Private Secretary to offer Mrs Crouch 'money or Bonds to the amount of £12,000'; at the same time, her allegedly outraged husband was given an annual stipend of £400 'to prevent His bringing an action against the Prince'. As was the case with the majority of his discarded women, however, George's monetary promises proved as worthless as his amorous protestations, and Anna Maria was forced to haggle for her money.[10]

Some of George's female victims found themselves with rather more than a pension. His affair with the society beauty Grace Eliot in 1781 purportedly left her with a daughter, born on 30 March 1782 and christened Georgiana Augusta Frederica Seymour. (Predictably, George always refused to acknowledge the child's paternity, but she became a celebrated figure in society and in 1808 married the Duke of Portland's son, Lord Charles Bentinck.) Ten years later George, supposedly still enamoured of Maria Fitzherbert, fell in love with the daughter of Lady Archer, a timid and credulous girl ('a perfect novice in the world') named Lucy Howard. Lucy subsequently gave birth to a child, George Howard, whom we may assume to have been the Prince's bastard son; he died when he was two, and was buried quietly at Brighton. Meanwhile, however, news of the affair had leaked out, and Lucy Howard's house was besieged by curious spectators. She fled to Richmond in Yorkshire, and there met and later married a local man rejoicing in the appropriately anonymous name of Mr Smith.[11]

Many of George's married inamorata were actively encouraged to respond to his attentions by complaisant husbands prepared to turn a blind eye in the hope that preferment would follow. For the most famous of these Court cuckolds, the Earl of Jersey and the Marquess of Hertford, the rewards were indeed substantial – at least, that is, until the affair cooled, at which time each salvaged what he could and ran for cover. Occasionally, however, this machiavellian ploy backfired. The Hanoverian envoy, Count von Hardenburg, was presumably aware that his flirtatious and attractive wife was having an affair with the Prince of Wales, but the *Morning Herald*'s exposure of the relationship, followed by the Countess's impassioned plea to her paramour to elope with her at once – which in turn prompted the faint-hearted Prince to confess everything in a theatrical audience with his mother – saw him returned in disgrace to Germany.

Writing nearly fifty years later, George's unsympathetic biographer Robert Huish nevertheless reserved most of his bile for 'the husband who would leave his residence at the door, while a prince entered it at another, and absent himself for the night'. Not all Huish's contemporaries were so censorious. William Cobbett impressively resisted the temptation to delineate the complex early love-life of his late sovereign, declaring that such revelations would 'only serve as an entertainment to the idle, encouragement to the profligate, and to fill the sensible and sober with disgust'[12] – a sentiment the truth of which has become only too obvious in the treatment of public figures in the late twentieth century.

The Countess von Hardenburg having been helpfully spirited away, by 1783 George's swiftly-moving affections had alighted on Maria Fitzherbert, a twice-widowed Catholic six years his senior. Mrs Fitzherbert's first husband, Edward Weld, had died shortly after their marriage in 1775; her second, Thomas Fitzherbert, perished of wounds inflicted during the anti-Catholic Gordon Riots of 1780. Soon after Thomas's death, Maria took a lease on Marble Hill House, the Palladian villa at Twickenham originally – and rather appropriately, given her future role – built for a mistress of a previous Prince of Wales, later George II.

Maria was by all accounts kind and attractive. Even Huish remembered her as 'unquestionably, a beautiful woman', although he was unable to resist the qualification that she was 'perhaps too much inclined to fulness of figure'. She was allegedly spotted by the Prince in Lady Sefton's box at the opera – or, alternatively, when out walking in Richmond. (Was Maria, one biographer wondered in 1925, really the famous song's 'sweet lass of Richmond Hill'?)[13] Mrs Fitzherbert might have proved merely the latest in an already long line of royal inamorata. The Duchess of Devonshire later recalled that 'In the Spring in 83 whilst I was at Bath I heard great reports of the Prince of Wales's attachment to Mrs Hodges and afterwards of his falling in love with Mrs Fitzherbert.' However, George's latest attachment seemed, in its cheap melodrama, to surpass even his relationship with Perdita Robinson. The story has often been told of how on 8 July 1784, Maria having declined his request that she live at Carlton House as his mistress, he further refined the tactic which had failed with Mary

Hamilton and attempted 'suicide' by stabbing himself – ineffectually. Again the lady was unimpressed: Maria fled to Holland and then to France, where she was pursued by the marquis de Bellois, a notorious rake, and discovered by an agent of George's friend the duc d'Orléans. George thereupon sent her a rambling, forty-two-page letter, meanwhile demanding that his father allow him to go abroad. Declaiming theatrically that 'I am ruined if I stay in England', and that by failing to follow her 'I disgrace myself as a man',[14] he thought of journeying to Holland in Maria's footsteps, but was dissuaded by the urbane envoy at The Hague, Sir James Harris. (Ironically, ten years later Harris, as Lord Malmesbury, was the intermediary between the Prince and his official bride.)

Despite the fact that any union with her would be illegal under the terms of the 1772 Royal Marriage Act, George now decided that matrimony was the only way to secure Maria's affections. As early as 17 July 1784 he signed a letter to her as 'not only your most affectionate of Lovers, but the tenderest of Husbands'. Following her capitulation in October to his epistolary entreaties – which had been accompanied by further threats of suicide as well as protestations of undying love – George assured Maria on 3 November that he would 'through life endeavour to convince [her] by his love and attention of his wishes to be the best of husbands' and that he would 'ever remain unto the last moments of his existence, *unalterably thine*'.[15]

Maria returned to England soon after receiving this note. Despite being warned against it by Fox, who pointed out the illegality of what he contemplated and the possibility that his father would transfer the succession to the Duke of York ('professedly his favourite'), George married Maria in a hastily-arranged ceremony on 15 December 1785. The union was illegal on two counts: under the terms of the Royal Marriage Act of 1772 any marriage of a member of the royal family under the age of twenty-six contracted without the sovereign's consent was void, while under those of the 1701 Act of Settlement no one married to a Catholic could succeed to the throne of Great Britain. Accordingly, it was difficult to find a respectable cleric to officiate: even the less than scrupulous did not wish to see what careers they had disappear in a flurry of litigation and consequent financial ruin. Eventually the Prince secured the services of a curate, Robert Burt, who had recently been in debtors' prison and to whom a fee of £500 and the promise (poor foolish Burt) of a position as one of the royal chaplains was extremely welcome. The couple were married by Anglican rites in the drawing room of Maria's Mayfair home and in the presence of her uncle, Henry Errington, her brother, John Smythe, and a friend, Orlando Bridgeman, who kept watch at the door. Husband and wife then set off for a clandestine honeymoon at a cottage on Ham Common in Surrey.

Clearly, George and Maria could never hope to enjoy a proper domestic home life. However, they attempted to create its semblance at Carlton House and Brighton Pavilion. Maria's own house at Brighton was hardly tiny (it would have suited a well-to-do middle-class family), but presented a cosy contrast to the neo-classical formality of the first Pavilion. The principal front was dominated by a long veranda overlooking the Steine, on which the Prince 'was often to be seen ... especially of a morning':

> All Brighton walked, rode, or drove on the Steine in those days ... [The Prince] would sit there talking to her by the hour together; sometimes he would honour with a bow or a smile some one of his acquaintance passing on the Steine below. How he got there was a mystery to many, [since he] was rarely seen to pass backwards and forwards between Mrs Fitzherbert's house and the Pavilion.[16]

Henry Singleton's undated painting now in the Baltimore Museum of Art shows a touching domestic scene, with Maria curtseying before a Prince dressed in the Whig colours of buff and blue. The room is certainly not one at Carlton House or the Pavilion, and the picture may well have been painted at Maria's home, Steine House: the room is small, with everyday floral fabric as the seat upholstery and floral paper borders on the walls. Despite the relative modesty of Maria's own surroundings, however, John Croker observed that at Brighton 'she is treated as Queen' and that 'When she dines out she expects to be led out to dinner before princesses' ('Mighty foolish this', he added).[17] In contrast, most of conservative London society refused to receive her – even after the bizarre rumour spread that she was to be made a duchess.

Inevitably, news of the marriage leaked out. In 1786 the radical Horne Tooke published a pamphlet on the subject, *The Reported Marriage of the Prince of Wales*, which named Maria as 'his lawful wife'. And the cartoonists proceeded to have a field-day. The majority stuck to the familiar theme of a credulous man dominated by a calculating widow, depicting George as a victim of feminine and Catholic wiles rather than the instigator of the relationship. In 1786 Maria was portrayed, breasts bared, forcing the Prince to take her to Court at St James's or, alternatively, as *The Kings Evil*, her garter a halter for her royal husband. One more flattering print of March 1786, *Tender Trim and Only Thirty*, gently compared the happy couple with the perennially dull but eminently respectable *Farmer George and his Wife*.[18]

Clear allusions were made to the illegal marriage during the House of Commons debates of April 1787 on the Prince's debts (the Prime Minister, Pitt, after an initial show of disgusted reticence, began to encourage the insinuations). Tory backwoodsman John Rolle, and Nathaniel Newnham, the City of London alderman who had first raised the issue on 20 April, both pressed the government for an answer on the question of the marriage. Sheridan replied to the charges evasively, reprehending Newnham 'for having taken notice of a report, calculated to injure a most amiable character and wound the honour and feelings of the Prince'.[19] Yet Fox, who appears to have genuinely believed what George had told him and on that basis declared that he spoke 'from the immediate authority of the Prince of Wales', assured the House of Commons on 30 April that no such marriage had taken place. The rumoured union, he added, 'not only never could have happened legally, but never did happen in any way whatsoever'; any suggestion to the contrary had from 'the beginning been a base and malicious falsehood'. Sheridan's subsequent attempt to remuddy the waters – leading Whig Charles Grey having sensibly refused this poisoned chalice – merely served to make Fox appear a liar (and later observers, Robert Huish among them, thought he had been exactly that[20]). George, duplicitous as ever, privately expressed astonishment to Maria that Fox should have denied their marriage. Gillray's memorable image of *Dido Forsaken* of May 1787, depicting Fox's realisation that he had no choice but to alienate either the Prince or his own followers, neatly encapsulated the Whig leader's predicament.

Hard on the heels of the exposure of the marriage came allegations that the union had produced children. Caricaturists were actually suggesting this as early as May 1786, and a harder-hitting satire of August 1786 had George offering to abandon his wife and their supposed child in the cause of retrenchment. By February 1787 the prints had become distinctly less deferential, with Maria frequently depicted in abject poverty, while prints such as *Love's Last Shift* of February 1787 included a neglected child along with the usual cast of Weltje and

Hanger. A satire of December 1789 drew a parallel between Maria and Mary of Modena, a century before: Maria was shown being offered a warming-pan, the notorious device by which it was popularly believed the infant Prince James (later the 'Old Pretender') was smuggled into Mary's bedroom – exploiting popular prejudice against Mrs Fitzherbert's Catholicism to associate her with the Jacobite descendants of the papist James II.[21]

Maria Fitzherbert's ward Minney Seymour is now, despite persistent rumours to the contrary, generally acknowledged to have been just that and no more. Nevertheless, Minney played her part in the small industry which grew up after Maria's death centred on attempts to prove a variety of claims regarding possible progeny of the illegal union. When asked in 1833 whether Mrs Fitzherbert ever acknowledged having any children by the late King, Maria's relative Lord Stourton declared that when he put this same question to her 'she smilingly objected on the score of delicacy'. Three years later, however, Maria signed an affidavit affirming that 'my union with George, Prince of Wales, was without issue'. This has not, however, dissuaded numerous individuals from requisitioning the Prince of Wales and Maria Fitzherbert as their ancestors. Since Mrs Fitzherbert's private papers were deliberately destroyed and the Royal Archive, unsurprisingly, contains little information regarding any illegitimate children of George IV, most musings on this subject must remain largely conjectural.

Perhaps the best claim to princely paternity lies with Mary Anne Smythe, who lived with Mrs Fitzherbert as an adopted daughter from 1812. Ostensibly she was the illegitimate child of Maria's brother John Smythe, witness it will be recalled to the 1785 'wedding'. In 1828 Mary Anne married Edward Stafford-Jerningham, and their two sons succeeded to the Stafford barony. In 1939 Mrs Fitzherbert's biographer Sir Shane Leslie (himself a descendant of Maria's adopted daughter Minney Seymour and her husband, George Dawson-Damer) enthusiastically endorsed Mary Anne's claim to royal paternity. Additional candidates suggested by Shane Leslie, Christopher Hibbert, the Foord-Kelceys, Cynthia Campbell and others as children of George and Maria include James Ord, Henry Hervey, Horace Wilson, George Lamb, Jane Bowman, Sophia Sims, and two John Smiths, both of whom emigrated to Australia. Ord, born in 1786, was allegedly brought up a Catholic, sent to Spain and educated at Georgetown College in Washington using funds provided by the nearby British

Embassy. (Campbell additionally points out the strange coincidence that Ord's passage to America in 1790 was arranged by the diplomat Alleyne Fitzherbert, a distant relative of Maria's.)[22] Henry Hervey was also born in 1786 (on 1 December) and at the age of seventeen joined the East India Company; letters from Hervey's sons in the possession of the Barnard family discuss the possibility of their father being the son of the Prince of Wales. Horace Wilson, too, was born in 1786, on 26 September. After studying medicine and music and, like Hervey, serving in the East India Company, he became the first Professor of Sanskrit at Oxford, and produced the first Sanskrit–English dictionary. In 1823 George IV reportedly told the Lord Chancellor, Eldon, that he 'thought himself bound' to leave a son who was an officer in the East India Company £30,000 in his will; this may refer to Hervey or Wilson, or possibly to George Crole (see below), who was then serving as an army officer in India.[23]

Leslie Grout has recently suggested that George and Maria produced no fewer than seven children, all of whom were given the surname of the Prince's Comptroller of the Household, Captain Jack Payne, who became their guardian:

> The Prince himself had adopted the name of Randolph Payne for his secret life and the baptism of Randolph, son of Randolph and Ann Jane Payne, is recorded in the register of St Thomas, Southwark on 18th October 1790. A secret trust fund was set up to provide for the children when they came of age; the Prince made payments into the fund which was administered by a private bank owned by Rene Payne who was a relative of Jack and acted as Chairman of the Trust.[24]

These are by no means the only illegitimate children allegedly fathered by the Prince of Wales. In addition to Grace Eliot's daughter Georgiana Seymour and Lucy Howard's son George there are numerous candidates for inclusion in the list of the Prince's putative bastards by women other than Maria Fitzberbert. George Lamb, ostensibly the fourth son of the first Viscount Melbourne (and brother of the future Prime Minister, the second Viscount), was widely believed to be the Prince of Wales's child: William Lamb, the second Viscount, later admitted that his mother had been 'a remarkable woman, a devoted mother, an excellent wife – but not chaste, not chaste'.[25] George Lamb married into the family of the Duke of Devonshire in 1809 and became MP for Westminster and the Devonshire pocket borough of

Dungarvan until his death in 1834, serving as Under-Secretary in the Home Office in Grey's ministry after 1830. Jane Bowman – who also went by the names Mills and Atkinson – born in 1801, was supposedly George's daughter, as was Sophia Sims who demanded financial assistance from the Lord Mayor of London in June 1839 on those grounds. The Lord Mayor refused, exclaiming 'What proof is there that there was any child at all resulting from ... the union, but what everybody knew could be no union at all?' and suggesting that, if she was indeed the late King's daughter, 'I am sure that he would have made provision for you.'[26] On 23 August 1799 a Mrs Crole, born Elizabeth Fox and formerly Lord Egremont's mistress, gave birth to a son, predictably named George, who from evidence in the Royal Archives has been assumed to be the Prince's offspring. Both the child and his mother received financial gifts from the Crown which covered, among other things, young Crole's Sandhurst fees and the purchase of a commission in the 21st Dragoons. In 1831 Knighton and the Duke of Wellington, as the King's executors, sent George – by now a major – the considerable sum of £10,000, and in the document recording this payment he is described as 'a natural son of George IV'.[27] Other children who may have been fathered by the Prince include William Francis, born in 1806 to a Mrs Davies of Parsons Green (provision for whom prior to 1823, when George disowned him, is also recorded at Windsor); George Seymour, son of a Mrs Crowe of St James's (and, interestingly, bearing the same surname as Grace Eliot's daughter), who was nicknamed 'Prince' by his mother and his schoolfriends and was provided with an army commission; William Hampshire, son of an East End publican's daughter, who rose to become Paymaster to the Royal Household in 1854; and Charles Candy, son of a Mademoiselle Candy who married into Queen Adelaide's household.[28]

Whether or not Maria Fitzherbert had any children by George, her position remained precarious. Following George III's illness of 1788–9 and the resulting Regency Crisis, James Gillray's print *The Funeral Procession of Miss Regency* of early 1789, showing Mrs Fitzherbert as chief mourner, rightly suggested that it was she who had most to lose from the King's recovery: the Prince had time on his side, and could afford to wait for his father's death or permanent incapacity. Given the already lengthy list of the Prince's discarded women, however, few would have bet on the longevity of any relationship he contracted, even one cemented by a formal ceremony. Although he was frequently complimented on his manners, when it came to people or principles he found it all too easy to abandon them, along with consideration and politeness. Barely a year after the Fitzherbert 'marriage' he was belittling the event to his drinking crony the Duke of Rutland, expressing surprise that, while he recognised the wedding as a convenient sham, his 'wife' apparently believed in it. As to the later suggestion that he had bought the lease of the hunting lodge Bagshot Park to provide a retreat from the nagging of his 'wife', certainly by January 1795, as the architect George Dance told Farington, Maria herself was complaining that 'she has expended £8,000 in entertainments &c provided for the Prince of Wales, and that if He would pay that sum, & trouble her no more she would be contented'; Dance apparently added, 'She says she has lived the life of a Galley Slave for 4 years past'. An anonymous cartoon of as early as April 1792 pictured Maria flinging a cup of tea in the Prince's face in a domestic brawl; other satirists, blatantly anti-Catholic, likened her to a papist Trojan horse, bent on converting the nation to her own faith, in the manner of Charles I's Henrietta Maria. (One snide pamphleteer of 1789 accused her of wanting to have her alleged children by the Prince 'educated ... in the principles of popery. And then the good People of England may be put to the expense and trouble of another REVOLUTION.')[29] By 1794 it was common knowledge that George's attention had wandered, and that Maria Fitzherbert had become a victim of his inconstant and erratic temperament. Crucially for her relationship with the Prince, Maria was on bad terms with Louis Weltje, the cook, confidant and quondam decorator who effectively ran the Brighton court. This posed an awkward problem for George, caught between the formidable appetites of penis and stomach: in the event, he found satisfaction for both.

The catalyst in the eventual separation of George from Maria was the beautiful but unprincipled Frances, Countess of Jersey. Lady Jersey was no novice in attracting lovers. In 1778 she had embarked on an affair with the husband of George's close friend the Duchess of Devonshire, and four years later rejected George's own advances. By the summer of 1794, however, she was evidently tiring of her current paramour, the Earl of Carlisle. She now thrust herself at her royal admirer, who at Weymouth on 24 August told the King (to his father's relief) that he had severed all connection with Mrs Fitzherbert and was now prepared to seek a Protestant bride – Lady Jersey having suggested that a marriage of convenience would provide a shield for their relationship. On 8 September 1794 Farington recorded that, as a result of her success with the Prince of Wales, 'Lady Jersey has at last accomplished her ardent desire to be admitted to the Queen's Parties at Windsor'. He hinted strongly that she and the Prince were more than Court acquaintances, and implied that negotiations for 'a separation between the Prince of Wales and Mrs Fitzherbert' were not unconnected with Lady Jersey's new-found favour at Court. More than a quarter of a century later, at the time of Caroline of Brunswick's divorce trial, her advocate Lord Brougham alleged that Queen Charlotte had encouraged the liaison with Lady Jersey in order to divide her son from Mrs Fitzherbert. The first inkling Maria had of George's new obsession was when, following 'a cordial note from Brighton', she dined at the Duke of Clarence's and found the Prince of Wales conspicuously absent. She later received a curt note from the 'husband' who had once sworn eternal love, stating bluntly that he would never see her again.[30]

George treated Maria with unfeeling coldness, directing Lady Cholmondeley to tell the Queen that her championing of Mrs Fitzherbert against Lady Jersey would never 'reconcile me to a person whose conduct I always must resent with just indignation'. (Lady Cholmondeley herself wisely refrained from ostracising the discarded mistress, sensibly allowing for the possibility of a future reconciliation.) Maria's friends reacted by organising a public display of support for Caroline at the opera in May, which in turn prompted a torrent of abuse from the Prince.[31]

Such charmless behaviour towards his paramours was entirely characteristic of George. Young Harriet Vernon, seduced by him in 1782, had soon found that he did not expect the relationship to last. In Huish's view, George showed Harriet only 'neglect and indifference ... after she had sacrificed to him all that was the most dear to her on earth'. Worse still, she found herself not only bereft of her virginity but out of a job, when the King brusquely sacked his wife's errant Maid of Honour. Twenty years later George's behaviour had not improved. Lady Massereene, with whom he had a brief affair in 1804, was 'soon discarded ... to make way for another whose chief recommendation was that of novelty', and he went on to pursue more amenable conquests such as the courtesan Harriette Wilson and one Madame de Meyer, installed in a Marylebone flat in 1805. 'Like the bee', declared Huish in 1830, 'he roamed from flower to flower, but never visited that flower again'; his Court became a place 'where many an ardent vow has been breathed of *everlasting* constancy and affection'.[32]

In contrast to George's boorish behaviour, and to their everlasting credit, his brothers continued to treat Mrs Fitzherbert with the utmost respect even after 1794, addressing her as though she were indeed the Princess of Wales. Though the new Duchess of York was markedly unsympathetic, her husband – who had been a regular guest at Marble Hill before marrying his Prussian princess in September 1791 – continued to visit her on his own.[33] Even George's uncle the Duke of Gloucester behaved chivalrously, and in May 1787 sent Maria a gift accompanied by an assurance of his support.

Brighton, too, maintained its loyalty to the woman who had made the fast-developing town her second home. On 30 July 1795 Lady Spencer wrote to the Duchess of Devonshire that 'a stuffed mawkin [scarecrow] with a feather had been carried round about two days before with Lady J— written at full length upon it, and it was afterwards burnt'. Even seven years after George IV's death the issue was still very much alive: the *Brighton Gazette* controversially reminded its readers that Mrs Fitzherbert 'was one of the first persons who attracted good company to Brighton', and that to her 'undoubtedly were due many of the first advantages possessed by this town'. (In reply to the *Gazette*'s airing of this sensitive subject, *The Times* fulminated pompously against those who were prepared to 'risk the honour of a deceased Sovereign, and the respect due to the Crown of England, by even an allusion to an event which every friend of monarchy, in the abstract or in the individual, must wish buried in oblivion'.) [34]

At Carlton House, Lady Jersey was now firmly in the ascendant, even as George prepared to marry Caroline of Brunswick. She was not, however, any more popular in London than in Brighton. Hissed and insulted on the streets – where walls were soon daubed with the graffiti 'No Lady Jersey' – her insults to the new Princess of Wales were widely reported and her husband's rapid advancement extensively ridiculed. Vivacious, wilful and beautiful, mother of eight and a grandmother, nakedly ambitious and strikingly seductive, she stirred passionate responses in her contemporaries, to whom she was alternately a 'bitch' ('a regrettable epithet for a bishop's daughter to attract', as Flora Fraser has commented), the personification of vain ambition, or a goddess. Two decades after her moment of glory, Farington gleefully noted the Countess's horror at being thought 'old and ugly', but James Gillray had depicted her in this guise as early as 1796, in his celebrated cartoon showing her as a wizened old crone awaiting the arrival of her corpulent Prince, who was riding to bed on the back of his new Master of the Horse, Lord Jersey. Huish later likened her to a serpent: 'beautiful, bright and glossy in its exterior – in its interior, poisonous and pestiferous'. Even in the twentieth century her reputation aroused strong opinions. Maria Fitzherbert's biographer designated her 'the most hated and abused woman in England'. Roger Fulford was more subtle in his condemnation: 'Lady Jersey was a skilled harpist, though by character she was perhaps ill-suited to twang this heavenly instrument.'[35]

His parents and the rest of the nation wanted the Prince of Wales to marry; as Sir James Harris had pompously but perceptively observed to him in 1784, 'till you are married, Sir, and have children, you have no solid hold on the affections of the people'. Home-grown candidates, among them dukes' daughters such as Lady Mary Osborne and Lady Charlotte Spencer and, more controversially, the Earl of Jersey's daughter Lady Caroline Villiers, were considered, though not very seriously, and dismissed. (Not surprisingly, perhaps, the Villiers match was George's own suggestion; in 1795 Lady Caroline married Henry Paget, future Waterloo hero, whom she divorced in 1810.) Fortified by his lust for Lady Jersey, George set about the business of choosing a bride from one of the Protestant states of Europe, in a denigrating parade of potential breeding stock which aroused sympathy for his plight even in the caustic Huish:

> That the heir apparent to the throne of a free country should be compelled, against his inclinations, to unite his destiny with an individual whom he did not love, is a circumstance which the statesman, the moralist, and the philanthropist must deplore.[36]

Princess Louise of Mecklenburg-Strelitz was rejected as unsuitable ostensibly because, as Queen Charlotte's niece, she was a close relative. In retrospect she, or even Lady Caroline Villiers, might have fared very well. The young woman finally settled upon, Princess Caroline of Brunswick-Wolfenbüttel (oddly, a niece of George III), was undoubtedly one of the worst choices that could have been made for a Prince so hypersensitive, finicky and faithless. Six years younger than George and brought up in the small and surprisingly lax Court of a minor German state, she had been allowed considerable freedom: as a result, London's polite circles considered her conversation salacious and vulgar, while her personal hygiene was not all that it should have been.

Inevitably, Caroline was widely rumoured to have been Lady

Jersey's choice – a tale Wellington later repeated, declaring that the Countess had chosen Caroline for her 'indelicate manners, indifferent character, and not very inviting appearance, from the hope that disgust for the wife would secure constancy to the mistress'. He additionally suggested that one of Lady Jersey's motives had been to reduce Maria Fitzherbert to the same level as herself. According to Farington, however, current gossip had it that 'the Prince was not induced to marry by Lady Jersey' but 'in consequence of violent quarrels with Mrs Fitzherbert'. George III, on the other hand, later told Lord Liverpool that his son, being extremely impatient to secure a marriage in order to have his debts paid off by Parliament, had chosen Caroline largely because her father was the Duke of Brunswick, who had recently led the allied armies against the revolutionary French and 'whose military, political and private character he admired'.[37]

In November 1794 Lord Malmesbury was sent to collect the bride-to-be from Brunswick. Initially he was diplomatically noncommittal, declaring that she had a 'pretty face – not expressive of softness – her figure not graceful – fine eyes – good hand – tolerable teeth, but going ... good bust, but with what the French call "*des épaules impertinentes*".' Meanwhile George, with astonishing effrontery (and with the scheming Queen Charlotte's blessing), appointed Lady Jersey one of Caroline's Ladies of the Bedchamber, while Lady Jersey succeeded in having her friends Mrs Pelham and Mrs Aston appointed Women of the Bedchamber. As a later commentator (possibly Robert Huish) wrote: 'What could be said for any man in private life, who should choose for the escort of his bride one of his former mistresses; who should place that mistress as an attendant on his young wife; should point her out as a sort of instructress in the ways of her newly-acquired country?' Learning of Lady Jersey and her machinations, Caroline bravely told Malmesbury: 'I am determined never to appear jealous. I know the Prince is *léger*, and am prepared on this point.'[38]

Caroline arrived at Greenwich on 5 April 1795. Lady Jersey kept her waiting an hour before presenting herself to greet her, then proceeded to belittle her appearance. She even attempted to sit in the position of honour in the carriage – claiming that she would feel sick if she sat with her back to the horses – and was only prevented from delivering this significant slight to the future Princess of Wales by Malmesbury's intervention. He himself was evidently growing increasingly anxious about Caroline's attitude and behaviour, confiding to his diary that he thought she had 'no fixed character [and] a light and flighty mind, but meaning well' and observing that 'my eternal theme to her is *to think before she speaks, to recollect herself*'. A few months later Malmesbury's patience was clearly becoming exhausted: his diary relates that he had repeatedly argued with the Princess 'on the toilette, on cleanliness, and on delicacy of speaking'.[39]

George , on meeting Caroline for the first time at St James's Palace, bade her rise from her curtsey, muttering memorably: 'Harris, I am not well; pray get me a glass of brandy.' Malmesbury had the presence of mind to suggest water instead; the Prince, however, left the room immediately, announcing that he was going to visit his mother. Not unnaturally, Caroline asked Malmesbury, 'Does the Prince always act like this?' and observed (in French), 'I think he's very fat, and he's nothing like as handsome as his portrait.' Malmesbury's diplomatic but unconvincing reply was that 'His Royal Highness was a good deal affected and flurried at his first interview, but she certainly would find him different at dinner.' That evening Caroline attempted to retaliate with 'flippant, rattling . . . sarcasms and vulgar hints about Lady Jersey', and what the unbending Malmesbury described in his diary as 'giddy manners and silly attempts at cleverness and coarse joking'.[40]

From the moment of their initial meeting George treated Caroline with disdain and rudeness. His calculated insults were undoubtedly extremely hurtful to a young woman 'who had as yet conducted herself with the utmost decorum and propriety'. More than thirty years later – and a decade after her death – Caroline's blatantly ungenerous treatment at his hands was still capable of infuriating commentators. In reviewing the quickly-penned panegyrics of the late King by H. E. Lloyd and George Croly in 1831, for example, the anonymous correspondent of *The Westminster Review* (the prose style suggests he was Robert Huish) contrasted the 'artificial courtesy' generally displayed by George towards women with 'his neglect of his wife'.[41]

The disaster of the marriage ceremony is a familiar story. At the wedding itself, staged in Inigo Jones's Chapel Royal on 8 April, the groom was visibly drunk and almost passed out twice. During his carriage ride to the chapel in the company of his confidants Cornet George Brummell and Lord Moira, the Prince professed his undying love for Maria Fitzherbert, a sentiment he had earlier vouchsafed to his brother William. At the altar, completely inebriated, 'he hiccupped out his vows of fidelity' while turning to gaze meaningfully at Lady Jersey and, in the anxious silence after the Archbishop of Canterbury asked whether anyone knew of 'any just cause or impediment', burst into tears. (The Archbishop was plainly terrified lest the rumoured marriage to Mrs Fitzherbert be divulged at this point: he stared directly at the Prince as he enunciated the word 'impediment', and repeated the passage regarding 'nuptial fidelity' twice.) Some hours later George became unconscious and, according to Caroline, 'passed the greatest part of his bridal-night under the grate, where he fell'.[42]

The honeymoon at Windsor and at Kempshott in Hampshire was, by Caroline's later account (and as might have been expected), a disaster. Kempshott, George's hunting retreat, was hardly the setting for a romantic idyll such as most newlyweds contemplate. The Prince had invited a number of his drinking companions, who allegedly lay about the house, 'constantly drunk and filthy, sleeping and snoring in boots on the sofas'. However, his friend and mentor George Brummell is recorded as recollecting it differently: 'He said nothing could go off better; that "the young couple appeared perfectly satisfied with each other, particularly the Princess: she was then a very handsome and desirable-looking woman".'[43] At some point during these few days George at least sobered up sufficiently to perform his dynastic duty and conceive a royal heir with the bewildered Princess (Gillray had pictured Caroline approaching her honeymoon bed to find Lady Jersey already there). Months later George ungallantly told Malmesbury how appalled he had been at the scars on the Princess's neck and thighs, and by the fact that, in his view, 'her manners were not those of a novice'. In a typical piece of male braggadocio he also recalled that Caroline had gasped, 'Ah mon dieu qu'il est gros!' In the weeks following his honeymoon he ostentatiously failed to attend his parents' celebration of his marriage, then invited Lady Jersey – but not his new wife – to accompany him on his next visit to Kempshott. Caroline later told Lord Minto that their period of genuine co-habitation had lasted only two or three weeks.[44]

Caroline was by no means everyone's idea of the perfect royal bride. Lord Malmesbury, horrified to receive as a mark of gratitude a tooth she had recently had pulled, subsequently judged that 'She had quick parts, without a sound or distinguishing understanding; a ready conception, but no judgement; caught by the first impression, led by the first impulse, turned away by appearances [and] loving to talk'; he also acknowledged her 'great good humour and much good nature'. She often dressed inappropriately – Farington later noted that she exhibited 'too much of her naked person'. It may have been his physical 'disgust of her person' which most discouraged George. Even in preparing for their first meeting on 5 April 1795, Caroline apparently ignored Malmesbury's advice to 'wash all over', and smelt horribly. As Saul David has discovered, a year after his marriage George confided to Malmesbury that on the three nights on which he admitted to having sexual relations with her, 'she showed ... such marks of filth both in the fore and *hind* part of her ... that she turned my stomach and from that moment I made a vow *never to touch her again*'. Nevertheless Richard Cosway, a fastidious man, 'spoke highly of her beauty and manners' and flatly declared that 'The Prince does not know Her'.[45]

Lady Charlotte Bury, who as the widowed Lady Charlotte Campbell was in 1809 appointed a Lady-in-Waiting in the Princess of Wales's household, later wrote that, from the moment she arrived, the Prince 'took every opportunity of wounding the Princess, by showing her that Lady Jersey was her rival. The ornaments with which he had decked his wife's arms, he took from her and gave to his mistress, who wore them in her presence.' Returning to London after the honeymoon, Caroline found there was, apparently, no room at Carlton House for the majority of her servants, and when she went to Brighton Pavilion (which, in its neo-classical incarnation, she admired), her Maids of Honour were dismissed without explanation. Lady Jersey, meanwhile, was continually in attendance, and gleefully advertised that she saw much more of the Prince, in every sense, than did his wife. Caroline even spent her pregnancy largely shut up with Lady Jersey. As early as July 1795 she was evidently dejected. 'I do not know how I shall bear the loneliness,' she miserably confided to a German friend; 'the Queen seldom visits me, and my sisters-in-law show me the same sympathy, [while] The Countess is still here. I hate her, and I know she feels the same towards me. My husband is wholly given up to her ...'[46] When on 7 January 1796 Caroline gave birth to a daughter, named Charlotte in honour of the Queen who had barely addressed her, George's reaction was cold indifference. To some observers it seemed as if he were more interested in the welfare of Lady Jersey's son, born four months previously. Whether the Prince, Lord Jersey or another was the boy's father is a matter of speculation.

By March 1796 George had resolved to separate from his wife, railing at Malmesbury about 'how I have been deceived, how I have been treated' and declaring he could not 'dwell under the same roof' as Caroline.[47] Conjuring up a barrage of slights and slanders which had never occurred he proffered them as evidence of his wife's preposterous nature and his own suffering. As to their correspondence, in May he told Caroline that 'this really is the last attempt I can make' (proclaiming that 'the discussion is too painful to be continued'), and warned his mother of the Princess's 'impracticable temper' – a fault more recognisable in himself. His astounding allegations included the assertion that Caroline was a 'designing woman' who sought to establish 'a decided political superiority in this country ... by the degradation of my character'. In a shameless bid to win his mother's attention and confidence he even suggested that she was a tool of Maria Fitzherbert's supporters. He also had the audacity to protest at Caroline's objections to Lady Jersey, 'a woman whom I declared on your arrival not to be my mistress, as you indecorously term her, but a friend to whom I am attached by the strong ties of habitude, esteem and respect'. When the Princess was enthusiastically applauded by Mrs Fitzherbert's friends at the opera on 28 May, he intemperately denounced her to the Queen as 'the vilest wretch [that the world] was ever curs'd with', and a 'monster of iniquity' having an 'entire want of all principle'. He even went so far as to suggest that any failure on his parents' part to support him in his dispute with his wife would result in a repetition of the recent events on the other side of the Channel:

> If the King does not now manage to throw some stigma, and one very strong mark of disapprobation upon the Princess, this worthless wretch will prove the ruin of him, of you, of me, of every one of us. The King must be resolute and firm, or everything is at an end. Let him recall to his mind the want of firmness of Louis 16 ... [and that] for the want of that true spirit everything fail'd in France.[48]

Later that year – for the first but not for the last time – George chillingly denied even that Princess Charlotte was his child.[49]

George III refused to entertain the idea of a formal separation, but his attempts to make of his eldest son's ruined marriage anything approaching the civilised, warm and respectful relationship he enjoyed with his own wife were doomed. Revealingly, it was the father and not the son who commissioned portraits of Caroline in her wedding robes. Like the marriage it was designed to celebrate, however, Gainsborough Dupont's picture was dogged with ill-luck: the frame was not ready in time for it to be exhibited at the Royal Academy in 1796, and it was not shown the following year because

Dupont had since died. Similarly fated was William Hamilton's wedding picture, which was still in gestation in February 1797; alleg-edly, Hamilton needed to borrow the coat George had worn at the cer-emony – yet 'so unpleasant is the subject supposed to be, nobody will ask the Prince for it'.[50]

In retrospect, it might have been better for the reputation of the royal family if the King had given in, and promulgated a divorce as quickly as possible. In May 1796 Farington heard a report that Caroline had demanded of the Lord Chancellor 'either to be sent to her own Country, or to be separated from the Prince here; or to be treated with more respect in her own house'. In the meantime, further abusing her position as the Princess's Lady of the Bedchamber, Lady Jersey intercepted her private letters. These came into George's hands and he, finding in them 'such a description of Lady Jersey as She [Caroline] merits', stormed into the Princess's apartments for the first time in weeks and lectured her 'with endeavouring to destroy the char-acter of Lady Jersey' – as if any such endeavour were necessary. Lady Jersey, however, was it seems beginning to overestimate her influence. Chafing at her public unpopularity, she sent her husband to seek an audience of the King; but he foolishly embroidered his case to such an extent (at one point swearing that Lady Jersey 'had been a most faithful and virtuous wife') that he left George III cackling with incre-dulity. What little sympathy the King had had for Lady Jersey had evaporated, and on 29 June 1796 he acceded to an ultimatum from his daughter-in-law and obliged the Countess to resign from her flagrantly anomalous position in the Princess of Wales's household.[51]

Lady Jersey was not finished yet, but even *The Times* censured her malicious letter of resignation as 'one of the most disrespectful we ever recollect to have read':

> Her Ladyship begins by stating that her wish was to have resigned long since, but that his Royal Highness would not suffer it on the ground that it would only tend to justify the calumnies reported of her. She then insin-uates who the person is who has propagated all the scandal against her, and concludes by assuring the Princess she shall to the last moment of her life be proud to serve the Prince of Wales. Throughout the letter there is not one word of respect towards her Royal Highness.[52]

For the time being, however, Lady Jersey could still count on George's slavish adoration. The day after her resignation, she met him in secret at Brighton; that September they escaped together for a few days of illicit pleasure in Bognor. According to Lady Jersey, the Prince intended to buy her an estate near Wimborne in Dorset – far away from the cat-calls of the London mob – and spend Christmas with her there. This plan never came to fruition, but the Jerseys were soon installed next door to Carlton House, from where George was able to reach his mistress 'by a private way'. Even the Queen could not believe the newspaper stories reporting this move, 'as [she stated with exaggerated irony] I have formed a great oppinion of your prudence'.[53] Nevertheless, both King and Queen lamely agreed to support George's insulting proposal to limit his wife's travel.

Rumours concerning Caroline's treatment at the hands of her husband and his mistress were soon rife. 'The behaviour of the Prince and Lady Jersey towards the Princess is spoken of as having been most scandalous,' reported Farington from Brighton in the summer of 1796; 'They sometimes mixed brandy with her wine intending to affect her, and then would laugh on the Stein [*sic*] (the walk) at the Princess being drunk.' Caroline stood up to it all remarkably well, clearly a girl of spirit. When the Duke of Leeds warned her during an opera performance that assassins lurked nearby, she wittily answered: 'When the daughter of a hero marries a zero, she does not fear gunfire.'[54]

It was only a matter of time before George wearied of the carnal attractions of Lady Jersey, however. By the end of 1797 the satirists were documenting liaisons with one Honor Gubbins of Bath, with Eliza Crole, and with the Duchess of Manchester. 'Some say she is youngish and pretty,' said Lady Stafford of Mrs Crole, 'others that she is oldish, fat and looks like a good House-Keeper.'[55] His mind had also been returning to past loves. Only days after the birth of his daughter – at a time when he was supposedly still enamoured of Lady Jersey – he had dictated his bizarre will of 10 January 1796. Imagining himself already dead, in the overwrought language of a cheap novel he assured 'my Maria, my wife, my soul' – 'my real and true Wife ... infamously traduced' – that:

> ... round thee shall my souls for ever hover as thy guardian angel, for as I never ceased to adore thee whilst living, so shall I ever be watchful over thee and protect thee against every evil. farewell, dearest angel, if I must quit thee and the whole world ... be it so ... but think of thy DEPARTED HUSBAND, shed a tear o'er his memory and his grave, and then recollect that no woman ever yet was loved or adored by man as you were and are by him.

By the terms of the will, Maria was to receive everything, while 'to her who is call'd the Princess of Wales I leave one shilling'.[56] George's actions were often attributable to a passion for self-publicising histrionics, but in this instance he controlled his habitual indiscretion enough to keep the will's terms a secret from Maria for three years. Its over-emotional prose seems more a product of excessive self-pity at having been forced (by his own indebtedness) to marry against his better judgement.

Two and a half years later, in August 1798, George suddenly sent Colonel MacMahon to Maria Fitzherbert with a request that they should kiss and make up. Recent commentators have suggested he was fearful that Mrs Fitzherbert was on the point of revealing the details of their marriage in 1785, but worries on that score are unlikely to have provoked such an emotional offensive. He professed to Maria that his relationship with Lady Jersey was over – 'so far that I think there is but little probability of my even visiting there in a common way much more' – and in 1799 advertised his new-found resolve by dismissing the Earl of Jersey as his Master of the Horse, on the spurious grounds of economy. The Countess herself was swiftly dropped, and George was subsequently furious with Lady Bessborough merely for visiting the Jerseys' son when he was very ill.[57]

At first, wisely, Maria held back. Her restraint prompted George to reveal the terms of the 1796 will and to shower her with presents – including, typically, a Cosway miniature of himself (or, rather, of one of his eyes) and a bracelet incised with the characteristically melodramatic legend *Rejoindre ou mourir*. A report that Maria had died in Bath left the Prince, in his own words, 'bereft of all sense'. The rambling letter he wrote her on 12 June 1800, after discovering the rumour to be untrue, was penned almost entirely in capitals and tediously repetitive (an increasingly common feature of his later correspondence). It was more like the rantings of a Bedlam patient than the confession of love of a prince in his late thirties. Once again George raised the possibility of his own suicide, shamelessly exerting emotional blackmail on the woman he had cheerfully abandoned for Lady Jersey:

IF YOU WISH MY LIFE YOU SHALL HAVE IT ... You know not what you will drive me to FROM DESPAIR, YOU KNOW YOU ARE MY WIFE, THE WIFE OF MY HEART AND SOUL, MY WIFE IN THE PRESENCE OF MY GOD: 'TIS THE ONLY ONLY REPRIEVE LEFT ... The wretched experiences of the last five years have MADE LIFE ONLY DESIRABLE IN ONE SHAPE TO ME, AND THAT IS IN YOU. I AM WRAPPED UP IN YOU ENTIRELY ... NOTHING CAN ALTER ME, SHAKE ME OR CHANGE ME. ALIKE YOURS IN LIFE AND DEATH ... YOU SHALL FIX MY DOOM.[58]

Helped rather by the intercession of his brother and Maria's friend, the Duke of Kent, than by his own rambling prose, George was formally reconciled with Mrs Fitzherbert within days. They celebrated the occasion with a party on 16 June 1800 which they referred to half-jokingly as their 'wedding breakfast'. Exhibiting a notable lack of diplomacy and tact – or perhaps to revenge herself on the King – the 'bride' invited a number of her Catholic friends and relations. This doubly enraged George III, who was not only rabidly anti-Catholic but also furious about Maria's readmittance into his eldest son's life.

Maria's relationship with her 'husband' never afterwards attained the same stability it had enjoyed fifteen years before, even though in the meantime, at Maria's request, the Pope had secretly confirmed her as the Prince's canonical wife. ('Time was to reveal, as usual,' Arthur Aspinall judged pertinently in 1967, 'the worthlessness of [George's] protestations.'[59]) In the ensuing years Maria tried not to presume too much. She continued to live alone at Brighton until 1811, and was only resident in the Pavilion itself during one of the Prince's bouts of illness in 1804.[60] She did enlist George's support after 1802 to regain the guardianship of Minney Seymour – whom she regarded as an adopted daughter, and many believed to be his child. (In ensuring that she remained with Maria, incidentally, George completely ignored the wishes of Minney's dead parents.) However, Maria was not blind to George's character and, determined to avoid the fate of various previously discarded and now penniless mistresses, encouraged him to raise her annual pension from £3,000 to £6,000.[61]

By 1807 the relationship was beginning to crumble, and Maria found herself being used to distract attention from George's embarrassingly obvious infatuation with the matronly Lady Hertford. She was now invited to Carlton House or to Brighton Pavilion merely 'to preserve Lady Hertford's reputation' – which all but the Prince recognised was already in tatters. Shane Leslie has suggested that 'It must have been a relief for Mrs Fitzherbert to find so collapsible a lover slowly drifting from her'; yet in truth Maria was understandably bitter over this new rival. Her first biographer observed how, so as not to offend Lady Hertford, 'When at Brighton, the Prince, who had passed part of his mornings with Mrs Fitzherbert on friendly terms at her own house, did not even notice her in the slightest manner at the Pavilion on the same evenings.'[62]

By the end of 1809 the breach between the Prince of Wales and his Catholic 'wife' was fully apparent. This did not necessarily mean, however, that Lady Hertford was the sole recipient of George's wayward affections. Hearing, for example, that Lady Bessborough had been deserted by her former lover, he cast himself at her in ridiculous fashion. 'Such a scene I never went through,' wrote Lady Bessborough later, recalling the spectacle of 'that immense, grotesque figure flouncing about half on the couch, half on the ground' who then

> threw himself on his knees, and clasping me round, kissed my neck before I was aware of what he was doing ... sometimes struggling with me, sometimes sobbing and crying ... The mixing abuse of you [her current lover, Lord Granville], vows of eternal love, entreaties and prom- ises of what he would do – he would break with Mrs F and Lady H, I should make my own terms!! I should be his sole confidant, sole adviser – private or public – I should guide his politics, Mr Canning should be Prime Minister (whether in this reign or the next ...); then over and over and over again the same round of complaint, despair, entreaties and promises ...

Lady Bessborough never forgot this farcical display.[63] Meanwhile, on 18 December 1809 Maria Fitzherbert sent George a 'farewell' letter expressing her determination not to subject herself to further humil- iations at his hands or those of his factotum Bloomfield, a letter which left a faint whiff of blackmail hanging in the air:

> The very great incivilities I have received these two years just because I obeyed your orders in going [to Brighton Pavilion] was too visible to everyone present and too poignantly felt by me to admit of my putting myself in a situation of again being treated with such indignity, for what- ever may be thought of me by some individuals, it is well known Y R H four-and-twenty years ago placed me in a situation so nearly connected with your own that I have a claim upon you for protection. I feel I owe it to myself not to be insulted under your roof with impunity. The influence you are now under, and the conduct of one of your servants, I am sorry to say, has the appearance of your sanction and support, and renders my situation in your house, situated as I am, impossible any longer to submit to.[64]

Maria's final humiliation at Carlton House in 1811 was widely observed and commented upon. Arriving for a dinner in honour of the exiled Louis XVIII, she found herself placed not on George's right, as had been his custom, but seated strictly according to prece- dence, far lower down the table. When she queried this arrangement, she was brusquely informed: 'You know, Madam, you have no place.' Maria left immediately, afterwards soothing her wounded dignity by announcing that she would never again 'submit to appear in your house in any place or situation but in that where you yourself first placed me many years ago'. Shortly afterwards she retired to Sherwood Lodge in Battersea and never returned to the Pavilion during George IV's lifetime, although Minney Seymour continued to be invited there.[65]

It is pleasant to note that Maria was not abandoned by her friends following this very public rejection. Once again George's brothers rallied round, both Kent and Sussex risking the Prince's wrath by remaining in frequent correspondence with her. While she was out of favour in 1798, the Duke of Kent had bought her a house, Castle Hill in Ealing; now, in January 1812, he wrote her a delightful letter promising his steadfast support. George, predictably, was never as mindful of his obligations to his 'wife'. In 1825 he went so far as to deny any knowledge of his 'supposed marriage' to an incredulous John Croker, who had previously observed that Maria Fitzherbert's presence in Brighton (at her own house) was considered by the King's circle to be both 'indelicate' and 'embarrassing to herself'. In spite of everything, however, Mrs Fitzherbert remained (in the words of Prince Pückler-Muskau in 1827) 'a very dignified and delightful woman' who was 'still universally beloved and respected' – something which could not be said of her sovereign.[66] Although she appeared genuinely upset by George's death in 1830, her annual pension was possibly more of a consolation than the revelation that the old reprobate had been buried with Cosway's miniature of her fastened around his neck.

Maria Fitzherbert was fortunate in her financial settlement, since George was notoriously bad about securing promised pensions for his rejected mistresses. Even she, however, felt obliged to complain to him about the vagueness of the financial provisions made for her after 1811, implying that he was reneging on previously-agreed arrangements.[67] And she was by no means the only former mistress to protest against her treatment. After numerous entreaties, her old rival Lady Jersey finally managed to extract a sum of money from George in 1813 (only to carp about 'how much I am distressed that what you sent came from a very different fund than I intended'). She subsequently made persistent attempts to secure a formal pension, moaning to the Prince in December 1813 that 'I have only £700 per annum which considering my former situation will scarcely afford me the necessaries of life'. In the meantime, George warned his daughter's Household against the evils even of speaking to her. 'He had observed Lady Jersey talking to Princess Charlotte the night before the ball, and said he did not choose she should be too intimate at Warwick House', declaring his close acquaintance with 'all the wickedness, perseverance and trick of that infernal Jezabel Lady Jersey, and of all her Jacobinal set of connexions'.[68] It will be recalled that Anna Maria Crouch, promised much during their brief liaison, was actually given a bond in the Prince's hand. Years later, Nathaniel Wraxall recorded how George, coldly calculating, sent Jack Payne to try to negotiate, or if necessary purchase, the return of the bond. Payne succeeded, paying the wretched Mrs Crouch only 1,000 guineas – considerably less than he had expected to have to give.[69]

Mrs Fitzherbert's replacement – Isabella, Marchioness of Hertford – was two years older than George and thus four years younger than Maria, having turned fifty in 1810. Originally she came to his attention during the battle over the guardianship of Minney Seymour, who was a distant relation. In 1806 Maria Fitzherbert won her case with the help of the Hertfords, who were nominated Minney's formal guardians, Maria being named only as their deputy. Maria herself had involved the Prince in the affair, bringing him into frequent contact with Isabella, who rapidly established a firmer hold on his affections than Mrs Fitzherbert was now able to maintain. Soon he was completely obsessed. In October 1807 Lady Bessborough was noting that he 'frets himself into a fever ... to persuade [Lady Hertford] *to live with him – publickly*!!' (Nor, incidentally, was Lady Bessborough the only contemporary to observe that the Prince's 'fretting', whether over Lady Hertford or the redecoration of Carlton House, was ominously reminiscent of his father's 'madness'.[70]) By 1811 it was clear to those close to him that the scheming Isabella (now privately designated 'Madame Maintenon', after the celebrated mistress of Louis XIV) had 'completely swayed the voluptuary of Carlton House', who was said 'to seek her company daily'. The caricaturists were a little slower off the mark; it was five years before they began to include her in their satires. The first print to feature Lady Hertford, published in February 1812, showed the Regent reclining against her knees, fast asleep, while she, as Delilah, prepared to shear off his Whig 'locks'.[71]

Like George, the Hertfords were keenly interested in paintings and in the decorative arts in general. Indeed, as we shall see, the passion of

Lady Hertford's son, Lord Yarmouth, for contemporary French furniture and seventeenth-century Dutch and Flemish pictures played its part in his own collecting. Yarmouth had in 1798 married Maria, daughter of the Marchesa Fagniani and either George's old drinking crony the fourth Duke of Queensberry or the wit and politician George Seymour, both of whom left her large sums. During the brief Peace of Amiens Yarmouth was in Paris, more with the object of buying paintings than of furthering Britain's diplomatic interests; when war with France resumed in 1803 he found himself imprisoned in the fortress of Verdun. George's personal intervention secured his release in 1806, and also helped to bring about a reconciliation with his parents, to whom he had not spoken for five years before his incarceration.

As early as December 1807 George admitted his reliance on Lady Hertford to his Private Secretary; Bloomfield, inexplicably, relayed the information to Lord Hertford. Without her by his side, George tended to wallow in self-pity, 'hardly speaking to friends, and sometimes sitting dumb and tearful in Carlton House for hours at a time'. Instead of the suicide threats with which he had attempted to win Maria Fitzherbert, the royal hypochondriac now indulged himself in (or perhaps simulated) a state of profound depression. Colonel Bloomfield wrote, at a time when the affairs of Britain and the rest of Europe were being decided on the battlefields of Spain and Austria, that the Prince Regent 'scarcely speaks a word' and was 'plung'd into a state of apathy and indifference towards himself'.[72]

George's fascination with Lady Hertford mystified many. While she was generally acknowledged to be remarkably attractive for a woman approaching fifty, commentators such as Mrs Calvert declared her 'the most forbidding, haughty, unpleasant-looking woman' they had ever met.[73] However, the Hertfords were more than comfortably off, so there was unlikely to be any undignified begging for pensions when the affair ended. In addition, as a grandmother Lady Hertford provided the Prince with a large, instant family, to which he could be as distant or as affectionate as the whim took him. Additionally, her political beliefs appeared to reflect George's developing conservatism. No Whig herself, she undoubtedly encouraged him to retain Perceval's Tory government at the beginning of his Regency in 1811–12, and effectively distanced him from those old Whig friends who still came to call at Carlton House. More bizarrely, she was even alleged to have 'infused some methodistical notions into the Prince's mind'.

The caricaturists were quick to make much of Lady Hertford's size, age and influence. As early as 1795 Isaac Cruickshank had illuminated George's apparent penchant for fat, middle-aged women, and the Marchioness's generous proportions, particularly when united with the portly figure of the Prince himself, presented an ideal subject for the cartoonists of the day. By 1812 Isaac Cruikshank was depicting Lady Hertford as a full-figured mermaid–siren, captivating the 'Prince of Whales' while her husband struggled to contain his cuckold's horns. Thereafter she was seen in motherly guise dandling the Regent as the Great Babe; as a political umpire deciding the fate of the 'ministerial races'; as an obese ghost whispering instructions into the sleeping Regent's ear; and as Pandora. A popular and much-imitated George Cruikshank print of August 1816 saw the Regent as a bomb, his sexual excesses liable to cause himself and his partner to explode at any moment. By the end of the Regency Cruikshank was picturing George transformed into a hobby-horse, his mistress astride, tugging on a bridle attached to the royal mouth. In subsequent prints these two images became fused, and Lady Hertford sat astride the Regent's Bomb.[74] In this context, George's gift to Lady Hertford in 1818 of Gainsborough's full-length portrait of 'Perdita' Robinson was perhaps a little unwise. While it could be seen as a well-chosen present from one connoisseur to another, the difference in girth and in age between Mary Robinson and Lady Hertford could hardly have been more pronounced. However complacent she felt, the Marchioness must have been aware of an unwelcome contrast.

Shortly after making Lady Hertford this present, George once again transferred his affections. Prior to his accession he was the subject of rumours linking him to numerous aristocratic women, among them the duchesses of Richmond and Marlborough.[75] Other satirists resurrected old flames such as Mrs Quentin.[76] In truth George had fallen for another portly, middle-aged woman: Elizabeth, Lady Conyngham, born a banker's daughter and fifty years old in 1820. Her former lover Lord Ponsonby had, interestingly, been involved with Lady Jersey some years before; her other past paramours, it was rumoured, had included the future Tsar Nicholas I, whom she captivated during his visit to England in 1816. In February 1819 Lady Charlotte Bury declared confidently that 'Lady Hertford's influence is quite at an end' and that 'Lady Conyngham is now the reigning favourite of the Regent'. As before, however, people in general were not immediately aware of George's fresh attachment. In a print of summer 1820 the satirist Lewis Marks, for example, was still portraying Lady Hertford as the new King's *éminence grise*, while in the tumult following his attempt to divorce Caroline of Brunswick it was Lady Hertford's windows rather than the Conynghams' that were smashed by the mob.[77]

By the time of his coronation George's relationship with Lady Conyngham was being conducted in public. Their juvenile behaviour encouraging contemporaries to liken them to elephantine stage lovers. Mrs Arbuthnot was disgusted by the kisses they sent one another in the middle of the coronation ceremony; she observed, too, that all the pages had been selected by Lady Conyngham. Princess Lieven was another who regarded their openly-expressed affection with distaste, but she saw it as part of the King's overall deterioration – noting that 'two smacking kisses' for each lady was now 'etiquette at official audiences'.[78] Lord Conyngham, like Lord Hertford before him, proved remarkably accommodating, and was assigned all Hertford's Court offices in return for his complaisance. Having successfully begged his Irish marquessate in 1816, he clearly saw his wife's affair as an effective path to advancement.

It was being widely asserted by early 1821 that the two love-birds were inseparable. Many observers, indeed, thought the principal reason for George's journey to Ireland in the summer of 1821 was to visit the Conynghams' Slane Castle. Countess Granville had told Lady Morpeth in February of that year that 'the King is more in love with your friend [Lady Conyngham] than ever ... and ... sits kissing her hand with a look of the most devoted submission'; six months later she declared that 'he is jealous of her as a boy of fifteen would be, and pouts and sulks if she does not follow him from room to room'.[79] Except for the size of his motherly mistresses, George's passive-submissive relationship with them was not unlike that between the Duke and Duchess of Windsor more than a century later; it helped to popularise the widely-touted caricatures of him as a child, or The Great Babe.

Lady Conyngham herself was charitably described by one observer as looking like Maria Fitzherbert when she was young. She was indeed candidly labelled by one cheerful cartoon of 1826 as 'Fair, Fat and Fifty', a conscious echo of the depiction of Mrs Fitzherbert forty years before as 'Fat, Fair and Forty'. Other satirists, as we shall see, were more brutal. Lady Conyngham's well-deserved reputation for avarice was savagely illuminated by artists such as Paul Pry, who depicted her in his *Sketch of a Lady – Playing with a Sovereign* of July 1829 perusing the lines 'When Kissing and Cooing and toying are done, 'Tis Gold must enliven the lover.' Her greedy appropriation of the priceless Stuart Sapphire which had belonged to Princess Charlotte and her venal conduct after George's death certainly seemed to vindicate these rumours. However, she did eventually have the grace – or perhaps the sense – to return the sapphire, which, she now realised (as she commented with a fine throwaway carelessness), 'his late Majesty ought [not] to have given away'.[80]

Lady Conyngham's influence was more pernicious than her predecessor's. Not for nothing was she being hailed as the 'Vice Queen' by the time of George's accession. In 1821 she attempted to have her children's former tutor, the Reverend Charles Sumner, appointed to a vacant canonry at St George's Chapel, Windsor. Although frustrated in her endeavours by Lord Liverpool's obstinate opposition, she did succeed in obtaining for Sumner first a canonry at Worcester Cathedral and later the bishopric of Llandaff.[81] More significantly, she also engineered the replacement of Sir Benjamin Bloomfield (himself Lady Hertford's nominee in 1817) as the King's Private Secretary by the silky physician Sir William Knighton. In January 1822 – reportedly at the behest of Lady Conyngham – George was contemplating Bloomfield's 'retirement', and suggested the Governor-Generalship of Ceylon as a fitting reward for his secretary's 'long, meritorious and faithful service'. Disingenuously proposing to Liverpool that the office of the King's Private Secretary might now be abolished altogether, he proposed that Bloomfield be given a title in the Irish peerage – an idea received unfavourably by the Prime Minister, who maintained that 'Irish honours should be confined to services and *personal consequence* in Ireland'.[82] Unsurprisingly, Bloomfield rejected the opportunity of expiring from disease in faraway Asia, and 'with considerable pertinacity', as Liverpool told the King on 7 March, continued to argue for an English title rather than a second-rate Irish peerage. Bloomfield certainly had as much right to an English peerage as any of the aristocratic numbskulls whom George had promoted or ennobled since 1820, even if his grasp of finance had been somewhat shaky, but his years of toil for the most capricious of royal masters suddenly counted for nothing. George's reaction to Bloomfield's plea was chillingly impersonal: 'I agree with you fully as to the impropriety of the English Peerage being granted,' he wrote to Liverpool, 'and never approved of it when his wishes on the subject were hinted to me.' He later explained to the Prime Minister that 'I could no longer with any prospect of comfort to myself go on with Sir Benjamin Bloomfield upon those terms of entire confidence and intimacy with which I had lived with him for many years' – a shameful abandonment of a faithful servant of which the servant himself was blissfully unaware. Bloomfield's salary was abruptly stopped, despite a suggestion by his probable successor Knighton that he should ostensibly remain as Private Secretary in order to save him from financial embarrassment.

Lady Conyngham's enmity and George IV's heartless betrayal relegated Bloomfield overnight to the status of inconspicuous pensioner. Princess Lieven wrote on 12 March 1822 that 'his name is never mentioned'. He was only partly appeased by the miserly compensation of the red ribbon of the Grand Cross of the Order of the Bath. When the likelihood of even an Irish title evaporated and with bankruptcy looming he was forced to settle for the sinecure of the Governorship of Fort Charles in Jamaica. Bloomfield continued to petition for a plum diplomatic post, however. The King reluctantly granted him a gift of £1,500 in May 1823, but in a manner which made it very obvious that further claims would be unwelcome:

> When ... I look back to the period when you were first introduced to me ... when I look to your situation and the date of your first becoming my servant, and compare it to your situation and income at this moment, neither you nor your family, I feel, can have the smallest reason to complain of my want of generosity to you.

Bloomfield finally achieved some sort of respectable retirement when he procured the appointment of Minister to the Swedish Court from Liverpool's government. His additional requests for consulships at both Florence and Turin were refused, but he was at last granted an Irish peerage in 1825.[83] The manner of his enforced retirement at the urging of an unsavoury mistress, and the great lengths to which he had been forced to restore both his reputation and his bank balance, did little to enhance his sovereign's image.

Bloomfield was not the only casualty of George's new obsession. Lady Conyngham allegedly had a hand in persuading the King not to return to Brighton – a town which still remembered Maria Fitzherbert with affection – after 1827.[84] She was also said to have been instrumental in engineering Viscount Goderich's tearful resignation as Prime

Minister in February 1828, and was regularly depicted by satirists as being the power behind the throne.[85] From the mid 1820s, royal appointments were effectively decided by the 'cottage coterie' of Lady Conyngham, Knighton and, occasionally, Wellington, meeting at the Royal Lodge in Windsor Great Park, where George now spent so much of his time. To Princess Lieven, Lady Conyngham was 'a fool', but 'just the kind of malicious fool who might do a great deal of harm'; observing that 'all sensible people regret Lady Hertford', she asked whether it was possible to imagine 'anything more absurd than an amorous and inconstant sexagenarian who, at the beginning of his reign, gives up all his time to a love affair? It is pitiable.' Yet by 1829 this 'malicious fool' was being cast as 'The Guard Wot Looks Arfter the Sovereign' – while Halford was telling Knighton that if *he* could stop the King consuming so much laudanum, he himself would endeavour to get rid of 'the Lady'.[86]

Lady Conyngham was particularly assiduous in finding places and titles for her friends and relatives. Some thought in 1821 that Bloomfield was being ejected to make way for her son, Lord Francis Conyngham. In 1823 the Foreign Secretary, George Canning, finally agreed to appoint Lord Francis an Under-Secretary at the Foreign Office[87], and despatched one of her former lovers as minister to the new Republic of Argentina (generous actions which did little to stop the coterie's incessant plotting against the embattled Foreign Secretary). Lord Conyngham himself had already, as we have seen, achieved advancement in the Irish peerage in 1816. His wife, abetted by the King, now sought to have him appointed Lord Chamberlain, on the Marquess of Hertford's diplomatic resignation from this post in July 1821. Liverpool's government, however, insisted that he receive no more than the Court Office of Groom of the Stole.

George also cheerfully helped broker advantageous marriages among his mistress's numerous family. Conyngham's daughter Elizabeth (whom some suspected to be the real target of the King's affections) was cast at the Earl Gower, wealthy heir to vast estates and the Stafford marquessate; Gower was even promised a dukedom if he would wed Lady Elizabeth. In the event, George was much put out when the couple, who cared nothing for one another, summarily rejected the proposed alliance.[88]

To her friends and acquaintances Lady Conyngham often assumed an air of political naïvety, informing Wellington, as he reported in 1821, that 'whenever the King spoke to her about Politicks she told him that she did not understand the subject'. (This while she was strenuously lobbying to have her husband appointed Lord Chamberlain.) Even the cynical and perceptive Princess Lieven accepted her play-acting at face value: 'Not an idea in her head; not a word to say for herself; nothing but a hand to accept pearls and diamonds with, and an enormous balcony to wear them on.' Clearly underestimating Lady Conyngham's ability to influence her royal lover, the Princess subsequently observed that 'the favourite does nothing but yawn'.[89]

According to Sir Thomas Lawrence, the King was not unaware of his mistress's scheming. He reports that George remarked to him in January 1823: 'You see how she takes advantage of her position to push her family. Oh, and she knows very well when she is well off.' Lawrence later quoted Lady Conyngham herself as candidly admitting, 'What a pity now if all this were to end'. Between January 1821 and January 1829 George spent £105,618 with the royal jewellers Rundell, Bridge and Rundell, most of which went on lavish presents for Lady Conyngham. One pearl necklace alone cost £3,150 – at least ten times the average annual salary for a respectable, middle-class professional man.[90]

Despite her age, inevitably there were rumours that the King would marry Lady Conyngham and try to conceive another heir. (It was already being whispered that her son Albert, born in 1805, was George's.) On returning from his visit to Dublin in 1821 George certainly intimated such an intention to Mrs Fitzherbert, while in 1822 he told Lawrence that 'If she were a widow, as I am a widower, she would not be one for long.'[91] Although the marriage never happened – there was the small matter of the lady's husband to be considered – George remained under Lady Conyngham's influence until his death. Wellington later recounted with distaste an interview of 1827 in which 'His Majesty with Tears in His eyes told him that he was more in Love with this Beauty than ever!' – adding as a postscript that neither he nor Knighton (whom he still called 'the Accoucheur', though Knighton had not practised as such for more than twenty years) believed anything the King said when he was in this mood. Princess Lieven cites a similar story: having played the piano for the King, she looked up to find him speechless and tearful at the thought of Lady Conyngham. 'I have never', she declared, 'seen a man more in love.' Robert Seymour had obviously heard a comparable tale: his incisively vicious print *The Great Joss and his Playthings* of 1829 shows the letter 'C' expelling the words 'Oh 'tis Love 'tis Love 'tis Love'. The Marchioness herself, however, was decidedly more pragmatic. Princess Lieven alleged that during the King's severe illness of spring 1826 'his mistress tried to desert him', and only the Duke of York's intervention persuaded her to stay.[92] And as we have seen, hardly was the King's body cold before the Conynghams were attempting to convey quantities of booty out of Windsor Castle. Lady Conyngham not only proved far more tenacious than any of her predecessors; she was, as a result of her labours, also far better off.

4

Dress and Militaria

Some monarchs take roundabout ways into note,
While *His* short cut to fame is – the cut of his coat;
Philip's Son thought the World was too small for his Soul,
But our R–g—t's finds room in a laced button-hole.
                    Thomas Moore, *The Twopenny Post-Bag*, Letter VII

IN CONTRAST TO what many of his twentieth-century biographers have implied, women were by no means George IV's only passion in life. Flamboyant and extravagant costumes were another significant, and lifelong, preoccupation. From his earliest years he enjoyed the feel, the colour, and the sheer thrill of expensive new clothes. Aged only two, he made an appearance with his baby brother Frederick at a royal ball dressed in 'rich blue and silver jammers [drawers], with new point lace tuckers and cuffs, diamonds round their tuckers and diamond belts and the Prince of Wales had diamond buttons down his petticoat'.[1] Johann Zoffany's group portrait of 1765, of Queen Charlotte with the young princes George and Frederick, shows the two little boys dressed as an ancient Greek hero (Telemachus) and a Turk, respectively. At the age of eight George was painted by Zoffany in a highly fashionable 'Vandyke' costume, while Richard Cosway's sketches for his 1788 portrait (since lost) featured George 'in Vandyke dress standing next to a rearing white horse' – or, as an alternative, as 'St George riding a horse, with an angel flying down to arm him with a shield'. By the late 1780s Cosway was drawing his royal patron in robes and regalia, which he evidently much enjoyed; Cosway's full-length drawing of 1787, depicting him again in Van Dyck dress – the over-prominent Garter star on his shoulder artfully balanced by his long cane – shows the young Prince as the epitome of sartorial confidence.[2]

As early as 1782 his friend the Duchess of Devonshire admitted that the Prince of Wales was 'fond of dress even to a tawdry degree' and that 'his person, his dress and the admiration he has met ... from women take up his thoughts chiefly', but predicted that his fascination with clothes, 'young as he is, will soon wear off'.[3] The Duchess's forecast was to prove wholly wrong, however; as he grew older, clothes, and the image they helped to create, became one of George's primary obsessions. In 1799 Farington noted that the Prince of Wales was 'very attentive to his person' and 'dresses surrounded by 3 glasses in which He can see his person'. Thirty years after his death, William Thackeray reminisced in some detail about the late King's passion for dressing 'in every kind of uniform and every possible court-dress – in long fair hair, with powder, with and without a pig-tail – in every conceivable cocked-hat – in dragoon uniform – in Windsor uniform – in a field-marshal's clothes – in a Scotch kilt and tartans, with dirk and claymore (a stupendous figure) – in a frogged frock-coat with a fur collar and tight breeches and silk stockings – in wigs of every colour, fair, brown and black'.[4]

In this, as in so many other aspects of his character, George inherited his enthusiasm at least in part from his father. George III also spent much of his time designing clothes – albeit less gaudy and more practical than those favoured by his eldest son. His greatest triumph was the 'Windsor uniform' he devised in the mid 1780s for everyday wear at the castle. Blue, red and gold, it borrowed its inspiration from the militaristic Court of Frederick the Great of Prussia and its decoration from the hunting livery his father Prince Frederick had designed in 1729 – and also, more pertinently, from the colours of the national flag. Its effect was to iron out social and hierarchical differences, in the manner of a school uniform. By 1786, Fanny Burney noted, it was being worn not only by the King and his sons but 'by all men who belong to his Majesty and come into his presence at Windsor'.[5]

Where his father had indulged his more expensive hobbies behind a façade of frugality, young George inevitably took his passions to excess. Where George III snorted at fashionable clothes, his son saw them as one of the reasons for his existence. He loved clothes for their colour or their cut, not for the uniformity they could impart. Unlike the fashionable 'macaroni' dandies of the 1770s, however, he did not intend his clothes to be excessively challenging or outrageous, and he never strayed too far beyond the parameters established by such arbiters of taste as George Brummell. Yet while many of his innovations were adopted by his personal Court, even his closest friends eschewed both the pseudo-military posturing and the boundless expenditure that accompanied his obsession with costume.

The cost of the Prince's vanity was indeed enormous. On coming of age in 1783, for example, he bought twenty-three pairs of boots, all from different makers. In June 1786 he spent £2,041 1s. 2d. on lace from Barrett, Sons and Corney and £38 10s. on perfumes, including '12 pints of Lavender water' and a spectacular seventy-two pounds of 'Perfumed Powder'; the following September he ordered a total of seventy-four pairs of white-and-tan gloves from Robert Bond – who was not paid for these items until July 1789.[6] By 1787 George owed his tailors nearly £17,000 – an astronomical figure, approximately equivalent to £750,000 today. By 1793 his unpaid tailors' bills topped £30,000. In 1802 Farington recorded that 'The Prince of Wales is profusely expensive in what relates to dress', and cited an alleged example of both his profligacy with clothes and the transience of his enthusiasms: 'At one time silver buckles were taken from him which sold as old silver for £150 – they must have originally cost £900.'[7] The Royal Archives record that in just one year, 1803, George spent £681 14s. 9d. (approximately £30,000 today) on clothing and related et ceteras, including regimental outfits worth £330 from Schweitzer and Davidson, £100 16s. for twenty-four 'fine Holland shirts' from Elizabeth Gordon, hats from K. Cater and Sons, spurs and buckles from Henry Vincent, swords and belts from John Prosser, perfume from Bourgeois, Amick and Son (with whom he had a quarterly standing order which amounted to goods worth more than £300 a year), plumes from Carbery, and 'satin cloth manufactured from the Fur of Seals' from John William Jacob. By 10 October of that year more than two-thirds of the sum owing for these orders was still unpaid. It did not help that everything was bought in huge quantities: 'perfumed powder was delivered in amounts of up to 36 lb at a time; tooth brushes came by the three dozen ... [and,] in need of a few walking sticks, he bought thirty-two in one day'.[8]

While by 1800 the 'bright colours and lavish trimmings' of George's former years were, in his middle age, being replaced by more sober, well-fitting clothes for everyday wear, his obsession with fancy dress persisted. In May 1802 he bought a 'Friar's dress' (and related 'equipment', including impeccably ecclesiastical 'fine pink Silk Hose') from Henry Wayte, together with 'a Henry 5th dress Richly Trim'd with gold Loops, Tassells and Bullions'. The purchases for 1804 included 'Henry IV's dress in white sattin' and costumes for a ghost, a skeleton and a Sultan. Four years later Meyer's supplied a 'Polish dress', in blue superfine cloth with silver trimmings and lambswool lining, for £98 16s. 9d.[9] His reputation as, if not the First Gentleman of Europe, then at least its Premier Dandy, was secured by outrageous costumes such as these.

London was well-equipped to satisfy George's sartorial extravagance. His adulthood corresponded to a period of what one fashion historian has termed 'the international recognition of the excellence of men's tailoring in London'. Firms such as Schweitzer and Davidson of Cork Street and John Meyer of Conduit Street were constantly patronised by the Prince, and he was perfectly familiar with the minutiae of the trade. (His wife famously commented that he 'would have made an excellent tailor, or shoemaker or hairdresser but', she added maliciously, 'nothing else'.)[10]

The royal brothers liked nothing more than to discuss the newest fashions in civil or military attire. In 1781 George's letters to his brother Frederick were filled with gossip about ideas for uniforms and the latest London fads. 'I hope you liked the frocks I sent you over,' George wrote to Frederick on 30 March,

and by the next messenger I will send you two new uniforms at least, with the dress and undress of my hunting uniform. It is called so and is universally admired thro'out London, tout ce qui s'appelle ton, has made it up by way of handsome Ranelagh frocks. If there are any other cloaths of any sort or kind besides these and your Vandyke dress, which you wish to be sent over, I will take care of it. I shall also send you some new buckles together with the sword you ordered. Grey humbly begged to make some alterations and improvements in it, to which I most graciously assented. He has sent it home; 'tis excessively pretty, a mixture of gold and steel beads. However, tho' it is so pretty I made him take it back immediately, as it was not near so pretty or so elegant as your sword, nor was it anything in your taste.[11]

The Prince's correspondence with his brothers is full of this sort of thing. On 10 April he described in enormous detail the imitation lace ruff ('with two little white strings and tassels') of the 'Vandyke' costume he was sending Frederick, and a month later was ordering his supposedly martial brother another Vandyke suit, this time in 'white sattin and pink ... with pink puffs and knots'.[12]

Dress was central to every aspect of George's life. His public displays of support for the Whig cause, and in particular for his friend Charles James Fox, can be interpreted by the cynic as little more than an excuse to dress up in buff and blue – the colours the opposition Whigs had borrowed from the uniforms of General George Washington's troops. As the King rode down the Mall to open Parliament in the aftermath of Fox's victory at Westminster in 1784, George donned buff and blue to host a loud garden party for Fox at Carlton House – directly on his father's processional route. For his first appearance in the House of Lords on 11 November 1783, however, the Prince acquired a costume more exotic by far than the sober colours favoured by Washington's army, arriving at Westminster 'attired in black velvet lined with pink satin and embroidered with gold and pink spangles, pink high-heeled shoes, his hair frizzed "with two very full curls at the sides" '.[13]

George was an exacting patron of fashion. He kept tradesmen waiting, constantly changed his mind, and rarely paid his suppliers promptly, if he paid them at all. On 27 July 1796 the painter Robert Smirke, father of the architect, told Farington that

> Rossi, the Sculptor, was with the Prince of Wales today modelling a small head of him in the Uniform of the 10th regt. of Dragoons. Rossi waited 3 hours today before he was admitted, during which time the Prince was entirely engaged by a Shoemaker, and two Taylors who succeeded each other. – The Shoemaker carried in at least 40 pairs of Boots – and was with the Prince an Hour while he was trying them. The first Taylor that was admitted, after many trials of patterns, & cuttings, was dismissed, not having given satisfaction: The other was then sent for. Rossi yesterday waited 5 hours in vain.[14]

Like a magpie, George could not resist glitter and sparkle. No doubt it was a reaction against the sober frugality of his parents' Court and way of life, but his eye could always be drawn to bright, gaudy objects, whether ruby rings, ormolu clocks, or gilded mouldings. Any excuse would do to purchase jewellery for himself or others. His marriage of 1795 and coronation of 1821 in particular provided ideal opportunities for him to surround himself with bright baubles at the taxpayers' expense. Farington noted in December 1794 that 'the Prince of Wales had given the most profuse orders for Diamonds &c in consequence of his intended marriage', while his augmentation of the royal crowns in 1821, on the excuse of affording spectators an appropriately dazzling display of precious gems at his coronation, was excessive even by his own standards. There were, he had decided, simply not enough diamonds and rubies on the regalia.[15]

Closely allied to this passion for jewellery was George's life-long zeal for the acquisition of military decorations and the insignia of chivalric orders. His ardour for uniforms persisted throughout his life, long past the stage when he could be squeezed into even the most gen-erously-cut field marshal's garb, and in his later years this predilection for donning military uniforms at the drop of a sabre had alarming consequences for his state of mind. Before 1811 George III had confined his eldest son to a very junior and ceremonial role in the British army, and by the time the Prince assumed the Regency and the power that went with it, he was too fat – and possibly too indolent – to take a more active role, supposing he had been able to persuade the government to allow him to do so. As he grew older, however, his addiction to uniforms encouraged his faltering mind to engage in senile military fantasies. In the late 1820s he frequently told dinner guests – who often included the Duke of Wellington himself – not only that he had helped to win at Waterloo, but that he had taken part in some of Wellington's hard-fought Peninsular War battles. (In a similar vein, the Alzheimer's-stricken President Reagan, having so often donned uniform to play army or naval officers during his film career, apparently came to believe he had genuinely served in the armed forces.) Such fictions perhaps reveal a consciousness on George's part of a need to justify his habitual flaunting of splendid orders and uniforms.

Most of George's knowledge of military apparel was gleaned from his family. While they learned their soldiering in Hanover or else-where, as he was forbidden to do, his brothers assiduously sent him details, sketches and even coloured drawings of the latest European uniforms. When the Duke of York visited Berlin in 1791, for example, George gave him a shopping list of information he wanted, which included descriptions of 'the compleat uniforms, accoutrements, saddle, bridle, &c, of one of Zieten's Hussars ... as well as one of the Officers compleat uniforms, cloathing, sword, cap, saddle, bridle, chabrack, pistols, in sort, everything compleat'.[16] In 1802, during the brief lull in the French wars which followed the Peace of Amiens, the Duke of Cumberland busied himself not with army reforms but with sending George sketches of the new Hanoverian uniforms.[17]

The following year the Duke of Clarence eagerly sent his brother details of the uniform he had devised for his absurdly-titled Royal Spelthorne Legion of Militia:

> The pantaloons are to be red, the officers to have felt caps with red and gold tassels, the privates leather caps like yours [for the 10th] and no helmets. The officers of the infantry will have a neat plain jacket with blue lappels with a gold epaulette blue pantaloons and Hussar boots with a black tassel in front and a plate to their back sword belt ... the Field Officers to have two epaulettes and to wear a sabre round the waist: the serjeants and privates to have jackets according to the regulation without any lace, and blue pantaloons and half black gaiters: the drummers laced down the seams and over the arms with white lace: the serjeants and privates of the troop the same in red and blue and white and silver as your regiment in blue, yellow and white and silver.

'I hope', William concluded optimistically, 'all the volunteers except the officers, the serjeant and drum majors will wear their hair round in their necks.'[18]

The origin of George's delight in uniforms is not difficult to fathom. It did not derive merely, as Oliver Millar has suggested, from the Hanoverians' traditional enjoyment of all things to do with soldiering. His martial fantasies far outstripped his father's taste for sober Prussian militaria, in terms both of imagination and of cost, and no doubt stemmed primarily from his frustration at being prevented from serving alongside his brothers on the Continent. By the time of his appointment as Regent in 1811 this long-standing grievance had become inextricably entwined with more complex ambitions – notably his desperate desire to eclipse Napoleon, or at least to emulate the Allied sovereigns who were leading their national armies into battle.

Undoubtedly George III's refusal to let his heir anywhere near a real army, either at home or abroad, in other than a ceremonial capacity, was a proscription which hit the Prince hard. He had been brought up to expect military service, and was from a very early age surrounded with the toys of war. In 1767, for example, he 'was given a battery of twenty-one one-pounder brass guns, complete with travelling carriages' on his birthday, in order to correct what his parents perceived as a tendency to timidity – not exactly a typical present for a boy of five. By the mid 1770s, however, it was clear that George III had earmarked Frederick for the army, preferring to direct his eldest son to more pacific studies. As Mark Evans has recently pointed out, this decision was sanctioned by the practice of centuries. The only post-medieval Prince of Wales to have seen active service in the army was Charles II, who attended his father at Edgehill in 1642.[19] Thus, while the Duke of York was made a colonel at the tender age of seventeen, and subsequently sent to Hanover for military training, the Prince of Wales languished at home, playing with his toy soldiers and his battery of brass guns.

By 1794 three of George III's sons were in the army. The Duke of York was commanding British forces in the Low Countries, and senior to the seventy-two-year-old veteran of the Seven Years' War, General von Freytag. Despite the abject failure of the ensuing campaign, in 1795 the Duke was raised by his father to the rank of Field Marshal and, three years later, to Commander-in-Chief of the British army. Prince Ernest, later Duke of Cumberland, was sent for military train-ing in Hanover after the outbreak of the French Revolution; serving with the Hanoverian forces in May 1794 he was seriously wounded in the left eye and arm and sent home to convalesce. Prince Adolphus, later Duke of Cambridge, was sent to join the Hanoverian army and, like Ernest, was injured in action. Also despatched to Hanover was their brother Edward, later Duke of Kent. Like York, he was destined for a military career from an early age; his temperament, however, made him signally unfitted for the variety of jobs with which he was provided. Having run up large debts in Hanover, he was sent in dis-grace to Geneva (which he found 'the dullest and most insufferable of places'). After a spell with the garrison at Gibraltar – where he earned a reputation as a mindless martinet – he was sent to join the army in Canada. He returned to Gibraltar as Governor in 1800, but his harsh conduct provoked a mutiny and his ignominious recall.

Of a similar disposition was Prince William, who, as we have seen, was sent to join the navy at the age of fourteen. In 1780 he was a mere midshipman during the relief of Gibraltar, but thanks to his royal blood he was promoted captain of the frigate *Pegasus* in 1786, aged only twenty. Here, as elsewhere, he showed himself to be essentially much like his brother Edward: an unnecessarily strict officer who dis-played little initiative or insight.

The Prince of Wales, in the meantime, was dressing up and indulg-ing in pretend-generalship. On 23 July 1792 the King and the Duke of York went to Bagshot Heath to watch him play at manoeuvres with two regiments of light cavalry:

The action began by the grand guard of cavalry being drove in after a good deal of skirmishing: a heavy cannonade commenced from the field pieces posted on the flanks of the three redoubts, and in half an hour's time the fire became general throughout the whole line for above twenty minutes, when the two regiments of cavalry on the left headed by the PRINCE OF WALES, charged the hollow-way about half a mile in front, which had a truly grand effect.

The fact that the guns set the heath alight only added, in the obsequious opinion of *The Times*, 'to the grandness of the occasion'.[20]

If he was grounded, the Prince had at least been given something to play with. In 1783 the new 10th Regiment of Light Dragoons was 'honoured' with the title of 'The Prince of Wales's Own', though even this crumb of comfort appeared likely to be withdrawn at a moment's notice. In 1788 the King turned down a request from the colonel of the 10th that 'as they bore the name of the Prince of Wales's Regiment, [the Prince] would do them the honour of appearing at their head'. In 1793, when Revolutionary France's declaration of war with Britain necessitated a considerable increase in the country's armed forces, the King finally relented, appointing George Colonel-in-Chief of the 10th (Light) Dragoons on 26 January. As a token gesture towards easing George's bruised pride this commission was backdated to 19 November 1782, thus making him the army's most senior colonel. Yet the King left him in no doubt that his colonelcy had only been bestowed 'on the solemn assurance ... that no higher rank was meant hereafter to be claimed from it'. The Prince's military position, it was clear, was devised by his father to be little more than a ceremonial sop, which enabled him to substitute real soldiers for toy ones. The King specifically stipulated that his rank 'should not be the forerunner of a military career', and that the Prince should attend the regiment in camp only – *not* on service abroad.

Given these immutable boundaries, and the natural predisposition of the regiment's colonel-in-chief to parties and play-acting, it was inevitable that the Prince of Wales's time with the 10th should have been largely spent in entertainments, parades, and pantomime battles. The regiment was customarily stationed either in London or near Brighton, and when at the latter was generally used for mock manoeuvres or for providing guards and escorts for social events. The regiment's programme of activities on arriving near Brighton in

August 1793 was typical of most of their summer assignments of the 1790s:

> When the regiment finally reached Brighton that morning it was met by the Prince in person and led to the camp ground. The Prince's 'tent' was put up and that night he slept in it. A week later, the Prince's birthday was celebrated in style, with the ringing of bells and the firing of salutes. He gave a 'very superb entertainment' to the officers of his regiment in the marquee and in the evening there was a ball at the Castle Hotel, which was 'numerously attended'. The next day the Militia arrived on the outskirts of Brighton ... and were 'formed in battalions, in which order they moved, keeping good wheeling distance'.[21]

Equally typically, George soon became bored with these goings-on, and when a September gale blew down most of the camp's tents he scuttled back to London. The next summer, however, the 10th returned to Brighton and George organised a mock-battle, leading the regiment against a notional enemy. His martial ardour was observed from horseback by Maria Fitzherbert – who, in a rather liberal interpretation of the King's Regulations, was herself dressed in a variation of the 10th's uniform.

These good-humoured war-games did little to compensate George for his relatively junior rank and his military quarantine. Early in 1795, therefore, he launched a persistent campaign to gain 'the rank of General, or Lt-General'. The withholding of his long-overdue promotion by the King, he declared in his usual melodramatic fashion, constituted 'a stigma ... too heavy to be any longer endured', one which he could 'no further suffer in silence'.[22]

His brothers did their best to help. In January 1795 Ernest had suggested that he might succeed Field Marshal Conway as Colonel-in-Chief of the Royal Regiment of Horse Guards. When Conway died in July, however, that appointment was presented by the King to the Duke of Richmond. George was doubly furious on discovering from the *London Gazette* of 28 February that his cousin Prince William of Gloucester, only nineteen years old and in his opinion 'a dull stupid boy', had been promoted major-general. Pleading with his father to relax his prohibition of overseas service, George disingenuously suggested that his reputation for women, drink and debt stemmed from the frustration this engendered. 'There ought to be some serious object to which my mind should be diverted,' he suggested reasonably, adding (untruthfully) that his father's stipulation that he should never be promoted beyond the rank of full colonel did not bother him unduly. Warming to his argument, the Prince began to compare Britain's resistance against the armies of Revolutionary France to her plight during the Hundred Years' War, and himself to the Black Prince. Could he and his father not command jointly, as Edward III and his son had at Crécy? ('The heroic Edward gave to the unexperienced Prince of Wales the command of the vanguard at Creçi, and the services of the son, not on the day alone but thro' life, repaid the confidence of the father.') The King did not reply to these embarrassing flights of fancy, leaving Lord Moira to point out the potential humiliation involved if the Prince of Wales were to serve as a colonel in an army commanded by his younger brother. George thereupon tried another tack, declaring that since 'I ... have the good fortune to possess so many brothers, the nation has the security of so many representatives of your Majesty to look towards, that the stake of my life can be of little political importance.' His central argument, that it was time he was allowed some degree of responsibility in order to prepare himself for the day of his accession, certainly seemed sensible:

> At a stage of life which calls upon others to incline themselves to serious pursuits, I find myself barred from the objects of application natural and becoming to my rank. The chain of public affairs, whence I might have derived instruction as well as occupation, has been uniformly withheld from me.[23]

As before, his entreaties fell on deaf ears. He therefore attempted to go behind his father's back and, in defiance of military precedent, applied to the former army Commander-in-Chief, Lord Amherst, for the rank of major-general. Amherst could clearly do nothing – he had been persuaded to resign to make way for the Duke of York – and George's request was, inevitably, passed back to the King, who once again refused to permit him any involvement at all in the expanding conflict with France. Insensitive as ever where his eldest son was concerned, George III certainly made his prohibition no easier to bear by choosing the Prince's wedding day to inform him that he could never expect promotion beyond his present rank. 'My younger sons can have no other situation in the State but what arise from the military lines they have been placed in,' he declared. 'You are born to a more difficult one, and which I shall be most happy if I find you seriously turn your thoughts to.' In conclusion, he trusted that the imminent

arrival of the Prince's future wife would calm his agitation. As it trans-
pired, of course, his pious hope that 'Princess Caroline's character
may prove so pleasing to you that your mind may be engrossed with
domestic felicity ... and that a numerous progeny may be the result of
this union' was to be disastrously disappointed.[24]

There came a day in 1797, however, when George thought his hour
had come at last. Returning from a day's hunting in Dorset, he was told
by an officer of the 10th that a French invasion fleet lay off the coast
nearby:

> Immediately he announced that he was going to join the regiment and
> galloped off towards Dorchester in the hope that he and his men would
> give the enemy a warm reception. Stopping at Blandford on the way he
> ordered a squadron of the Bays who were in quarters there to hold them-
> selves in readiness. The he rode off again, arriving in Dorchester after
> dark. The place was quiet, and the major-general in command of the dis-
> trict had gone to bed. The King, who received his son's hasty message that
> he was 'instantly' joining his regiment early the next morning, could not
> credit the report of a French fleet in English waters; and soon it was,
> indeed, confirmed that the supposed French fleet was not a French fleet
> at all but an English one.[25]

This embarrassing mistake deterred George not at all. His request
of February 1797 that Pitt appoint him to the Lord-Lieutenantcy of
Ireland in order that he might pacify the restive Irish Catholic population (with whom he then professed much sympathy) having been
turned down by both Prime Minister and King, George returned to
the subject of his military service, asking his father yet again 'to call
me forth to a station wherein I may prove myself worthy of the
confidence of my country and of the high rank I hold in it, by staking
my life in its defence!'[26] George III eventually replied in wearily measured tones that 'the approbation of the public' – rather than such fantasies as reincarnating the Black Prince – 'should be your first object'.

When war with France was resumed in 1803, George vigorously
renewed his own campaign. The peace brokered by Britain with
Napoleon's France the previous year had already begun to break down
when he wrote to Henry Addington, then Prime Minister, beseeching
an active military commission. 'I feel myself exposed to the obloquy
of being regarded by the country as passing my time indifferent to the
events which menace, and insensible to the call of patriotism,' complained the Prince with surprising self-awareness, and considerable

justification, on 18 July. (This plea raises the question of what would have been the consequences had George III involved his eldest son in national affairs of a military or civil nature. Would his Regency and reign have been a more productive era for the monarchy if he had had prior experience of government? Would he have revealed hidden military aptitude in serving with Moore or Wellington?) A week later, however, George was casting himself once more as a Hanoverian Arthur, destined to save not only Britain but the whole of Europe from the French. The language of his plea to the government and his use of the third person hinted at delusions of grandeur to come:

> He has, at a moment when everything is at stake that is dear and sacred to him and to the nation, asked to be advanced in military rank, because he may have his birth-right to fight for, the throne of his father to defend, the glory of the people of England to uphold, which is dearer to him than life, which has yet remained unsullied under the Princes of the House of Brunswick, and which he trusts will be transmitted pure and uncontaminated to the latest generations ... In making this offer, in again repeating it, the Prince of Wales considers that he has only performed his duty to himself, to the State, to the King, to Europe, whose fate may be involved in the issue of this contest.

George attempted to use the same language with his father. In August 1803 he wrote from Brighton yet another entreaty, in which he painted a breathlessly dramatic but essentially accurate picture of the current situation in Europe ('Hanover is lost, England is menaced with invasion, Ireland is in rebellion, Europe is at the foot of France'), and concluded that his personal service was vital to turn back the Napoleonic tide. George III simply replied that nothing further was to be said on the subject. He did hold out a crumb of hope – 'Should the implacable enemy so far succeed as to land, you will have an opportunity of shewing your zeal at the head of your Regiment' – but that was not enough for his restless son. In retaliation George adopted a tactic which has become tiresomely familiar two centuries later, and decided to tell his side of the story to the press. Favourable comparisons between the two 'great' Princes of Wales, of the 1340s and the 1800s, began to appear in the newspapers, along with helpful forecasts of how the present one might single-handedly determine the fate of Europe. Such deliberately planted stories indicated that George's imagination was already worryingly vivid. He was even reported as having boasted to Fox that the King 'desired me to be on his right hand whenever he took the field'.[27]

In the autumn of 1803 the Duke of Clarence, unwisely fanning his eldest brother's military expectations, wrote to George that 'We may perhaps meet in the field. I really believe at last the French will come.' The Duke of York was not so optimistic. Repeating his offer of service to his brother, now Commander-in-Chief, in October 1803, George maintained that his 'idle, inactive rank' was no help to anyone, and pointed out that he had been consistently passed over in rounds of army promotion. Frederick, however, politely declined his brother's offer, reminding him that he had supported his case for promotion in the past, but taking convenient refuge behind their father's known wishes. The result was an increasingly acrimonious correspondence between the two brothers, George tartly concluding that 'nothing could be more distressing to me than to prolong a topic on which it is *now clear* to me, my dear brother, that you and I can never agree'. He then resorted to an act calculated to enrage his father, and in December 1803 published their correspondence on this issue. George III's reaction was predictable, and in the ensuing weeks he publicly referred to his son and heir only as 'the publisher of *my* letters'. Christopher Hibbert has recently suggest that this flouting of estab-lished royal protocol was a principal factor in prompting the King's relapse into 'madness' in the following year.[28] It certainly tended to convince Queen Charlotte that she could not trust her eldest son with the safety of the King's person: at the onset of her husband's illness in 1804 she preferred to place her faith and the care of the royal family in the hands of Addington's tottering government, rather than those of the heir to the throne, her own son.

For George, the posting of the 10th Dragoons from their encamp-ment outside Brighton to a site near Guildford, miles away from any possible invasion target, piled insult upon injury. He told Frederick it was a slight he could never forgive, and in January 1804 refused him admission to Carlton House (almost the only sanction he could impose). In a further show of childish petulance, which did his cause no good, he refused to attend his mother's birthday celebrations in May of that year.[29]

During these years George consoled himself for his military disap-pointments as he always did, by dressing up as a soldier – not, of course, as a common foot-slogger, but as a glorious officer-of-paradise. At Schweitzer and Davidson early in 1799 he spent £178 on regimental wear for himself, including a blue superfine cloth coat trimmed with silver braid and plumes. On 22 May of that year he ordered 'a very curious Spanish Dress Sword Blade studded with silver' and 'An Asiatic Scimitar Blade with Inscription' from the sword-cutler Henry Tatham. In January 1800 he ordered not one but two field marshal's full-dress uniforms, and spent a further £187 on regimental wear for himself and the officers of the 10th. Late in 1803 he ordered new uniforms, including 929 privates' caps, at a cost of £305, and the next year treated himself to a 'Hungarian Hussar's cap' from Caters. The new regimental uniforms of 1805 cost a startling £722 7s. An order of July 1806 to Steinbach's for a single 'Rich Hussar Sash in Gold and Crimson' was billed at £40. Altogether, George's colonelcy of the 10th Dragoons served as the excuse for an outlay of hundreds of pounds on fancy trimmings for himself and for his men, pounds that would have been better spent on workaday uniforms and equipment for troops fighting in the front line.[30]

George's toy-soldier fantasies were frequently translated into paint. As early as 1782 Thomas Gainsborough was commissioned to portray him in a specially-invented and wholly unauthorised military uniform, later adapted for his own 10th Dragoons.[31] (The brushwork of Gainsborough's rapid technique makes it difficult to decipher the detail of the uniform – a factor which may help explain the Prince's lukewarm regard for this painter.) Most revealing of these early depictions was Joshua Reynolds's portrait of 1784, which featured George in uniform, with drawn sword, about to mount his horse. Reynolds's image of a royal hero caught on the point of dashing to his country's defence in the manner of a battle-hardened Plantagenet clearly made a deep impression on George, who subsequently commissioned other equally evocative pictures of himself as Britain's courageous inspiration. William Beechey's equestrian painting of him of 1798, which employed a composition similar to Reynolds's, conveyed the Prince's martial affectations so explicitly as to prompt George III to denounce his son's abhorrent military posturing.

Not all the pseudo-military portraits George commissioned were as successful as those by Reynolds and Beechey. Mather Brown's 1791 depiction of him in another imaginary uniform was clearly intended as a riposte to Benjamin West's 1779 portrait of the King in his simple Household attire, but the outlandish accoutrements of the Prince's costume look more appropriate to the stage than to the battlefield. Equally risible was John Russell's full-length portrait of 1792, depicting George squashed tightly into the Lincoln-green uniform of the Royal Society of Kentish Bowmen, of which he had been patron since 1788. Instead of a legendary figure from the pages of history, he cut an unintentionally comic figure, more Friar Tuck than Earl of Locksley.

Nevertheless, George was prouder of his military portraits than of almost any others in his collection. Gainsborough's depiction of him in the uniform of the 10th was indeed given away to Lord Heathfield in 1810, but not before George had authorised it to be engraved. Beechey's stirring image of 1798 was copied for the Duke of Kent in 1803. Élisabeth Vigée-Le Brun's 1804 portrait of the Prince in a later Hussar uniform was also copied, on his instructions – this time in miniature by his enamellist, Henry Bone. The original was then presented to Maria Fitzherbert.

The Prince tended to favour painters who specialised in the precise delineation of military attire. Equestrian and military portraits by, or in the manner of, David Morier were more consistently popular with him than, say, Gainsborough's hazier impressionism. Morier, who had died in 1770, was a military portraitist at one time retained by 'Butcher' Cumberland, George II's brother. Between 1812 and 1818 the Prince Regent bought thirteen of Morier's pictures: nine of Cumberland in various uniforms, two of George III in uniform on horseback, and two of the Seven Years' War heroes Granby and Ligonier. From 1803 the painter Robert Dighton produced more than thirty coloured drawings of British soldiers for the Prince, who at the same time bought more than four hundred drawings and water-colours of uniforms and of soldiers of foreign armies by the Dutch military artists Dirk and Jan Anthonie. Some of his purchases featured more lively military subjects, such as Swebach's melodramatic 1801 canvas of *The Death of General Desaix at the Battle of Marengo* and the drawings and memorabilia associated with the final defeat of Tipu Sultan at Seringapatam in 1799.[32]

Inevitably, George's predilection for military posturing and posing was a gift for the cartoonists. James Gillray's famous satire on the Jerseys and their royal patron of June 1796, *Fashionable Jockeyship*, cruelly caricatured not only that relationship but particularly the Prince's corpulent figure in the ridiculous dragoons uniform he had invented, its comical bag-busby falling over his eyes. However, notwithstanding the money he unquestionably wasted, not all the equipment George bought was destined merely for parade-ground show and fodder for the print-makers. In addition to ever more ostentatious uniforms and accoutrements, deemed necessary to fit the 10th for its new billing as Hussars after 1803, George also acquired forty of Ezekiel Baker's new rifled carbines, making the unit the first British cavalry regiment to be armed with them.[33]

The conversion of the 10th Dragoons into Hussars reinvigorated George's interest in his pet regiment, at least for a year or two. The new uniforms, which he naturally took it upon himself to design, gave him an opportunity not only to indulge in exotic militaria but also to exact further indirect revenge on his sober, straightlaced father for all those years of unfulfilled dreams. As military historian John Mollo has remarked:

> Hussar dress – outlandish, outrageous and foreign – was an ideal vehicle for the expression of his opposition to his royal father. Led by him, the 'hussar craze' became the military manifestation of the same desire for 'exclusivity' that pervaded the upper realms of London society ... and was responsible for the rise of the 'Dandy'; in fact, the two were inextricably bound up, as many of the leading dandies had, at one time or another, been hussar officers.[34]

In later years, after his love-affair with the 10th had cooled, George became an enthusiast for the new concept of lancers (they had been very successful on the French side at Waterloo), and devised equally elaborate outfits for the lancer regiments he now urged the army to create. The Royal Collection is still crammed with items designed by the Prince, from leopard-skin sabretaches – the sort of satchel hanging from a cavalry officer's sword – to gold epaulettes. In 1991 the keepers of the Collection were prepared to admit that the 'richly covered and decorated items of equipment' designed or bought by him were 'probably used by the Prince and his circle almost as a form of fancy or theatrical dress, in which they could imagine themselves in the roles of romantic, savage, warrior kings and princes.'[35]

As long as the 10th Hussars were in Britain, George was able to play at soldiers. When they went abroad he was of course forbidden to accompany them and thus took no part in their Spanish campaign of 1808–9. His only involvement with the 10th at this time was after their return, when he had Colonel Leigh dismissed from the regiment for supposedly cheating him over the sale of a horse, and allegedly defrauding his men over the purchase of equipment – a bathetic contrast to the regiment's recent experience of the ardours of service in the Peninsula. During 1811 George's easily-diverted attention was deflected to the task of helping the Duke of Cumberland devise new uniforms for the army. The 10th were immediately re-equipped, and the subsequent regimental review was the first occasion on which he saw them following their return from Spain. A witness to the ceremony, Berkeley Paget, commented of the Prince that 'I fancy his whole soul is wrapped up in Hussar saddles, caps, cuirasses, and sword-belts', and ridiculed his manner of 'dismissing each horse with a "tap of his cane"'. Paget subsequently learned that the rest of the cavalry, the Prince's pampered Hussars excepted, were 'amazingly disgusted' with the new uniforms, which were needlessly expensive and too closely resembled those of their German or French contemporaries.[36]

Unfortunately for George's fitful military ambitions, the 10th, already irreparably tainted with the stigma of being mere royal clothes-horses, failed to cover themselves with glory in Portugal, Spain or France. (At Waterloo they were largely occupied in ensuring that the Duke of Brunswick's infantry regiments did not retire prematurely from the field.) To make matters worse, when they were in Britain in 1814 a number of senior officers involved George, as the Colonel-in-Chief, in a very public attempt to rid the regiment of their commanding officer, Colonel Quentin. The affair resulted in a court martial and the subsequent dismissal of most of the regimental officers; it also led to a new wave of satirical prints linking the Prince with Quentin's allegedly amenable wife.

In the face of this well-publicised embarrassment, and the Hussars' disappointing showing at Waterloo, George began to transfer his allegiance to more fashionable units. On 2 August 1815, the Military Register noted that the Prince Regent 'has appointed himself Colonel of the 1st and 2nd Regiments of Life Guards, as a mark of peculiar approval and censure [of the Hussars]'. Wellington was distinctly reluctant to review the 10th ('Quite irregular,' he snorted when that notorious outfit cheered its exceedingly portly Colonel-in-Chief),[37] and on 25 December 1819 George resigned the colonelcy to Lord Stewart. By then, his ambition to be regarded as the Nemesis of Napoleon more than eclipsed the fostering of any mere regiment.

The 10th gave George an opportunity to play at soldiers with real men, and also provided him with a number of his closest friends. Through it he met Benjamin Bloomfield, the Irish captain who became his Private Secretary. The regiment was also responsible for bringing to his attention a larger-than-life figure who for a few years at least became his principal mentor in matters of taste, manners and, most importantly, fashion. Although Brummell later claimed to have met the Prince of Wales while he was a schoolboy at Eton, it is likely that they first spoke soon after Brummell was gazetted a cornet in the 10th, on 17 June 1794. Brummell was far from a model officer, as evidenced by the well-known story that he could only recognise his troop on parade by looking out for an old soldier with a famously red nose. In the event, he left the 10th when the regiment was ordered to Manchester in 1800 – impudently declaring that he could never go on such 'foreign service'.[38] From 1804 he was occasionally called upon to serve as a major in the Belvoir Volunteers of George's friend the Duke of Rutland, but this was more to ensure his attendance at the duke's Belvoir Castle parties than for the sake of his military assistance. If he was a failure as a soldier, however, Brummell was perfectly suited to be a companion of the Prince of Wales.

Unusually for one his social advisors, Brummell was considerably younger than the Prince; he was only sixteen in 1794, to the Prince's thirty-two. However, the attraction was clearly mutual. Brummell was the drunken groom's personal attendant during the marriage ceremony of 1795, and the 10th Dragoons formed the Prince's personal bodyguard. By this time, 'Beau' Brummell was his impressionable Prince's consultant on all aspects of fashion. Thomas Raikes described George's studious pupillage under Brummel: 'His Royal Highness would go of a morning to Chesterfield Street to watch the progress of his friend's toilet, and remain till so late an hour that he sometimes sent away his horses, and insisted on Brummell's giving him a quiet dinner.' Brummell introduced the high, tasselled boots known as 'Hessians', and his innovations in pantaloons and neckcloths were studiously copied by his eager pupil. Under Brummell's guidance, George learned the most elegant way of opening a snuffbox, and followed the lead of the Duke of Bedford in casting aside his old-fashioned, white-powdered wig in favour of cropped, natural hair. This was more than a simple rejection of the staid fashions of his father's Court; it was also a political protest against Pitt's imposition of a tax on hair powder (usually made of flour) in 1795.[39] George, like his brothers, soon began to lose his own hair; by 1800 he was wearing false hair, and by the time of his coronation it was being ordered by the yard.

George Bryan Brummell was, briefly, one of the celebrities of his age. His daily dress was widely reported, his accessories and manners were aped by the *cognoscenti* of fashion. His reputation as a trend-setter eclipsed even that of his royal pupil. Recently, Saul David has speculated that Brummell may have been homosexual, which would cast an interesting light on his intense and fashion-centered relationship with the Prince of Wales, and suggest a new approach to interpreting the latter's relationships with women.[40] Certainly Brummell's recorded behaviour approximates to the modern stereotype of the 'bitchy queen'. His scalpel-sharp dissections of the clothes and manners of his contemporaries won him many enemies, and were perhaps less than wise in view of his own humble origins and his increasing reliance on the continued support of the Prince.

Given Brummell's arrogant, lacerating wit and George's tendency to tire even of his dearest companions, there was bound to be a falling-out. Perennially vain and envious, George was probably also jealous of Brummell's popularity with both men and women, and of the public acclaim he enjoyed as a dandy. (Thomas Raikes later wrote of Brummell that there 'Never was a man who during his career had such unbounded influence and, what is seldom the case, such general popularity in society.') Worse still, for George, was the fact that people were beginning to confuse him with Brummell: Captain Jesse relates the celebrated incident at Belvoir Castle in 1799, when 'Brummell, in going down the hill ... clad in a pelisse of fur, was one morning mistaken by the people, who had assembled in great numbers, for the Prince of Wales.'[41]

Ultimately, Brummell's arrogance and presumption broke him. MacMahon reported his public declaration that 'I made [the Prince of Wales] what he is, and I can unmake him': in the event, it was the Prince who unmade Brummell. In the manner of Shakespeare's Henry V – one of the medieval monarchs with whom he liked idly to compare himself – George cast off some of his disreputable companions, as he did some of his former beliefs. So it was that the Carlton House fête of June 1811, designed to celebrate the new Regency, was the last royal event to which Brummell received an invitation. In his declining years, he repeatedly denied that the cause of the final breach in 1812 was his peremptory command 'Wales, ring the bell!', and this entertaining anecdote is possibly apocryphal. More likely to have aroused the royal ire were Brummell's constantly disparaging remarks about Mrs Fitzherbert, in particular the nickname 'Benina' he coined for her. (This derived from the massively-built porter at Carlton House, known popularly as 'Big Ben', a label Brummell had also begun to use for George as he became increasingly portly.) It has been widely recounted how in February 1812 Brummell, having been cut dead by George, was prompted to enquire loudly of his companion, 'Who's your fat friend?' He was cut by the Prince again at a fête in July 1813, fell deep into debt, and fled from his creditors to Calais in 1816. The Duke of York maintained a correspondence with him even in his French exile, but terminated it on George's accession to the throne in 1820. As a contemporary noted, George was prepared to send Brummell small financial gifts, and even to offer him a token post as consul at Calais, but was clearly unwilling to renew their former relationship:

> For a trifling folly you chase your friend from your presence – you forget his very existence for something approaching to a quarter of a century, and then by accident hearing that he is starving, you give him two hundred a year out of the pockets of the people, for filling a situation, the duties of which he is totally unfit to perform!

Passing through Calais in 1821 on his way to Hanover, and pausing at the Hôtel d'Angleterre for a glass or two of his favourite Maraschino brandy, George ostentatiously refused to visit Brummell, who had advertised his wish to be reconciled by signing his name in the hotel's visitors' book.[42]

With Brummell gone, George was able to cast himself as the nation's principal arbiter of fashion – at least until his increasing girth put an end to his extravagances. He can be held at least partly responsible for the abandonment of knee-breeches and the popularisation in their stead of pantaloons and trousers – looser than pantaloons, and working-class in origin – and of the starched neckcloth. The neckcloth was an invaluable accessory for the amply-proportioned, in helping to conceal a multiplicity of chins; in the Prince's case, it enabled Thomas Lawrence to depict him at the close of the Napoleonic Wars as a firm-jawed hero.[43]

George was beginning to try to disguise his increasing bulk. The sombre colours he now wore in public – dark blues and dark greens, greys and browns – were certainly 'more flattering to the fuller figure'. Robert Dighton's print of 1804 of the Prince on horseback, in a pallid imitation of David's *Napoléon*, shows him crammed into a fashionably high-collared coat – and that collar, like the neckcloth, helped hide his assemblage of chins. As Aileen Ribeiro has commented, 'Dighton's image of the Prince is fairly flattering, or at least a tribute to the skills of his tailors, whose subterfuges to restrain the royal belly (clever interlining of coats, the use of "belts" or corsets) are also revealed in the [royal] accounts.'[44] The clothing orders for the summer of 1806 surviving in the Royal Archive at Windsor almost entirely concern alterations to George's existing wardrobe, to accommodate his increasing waistline, rather than additions. (The clothes so altered included his sizeable collection of field marshals' uniforms.) Over the next few years, the pattern revealed by this archive is much the same – alterations to his existing wardrobe, rather than lavish new commissions. After 1815 his expanding girth seems to have prompted George to spend enormous sums on military goodies instead, including £904 3s. 1d. on re-equipping the 10th Hussars. Typically, payment for much of this latter expenditure – such as the £350 for new pantaloons in 1815 – was still owed to the regimental agents Greenwood Cox and Company at the time of George's death.[45]

Neither resignation from 'his' regiment nor his increasing size and ill-health, nor indeed the Guards' well-publicised and shocking mutiny at the time of Queen Caroline's trial in 1820,[46] served to quench George's obsession with militaria. In 1823, for example, he spent £1,912 'For the State Cloathing of Bands'. Indeed, most of his expenditure on tailoring during the 1820s was with the army clothiers John Prosser and John Meyer, who during 1828 alone provided new uniforms worth £869. He was even ordering new equipment for the army on his death-bed. Almost his last conscious act in June 1830, when his eyesight had failed and as his body was swiftly deteroriating, was to order new helmets and uniforms for the Gentlemen Pensioners at Chelsea from F. J. Cater and John Meyer.[47] George's love of the evocative image conjured up by well-designed uniforms was a passion that stayed with him until the very end.

5

Architectural Patronage

... when Fum first did light on
The floor of that grand China-warehouse at Brighton,
The lanterns, and dragons, and things round the dome
Were so like what he left, 'Gad,' says Fum, 'I'm at home.'
Thomas Moore, *Fum and Hum, The Two Birds of Royalty*

PREVENTED FROM SERVING beside his brothers in the army, the
Prince of Wales found an outlet for his ambitions and aspirations
in the visual arts instead. In the creation of a series of spectacular residences his aesthetic flair and his eclectic connoisseurship were given
full rein – at the taxpayers' expense. Nevertheless, Holland's Carlton
House and Brighton Pavilion, as they stood in 1800, were two of the
most exquisitely tasteful expressions of French neoclassicism ever to
be executed on this side of the Channel, while the subsequent reincarnation of the Pavilion in 'Oriental' guise involved the concoction of a
series of breathtaking interiors unique in western Europe.

It was in his homes and their decoration that George's character
was most revealingly expressed. Erecting or merely remodelling buildings was a lifelong obsession, and one of his favourite occupations.
However, like his personality, George's architectural achievements
were invariably flawed and, like all his enthusiasms, also often remarkably short-lived. His reckless expenditure, and the failure of his architects to supervise and check the escalating costs of his architectural
whims, laid him open to justifiable charges of fiscal irresponsibility.
His eclectic taste, which when adequately harnessed could inspire
interiors of unparalleled interest and innovation, led him as he grew
older into increasingly bizarre and seemingly contradictory flights of
fancy in decoration and collecting. Most significantly, his inability to

concentrate on anything for long meant that all his homes were subjected to a bewildering succession of expensive reincarnations. By 1815 Holland's tasteful neo-classical vision had been fatally compromised both at Carlton House and, more obviously, at Brighton. A decade later, George's notorious susceptibility to peevish boredom, allied to an increasingly reclusive nature, led him to raze Carlton House to the ground and to disperse or store its exceptional contents. What was perhaps the greatest testimony to royal taste and royal patronage thus perished at its begetter's own command. The wilful destruction of his achievement at Carlton House is possibly one of the best illustrations of George's persistent inability ever to remain faithful to any one thing, whether building or individual. His tendency to indulge every whim, regardless of its physical or emotional consequences, was never so apparent.

Few would deny that George was a compulsive builder. Here again, although the scale, vision and expense of his numerous projects far exceeded the modest schemes commissioned by his father or his Hanoverian ancestors, the passion for architecture was inherited. George III had studied under his mother's architect, William Chambers, and attained a reasonable level of skill with the draughtsman's pencil. In gratitude, after his accession in 1760 he rewarded Chambers with a shower of official appointments – Joint Architect (1761), Comptroller (1769) and finally Surveyor-General (1782) of the Royal Works – and with much-envied commissions to remodel Buckingham House, to build new royal residences in Richmond and Windsor, and to redevelop the site of Somerset House in part as a home for George III's cherished Royal Academy of Arts. The King himself dabbled on the periphery of architectural design, much as his son later did. The student who faithfully reproduced plates from Chambers's *Treatise on Civil Architecture* became the monarch who reputedly designed Chambersian doorcases at Buckingham House after 1762 and a farm worker's cottage for Windsor Great Park in 1793. George III's prejudice against Chambers's talented rivals, the Adam brothers, mirrored Chambers's own poor opinion of the clan, expressed in a sour diatribe in the third (1791) edition of his *Treatise*, in which the old architect railed, too late, against the Adams's 'boyish conceits, and trifling complicated ornaments', which 'open a wide door to whim & extravagance', leaving 'a latitude to the composer, which often betrays, & hurries him to ridiculous absurdities ... and an ocean of extravagance'. Sounding exactly like his architectural mentor, the King firmly declared that Robert Adam had 'introduced too much of neatness and prettyness' into British architecture.[1]

By 1800 George III' s architectural commissions were few and far between, however. Chambers's death in 1796, the King's own periodic illnesses and the financial burdens of the war against France all discouraged him from instituting any significant building projects. The cost of his own modest alterations to existing royal residences had by this time been far surpassed by that of his eldest son's architectural extravagances. Revealingly, the Prince of Wales chose not to replicate the close bond that had existed between his father and William Chambers – despite the fact that Chambers, as Surveyor-General of the Royal Office of Works, was technically responsible for the Carlton House site. George preferred to eschew a master–pupil relationship in which he was the junior partner in favour of dialogue with more malleable professionals who would execute his whims without demur. Deliberately ignoring the tried-and-trusted talents of Chambers and even of his rival Robert Adam – whose delicate synthesis of traditional Palladianism, contemporary Italian and neoclassical styles was anyway beginning to look a little old-hat by the mid 1780s – the young Prince turned to one of the most sophisticated proponents of the neoclassical style in Britain, and the unofficial architect of the Whigs: Henry Holland.

Carlton House as devised by Holland and the Prince was a homage to the contemporary French taste of the *ancien régime*. The creation of what Horace Walpole admiringly termed a 'chaste palace [of] august simplicity . . ., taste and propriety' has often been used as a convenient point from which to date the inception of the so-called Regency period in architecture and the decorative arts – a period in which French-inspired neo-classicism, allied to a more daring use of new technology, significantly altered the way Britons of all classes regarded their built environment.[2] This new idiom, as expressed in the decorous exterior and sumptuous interiors of Holland's Carlton House, caught the imagination of a generation. By the mid 1790s George's London home was, in the opinion of Walpole, a royal palace without parallel – 'the most perfect in Europe'. Never was any of his subsequent creations so unreservedly admired.

The site of Carlton House originally came into the royal family's possession when Prince Frederick bought it from the third Earl of Burlington's mother in 1732. Frederick had commissioned Burlington's protégé William Kent and his Palladian cronies in the Office of Works to remodel the red brick house of 1709 into a properly-proportioned Palladian villa. Kent had been appointed Architect to the Prince of Wales that very year; the finished residence was hidden in a Kent-designed 'English garden' complete with a typically Kentian octagonal retreat.[3] Fifty years later, George III gave this unremarkable but excellently situated house to his eldest son as a coming-of-age present.

George's first thought was to transform his staid Palladian mansion into something far more up-to-date. His chosen architect, Henry Holland, was a bricklayer's son who had recently shot to prominence with his reticent but daringly brick-faced neoclassical design for Brooks's Club in St James's, a haunt of Whig politicians which George himself frequented in the company of Charles James Fox. Holland's Whig connections and his evident admiration of French design and French taste were instant recommendations, and George commissioned him to remodel the setting for his princely Court in a fashionably Francophile neoclassical idiom.

In England, unalloyed admiration for things French has always been apt to invite charges of lack of patriotism. When work began on Carlton House in 1783, Britain had only just made peace with France; ten years later, when the building was being extended and redecorated, the nation was once again at war with her traditional enemy. George, however, exhibited his customary disregard for other people's sensibilities and gave no thought to issues of political propriety, happily indulging his Francophile enthusiasms as freely as possible. While Holland was his architect for the first fifteen years of the project, George's principal advisors on decoration were consistently French: initially the barely-qualified decorator-cum-cook Guillaume Gaubert, and after 1787 the *émigré* furniture dealer Dominique Daguerre. During his eight years at Carlton House Monsieur Daguerre established a good working relationship with the amenable Holland. As Hugh Roberts has observed, 'The combination of Daguerre's stylish opulence and Holland's classical restraint produced some of the most perfect and refined Anglo-French interiors ever realised in England'.[4] Daguerre's own preference was for showy pieces of furniture set with Sèvres porcelain plaques or panels of old *pietra dura*. George, always ready to conform with those of decided opinions, accordingly adopted this taste, too – at least until he was persuaded otherwise by later advisors.

Many of the key elements of Carlton House, borrowed as they were directly from contemporary French projects, appeared markedly innovative in 1780s Britain. The forecourt was modelled on that at Rousseau's widely-admired Hôtel de Salm in Paris, a building begun in the same year as Carlton House which by 1786, when Thomas Jefferson was charmed by its neoclassical elegance, had achieved an international reputation. After crossing the forecourt, visitors passed through Holland's impressively austere Grecian portico into the noble and unmistakably neoclassical hall. From the principal entrance on Pall Mall the portico, hall and other principal rooms appeared to be situated on the ground floor and not, as was more usual, on the first, or *piano nobile*. The site actually sloped to the south, however, and from the garden the main apartments could be seen to stand upon a 'basement' floor. The severe lines of the rectangular hall were offset by the vibrant, summery yellows and ochres of its bold colour scheme. The marble floor and the enormous brass lanterns which hung from the top-lit, coffered ceiling cupola were framed by Ionic columns in yellow brocatello marble with bronzed bases and capitals, and the walls were painted in yellow, Siena ochre and green. From here visitors passed between two of the columns to reach an octagonal vestibule painted a 'granite' green to match that in the hall, lit by a glazed skylight and framed by modern marble busts and bizarre, Holland-designed lights (in the shape of Classical terms with bronze oil lamps upon their heads).[5] Once here they could, again unusually, descend Holland's superbly theatrical grand stair, adapted from Bélanger's published plans for the Pavillon de Bagatelle near Paris (Holland may well also have seen Bélanger's scheme when he visited Paris in 1788). Begun in 1786 but not finished until 1795 (when Britain had been at war with France for two years), the staircase's sumptuous iron-and-brass balustrade originally terminated opposite two enormous caryatids, each more than seven feet in height, which supported an allegory of Familiarity – an ambitious feature later replaced by a prosaically empty niche. From here guests could visit the bizarre Chinese Room, complete with its gilded French furnishings in a clumsily oriental manner. Alternatively, they could proceed through the vestibule to the glittering apartments on the north side, those which later became the Rose Satin Drawing Room and the Blue Velvet Rooms, the circular Music Room, the two Throne Rooms (old and new) and the Crimson Drawing Room.

These sumptuous interiors became bywords not only for George's taste but also for his fickle nature. Between 1784 and 1819, the bowfronted Rose Satin Drawing Room, on the ceiling of which Pegasus rode across a clouded sky surrounded by the Muses, was provided with four different chimney-pieces. The colour of the silk wall-hangings and seat upholstery was also changed from lemon yellow to green to crimson within the space of ten years. By 1811 the seats were covered in blue silk, although the walls were still red; later that same year, however, George changed his mind yet again and had them recovered in crimson damask. However, the gold-coloured taffeta ordered for this room in 1818 was never hung, nor was the green silk bought in 1821 (it was instead diverted to Brighton).[6] Holland's circular Music Room fared better, and retained its elegant, red-and-white scagliola columns until the end of its life. However, by 1794 it had become another Drawing Room, and after 1804 was converted into the Dining Room (while the old Dining Room became the Crimson Drawing Room). The handsome, richly-gilded (new) Throne Room also managed to remain much as Holland had originally devised it, although again the seat upholstery underwent various changes of hue.

Holland's new rooms at Carlton House were the acme of late eighteenth-century taste: restrained, elegant and knowingly francophile. That ageing wit, connoisseur and collector Horace Walpole was so delighted with Holland's creation as to compare it favourably with Robert Adam's interiors of the previous two decades, famously observing: 'How sick one shall be, after this chaste place, of Mr Adam's gingerbread and sippets of embroidery.'[7] However, restraint was not a concept with which George was overly familiar, and he rapidly tired of all this cool classicism. He callously dropped Holland in 1802, following an entirely unnecessary altercation over the ownership of a parcel of land in Okehampton in Devon, and Holland never again communicated with his former patron.[8]

After Holland was removed from the equation, his work at Carlton House was largely obliterated. After 1805 most of the interiors were completely recast – not by an architect, not by an interior designer (French or otherwise), not even by an acknowledged furniture expert, but by a picture-dealer. Walsh Porter had come to George's attention through his eccentric Gothic design for his own home, Craven Cottage, which was worked up with the help of the professional architect Thomas Hopper and built on the Thames next to the Bishop's Palace at Fulham. By the time Craven Cottage was completed in 1806 (on a site today synonymous with football rather than finials), Porter, although largely unqualified, was engaged in a vague but important capacity at Carlton House. That same year, as Farington commented, the Prince and Porter 'destroyed all that Holland has done', and Porter was busily 'substituting and finishing in a most expensive and motley taste'.[9]

Porter's gifts lay not so much in his eye for decoration or in any flair for architectural planning as in his general enthusiasm and entrepreneurial self-confidence. His belief in himself certainly appears to have bowled George over. The eminent dealer–collector Francis Bourgeois sniffily dismissed Porter as no more than 'very eccentric and entertaining', but was forced to admit that 'His Society was much relished by the Prince of Wales' – 'who, in His associations,' he added cattily, 'was sure to fix upon [such] a man.' Porter's greatest ability, his critics opined, lay in his 'delicacy in entertaining'. As for his professional qualifications, Lord Dunstanville 'thought him to be "a very slight man [and] that there was nothing in Him either of knowledge or understanding"'. Bourgeois snobbily denigrated Porter as 'a dealer' (a term which could also have been applied aptly enough to himself), and a man who 'had not the least real knowledge of pictures'. Another, less refined critic of 1806 wholeheartedly agreed with Bourgeois's diagnosis, accusing the Prince directly of 'pulling to pieces [Carlton House], under the direction of a gentleman, called, an *amateur architect*'.[10]

Porter's unprofessional conduct on site fully merited these unflattering judgements. His amateurism and arrogance are revealed in his indignant reply on being asked in August 1805 to give precise estimates for the work yet to be done at Carlton House. Refusing to admit that his financial forecasts were completely unreliable, he quickly transferred the anticipated blame onto his employer: 'I have not', he remonstrated, 'added or branched out into a single thing that was not plan'd by the Prince himself.' Not once did Porter admit that it was his responsibility to provide costings of the projected alterations.[11] In the last analysis, of course, the Prince alone would be held accountable – a fact of which Porter was clearly all too well aware.

In his attitude to the aesthetics of redecoration, as in his carelessness over finance – and, in particular, when the use of public money was involved – Walsh Porter's own enthusiasm and strong convictions tended to sway the Prince's always impressionable judgement. Porter's dramatic use of bright colours to create ensembles of 'opulence ... and barbaric splendour' certainly appears to have captured George's imagination. Under Porter's direction a new (and short-lived) Chinese Room in an eye-catching scheme of carmine, black and gold was created on the principal floor, while in the new, circular Dining Room – formerly Holland's coolly elegant Music Room – he introduced sky-blue walls and draperies together with a bright orange carpet. These must have clashed as horribly with the Sèvres dinner services, the gold plate and Boulle furniture which now filled the room as with Holland's scagliola columns, silvered capitals and lavender cornice. George, however, appears to have been perfectly happy with the result.

Porter, ever the inventive courtier, skilfully played to George's enthusiasms and partialities in a way Holland had not. Recognising his patron's abiding passion for play-soldiering, he inserted both an Admiral's Room (adapted from Holland's Small Blue Velvet Room) and a 'Military Tent Room' into Carlton House. The ceiling of the Admiral's Room was decorated by Porter with evocations of great British naval victories – battles which the Prince, as he dozed, could pretend he had won. These martial images were far more soothing than memories of his wife, for whom the room had been redecorated in 1795. All traces of her taste were now successfully expunged. Stretched velvet panels of Garter blue replaced Caroline's wall-hung tapestries – the gold-embroidered ornaments for these fabric panels featured 96 gold oak leaves and acorns, 170 roses and 11 large anchors. The Plate Closet was calculated to appeal directly to George's acquisitive appetites: devised by Porter as the most sumptuous room of all, it was stuffed with silver, silver-gilt and gold plate supplied by the royal jewellers and goldsmiths Rundell, Bridge and Rundell, all arranged in 'a magnificent exhibition of taste and expense'.[12]

The rapid metamorphoses of the Carlton House interiors bewildered all but the most sycophantic observers. After Walsh Porter's death in 1809, rooms were frequently replanned and redecorated in the complete absence of any overall philosophy or consistency of vision. Sometimes a principal interior was simply gutted. For example, the Chinese Room, the decor and fittings of which had originally been assembled with great care and at considerable expense by Holland and Daguerre between 1787 and 1790, and which had so recently been remodelled by Porter, had been largely dismantled by 1811. George was happy to countenance the orientalisation of Brighton Pavilion, but had evidently grown bored with the Chinese style in his London home.

This propensity to lose interest in familiar objects both accelerated and grew more pronounced as George grew older. On 2 May 1810, for example, he took delivery of a gilt-bronze mantel clock by

Napoleon's master-clockmaker, Pierre-Philippe Thomire, upon which Apollo's chariot rode over Heaven's arch. This costly piece was placed in one of the most important spaces at Carlton House, the Crimson Drawing Room. Eighteen months later, however, it had disappeared into store, having been replaced by another French clock.[13] The most expensive acquisitions were it seemed just so many toys, to be disposed of once the Great Babe had tired of them.

The vulgarity and capriciousness of it all did not go unremarked by contemporaries. A friend of Joseph Farington's, on attending the new Regent's first levée at Carlton House in February 1811, condemned the 'very expensive manner in which the apartments are fitted up':

> ... not a spot without some finery upon it, gold upon gold – a bad taste. Smirke had seen the apartments, and said, they are so overdone with finery, and superfluous as, supposing the owner not to [be] known, would give an unfavourable idea of the kind of mind He must have who could have pleasure in such scenery.[14]

More recent commentators have tended to echo this judgement on the post-Holland Carlton House. Sir Oliver Millar has described with distaste how the interiors of the house 'were continually being re-arranged, the hangings, the curtains and carpets constantly renewed, the colour schemes endlessly altered: blue and gold, red and gold, scarlet, pale yellow, salmon, lemon or green'. Nash's greatest biographer, Sir John Summerson, firmly believed that the Prince never commissioned 'anything as good as Henry Holland's work in Carlton House', and that Walsh Porter's exotic redesign amounted to wanton disfigurement of a work of genius. Summerson's magisterial conclusion was that, as George grew older, 'Both his love affairs and his architecture declined in distinction.'[15]

While Walsh Porter was employed in tarting up its interiors, the comparatively unknown architect Thomas Hopper, recommended by Porter, contributed perhaps the most eccentric of all the spaces at Carlton House: the Gothic conservatory of 1807–9, which projected from the new Dining Room on the basement side of the building. While Hopper's fantasy-Gothic design, based on the impressive fan-vaulting of Henry VII's Chapel at Westminster Abbey, appears to have been deliberately frivolous, the construction was nothing if not avant-garde. The revolutionary iron frame, which Hopper filled with stained glass, anticipated the great glazed sheds of the 1840s and 50s at

Paddington Station and the Crystal Palace. Even the candelabras were made of an emphatically modern material: Coade stone. The glass, however, was designed to evoke past centuries. Echoing the Prince's laudanum-fuelled visions of himself as a reincarnation of the great medieval warrior-sovereigns of yore, it featured the arms of all the English monarchs since William the Conqueror and all the Princes of Wales since Edward II. Alas, Hopper proved perhaps a little *too* far ahead of his time: the glazed iron vault constantly leaked, and soon became infested with rust.

The building and decorating at Carlton House did not merely strain the Prince's relatively limited budget; more than any of his extravagances, they served to unbalance his always precarious finances. When the house was given him for his London residence, he was hoping for an allowance as Prince of Wales of £100,000 a year from Parliament. In the event, as we have seen, he received only £62,000 – £50,000 from the Civil List, the rest from his own Duchy of Cornwall. And only £30,000 of this was allocated for 'repairs' to Carlton House. His ambitious new works were thus substantially under-funded from the very beginning, and his cheerful profligacy in commissioning new interiors only served to make matters worse. Holland originally estimated that £18,000 would be needed to rebuild and refit the existing house; by 1784, however, £30,250 had already been spent, and an extra £35,000 had been assigned to fund the interior decoration. The economic context of such expenditure – a severe slump occasioned by bad harvests and the delayed fiscal effects of the ruinous American War – merely underlined George's blithe unconcern for the ramifications of his self-indulgence, and ensured that Carlton House became more a popular symbol of heedless intemperance than of exquisite taste. George himself, however, refused to acknowledge his mistake, spluttering ineffably pompous protests at the 'absurdity as well as impossibility' of acceding to his father's request that work be curtailed, and feigning shock at the very notion of 'the Heir Apparent to the Crown of Britain' having to 'dismiss his servants, sell his horses, and part, in short, with every magnificence annexed to his situation in life'. Betraying, as ever, an over-inflated view of his own worth to the nation, George concluded that 'it would be improper for me to live with a less degree of magnificence than I hitherto have done'.[16]

In spite of George III's protests, the escalation of costs at Carlton House continued. In 1785, they amounted to £147,293 – the new stables alone, at £31,000, accounted for more than Parliament's designated £30,000. In 1786 Holland's estimate for work 'necessary to be done in order to Compleat the palace for Habitation' and to 'render [it] compleatly Magnificent' amounted to a substantial £69,700, while Gaubert's interior decoration had already cost £38,021. The following year the Prince asked his father for an additional £20,000 from the Civil List to complete the works. This was voted by the House of Commons in May 1786; however, in return George was compelled to make drastic economies – despite his disingenuous claims to his father that any reduction of expenditure would merely be 'a drop of water in the sea'.[17] Work did stop for a few months (though as we have seen, the cuts imposed were little more than window-dressing), but George never curbed his grand vision, and building work began again as soon as was decently possible. The prospect of a Regency caused a quickening of the pace: the principal rooms, George declared in eager anticipation, must be redecorated 'with the greatest haste possible ... for a very approaching Epocha'. No expense was to be spared; thus Holland's revised estimate of early 1789 was a staggering £110,500. Faced with the need to secure government support for the proposed Regency Bill in February, George felt obliged to pare this down to £56,950. This figure was still, however, ten times the original estimate for repairs, which had been set at a mere £5,500.[18] By March his father had recovered and Pitt's government was safe: both, unsurprisingly, rejected these inflated estimates. In place of the funds anticipated from Parliament, revenue from the Prince's increasingly overburdened Duchy of Cornwall paid for much of the work. In 1792 George III, by now thoroughly exasperated, flatly refused to allow Parliament to vote any more money for the project.[19]

Carlton House was by no means the only property George transformed during these years. Despite the ostensibly strict limitations on his funds, he persistently diverted substantial resources to his hobby of buying or leasing houses – trying them out for size, altering them at great expense, and then selling or demolishing them when he had tired of their charms. In 1795, for example, he abandoned his Hampshire hunting retreat at Kempshott, near Basingstoke – which he had rented from the banker Henry Drummond and on which he had already spent considerable sums – in order to lease The Grange, ten miles to the south near Northington. The Grange was a house of 1664, originally built by the Restoration architect William Samwell. Here George could hunt and shoot to his heart's content in the company of Lady Jersey and his reprobate friends, sixty good miles away from his hated spouse. Within two years he had hired Holland to make repairs at The Grange and to introduce five thousand pounds' worth of new fittings. Inevitably, however, he soon became bored with both site and decor. (He was also being hounded by local tradesmen; two years after leaving The Grange, he was still £757 in arrears for wine supplied to the house.) In 1797 The Grange was sub-let to Lord Lonsdale, and in October 1800 the Prince announced that 'the place is no longer mine, having entirely got rid of it'.[20]

George's decorative restlessness was by no means confined to Carlton House or his country retreats. In 1808, at Kensington Palace, £14,104 was spent by the Office of Works in fitting out rooms for him, but in subsequent years he was rarely there. In 1818 he bought three houses on the north side of Kew Green and converted them into one, at a cost of £16,000. A surveyor's report of 1823 noted that 'The house has ... been considerably enlarged, and attached thereto are a set of offices principally new built consisting of a large kitchen, confectionaries and other domestic accommodations, replete with useful fittings up, besides apartments adapted to the particular convenience of a part of the Royal Household upon his Majesty's occasional resort to Kew.' (Although His Majesty's visits to the house were very occasional indeed, it is interesting to learn that he had made a point of adding 'confectionaries' – an equally important feature of the plans of Nash's roughly contemporary alterations to Brighton Pavilion. George clearly had a very expensive sweet tooth.) The Kew Green house was only a few hundred yards away from the so-called Kew Castle, a bizarre castellated folly begun by James Wyatt for George III after 1802 and still incomplete in 1811. One of George's first acts as Prince Regent was to stop work on Wyatt's 'bastille'; sixteen years later, in a fit of malice, he ordered the unfinished building blown up. Some of the materials were salvaged for re-use at Buckingham Palace and Windsor; one Gothic window from the castle has been tracked down to a shed in Kew Gardens. The castle's fate was ominously indicative: it was evident that George knew no qualms when it came to remodelling or even destroying his parents' homes.

Other royal residences almost went the way of Kew Castle. When George demolished Carlton House after 1826, many feared the adjacent and venerable pile of St James's Palace would also be razed to make way for yet another pompous edifice by Nash or Wyatville. George realised, however, that while Buckingham Palace was being rebuilt he needed somewhere to stay during his increasingly brief sojourns in his capital, and chose instead to lavish considerable resources on refitting 'the only apartments in which he can at present hold his Court in London'. Meanwhile Windsor Castle was equipped with elements rescued from Carlton House, including 23 chimney-pieces with their grates, fenders and fire irons, and whole floors from the Great Drawing Room, the Circular Dining Room, and other key interiors.[21]

We have seen how the decoration of Carlton House was propelled in a new direction after George's abandonment of Holland. In 1804 the prolific if careless architect James Wyatt was directed to 'repair' the building. Given the ambitions of both Prince and architect, it is hardly surprising to find that the parameters of Wyatt's commission were soon extended, and estimates for what was effectively a complete rebuilding once again soared – from an initial £5,000 to £8,500 and beyond. After Porter's death in 1809, the eager Wyatt was brought in once more. He was initially asked to design the temporary buildings needed for the great fête to celebrate the Regency held in the Carlton House grounds in June 1811 (at which Hopper's Conservatory was centrally cast as the royal supper room); subsequently he was employed making additions to the main house. In 1812 Wyatt built a new Library; a Strong Room soon followed, deemed necessary to hold the quantities of gold and silver plate the new Regent was greedily amassing.[22]

Wyatt's increasing influence came to an end with his sudden death in a carriage accident on 18 September 1813. George cried on hearing the news: he had, he blubbed, 'just found a man suited to his mind and was thus unhappily deprived of him.' However, this did not prevent him from dismissing Wyatt's importunate son, who had broken the news to him. Philip Wyatt, extracting every ounce of drama and seizing every opportunity, had burst into the royal bed-chamber at three in the morning. After reducing George to tears, he had 'proceeded with the real business which ... was to solicit the Prince Regent to bestow upon Him such of the advantages possessed by his late Father as His Royal Highness might think proper' – a request which met only 'with a civil answer in a general way'. Far more successful in this regard was Philip's cousin Jeffry Wyatt, who wrote fifteen letters to suitable targets 'soliciting their interest to get something that His uncle enjoyed'.[23] Although Jeffry Wyatt failed to secure the appointment of Surveyor-General his uncle had held, George patently did not forget him, and a decade later was employing him at Windsor Castle.

James Wyatt's place at Carlton House was instead filled by his slightly younger rival John Nash. He was neither the most original designer of his day, nor the most competent, but Nash's flamboyant and theatrical approach nevertheless coincided with George's own taste. Equally importantly, in personality and temperament he was more pliable than better-known practitioners such as John Soane or Robert Smirke. To the Prince Regent, such qualities mattered more than uncompromising vision, or even mere skill.

When the Prince of Wales came of age in 1783, Nash was a relatively unknown architect and speculative builder who had fled to Wales when he was declared bankrupt. He returned to London in 1796, and planned his social ascent with great care. At first he failed to win any commissions, and though in 1798 he submitted to the Prince a design for a conservatory at Brighton, it was not executed. Four years later he married his second wife, Mary Anne Bradley, who was widely believed – with no apparent foundation – to have been at one time a mistress of the Prince of Wales. At the same time he insinuated himself into friendships with the Prince's current confidant and advisor, Lord Yarmouth, and with his Private Secretary, Sir Benjamin Bloomfield. Nash was soon reported to be 'in constant habits of intimacy' with Yarmouth; royal preferment, he presumably hoped, could not be long in coming. Private commissions did indeed begin to come in, but Nash hoped for greater things. In 1806 his courting of the Prince's circle finally bore fruit, and he was appointed architect to the Department of Woods and Forests – in which capacity he later planned the development of what had been known as Marylebone Park and is now Regent's Park. His intimate relationship with the Prince thereafter prompted a good deal of popular speculation, which included the rumour that Nash's pupil James Pennethorne was actually George's bastard son. Certainly by 1813 Nash was close enough to the Regent to be employed as an intermediary with Sir Samuel Romilly, the Solicitor-General, in negotiations concerning the future position of the Princess of Wales – in which unlikely and unedifying role he was directed to offer Romilly the Lord Chancellorship (an appointment over which George in truth had little control). The same year he was asked to do some work on what was then known as the Lower Lodge in Windsor Great Park, and which became that bizarre Gothic retreat, the Royal Lodge. Here, as with so many of George's architectural whims, what was originally characterised as a modest repair scheme swiftly ballooned into something far more ambitious and expensive. Nash's 'repairs' alone cost £35,243, another burden to be borne by the taxpayer and by the Prince's luckless Cornish tenants.[24]

Nash's first major royal architectural commission, offered to him at the very outset of the long-awaited Regency, was a wholly unnecessary and outrageously expensive project: the rebuilding of Carlton House from scratch. George asserted that what had been suitable as his private home now required conversion into a palace fit for State functions. He of course saw no reason why government funds should not instantly be made available for this purpose. Fortified as he was by his new position and its anticipated income, his decorative dictates became even more imperious and whimsical. One of his first acts as Regent was to reject new blue upholstery designed by C. H. Tatham for the former Chinese Drawing Room at a cost of £285, ordering something equally expensive in its stead. Tatham's workmen began at once, 'ripping the blue satin off [the chairs] and recovering with HRH's Crimson Damask decorated with rich Chinese Tassels Cord Gymp etc'. However, Perceval's government was quick to warn the new Regent that the funds available for the rebuilding of Carlton House were not inexhaustible. Accordingly, Nash was directed to scale down his commission. This did not mean that the rooms he did create were any less sumptuous or extravagant: the Gothic Dining Room of 1814, for example, cost almost £9,000. Nor were the new interiors any less imaginative than their predecessors: they epitomised George's increasing tendency to favour a bizarre mixture of styles and periods. The peculiar Gothic piano in the Gothic Dining Room, for example, had little in common with the Louis XVI tables George was avidly acquiring at this time, and none of this furniture had much stylistic affinity with that in the nearby Old Throne Room, which was redecorated and furnished by C. H. Tatham in the latest 'Greek' fashion.[25] The Prince Regent was clearly not concerned with visual coherence, but preferred instead a liberal, 'mix-and-match' approach which anticipated by fifty years the eclectic aesthetic philosophy of the mid-Victorians.

If Nash was never asked to standardise the decorative schemes running through Carlton House, he was allowed to temper the vibrant and often clashing colours of Walsh Porter's day. By 1819 he had reduced Porter's over-imaginative palette to three principal colours, crimson, blue and white, each invariably overlaid or framed with gold. During the last decade of George's life these were the principal colours used not only at Carlton House before its demolition but also at Buckingham Palace and Windsor Castle. Red, white and blue were additionally the predominant colours at the Coronation of 1821 and the Edinburgh pageant of the following year. Blue, fortuituously, was the colour of the Garter, the pre-eminent English chivalric Order with which George so closely identified: at his Coronation, Westminster Abbey was swathed in Garter blue. White and gold were the colours of Bourbon France, whose rulers and decorative arts he so much admired. Crimson provided an excellent foil for his numerous gilt-framed pictures. (Red was the colour generally preferred by the early nineteenth century for drawing room and dining room walls – the spaces in which the most important pictures were customarily hung. J. M. W. Turner himself stipulated that his oils should always be hung against a dark red background.) And George's lavish use of gold was an expression of his predilection for surface glitter and his delight in conspicuous expenditure.

The red, white and blue walls of Carlton House also had a more telling significance. In his choice of this particular combination, George can be seen as attempting, consciously or unconsciously, to wrap himself in the British flag. This was not a novel concept: like so much else in George's life, it derived from a precedent set by his father. Crimson, blue and gold were the colours adopted by George III for his 'Windsor uniform', which his son had been obliged to wear as a youth. Predictably, however, in George's hands the colours of the national flag were employed far more audaciously, and more portentously, than his father had ever wished or dared to use them. In selecting this colour scheme for his royal residences after 1819, George was presenting himself as the embodiment and cynosure of the British nation, a pose he had begun to appropriate even before Waterloo. In truth, of course, the self-appointed Saviour of Europe and Vanquisher of Napoleon, for whom Nash rebuilt Carlton House and Brighton Pavilion and whom Lawrence commemorated so vividly in oils, was seen by most of his subjects as little more than a profligate, guzzling adulterer. Filling his palaces and swaddling his officials with the colours of the national flag would not of itself earn him the genuine affection in which his father had been held.

The newly-refurbished walls of Carlton House were soon covered with paintings. Indeed, by the time of the Regent's accession in 1820,

John Nash, working closely with George and with Lord Yarmouth, had made Carlton House into one vast exhibition gallery. The picture hang, like the decorative treatments, changed constantly, lest the capricious monarch grow bored. There was no separate gallery here: instead, George's numerous pictures – and as well as those 'in use' there were 250 in store in 1819 – were an integral part of the overall effect. In the manner of the Adam brothers or of Meissonnier and the great Rococo decorators of Louis XV's France, Nash was required to devise schemes for each wall which embraced not only the surviving architectural details, fittings and finishes but every aspect of that room's contents, including paintings and prints.

Sadly, we can now only imagine how the interiors were transformed by Nash's improvisatory and pragmatic genius. During the decade after 1810 George grew increasingly uncomfortable with Carlton House – in particular, with its proximity to the street and thus to his ever-curious subjects – and thought of moving elsewhere. In 1818 he suggested buying Wren's adjacent Marlborough House, and by 1821 had resolved to leave Carlton House for the now-empty Buckingham House. In 1826 demolition of Carlton House began, at George's behest, and its carefully-collected contents were dispersed to his other residences.

While the building on the receiving end of the breaker's ball in 1826 was externally still recognisable as Holland's austerly neoclassical composition, the same could not be said of his other principal commission for George, Brighton Pavilion. George first visited the tiny fishing village of Brighthelmstone in September 1783 in the company of his notoriously dissolute uncle Cumberland, both seeking escape from the stultifyingly dull and morally repressed Court of George III. In the best Hanoverian tradition, Cumberland was soon suggesting how his precocious nephew might create an alternative Court there, one where lapses of etiquette, to say nothing of gambling, drinking and the flaunting of mistresses, were not just permissible but the rule. In 1784 the Prince returned to Brighton to take Dr Richard Russell's famous cure – which involved not only bathing in sea-water but actually drinking it – to soothe his throat. (Between them Russell, who had first arrived in 1753, the old Duke of Cumberland and the Prince of Wales effectively created the modern town of Brighton.) Happy at being able to flirt with the local women, to gamble, watch prize-fights and play cricket far from the censorious gaze of his parents, George took to Brighton whole-heartedly. At first he stayed at George

Wyndham's Grove House, on the Steine in the centre of the village; as his visits grew more regular, however, he began to contemplate building for himself.

Robert Huish, tongue firmly in cheek, later suggested that the Prince had been drawn to Brighton 'by the angelic figure of a sea-nymph whom he one day encountered reclining on one of the groins of the beach' – a delicious image which a century or so later became the basis of Rex Whistler's famous mural, still at the Pavilion. In truth, the sea-nymph was the decidedly earth-bound Maria Fitzherbert. At Brighton, George and Maria could live as man and wife, basking in the support of the local people and far from the disapproving mutterings of the royal family or Pitt's government. With the resolution of making his visits a fixed part of his social calendar, George hired the architect of Carlton House to furnish him with a permanent home. Between 1785 and 1795 Henry Holland created a small, exquisite neo-classical villa which would not have looked out of place in pre-Revolutionary or later Napoleonic Paris. As at Carlton House, the composition essentially followed that of Pierre Rousseau's Hôtel de Salm: a central, circular saloon, emphasised by a colonnade, between two low wings. Also as at Carlton House, the principal rooms at the Pavilion were on the ground floor. This departure from the Georgian custom was not here dictated by the site's topography, however; in this case the arrangement was instituted so that George, who was growing increasingly obese, would not have to mount tiresome flights of stairs after dinner.

As Guillaume Gaubert initially controlled the furnishing of Carlton House, so another cook, Louis Weltje, directed the internal works at Holland's Brighton villa. In a complicated legal and financial arrange-ment, Weltje sub-let the Pavilion to the Prince of Wales in 1786, and during 1787–8 spent £21,454 on decorating what was supposedly a modest seaside villa, buying quantities of expensive French furniture in Paris. As at Carlton House, contemporary France was once again the principal inspiration; the library and dining room, for example, were fitted out in 'French style' and lined with yellow wallpaper. And to ensure that neither the Office of Works nor His Majesty's Treasury could interfere, by insisting, for example, that the works be carried out properly and professionally, the fiction was maintained that the villa was Weltje's personal project. Only in 20 September 1793 did his favourite cook formally lease George the almost-completed Pavilion, at £1,000 a year for twenty-six years.[26]

By 1800, the year Weltje died, George had tired of Holland's undemonstrative interiors at Brighton, exactly as he had of the cool elegance of Carlton House. Now he went to the opposite extreme, inviting designs for a remodelling in the 'Chinese' style. The Chinese taste had been markedly popular in the middle of the preceding century, when its more outrageous manifestations were tamed and ordered in William Chambers's book on the subject of 1757. From his earliest years George must have been very familiar with the Chinese Pagoda and other 'Chinese' structures erected by Chambers in the gardens at Kew. There is unmistakable irony in his return, so many years later, to a style pioneered by his father's architect – a man whom, when alive, he had so studiously ignored.

Shortly before Chambers's death in 1796, chinoiserie – the evocation of Chinese forms and designs by English craftsmen – was again briefly fashionable, following Lord Macartney's embassy of 1794 to the Pekin court of the Emperor Ch'ien Lung. The public imagination was not caught, as it had been half a century before, but George was obviously enraptured by its daring exoticism (E. W. Brayley suggested in 1838 that he had been particularly impressed by a gift of some 'very beautiful' hand-painted Chinese wallpaper[27]). Holland was accordingly invited to disguise his quintessentially Graeco-French villa in an approximately 'Chinese' idiom – a task which must surely have appalled his neoclassical soul, and may have been a contributory factor in his subsequent break with the Prince. Holland's departure in 1802 made little difference to the progress of the work, which continued under the direction of his nephew and pupil, P. F. Robinson. By 1803, £12,799 had been spent on the orientalising of Holland's villa. In this year James Wyatt's former pupil, William Porden, was hired to build stables (costing £49,871) and to continue recasing the main building (at an estimated cost of £25,758). Porden had recently remodelled Eaton Hall in Cheshire for George's racing crony Earl Grosvenor, and Grosvenor probably brought him to the Prince's notice. As ever, George's architectural ambitions bore no relation to the size of his purse. Income from the Duchy of Cornwall and from sales of some of his other properties would, his advisors calculated, raise only £14,348 towards Porden's estimated costs,[28] leaving a hefty sum to be found from public money.

In 1805 the architect, designer and landscape gardener Humphry Repton was asked to prepare some 'oriental' designs for the main Pavilion. Like similar schemes prepared by Porden at this time,

Repton's reflected 'the architecture of Hindustan' – even though neither man (any more, of course, than their royal patron) had had first-hand experience of genuine Indian design. Porden had been interested in 'Hindu' architecture as early as 1797, when he exhibited a design in this tortuous style at the Royal Academy, and his Brighton stables and riding school or 'riding-house' were certainly more 'Indian' in character than Nash's subsequent Pavilion. Porden's basic plan nevertheless remained classically orthodox, while much of the external decoration was more reminiscent of Nicholas Hawksmoor's strange hybrid Gothic of the 1720s than of contemporary Indian forms. The centre-piece of Porden's new stable complex was a massive glazed iron roof, sixty-five feet in diameter and modelled on the domed trading floor of Bélanger's Halle au Blé of 1805–11. Contemporaries were mightily impressed, but its erection necessitated obliteration of the charming Promenade Grove pleasure gardens, laid out in 1793 in imitation of those at Vauxhall, while the great dome dwarfed Holland's adjacent Pavilion. This, with its quiet and dignified classical façade, now looked wholly out of place beside Porden's Brobdignagian pantomine set. Repton commented that he thought Porden's block resembled 'rather a Turkish mosque than the buildings of Hindustan'. Nevertheless, the new complex won general acclaim. Lord Thomond declared that he thought the facilities too good for their purpose: 'the Stalls for the Horses were so fine, that at the head of them instead of a rack for Hay, there ought to be a looking glass'.[29]

George's habit of going ahead with projects he patently could not afford inevitably left personal as well as architectural casualties in its wake. Among the former was the principal builder at the Pavilion, Edward Gray Saunders. Having long complained of 'Mr Porden's departure from the best and most approved practice in settling the prices of Works', Saunders died in embarrassed circumstances in December 1810, still owing large sums to tradesmen supplying the works at the Pavilion. His demise meant financial disaster in turn for many local timber merchants, who subsequently petitioned the Prince himself for the £11,000 they were owed.[30] Porden, as is clear from what Edward Saunders says of him, was part of the problem; but, if he was prone to delays and sloppy tendering practices, he was never provided by the Prince with enough money to pay his subcontractors. He was not even given enough to cover his own fees; at Christmas 1806, for example, he was warned that he would not be paid at all for work already completed. He was probably well aware that, having no formal contract for his work at Brighton, he might face financial ruin. He was, however, sufficiently businesslike to warn his patron, rather wearily, of the danger of proceeding with the works 'more rapidly than the finances would discharge', reminding him that 'the naked timbers of the Riding House stand exposed to all weathers, a monument of disgrace to His Royal Highness and all concerned'. Nor was Porden unaware of the problems of such as Edward Saunders, for when this admonition fell on deaf ears, as he had no doubt anticipated it would, he wrote to a friend that 'The distress of these [local] Creditors is I believe very great; and the clamour against His Royal Highness will be in proportion.'[31] Unsurprisingly, this realistic appraisal did not endear him to George: after completion of the riding school in 1808 and a house for Mrs Fitzherbert on the Steine, to the south of the Pavilion, Porden was not asked to execute any of the schemes he had prepared for the main house. Repton was equally disappointed: 1808 also saw the publication of his designs for the Pavilion, for which great royal enthusiasm had originally been expressed; he soon found, however, that the moment had passed, and he and his ideas were no longer favoured by the Prince – who had the effrontery to plead poverty as his excuse.

In place of Porden and instead of Repton, George turned first to James Wyatt – whose 1812 scheme for a drastic remodelling of the Pavilion would have cost a staggering £200,000 – and after Wyatt's death to his new architectural favourite, John Nash. The latter was extremely fortunate: the powers afforded by the Regency meant that funds were readily available for his project that had never been forthcoming for Holland or Porden. However, Nash was even more lax than Porden in his financial regulation of work in progress – no great matter in the carefree atmosphere of the Regency. The fact that the costs of work at the Pavilion during this period rose to over £12,000 more than Nash's original estimate was not something which unduly worried either the architect or his royal patron, and there was no real attempt to control expenditure. Even a short ornamental wall designed to enclose the area to the east of the stables cost £2,445 – more than £100,000 at present-day values.[32]

The rebuilding of Brighton Pavilion was particularly ill-timed. The fact that his country was suffering the effects of a severe post-war slump appears, indeed, to have wholly escaped George. In March 1816 the Tory leadership felt impelled to minute him as to the inadvisability of undertaking ever more ambitious works at Brighton 'at a time when most of the landed gentlemen of the country are obliged to submit to losses and privations'. The Prime Minister, Lord Liverpool, together with the Foreign Secretary, Lord Castlereagh, and the Home Secretary, Nicholas Vansittart, advised him in plain language to desist from future construction or redecoration at the Pavilion. To forestall criticism in Parliament – where George Tierney, one of the chief opposition Members in the House of Commons, had already demanded an inquiry into the Regent's finances, singling out for particular condemnation the excesses at Brighton – in May 1816 he agreed to bring work at the Pavilion to a temporary halt. Yet once Liverpool's government vote had contrived to save George the embarrassment of a detailed examination of his profligate expenditure, the reprimand was conveniently forgotten, and work began again. Three years later George again revealed his disdain for prevailing economic conditions and the attitude of his subjects. In May 1819 Liverpool's government, seeing no obvious way out of the country's economic malaise, considered a proposal to levy £3 million in new taxes. Three months later, on 16 August 1819, a crowd perhaps 80,000-strong was peacefully assembled in St Peter's Field, Manchester to hear the reformer Henry Hunt; the magistrates, alarmed by Hunt's fiery eloquence, sent in forty scarcely-trained militiamen to arrest him. They were engulfed in the crowd, and it was thought necessary to send in the 15th Hussars to rescue them. In the ensuing mêlée eleven of the crowd were killed and about four hundred wounded. The fact that a quarter of the injured were women prompted the Opposition press and the print-makers to ever greater heights of indignation. Meanwhile, news of an ill-conceived message of congratulation George sent to the Manchester magistrates served to associate him closely with the outrage.

It was against this background of unrest and disquiet that the government was notified of a further sizeable increase in expenditure on Brighton Pavilion. (Maintained directly by the Regent's Privy Purse, the Pavilion lay outside the remit of the Office of Works, itself now under direct Treasury control rather than that of the Regent's Household.) 'We were shown a chandelier which cost eleven thousand pounds sterling,' Princess Lieven told Metternich after a visit to Brighton in 1821. She subsequently reported that although Nash's work 'has already cost £700,000 ... [the Pavilion] is still not fit to live in'.[33]

Nash's dramatic new master-plan for the Pavilion obliterated almost every trace of Holland's reticent neoclassical villa. The Marine

Pavilion was now to become an oriental fantasy-palace. Outside, the walls were dressed in an exotic Indian guise, the detailing loosely based on the plates in Thomas and William Daniell's *Oriental Scenery*, a compendium of views of India published from 1795 (borrowed by Nash from the Carlton House library in 1815), and on S. P. Cockerell's recently-completed 'Hindu palace' at Sezincote in Gloucestershire. While Sezincote's modelling at least attempted to reflect genuine Indian practice, however, neither the Pavilion's 'Hindu' motifs nor the materials used were intended to be at all authentic. Externally, Holland's glazed, cream-coloured mathematical tiles were replaced by bizarre adaptations of Eastern motifs executed in stucco or (in the case of a few of the finials and surrounds) of Bath stone. Nash's evocation of the architecture of eastern Asia was never intended as an academically-correct exercise, as was the case with A. W. N. Pugin's Gothic churches of the 1830s and 40s. His lax attention to accuracy and casual mixing of styles later appalled Pugin and his fellow Goths, and signally failed to impress Queen Victoria.[34]

Nash did not stop at submerging the Pavilion's classical lines in honey-painted stucco. In place of Holland's slender, floor-length sash windows he inserted a theatrical fenestration more Gothic in character than Chinese or Indian. Above what had been Holland's restrained parapet, lofty minarets and bulbous onion domes now littered the skyline. Beneath these playful features, however, lurked some remarkably advanced technology: the domes and much of the rest of the building were framed internally in cast iron, an innovation some years ahead of its time which gave great structural strength to what appeared to be a frail assembly of over-large elements. As had been the case with Porden's adjacent stables, Bélanger's iron-framed Halle au Blé in Paris was once again the inspiration.

Inside, Holland's Pavilion was completely redecorated and refurnished by the firms of Frederick Crace and Robert Jones in a bizarre mixture of Chinese, chinoiserie, Indian and Gothic elements, all stuffed into a shell still recognisably based on classical precepts and proportions. The result, oddly enough, was remarkably successful; even visitors who found the interiors overstated and vulgar were forced to acknowledge the brilliance of the craftsmanship and the power of the decorators' vision.

In remodelling the principal rooms in the centre of the building, Nash did little to alter Holland's plan, straying beyond the original footprint only at the northern and southern (sea front) ends of the site in order to add the Music Room and new private apartments for the Regent to the north and, to the south, a new wing incorporating the Banqueting Room, the kitchen, services and visitors' apartments.[35] What was wholly different was the new emphasis on cheerful eclecticism. The entrance hall, for example, retained Holland's classical proportions, together with his Georgian eight-panelled doors in their restrained surrounds; however, superimposed on the walls after 1815 were a dado of 'Chinese' fretwork, a Gothic-Chinese cornice, pale green dragons (expertly imagined by Frederick Crace's gifted craftsmen), and a classical chimney-piece with applied chinoiserie motifs. The room's furnishings, equally diverse, included a French clock, contemporary sabre-leg chairs, and a locally-made, classically-styled grand piano. In the principal corridor or 'long gallery' to which the hall led, the overall effect was more consistently 'Chinese'; even here, however, genuine Chinese vases and sculptures imported from China by Crace and Sons – prominent among which were the celebrated 'nodding men', jointed figures of Chinese court officials – jostled with chinoiserie seat furniture made from Buckinghamshire beech but turned and carved to resemble bamboo, a Brussels looped-pile carpet with an abstract geometric pattern, and William Stark's revolutionary, locally-made iron staircase, cast and painted to resemble bamboo. In 1822 Nash diluted the Chinese character of the gallery still further by introducing chairs which, though designed in early-Chippendale style, had been manufactured in Madras and veneered in ivory.

On the opposite, eastern side of the building, Holland's graceful circular Saloon had already been completely altered in 1802–4. Soon after 1815 the decorative scheme was changed again, Frederick Crace devising a light-hearted 'Chinese' theme which, delightful as it was, jarred with the neoclassical furniture used in the room. Eight years later George, clearly tired of Crace's chinoiserie, asked Robert Jones to concoct something new. Jones's solution was a wholly unorthodox but strangely successful synthesis of French Empire and 'Indian' styles, complete with subliminal allusions to two of George's favourite motifs, the Garter star and the sunflower of Louis XIV.

The plan of the new Pavilion was a reflection of George's priorities. The hall and Saloon – frequently the largest rooms in a great house – were relatively small. Far larger, and far more expensive, were the Music and Banqueting Rooms, which cost £45,125 and £41,887 respectively. Not only did these two rooms dominate the plan of the building: their sumptuous decoration was intended to outshine that of the other apartments in the Pavilion and of any other interior in the country. The walls of the glittering Music Room were dominated on the west side by a huge chimney-piece by Richard Westmacott and large red-and-yellow painted panels featuring Chinese scenes. (The panels had been adapted by Robert Jones from plates in William Alexander's *Views of China* of 1805.) On the eastern wall, huge silvered flying dragons at pelmet height appeared to support lush swathes of silk drapery framing the floor-length French windows; to the north was placed a large organ ('borrowed' by Queen Victoria in 1847 and replaced in 1850). Above the visitors' heads, spectacular lotus-flower-shaped lamps led their eyes to the domed ceiling, encased in plaster cockleshells laid in courses of receding size and gilded in four subtly different shades of gold leaf. Beneath this ceiling, chairs by Bailey and Saunders, fusing Chinese motifs with the strong Grecian profile popularised by the designers of Napoleon's Paris, sat on a colourful hand-woven Axminster carpet.

The Music Room, like its partner the Banqueting Room, was explicitly designed to be seen at night – the time at which it was usually used. Like all the rooms in the Pavilion, by the standards of the day it was extravagantly over-lit, the large lotus-flower chandeliers originally burning colza oil (rape-seed oil: an oil cellar in the basement below could accommodate nine huge oil vats). Together with the principal ceiling lights in the other public rooms, however, the chandeliers were converted to gas in 1821, an innovation which saved the Pavilion's shimmering finishes further damage from oily soot.[36] Gas lighting had been used to illuminate the exterior of the Pavilion since at least 1815. George was an enthusiastic champion of this technological break-through, and his personal support did much to promote the wide-spread domestic adoption of gas. The pioneer of its provision in Britain, Frederick Winsor, was commissioned to illuminate the façade of Carlton House with gas-lights as early as 1808, and the Prince enthusiastically backed his subsequent Gas-Light and Coke Company, which pumped gas from a works in the heart of Westminster to key streets and important public buildings throughout London.

Although George was proud of his talents as a musician, food and drink were more central than music to his way of life. The Banqueting Room, more glittering even than the Music Room, was intended as the heart of his new Pavilion, and the decor, again devised and executed by Robert Jones and the Craces, was more remarkable still. The stu-pendous one-ton central chandelier, with its six lotus-flower lamps issuing from the mouths of silvered dragons, was itself suspended from a single winged dragon, from whose jaws protruded an alarmingly realistic red tongue and above which hung a copper-leaved 'plantain tree'. The smaller lotus-lamps in the room were carried by four 'F'eng' birds (from Chinese mythology); below them stood four torchères of Spode porcelain in a blue imitating the distinctive shade exclusive to the pre-Revolutionary Sèvres factory. The result was one of the most breathtaking interiors in Europe; its lustrous appeal managed to charm more often than it appalled, and its studied eclecticism helped to make it perhaps the most successful, and certainly the most modern, of all George's many creations.

The Banqueting Room was where George spent most of his time when he was not resting or sleeping in his private apartments. As at Carlton House, these were situated on the ground floor, only a short stagger from the Banqueting Room and behind rather than above the principal rooms and public areas. Unlike the interiors of Carlton House, however, the rooms of the Pavilion were designed to be frequented only by the chosen few – and a good many of these would have been members of The Craft. George had been a Freemason since his coming-of-age (like the old Duke of Cumberland who had introduced him to Brighton), and in 1787 had founded his own Lodge, of which he naturally made himself Grand Master. It was packed with his own cronies and hangers-on, many of whom were frequent visitors to Brighton and guests in the Pavilion's Banqueting Room. Hijacking the iconography of an institution supposedly devoted to selfless brotherly commitment, George had Robert Jones incorporate such Masonic symbols as the all-seeing eye and the moon into the decorative scheme.

Brighton Pavilion and Carlton House have been justly celebrated as two of British royalty's most outstanding architectural achievements. The power, expense, diversity and sheer scintillation of the interiors created by Nash and his predecessors remain as unrivalled testimony to the skill of the professionals involved in their creation, to the technologically-enhanced capabilities of Regency manufacturers, and to the indulgent, exuberant taste of their royal progenitor. Yet, as we have seen, George all too often discarded the things he had loved best, and even these spectacular residences in the end fell victim to his self-centred caprices – more precisely, to a combination of his easily-diverted attention and his growing propensity for seclusion. By the spring of 1827 he had abandoned Brighton Pavilion –

widely caricatured as a symbol of his remoteness and irrelevance – and Carlton House lay half-demolished. Brilliant exemplars though they were of the vanguard of contemporary taste, even their gorgeous walls and glistening contents seem not to have inspired in George any consistency of commitment. Like the small boy he remained at heart, he was always wanting new toys, new vistas, and new experiences. Once sampled, any novel phenomenon – whether a fresh mistress or a remodelled room – was always liable to be repudiated without warning.

6

Connoisseur of Fine Art

What falsehood rankles in their hearts,
Who say the P—e neglects the arts ...
Thomas Moore, *The Twopenny Post-Bag*, Letter VIII

CONTEMPORARY OBSERVERS WERE constantly surprised by the depth of George's connoisseurship, and by his evident eye for a good painting. On 12 July 1816 Thomas Lawrence arrived at Carlton House to find the Regent 'arranging Pictures'; his attention was drawn to the enamels, and he went away with his opinion of the Regent's principal enamellist, Henry Bone, much altered. 'On seeing these pictures today,' Lawrence admitted, 'Bone rose in [my] estimation as an artist.' Farington was impressed that, attending the Royal Academy's annual exhibition of 1812, the Prince Regent 'staid full two hours' – paying particular attention to the portraits. (More typically, he also 'seemed much delighted with a drawing by Craig of a Cook in His Shop'.[1]) Buchanan's *Memoirs of Painting* of 1824 predicted that George IV's reign would 'rival the period of Lorenzo de Medici' and that the King's artistic influence would 'be to ENGLAND what that of FRANÇOIS PREMIER was to France'.[2]

George's love of art was yet another characteristic undoubtedly inherited from his father and, more particularly, from his grandfather. Earlier in the eighteenth century Frederick, Prince of Wales had bought six Van Dycks and three Rubens portraits (plus three other paintings now assigned to Rubens's studio), two paintings by Guido Reni, two by Jan Brueghel the Elder (*Flemish Fair* and *The Garden of Eden*) and four landscapes by Claude Lorraine. His favourite artist was the French émigré Philippe Mercier, who was briefly his Principal Painter after 1727 and who painted no fewer than eight portraits of

Frederick between 1716 and his untimely death thirty-five years later (in addition to his three versions of the celebrated picture of the Prince playing the cello with his sisters at Kew, *The Music Party* of 1733). Frederick also patronised such contemporary British artists as Joseph Highmore (who painted three portraits of him in the early 1740s), John Wootton and William Aikman. A passion for Dutch and Flemish pictures of the seventeenth century was a clear legacy across the generations: by the time of his death in 1751, Frederick owned eight pictures by David Teniers the Younger, a Dutch painter also admired by his grandson.[3]

George's love of collecting, may have been inherited equally from his father and grandfather, but the pictures he collected were both a tribute to the latter's connoisseurship and an implied rebuke to the former's taste. George III was less keen in his support of living British artists, preferring to buy Continental art, especially from Italy. Awareness of his patriotic obligations as sovereign prompted him nevertheless to ostentatious commissions from such native artists as Thomas Gainsborough, William Beechey, Francis Cotes, Paul Sandby, John Hoppner and (reluctantly) Joshua Reynolds, as well as from naturalised Britons Johann Zoffany, Benjamin West and John Singleton Copley. George's complete indifference to contemporary Italian paintings, his lukewarm attitude to Gainsborough, his championship of Reynolds and his rejection of West all seem to indicate a deliberate repudiation of his father's tastes.

While George's ability to recognise high quality in works of art was at least as developed as that of his ancestors, he came increasingly to rely on others to guide his purchases, from perceptive connoisseurs and well-trained agents like Lord Yarmouth and Charles Long to such barely-qualified personal friends as the cook Louis Weltje and the confectioner François Benois. Always most amenable to the ideas propounded by the last person he had consulted, George happily acceded to the suggestions of even the most amateur of these advisors. By 1806 he was excessively dependent on the art dealer-turned-interior decorator Walsh Porter; and following Porter's death, Lord Yarmouth often acted for him at major sales.[4] After 1820 Charles Long and, later in the decade, William Seguier were apparently in complete control of royal art purchases, even to the extent of opposing George's own requests. A few months before George III's death, Farington reported a member of his son's household as having declared that 'in matters respecting Art "the Prince Regent saw through Mr Long's spectacles"', while a recent historian has termed Long 'the *éminence grise* behind much of George IV's activity as a connoisseur of art and patron of architecture'.[5] The artist Benjamin Haydon certainly always believed it was Seguier and not the King who rejected his picture *Punch* when it was sent to Windsor in 1830. Haydon's principal evidence for this was that George had bought his picture *A Mock Election* two years before, calling it 'a damned fine thing'. Somewhat paranoid, and quick to spot conspiracies where none existed, Haydon later suggested Seguier was afraid that if he (Haydon) 'once got to the King he would so interest his Majesty that Seguier's own position about the person of the Sovereign would be in peril'.[6] Haydon seems not to have realised that consistency was never George's strong point.

George's earliest artistic mentor was the miniaturist Richard Cosway. Like himself, Cosway was witty, foppish and extravagant; and, like so many of the other men and women who were to be influential in his life, somewhat older – twenty years older, in fact, and thus the first obvious substitute father-figure. Perhaps Cosway's most important qualification, however, was that his talents had been wholly ignored by George III and Queen Charlotte, who both preferred the German-born miniaturist Jeremiah Meyer to this showy and self-advertising Englishman. Cosway thus became automatically eligible for George's alternative Court.

The young Prince's patronage went straight to Cosway's vain head. By 1785 he was signing himself, somewhat prematurely, 'Primarius Pictor Serenissimi Walliae Principis'; in the same year he was created the first Surveyor of Pictures at Carlton House, having found accommodation round the corner at Schomberg House in Pall Mall. Under Cosway's tutelage, George began to re-evaluate the Italian Old Masters his father had bought and, more significantly for his personal collection, to appreciate the Dutch and Flemish seventeeth-century landscapes, portraits and domestic scenes his grandfather had collected and which were then so popular in Louis XVI's France. In 1795 Cosway was commissioned to paint miniatures of the entire royal family – a gesture clearly designed to rival the series Gainsborough had executed for George III thirteen years before. He did work during that year to the value of 557 guineas, only to find that George had meanwhile turned his attention to other projects. He also most unwisely lent his patron the considerable sum of £1,500, which was never completely repaid. And in 1808 he suddenly found himself excluded from George's ever-changing inner circle.

Admittedly, the behaviour of the 'foppish little miniaturist' had become extremely eccentric. Stephen Lloyd suggests that an over-estimation of his place in the Prince's affections lay behind his precip-itous exclusion – a particular instance of which is explained in an unfinished manuscript biography of the artist by William Combe:

> The Prince of Wales sent to Mr C— that he wished him to accompany him to a collection of Pictures as he was anxious of his oppinion, Mr C— neglecting the ... respect due to Royalty, sent word he was engaged[;] the Prince order'd his Carriage and drove to Stratford Place [where Cosway had moved from Schomberg House], he there told the Servant to tell his Master he wished to see him[.] the Servant brought down word that his Master has company ...

If Combe's anecdote can be believed, Cosway failed to appreciate that the engaging and liberal young Prince of the 1780s had been replaced by an increasingly self-important reactionary. By 1812, however, real-isation had clearly dawned, and Cosway declined an invitation to yet another royal banquet celebrating the Regency, on the grounds that 'I have long done with these vanities, [that] I have no leisure for such visits, and that I am better employed'. In a splendidly stylish and deli-ciously apposite reversal of the Shakespearian Henry V's celebrated repudiation of Falstaff, the failing artist declared that he felt com-pelled 'to admonish [the Prince] it were well to think the time for such follies were past'.[7]

Cosway never received another royal commission; nor indeed was he paid for work already completed. After he was paralysed by a stroke in 1819, it was left to his estranged wife Maria, returning from Italy, to remind the Regent's Household of the 'very trifling sum' owed to her husband from a 'distant date'. The money was grudgingly paid shortly before Cosway died, in straitened circumstances, in 1821; George's only comment was condescending: that the sum was correct 'as far as His Royal Highness's memory serves him'.[8]

By 1805 the extrovert art dealer Walsh Porter had replaced Cosway as George's artistic confidant. The characters of the Prince and his new mentor were clearly similar. Like his patron, Porter never let one word suffice when ten could be used, and was never one to shrink from wringing every possible iota of emotion from the most trivial event or concept. In 1806, for example, he wrote to George concern-ing 'The very delicate matter in which yr Royal Highness has occasion-ally *hinted* at my procuring you a few fine pictures to add to those you already possess'. His manner was strikingly reminiscent of George's own over-inflated and over-emphatic epistolary style:

> I flatter myself you will give *me* some credit for *my reserve*, as well as for the manner in which I am *now* about to act. The moment is however arrived to throw off that reserve, it being absolutely necessary to receive yr R Hss *final* commands and to decide one way or the other before I *can* proceed in finishing that appartment which, if it is to contain pictures, ought assuredly to contain such *only* as are of the rarest quality and consequence ... I do flatter myself I have succeeded in culling a small but rare assemblage ... and this I have done, Sir, *solely* with a view of endeavouring silently to accomplish what I conceived to be the *wish* of yr Rl Hss of making that appartment refined and *classical* as possible ... and I pledge my *word* to yr Rl Hss there is not a single picture that has ever been in *any* Collection in this country: they have all been either imported by myself or I have directly purchased them ... from those who *did* import them, & are (of course) all *undoubted* originals and by the scarcest Masters.[9]

Walsh Porter, and later Lord Yarmouth, encouraged George's passion for seventeeth-century Dutch and Flemish pictures. As we have seen, it was an enthusiasm his grandfather had also expressed; yet while many great late-Georgian collectors acquired Dutch or Flemish paintings of the previous century, such an acquisitions policy was undoubtedly less usual in British aristocratic circles than in French. The high prices George was prepared to pay for these paintings tended eventually to make such tastes even more exclusive. Significantly, at Carlton House those royal purchases originating from the Low Countries were generally hung adjacent to items from George's collection of Sèvres porcelain, in the manner fashionable in French royal and aristocratic circles before 1789.

With the French Revolution and the consequent dispersal of many French collections, George was able through his agents to secure some splendid bargains among the flood of cut-price paintings which entered Britain after 1789. Indeed, the very availability of so many high-quality seventeenth-century works from the Low Countries during the period of the Revolution and Directory may have fostered his enthusiasm. Particular favourites were Aelbert Cuyp, David Teniers, Jan Steen and Adriaen van Ostade. During the 1790s he acquired numerous pictures by these artists from the great Amsterdam collections of Braancamp and Gildemeester, sold to avoid capture by the invading French Revolutionary armies, and from the collection of Louis XVI's former finance minister Calonne, sold at Christie's in 1795 to raise money for French émigrés (Revolutionary France having declared war on Britain in 1793). George had failed, however, to acquire anything from the fabulous collection of his friend the duc d'Orléans, when this was sold in 1792: no one else would join his purchasing syndicate, realising that he would always reserve the best pictures for himself.[10]

The few Rembrandts George owned appear to modern eyes to be the crowning glory of his collection. His first Rembrandt was acquired as late as 1811, and he bought no more after 1819. He also owned very few seventeeth-century French pictures, despite being an avid, indeed an obsessive, collector of seventeenth- and eighteenth-century French furniture. The best of the few he did buy, Claude's *Rape of Europa*, was acquired only a year before his death, in May 1829. Indeed, it is perhaps worth noting those pictures which George did *not* buy during this period. Although many Old Masters and contemporary paintings from southern European national schools were available on the market as a result of the upheavals of the recent past, many of them were based on religious themes, and religion was a subject about which George was always reluctant to concern himself. Both he and his agents preferred those tightly-composed, cheerfully domestic and distinctly secular products of the Low Countries in the seventeenth-century.

The advisor who secured George most of his Flemish and Dutch paintings during the Regency period was Lord Yarmouth, son of George's confidante and mistress Lady Hertford and himself later the third Marquess of Hertford. Yarmouth was eminently qualified for membership of George's inner circle. In the opinion of art historian John Ingamells, he was definitely 'not a likeable man', being 'a wayward son, a wretched husband, a feckless Irish landlord, a Tory autocrat abusive of reform, and an example ... of undisguised debauchery' – in short, irresistible to the Prince. 'His redeeming characteristic', Ingamells remarks, 'was the sensibility which he exercised in the sale-rooms of London and Paris' – the results of which formed the backbone of what is today the Wallace Collection, to be seen at Hertford House in London.

George readily acknowledged Yarmouth's abilities, declaring that 'his sense and his information and the accuracy of his judgement and of his discrimination is really quite wonderful, and he is indeed in point of talent very superior to all the young men of the rising generation at least to any that I know.' Yarmouth's passion for pictures was clearly infectious, and over a period of nine years his nose for a bargain secured for his royal master a large number of Dutch and Flemish 'cabinet' paintings. Among his early successes when he was acting on behalf of the Prince was at Christie's 1810 sale of the personal collection of George's former advisor Walsh Porter. Here Yarmouth snapped up van Ruisdael's *Evening Landscape*, and it subsequently adorned the walls at Carlton House on which Porter himself had worked so enthusiastically. In June 1811, the month of the great Carlton House fête, Yarmouth bought a number of outstanding Dutch and Flemish pictures at Christie's, among them Rembrandt's *Ship-Builder and his Wife* of 1633 (for £5,000) and van Ostade's *Interior of a Peasant's Cottage* of 1668.[11]

Yarmouth's finest hour came in 1814, when at relatively modest cost he acquired eighty-six Dutch and Flemish pictures from the Baring Collection. Only three weeks later, however, George demonstrated just how capricious he was becoming by ordering the immediate sale at Christie's of seventy-seven Dutch and Flemish pictures from his own collection, among them many from Yarmouth's recent coup. For good measure he also included a number of George III's Italian purchases in the sale – his ready disposal of such cherished canvases demonstrating his disdain for both his father and his father's taste.

During his years of influence Yarmouth was showered with gifts and offices. In 1810 he was given Hoppner's recent portrait of the Prince, presented to George by Hoppner's widow, and was provided with his own bedroom at Carlton House. In 1812 he was made Vice-Chamberlain of the Regent's Household, a Privy Councillor, and Lord Warden of the Stannaries (effectively, head of the council which administered the rich revenues of the Duchy of Cornwall). Unsurprisingly, 'It was noticed that when Parliament debated the Regent's allowance later that same year, Lord [Yarmouth] became very fidgety at the mention of the Regent's *minions* receiving improper rewards.' However, his mother's replacement as George's mistress by Lady Conyngham effectively ended Yarmouth's tenure as artistic advisor and agent. After 1819, the year in which it became widely rumoured that Lady Hertford had lost her place at the Regent's right hand, he bought nothing on George's behalf. The link with his royal patron was not entirely severed, however; in 1826 Yarmouth, who had by then succeeded his father in the marquessate, bought one of the first villas to be completed in the new Crown development of Regent's Park.[12]

Yarmouth's role was henceforward filled by Sir Charles Long – created Lord Farnborough in 1826 – and Long's friend William Seguier, appointed Surveyor of Pictures in place of West in 1820 and, after George's death, first Keeper of the new National Gallery. While the pace of collecting was not as frenetic as during Yarmouth's heyday, the importance of Long and Seguier should not be underestimated. Long, indeed, quickly became George's advisor in matters other than art, and can fairly be said to have been the primary instigator of the ambitious royal building programme of the 1820s. As we will see, the form and detail of the new Windsor Castle owed a little to the King and much to Long, who was largely responsible for the architect's brief and the direction of the works.

George always wished to be regarded, like his father and grandfather, as a significant patron of contemporary British art. Yet in truth he was a rather fitful supporter. After his coming-of-age he liked to claim to be British art's greatest promoter, yet he went to the races rather than the annual Royal Academy dinner of 1784. Of the native painters he professed to admire, only Thomas Lawrence, fashioner of his idealised image, received his uninterrupted and unqualified support. Thomas Gainsborough, for example, never enjoyed his consistent patronage – principally, no doubt, because of his popularity with George III and Queen Charlotte. The full-length portraits of the King and Queen delivered in 1781 were the first of many commissions Gainsborough received from George III, most celebrated of all being the series of miniatures of the King and his immediate family he painted between September and October 1782. By the mid 1780s Gainsborough was on very familiar terms with his royal patron and clearly saw no need to cultivate the young Prince. Farington noted that Gainsborough 'talked bawdy to the King, and morality to the Prince of Wales' – a habit which, while it may have amused the King, probably enraged his dissolute son. Nor was Gainsborough's custom of painting his subjects only in their normal dress likely to have endeared him to George, whose love of role-playing was already very evident. For a full-length portrait of 1782 he did, however, as we have seen, allow George, to pose leaning languidly against his horse, wearing an invented military uniform. The Prince thought highly enough of the result to have it engraved by John Raphael Smith in 1783. Copies were subsequently sold at the considerable price of one guinea each,[13] and the following year Smith was appointed Mezzotint Engraver to the Prince of Wales. However, other commissions executed by

Gainsborough at George's behest – portraits of Mary Robinson, Maria Fitzherbert and Colonel St Leger – had not been paid for in full at the time of the artist's death in 1788.[14]

In later years George's opinion of Gainsborough's talents appeared to remain equivocal. A special niche was created at Carlton House for *The Three Eldest Daughters of George III and Queen Charlotte*, painted in 1784, but by the time of the 1816 inventory it had been relegated to store (and seventy years later, in an appalling act of vandalism, it was savagely cut down to fit a Buckingham Palace overdoor). Gainsborough's 'exquisite' *Diana and Actaeon*, which George had bought in 1797, also went into storage, as did his celebrated double portrait of the young Duke and Duchess of Cumberland walking in the woods.[15]

After Gainsborough's death, Benjamin West became George III's favourite contemporary painter. West received more money from the King than any other living artist – despite the fact that the friendship had cooled by 1803, allegedly on account of West's republicanism. Thus, although his historical pictures should in theory have appealed to the Prince of Wales's dramatic sense of his royal heritage, West was rarely, if ever, employed by him. A further factor in West's rejection may have been his close friendship with George's former tutor, Dr Hurd, who helped the artist plan a Chapel of the Revealed Religion at Windsor Castle, which was never executed; his predilection for religious subjects told against him.[16] Certainly, as President of the Royal Academy, West's advice was heard by the Prince, but rarely followed.

Once his father was safely ensconced with his mad-doctors in December 1810, the new Regent, in a remarkable act of mean-minded filial spite, refused to renew West's royal pension, despite numerous pleas from the art world that he should do so.[17] Furthermore, he made no attempt to rescue from West's studio the huge religious canvases George III had commissioned for the Royal Chapel at Windsor Castle. His presentation of one of these forgotten pictures, *The Last Supper*, to the new National Gallery in 1828 was little less than an insult to an institution he had otherwise signally failed to support with either funds or gifts. Deprived of the sun of royal patronage, West's reputation rapidly withered; the other Royal Chapel pictures remained in his studio until his death in 1829, when they were sold at auction for a fraction of the price originally agreed. In further acts of petty spite, George broke up West's series of paintings depicting the life of Edward III which hung in the Presence Chamber at Windsor Castle, and destroyed his ceiling in the Queen's Lodge in Windsor Great Park. (West's half-finished west window in St George's Chapel at Windsor had already been put into store, some time after 1813; reassembled at St Paul's Cathedral in Calcutta, it was destroyed in 1864. West's remaining windows in St George's Chapel were replaced after 1862 with work by Clayton and Bell and other fashionable firms; his altar-piece there was also removed.)[18]

If Gainsborough and West, his parents' favourite artists, were viewed with less than wholehearted enthusiasm by the young Prince while they were alive, the outstanding British painter Joshua Reynolds, regarded with suspicion and even loathing by George III, was eagerly embraced by the Carlton House set. In spite of Reynolds's obvious talents, George III had taken a pronounced dislike to him by the time of the Prince's coming-of-age, by which time Reynolds was firmly established as the 'house artist' of the Foxite Whigs. His series of portraits of Whig heroes culminated in an iconic full-length of Fox himself, painted in December 1783 – after the failure of the India Bill (which the obdurate Whig nevertheless still grasps in his hand) and George III's subsequent personal intervention to oust his ministry, and shortly before the general election which Fox knew he would lose. Gossips such as Joseph Farington suggested that it was Reynolds's hesitation in accepting the presidency of the new Royal Academy in 1768 – an institution George III had backed with great enthusiasm from its original conception – which had earned him the King's lasting enmity, but his close association with the hated Fox seems to have been the real reason. During the 1780s, when Gainsborough was the Court painter at St James's Palace and Buckingham House, Reynolds fulfilled an equivalent role at Carlton House, his portrait of Fox the tragic hero representing the proud emblem of the Foxite Whig cause.[19]

George III never forgave Reynolds for embracing the Foxite creed, which after the turbulent events of 1783–4 had placed the King himself squarely at the centre of its demonology. (Reynolds died in 1792, before Burke and other moderate Whigs – and the Prince himself – had begun to desert the Foxite camp in the wake of the excesses of the French Revolution.) The King told William Beechey that he found Reynolds's canvases 'coarse and unfinished', and later declared the painter himself to be 'poison in my sight'. It did not help, Beechey emolliently suggested when recounting these remarks, that the near-sighted King was always in the habit 'of looking at his pictures closely', which did Reynolds's ambitious and not always successful painting technique no favours. As late as 1805, thirteen years after the artist's death, George III remained as adamant in his distaste for Reynolds as for Fox. In an act of the sort of malicious spite more readily associated with his eldest son, the King vehemently opposed plans to erect a monument to the great artist in St Paul's Cathedral. George III insisted, moreover, that his implacable opposition be noted in the Royal Academy's Minutes, which duly recorded that the sovereign 'would not suffer the money of the Academy to be squandered for purposes of vain parade and Ostentation'.[20]

By the mid 1780s – at the time when his sight was, sadly, beginning to fail – Reynolds's chief source of patronage lay firmly in the circle of the Prince of Wales and his Foxite friends. George commissioned from him a painting of his brother Frederick in Garter robes, executed in 1787–8; of his friends the duc d'Orléans (1785) and Lord Moira (1786); of the Whig naval heroes Rodney (1786) and Keppel (1788–9); plus a full-length of himself, which was completed in 1787.[21] Another princely commission, for a portrait of Maria Fitzherbert, was left half-finished by Reynolds at the time of his death in 1792. It remained in store at Carlton House and at St James's Palace until 1830, when William IV, clearly embarrassed, gave it to Mrs Fitzherbert.

After Reynolds's death, George acquired fourteen more of his paintings, and even after his personal political beliefs had veered sharply to the right, continued to publicly revere both Reynolds and Fox. Hanging his walls with Reynolds canvases reminded him of the carefree days of the 1780s, when he was young, slender, relatively athletic, and unencumbered with his hated wife. It was also on a par with the way his Tory Ministers of 1811 were compelled to stare at the bust of Charles James Fox at Carlton House: a theatrical evocation of a political creed long since abandoned and of a time long since past. Two of the Reynolds portraits – of the Seven Years' War heroes Granby and Schaumburg-Lippe – were given to him by Lady Townshend in 1810 and placed in prominent positions in the Crimson Drawing Room at Carlton House. Another Reynolds was presented to him by Lord Erskine in the same year. Erskine regretted this gift after George's betrayal of his Whig 'friends' the following year, and in 1820 emerged as one of Queen Caroline's leading supporters. Four more works by Reynolds were presented to the Regent in 1812 by the artist's niece, Lady Thomond, in recognition of his unflinchingly consistent support of her uncle. In 1813 George agreed to become patron of the ball held to mark the opening of the first Reynolds retrospective exhibition, staged at the British Institution (of which he was now President); he also lent some of his own Reynoldses. In 1822 George acquired Reynolds's portrait of Lord Southampton, partly because of the identity of the artist and partly from a sentimental respect for Southampton himself, who had once acted as intermediary between him and his father over his perennially-mounting debts.[22]

Reynolds's canvases were also immortalised by being copied as small enamels by Henry Bone, who was appointed Enamel Painter to the Prince of Wales in 1801. These miniatures were placed in George's own bedroom at Carlton House, where he could gaze at them in private and fantasise fondly about his past life. Bone, meanwhile, was delighted with this burst of royal patronage and could not resist broadcasting his good fortune. 'Bone told me that the Prince of Wales is very favourable to him, and employs him much,' recorded Farington wearily in June 1803; 'Were I a rich man,' he reported Bone as exclaiming, 'I would rather work for the Prince for nothing than for many another for money.'[23] As Bone was to discover, artists in George's employ invariably tended to find that they had indeed worked for nothing, when their repeatedly-presented invoices went unpaid.

If his politics made Reynolds attractive to the young Prince, George was equally happy to support artists whose works featured another of his great enthusiasms, sport. After his withdrawal from horse-racing in 1791 the Prince concentrated on having his favourite animals immortalised by such leading exponents as Sawrey Gilpin, a former protégé of his uncle Cumberland, who was still at work on sporting pictures for the Prince shortly before his death in 1807; George Garrard, who painted seven large studies of horses for George's hunting retreat at Kempshott in 1792; Benjamin Marshall, who in 1794 painted George's favourite Kempshott hack, Tiger; and the animal painter James Ward, who in 1794 was appointed George's Painter-in-Ordinary and Engraver in Mezzotint.[24] He also employed the most famous of all sporting artists, George Stubbs. His first Stubbs canvases were commissioned in 1791: a charming picture of two dogs, *Fino and Tiny*; a depiction of his leading jockey, Sam Chifney, with his horse Baronet at Newmarket; and a portrait of George himself on horseback. Stubbs felt sufficiently proud of the last to exhibit it at the Royal Academy in that year. Two years later, he was engaged to paint three of George's pet enthusiasms: *The Prince of Wales's Phaeton*, a group of NCOs and men from his tame regiment, the 10th Light Dragoons, and the notorious Lady Lade on horseback.

Laetitia Lade was in storage at Carlton House by 1816, but found herself back in favour in 1822, when Stubbs's portrait was hung at the Royal Lodge in Windsor Great Park; two years later George even commissioned an engraving of it.[25]

After 1815 George turned to the new generation of horse painters led by Charles Schwanfelder and Henry Bernard Chalon, appointed royal Animal Painters in 1817 and 1820 respectively, although he still regularly employed James Ward, an artist by now increasingly out of favour with his other patrons. In 1824, for example, Ward was commissioned to paint George's 'favourite charger', Nonpareil, and was offered three further similar commissions the following year. The success of these pictures at least partly made up for the critical and financial failure of Ward's ambitious *Waterloo Allegory*, which had been commissioned by the British Institution in 1815 and which occupied him for much of the next six years.[26]

Not all British artists profited as handsomely as Ward from the Prince's patronage. Principal Painter to the Queen from 1793, William Beechey had been a great favourite of George III and Queen Charlotte, and about 1800 was responsible for their last official portraits. However, by 1804 he had fallen out dramatically with the King, who in that year declared that he 'wanted no more of his pictures', an abrupt breach that has never been explained. It may be that the King was steered away from Beechey by jealous rivals such as West, who frequently criticised his works; more probably, he was alarmed by Beechey's growing friendship with the Prince of Wales, and the tale that Beechey had lent him money. (In 1801 George was indeed in Beechey's debt to the tune of £390 12s.)[27]

In the circumstances, Beechey might have expected to benefit from the support of Carlton House. He had, after all, already produced one of the most flattering images of the young Prince yet committed to canvas – a celebration of George's egotistical aspirations which in its shameless militaristic posturing rivals the post-Waterloo images created by Thomas Lawrence. Having painted a series of portraits of George's sisters for him in 1797, the following year Beechey was commissioned to paint the Prince himself, in the striking uniform he had devised for his Dragoons. The pose is compellingly martial: with his beloved Garter Star shielding his breast, George's hand rests lightly but menacingly on the hilt of his sabre. The inference was clear: at a time when Nelson had soundly defeated the French fleet in the Battle of the Nile but Britain still feared invasion across the Channel, her

Prince of Wales – a latter-day Black Prince – stood ready to unsheath his trusty sword in the defence of the nation.

George was delighted with Beechey's portrait – though his father was apparently disgusted by such absurd posturing on the part of a mere honorary colonel. Presumably regarding the picture as an excellent advertisement for his much-vaunted desire to serve in the field, George commissioned an engraving to be made of it, together with a copy in oils for the Duke of Kent (still in the Royal Collection). But the King remained steadfast in his refusal to allow his son any experience of active service, and after Beechey had made the Duke of Kent's copy in 1803, the Prince never employed him again. Unlikely as it seems, it would appear that George, usually so eager to cross his parents in every possible way, bowed – for once – to his father's dictates and summarily dispensed with Beechey's talents.

In contrast, Beechey's great rival John Hoppner – an artist who was also brusquely dropped by George III – benefited greatly from the support of the Prince of Wales. In 1795 Hoppner was commissioned by the King to paint his daughters, but saw the job reallocated to Dupont. To add insult to injury, a few weeks after April 1795, when George had agreed to his father's suggestion that Hoppner should paint the new Princess of Wales 'in the robes in which she was married', the King changed his mind and offered the commission to Beechey. If he was unable to undertake it, George III was adamant that the project should not go to Thomas Lawrence, before whose recent portrait of Lord Mountstuart he had 'started back in disgust'.[28]

Fortunately for Hoppner, by 1793 he had been appointed Principal Portrait Painter to the Prince of Wales, so was able to take refuge in George's patronage. By the summer of 1805 he was sufficiently confident to lobby George for help in his bid for the presidency of the Royal Academy. (In the event, the architect James Wyatt temporarily wrested it from West.) In 1807 Farington observed the Prince's familiarity with Hoppner at an Academy dinner: warning that his 'bodily health did not enable [him] to make great exertions ... the Prince put His hands to Hoppner's cheeks and patting them said, "Oh! you have constitution enough to do anything".'[29] Before his untimely death in 1810, Hoppner had been commissioned by George to paint numerous family portraits, including the dukes of Clarence (*c.* 1794) and Kent (*c.* 1797), and many of his intimate friends, among them Lord Moira, Jack Payne, Charles James Fox, the Duchess of Devonshire and George Hanger.

Hoppner was not the only artist with whom George appeared to be on close terms. He was likewise 'easy and familiar' with William Owen, 'putting His hand upon Owen's shoulder [so] that it required constant guard not to forget His situation'. Owen, formerly a royal coach painter, succeeded Hoppner as George's Principal Portrait Painter. George was pleased with his portrait of Sir David Dundas of 1813, which still hangs at Windsor, but becoming enraptured by Lawrence's talents after 1814, never actually sat to him. When James Ward, by now an acquaintance of more than thirty years' standing, was invited to Windsor in 1824 to paint various favourite royal horses, he too found George flatteringly informal in his ways, resting a podgy royal paw on his shoulder. Three years later the sculptor Francis Chantrey, during one of his visits to Windsor, was told by the King to 'do here, if you please, just as you would if you were at home'.[30]

We have seen how George's patronage ebbed and flowed according to the whims of his capricious nature, and how even those reputed to be his favourite artists were often treated dismissively. Canova's sculpture of *Mars and Venus*, commissioned with great fanfare in 1815, was immediately relegated to the leaking conservatory at Carlton House on its delivery in 1825. Similarly, George had announced in 1814 that he would not after all buy J. S. Copley's portrait of himself, dressed as a field marshal and with the 10th Light Dragoons capering about purposefully in the background, for which he had sat almost five years before. Copley was instead brusquely informed that 'His Royal Highness never intended to purchase the picture, having sat merely at the request of the artist, and understanding it to be a public work, like the Death of Lord Chatham'. And only months after so cordially receiving James Ward at Windsor in 1824, George impugned Ward's finished works and refused him any further interview.[31]

If he was inconsistent in his patronage of native artists, George was a predictably enthusiastic supporter of the French artist Marie-Louise Élisabeth Vigée-Le Brun, who was in Britain in 1803–4. Not only was she an 'older woman' (more or less a contemporary of Lady Hertford) but, as the artist who had painted Marie-Antoinette before the Revolution, she represented a direct link with the Prince's beloved Bourbons. George attended evening parties at her Maddox Street house – on one occasion telling her: 'I flit about from one soirée to the next, but at you I stay put' – and exempted her from the regulations restricting the movements of French visitors to Britain which followed the collapse of the Treaty of Amiens. As Madame Le Brun later recorded,

> The Prince of Wales ... assured me that I was not to be included in this edict, that he was opposed to it, and that he was going immediately to ask his father for permission for me to stay. This permission was granted with all the necessary details, mentioning that I could travel all over the interior of the kingdom, staying wherever I wanted ... The Prince of Wales put the seal on his obligingness by bringing me this paper himself.

The Prince also sat to Madame Le Brun before she left England – a commission which appears to have aroused Hoppner's ire (in 1805 he savaged her lack of 'smoothness and finishing', and disparaged her studio-cum-gallery in Paris as a 'shop').[32]

Although in his capacity as its patron the Prince attended nearly every annual exhibition at the Royal Academy, where he frequently demonstrated his appreciation and knowledge of contemporary British painting, small benefit accrued to the institution from this connection. In 1816 he did give the Academy the Raphael cartoons from Hampton Court; yet the gift was made at Lawrence's request, and its apparent generosity is tempered by the fact that the royal family had not occupied Hampton Court since 1737. (George had never lived there, and was a rare visitor.) Nor was the Prince's bounteous presentation of a new chandelier to the Royal Academy, accompanied by the remark that the annual exhibition's pictures 'would be much better seen than they were by Candle light at present', quite the splendid donation it initially appeared to be. The chandelier cost £2,500, of which George provided but £500. He had also previously promised to find the Academy a better venue than the cramped rooms of Chamber's Somerset House, and in February 1812 Farington reported a rumour 'that the Prince Regent intended to give Carlton House to the Royal Academy'.[33] Typically, nothing came of it, and when the decision was taken after 1826 to demolish Carlton House, it was apparently without a thought that it might have provided a suitable home for an institution such as the Royal Academy or the National Gallery.

More serious was George's failure to honour his promises regarding the creation of a national art collection. In 1810 he intimated to Benjamin West that he was 'much disposed to make a Collection of the Works of British Artists', of which he intended the first should be Edward Bird's *Country Choristers*, for which he now sought a companion by David Wilkie. Wilkie's response was the popular *Blind Man's Buff*; however, Bird was quietly dropped. (Six years later he presented George with his *Embarkation of Louis XVIII at Dover*, for which the corpulent Bourbon monarch had sat both at Calais and in the Tuileries, and which was explicitly designed to appeal to the Regent's known taste for images of Napoleon's defeat; nevertheless, George rejected it. Bird's appointment as Historical Painter to Princess Charlotte was small comfort to him, and of course short-lived; he died impoverished in 1819.)

George's speech at the Academy dinner of 1811 lauded British art in general, comparing contemporary native practitioners with Van Dyck and Claude:

> In expressing the pride and satisfaction He felt as an Englishman while sitting in that room wherein He saw exhibited works of art which would have done Honor to any country ... [and] which manifested the great improvement in Art[,] He felt proud as an Englishman that He might with confidence expect that as this country had risen superior to all others in Arms, in military and naval prowess, so would it in Arts.[34]

During 1819 it seemed likely, from the evidence of his throwaway comments, that the Prince's embryonic British collection would go to the Royal Academy rather than to the more recently-founded British Institution, whose patron he had been since 1806. In July 1819 he promised the Academy a bigger and better site, leading its members to anticipate a sizeable donation of pictures.[35] In December 1820 Farington heard a rumour that Nash had been approached to design 'a new *Exhibition Building*' to hold, among other things, the Wests commissioned by George III which his son had rejected. Nothing, however, was subsequently heard of this project. Two years later George gave a categorical assurance that he would present much of his own collection as the nucleus of a new national gallery. Yet although he encouraged the government's purchase of John Julius Angerstein's collection, which became the foundation of the new National Gallery in 1824, he himself provided neither funding nor pictures. The £57,000 Liverpool's government gave for the Angerstein collection came from public money, not from the King's Privy Purse. But George did make sure that the new gallery's Managing Committee was dominated by his personal advisor, Sir Charles Long.

In 1826 George lodged all 164 pictures from Carlton House with the British Institution, using it as a temporary repository for his collection while he razed his old home. But the widespread expectation that these pictures would be subsequently presented to the fledgling National Gallery proved over-optimistic.[36] At the time of George's death the pictures were languishing in storage at 105 Pall Mall – almost opposite William Wilkins's unfinished National Gallery building – waiting to grace the walls of the private picture gallery Nash was creating at Buckingham Palace, rather than those of the nation's art museum.

George's greatest contribution to the National Gallery was, in the event, both indirect and strangely apposite. The Ionic columns Wilkins used to flank the entrance of his strangely unheroic composition actually came from Carlton House. Originally they had supported the portico through which Maria Fitzherbert, the Countess of Jersey and the marchionesses of Hertford and Conyngham had passed on their way to furtive assignations; after George's death, they became the gateway through which thousands of ordinary Britains flocked to see John Julius Angerstein's masterpieces.

As George grew older, his fondness for narrative 'genre' pictures grew more pronounced. In addition to his Dutch and Flemish purchases, he bought pictures from the artist many regarded as the British heir to the seventeenth-century masters: David Wilkie. In 1818 George bought Wilkie's sentimental *The Penny Wedding*, companion piece to his earlier *Blind Man's Buff* and the first of many royal purchases from this Scottish artist. The British countryside, as portrayed in such pictures as *The Penny Wedding* and the luckless Bird's *Country Choristers*, was a semi-mythical land of happy peasants, church bells and warm beer – of 'domestic scenes of English cottages', as the *New Monthly Magazine* put it in 1829. This unrealistic rural environment was one in which George presumably believed most of his subjects lived, and seems to have inspired his remodelling of the Royal Lodge, his 'country retreat' in Windsor Great Park, after 1824.

If, as we have seen, George's collection of Continental paintings was unrepresentative in that it contained no Italian pictures and none by any of the Renaissance or Baroque Masters (in 1816 he had turned down an opportunity to acquire what is now one of the most celebrated of Renaissance canvases, van Eyck's *Arnolfini and his Wife*), in the same way his collection of pictures by contemporary British artists was, as Oliver Millar has noted, 'very unbalanced'. Not for him naturalistic Constable landscapes, not for him the increasingly innovative atmospheric oils of J. M. W. Turner – although he did commission a painting of the Battle of Trafalgar from Turner in 1823. (After hanging in St James's Palace for two years, Turner's great work was put into store, and in 1829 given to the Royal Naval College at Greenwich.) George preferred to cover the walls of his palaces with portraits by Thomas Lawrence (whose impossibly heroic images of himself and his family so reassuringly ignored the ignominious truth), with the sort of sentimental village panoramas in which David Wilkie specialised, and with dramatic evocations of the Napoleonic battles he increasingly liked to believe he had personally won. His later purchases were thus dominated by commissions from Lawrence and Wilkie.[37] Returning to Britain in 1828 after three years in Spain and Italy, Wilkie was delighted to find his royal patron as enthusiastic about his vivid, Mediterranean-influenced pictures as he had been about the earlier *Blind Man's Buff*. George particularly admired Wilkie's *Defence of Saragossa* of 1828, and relished his other recreations of alleged episodes from the Peninsular War of twenty years before. Through David Wilkie, George could both pretend to live a simple country life, and also imagine himself winning great military triumphs.

In 1830 Wilkie's reputation was at its zenith. Lauded by one of his rivals as 'the greatest genius in his walk that ever lived', in George's eyes he could apparently do little wrong. The sculptor Francis Chantrey told Walter Scott's biographer that 'the King's kindness to Wilkie was beautiful'. Wilkie's Scottish tableaux reminded George of the Dutch and Flemish scenes so avidly collected in his Regency. The 1829 full-length of him in Highland dress, though it shows him tightly bound into his ludicrous costume, clearly approximated to the ailing monarch's highly romanticised view of himself as heir to the Scottish sovereigns and Jacobite claimants of old. In 1829, having shown George some of his new 'Spanish' pictures, Wilkie recorded that he was 'much satisfied with the impression they appeared to make upon his Majesty, who commanded me ... to complete the series of four', and 'pleased by the resemblance remarked to Rembrandt, to Murillo, and Velasquez. Nothing seemed to escape.'[38]

Following Thomas Lawrence's death early in 1830, George made Wilkie his Principal Painter in Ordinary. (A knighthood had to wait until 1836, however, when it was bestowed by William IV.) Yet this royal appointment did Wilkie few favours in the race for the presidency of the Royal Academy later that year. The Academicians plumped instead for Martin Archer Shee – an artist famously but unfairly termed by his embittered and unhinged rival Haydon 'the most incompetent painter in the solar system' – by the wide margin of eighteen votes to two. Haydon cannot have been the only artist to consider that Wilkie's close links with the King had cost him the office. Clearly the Academy had learned how fruitless it was to put their trust in the self-styled champion of British art. As far as Wilkie's own fortunes were concerned, the King's death perhaps saved him from inexplicable rejection in the manner of Beechey or Bird.[39]

A delight in Wilkie's pictures was not the only taste which separated George from the conventional aristocratic patrons of his time. Unlike many of his wealthy subjects, for example, he never evinced any interest in sculpture from the ancient world. He was drawn, more predictably, to what Mark Evans has called 'the fabulous polish and sensuous lines of Canova'.[40] Antonio Canova, having been the sculptor Napoleon most esteemed, accordingly possessed a special appeal for George. In August 1815 the British sculptor John Rossi reported that the Prince Regent 'was intending to employ Canova', and in December Canova attended a levée at Carlton House, where he was presented with a gold snuff-box set with diamonds and (inevitably) a royal portrait. (Arriving back in Rome in January 1816, Canova discovered a five-hundred-pound bank note hidden inside the box.) It was probably at this time that George commissioned from Canova the group *Mars and Venus*, now at Buckingham Palace, though the finished piece only arrived at Carlton House in 1825, two years after the sculptor's death. George also made use of Canova as an *ad hoc* diplomat, entrusting him on his return to Italy with letters to Pope Pius VII; in 1817 Canova supervised the Pope's despatch to the Regent of a large number of antique casts, which were subsequently exhibited at the Royal Mews Riding School under Rossi's direction. Two years later George bought the *Reclining Nymph*. Small wonder that Canova should later have claimed: 'In his present Majesty, the fine arts have ever found an enlightened and generous patron.'[41]

At home, it was Francis Chantrey who won the most important sculptural commissions from the royal patron. Chantrey was introduced to George in 1819 by Sir Charles Long, who had recently sat to him for a bust – yet another instance of Long's all-pervading aesthetic influence over his royal master. In 1820 Chantrey was commissioned to carve a bust of the new King, the first of many he was to execute over the next decade. (Predictably, one of the first was delivered to Lady Conyngham.)[42] Chantrey's biographer later asserted that the

King 'evinced an affability towards him, which he often mentioned with plesure', and cited the sculptor's observation that George 'was a great master of that first proof of good breeding, which consists in putting every one at their ease'. After Chantrey had completed the statue of the King intended for the Grand Staircase at Windsor Castle, George congratulated him: 'I have reason to be obliged to you, for you have immortalised me.'[43] Chantrey certainly had cause to be obliged to George, since the busts and monumental statues he carved of him provided a steady source of income throughout the 1820s and helped to make him, in the words of a recent expert judgement, 'the established portrait sculptor of the great and the good'.[44] Chantrey was in effect the sculptural equivalent of Thomas Lawrence, ready and able to fashion a svelte and heroic image wholly at variance with the reality of the fat, slovenly man dressed 'in a dirty flannel waistcoat and cotton nightcap' who once met him at Windsor. Significantly, it was one of Chantrey's highly flattering busts that George chose as the basis for his profile portrait on the new coinage of 1826.

Chantrey was not the only native sculptor provided with a reasonable living by George's patronage. Buckingham Palace, only half-finished at the time of the King's death, was intended to be a splendid showcase for contemporary British sculpture, including pieces by Edward Baily, John Carew, William Croggan, William Pitts, John Rossi and Richard Westmacott. (In the event, the cessation of work and dismissal of Nash after George's death resulted in some of the planned sculptural decoration being abandoned, or diverted to other sites.) Westmacott was especially favoured: tipped as the man to succeed Chantrey as the King's unofficial sculptor, he was commissioned to create pieces as various and substantial as the Music Room chimney-piece at Brighton Pavilion (which cost £1,244), the massive Waterloo Vase, and an equestrian statute of George III for Windsor Great Park.

Of all the sculptors employed at Buckingham Palace, John Rossi was the most dependent on George's favour. The son of an Italian from Siena, his early career was spent modelling patterns for Coade stone, the highly durable architectural ceramic manufactured at Eleanor Coade's Lambeth factory. Although to everyone's surprise – including, probably, his own – Rossi was appointed the Prince of Wales's principal sculptor in 1797, he then made a number of false starts. In 1816 he almost went to Haiti, having been appointed sculptor to King Christophe; thereafter, however, he found employment under Nash at Buckingham Palace, designing friezes and ornaments to be executed both in marble and in Coade stone.[45] His early friezes so impressed George that Nash was directed to 'give Rossi any part of the sculpture he wanted' at the site. Rossi certainly needed the money: having married twice and fathered eight children by each wife, he was constantly in debt, and by 1834 was appealing to the Royal Academy to alleviate his 'great distress'. However, his close identification with George IV was of small use to him after the King's death. Many of his better-known contemporaries, men like Flaxman and Banks, had deeply resented Rossi's royal commissions, and had been highly critical of his often quite mediocre work. He was appointed principal sculptor to William IV in 1830, but since William had almost no interest in the visual arts, his career collapsed as quickly as that of Nash – whom he had immortalised in marble in 1823. After his death in 1839, the *Art Union* magazine sniffed that 'Mr Rossi found but few patrons ... and he bequeathed nothing to his family but his fame.'[46]

Rossi's story illustrates an aspect of George's patronage which has rarely been highlighted. As with painting and architecture, the nature of his patronage of sculpture was to pass over unmistakable gifts in favour of the second-rate. The galaxy of British sculptural talent assembled at Buckingham Palace was somewhat deceptive. John Flaxman, for instance, although widely regarded as the greatest British sculptor of the age, was never employed by George; he did, however, design silverware for goldsmiths Rundell, Bridge and Rundell.[47] Lesser talents such as Nash, Wyatville, Hoppner and Rossi were perhaps more 'clubbable' than palpable geniuses like Soane, Turner or Flaxman. Their lack of professionalism and, in particular, of financial acumen (a failing certainly evident in the case of Nash and of Rossi) also doubtless made them more amenable to a patron to whom fiscal probity was an irritating irrelevance, and who was also notoriously lax about paying his bills.

Equally importantly, artists, sculptors and architects not at the summit of their profession were often more ready to comply with the requirements of their royal patron and his powerful advisors. Nor were they in a strong position to demand a more public recognition as of right. George was indeed notably miserly when it came to rewarding his creatures with honours. It is surely significant that, while his cultural advisors enjoyed titles and wealth, his artists fared poorly. The quondam politician Sir Charles Long, for example, was created Viscount Farnborough in 1826, but by the end of the King's reign neither Chantrey nor Rossi nor Westmacott – supposedly George's favourite British sculptors – had received so much as a knighthood. Nor, more surprisingly, had John Nash or David Wilkie. Like Wilkie, Westmacott had to wait to be knighted by William IV, in 1837. George had certainly floated the idea of making Nash a baronet, but gave in to Wellington's demand that the honour be postponed until Nash had completed his work at Buckingham Palace.[48] Obsessed as ever with his own appetites and his own pleasures, George failed to recognise that his favourite practitioners might deserve a more lasting expression of his gratitude than a mere pat on the arm. It was, after all, Nash, Rossi and Wilkie, rather than the outstanding prodigies of the day, who wrote the visual history of his Regency and his reign.

7

Conspicuous Consumption

Nay, I do not see why the great R–g—t himself
Should, in times such as these, stay at home on the shelf:
Though through narrow defiles he's not fitted to pass,
Yet who could resist, if he bore down *en masse?*
Thomas Moore, *Reinforcements for Lord Wellington*

ONE OF GEORGE IV's abiding pleasures was the prodigious consumption of food and drink. When such indulgence was combined with a growing reluctance to take even the most moderate
exercise, with hypochondria and a capacity for self-dramatisation –
and, possibly, with an inherited and debilitating porphyric condition –
the inevitable results were not only bouts of apparent severe ill-health
but a consequent destabilisation of the monarchy. On numerous
occasions after his assumption of the Regency – and indeed many
times before – George was rumoured to be on the point of death.
Such tales, exaggerated though they proved, led many to dismiss him
as an essentially transient phenomenon. When allied to anecdotes
highlighting his over-indulgences and his burgeoning weight, they
further eroded respect for a man who, by the time of his accession,
had become to many a figure of fun.

George's excessive intake of alcohol did much to accelerate a
genuine deterioration in his health, and was often commented upon.
As early as May 1792 the cartoonist James Gillray had cast him as
'Drunkenness' in his gallery of royal rogues – his brothers Frederick
and William being allotted the roles of 'Gambling' and 'Debauchery',
respectively. His celebrated demolition of the Prince as *A Voluptuary
Undergoing the Horrors of Digestion*, designed as a scabrous comparison
with his parents' equally reprehensible cheese-paring austerity, fol-

lowed two months later. George's excessive drinking was already so widely renowned as to require no more than allusion on Gillray's part, the print's symbolism of decanters of port and brandy and empty wine bottles needing no further explanation.[1]

Food was another central facet of George's life. Cooks certainly played a key role in his day-to-day activities. During the 1780s, as we have seen, Weltje was not only George's cook but also his gambling associate, drinking companion, political advisor, picture agent, arbiter of taste and Brighton estate agent; and until 1787 the French chef Guillaume Gaubert, no more qualified than Weltje, supervised the interior decoration at Carlton House. In December 1809, Farington noted that the Prince was prepared to pay the considerable sum of £200 a year to secure the services of the late Duke of Portland's 'French cook'. Three years later, it was the picture of *A Cook in his Shop* which most attracted George's attention at that year's Royal Academy exhibition. And when he visited Nash at East Cowes in 1817, it was his personal cook – not his Private Secretary, nor any other Household official – who was sent to the Isle of Wight three days beforehand to prepare for the royal arrival.[2]

George's celebration of food reached its apogee after Waterloo, with his recruitment in 1816 of the internationally-acclaimed French cook Antonin Carême – recently described as 'probably the greatest cook of all time' – at a salary of no less than £2,000 a year. While working under the Parisian *pâtissier* Bailly Carême had learned not only to prepare pastries and confectionary but also to read and write. By 1815, aged thirty-two, he had published his first two books, *Le Pâtissier royal parisien* and *Le Pâtissier pittoresque*, and had spent twelve years in the service of Napoleon's foreign minister, Prince Talleyrand. In 1816, with Napoleon exiled to St Helena, George managed to entice Carême to England. He was delighted: the best chef of the day was not only working exclusively for him, but in his person provided a tangible link with the First Empire and (clearly an additional *frisson*) with the assembled European statesmen, for whom he had cooked at the recent Congress of Vienna.

By January 1817 Carême was preparing hundred-dish dinners at Brighton for guests such as the Grand Duke Nicholas, heir to the Russian throne. Such complex and lavish concoctions did nothing to reduce George's waistline. When the Regent complained that the temptation was too great and Carême would kill him with a surfeit of food, the chef responded (as he records in the preface of another book, *Le Cuisinier parisien*): 'Your Highness, my concern is to tempt your appetite, not to curb it.'

At Brighton, Carême was equipped with one of the most techno-logically-advanced kitchens of its day. It compared favourably in size with many of the principal rooms, being almost as large as the Banqueting Room itself. If the four cast-iron ceiling supports topped by painted copper palm leaves imparted an air of frivolity, the 'King's kitchen' was no mere folly; its construction was, after all, one of George's first priorities when he rebuilt the Pavilion after 1815. Copper awnings drew away smells and smoke from the ultra-modern cooking ranges below, while an impressive battery of smoke jacks and clockwork jacks allowed several joints of meat to be mechanically spit-roasted simultaneously. Above the centre of the room a tall, glazed clerestory further aided the dissipation of heat and fumes. Directly beneath it was a large, oval 'steam table'. An invention of a local man, William Stark, this iron-topped, brass-bound table enabled prepared dishes to be kept warm by means of steam heat piped into its innards from a boiler hidden behind the range.

The kitchen was not the only space at Brighton Pavilion devoted to food. We have already noted the 'confectionery', three rooms devoted to the preparation of desserts, and two 'pastry rooms' further catered to George's incorrigibly sweet tooth. Sorbets and ice-creams were made in the confectionery, using ice from the adjacent 'ice room', which was drawn in turn from the straw-lined ice-house sited to the south-west of the building.

The expense involved in gratifying George's robust interest in dining was predictably over-scaled – Stark's kitchen fittings alone cost more than £6,000 – but the result was an impeccably modern kitchen suite which was the envy of Europe. The local newspaper was for once not exaggerating when it commented, in 1818, that the Pavilion's kitchens formed 'one part of the most useful and convenient append-ages to a mansion that is to be seen in the British Empire'.[3] Sadly, life in England in general, and on the Sussex coast in particular, failed to impress the man for whom this fabulous cockpit had been created. Carême found the English climate depressing, the level of knowledge of his English fellow-cooks woeful, the English preference for 'the roasts of beef, mutton and lamb [and] the various meats cooked in salt water' pitiable, and the traditional antipathy of the English towards the French distasteful. In 1818 he returned to Paris.[4]

The diary of the artist Joseph Farington is peppered with references to George's dietary and drinking habits. On 2 April 1799, for example, he records that the Prince of Wales drank barely-diluted spirits – often gin and water – in half-pint measures, and that he was an habitual smoker.[5] He also reported that the Prince took snuff – 'sensual snuff' from Spain, which he apparently judged 'highly inspiring'. More sceptical observers, however, were inclined to suppose the princely snuff-taking a mere following of the fashion set by such dandies as Brummell and Lord Petersham, and more than one court commentator noted that the Prince appeared more interested in the workmanship of the gold and silver snuff-boxes he was offered than in their contents.[6] By the time of his accession George was drinking not only half-pints of gin and wine by the bottle, but also copious quantities of whisky, a particular favourite during his visits to Ireland and Scotland in 1821 and 1822. As he grew older, this was regularly supplemented by glass upon glass of the cloyingly sweet cherry liqueur which became his preferred tipple, 'Maraschino'. His apparently limitless consumption of Maraschino during the 1820s, allied to his laudanum-taking, his enthusiasm for being bled, his porphyria, and all the other problems to be expected by a man in his sixties, could not but have a deleterious effect on a constitution already over-strained by dissipation. As early as 1800 the Princess of Wales – admittedly not the most neutral of observers – had observed how physically changed her husband was since their first meeting five years before. Farington reported that Caroline, catching sight of a picture of her husband in Hoppner's studio, asked when it had been painted: 'Hoppner replied 4 or 5 years ago – *Twenty years ago I should think*, she rejoined, alluding probably to his different appearance now.'[7]

George's inordinate love of food and drink and reliance on laudanum apart, it is difficult to know exactly what caused the obvious physical pain which periodically wracked George's body. No medical records exist, except what is contained in the surviving correspondence of his physician Sir Henry Halford. Knighton's papers were burnt by his widow, and most of George's correspondence with Mrs Fitzherbert suffered a similar fate. Thus the conclusions drawn by medical historians concerning the nature of his many illnesses – never mind whether these were genuine or imagined – have necessarily been speculative.

Macalpine and Hunter's diagnosis in 1969 was that the medical histories (such as they are) of George III and his son 'show much similarity, save only that George IV did not suffer from episodes of obvious derangement'. His general debility and occasional near-paralysis, they suggested, indicate that George IV, too, suffered from porphyria. In particular they noted the strange lassitude which followed the Prince's more serious attacks – a lassitude with which, they pointed out, Princess Charlotte was also afflicted shortly before her death.

Macalpine and Hunter argued that George tried to conceal the seriousness of his sufferings, wishing to avoid another Regency. The symptoms of his poor health were quickly recognisable by observers, however – and, actor *manqué* that he was, George could seldom resist the histrionic opportunities afforded by suitably dramatic revelations of his condition. As with George III, however, porphyria did not in itself prove fatal. What helped to kill off George IV was heart disease and other ailments associated with the excesses of his way of life – in particular, his reliance on alcohol and laudanum, often taken at the same time. It is certain that the shadow of his father's 'madness' clouded George's thoughts, and throughout his adult life both he and the nation tremulously awaited signs of the 'dementia' that had so thoroughly debilitated George III after 1810. Such fears remained largely unspoken, but the least allusion to the terrifying spectre caused George to fall into fits of ungovernable fury which served only to convince spectators that he would, after all, end up as mad as his father. In 1816, for example, he became livid with rage on learning of a rumour, supposedly circulated by the Duke of Cumberland, that the source of his current ailment was *'no other* than that he *was mad'*. George IV, wrote Charles Greville in 1829, was 'in a great fright with his father's fate before him, and indeed nothing is more probable than that he will become blind and mad too; he is already a little of both'.[8]

The question as to which of his uninspiring brothers would succeed George was thus always under discussion, in public or in secret, following George III's incarceration in 1811 and particularly after Princess Charlotte's tragic death in 1817. When George IV was dangerously ill following his accession, it was widely expected that the Duke of York – whose wife, Frederica, had recently died – would remarry and try to beget an heir, so that the unpopular Duke of Kent's daughter (the future Queen Victoria) should not inherit the throne. With typical insouciance, York ignored the advice he was repeatedly given and, behaving in a way which had become virtually axiomatic with the sons of George III, took up instead with the Duchess of Rutland, wife of one of the new King's drinking companions.

By 1820 George's increased weight and accompanying illnesses were being frequently noted. John Russell's picture of the Prince of Wales of 1792 showed his face to be already fat and florid, with obvious double chins – a dramatic and revealing contrast to the flatteringly idealised full-lengths by Reynolds and Gainsborough. Élisabeth Vigée-Le Brun, who painted George in 1804, commented that, although he was undoubtedly 'tall and well built' and had 'a fine face', he had 'gained too much weight for his age': but three years later, at a Royal Academy dinner, 'The Prince buckled on a belt ... and found it too wide by 10 or 12 inches, so much had He shrunk in size.' The reason was not careful dieting, but ill-health (the Prince did not, Farington explained, 'abstain from meat and wine' at that time 'from their being forbidden by His Physicians but from nauseating both'). George himself 'seemed sensible that His constitution was in a bad state', and his habitually indiscreet brother William blurted out that 'He would not live three months'.[9] In 1809 Farington's brother thought the Prince 'much altered in His appearance', having 'a shattered look', and that the contrast between George and his brother York – 'who had all the fulness and elastick vigour of a strong man' – was very marked, the Prince appearing 'to great disadvantage'. The following year Benjamin West noted of George that '[he] is grown enormously large; a figure like Henry 8th'. By 1821 he was wearing a 'Bastille of whalebone' to encase his burgeoning body, which weighed as much as twenty stone. In 1824 his corset was made to fit a waist of fifty inches; by 1830 the Duke of Gloucester was comparing the King's body to 'a feather bed'. Even the sympathetic David Wilkie, painting George at Windsor in the last year of his life, found his sitter grossly overweight and sadly deteriorated. It took three hours, he related, to dress the King in his costume and 'to lace up all the bulgings and excrescencies'. Even then, he lamented, the end result looked only 'like a great sausage stuffed into the covering'.[10]

George was not only overweight but also often 'overwrought', a condition probably exacerbated by, or even the direct result of, the immoderate quantities of alcohol and laudanum he was ingesting. Increasingly, these attacks of panic or emotion made him physically sick. They also clouded his judgement, in a manner not dissimilar to the effects of porphyria on his father.

George suffered from gout from an early age, and by 1826 his bed at Carlton House was furnished with no fewer than '11 gouty pillows'. He was also often virtually paralysed by what he described as 'violent bilious attacks', which may well have been symptoms of porphyria. He was seriously ill in 1781 and again in 1787 – 'with an inward complaint', the *Gentleman's Magazine* opined. During much of 1791 he was a victim of the same 'violent complaint', which, he admitted, left his nerves 'in a shatter'd state'. These attacks continued throughout the 1790s, and the pattern was always much the same: biliousness, pains and even semi-paralysis, followed by 'extreme weakness and lassitude'. More often than not these attacks were treated by 'profuse bleeding'.[11] In 1800, believed to be near death, George was copiously bled. More seriously, in 1804 he was taken ill 'with one of those sudden and mysterious attacks', characterised by 'violent cramp and a bowel complaint'. It seemed likely at the time that he would be offered Regency powers, since his father's illness had reasserted itself. Yet it was also a time of international crisis: war had broken out again, Napoleon had crowned himself Emperor, and the prospects for an anti-French alliance looked grim.

There certainly seems to have been a correlation between George's 'bilious attacks' and occasions of great stress, his illnesses appearing particularly prevalent at times when he was most anxious or apprehensive. Shortly after he assumed the Regency in February 1811, for example, an observer noted that the Prince had 'had three epileptic fits' and had 'been very ill with sickness, swelled legs, etc'. By November George was complaining that he was 'incapable of moving a single joint in my whole frame', and the following month told MacMahon that he was unable 'to stand on the left foot'. For much of the winter of 1811–12 he was afflicted with severe pains in his arms and legs, at times almost amounting to the paralysis which had affected his father. Macalpine and Hunter associated these possibly porphyric symptoms with his frequent admission of 'shattered nerves' and his increasing tendency, as he grew older, to languid indolence. Early in 1812, one doctor was wondering whether George III or his eldest son would die first.[12]

These ailments were not helped by George's pronounced disinclination to stir himself. As early as 1811 he was reported to be taking 'little exercise, not such as his bulk requires'. Ordered by his doctors to compensate for this by a diet of French beans and barley-water, George proceeded to a public dinner where he made 'great havoc of sundry savoury meats and much champagne, claret and burgundy'. Even the athletic pleasures of his youth, such as riding, were now most often deemed hardly worth the effort. 'He seldom rides on

Horseback,' said James Boswell the younger, 'never walks and only has the exercise which a Carriage gives Him.' A few months later the sculptor Joseph Nollekens was outspoken enough to tell the Regent: 'Your Royal Highness has increased in fullness of face the thickness of two fingers since I first modelled your face.' The Prince merely smiled enigmatically.

By the beginning of his Regency George was prepared, at least in private, to admit to his increasing reliance on laudanum – opium in an alcohol solution, a widely-used drug popular long into the nineteenth century. To deal with his 'sprained ankle' in 1811, George's doctors prescribed prodigious doses – 250 drops at one sitting, according to Farington, or a hundred drops every three hours, according to Fremantle. Sir Henry Halford later suggested that such excessive use of laudanum would drive him mad.[13] The reality of George's indispositions, however, made laudanum increasingly essential. According to one account, the 'agony of pain' he was enduring caused 'a degree of irritation on his nerves nearly approaching delirium'. The Duke of Cumberland publicly demonstrated his typically Hanoverian want of tact and sympathy by suggesting that his brother's illness was all in his mind, and that 'a blister on the head might be more efficacious than a poultice on the ankle'.[14] Whatever George's state of mind, it was scarcely aided by his heavy reliance on laudanum.

Nor was laudanum George's only injurious addiction. In common with those of his subjects who could afford medical attention, he was frequently subjected to the ordeal of cupping, a procedure designed to produce blisters and so rid the body of deleterious humours. He also appeared to relish the languid torture of being bled. Neither of these dubious panaceas did much to balance his already precarious constitution, of course, but his enthusiasm for them, and in particular for being bled, amounted to what has been called a 'sport'. The doctor who cupped George in March 1813 told Farington that 'the Prince Regent has been in the habit of being cupped for more than twenty years past, and has been cupped more than a hundred times', not always merely at his doctors' instigation; moreover, he continued, 'Such is the fullness of the Prince's habit that He ... takes from Him twenty ounces of blood at a time'. He added by way of an afterthought that to take more than eight ounces at a time from anyone else 'might do harm by causing debility', a shocking revelation dismissed by Farington as simply 'the consequence of the Prince's mode of living'. Yet this obsession certainly contributed to his general ill-health. When William Knighton first met him in 1811 he was struck by the Regent's 'copper colour', which he attributed partly to 'the excessive free living of his early years' and partly to his penchant for being bled.[15]

As his Regency progressed, George's attacks grew increasingly frequent. In January 1814 he suffered another 'long and painful confinement', and in the words of his daughter was 'alarmingly ill'. In 1815 he was described as being 'in a very nervous state', and later 'quite struck down'. By 1817 observers like Creevey were once again despairing of his life: 'We have been losing our Regent,' Creevey wrote in September of that year, suggesting (probably correctly) that his doctors had 'curtailed his length of life'. The usual solution, 'laudanum and cordials', was having little effect. 'The consequences are likely to produce dropsy,' suggested Creevey. Indeed, so serious was George's indisposition and 'disinclination to all business' that, it was reported, 'there have been serious thoughts of a Council of Regency to assist in the dispatch of affairs.' The prospect of a Regency for the Regent himself, while the mad old King was still alive, must have horrified Liverpool's government, as they saw George deteriorate even further after the death of Princess Charlotte in November 1817. Macalpine and Hunter have suggested that the results of the Princess's *post mortem* examination 'indicate a general paralysis of the vital nerves, that is of the autonomic nervous system', and are thus also 'consistent with the diagnosis of porphyria'.[16]

George was so unwell at the time of his father's death on 29 January 1820 that few believed his reign would last more than a few months. His doctors announced simply that he had an 'inflammation of the lungs'; privately, they thought it might be pneumonia. He had been taken ill the day before George III's death and was not, his doctors insisted, in a fit state to attend the funeral on 15 February. Again, stress – possibly guilt-induced, and connected with his father's demise – may have been a factor. Charles Greville reported on 4 February 1820 that 'The new King has been desperately ill. He had a bad cold at Brighton, for which he lost eighty ounces of blood; yet he afterwards had a severe oppression, amounting almost to suffocation, on his chest.' Despite the extraction of approximately 150 ounces of blood, George had apparently recovered somewhat by March, although the trial of his wife ensured that he remained 'a little nervous' throughout the summer. In September 1820 Farington's brother, turning out to see the new King when he attended Cowes Regatta, 'thought he looked much worse than He did last year – his flesh more sodden and of bad colour'. The sculptor Stothard's report of June 1821 that 'the King is very ill and that *his head* is *affected*' clearly encouraged Farington, and doubtless many others, to speculate whether he was becoming afflicted with his late father's malady.[17] Queen Caroline's sudden death on 8 August helped to lift the clouds of depression considerably, but a relapse could never be ruled out.[18]

Matters all but came to a head during George's visit to Ireland in 1821. At a grand dinner on 5 September for the Order of St Patrick (or the 'Knights and Todies', as Creevey called the Order's members), he 'showed evident signs of uneasiness in his Royal stomacher'. Next day he was too ill to attend a banquet on which Lord Portarlington and others had spent nearly £5,000. In Scotland the following year, the *Observer* noted how tired the King looked, and judged him little more than 'an ugly old man'.[19]

After his return from Scotland, Princess Lieven reported that the King was 'very ill' and 'looks ghastly', was 'tortured by gout, ... is plunged in gloom' and 'talks about nothing but dying. I have never seen him so wretched.' In April 1823 she wrote that he was bed-ridden, 'and sees nobody but his doctors'. His birthday celebrations of 1823 were cancelled due to his 'flying gout'. By mid May his condition was more accurately described as an 'inflammation ... from his toe nearly to the top of his thigh', allied to the 'great irritability upon his stomach being literally soused with Opium and Bark Brandy and Wine', which he drank 'like mother's milk'. Two years later Creevey was predicting that he would expire before long – 'From the Apothecary's department it is said there is a general regular declining in strength and flesh' – while even the mealy-mouthed Halford publicly admitted that 'his present extreme inactivity is very unfavourable to the continuance of his health'.

Plagued as he was in his late years by debilitating ill-health, George's temper was becoming increasingly unpredictable. At times he even went so far as to abuse Sir William Knighton in public.[20] It is surely more than coincidental that this indispensable (if Machiavellian) right hand, effectively George's last Private Secretary, was a medical doctor by training. Knighton was thus well-equipped to sympathise with his royal master's perpetual infirmities, whether real or imaginary.

8

Political Posturing

Now you have the triple feather,
Bind the kindred stems together
With a silken tie, whose hue
Once was brilliant Buff and Blue;
Sullied now – alas, how much!
Only fit for Y–rm——th's touch.

Thomas Moore, *Anacreontic*

O NE OF THE least attractive aspects of George's character was his propensity to abandon both his political principles and his friendships with barely a backward glance. As he grew older, this disregard for people and causes became more pronounced. One obituary attested that 'At an age when generous feelings are usually predominant, we find him absorbed by an all-engrossing selfishness; not merely careless of the feelings of others, but indulging in wanton cruelty.' While this judgement is harsh, George was certainly heedless of the feelings even of those closest to him. It is hard to quarrel with the obituarist's subsequent comment that the late King 'was essentially a lover of personal ease', and that 'during the later years of his life, a quiet indulgence of certain sensual enjoyments seemed the sole object of his existence'.[1]

As far as George was concerned, everything revolved around his own whims, and if these altered, so the attitudes and actions of his friends, his household and his government were expected to follow suit. Not least among those he managed to exasperate, despite his incontrovertible charm, were his political supporters. In 1829, by which time his early admiration had wilted in the light of George's lamentable reaction to the Catholic Emancipation Bill, Charles

Greville put his finger on it: 'He has a sort of capricious good-nature, arising however out of no good principles or good feeling, but which is of use to him, as it cancels in a moment.' Greville concluded that 'a more contemptible, cowardly, selfish, unfeeling dog does not exist'.[2] The artist Thomas Phillips also testified to George's tendency to forget or dismiss obligations and to his inability, despite his obvious natural intelligence, to concentrate on any one matter or person for even a reasonable length of time:

> [The Prince of Wales] is influenced by caprice, and has no steadiness ...
> He has the power of giving a proper answer to whoever addresses him
> upon any subject, but nothing fixes him. The person who last spoke to
> him makes an apparent impression, but it is gone when another person
> or subject comes before him, and His Taylor, or Bootmaker will occupy
> his mind to the doing away any other consideration to which His atten-
> tion might before have been drawn.[3]

Robert Huish's judgement on George IV's character was, predictably, equally severe: 'notwithstanding the principles inculcated in his youth ... his subsequent conduct proved that he rather upheld the men than valued their principles, and that he repudiated their principles as soon as he had abandoned the men'. As the *Westminster Review*'s obituarist bitterly proclaimed in 1831: 'no act of the King's life seems to have been guided by any principle but that of self-gratification'.[4]

This selfishness moved George to outbursts of incredulous anger when he was thwarted. A prominent instance of this was his increas-ingly petulant and hysterical reaction to the likely collapse of Queen Caroline's trial in 1820, when he behaved like a small child robbed of his toys. On 22 July Lord Harrowby confidently told Princess Lieven that, should Caroline win, 'The King would go to reign in Hanover'.[5] Clearly, the prospect of having his wishes frustrated in a very public loss of face was enough to make George, so eager at other times to profess his undying commitment to the safety and welfare of his realm, consider sacrificing all thought of family or nation. (A parallel with Edward VIII's conduct in 1936 comes readily to mind.) There are few better examples of his boundless capacity for self-absorption.

Political principles were, George found, remarkably easy to discard should circumstances require. Even his much-trumpeted youthful alliance with Charles James Fox and his Whig friends was always, as Thackeray observed much later, something of a 'hollow compact'.

George often seemed to regard Fox's radical Whiggism more as a fashionable pose than as a catalyst for necessary reform. Walter Sichel drew an evocative picture of the Foxite Prince wearing 'the cockade of a fox's brush entwined with sprigs of laurel (as contrasted with the Pittite wreath of oak-leaves), and a black coat-collar as against the gaudier blue ones'. More recently, even E. A. Smith grudgingly admitted that 'His association with the Whigs was social and selfish'.[6] In public, however, George behaved as though Fox's politics were his own. In his first speech in the House of Lords, he announced to the assembled peers: 'I exist by the love, the friendship, and the benevolence of the people, and their cause I will never forsake as long as I live' – a Foxite sentiment that was to prove, as it turned out, a hostage to fortune.

Though George was undeniably good at giving parties, this was too often the sum of his contribution to the Whig cause. As Amanda Foreman has noted, although he and the Duchess of Devonshire sallied out to greet the pro-Fox mob before the Westminster election of 1784, George was 'too drunk for most of the election to be of any help'.[7] He generally managed to bestir himself however, if required, for a social event; on 19 May 1784, for example, he gave a fête in the garden of Carlton House to celebrate Fox's Westminster victory, proposing the celebrated Whig toast 'True Blue and Mrs Crewe'. But he infinitely preferred his support to take the form of alcohol consumption rather than active lobbying. Fox's biographer Leslie Mitchell has suggested that George was principally drawn to Fox and the Whigs from a wish to irritate his father and because he was attracted by the melodramatic 'celebrity' politics of 1784, when Fox and his glamorous allies were martyred on the altar of monarchical power. Once politics stopped being about drunken parties and duchesses selling kisses for votes, he rather lost interest.

As long as Fox lived, George continued to play the part of a Foxite Whig. Yet his illegal marriage to Maria Fitzherbert in 1785 was an early signal that he was ready to sacrifice both Fox's friendship and his own professed Whig principles if they were in conflict with something he badly wanted. As in every great crisis of his life, from the time of the Fitzherbert 'marriage' to his resistance to the Catholic Emancipation Act forty years later, George told his friends and allies what they wanted to hear, and then proceeded to satisfy his own whims. On 10 December 1785 Fox implored him not to contravene his father's Royal Marriage Act: 'A mock marriage ... is neither honorable for any

of the parties, nor, with respect to your Royal Highness, even safe.'
The next day the Prince wrote to assure his friend that 'there was no
cause for alarm'; four days later, however, he married Maria in secret.
As one of Mrs Fitzherbert's biographers has said, 'It is impossible to
acquit the Prince of the intention to deceive Fox by this disingenuous
epistle.'[8]

The repercussions of the marriage surfaced eighteen months later,
when George's spending excesses left him no option but to appeal to
Parliament to pay off his mounting debts. As noted earlier, Fox denied
in the House of Commons on 30 April 1787 that any such illegal marriage had taken place. To George, no stranger to duplicity, this was
doubtless perfectly acceptable; his 'wife', however, whe she read newspaper reports of Fox's speech the next morning, demanded furiously
that he compel Fox to retract. Fox refused: to retract was in effect to
admit that he had lied to the House. (He later claimed that he had been
informed of the truth by a fellow MP shortly *after* making his denial.)
Richard Sheridan failed to achieve a compromise, and Prinny let the
matter drop, preferring to concentrate on his campaign to have his
debts relieved. However, the issue further divided the Whigs, as
leaders such as Portland sought to distance themselves from a Prince
who heedlessly amassed debts assuming they would be relieved at
public expense, contracted an illegal marriage, and then attempted to
use his political influence to escape the consequences of his mistakes.

Mrs Fitzherbert's animus against Fox played its part in creating a
breach between George and his political mentor. For a time the two
men met in secret, for fear of enraging the 'Princess of Wales'. In 1788
George's Private Secretary noted that she 'would never forgive [Fox's]
public declaration on her subject in the House of Commons, and had
taken every opportunity of alienating the Prince's mind from him'.[9]
Decades later Brougham, writing to John Croker, noted that even in
her old age Mrs Fitzherbert still resented Fox's denial of her marriage,
believing (it seems wrongly) that he had already been told the truth by
the Prince.

For his part, Fox was quick to realise that once the marriage had
become public knowledge the Whig party stood to be fatally compromised by its connection with the Prince of Wales. However much
he might enjoy George's company, he was realistic enough to be
aware that any radical programme of reform and emancipation the
Whigs might espouse would always be in danger of eclipse by the
conduct of their royal patron. He was also acutely aware that he

himself would be blamed for any public revelation of George's disreputable conduct. As Dr Mitchell has noted, 'many people, including the King, regarded [Fox] as the Prince's tutor in debauchery'. George III certainly 'held Fox principally responsible for the Prince's many failings' (beginning with his habit of vomiting in public), a point of view which seemed to be buttressed by the fact that Fox's 'indebtedness mirrored that of the heir apparent'. Accordingly, after 1787 Fox attempted to keep Carlton House at arm's length. He was quickly replaced as George's political 'errand boy' by the more malleable Sheridan, who 'appeared happy to abet the Prince in any scheme, however unprincipled'.[10]

The Regency Crisis of 1788–9, during which the tantalising prospect of a return to power seemed for an instant to be within Fox's grasp, in the end merely served to realise many of his fears concerning his royal patron's political irresponsiblity. George's principal interest proved to lie not, as Fox had hoped, in exploiting his father's seemingly permanent debility to unseat Pitt and propel the Foxite Whigs into government, but rather in ensuring that his Regency would afford him powers equivalent to those enjoyed by the King. Some years later the Duchess of Devonshire dated the beginning of the decline of the old Whig party not to the outbreak of the French Revolution but to the events of the Regency Crisis, some months earlier.[11]

At first developments unfolded to the Whigs' advantage. George, learning of his father's illness in December 1788, immediately sent for Fox, recognising that Sheridan was not the man to lead a government. In January 1789, when there had been no apparent improvement in the King's condition, George and his chief advisors – Sheridan, Burke and Fox – began confidently to allot posts in a new Whig government. However, Pitt successfully stalled the passage of the Regency Bill, and the King suddenly recovered in February. All Whig hopes of terminating Pitt's administration were at an end, and George's Regency was indefinitely postponed.[12] Not only were the Foxite Whigs flung back into the political wilderness in which they had languished since 1784, but the previously close bond between Fox and the Prince was put under further severe strain. Some felt that Fox had 'fail'd in judgement', while Burke, in an implied criticism of the Prince, lamented that the Whigs had not beaten 'an honourable retreat'. In March George and his old friend quarrelled publicly at Almack's, and Fox grew increasingly frantic trying to quash some of the Prince's more harebrained schemes, such as borrowing money from the duc d'Orléans (which he failed to prevent) and retiring to Hanover (which he was successful in frustrating).[13]

Fox's enthusiastic espousal of the French Revolution proved the final straw, though it should not have surprised George. Foxite Whiggism, defined by the interpretation of the King's dismissal in December 1783 of a legitimately-formed government in favour of a ministry friendly to the Crown as a blatant betrayal of parliamentary democracy, was predicated on the assumption that monarchical influence was inherently despotic, and should be curbed wherever possible. George continued to pay public lip-service to the Foxite creed, which led him to dismiss Burke's *Reflections on the French Revolution* – a critical appraisal of events in France which sundered its author from his former colleagues Fox and Sheridan – as 'a Farrago of Nonsense'. Privately, however, he realised with growing dismay that any connection with the Whigs, even those such as Sheridan, implied his approbation of the revolutionaries' programme. In deciding that he had no option but to support the execution of Louis XVI and his Queen in 1793, Fox laid the Whigs open to a charge of being guilty of regicide by association. George thereafter kept his distance from the Foxites, and aristocratic Whigs also began to desert the sinking ship. By May 1793 the Whig leader Lord Malmesbury admitted that the party was now 'dispersed and broken'.[14] Pitt was to remain in power for another eight years, and when he did go, it was by his own choice.

In March 1793 the caricaturist George Cruikshank lauded the Prince for his attack on the Foxite Whigs' continued support for the regicide French regime. His rival satirist James Gillray was too optimistic when he once again associated the Prince with Fox and Sheridan in a print of November 1795: Fox had languished in George's disfavour for some time. On 26 March 1797, however, Farington reported that 'Fox and the Heads of Opposition dined with the Prince of Wales a day or two since for the first time in 5 or 6 years'. This dinner clearly inspired George to renew his political career, since when Fox decided to secede from Parliament after the failure of his reform attempts early in 1797, he actually offered to lead the sadly depleted and disorganised Whig opposition. Yet again, however, his personal concerns triumphed over issues of principle and patriotism. In December 1797, for example, when a Service of Thanksgiving for Admiral Duncan's victory over the Dutch fleet at Camperdown was held, George tried to prevent his wife's attendance, a tawdry attempt to hijack a solemn national occasion which met with failure.[15]

As the horrors of the French Revolution receded into the past, Fox was once more restored to George's pantheon of heroes. However, while he continued to pay homage to the idea of Fox the Mentor, he kept the reality of Fox's politics at arm's length. Thus, when the King again fell seriously ill in 1801, Fox was once again subtly ignored and George instead consulted with Pitt, who seemed likely to remain in office in the event of any Regency. The Prince and Mrs Fitzherbert had lately been reconciled: given that Maria had never forgiven Fox for his public denial of her marriage, it is possible that her influence was at work. It is equally likely that, while England remained at war with France, Fox's enduring francophilia was an insurmountable obstacle. In any event, as ever, personal considerations appeared to be far more important to George than any furtherance of Whig policies. Even when Pitt resigned and the tremulous, unlikely Henry Addington was invited to form a ministry, George elected to open negotiations with the new government rather than appeal to Fox and his former Whig friends for support in his all too characteristic attempts to secure the arrears of the Duchy of Cornwall to help pay off his debts. His efforts were doomed to failure, however, and even the Whig leader Lord Grey, disgusted with such selfish machinations at a time of international crisis, voted with the government to prevent any wholesale relief of the Prince's debts (George's dislike of Grey, plainly evident in his failure to bring him into government on assuming the Regency in 1811, may date from this incident). It was two years before Fox resumed a friendly correspondence with him, but thereafter, whenever George fantasised about an ideal Whig alliance, it was Fox and William Grenville – not Fox and Charles Grey – who were the chief figures.[16]

George III's refusal to have Fox serve in the national government following Addington's fall in 1804 was one of the rare occasions when the Prince of Wales publicly stood by his friend. His motive, however, as with his simultaneous establishment of anti-Pitt 'political dinners', was probably less a desire to vindicate Fox's principles than simply to oppose and annoy his father. George III's continuing antipathy to Fox enabled the Prince to make a grand but empty gesture, one which involved few political repercussions and committed him to nothing. In similar vein was his support of Sir Francis Burdett's radical candidature in the Middlesex Election of 1804. (At this time he was still petulantly smarting over his father's refusal to permit him to play any active part in the war against Napoleon, or even to advance his military rank. It will be recalled that in December 1803 he had gone so far as to publish his correspondence with the King on the subject, a proceeding which even many of his closest supporters thought inadvisable and in poor taste.) And while George now ignored many of Fox's political pronouncements, he ostentatiously consulted him concerning Princess Charlotte's education – a move particularly calculated to infuriate the King.[17]

Charles James Fox's eventual if tantalisingly brief attainment of office, as part of the new Whig government formed following the death of Pitt in 1806, was seized upon by George as a means of finally exercising a degree of genuine political influence, at least in the sense of rewarding his friends with offices and pensions. He found, however, that most of his attempts at patronage were subtly but effectively blocked by William Grenville, the new First Lord of the Treasury. All his complaints that his wishes had been disregarded fell on deaf ears. His only ally in the cabinet was effectively Lord Moira, who occupied the relatively minor post of Master-General of the Ordnance. Meanwhile Fox, the new Foreign Secretary, discovered with some curiosity that the Queen was prepared to speak to him for the first time since the Regency Crisis of 1788–9. As he wrote subsequently to Grenville, having been accused in the past by both King and Queen of corrupting the Prince of Wales and turning him against his parents, he had now had the chance to defend himself vigorously to the Queen's face, 'arguing with some justice that Prinny was quite able to find his own way down the primrose path without assistance'.[18]

Fox's death on 13 September 1806 presented George with an outlet for melodramatic expressions of grief. On hearing the news, 'he flung himself on a sofa and burst into passionate tears' – even though it was not at all unexpected.[19] Writing to Fox's nephew Lord Holland three days before the event, he could not resist exploiting the imminent sad prospect, expressing no hint of concern about what Holland himself or other members of Fox's family might be feeling, and at the same time inadvertently exposing the innate superficiality of his own political commitment:

My feelings are not to be describ'd; the loss of such a man, such a friend, to myself in particular, is so incalculable, and such a stab that I candidly acknowledge to you that I have neither resolution nor spirits sufficient to stand up against it, and the only wish I now feel remaining, is that of retiring entirely from all my political career, for in losing Fox, we lose everything.

Having cast himself as Fox's greatest friend and most intimate political ally, two days later George clumsily excused himself from attendance at the death-bed:

> Could I be of the smallest use I would fly, but to come merely to see him expire is more than my nature could endure, the blow is too severe; without him I can neither be of use to the country, to my friends nor to myself ... What am I then to do without my friend, my supporter ...?[20]

Happy to be unequivocating in his praise of the Whig statesman once he was safely in his grave, to George's intense frustration the King forbade him access to the platform from which most attention could be gained: Fox's funeral. (He did manage to send his Volunteer regiment to marshal the crowds, however, and to pay £500 towards the costs of the ceremony.)[21] The mourning he adopted as a mark of respect soon became a mere matter of fashion – George wore black far longer than custom dictated, finding that it helped to disguise his increasing girth – rather than a genuine expression of sorrow. Many attributed his subsequent loss of appetite (and his even more shocking decision to drink nothing but water) to his distress over Fox's death. Lord Holland, however, suggested perceptively that the Prince's condition was not a consequence of despair at Fox's demise, but feigned to impress the latest object of his desires, Lady Hertford, with the sincerity of his attachments, and encourage her 'commiserations for his sufferings and ... apprehensions for his health'.[22]

After Fox's death, George gave up even pretending to be interested in politics, announcing in 1807 that henceforth he would be politically neutral. The reaction to this statement was predictable. Many Whigs held that he had 'deserted his friends', while to Whig leaders such as Grenville and Tierney his behaviour was simply 'offensive'.[23] Few were either surprised or perturbed when in 1808 his drinking cronies the dukes of Norfolk and Northumberland, following his lead, withdrew their MPs from the Whig camp. Having now openly abandoned the party of Charles James Fox, George was said to be constantly in the company of his reactionary brother Cumberland. By early 1809 it was also widely rumoured that any interest in politics he retained took second place to his obsession with Lady Hertford. In 1809 he was happy to donate a thousand pounds towards the cost of Westmacott's statue of Fox (the idea for a monument to commemorate the late politician did not, it may be noted, originate at Carlton House),[24] but this gesture apart, his previously-professed Whig principles withered and died.

His father's illness of December 1810 roused George from his political lethargy. The events of 1788–9, 1801 and 1804 having taught him the wisdom of at least appearing to watch and wait, he stood by until his father's deteriorating condition left Perceval's government no option but to draw up a Regency Bill. Although such a Bill was clearly necessary, neither Perceval nor his Tory colleagues felt inclined to trust the Prince – particularly after receiving, on 19 December, a hideously clumsy and ill-advised protest from his brothers, clearly sent at George's suggestion, in which they fulminated against the proposed restrictions on the Regency as 'perfectly unconstitutional' and 'subversive of the principles which seated our family upon the throne of these realms'.[25] Even after George had assured him on 4 February 1811 that he would not be evicted from office, Perceval fully expected to be dismissed to make way for a Whig government once George had been sworn in as Regent on 6 February. He had clashed with the Prince over those restrictions which both Whigs and Tories felt should be imposed as a check upon his notorious fecklessness, and he had persistently obstructed the Prince's attempts to exercise political patronage. One of George's candidates for clerical office, for example, was vetoed by Perceval on the grounds that 'He is a notorious bon vivant' (a description readily applicable to many Anglican incumbents of the time).[26]

The new Regent disliked the Whig leader Lord Grey, and by this time in any case had few personal allies in either party. It seems instead that his correspondence with his mother and his conversations with his principal doctor had the greatest effect on his political doctrine and strategy. The old Queen strongly advised her son to keep the party of Fox and Sheridan out of office, and to continue with Perceval's Tories; at the same time, Sir Henry Halford cunningly suggested that a dismissal of the Perceval government followed by an invitation to Grey to form a new ministry would undoubtedly prompt a sharp decline in the King's condition and probably result in his death. Queen Charlotte having eagerly seized on Halford's Cassandra-like prophecy to exacerbate her son's feelings of guilt and apprehension still further, George accordingly began to talk of the need for 'caution' in contemplating a change of government. Grenville was not the only observer to report a 'total want of confidence in the Prince's steadiness and good faith'. Grey was shocked by what he saw as 'the Prince Regent's duplicity in all companies', and famously informed the Duke of York (in rather more measured language) that 'Our differences of opinion are too many and too important' for him to even consider the bipartisan coalition which George was now vaguely suggesting. George's former support for the Whigs was, in Roger Sales's words, now confirmed as 'a largely theatrical act of defiance towards his father rather than the product of any deep commitment'. Those Whig colours were 'just another theatrical costume that he had worn'.[27]

Robert Huish's unflinching pen put the Whig view of this distressing turn of events in a nutshell: 'Incapable of a durable friendship, [the Prince Regent] abandoned his early counsellors, in the same heartless manner as he did his successive mistresses.' At the time, Joseph Farington recognised that he was 'playing between the two Political parties ... in order to obtain payment of His debts and whatever He wants' but still found it difficult to believe that the new Regent, who had 'so much pledged himself' to the Whigs, would now desert them. Lady Mary Lowther, too, reported that Grey and Grenville still 'expected to tie the Prince Regent Hand and foot'.[28] Certainly the early weeks of the Regency appeared to augur a change of ministry. George, who had salved what there was of his own conscience by affecting to consider the Tories as the 'de facto government', was nevertheless publicly rude to Perceval, and in a characteristic display of pique kept the first meeting of his Privy Council waiting an hour and a half – largely, so it was rumoured, in order that they might be discomfited by the sight of the bust of Fox by Nollekens, prominently placed in the Carlton House Throne Room in which they were forced to loiter.

That the new Regent could accommodate himself not simply to a Tory government but to the Tory government of Spencer Perceval was particularly galling to the Whigs. It was Perceval who had been the most vehement defender of Princess Caroline only a few years before, and who had been responsible for the suggestion not only that the Prince was seeking to imprison his wife in the Tower but that he was a liar and a bankrupt. Informed of these accusations, George had allegedly sworn 'with most offensive personal abuse, and an oath which cannot be recited'. Even more damagingly, Caroline had agreed to act as godmother to Perceval's youngest son, Ernest. Now, to the general astonishment, the new Regent was apparently prepared to allow the man who in his view had traduced his reputation to remain in office, and moreover was seen to become increasingly cordial towards him. Some observers continued to express disbelief at this turn-around. William Cobbett later alleged that Perceval had only maintained himself in office after 1811 by blackmail, threatening to publish further details of the recent and highly embarrassing 'Delicate Investigation' of Caroline's supposed affairs, should he be replaced. The *Westminster Review* later asserted that 'either the Prince changed his opinions without reference to the interest of the people, or if he did guide his conduct with reference to the general welfare, he must have discovered that his political doctrines up to the mature age of forty-nine, were utterly erroneous'. More probably, George felt at ease with a highly capable prime minister who mirrored his own increasingly conservative instincts and whom a now disillusioned Princess of Wales had recently denounced as unfit to govern.[29]

The Prince Regent and his Prime Minister having come to an understanding, social engagements at Carlton House were balanced between Whigs and Tories. It soon became clear that George's immediate preoccupation was not the admission of his old political allies into a coalition government but the clearance of his embarrassing personal debts. In the event, Perceval's government could only secure a vote of £100,000 against a grand total of £552,000. The Whigs cursed the Regent, and cartoonists showed the ghost of Fox lamenting his desertion.[30]

Hardly had George reached an accommodation with Perceval, however, when the unfortunate premier was assassinated in the Central Lobby of the Palace of Westminster, on 10 May 1812. The Regent's relationship with the Earl of Liverpool, who succeeded Perceval as Prime Minister, was never as smooth. He delighted, for example, in rebuking Liverpool for trifling mistakes in form, and the 'cottage coterie' of foreign diplomats and disgruntled Tories who met at the Royal Lodge in the 1820s sought to undermine Canning's liberal foreign policy and Liverpool's leadership by advocating closer ties with the ultra-conservative powers of the Holy Alliance. In January 1825 George launched a vehement public attack on Canning, comparing his policies unfavourably with Pitt's resistance to revolutionary ideas in the 1790s and declaring that the independence of Spain's South American colonies – formal recognition of which Canning had urged – 'threatened the destruction of our happy Constitution and the peace of the world'. Typically, however, by 1826 the coterie's programme was forgotten, and Canning himself was being invited to weekend parties at the Royal Lodge.[31]

By the 1820s George IV saw himself as the enemy of 'the new political liberalism'.[32] His Foxite Whiggism of the 1780s had evaporated and he now began to reinvent himself as a born-again reactionary. He praised Pitt – the political foe of his friend Fox, and a man whom he had denounced in no uncertain terms forty years before – and applauded the firm support given him by his own 'revered and excellent father'.[33] It was as if Fox and Sheridan had never lived, and the young Prince in buff and blue had been no more than an artist's fantasy.

One issue in particular demonstrated how much George had changed in the course of forty years. During the 1780s he had been quick to advertise the pro-Catholic sentiments he ingested at the feet of Fox. His 'wife' Maria Fitzherbert – herself, of course, a Catholic – had witnessed the fruits of religious intolerance at first hand, her second husband having died of wounds inflicted during the anti-Papist Gordon Riots of 1780. In 1797 George went so far as to petition Pitt for a Catholic Emancipation Bill for Ireland, and was invited by the Irish Whigs to promote himself as the next Lord Lieutenant of Ireland. The invitation came to nothing, but George impressed upon his own nominee, his bibulous companion the Duke of Norfolk, the necessity of bringing forward measures for Catholic Relief. Fox suggested that the Prince should lead a pro-Emancipation coalition;[34] Pitt, his own liberal instincts on this question frustrated by the King's intransigence – and doubtless suspicious of the strength of his son's convictions – made no response. In the event, of course, Pitt resigned as premier over the issue in 1801, making a sacrifice for the Catholic cause far greater than anything George was ever to offer.

After the deaths of Pitt and Fox, George's opinions on the Catholic question moved gradually in the opposite direction. In the 1830s Creevey recalled a dinner in 1805 which the Prince of Wales had spoiled by making speeches which were 'very prosy as well as highly injudicious', concluding with 'a long harangue in favour of Catholics'. In 1807, however, the banker John Julius Angerstein declared that he 'knew the Prince of Wales disapproved of the Catholic question having been brought foward'. Trotter's memoirs of Fox published in 1811 toed the Regent's current line in alleging, with a sad want of truth, that George had *always* opposed Catholic relief, and that Fox's 'dutiful feelings to a venerable sovereign' had prevented him 'from rudely intruding matters upon him, on which it was understood he had a fixed and strong opinion'.[35] To avoid a straightforward betrayal of his former promises to Irish Catholics, George took refuge in muddied prevarications – announcing, for example, that his reverence for his father prevented him from introducing a Catholic Emancipation Bill while George III lived and, in January 1813, that the passage of a toleration bill 'would endanger the safety of the Country'. When in May 1813 the Whigs' ambitious Catholic Relief Bill was defeated, Grey declared that this was largely due to the 'undisguised and indecent canvass made by Carlton House' against the measure, the Regent having publicly announced that a vote for the Bill was a vote against the Crown.[36]

By the time of his vain protestations of 1824 against Canning's proposal to recognise the newly-liberated South American republics, George was willing to denounce those who promoted Catholic emancipation, including his former Whig friends, in public. Assuming the mantle of Shakespeare's Henry V – and speaking of his father with an exaggerated respect he had never accorded him when he was alive and in good health – he minuted the Cabinet that:

> When the Prince of Wales undertook the Regency of this Kingdom, during the indisposition of his revered father, the Prince abandoned all those friends, with whom he had lived in terms of the most unqualified friendship during the best years of his life; because the Prince, as Regent, thought their liberal & anti-Monarchical sentiments, unfavourable to the good government of his father's dominions; but the King now finds, that the opinions of the Opposition & liberals are uniformly acted upon.[37]

On 25 March 1827 Charles Greville declared that the King's 'opinions on the Catholic question are just the same as those of the Duke of York, and equally strong'. In November 1826 the ailing Duke had written both to his brother and to Liverpool, expressing his alarm at 'the very critical situation in which this country stands' and beseeching King and Prime Minister not to deviate from 'those principles in which we have gained honor and security since the year 1688'. Liverpool had in fact proposed a Catholic Relief Bill as early as March 1821, but George, as Creevey wrote on 10 April 1827, remained ostensibly 'a true Protestant' who would not give way to the emancipators.[38] Soon Greville's confidence in the staunchness of the King's Protestantism was seriously undermined: 'All his ministers', he reported on 13 April, 'are disgusted with his doubting, wavering, uncertain conduct, so weak in action and so intemperate in language.' Significantly, satirical prints of the time depicted the Duke of York and other Ultra Tories, rather than George himself, leading the attack on the would-be emancipators.[39]

While those who favoured Catholic emancipation tended to blame Lady Hertford or the King's brothers for his seemingly intransigent anti-Catholicism, those of an anti-Catholic bias, such as Greville, considered that Canning or Knighton was responsible for weakening the King's resolve. Knighton was viewed by many Ultras as the real architect of Canning's ministry of 1827, even after George revealed on 8 August that he had directed his new Prime Minister not to raise the issue of Catholic emancipation ('that painful question, upon which the King's opinions are unalterably fixed'), and that Canning had acquiesced in his wish.

After the Duke of York's demise early in 1827, his brother Cumberland assumed the role of George's Protestant conscience. The Duke of Cumberland detested Canning (who he declared had 'violently offended every foreign Cabinet'), and rejoiced at his premature death in August 1827. Yet his successor Viscount Goderich – whom George had, after all, specifically asked to form a ministry – appeared to be even more suspect on the Catholic question. At the beginning of what was to prove a very brief tenure of office, Goderich attested that as far as his government was concerned the issue remained an 'open question, upon which each member of the Cabinet should be at liberty to exercise his own judgement'. Even though Goderich's ministers had 'at no time entertained the thought of bringing forward or supporting' a Catholic bill, they were making it clear that George IV, unlike his father, was not going to be allowed to dictate government policy.[40]

From Hanover, Cumberland continued to sound apocalyptic alarms. On 15 September 1828 he warned Knighton that 'a single spark may set all in a blaze'; a month later that 'Never was any man's life more necessary than [George IV's] at this extraordinary crisis in which our wretched country is placed, for to judge from all that appears in the public papers, the moment is nigh at hand, that a Civil War is ready to break out in Ireland, when it has not already.' Princess Lieven, however, considered it was the 'infamous' Cumberland himself who sought civil war.[41] Incensed by the news that Wellington (who had replaced the lacklustre Goderich as Prime Minister) had reluctantly decided to support Catholic emancipation, Cumberland returned to England on 14 February 1829.

Caught between Cumberland's vociferous championing of the

Protestant cause and the need to support Wellington's government lest anything worse (or Whig) appear in its place, George appeared alternately confused, belligerent, and panic-stricken. Cumberland was puzzled to be assured by his brother, 'but a few hours before, that there was not the least idea of Catholic Emancipation, rather intimating that it was a phantom that I had conjured up in my own head', only to discover at a dinner with Wellington later that day that his government was confident the Emancipation Bill would pass both Houses. Cumberland was widely assumed to have the King's confidence – Princess Lieven reported that George was more than willing to 'give audiences to the Ultras among the peers who ask for them'. As the debates on the Bill progressed, however, it became clear that George had in fact no strong feelings on the subject and that, as ever, he would agree with the opinions of his loudest or most recent interlocutor. (As early as 1808 Lord Holland had noted astutely that the Prince was always 'notoriously influenced by the sentiments of his last conversation'.) Lord Mount Charles, it is true, 'verily believed the King would go mad on the Catholic question, his violence was so great about it', but he was never a reliable source – he also believed that the King abhorred Knighton 'with a detestation'. Meanwhile, Lady Conyngham disloyally told Cumberland she thought the King's considerable daily intake of laudanum had so disoriented him that he knew nothing of the contents of his own King's Speech, delivered at the opening of the current session of Parliament, and thus had no idea of what bills were due for debate.[42] In March 1829 George made a feeble attempt to convince Wellington that his indecision derived from his respect for the workings of the British constitution – 'I have decided to yield my opinion to that which is considered by the Cabinet to be for the immediate interests of the country' – or, alternatively, from the tortured agonies of his conscience ('God knows about what pain it causes me to write these words').[43] As Cumberland presented 200 anti-Catholic petitions to his brother and another 150 to the House of Lords, other anti-Catholics, such as Lord Eldon, still hoped the King himself would make a definite stand against the measure, and circulated a rumour that, rather than sign the Act, he would flee with Cumberland to Hanover. (Disgusted and disillusioned, Cumberland did indeed depart for Germany in June 1829.)

The passing of the Catholic Emancipation Act in 1829 was inevitably recognised by both its supporters and its opponents as an indication of the supremacy of Parliament over an indolent and irrelevant monarch. Wellington was repeatedly depicted in caricatures of the time as 'The Man Wot Drives the Sovereign' – a task in which he was often shown being aided by the odious Lady Conyngham. It was not only Huish who thought that at this date 'the Duke of Wellington acted the King'. Some cartoonists now even dared to attack George directly, and more than one summoned the ghost of George III to denounce the betrayal perpetrated by his son.[44] Never was a British monarch so bitterly assailed by the prints of the day.

9

The Ancien Régime

You prove that we can ne'er intrench
Our happy isles against the French,
Till Royalty in England's made
A much more independent trade ...
Thomas Moore, *The Twopenny Post-Bag*, Letter II

O N A VISIT to Paris in 1786, the artist Richard Cosway presented
the French Queen Marie-Antoinette with a miniature portrait of
the young Prince George, and her husband with a set of tapestries by
Giulio Romano. Louis XVI responded with a gift to Cosway of four
pieces of Gobelins tapestry from the *Don Quixote* series begun in 1714;
on his return to Britain, Cosway diplomatically presented the
Gobelins to the Prince, and they are still at Buckingham Palace.[1] Seven
years later, both Louis XVI and his wife were dead, executed by the
guillotine of the Revolution. However, the memory of that exchange
of gifts in 1786, allied to the affection and admiration he already felt
for the *Ancien Régime*, sparked in George an obsession with the French
royal family that was to last for, and deeply affect, the rest of his life.

Linda Colley has rightly labelled George 'a man bent on championing the old France against the principles and ruling personnel of the
new'.[2] Yet his passion for Bourbon memorabilia stemmed from no
desire to emulate the absolutism of the French kings – though at times
observers did fear this to be his hidden goal. He had not been a particular friend of Louis XVI; indeed, as we have seen, prior to 1789 his
affections lay with Louis's cousin, the notorious duc d'Orléans, whose
libertine way of life and apparent desertion of the royal cause in 1789
so scandalised the Bourbon Court. After the restorations of 1814 and
1815 George maintained no close ties with the courts of Louis XVIII

or (after 1824) of Charles X, even though he had personally super-vised Louis's departure for France in 1814 and his friendship with Charles predated the Revolution. Dead Bourbons, it seemed, were preferable to their restored successors. As we shall see, George did not even take advantage of the Peace of 1815 to visit the French capital he professedly so admired.

In truth, George's energetic promotion of the Bourbons' memory was rooted not in any burning espousal of a particular political creed but in two more predictably pragmatic factors: his admiration for the fashions and tastes of the French Court of the *Ancien Régime*, and the possibility of personal gain. The interiors of the French aristocracy, characterised by sinuous lines, lavish upholstery, profuse drapery and acres of gilt, were much more to George's taste than the neoclassicism of his insipid Hanoverian predecessors or the restrained, geometric elegance of contemporary British designers such as Holland, Soane or Hope. Increasingly, therefore, it was to the *Grand Siècle* and the *Siècle des lumières* that he looked for decorative inspiration and motivation. And as we have seen, in the aftermath of the executions and exiles of the French Revolution many desirable mementoes of seventeenth- and eighteenth-century Bourbon French taste found their way onto the market.[3]

If George's close identification with *Ancien Régime* France helped lend character and class to the interiors of his newly-remodelled resi-dences, it was nevertheless a singularly unfortunate enthusiasm in terms of the contemporary political world. By some it was seen to imply that, not content with aspiring to be 'the first gentleman of Europe', and despite the liberal protestations of his youth, George secretly coveted the exercise of absolute power, without recourse to any representative body, which Louis XIV and his immediate succes-sors had enjoyed.[4] The French government's declaration of war in 1793 and the subsequent execution of those Bourbons who remained in France rendered any public celebration of the delights of eigh-teenth-century France even more unwise. George thereby laid himself open to being branded unpatriotic, because of his acutely francophile aesthetic leanings; a potential revolutionary, because of his friend-ships with Fox (who continued to issue apologia for Revolutionary France throughout the 1790s) and the duc d'Orléans (who actually sided with the Revolution on his return to France); or a dangerous reactionary, because of his apparently unqualified admiration of the Bourbons. Yet he hardly seemed aware of the predicament in which his love of all things French placed him. In 1797 *The Times* reported with satisfaction that he was to dismiss all Frenchmen from his service, citing this patriotic act as a suitable model for others to follow. In the event, of course, George did no such thing, but with the petulant astonishment of a spoiled child complained to Lady Bessborough that 'there was such a cry against French things etc, that he was afraid of his furniture being accus'd of Jacobinism'.[5]

From his coming-of-age in 1783, when he daringly fêted the duc de Chartres (later duc d'Orléans) at Carlton House only days after the conclusion of the Treaty of Versailles with France, George was fascinated by the French royal family and passionate about French décor. As early as 1784 he was buying quantities of French pieces for Carlton House: armchairs by Georges Jacob, remarkably similar to those supplied by Jacob to Louis XVI; Sèvres chinoiserie vases; clocks by Lépine, Lignereux and Latz. When Horace Walpole visited Carlton House in 1785 he was reminded not of any London equivalent, nor even of Holland's other interiors, but of fashionable Parisian buildings such as the Hôtel Bourbon-Condé. Between 1798 and 1808 – a decade during which Britain and France were at war for eight years – George bought thirty thousand pounds' worth of mostly French furniture from Tatham, Bailey and Saunders.[6]

Many of George's acquisitions were especially prized for their direct or indirect links with Louis XIV and his progeny. The most resonant was perhaps van der Meulen's large canvas showing the building of Louis XIV's Palace of Versailles, painted around 1680 and bought in 1809. Its purchase was not only an expression of admiration for the Bourbons in general – and, perhaps more importantly, of George's devotion to the principle of hereditary monarchy, so recently demolished by Napoleon. Its arrival at Carlton House also signalled his desire to emulate the Sun King by building a new royal palace on a scale as heroic as that of Versailles. Nash's Buckingham Palace was his attempt to realise this ambition, and was well under way when the picture was exhibited at the British Institution in 1822, a coincidence doubtless noted by a number of visitors.[7] George's fondness for the imagery of van der Meulen's painting is testified to by the fact that it was subsequently removed to the Royal Lodge, where there was not room for many pictures of this size. His appreciation of the picture as it hung in the Lodge and his personal identification with the Sun King can only have been enhanced by the figure of Louis XIV himself, shown visiting Versailles by carriage in van der Meulen's canvas. At this time George himself often journeyed from the Royal Lodge to visit Wyatville's building works at nearby Windsor Castle – an obvious parallel with the painting which he no doubt relished. The epic imagery was however somewhat marred by George's preference for an undersized pony-drawn phaeton, rather than the grand carriage depicted by van der Meulen.

Van der Meulen's picture was by no means the only memorial of Louis XIV's France which George acquired. He bought a water-colour of the young Louis XIV enthroned as Apollo, Pierre-Denis Martin's *Funeral of Louis XIV* (from Richard Cosway), a sword once owned by the Sun King himself, and in October 1817 an equestrian statue of Louis XIV of *c.* 1700, secured on his behalf by Sir Charles Long. (Originally George's French 'confectioner' François Benois had been sent to Paris to examine this statue; but Benois, not having the measure of his master's Bourbonophilia, judged it aesthetically 'unworthy' of Carlton House.[8]) The Regent also bought a number of other van der Meulen canvases on subjects connected with Louis XIV, including his recreations of the Sun King's military campaigns.[9] Into the Saloon at Brighton he had Robert Jones introduce suitable refer-ences to the illustrious monarch by reproducing Louis XIV's favourite sunflower and sunburst devices in the plaster ceiling and the Axminster carpet. The very furniture was a homage to George's hero. George was also particularly fascinated by Boulle furniture, veneered with brass or pewter set in red-stained tortoiseshell (or vice-versa), first popularised by Louis XIV in the late seventeenth century. A pair of early eighteenth-century cabinets for which he paid the outrageous sum of £840 in 1813 may even have been the work of André-Charles Boulle himself.[10]

George's enthusiasm for the Bourbon line extended to Louis XIV's heirs, notwithstanding the inescapable fact that every one of them during the previous hundred years had at some time been at war with Britain. His passion bordered at times on the obsessional. He bought a Charles Boit enamel of Louis XV, and his agents even bought Louis XV's coronation guide for him, in readiness for his own coronation of 1821.[11] He bought an equestrian statue of Louis XV after Bouchardon – a reduction of Bouchardon's original which stood in the Place Louis XV (now the Place de la Concorde) – and the com-tesse de Provence's Riesener jewel cabinet (rejected by Napoleon as too old-fashioned).[12] His eighteenth-century Chinese and Japanese vases, while having no direct Bourbon provenance, nevertheless 'closely resembled the oriental porcelain collections formed by the great French eighteenth century patrons of the arts'.[13] Even the 'Chinese' upholstery in the Chinese Drawing Room at Carlton House was in the style of Louis XVI. George was delighted to secure four gilt-bronze candelabra originally made by François Rémond in 1783 for the comte d'Artois's apartments at Versailles, and in 1816 a long-case clock from Versailles was installed prominently on the Grand Staircase at Carlton House.[14] The Riesener roll-top desk of *c.* 1775 now in the White Drawing Room at Buckingham Palace was, accord-ing to the stories of the time, made either for a daughter of Louis XV or for Louis XVI, and the pair of marquetry pedestals now in the Picture Gallery at Buckingham Palace was originally delivered to Versailles in 1762, intended as supports for clocks in Louis XV's *appartement intérieur.* The 1739 Gaudreau commode now in the Picture Gallery was once owned by Louis XV,[15] and the remarkable *pietra dura* plaques of fruit and flowers on the Martin Carlin commode now in the Green Drawing Room were devised in 1680 by Gian' Amrogio Giachetti to adorn one of Louis XIV's cabinets. (The plaques were re-affixed to a contemporary gilt ebony cabinet by Dominique Daguerre sometime during the 1760s. By 1782 Daguerre's preposterous confec-tion had passed to a member of the Paris Opéra chorus, Marie-Joséphine Laguerre, as a present from one of her numerous lovers.[16]) In a sale in 1813 Lord Yarmouth acquired for the Regent a three-foot-high patinated bronze of Louis XV, dating from 1776, a reduced version by Jean-Charles Delarche of an unexecuted statue, intended for Rouen, by Jean-Baptiste Lemoyne. Louis XV, hardly famed for martial enthusiasm, had been depicted by Lemoyne in the highly unlikely and decidedly camp pose of a contemporary general, the shield beneath his feet rather unsteadily supported by four Roman warriors. A smaller cast, also by Delarche, of this same subject had been presented to Louis XVI in February 1777 as a mark of respect for his dead father, and was much admired by Marie-Antoinette. Such *Ancien Régime* memorabilia were not the least fashionable by the time of George's Regency, and Yarmouth secured the bronze for a mere 130 guineas – a fraction of the 6,000 livres at which it was valued in the French royal inventory of 1788.[17]

George felt particularly drawn to the tragic figure of Louis XVI and was, like him, a passionate collector of clocks and Sèvres porcelain. The singularly unfortunate comparisons such shared passions were likely to invite, in view of this Louis's incompetence and untimely end, probably bothered the Prince not at all: no doubt he would have viewed *any* analogy with the late King as a compliment.

As his wife famously declared, Louis XVI would have been better suited to life as a clockmaker than as King of France. George bought large numbers of French clocks, and liked them most of all when they had a Bourbon provenance. One sumptuous late seventeenth-century pedestal clock inlaid with pewter Boulle marquetry which he bought in 1820 was believed to have belonged to Louis XIV. As so often happened, however, George swiftly lost interest in the piece, and it was never exhumed from storage at Carlton House. In 1790 he had bought two clocks directly from Jean-Antoine Lépine, who by January 1788 had supplied Louis XVI with no fewer than thirty; typically, George was undeterred by the immense cost, £3,250.[18]

Initially attracted by the sumptuous and often bizarre cases of his French clocks, George became increasingly interested in their mechanisms. However, as John Whitehead has noted, this passion for clocks rarely involved any respect for their integrity. George thought nothing of commissioning Britain's leading decorative experts, the Vulliamys, to add or regild gilt-bronze mounts, to replace original movements, or to ensure that even his most expensive examples corresponded to the ever-changing decorative schemes of the rooms in which they were placed.[19]

George was as keen to purchase mementoes of Louis XVI as he was to obtain items associated with his own 'martyred' ancestor, Charles I. In 1803, for example, Walsh Porter procured for him Louis's copy of Schalcken's painting *The Game of 'Lady, Come into the Garden'*,[20] and eight years later he added porcelain busts of Louis XVI and Marie Antoinette to his growing Sèvres collection, which by the time of his death in 1830 was the largest in the world.

George's infatuation with Sèvres was in itself a tribute both to the taste and manners of *Ancien Régime* France and to the Bourbon monarchs who had been the factory's most consistent and lucrative patrons – and who, by the time of the Revolution, actually owned the firm. Queen Charlotte collected Sèvres on a small scale, but George's interest was first piqued in 1784, when the minister responsible for Sèvres production, the comte d'Augiviller, astutely made him a handsome gift of various tea-wares and table-decorations. George took the bait, and presented d'Augiviller with a generous order for more.[21] The King and Queen were careful to patronise English porcelain manufacturers such as Worcester and Derby, but George clearly had no qualms about supporting their French rival. While he was happy to imagine himself as the nation's Patriot Prince, George failed to acknowledge the poor impression created by his ostentatiously unpatriotic collecting.

Of the numerous items of Sèvres porcelain acquired by George, the most significant was the service which had been commissioned by Louis XVI in 1783 for his personal use at Versailles. Hand-painted by eight different artists with scenes from Greek and Roman, its production was personally supervised by the King himself. Piece for piece, the service was the most expensive set of porcelain ever made. Louis was so proud of it that each year's new additions to the service were put on public display at Versailles, becoming in effect the centre-piece of an annual 'trade show' for Sèvres products. It is no surprise to learn that manufacture proved so slow that the service was only half-finished at the time of Louis's execution in January 1793. Auctioned by Robespierre's government the following year, it passed through various hands until the majority of its pieces were bought by George when he had secured his Regency funds. Once again, the price paid was astronomical – £2,130 14s. 8d.[22] And once again, the objects of his desire lost their appeal as soon as another dazzling toy appeared on the horizon, since it seems that George never actually put the Louis XVI service to use.

It was not only in decorative objects that George sought to emulate the Bourbons' taste. He also liked to collect people who had been in some way connected with the *Ancien Régime*. He was undoubtedly impressed by the fact that the Paris dealer closely involved in the furnishing of Carlton House after 1787, Dominique Daguerre, had previously worked for Marie Antoinette. He was clearly delighted to sit in 1804 for Élisabeth Vigée-Le Brun, who had painted the ill-fated French queen. And the principal guest at the fête he gave in 1811 to celebrate the new Regency, but dedicated to Louis XVIII and his Bourbon ancestors, was the duchesse d'Angoulême, the last surviving child of Louis XVI. She, rather than any of George's own relations, was placed on his right hand at the principal table. Even Maria Fitzherbert's allure may have derived at least in part from her alleged Bourbon associations: as Edward Parry noted long ago, her Smythe forebears had served in the Austrian army against Louis XV's troops in the 1740s, and she herself (then plain Mary Anne) had been educated in a Paris convent. The possibly apocryphal story that Louis XV sent her a dish of sugared plums on hearing her laugh during a public royal dinner (she was supposedly amused by the way the elderly King attacked his chicken) must have appealed to George enormously.[23]

After Waterloo the pace of French purchases quickened. If George's public pose was as the victor of 1815, his private aim appears to have been to exploit the opportunity to acquire French pieces on the open market more confidently than ever before. In 1818, through the agency of Lord Yarmouth, he bought not one but four French bow-front commodes of the late Louis XV period. In 1823 he purchased decidedly eccentric marble and gilt side tables by Bellangé, which like the commodes were destined for Windsor. In September 1828 Knighton bought him a Paris cylinder-top desk by F.-G. Teune, made in the 1780s for Louis XVI's younger brother the comte d'Artois, the rakish yet reactionary friend of George's pre-Revolutionary days who now occupied the French throne as Charles X.[24] Whatever the vagaries of fashion might dictate, George retained his deep attachment to the style and the cause of the Bourbons, happily abandoning the traditional British preference for mahogany furniture in favour of unmistakably French ebony and gilt.

Surprisingly, perhaps, George did not take advantage of the peace which followed Waterloo to visit France personally. Possibly an awareness of the pathetic spectacle he had presented when bidding farewell to Louis XVIII at Dover in 1814 – much to the crowd's amusement, the stout Regent found that he could barely tie the Order of the Garter around Louis's expansive thigh – made him reluctant to renew their acquaintance. (Painful recollections of this farce may also explain why George, who in 1813 had appointed Edward Bird as Princess Charlotte's Historical Painter, later rejected Bird's 1816 canvas of *The Embarkation of Louis XVIII at Dover* though he was quite happy to buy Pécheux's water-colour of Louis XVIII entering Paris.[25]) Additionally, it was soon widely rumoured that he was indignant because Louis XVIII failed to shower him with the presents and other tangible expressions of gratitude he had anticipated.[26] George's reluctance to travel to Paris may, however, have been based on a deep-seated aversion to facing reality. At no time had George ever suggested actually visiting the city whose products filled his palaces, even in the years before the Revolution. During the two-year respite following the Treaty of Amiens in 1802 he had merely directed his agents to make what acquisitions they could; and when he travelled to the Continent in 1821, he landed at Calais and proceeded directly to Hanover via

Brussels. Clearly, he preferred that his fantasy-image of *Ancien Régime* Paris should remain unsullied.

His reluctance to visit France notwithstanding, George's fixation with the Bourbon monarchs lingered into the twilight of his reign. The inspiration for the bronze of him by Francis Chantrey which was placed at the north entrance to Brighton Pavilion in 1828 was the Lemoyne statue of Louis XV, while the pose of Chantrey's great equestrian statue, commissioned by the King himself in July 1829 for the summit of Nash's gateway to Buckingham Palace, was borrowed directly from Girardon and Bouchardon's equestrian statues of Louis XIV. In the event, during George's reign this particular commission got no further than Chantrey's studio, and at the end of the 1830s it was dumped on a conveniently empty plinth in newly-completed Trafalgar Square.[27]

Francis Chantrey was not the only Briton to recognise George's predilection for the Bourbon dynasty. In his post-Waterloo eulogy of 1815, the MP and sycophant Nathaniel Wraxall explicitly, and apparently without irony, likened the Regent to the 'martyred' Louis XVI.[28] Less hagiographical was Prince Pückler-Muskau's judgement of 1826, in the course of which he compared George's reclusive and torpid Court with that of Louis XV. Such pejorative comparisons became more common after George's death and the Bourbons' ejection from the French throne. Robert Huish, for example, likened George to Louis XIV, ascribing the late King's excessive building programme to a wish to emulate Versailles, and equating his public opposition to Catholic Emancipation with the Sun King's notorious persecution of the Protestant Huguenots. Both George IV and Louis XIV, Huish concluded, had erected 'several royal palaces, the building of which [was] at the expense of the tears and happiness of his people', yet both, he judged, were 'revolting ... vainglorious and indifferent'.[29]

That the heir to the British throne chose to publicly parade his unceasing admiration for a French monarchy against the forces of which his country had been at war for much of the preceding hundred years emphasises the degree to which George valued his personal tastes above political wisdom. His passion for French furniture, gratified even when his country was at war with France and in hourly expectation of invasion, was at best a naïve, at worst a myopically selfish indulgence. The vast sums spent on French furnishings certainly undermined his claims to be the champion of English manufacturers, which grew more strident after Waterloo. He could not see that the ostentatious substitution of Wedgwood cameos for the Sèvres plaques on his French furniture at Carlton House did not automatically qualify him as the saviour of British decorative art. Throughout his adult life, George's unabashed francophilia continuously subverted his portrayal of himself as the incarnation of the British nation. Had George IV lived even a month longer, he would surely have been mortified by the relief with which his own subjects – and even Wellington's Tory government – greeted the fall of Charles X's reactionary regime during the July Revolution. He was perhaps fortunate in the innate patience and conservatism of his own subjects, thanks to which even the most unpopular of the Hanoverians never suffered the fate of the restored Bourbons.

George's fertile historical imagination was by no means limited to adulation of the Bourbon dynasty. He was also attracted by the romance of the Stuart cause and by the colourful histories of its family members, whose incident-filled lives contrasted so sharply with the dullness of his Hanoverian ancestors. As he grew older this interest increasingly focused on James II and his Jacobite descendants, giving rise to concern over George's political ambitions as well as his religious leanings and thus offering further proof of his complete indifference to any offence or embarrassment such obsessions might provoke.

The parallels between George IV and his Stuart ancestor Charles I were readily apparent. Both were keen and inspired collectors. George's patronage of Thomas Lawrence – whose flattering virtuoso brush made romantic heroes of even the most stolid members of the royal family – recalled Charles's employment of Anthony Van Dyck as Court Painter during the 1630s. Each artist provided audaciously stylish and flattering portraits of his patron and his immediate circle, executed with a flair and dash which few other painters could rival; and each was knighted by his grateful sovereign.

George's admiration for Charles I and the splendid picture collection dispersed after his execution extended to the retrieval or resiting of items the 'martyr-king' had owned. He was particularly pleased to have Rubens's self-portrait of 1622, sold by the Commonwealth in 1651 but recovered for the Royal Collection after the Restoration of 1660. Assured and confident, Rubens's *Portrait of the Artist* epitomised the exquisite artistic taste and cultural appreciation of his forebears, which George yearned to be thought to reincarnate. Accordingly, in 1816 he rescued the picture from ignominious exile in the Upper

Library at Buckingham House – it was one of the few items he physically removed from the Royal Collection prior to his accession – and
hung it prominently at Carlton House. Two years earlier, in 1814, he
had acquired a picture of Charles I, Henrietta Maria and their eldest
son (then believed to be by Daniel Mytens, but now assigned to
Hendrik Pot) as part of his purchase of the Baring Collection.[30] In the
same year Farington recorded George's enthusiasm for Van Dyck's
celebrated study *Three Heads of Charles I*, now at Windsor, eventually
purchased in 1822 for the considerable sum of one thousand guineas.
To such splendid portraits as these, noted W. H. Pyne somewhat
bathetically in 1819, he added 'a collection of boots and spurs from
the time of Charles I'.[31]

George's admiration for the Court of Charles I, and particularly for
his Court Painter, was another defining element of how he saw
himself. During the 1780s he sat to Richard Cosway for two full-length
oils, both since lost; one showed him as St George, while in the other
he wore the 'Vandyck' dress popular at the time. In both he was seated
on a rearing white charger – a direct reference to Rubens's portrait of
the Duke of Lerma (the pose of which was also borrowed by
Reynolds for his 1784 portrait of the Prince) and to Van Dyck's
famous equestrian portrait of Charles I, which itself was based on
Titian's imposing study of the Emperor Charles V on horseback. A
Cosway portrait miniature which does survive shows George, once
again in Van Dyck dress and with his Garter star prominently displayed, unmistakably posed as Charles I.[32]

George's pretensions to equal Charles I as a patron of the arts can
be amply vindicated. Both were refreshing exceptions to the general
run of British monarchs, so many of whom have, by and large, shown
little interest in the visual arts. Both displayed a real understanding of
the creative process, and a keenly developed eye for quality. Of the
two, George may be acclaimed the more complete patron, from his
abiding interest in architecture and the decorative arts as well as his
love of painting. Such superficial comparisons are invidious, however.
Charles I, perennially and disastrously short of money, never embarked
on great building projects – not that lack of money ever deterred
George – and his collecting came to an abrupt end on the outbreak of
the Civil War in 1642.

George's self-identification with Charles I did not go unnoticed. In
1813 the cartoonist George Cruikshank publicly reminded him of his
ancestor's fate[33] – ironically, only a few months before Charles's body

was discovered in the crypt of St George's Chapel at Windsor Castle. The obvious delight George took in this find in turn encouraged the opposition Whigs to link his increasingly evident reactionary tendencies with Charles's notorious experiment in Personal Rule, when he dispensed with Parliament for eleven years. In the House of Commons in 1816 Brougham attacked George's profligacy by associating his excessive personal expenditure – and, by implication, his political programme – with that of the ill-fated Charles I.[34] At a time of international revolution, when George felt himself constantly in fear of assassination, neither civil war nor regicide could be absolutely dismissed as mere far-fetched possibilities.

George's fascination with James II, whose reign had been one of the most disastrous in British history, was less excusable than his identification with Charles I. That James had been rejected by his country in 1688 for attempting to drag it back into the Catholic fold should have been enough to deter George from inviting direct comparisons, particularly since in middle age he had professedly become a staunch opposer of Catholic relief. However, George was always full of praise for his rash and arrogant predecessor, and even based elements of his Coronation spectacular of 1821 on that of James II, as recorded in print by Francis Sandford in 1687. Not only did he attempt to rehabilitate James: he also helped to perpetuate the whole tangle of romantic nonsense and unsubstantiated myth which surrounded the failed attempts of James II and his successors to wrest back the crown by force. That disappointed Scotsmen should have muttered into their whisky about the Lost Cause and toasted the King over the Water was understandable; that someone whose great-grandfather's throne had been seriously endangered by Bonnie Prince Charlie's French-backed invasion of 1745 should actively encourage the idealisation of the Jacobite cause was in downright poor taste. Possibly George's Jacobite enthusiasms arose in part from his awareness that he himself was the first child to be born to a reigning monarch since 1688 – when the child in question was James II's son James Stuart, 'James III' to Jacobite adherents and 'The Old Pretender' to his opponents. That this child's birth was the catalyst that sparked the Glorious Revolution, and that he was living in exile in France before his first birthday, should perhaps have given George food for thought. Similarly, the knowledge that the Old Pretender's son 'Bonnie' Charles Stuart had spent much of his life as a maudlin and bitter drunk should possibly have dissuaded him, when his own considerable alcohol consumption was being widely reported, from too blatantly advertising his Jacobite sympathies.

In purely political terms, by 1800 the Jacobite threat was effectively non-existent. The last Stuart heir, styled by his supporters Henry IX, was not only a Cardinal but, moreover, a Cardinal who unlike many of his saintly colleagues practised the morality he preached. As a result, Henry, Cardinal Duke of York was childless, and the Jacobite claim to the British throne perished with him in 1806, passing eventually to the Bavarian royal house. Furthermore, at the time of his death Henry was receiving a generous pension of £4,000 a year from the Crown. As a mark of gratitude, under the terms of Henry's will George was offered the splendid 'Stuart Sapphire', part of the Coronation jewels of the Scottish Kings, together with the diamond saltire worn by Charles I at his Scottish coronation of 1633 and, a little more than a century later, by his ill-fated descendant Charles Edward Stuart during his invasion of Britain. What must also have appealed to him, on several levels, was the additional offer of the 'George' worn by Charles I on the scaffold.[35]

Royal connivance at, and encouragement of, the transformation of embittered Jacobites into Walter Scott's loyal, romanticised Highlanders may not have been in the best interests of the later Hanoverians, but George never shrank from exploiting Jacobite memories and Jacobite symbolism to underline his claim to the hearts of *all* Britons. At the time of his illegal marriage in 1785 he called Maria Fitzherbert his 'white rose', and at the public breakfast to celebrate his reunion with her in 1800 the tables were strewn with them. The white rose being a notorious Jacobite badge, its adoption in this context perhaps fed some princely fantasy of his relationship with his Catholic mistress as a Jacobite romance. Jacobite imagery also abounded during his visit to Edinburgh in 1822. George made sure, for example, that he prominently displayed the Order of the Thistle, founded by James III of Scotland but only formally organised in 1687 by James II.[36] Indeed, as we shall see, one of the underlying purposes of this visit, as devised by Sir Walter Scott and his advisors, was a theatrical reclamation by George of his supposed Jacobite inheritance.

Most ostentatious of all George's tributes to the exiled Stuarts was his proposal of 1816 to erect a monument in St Peter's Cathedral in Rome, over the bodies of the Old and Young Pretenders and Cardinal Henry. The monument was executed by Canova, and was largely paid for by George.[37] And when a casket containing James II's entrails was discovered during the rebuilding of the church at St Germain-en-Laye outside Paris in 1824, it was George who directed that the remains be ceremonially reinterred in the new church three years later.[38]

George also went to great pains to acquire physical mementoes of what he regarded as his Jacobite heritage, and was particularly delighted to add a broadsword that had belonged to the Young Pretender to his growing collection.[39] In 1804 he asked one of his agents in Italy, Sir John Hippisley, to retrieve the Stuart family papers. These had accompanied James II to France, then followed the Jacobite claimants to Rome and finally come to rest in Civitavecchia, where they had been deposited with a British merchant. George was not, however, immediately disposed to share this controversial treasure with his father's subjects: in 1813 he actually directed his librarian to refuse Sir James Mackintosh's request to research the newly-acquired papers.[40] However, the more palatable parts of them – those dealing with the life of James II, rather than with the declining fortunes of his successors – were published in two volumes by Longmans in 1816. One of George's last acts as King was to ask Sir Walter Scott, then himself in poor health, to head a new commission to examine and edit the Stuart papers.

That George was a man who preferred to live in the past – a past which was often absolutist, papist, and irredeemably foreign – became increasingly obvious as he aged. Having invoked history's ghosts, however, he found that he could not readily consign them back into oblivion; instead, the spectres of Louis XIV, Charles I, Louis XVI and James II continued to haunt him. While these sovereigns had provided him with inspiration for his constitutional and decorative fantasies, his growing band of critics found in them ready ammunition for their satires. Few British monarchs have been so unfortunate and so misguided in their choice of kingly exemplars.

PART III

Family Affairs

The young Prince George's vanity, self-confidence and fondness for outrageous militaria are already very evident in this full-length portrait, showing him in an invented uniform, by Thomas Gainsborough, of 1782

George's parents, George III and Queen Charlotte, undoubtedly meant well, but they were unremittingly harsh in their treatment and judgement of the eldest son. They are seen here in portraits by Benjamin West and after Thomas Gainsborough. W shows the parsimonious German queen in an unusually glamorou light

The Prince of Wales's closest intimates at his coming-of-age in 1783, Charles James Fox and Mary 'Perdita' Robinson, both painted by the Whigs' semi-official portraitist, Joshua Reynolds, in 1784. By the time Perdita's painting was completed, however, she had not only been discarded by George but was also crippled from the waist down following a disastrous miscarriage

The Prince had many affairs during his twenties and thirties. However, two women dominate this period of his life, for very different reasons: his wife, Prince Caroline, shown here in the celebrated portrait by Thomas Lawrence of 1804, and his first serious mistress, Maria Fitzherbert, shown in an engraving after Richard Cosway

The Prince's enormous debts were public knowledge long before his Regency, and were frequently alluded to in the prints of the day. William Heath's *Regency à la Mode* of 1812 shows two files on the wall bracket: that for bills is full while that for receipts is empty. That the Prince incurred much of this debt by spending vast sums on clothes and perfumes is also made very apparent. Colonel MacMahon laces the Prince's stays as he rouges his cheeks, while the monkey atop the mirror sports the same ludicrous hairstyle as his royal master

After 1802 the interiors of the Prince's London home, Carlton House, were frequently replanned and redecorated with no overall philosophy or consistent direction. After 1814 John Nash at least ensured that the 'opulence and . . . barbaric splendour' of the most recent schemes was toned down, preferring to employ the colours of the national flag, as well as the inevitable gold-leaf. W. H. Pyne's views of two of Nash's redecorated interiors, the Crimson Drawing Room and the Blue Velvet Room, are shown here, as published in 1819

The key to Brighton Pavilion's replanning after 1815 was the prominence afforded to the Banqueting Room and Kitchen, seen here in A. C. Pugin's water-colours commissioned by Nash for his publication of 1826. The Kitchen was one of the most technologically advanced in the world, while the Banqueting Room, with its stupendous one-ton central chandelier suspended from an enormous winged dragon, was one of the most breathtaking interiors in Europe – a room whose lustrous appeal managed to charm more often than it appalled

The apparent end of the Napoleonic Wars in 1814 provided the Prince Regent with a splendid excuse for parties and pageantry. George Cruikshank's *The Grand Entertainment* of 1814, below, shows the Prince celebrating in front of the Carlton House screen in the company of Lady Hertford and her cuckolded husband. Above is Edward Bird's ambitious depiction of *The Embarkation of Louis XVIII from Dover*. Bird had to follow the restored French king to his Tuileries palace to complete the picture. The Prince Regent, no doubt embarrassed by the memory of his bathetic send-off – and by the fact that Louis's restoration had, thanks to Napoleon's Hundred Days, proved somewhat premature – brusquely refused to accept it

James Whittaker's depiction of *The Coronation of George the Fourth* of 1821 shows the new King at his long-awaited anointing, which many believed he would not live to enjoy. Below is Whittaker's view of the 'King's herb women', one of the many pieces of George's ceremonial jigsaw that subsequent monarchs were to eliminate

By the time of his accession to the throne, George IV was consuming vast quantities of alcohol and laudanum. J. L. Marks's bitter print *The Coronation of King Punch* (1821), portrays the sovereign as a rollicking drunk

Thomas Lawrence's luscious Coronation portrait of 1821, Napoleon's 'Table of the Grand Commanders' prominently installed stage-left. This full-length portrait was deemed, as Sir Oliver Millar has noted, 'the perfect image of the hero of the alliance to be sent overseas', suggesting as it does that George had played a central role in the defeat of the French. This is perhaps the best example of Lawrence's splendid talent for substituting an alluring image for the disappointments of reality

Princess Charlotte's short life was a frustrating and frequently unhappy one, her propitious marriage being swiftly followed by her tragic death in childbirth. This portrait by Woodman shows how much she resembled her father; despite this evident family resemblance, however, the Prince rarely appeared to concern himself with his daughter's welfare

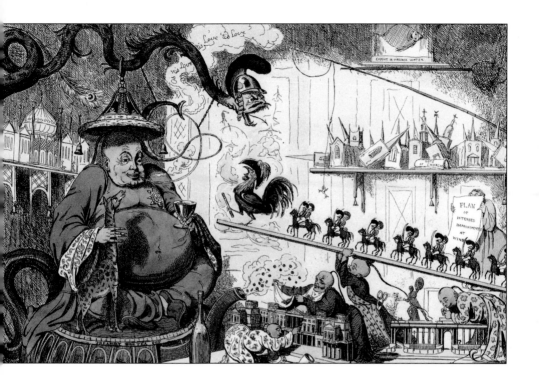

Robert Seymour's cruel satire, *The Great Joss and His Playthings* of 1829, shows the ageing King as a fat Chinese mandarin, surrounded by evidence of his extravagantly wasteful building projects. At the bottom of the scene is a model of Nash's new Buckingham Palace, the principal front of which is shown below in an engraving of 1825. George IV's enthusiasm for the 'Chinese' manner was increasingly used by the print-makers of the 1820s as an allegory of his irrelevance and reclusiveness, his unprincipled behaviour and his vast expenditure

Windsor Castle was rebuilt by Jeffry Wyatville to accord with his royal master's historical fantasies: *left,* the Waterloo Chamber – George's attempt to appropriate the defeat of Napoleon for himself and his family; *below,* the castle seen from the Long Walk to the south, as wholly remodelled by Wyatville. Despite the vast resources expended on this project, however, in 1829 the King announced that he would not, after all, actually live in the new castle

n the anonymous *Brobdignag Cottage,* a print of 1824, George and the Conyngham family
(Lady Conyngham with her prodigious back to us) are seen in blissful seclusion at the
Royal Lodge in Windsor Great Park. After 1822 the increasingly reclusive King spent
much of his time at this overblown rural retreat

While painting this official portrait of the King in Highland dress in 1829, David Wilkie reported that it took three hours to dress the King in his costume and 'to lace up all the bulgings and excrescencies', the end result resembling nothing so much as 'a great sausage stuffed into the covering'. An irreverent sketch he made at the same time, shown on the front dust-jacket, shows the artist's real impression of his subject's figure

10

Separation and Divorce

At the smallest hint in life,
You forsake your lawful wife.
Thomas Moore, *Dialogue Between a Sovereign and a
One Pound Note*

WHEN, IN A letter of 30 April 1796, the Prince of Wales expressed to his wife the pious hope that 'the rest of our lives will be passed in uninterrupted tranquility', his unstated presumption was that he would be allowed to dictate the terms of their relationship and the treatment of their daughter. Already, however, his demands and complaints were becoming unreasonable. Almost from the moment Princess Charlotte was born, George had exaggerated – or simply invented – slights perpetrated by Caroline against himself. On 31 May 1796 he wrote hysterically to his father alleging that Caroline was guilty of 'cruel calumnies' and 'odious endeavours' towards him, and declared that he would cease corresponding with her altogether on the King's Birthday.[1] (Already he was refusing to see her except on the most pressing formal occasions; they communicated by writing to one another from their separate apartments at Carlton House.) George III's patient and measured reply reminded his son that 'your marriage is a public act' and asked that he at least try to 'keep ... up appearances', but this only resulted in a stream of breathless and confused diatribes from the Prince during the course of the summer. By January 1797 Queen Charlotte was complaining to her husband that 'Since the unpleasant affairs of the Prince and Princess of Wales began I will own ... that my dislike to everything public is greatly increased.'[2]

Initially the King and Queen failed to grasp the seriousness of the situation. Queen Charlotte was no help whatsoever to Caroline, although she had been in approximately the same position herself forty years earlier: a German Princess in a foreign land struggling for survival in a potentially hostile Court. As early as May 1796 Caroline is reported to have observed that 'the conduct of the Queen' had left her 'with no hopes from that quarter'; by the same time the next year it was obvious not only that the Queen viewed her with contempt, but that this attitude had similarly infected her daughters. Only Princess Sophia admitted to 'a partiality for the amiable princess'.[3]

Writing in 1830, William Cobbett was in no doubt as to who had been the injured party. The 'cruelly-treated princess was, during the whole of her married life, dogged by spies, and beset by perjurers and traitors', he fulminated – a partisan judgement which nevertheless appears to have been largely justified. Not content with subjecting her to a tirade of unfounded and inflated accusations, George also sought to restrict his wife's freedom of movement, even of choice, wherever possible. When he was absent from Carlton House, for example, he insisted that Caroline submit every detail, no matter how small, to his Private Secretary for approval. Even her daily menus and proposed dinner guests were to be vetted. Unsurprisingly, this treatment stirred the Princess to rebellion, and on 4 December 1797 she announced: 'I regard myself as being no longer subject to your orders, or your rules'.[4] Yet George continued to pursue his quarrel at every opportunity; minor issues were blown up to ludicrous proportions while other more important concerns, such as the welfare of his daughter and heir, were overlooked. The Duke of York's invitation to Princess Caroline to attend a fête in the grounds of the Yorks' Surrey home in June 1799, for example, goaded George into an irrational frenzy; he fumed over 'the continual provocation and insult I am exposed to from the most unprincipled and unfeeling person of her sex' and claimed that 'there is no end to her wickedness, her falsity, and her designs'. His mother's invitation to the Princess to visit her at Frogmore in June 1802 met with a similarly histrionic outburst, to which the Queen wisely did not reply:

I can only consider [the invitation] as highly prejudicial to the interests of the family by disturbing its tranquility in endeavouring to establish *a censure upon me* which I cannot pass over unnoticed, as it actually and *wantonly* revives topics of a domestic and too delicate a nature which had long, and ought ere that, to have been long committed to oblivion, and by which I have so *cruelly and unjustly* suffered ... I can see it but in one and in one only point of view, as an *interdiction to me*, under the *present* circumstances, to associate again with my own family as I have hitherto done; for her *triumphant and publick disclaim* of all duty to me, besides the insolence and insincerity I have in every one instance experienced from her, is alone sufficient to justify my total deriliction [*sic*] of a woman I never consequently can esteem.[5]

Any attempts at *rapprochement* initiated by George invariably cloaked some other motive. His suggestion in December 1798 that he and his wife dine together at Carlton House, for example, was in furtherance of a scheme to secure a loan from the Landgrave of Hesse, to whom Caroline was related. When in 1802 the King increased his son's allowance to £100,000, he assumed some of the increase would be passed on to Caroline, but George made no effort to help pay off her debts – currently £4,000, paltry in comparison with the hundreds of thousands he himself owed – and instead raised Maria Fitzherbert's pension by £1,000 a year. When Caroline finally reacted to the constant barrage of insults and slights by proposing that she return to Brunswick, George was livid, and demanded alternately that she be charged with high treason, or that the King secure Parliament's facilitation of a divorce.

George III's clumsy but well-intentioned attempts to avoid any step, such as divorce, that might culminate in the forcible separation of his granddaughter from her mother, and to ensure that incessant marital warfare did not affect the small Princess's education and well-being, merely served to make his over-sensitive, self-obsessed and hypochondriac son 'ill with rage'. Although the Prince of Wales rarely exhibited any great love for his only child, he nevertheless stubbornly refused to relinquish her into her grandparents' care. The King's unhelpful response was to reaffirm that his son was responsible for his wife's debts (which by 1808 had risen to £40,000). Reluctantly, George allowed her an extra £5,000 a year – a sum palpably insufficient for her needs. However, in 1805 the King provided his daughter-in-law with greater material security by appointing her Ranger of Greenwich Park. This gave her a house close to the river and thus within easy reach of Central London by boat as well as by carriage, but sufficiently far from Carlton House to secure her independence of action.[6]

At Blackheath, where she lived at Montague House during the winter of 1801–2, Caroline had meanwhile contracted an unfortunate friendship with Major-General Sir John Douglas and his wife

Charlotte, 'a showy, bold woman [who] wanted to be placed in a situation of higher respect than she was entitled to'. Caroline frequently entertained her friends and even looked after the Douglas children on occasion, and during February 1802 Lady Douglas temporarily acted as her lady-in-waiting. The two women soon fell out, however – each deciding that the other was an unsuitable companion. Lady Douglas now openly declared that she had found the Princess 'a person without education or talents, and without any desire of improving herself', whose conversation was 'very loose, and such as I have not been accustomed to hear'. She even went so far as to insinuate that Caroline had made lesbian advances to her. Worse was to come: Lady Douglas then spread the rumour that Caroline, pregnant by an unknown lover, had given birth some time late in 1802 – a charge which led Sir John to distance himself from his wife's allegations. Caroline's initial reaction was to send Lady Douglas long, anonymous, accusatory letters; she may also have been the author of an obscene sketch Lady Douglas received, imputing that she had had sexual relations with her lodger, Admiral Sir Sidney Smith. Far more effective was the notice to quit their Greenwich house which Caroline sent to the Douglases on 23 October 1805, following her appointment as Ranger of Greenwich Park. This prompted the Douglases to appeal for help to the Duke of Kent and the Duke of Sussex (Kent had already been approached by Admiral Smith, but to no avail) and ensured that by November George himself had heard of the allegation concerning the illegitimate child, which Lady Douglas put in writing on 3 December.[7]

The ensuing enquiry into the Douglases' allegations was unofficially entitled the 'Delicate Investigation' – the term 'delicate' generally implying, as Louis Mazzini so astutely remarked, a matter of extreme *in*delicacy. Certainly much of the 'evidence' collected was far from decorous. Her footman, Samuel Roberts, testified that the Princess of Wales was 'very fond of fucking'; other servants were similarly free with their opinions.[8] Seeing a possibility of permanently wrong-footing his wife, George deputed senior lawyers Sir Samuel Romilly and Lord Thurlow, a former Lord Chancellor, to examine the matter. By May 1806 they had elicited a report from the Douglases' solicitor which randomly implicated figures as diverse as the naval officers Captain Thomas Manby and Admiral Sir Samuel Hood, rising Tory politician George Canning, and the painter Sir Thomas Lawrence in Caroline's amorous adventures. Of this illustrious list,

Manby was the only individual against whom definitive charges could be levelled (his affair with the Princess had been bubbling away since 1802, when his ship HMS *Africaine* was fitting-out at nearby Deptford).[9] However, closer examination by officers of the Whig cabinet revealed that the child seen playing outside Montague House, alleged by Caroline's accusers to be her own, was William Austin – son of a Deptford docker, who had, so his natural mother averred, been legally adopted by the Princess. Even the authorship of the anonymous letters the Douglases had been so certain were from Caroline was now called into doubt.

While officially the Delicate Investigation was conducted in secret, Chinese whispers concerning the story and its implications inevitably began to circulate. The nature of the gossip revealed as much about the dismal reputation of the Prince of Wales and his brothers as about the Princess's. While Farington reported that Caroline 'had lately been delivered of a female Child, and that the father of it, an Irishman, was gone off', and the jeweller Nathaniel Jefferys in a rambling diatribe alleged that the Protestant Princess had been deliberately smeared by the Catholic apologist Mrs Fitzherbert (the *Morning Post* added the refinement that the Douglases had been supported both morally and financially by Mrs Fitzherbert), other rumours named the Duke of Cumberland as one of the Princess's lovers.[10]

At this critical juncture Caroline contemplated fleeing to Brunswick, but she was not without her supporters. The Tories, whatever their suspicions of the Princess, saw that the Delicate Investigation might be used to embarrass both the government and the Prince of Wales. Lord Eldon and Lord Malmesbury were prominent in the Princess's defence, and the ambitious Tory lawyer and politician Spencer Perceval (by March 1807 Chancellor of the Exchequer, and in October 1809 Prime Minister) was particularly outspoken. He described the Princess as 'a much injured lady' and, according to Brougham, labelled her husband a liar and a bankrupt.[11] He also cleverly outflanked government attempts to keep the investigation as secret and tightly-controlled as possible, repeatedly appealing to George III for a fair hearing. The commission handling the Delicate Investigation repudiated the charges against the Princess, but the King's decision to readmit her to Court, on the understanding that she should be 'circumspect in her future behaviour', did not go far enough for Perceval. Early in 1807, and despite the opposition of Portland, Canning and other leading Tories, he proposed that, unless the

Princess be immediately received at Court and allowed into her old rooms at Carlton House, full details of the Investigation should be made available as a published work.

Government, Prince and King were paralysed by this ultimatum. Printing, though not publication, duly went ahead, the offending volume being known simply by the ominous title *The Book*. Events subsequently moved swiftly. In March 1807 Addington's ministry fell on the issue of Catholic rights – Perceval's attacks were a contributory factor – and was replaced by a Tory administration, nominally led by the ailing Duke of Portland. In practice Perceval, who now combined the offices of Chancellor of the Exchequer and Chancellor of the Duchy of Lancaster, dominated the new cabinet, in which sat acknowledged supporters of the Princess such as Canning and Eldon. They dined at Montague House, and Caroline was present in the House of Commons to hear Perceval's maiden speech as Chancellor. In a great bonfire in Lincoln's Inn Fields Perceval burned all the copies of *The Book* he could find, with his own hands, then drafted a cabinet minute acquitting the Princess of all charges and recommending that the King receive her with 'as little delay as possible'. George III, protesting that such an interview 'cannot in its nature be very pleasant', graciously acquiesced, and by June the Princess of Wales was to be seen regularly at Court.[12]

Unfortunately, Perceval had already proudly distributed copies of *The Book* to cabinet colleagues, friends and family. Worse still, the printer, Richard Edwards, had surreptitiously leaked copies to interested parties. As early as 27 March 1807 the bookseller W. Lindsell, prompted by the Prince's Private Secretary Colonel MacMahon and the Treasury's solicitor, had advertised in *The Times* desperately promising 'a handsome gratuity' for any returned copies of 'a CERTAIN BOOK, printed by Mr Edwards in 1807'. Cobbett later claimed that the Prince's agents spent as much as £3,300 in securing a mere five copies.[13] Despite these efforts, on 14 February 1808 a journalist on the *Sun*, Francis Blagdon, announced in his own newspaper the *Phoenix* that he intended to begin serialisation of *The Book*. Eldon secured an injunction against publication which, combined with Treasury support for another of Blagdon's papers, staved off this particular threat (both Blagdon's newspapers had failed by 1812). However, at the Princess's insistence an adaptation of *The Book* was published late in 1811, in the guise of Thomas Ashe's *The Spirit of the Book*. By this time Caroline had broken publicly with Perceval, now as Prime

Minister too sensibly circumspect to involve himself in her volatile affairs, and had also turned against former supporters like Eldon. From the beginning of the Regency, when it became clear that George did not propose to eject Perceval's Tory administration, it was the Whigs who in their turn sought to exploit Caroline's cause for political advantage. Nor was the saga of *The Book* yet over, for in March 1813 the *Morning Post*, shedding crocodile tears, began – 'God knows, with an aching heart' – to serialise the text of the original volume, prompting the publication of a pamphlet on the same subject by Blagdon.[14]

At intervals from 1807 onwards George protested formally and at great length to his father about the survival and propagation of *The Book* and the publication of pamphlets taking his wife's part. Casting himself as a great figure on the European stage brought low by petty jealousies, he made the remarkable claim that he needed to be free of his matrimonial ties in order to 'discharge momentous public affairs' – as if, rather than playing cards at Brighton Pavilion, he were about to embark single-handedly upon the defeat of Napoleon.[15] His advisors warned him, however, that any attempt to use the matter or text of *The Book* in his own interests would undoubtedly damage his reputation more than Caroline's.

By this stage George seemed to care little how his own standing would be affected by his vendetta against his wife, which had now become an obsession. Farington reported that 'The Prince of Wales is inveterate against the Princess of Wales' and 'believes everything to be true that has been alleged or insinuated against Her':

> ... she is so much upon His mind that he lately introduced the subject unexpectedly to a Gentleman who mentioned it to Lord T[homond]. The Prince said He had formed an unchangeable resolution never to set His foot in a House in which she dwells.[16]

By the time George assumed the Regency in 1811 the disputes between 'the tarnished Prince and his dingy Caroline' had become the equivalent of a long-running soap opera. Rumours abounded – that he was about to divorce his wife with Parliament's assistance, that he had secretly married his cousin Princess Sophia of Gloucester.[17] Meanwhile, Caroline was attempting to retrieve her reputation and deny her enemies any excuse to renew their attacks. Shrewdly, she praised Maria Fitzherbert in public: 'The Princess of Wales speaks highly of Mrs Fitzherbert', Lady Charlotte Bury wrote in 1811, '[and] always says "that is the Prince's true wife; she is an excellent woman".' At the same time, she cultivated the leaders of the Whig opposition and made some effort to ensure that her stable of lovers – who allegedly ranged from Captain Manby and Sir Sidney Smith to the radical Irish politician Lord Henry Fitzgerald – kept quiet. In February 1813 she even employed an old trick of her husband's, and published her most recent appeal to him.[18] Predictably, George was outraged. Incensed by Caroline's growing popularity, and deluding himself that a public revelation of the case would earn him sympathy, he resolved in retaliation to publish the evidence against his wife collected by Romilly and Thurlow in 1806–7.

George employed ever more desperate measures to undermine his wife's position. In 1813 his agents offered the owner of the *Evening Star* £300 a year to target his paper against the Princess; when money failed, Colonel MacMahon resorted to outright bullying.[19] In June 1814 Caroline again demonstrated how cleverly she could play the game of politics and reputations. Her response to the Regent's ban on her appearance at Court – lest she influence or even meet any of the Allied leaders and sovereigns due in London in the wake of the fall of Paris – was to write a well-phrased letter to the Speaker of the House of Commons suggesting that, in view of the heavy burden of wartime taxation, her annual allowance should be reduced from £50,000 to £30,000. George, of course, had never any thought of making such a gesture: Caroline's assumption of frugality was in welcome contrast to his needlessly lavish expenditure, and a further gift to the satirists.

The incessant feuding had taken its toll on both combatants. Caroline, worn out by matrimonial strife, sought and was granted leave to travel on the Continent – now supposedly purged of Napoleonic influence. On 8 August 1814 she sailed from Lancing in a Royal Navy frigate, accompanied by her ladies-in-waiting, her servants, and fourteen-year-old William Austin, and wearing a cap similar to the one she had donned on her arrival in England nineteen years earlier.[20] Hardly had she set foot in Germany, however, than she proceeded to undo all her good work of the last few years by sacrificing what remained of her reputation on the altar of sensual gratification. From her brother's Court she moved on to Italy, and her increasingly outrageous behaviour in the months that followed led to the resignation one by one of almost all of her English retinue, their places being taken 'by an extraordinary collection of retainers including French chambermaids and French cooks, Arab footboys, Austrian postillions and Italian footmen'.[21] Behaviour such as this only played into George's hands and helped him win support for the idea of a divorce.

Shortly after Caroline's departure, Liverpool admitted to Canning that 'only proof of adultery' would secure the Prince a divorce; he referred, of course, to Caroline's adultery – there was proof enough of George's serial infidelities. Furthermore, as he told the Prince, there was 'no power to prevent her Royal Highness's return to this country'.[22] At a time when all Allied diplomats would have been most constructively employed helping Castlereagh redraw the map of Europe at the Congress of Vienna, George ordered the Hanoverian Court's envoy at the Vatican, Count Ompteda, to gather as much damning evidence as possible about Caroline's activities in Italy. Foreign Office officials in Vienna – who possibly considered the Prince's employment of a Hanoverian diplomat somewhat galling, and who certainly had more pressing issues to deal with – were charged with relaying the 'evidence' to London.

Caroline recklessly furnished her husband's spies with all they sought. Her affair with the young Milanese 'aristocrat' Bartolomeo Bergami (or Pergami, as he preferred to be known), which began in the autumn of 1814, was conducted without the least discretion. The smooth-mannered Pergami came from an impoverished family, but soon found himself appointed the Princess's equerry and, through her direct influence, the proud owner of a Milanese estate and the title of Baron della Francina – which qualified him to serve as her Chamberlain. Described by Ompteda as a 'sort of Apollo, of a superb and commanding appearance more than six feet tall' (his 'physical beauty', he added, 'attracts all eyes'), Pergami certainly captivated Caroline. She took him with her to Rome, and from Rome travelled to Naples; there, according to the zealous Ompteda, she 'raped' the King, Napoleon's former marshal Joachim Murat. Her behaviour, even for 'a town where chastity has never had much of a ministry', was quite unguarded.[23] Having toured the eastern Mediterranean, in August 1815 she settled into a villa by Lake Como. By this time, Pergami effectively controlled her household: he had appointed his brother, his sister and his cousin to key posts, and for good measure had brought along his mother and the daughter from his previous marriage. When the captain of a Royal Navy frigate on which Caroline hoped to travel objected to Signor Pergami joining them for every meal, she simply abandoned the warship and hired a private vessel.

George, fortified by Ompteda's colourful accounts and eager to proceed, was heedless of either parliamentary procedure or the government's convenience. Numerous times after 1816, the cabinet was reluctantly forced to discuss the question of divorce when it had more urgent matters to deal with. Rebuffs in 1816 and again the following year did not deter George. In August 1818 he sent his own trio of 'commissioners' to Milan to assemble evidence which might be used against Caroline in future litigation. The commissioners, two lawyers and the Italian-speaking military attaché from the Vienna embassy, presented their findings on 13 July 1819. Having interviewed eighty eye-witnesses, they judged that the Princess's adultery provided ample grounds for divorce. The witnesses were nothing if not graphic and their statements were luridly explicit. Former servants testified that Pergami had often entered Caroline's room late at night, that she had been seen fondling him in public; according to her former postilion, Pergami had frequently joined the Princess in her bath (although, as David Levy has pointed out, 'if her normal routine was anything to go by, [it] cannot have been that often').[24]

Having examined the commission's sheaves of testimonies, however, Liverpool's cabinet once again declared there to be insufficient evidence in the wild allegations and unsubstantiated rumours to support a parliamentary proposal for a divorce. Were the evidence even conclusive, the ministers argued, it would be impossible to institute proceedings while Caroline remained abroad. Yet George continued to demand that his divorce be considered the most important issue of the day, raising the question again inopportunely late in 1819, just as Parliament was breaking up for its July recess. Not for the first time, he was only too ready to sacrifice constitutional courtesies to an all-consuming obsession.

When George III died in January 1820, Caroline technically became Queen Consort of England, and the cabinet had no option but to give serious consideration to the question of a divorce. With commendable foresight, Henry Brougham, the ambitious Whig politician and lawyer whom Caroline had appointed as her attorney-general, had already tried to defuse the issue by proposing a formal separation. But George saw this as nothing less than an acknowledgement of guilt, and a vindication of his campaign. His vindictiveness knew no bounds: on 14 February 1820, in response to his ministers' advice that the Queen should, as was customary, be included in the Church liturgy, he 'peremptorily refused, and said nothing should induce him to consent'.[25] (At the same time, alternative versions of the national anthem were going the rounds, in which Caroline's name was substituted for George's.) When the Prayer Book containing the liturgy for the new reign was published in February 1821 without the Queen's name, Liverpool's government feared a violent response from the mob, but hoped to soften the blow as far as Caroline was concerned by persuading George to increase her annuity to £50,000. Brougham's attempts to have her name reinstated met with obdurate refusal.[26]

Until the last minute Brougham did what he could to dissuade Caroline from crossing the Channel to claim her position as Queen Consort. He suggested instead a compromise by which 'an annuity should be granted without any renunciation of rank or title or rights, and with a pledge on the part of the Government that your Majesty should be acknowledged and received abroad by all the diplomatic agents of the country according to your rank and station', always provided that 'your Majesty should not go to England'. Brougham envisaged that in her absence (she was, after all, a liability to her own cause, with her lack of discretion and her Italian lovers) he could negotiate 'all that it is possible to wish'.[27] But Caroline was adamant that she would face her accusers in person.

The instant Caroline landed at Dover on 5 June 1820, claimed William Cobbett, 'the exultation of the people began'.[28] She was fortunate in that George's unpopularity automatically assured her considerable public support. Soon after his accession the radical newspaper *The Republican* roundly damned Carlton House as 'a complete brothel', compared George's conduct with that of Henry VIII towards Anne of Cleves. The paper urged women in particular to demonstrate their detestation of his unprincipled actions: 'We are aware that every virtuous female in the country already feels indignant at the treatment the Queen has uniformly received, and we trust that they will not fail to lift up their all-powerful tongues in her behalf.'[29] Linda Colley has highlighted the enthusiastic sympathy Caroline's predicament evoked in women nationwide, and from the middle and working classes in particular:

14,000 Bristol women, more than 9,000 women from Edinburgh, 11,000 women from Sheffield, 17,600 married women from London, 3,700 'ladies' from Halifax, 7,800 from Nottingham, 9,000 from Exeter and tens of thousands more signed addresses in support of the queen. In Newcastle-upon-Tyne, where the pro-Caroline address was confined to men, one woman brought along her five sons and made them all sign, complaining to the organisers at the same time about her own exclusion: 'for it was a woman's cause'.

On 20 September 1820 *The Times* was forced to publish a recantation of a report the previous day concerning the number of 'married ladies' of London who had signed in support of the Queen: 'The number to the Address of the Married Ladies of London is there stated to have been 8,500. The fact is, Sir, that there were 17,652 respectable names to that Address ...'[30] These women did not merely consider it disgraceful that a King who was notorious for his succession of mistresses should be able to abjure his wife for as yet unproven affairs; the weakening of the divorce laws presaged by making such hypocritical male-initiated divorce easier had disturbing implications for women still financially dependent on their husbands. Fortunately for Caroline's cause, before embarking for England she had heeded Brougham's pleas to send Pergami and his relatives back to Italy.

One 6 June, just as the Queen was reaching London, two green legal brief bags containing the evidence collated by the Delicate Investigation and the Milan Commission were deposited at the House of Lords. George was placing the problem firmly in Liverpool's lap.

The very bags themselves were soon featuring in contemporary prints. On 23 June George Cruikshank used a line from an old play of Sheridan's to accompany his image of the royal couple sealed up in two such green bags: 'Ah! sure such a pair was never seen so justly form'd to meet by nature.'[31] Threats to public order multiplied as the Queen's arraignment neared. Mobs rioted; the Hertfords' house was ransacked; Wellington's carriage and Castlereagh's house were attacked; threatening crowds gathered in Mayfair, poised to attack Carlton House (defended by a motley collection of soldiers and constables); and twenty-four regiments of soldiers were despatched to London in case of an insurrection. The climax came with an actual mutiny in support of the Queen: on 15 June the 1st Battalion of the Scots Guards refused to give up their ammunition when coming off duty, partly out of sympathy for the Queen, but partly too in protest over pay and conditions. Half the battalion were left shut up in their King Street barracks, while a mob tried to batter down the gates to let them out. As Henry Luttrell noted memorably at the time: 'The extinguisher is taking fire.'[32] Seven weeks later, on 3 August, as the Queen passed the Kensington barracks in her carriage on her way to her new home at Brandenburg House, Hammersmith, 'a great number of the military joined in the general shout; they took off their hats, and waved them in the air as her Majesty passed'. On 30 August Sir Thomas Lawrence told Farington that no less a personage than the Duke of

Wellington had been pelted with stones by the mob, who 'endeavour'd to pull him from His Horse' – small gratitude, judged the King's portraitist, 'from ... the Country he has sav'd'. Other observers noted that, while Wellington was being 'terribly booed', the mob was hailing the Duke of York as King. Liverpool commented ominously that 'the Queen's popularity was at its zenith', noting that 'Now a new spirit [of disaffection] was at work in London and in provincial centres'.[33]

The preamble to the 'trial' began on 5 July 1820, when Liverpool proposed the introduction of a bill entitled an 'Act to deprive her Majesty, Caroline ..., of the Title, Prerogatives, Rights, Privileges, and Exemptions of Queen Consort of this Realm, and to dissolve the Marriage between his Majesty and the said Caroline' – popularly known as the Bill of Pains and Penalties. The medieval law which characterised adultery by a queen consort as treason had never been repealed, so that, if the case against Caroline was proven, she might in theory lose not only her title but also her life. If this thought worried her, however, she did not show it. On arriving at the House of Lords for the first day of the formal proceedings, on 17 August, she asked the Usher of the Black Rod ironically whether she was being tried 'for intermarrying with a man whose first wife I knew to be alive'.[34]

The tale of this trial has been often retold.[35] The compelling evidence of her affair with Bartolomeo Pergami was rehearsed once more, her former servant Teodoro Majocchi being brought from Italy to repeat the damning evidence he had given the Milan Commission. However, Majocchi's testimony was successfully, and wittily, undermined during cross-examination by Brougham. Fully aware of the power of the popular press and the print-makers, he contrived to make Majocchi's repeated and flustered protestation '*Non mi recordo*' ('I don't recall') a national catch-phrase.[36] Liverpool was so worried by this failure of supposedly irrefutable first-hand evidence, and by the advantage the Opposition was deriving from the affair, that he recommended to the King that the divorce clauses of the bill be dropped. George, in the grip of his obsession, demanded that the measure go forward in its entirety.

As the proceedings continued in the House of Lords the mob bayed outside, hissing the King's officers and government officials and applauding those likely to support the Queen. The Duke of Sussex received an exceptionally hearty cheer from the crowd, to George's intense chagrin. The majority of print-makers, having caught the public mood, were fully behind Caroline. One anonymous satire declared her to be 'Britain's best Hope' and 'England's Sheet-Anchor'; another showed the 'sun' King, his green legal bag full of 'SLANDER', being eclipsed by the 'Caroline' moon.[37]

Brougham's opening of the case for the defence on 3 October helped sway opinion even further in the Queen's favour. His warning that to punish her publicly would be to jeopardise both Crown and Constitution was put so forcefully and persuasively that even reactionary Tories like Lord Lonsdale 'were struck with admiration and astonishment'. Charles Greville judged the speech 'the most magnificent display of argument and oratory that has been heard for years'. Brougham's assistant Thomas Denman perhaps went a little over the top in comparing George with the Emperor Nero, but while he was subsequently forced to apologise, the mob cheerfully renamed Carlton House 'Nero's Hotel'.[38]

On 6 November 1820 the Bill passed its first reading in the Lords with a majority of only twenty-eight, Whig peers having been joined by some of their Tory colleagues who, whatever their opinion of the Queen, thought the proposed legislation inadvisable at this time. Meanwhile, Brougham had obtained a copy of George's eccentric will of 1796 (in which, it will be recalled, he had bequeathed everything to his 'dear wife' Maria Fitzherbert), and now threatened to expose both this document and a handful of George's more embarrassing past affairs. This provided Liverpool with just the excuses he needed to abandon the Bill and at the same time save his ministry. After the Bill passed the motion for a third reading on 10 November by a majority of only nine, Liverpool announced that the government was postponing the measure for six months – a face-saving way of indicating that the Bill was being quietly dropped.

Effectively, Caroline had been acquitted: the government, if not the King himself, was throwing in the towel. George reacted to Liverpool's decision with predictable petulance and spite, immediately threatening to abdicate in favour of the Duke of York and 'retire' to his Kingdom of Hanover. Many of his subjects would have been quite happy with this solution; the cartoonist William Heath, for example, quickly composed a print in which demons dragged the King away to Hanover while Caroline sat on the throne, attended by Justice and Truth. A reminder from the cabinet that he would thereby forfeit much of his income, not to mention his palaces and his paintings, prompted George to reconsider. (On 14 November Mrs Arbuthnot, with whom the Duke of Wellington was in frequent correspondence, noted that 'The King had talked of going to Hanover, but the Duke says there is not much chance of that unless we allow him to take his eating and drinking money, his money for buhl furniture & for buying horses, which we could not think of doing.')[39]

Frustrated in his dream of absolute sovereignty in Hanover, George briefly considered alternative strategies of revenge. He was dissuaded from dismissing Liverpool's government in favour of the Whigs not only by Grey's support of the Queen following her 'trial' but, more importantly, by the reluctance of Lord Grenville and his moderate Whig supporters to contemplate the necessary coalition with more acceptable elements of the Tory party. He was also dissuaded from publishing a note he had received in 1814 from Princess Charlotte detailing her mother's connivance in and encouragement of her love affair with a Captain Hesse. Had he done so, he would surely have wounded his late daughter's reputation far more than his wife's.

Caroline, meanwhile, with an excellent sense of self-promotion, gave public thanks in St Paul's Cathedral on 29 November 'for the defeat of the late conspiracy against her honour'. Her progress to the City from her home in Hammersmith had something of the flavour of a coronation procession. *The Times* noted that

> The richness of the royal liveries, the number and respectability of the equestrian escort, the handsome decorations of the horses, and the tasteful knots of white favours (added, in very many instances, to medallions of her Majesty, suspended from the neck by blue ribands), gave the entire spectacle a splendid and interesting appearance.[40]

As Cobbett observed nine years later, following the 'trial' Caroline was 'on the pinnacle of fortune, where she might have stood, and where she would have been sustained by the people; but alas! down she came as rapidly as she had risen.' By early December, Loyal Addresses to the King were reported to be 'pouring in fast', while for the Queen 'the cheering was flat'. Caroline failed to make the most of her popularity; George did not. That same December, having taken the precaution of notifying the townspeople beforehand that 'he would condescend to permit them to hail his approach with public expressions of their unalterable attachment to his person', George made what amounted to a State Entry into Brighton. Formerly his visits had officially been private: now, by clever manipulation of the inhabitants of a town which owed its prosperity to his personal patronage, he engineered a public confirmation of his own celebrity.[41]

But popularity was as fickle as George himself. At the opening of Parliament on 23 January 1821, as Thomas Creevey observed, although the King 'was received with very considerable applause … his admirers were as drops in the ocean compared to those of his Wife'. Nor was his reception enhanced by the curious manner in which he delivered his Speech from the Throne – disjointedly and, when he was coherent, with theatrical over-emphasis; 'all *muggery*', in Creevey's opinion. Yet when at a public dinner in May the Duke of Sussex 'committed the impropriety of giving the Queen's health with that of the Royal Family', he was hissed for his pains.[42]

Caroline notoriously failed to gain admission to George's Coronation on 19 July 1821, and this seems to have brought on a severe illness 'which she made worse by taking opiates to relieve the great pain she suffered'. A few days later she told Brougham: 'I shall not recover; and I am much better dead, for I be tired of this life.' She appears to have recognised that she was on her deathbed; 'they have killed me at last!' she is said to have exclaimed. Yet she made no mention of her own dead daughter Charlotte, talking only of 'Petite Victorine', Pergami's daughter, and 'the child of Parson [Alderman] Wood'.

Caroline finally died on 8 August 1821, in considerable pain. Her estate was willed to her adopted son, William Austin (Brougham having sensibly removed the provision bequeathing some diamonds to Victorine – although the jewels were eventually sent); but since she died deep in debt, the gesture was an empty one. Austin received none of her possessions, only £200 annual rent from the tenants of Montague House, which Coutts the bankers were instructed to invest on his behalf.[43]

London society had relished the story that when George was informed, following Napoleon's demise on 5 May 1821, that his 'greatest enemy' was dead, he promptly replied, 'Is she, by God!' He was told of Caroline's death on 11 August, while he was on his way to Ireland, and having taken care to rehearse a seemly response to the long-awaited news, tried to hide his elation – although John Croker reported subsequently that 'the King was uncommonly well during his passage and gayer than it might be proper to tell'. He had ordered the flags of the royal squadron to be lowered, as a belated mark of respect, and on the cabinet's advice had stayed a day or two with the Marquess of Anglesey at Plas Newydd before embarking for Ireland. He rather spoiled the intended effect, however, by disembarking at Howth apparently dead drunk, barely able to stand upright; he was heard singing songs and observed drinking successive glasses of whiskey – hardly a convincing imitation of a sad or penitent man. Meanwhile, he had ordered the Court into mourning for the shortest time possible, and Liverpool had concurred in his wish to dispense with mourning altogether for the public celebrations of his Irish visit.[44] Clearly, George could not wait to rid himself of his wife's ghost.

Shortly before Caroline's death at Brandenburg House her papers were burned, partly by her own hand. This removed one potential problem, but her directions regarding her funeral posed the government a number of others. Her will stipulated that her body was to be returned to Brunswick, and trouble along the coffin's route was foreseen. George flatly rejected Liverpool's sensible suggestion of a private funeral in Westminster Abbey, and proposed instead that the coffin be quietly taken from Brandenburg House to the nearby Thames, and conveyed thence by water to Germany – an unduly secretive manoeuvre which, should it have become public knowledge, would have prompted widespread protests. Even more inflammatory was Caroline's directive that her coffin be inscribed 'Caroline of Brunswick, the *injured* Queen of England'. In this instance, Liverpool and his cabinet were ready to support the King's judgement 'that the offensive inscription which the Queen has decided to be placed on her coffin, cannot be acquiesced in'.[45]

Whatever the precautions taken, it was probably inevitable that Caroline's funeral procession would be sensational in some degree. The chaos and violence surrounding her coffin's passage were, however, more pronounced than many had anticipated, degenerating into an undignified spectacle which one modern commentator has designated 'the nadir of the British Monarchy'.[46] Liverpool's revised plan was to have the body conducted to the port of Harwich, and from there transported across the North Sea to Germany. From Brandenburg House it was to follow a circuitous route using the northern New Road (now Marylebone and Euston Roads) rather than the more populous City streets, but at Hyde Park Corner a mob overpowered the cortège and diverted the Queen's coffin through the centre of London. Once again, some of the regular soldiers deputed to guard the procession sided with the protesters, and in the ensuing confusion at least two bystanders were killed.[47]

Caroline's body was finally interred in a Brunswick church on

24 August 1821, in the presence of her closest friends and of the small figure of William Austin, her adopted son. He was perhaps the saddest casualty of the whole sordid struggle. A docker's son whose parentage was constantly questioned and challenged (before 1806, Caroline herself had mendaciously asserted that he was the child of Prince Louis Ferdinand of Prussia), Austin achieved little after Caroline's death, and died insane in a Chelsea lunatic asylum in 1849.[48]

I I

The Immense Girl

All that's bright must fade —
The brightest still the fleetest.
All that's sweet was made
But to be lost when sweetest.
Thomas Moore, *All That's Bright Must Fade*

GEORGE IV HAS always found too-ready forgiveness for his failings and inconsistencies. His charm, his intelligence and his aesthetic vision, combined with the glittering aura of monarchy, have encouraged historians and commentators to overlook his foibles and give him the benefit of the doubt. Even his shabby treatment of friends, lovers and adherents has been excused and held to be outweighed by his achievements in the cultural sphere. It is very difficult, however, to absolve him of lack of consideration for his only child. The cold indifference he consistently demonstrated during her lifetime, and his attempted exploitation of her memory after her death, reveal him to have been deeply concerned only with his own welfare.

Princess Charlotte of Wales was a public figure about whom there was much speculation and on whom countless hopes were pinned, but of whom her ordinary contemporaries actually knew very little. All too often, her identity has been defined only in terms of her premature death. However, the circumstances of her brief life illuminated some of the most unappealing aspects of her father's character – his ability to dismiss, forget or injure those nearest to him, as well as his profound self-absorption – while the aftermath of her death revealed his awesome ability to purloin the emotions of others and project them as his own.

Charlotte's very birth was difficult, presaging the pain to come.

Princess Caroline endured 'upwards of twelve hours in constant labour' before giving birth to her on 7 January 1796. Notwithstanding his wife's sufferings, George's reaction was cold-blooded even by his standards. 'We might have wish'd for a boy,' he murmured with callous indifference when told of the birth, referred to the baby slightingly as an 'immense girl', then moaned in a letter to his mother that he was 'so fatigued' that he could scarcely sign it. George III's response, however, was typically and contrastingly considerate: he chivalrously announced that he did not in the least mind that his grandchild was a girl, having 'always wished it should be of that sex'.[1]

The Prince's behaviour deteriorated even further. Only three days after the birth, having evinced little concern over the health of mother or daughter, he insisted that he himself was seriously ill – actually on the point of death. Wallowing in his customary self-pity, he dictated the notorious will of 10 January 1796 in which all his 'worldly property' was left to Mrs Fitzherbert – not to Caroline, not even to his newborn daughter: Charlotte was only to receive her mother's jewels. With effortless brutality, he further instructed that 'the mother of this child, called the Princess of Wales, should in no way either be concerned in the education or care of the child, or have possession of her person'.[2]

The unnecessarily cruel and inhumane regime George insisted upon for his daughter suggested a singular lack of interest in her as a person, and that he had learned nothing from his own upbringing. He pompously declared that 'the most essential point in a nursery' was 'order and regularity', and a litany of pettifogging regulations included the proviso that the infant's attendants be forbidden to talk to any other servants of the Royal Household. Charlotte's sub-governess, Miss Hayman, recorded in June 1797 that the Prince had only seen his little daughter 'when dressing, or at breakfast'. He had not, she added, been up to the nursery in a long while, 'having dropped that custom many months'. Protestations of paternal affection were evinced only when George was attempting to use his daughter as a pawn in his increasingly acrimonious disputes with his wife. As early as May 1796, having denounced to his mother Caroline's 'impracticable temper' and her supposed plan to establish 'a decided political superiority in this country ... by the degradation of my character', he concluded his ludicrously unbalanced outpourings (the discussion of which, he alleged at the commencement of his protracted harangue, would be 'too painful to be continued') with a reference to his daughter which was breathtaking in its disingenuousness: 'I cannot close this letter without advertising to the situation of my poor little girl'.[3]

As her daughter grew older Caroline naturally wanted to see her, and appealed to her father-in law for help. Following a personal interview with Caroline, which he judged 'gave the greatest satisfaction', George III announced that Princess Charlotte's future would henceforth 'entirely be guided' by himself. Yet Colonel MacMahon persuaded the Prince of Wales (whom news of the interview had made 'ill with rage') that his father was determined to 'get the little Princess entirely to himself'.[4] Though George scarcely saw his daughter, his father's interference in her upbringing was hardly more welcome than his wife's: Princess Charlotte's best interests had little to do with it. George III's compromise settlement of 1805 – by which Charlotte was to remain at Warwick House (adjacent to Carlton House) while the Prince of Wales was in London, and at Windsor the rest of the year, when her mother was to have visiting rights – was immediately represented by his son not as establishing a degree of stability in her life but, in typically overwrought and selfish fashion, as the triumph of his wife's implacable will over that of his ailing and possibly insane father.

As a small child, Charlotte was much praised by commentators wearied by her parents' ill-tempered bickerings. Lord Minto declared her a 'lively, intelligent and pleasant' toddler, while her royal grandmother was almost doting. In March 1799 Queen Charlotte declared that 'anything so good or so engaging I never saw before' and goodhumouredly described her granddaughter as 'unique' and 'delightfull'. Twelve years later, she was still writing fondly to George of her now adolescent namesake:

> You have indeed in this child every hope of comfort and delight to come. She is blessed with an uncommon share of good sense; she has talents and facility to learn anything, is easily led to follow good advice when treated with gentleness, desirous to oblige when an opportunity offers, and capable of very strong attachment. She is very sensible of any the smallest attention shewn to her, and ... seems, notwithstand[ing] her great liveliness and spirit, very desirous of improving herself. She is blessed with a very retentive memory, which is of great assistance to her, and her pursuits when not at her lessons are of that kind to convey information of all kinds necessary to know in her situation.[5]

Soon, however, it became apparent that the cunning old Queen was as ruthlessly adept as her son when it came to using Princess Charlotte as an innocent pawn in the game of family 'honour'. She exploited her position and vulnerability when appealing to George to prevent the Duke of Cumberland bringing his wife (whose German marriage the family refused to recognise) to Britain, on the grounds that 'as [Charlotte] leans very much towards her mother, the receiving the Dutchess [*sic*] of Cumberland, of whose history she is not ignorant, will arm her with not an unjust argument in favour of the Princess'. Alerting George to 'the opportunity looked for by the Princess of Wales to return and to make another clamour (which I know she intends)' was a sure-fire way of focusing his full attention. No wonder Caroline eventually came to regard the Queen as 'her greatest enemy'.[6]

In the cross-fire of her parents' battles, Charlotte's education suffered. She 'never learned to write legibly', and her spelling mistakes, her tutor Dr Nott informed her, were such as 'a common servant would have blushed to have committed'. The historian Sir Arthur Aspinall, cataloguing the papers of this period, found that 'Charlotte's spelling remained to the end inconceivably bad'. In 1808 Charlotte's German tutor summoned up the courage to inform the Queen that her granddaughter was not 'receiving the useful instruction requisite for her age and situation'. Intellectual accomplishment had never ranked high among the priorities of the House of Hanover, however; Queen Charlotte merely replied that 'it was of little consequence whether she learned a little more or less'.[7] In 1811 Mary Berry recorded a visit to Charlotte at her home during which the fifteen-year-old spent most of her time playing cards: 'She knows no creature, but the royal family and their attendants,' Miss Berry noted, and 'she has never yet seen a play or an opera.'[8] She was not even invited to her father's famous fête of June 1811. That he invited Princess Caroline's ladies-in-waiting but not Princess Caroline was insulting, but to be expected; that he did not invite his daughter and heir was shocking.

Ignored by her father and largely separated from her mother, the young Princess paid little heed to her stable of mediocre tutors and governesses, headed by Bishop Fisher of Salisbury and Lady de Clifford, who could not stand one another. Miss Knight, who replaced Lady de Clifford in 1813, later said of the ineffably pompous Bishop that she 'could not but see how narrow his views, how strong his prejudices, and how unequal his talents were to the charge with which he had been entrusted by the good old King', and alleged that he spent much of his time ranting 'against the encouragement of Popery and Whig principles (two evils which he seemed to think equally great), and endeavouring to appear himself a man of consequence'. The one tutor Miss Knight had approved of, Dr Nott, was summarily dismissed in 1809, largely it seems because of Charlotte's too-evident affection for him.[9] Not surprisingly, such useful homilies as those delivered by Hannah More in her *Hints towards Forming the Character of a Young Princess* of 1805 were wholly ignored by the other tutors.

As a result of this fitful training, Charlotte's mistakes often went uncorrected, and her social inadequacies were ignored. She stammered badly, a common Brunswick affliction which, revealingly, became more pronounced when she was in the presence of either parent. Visitors 'were unanimous in expressing their surprise that the future Queen of England was so deficient in manners'. She swore profusely – being likened by one Dutch diplomat to 'a mutinous boy in skirts' – and though Bishop Fisher complained of her dreadful manners, his chosen example was hardly apocalyptic: 'when her nose requir[ed] to be wiped, she did not apply her handkerchief, but wiped her nose with her sleeve as vulgar people do'. Household confidante Cornelia Knight saw this all as an inevitable consequence of the Prince 'pursuing the plan of protracted infancy, [which] was to be grafted on the education of a schoolboy':

> Princess Charlotte, in understanding, penetration, and stature, was become a woman, desirous to acquire more knowledge of public affairs and general society, alive to everything, and capable of forming a judgement for herself, [yet] the new plan of sending her back to the nursery was adopted, and everything was done to promote it.

George's own glib comments to Miss Knight, that 'Charlotte must lay aside the idle nonsense of thinking that she has a will of her own' and that 'while I live she must be subject to me as she is at present, if she were thirty, or forty, or five-and-forty', seem to vindicate the governess's unfavourable opinion.[10]

What we know of Charlotte's character does not seem particularly encouraging. Like her father, she was careless with people and with possessions. She had a vicious temper (which appears to have caused Nott something akin to a nervous breakdown in 1806); worse, from an early age she displayed a propensity for lying and, like her father, apparently believed her lies to be truth immediately they were uttered. Like him, too, she was impetuous and headstrong in love. Her rumoured liaison with army lieutenant Charles Hesse (allegedly the illegitimate son of the Duke of York) during 1812–13, when she was just sixteen, prompted much gossip, and sly comparisons between the proclivities of father and daughter. The Princess of Wales allegedly encouraged the affair, shamelessly contributing to her daughter's disgrace in her all-consuming desire to embarrass her husband. Charlotte later told George that on one occasion her mother had locked her in a bedroom with Hesse, murmuring as she departed, 'I leave you to amuse yourselves'. George thundered that Charlotte was 'on the brink of utter destruction and ruin in point of character' – something with which he was himself all too familiar. Rumours of this affair engendered others. A George Cruikshank cartoon of June 1814 – in which the artist was noticeably more sympathetic than he customarily was to her father – implied that the young Princess had fallen for the Marquess of Lansdowne, whose portrait miniature rested on her thigh and in whose chair she sat.[11]

Such minor scandals were largely disregarded by a public who, dismayed by the manifest failings of the Prince Regent, preferred to imbue his daughter with qualities she had so far failed to demonstrate, seeing her as a beacon of hope and a refuge. In the second decade of the nineteenth century, as at the dawn of the twenty-first, perceived imperfections in the immediate heir to the throne were countered by a naïve faith in the suitability of the sovereign's grandchild. Had Byron's 'love of millions' lived, however, it is doubtful whether she would have fulfilled those expectations. Thackeray acknowledged this twenty-odd years after her death, when with his customary acidity he put his thoughts into the mouth of the eccentric Mr Yellowplush:

> We called her the Princis Sharlot of Wales; and we valyoud a single drop of her blood more than the whole heartless body of her father. Well, we looked up to her as a kind of saint or angle, and blest God (such foolish loyal English pipple as we ware in those days) who had sent this sweet lady to rule over us. But heaven bless you! it was only souperstition. She was no better than she should be, as it turns out …[12]

Shelley, too – more realistic than the adoring Byron – wrote after Charlotte's death that in truth 'she had done nothing either good or evil'.[13]

In general, Charlotte's uncles Frederick, Augustus and Edward paid more attention to her than did her father. In October 1812 she described the Duke of Sussex as 'a *sincere and true* hearted creature', and noted that the Duke of Kent 'has always been *uniformly* kind to me since I have been here [at Windsor] ... and when it has been in his power to do [a] good natured thing by me or for me, he had been always ready and happy to do it'. In November 1812, at Windsor, she complained that 'The Regent has been down only once since I wrote last, and then did not say 5 words to me.' On 16 August 1813 George's excuse for not travelling the short distance between his party at Frogmore and his daughter's household at the Great Park's Lower Lodge was that he could not bear to see her ladies-in-waiting. Charlotte received not one letter from her father until her nineteenth birthday, in 1815, when she astutely dismissed his professions of affection as 'sugary' emotions 'which, after all, were but *des phrases, without* any meaning'. His irregular visits, she confided, '*strike* a *damp*, and *create fears* for a long time after they are over'. On the few occasions she was invited to Carlton House she was largely ignored, though as early as 1811 Maria Fitzherbert had urged George to treat her with more kindness – an overt reminder of his shameful neglect which may have contributed to Maria's final public humiliation at Carlton House a few months later. Lady Rose Weigall's suggestion, in her 'Memoir' of the Princess published long after the event, in 1874, that 'The Regent had reason to fear that [Charlotte's] appearance in public would give a fresh stimulus to the widespread feeling in favour of herself and her mother' is a rather lame and over-generous interpretation of his behaviour.[14]

Much as George had espoused Fox's Whig politics largely to annoy his father, so after 1811 his daughter condemned her father's retention of Perceval's Tory government and openly sided with the opposition. Hearing George denounce the Whigs at a Carlton House dinner she burst into tears, prompting Byron to write his savage lines on the Regent's 'disgrace'. Her Whig friends, including her much-loved companion Margaret Mercer Elphinstone, were banished from Court after her father's assumption of full Regency powers in February 1812, and she was effectively exiled to the Lower Lodge in Windsor Great Park – and watched over by the grandmother she loathed.[15] These were the actions of a man who, drinking the Princess's health eight years earlier, had declared that 'he had made it his first care to instil into the mind and heart of his daughter the knowledge and love of the true principles of the British constitution' and that he had recommended Fox to her 'as a model of study'. Charlotte clearly found it difficult to forgive such hypocritical contradictions and such a betrayal of the late Whig leader's radical idealism. She expressed her abhorrence of her father's incremental conservatism none too subtly, by giving friends small busts of Fox. In January 1812 she archly informed Lord Albemarle that 'Happy, thrice happy will the moment be when the plans Mr Fox pursued and planned are put into *full force*'.[16]

Commenting later on life at Carlton House during the first months of 1813, Cornelia Knight wrote of George that 'He talked but little of Princess Charlotte, and not with the manner or voice of affection', and noted that 'Every consideration was to be sacrificed to the plan of keeping the Princess Charlotte as long as possible *a child*.' Taken aside one evening by the Prince, Miss Knight was distressed to find herself the recipient of a spiteful and inaccurate diatribe contrasting his own devotion to Charlotte with her mother's neglect:

> The Prince ... talked to me for a long while against the Princess of Wales, and the little regard she had shown for Princess Charlotte when a child ... whereas *he* used continually to watch beside her cradle. He said very severe things of the Princess of Wales in every way, and even accused her of threatening to declare that Princess Charlotte was not his daughter.

Charlotte's request of January 1813 to be given her own household provoked her father's uncontrolled fury, and a scene in which she was dressed down before the Queen in front of all the Court. Lord Eldon subsequently pronounced, at the Prince's behest, that he 'would have her locked up'. George was determined that Charlotte should have no opportunity to take her mother's side, and by February 1813 had taken steps to prevent her seeing Caroline at all – on pain of 'losing my Balls or gaities'. When feuding with his father, George had published their correspondence: now Charlotte had her letters of appeal to the Prince and Lord Liverpool published in the *Morning Chronicle*. Following this act of bravado, George refused to see her at all.

Even more unpaternal was George's refusal to let Charlotte travel to the seaside when she was seriously ill in July 1813 – a trip recommended by the royal physician, Sir Henry Halford. George, who had little sympathy for anyone's ailments but his own, dismissed her request with the curt observation 'that she was quite well'. A few months later he had the effrontery to accuse his daughter of 'spending too much with the jewellers'. That summer, furious because Charlotte proved more popular than himself with the distinguished foreign guests who crowded London after the fall of Paris, he sent the ubiquitous Halford to her with the rather pathetic and childish demand that she see less of the Grand Duchess Catherine of Oldenburg, Tsar Alexander's sister.[17]

The ageing Queen Charlotte dealt little better with her namesake's popularity. Feeling betrayed when Cornelia Knight left her service to join Princess Charlotte's, she sent her former companion a series of 'resentful and bitter' letters, made no reply to her explanation, and barely spoke to her when the young Princess visited Windsor the following April. This spiteful behaviour was extended to her grand-daughter, and she firmly quashed the Duke of York's sensible and considerate suggestion that the young Princess should be 'enjoying more liberty and passing a part of her time in London', possibly chaperoned by her aunts, since she 'was to all intents and purposes without a mother ... and therefore ... required the full support and protection of the female part of her family.'[18]

Although George had, as he saw it, suffered immeasurably from an arranged marriage, he did not hesitate to subject his daughter to a similar fate. From December 1813, aided by the oily diplomatic skills of Sir Henry Halford, he attempted to hustle her into a marriage with Prince William of Orange, a 'short and skinny and indecisive' youth (and in later life a notoriously dull drunk) invariably known as 'Silly Billy'.[19] The fact that Charlotte would inevitably have to spend most of her time in Holland after her marriage worried him so little that he initially refused to consider the insertion in the marriage contract of a clause guaranteeing her right to return to Britain whenever she wished; at the same time, he avoided recognising her as the heir presumptive, gleefully pointing out that if Caroline left England and he divorced her and remarried, any subsequent male child would be the heir and 'the young Princess's title to the throne be gone' ('This has had an effect upon the young one almost magical', he gloated ghoulishly). Instead, George demanded that his daughter 'conquer her prejudices', and marry a man she despised. Lady Charlotte Bury, a lady-in-waiting to the Princess of Wales, recalled Caroline telling her a year later that her daughter was 'outrageous [sic] at the thoughts of leaving this country, and her unnatural father assured her that she would never have an establishment in this country'.[20]

Charlotte was adamant that she should never be obliged to leave England against her will, and the marriage negotiations faltered. Then in 1814 the Princess became infatuated with Prince Augustus of Russia, in London with the Allied rulers and generals, and on 10 June 1814 peremptorily informed Prince William that the engagement her father had brokered was at an end. Retribution was swift, and severe. On 12 July the Princess's adored Lady Companion, Cornelia Knight, her Lady-in-Waiting the Duchess of Leeds and all but one of her servants were dismissed. Spitefully, as she left, George told Miss Knight 'he was glad that every one would now see what the Princess was; and that it would be known on the Continent, and no-one would marry her'.[21] Ancient pillars of respectability, Lady Rosslyn and Lady Ilchester, were appointed in their stead.

Charlotte's reaction to this was melodramatic flight. On 14 July she jumped into a hackney carriage in Cockspur Street, promising the driver 'a sovereign if he hurried' to her mother's house in Connaught Place. It was left to Henry Brougham and the Duke of Sussex to remind her that the Regent had absolute control over her actions until she was twenty-one. Bitterly disappointed in her mother, who supported their position and coldly suggested that she leave her house – the mother who only months before had protested to the Regent at being 'cut off from one of the very few domestic enjoyments left me – ... the society of my child' – Charlotte was unceremoniously taken back to Warwick House at two o'clock in the morning by a not unsympathetic Duke of York.[22] Thereafter she lived virtually as a prisoner, surrounded by elderly attendants she heartily disliked and forbidden to travel further than her own front porch.

Lady Charlotte Bury later firmly attributed the Regent's hasty actions to his jealousy of any rival's popular ascendancy – even when that rival was his own daughter: 'The Prince of Orange, it is said, wishes his wife to go with him to his own Dutch land; and so does the Prince Regent, who does not like a rising sun in his own.' George Cruikshank depicted George as the murdering pirate Bluebeard, boasting of having 'Lock'd my Daughter up & driven my Wife out of the Country'.[23]

Her mother was little better, her refusal to support Charlotte in her flight being merely the latest in a series of disappointments. Charlotte complained that her mother's letters to her were 'the shortest, driest things in the world, and consist of 5 lines at the utmost', and Caroline rarely enquired about her daughter's health or situation. In that summer of 1814, before her summary dismissal, Cornelia Knight noted that Charlotte had received 'very little communication [from her] this year'. And Caroline's subsequent conduct abroad horrified Charlotte: 'It sinks her so very low in my opinion.' By the end of 1814, however, the Princess had generously concluded that her mother was 'a *very unhappy* and a very *unfortunate* woman who has had great *errors*, great *faults*, but is really oppressed and cruelly used'. Grey was probably nearer the truth when he noted in August 1814 that Caroline appeared to be playing off her husband and daughter against each other, neglecting to answer her daughter's letters and 'treating her daughter's complaints as trivial' while 'evidently playing the game of the Queen and the Regent'. Just two weeks before her death Princess Charlotte wrote to Cornelia Knight that 'I have not heard from my mother for a long time', and to Lady Charlotte Bury, 'If you can give me any intelligence of her, I should be much obliged.'[24]

The dismal example of her parents' marriage notwithstanding, Charlotte stumbled into what was apparently a love-match with Prince Leopold of Saxe-Coburg-Saalfeld. She had first attracted the attentions of Leopold, an uninspiring but good-looking and studious German princeling, in 1814 when, as a senior officer in the Russian army, he accompanied Tsar Alexander I to London. When Leopold returned to Britain in March 1815, Charlotte – recently rebuffed following a tactless overture to Prince Frederick of Prussia – was evidently prepared to return his feelings. George was reluctant to drop his advocacy of the Prince of Orange and Charlotte, writing at the end of that year to Margaret Mercer Elphinstone, wondered whether 'it is a bad thing that my liking Leo should be a little talked of', despairing of her father, who was 'so *afraid of him* and of my liking him'. In February 1816 George gave his consent (the Queen told him that Charlotte had greeted the news 'with the happiest face imaginable'), but he was not interested enough in his daughter's concerns even now to return from Brighton so that arrangements for the marriage could proceed. The rest of the royal family was, Charlotte asserted, 'much *alarmed* ... and in despair at the idea of my being married there [in Brighton]'; eventually the Regent was persuaded out of his lethargy and off to London.[25]

Already, however, there were signs that all was not well physically with the Princess. In the month her engagement was officially announced, Charlotte admitted to her mother that she was suffering from 'bilious complaints (which I am sorry to say I am but too liable to)' – possible indications, according to Hunter and Macalpine and to more recent medical opinion, of inherited porphyria. The premarital worries expressed to her mother shortly before her marriage on 2 May 1816 demonstrate an anxious morbidity reminiscent of her father and grandfather. And in her autobiography Cornelia Knight often noted symptoms indicative of the presence of porphyria, describing the Princess as 'pale and ill', 'agitated' and over-emotional.[26]

Nevertheless, Charlotte and Leopold settled down to domestic bliss at Claremont in Surrey. The house had been built in 1771–4 for Clive of India by Lancelot Brown and Henry Holland, and the young couple now commissioned the architects J. B. Papworth and John Hiort to add a number of ancillary buildings, including a conservatory and a Gothic summer-house. Delighted by her new-found freedom, the Princess invited her friends to Claremont, promising that they would find it to be 'Liberty Hall'. Thomas Lawrence thought the scenes he observed over dinner at Claremont indicated a genuine attachment:

> His address to the Princess was 'my Dear Charlotte' and She always called Him 'My Love'. – Their manner to each other was affectionate, and it was manifest that by the equality of His temper and His good sense He had great influence over Her which He used with discretion, never directly shewing it, but always at a time to have effect in a gentle manner.

In its evident mutual affection, Charlotte and Leopold's relationship seems to have presaged that of Victoria and Albert – Leopold's niece and nephew – a generation later. Certainly their publicly expressed love for one another, and Leopold's calming influence on 'her quickness and wilfulness of temper', made Claremont a happy place to visit. Lawrence commented that he 'never before was in a House where there was such uniform civility and attention shewn by all the Servants'.[27]

Relations were also unusully cordial between Charlotte and her father after her marriage, and the Princess managed to spend the Christmas of 1816 at Brighton Pavilion without stammering unduly. In the spring she discovered she was pregnant again – after two miscarriages – and even endured old Queen Charlotte's unsought advice concerning the appropriate regime for the expected child.

All this new-found happiness came to a tragic and poignant end. When Charlotte's labour began on 3 November 1817 it was pronounced 'good' and 'in every respects favourable' by her doctors. But it dragged on for forty-six hours, at the end of which, on 5 November 1817, a still-born male child was delivered. The Princess might have recovered from her ordeal, but fell into a strange lassitude (which more recent medical experts have identified as porphyric) and, following what appears to have been a postpartum haemorrhage, died at 2.30 a.m. on 5 November. Her accoucheur, Sir Richard Croft – the first of his profession to assist at a royal birth – appears to have been innocent of any blatant malpractice, but inevitably was widely blamed: he shot himself the following February.[28]

The public reaction to Princess Charlotte's death in 1817 – recently adjudged 'out of proportion to the event, whether by modern or by contemporary standards' – found an echo not quite two centuries later when another Princess died and was invested with a quasi-mythological status she herself would possibly have found unwarranted. Charlotte was seen as such a welcome and wholesome contrast to her father that her 'martyrdom' aroused sympathy across all levels of society; women in particular identified with a victim of 'that most common of Regency women's experiences, death in childbirth'.[29] To George Cruikshank she had been 'England's ONLY Hope', and 'a Lesson to Princes'. Even Leigh Hunt's fiercely anti-government *Examiner* rushed into print a sickly 'Elegy on our Lost Princess', in which Hunt lauded the character of a woman of whom he actually knew very little:

> For she was nothing falsely proud,
> Nor inhumane; but sweetly bowed
> To all kind pleasures and glad hours,
> And loved the green leaves and the flowers,
> And, wanting flowers, could make her merry
> With the holly and its blithe berry.

Rather more perceptive was Hunt's subsequent more considered piece in *The Examiner* of 8 November, which remarked on the contrast between the hope invested in the late Princess and the disappointing conduct of her father:

> The first and greatest feeling of the country on this occasion is certainly not a political one: it is real sorrow and sympathy, and no mourning for a Prince will have been so genuine for a long series of years ... If any dreary sceptic in sentiment should ask why the sorrow is so great for this young woman, any more than another, we answer, because this young woman is the representative of all the others – because she stood on high, in the eyes of us all, embodying as it were the ideal as well as actual images of youth, and promise, and blooming womanhood – ... images of happy love ... and approaching maternity.[30]

Predictably, George failed to rise to the occasion, or to take advantage of the ensuing national anguish to enhance his own reputation. Prince Leopold was grief-stricken and ordered that none of Charlotte's clothes or personal belongings be touched, before retreating into a private room. His subsequent incapacity ensured that Princess Caroline, then in Pesaro, was informed of her daughter's death only by a passing government courier, on his way to tell the Pope. (Later, reliable observers reported that Caroline had been severely depressed for months afterwards, a state she attempted to mask by a show of 'jocularity and indifference' which many of the less perceptive interpreted as callous heartlessness.[31]) George's reaction, however, was typically self-centered and melodramatic. According to Thomas Lawrence he 'appeared pale and spoke in a low tone of voice, seeming to subdue the expression of His grief. He said nobody could so feel the loss which Himself and the Public had sustained so deeply as Himself.' He quarrelled with Prince Leopold over possession of Lawrence's portrait of the late Princess – having claimed 'he was so much affected' by the picture that he could not look at it except in Lawrence's presence (Lawrence also privately noted that he felt 'very disagreeably circumstanced' in the whole tasteless affair). George's request that the grieving husband return his late wife's 'remarkably fine sapphire' – the Stuart Sapphire which had belong to the Cardinal-Duke of York – might in another man be put down to distraught and clumsy tactlessness, but coming from him seems but another example of his greed and callous insensitivity. Croker noted in his diary on 17 June 1821 that 'Lady Darnley ... has recognised [the sapphire] on Lady Conyngham's neck'. This relic of the Stuarts, which had been one of his dead daughter's favourite jewels, now cavorted in the ivory chasm of his mistress's cleavage.[32]

Within a month, George's grief was becoming diluted by concern over his own ailments. 'I have been ... still very much and very truly indispos'd for the last ten days,' he whimpered to his mother on 16 December, with 'a good deal of rheumatism, as much of cold, with a little touch of bile to boot ... compos'd of as unpleasant ingredients, as can well be thought of or imagin'd.'[33] Nevertheless, that same month he was well enough, both physically and mentally, to entertain lavishly at Brighton Pavilion, making full use of the talents of his expensive chef Antonin Carême.

A year after Charlotte's death, while declaring himself to have been most upset on seeing Dawe's portrait of her, George managed to stifle

a proposal to erect a monument to the Princess, and himself appropriated the money raised for this noble project. Robert Huish was not
the only one still asking, after George's own death, 'What is become
of the enormous sum which was contributed in this country for the
erection of a cenotaph to the memory of the Princess Charlotte?'[34] A
father's distress clearly did not extend to spending money on monuments to his dead daughter if it could be diverted to buy furniture and
fittings for his own palaces. He also continued for years to carp privately about his son-in-law – informing Wellington in January 1830
that he could not 'but deeply regret the selection made by France and
Russia of Prince Leopold to be placed at the head of the Greek
Kingdom' – while affecting in public to admire him.[35]

Charlotte's death was not uncommemorated, however. Matthew
Cotes Wyatt's fittingly sensational monument – in which the attendant
mourners and the Princess's earthly body on the bier are draped in
shrouds – was financed by means of a public subscription initiated not
by her father but by the Duchess of York.[36] The reaction to the appeal
was overwhelming; by 1819, the *Gentleman's Magazine* recorded,
£12,346 had been raised, for a figure or group to be erected in Hyde
Park. When it was announced – very belatedly, in 1823 – that the monument would be erected not in London but in St George's Chapel at
Windsor Castle, *The Literary Chronicle and Weekly Review* protested 'with
amazement' that 'a monument to which fifteen thousand Britons, in
various parts of the globe' had contributed 'is to be placed in ... the
private chapel of his Majesty, where it will be as completely secluded
from public view as if it were closeted in Carlton House'. The *Chronicle*
snorted indignantly that George IV was treating as private property
and concealing from the public 'the only monument of a princess they
adored – a monument not paid for out of the privy purse – not paid
for by a vote of Parliament, but raised by a voluntary subscription'.[37]
The intimation was clear: the King should not be allowed to appropriate his daughter's death as he had her life. George, however, had the
final say, and the monument was duly unveiled at Windsor in 1824.

Shelley's swiftly-composed *Address to the People on the Death of the
Princess Charlotte* bemoaned the demise of 'a woman young, innocent
and beautiful' who 'should have been the Queen of her beloved
nation, and whose posterity should have ruled it for ever', and who
was 'amiable and would have become wise'. At the same time,
however, he reminded Charlotte's more hysterical admirers that 'She
had accomplished nothing, and aspired to nothing, and could under-

stand nothing respecting those great political questions which involve the happiness of those over whom she was destined to rule'. For him, Charlotte's death, and her father's survival, were 'a national calamity', and he took solace in the imagined transformation of the dead princess from 'the corpse of British Liberty', carried 'slowly and reverentially to its tomb', into 'the Spirit of Liberty ... arisen from its grave'.[38] The close similarity between Shelley's lines and the composition of Wyatt's Windsor tomb suggests more than mere coincidence.

The posthumous adulation of Princess Charlotte served to throw her father's way of life and his excesses into sharper relief. As the nation's journalists and literati canonised the late Princess (remarkably foreshadowing the printed reactions to the death of Diana, Princess of Wales in 1997), the realisation that the monarchy's future was represented by the Prince Regent and his unsavoury brothers cast a chill over many hearts. Accordingly, although the birth of a daughter to the unpopular Duke and Duchess of Kent in 1819 was not immediately recognised as a significant event, the few commentators who reported it did so with a sigh of relief. The press could now begin its self-appointed task of transferring to another royal infant – the future Queen Victoria – the widespread affection which Charlotte had enjoyed.

PART IV

The Image of Royalty

12

Image and Reality

Some sprats have been, by Y–rm—th's wish,
Promoted into *Silver* Fish ...
Thomas Moore, *The Twopenny Post-Bag*, Letter VIII

IN OCTOBER 1810 George III began to experience a recurrence of
the 'symptoms of disorder' – now largely attributed to the metabolic disorder porphyria – which had almost precipitated a Regency
during the winter of 1788–9, returning ominously in 1801 and again
in 1804. This time there was to be no remission. On 29 October 1810
Lord Grenville told Lord Grey that the King had 'a decided return of
his former malady'; the same day the Tory Prime Minister, Spencer
Perceval, observed of the King that 'his conversation was prodig-
iously hurried, and ... extremely diffuse, explicit, and indiscreet'. Sir
Henry Halford and his colleagues agreed that, since the King was now
an old man, the physical restraints employed during his previous
attacks would not be required. The death of his beloved daughter
Princess Amelia on 2 November accelerated his decline, however, and
restraint became necessary after all. On 13 December Perceval moved
the questioning by a House of Commons Select Committee of the
royal physicians. R.D. Willis, son of the doctor who had 'cured'
George III in 1789, reported perceptively that 'the King's derangement [was] more nearly allied to delirium, than insanity', but preparations went ahead for the establishment of a Regency. On 19
December Perceval informed the Prince of Wales that he proposed
to introduce a Bill for his formal appointment as Regent which would
guarantee him some (but not all) sources of revenue, while not per-
mitting him to dispense titles or offices. George, having seen three
such 'regencies' escape from his grasp, cautiously referred the Prime

Minister 'to his answer in 1788, upon receiving a similar communication from Mr Pitt'. At the same time, however, he encouraged his brothers to write to Perceval protesting vehemently that any limitations on the Regency would be 'perfectly unconstitutional as they are contrary to and subversive of the principles which seated our family upon the throne of this realm'.[1]

By Christmas Day 1810 the King, now seventy-three, was widely believed to be 'at the last gasp', but just when most had given up hope his health began to improve perceptibly – though not enough, reported Halford to the Lord Chancellor on 15 January, for him to understand what was happening in Parliament, or to comprehend the passage of the Regency Bill. On 29 January 1811 the King intimated to Perceval that he was considering abdication ('retirement'). Two days later the Regency Bill was passed in Parliament, and on 6 February the Prince of Wales took the oath as Regent.

The domestic and international political climate of 1811 was decidedly precarious. British politics had never fully recovered from William Pitt's resignation as Prime Minister in 1801 over George III's refusal to grant civil rights to his Catholic populations in Britain and Ireland – a resignation which brought to a close seventeen years of relatively stable government. Addington's ministry of 1801–4 won temporary acclaim by concluding the Peace of Amiens with Napoleon's France in 1802 but was beset by divisions and uncertainty, exacerbated by Addington's own agonising indecision and the glaring omission of Pitt himself. War with France was renewed in 1803, and when Addington fell in April 1804, Pitt's hopes for a grand coalition government were frustrated by George III's implacable refusal to sanction the inclusion of Charles James Fox, whom the King regarded as his 'personal enemy' as much now as he had twenty years before, at the time of Fox's Westminster election victory. Pitt thus battled on with a weakened ministry until complex negotiations resulted in a shaky agreement with Addington in January 1805. Yet though he was only forty-five, Pitt had not been well since 1797; he was now terminally ill from alcohol-related afflictions, and died on 23 January 1806. The ensuing Whig administration – which George III was forced to approve, and over the composition of which, as we have seen, the Prince was shocked to find he had little say – staggered on for only a few weeks after the death of Fox in September 1806. Its replacement, an ostensibly Whig government led by Lord Grenville and optimistically labelled 'the Ministry of all the Talents', had an equally tenuous grip on power, and foundered in March 1807. Thereafter the British government – now a Tory administration – was led by the ineffectual and ailing Duke of Portland until his enforced retirement in September 1809, after which George III's choice of Spencer Perceval as Portland's replacement split the Tory party and prompted the resignation of Canning and Castlereagh. To everyone's surprise, Perceval's embattled ministry lasted three years; in 1812, however, he became the first – and, so far, the only – British Prime Minister to be assassinated. There was no indication at the time that his successor Lord Liverpool, a taciturn and private man, would survive in government for fifteen years.

The international situation at the beginning of the Regency appeared equally uncertain. Napoleon's grip on the continent of Europe seemed unshakeable. Nelson's famous naval victory at Trafalgar in 1805 had so far proved a rare British success, and it was not appreciated until long afterwards that it had destroyed all threat of a French invasion of Britain. Trafalgar was followed by a series of crushing military defeats for Prussia, Austria and Russia during 1806–8, culminating in Tsar Alexander I's accommodation with Napoleon at Tilsit in 1809. Austrian attempts to revive the Allied coalition resulted only in a French army parading through the streets of Vienna and a Habsburg marriage for the French Emperor. Moreover, Britain's martial contribution to the continued struggle against Napoleon during this period was less than impressive. In January 1809 a small British army led by General Sir John Moore was forced to evacuate Spain from the port of Corunna, and during a rear-guard action fought against superior French forces the brave and talented general was killed. Months later a British expeditionary force of 40,000 led by the incompetent Lord Chatham was sent across the Channel to occupy Walcheren off the Dutch coast but achieved nothing, at the cost of numerous lives (most lost to sickness rather than battle). As a recent military historian has commented, 'Britain's finest army was allowed to rot in the unhealthy marshes of that notoriously unhealthy island.'[2] Hard on the heels of these ignominies came the Duke of York's dismissal as Commander-in-Chief following public revelations that his mistress, Mary Anne Clarke, had been selling army commissions, and Joseph Sellis's attempted assassination of the Duke of Cumberland. At the time the Regency was established in Britain, the bulk of Wellington's successes in the Iberian peninsula, Napoleon's invasion of Russia and his army's disastrous winter retreat,

Leipzig and Waterloo, were all in the future. In the winter of 1810–11 there were not many who would have put money on a successful outcome for the Allied cause.

Probably not many more would have bet on the longevity of the new Regency. The Prince of Wales, as we have seen, was seriously ill, reputed on more than one occasion to be at death's door, and the succession thereafter lay with his unmarried fifteen-year-old daughter and his disreputable brothers. His father, meanwhile, showed no further signs of recovery, becoming ever less aware of the outside world. By July 1811 George III's death was 'hourly expected', and the King was reported to believe himself already in Heaven – 'having long conversations with Lady Pembroke, Lord Weymouth and Handel'. Six months later, in January 1812, the House of Commons again questioned the King's doctors, and they confidently declared a recovery to be 'highly improbable' and 'all but impossible'. The restrictions on the Regency were accordingly removed, and George was accorded all royal revenues, and the power to dispense titles and offices. At the same time, the King was increasingly shunted into the shadows, and the weekly bulletins on his health were reduced to monthly. He was soon in a 'pitiful' state, by now probably genuinely senile. The new Regent staunchly refused to give credence to Delahoyde and Lucett's alleged 'cure for insanity' – a physical regimen which, before it was revealed as a sham in 1814, was energetically promoted by his more optimistic brothers Kent and Sussex. Among other symptoms, the King was insisting – as he had in 1788 – that the Countess of Pembroke had all along been his real wife. Already virtually blind, in 1817 he became quite deaf as well, 'his last source of impressions from the outside world ... coming to an end'. In November 1819 the Duke of York reported to his brother the Regent that their father was 'greatly emaciated'; two months later he died.[3]

Political instability threatened at home, peril abroad. Nevertheless, George was determined to celebrate his Regency. The poet Thomas Moore perceived the incongruity of the extravagant fête which was the result, but could not help being impressed by it:

> Nothing was ever half so magnificent; it was in *reality* all that they try to imitate in the gorgeous scenery of the theatre; and I really sat for three quarters of an hour in the Prince's room after supper, silently looking at the spectacle, and feeding my eyes with the assemblage of beauty, splendour, and profuse magnificence which it presented.[4]

Three days after the fête the doors of Carlton House were opened to the public, and thousands crowded in to see those fabled interiors. On 25 June alone more than 30,000 visitors tramped through the hall; the Duke of Clarence attempted to regulate the tide from the top of the garden wall.[5] The resulting mayhem and damage convinced George that his London mansion should never be made accessible to his people again, and surely contributed to that marked distaste for public appearances which was a feature of his later years.

The early years of the Regency were, as far as Carlton House was concerned, one long party. As David Cannadine has remarked, the Regent could hardly present himself as the incarnation of family values in the manner of his father, George III; instead, he became the cynosure of a succession of glittering pageants. After the fête of June 1811 there were further celebrations, to mark his accession to full Regency powers in January 1812, Wellington's Spanish victories of 1812–13, Napoleon's defeat at the Battle of Leipzig in 1813, Napoleon's subsequent exile to Elba and final defeat at Wellington's hands at Waterloo, royal birthdays, and even the twice-attempted restoration of the French Bourbons. Any excuse served, it seemed, to spend money on parties and on clothes. The austere ways and rigid teutonic etiquette of his parents' Court were things of the past; in 1812, indeed, his Chief Equerry complained that those invited to the Regent's parties 'were of all ranks and in no respect select', and privately condemned him for breaking down social barriers by consorting with 'low blood blackguards'.[6]

The official image of the new Regent was carefully contrived by Thomas Lawrence's skilful brush. Lawrence had been appointed Principal Portrait-Painter in Ordinary to George III in 1792, having come to public notice two years before with his innovatory and controversial portraits of the actress Elizabeth Farren, later Countess of Derby, and Queen Charlotte. His father's favour and rumours of a liaison with the Princess of Wales – probably unfounded, although Lawrence had it seems been foolish enough to remain alone in a room with the Princess on more than one occasion in 1804 – were enough at first to make the Prince keep his distance. On 24 September 1806, however, during the 'Delicate Investigation' into Caroline's affairs, Lawrence swore an affidavit that while he had indeed been alone with the Princess for sittings, 'I never was with the door locked, bolted or fastened, otherwise than in the common or usual manner.'[7] In 1814, by now convinced of his innocence in this matter, George offered

Lawrence a commission to paint one head-and-shoulders portrait and one full-length of himself; the spectacular results can be seen in the National Portrait Gallery in London. Lawrence magically reduced the Prince's bulk – in the case of the unfinished profile, partly by means of a generous neck-cloth – and transformed him from a self-indulgent spoiled child of fifty-three into a dashing Instrument of Destiny with the Fate of Europe in his hands.

William Hazlitt, writing in *The Champion*, was impressed with the sleight-of-hand of Lawrence's full-length:

> Sir Thomas Lawrence had with the magic of his pencil recreated the Prince Regent as a well-fleshed Adonis of thirty-three; and ... we could not ... but derive a high degree of goodnatured pleasure from imagining to ourselves the transports with which his Royal Highness must have welcomed this improved version of himself. It goes beyond all that wigs, powders and pomatums have been able to effect for the last twenty years. Talk of the feelings of Bonaparte as he re-entered the Tuileries – psha! nonsense! Think of the feelings of the Regent when he saw himself in this picture!

The Times, however, was not so amused by Lawrence's skilful flattery, and suggested that the artist should 'add to the merit of his beautiful portraits that essential one of resemblance':

> In general his portraits have scarcely a shadow of likeness; witness his last portrait of the Prince Regent, who was represented, not as a staid and manly Prince of fifty-five, but as a mere foppish youth of twenty-five, who had no cares but of wearing his regimentals sprucely.[8]

George himself was delighted, however, and from 1815 Lawrence was repeatedly called upon to paint him in a variety of elaborate costumes and heroic poses. Unsurprisingly, George's favourites were those in which he was most luxuriantly costumed: the full-length portrait in Garter robes of 1818, and the Coronation version of 1821, in which he wore not only his cherished Order of the Garter but also the Order of the Bath, the Guelphic Order and the Collar of the Golden Fleece. In Lawrence's thickly-painted confections, the man inside these robes and orders retained the trim calves and visible jawline of his youth.[9] Increasingly, of course, these silky images were quite divorced from reality, a discrepancy Lawrence himself was happy to acknowledge in private. In 1825 he confided that 'The Countenance of His Most Christian Majesty', while of 'much Character ... presents some difficulty from its varying action.' Nevertheless, he concluded, 'I have little doubt of finally succeeding.'[10]

Lawrence certainly benefited from George's patronage during the nine years of the Regency. Knighted in 1815, in 1817 he set out for the Continent to complete his series of portraits of European statesmen begun in 1814, and on his return in 1820 was made President of the Royal Academy – Benjamin West having died nine days before. A year later, he was the only artist permitted to walk in the new King's Coronation procession of 1821.[11] By this time George had long been on cordially familiar terms with him; in July 1816, for example, as Farington noted, 'While the Prince Regent was with Sir Thomas, He did not keep him *standing*, but desired Him to sit down which of course He did, and they continued to converse together.' It was, Farington added, 'the same at Carlton House on the day of the Grand Ball ... Sir T. Lawrence was with Him at 3 o'clock that afternoon, and remained with Him an Hour and a half in conversation, chiefly about pictures and the arrangement of them.'[12] Lawrence was also paid handsomely – and, perhaps uniquely, on time – for his services. When he died in 1830 he had received a total of £25,417 10s. from the Privy Purse for his portraits; only £315 was outstanding.[13] For a man who had faced ruin at the beginning of his career – on 18 March 1801 Farington reported his circumstances to be 'so notoriously bad ... [that] it must end in Bankruptcy'[14] – this was an impressive achievement.

His disappointed rival Benjamin Haydon was predictably scathing about the flattery of Lawrence's compositions and his technical virtuosity. Tempting fate, he snorted that Lawrence would 'not rank high in the opinion of posterity' (adding that 'He had smiled so often and so long, that at last his smile had the appearance of being set in enamel'), and pronounced his overwhelming election to the Presidency of the Royal Academy 'a blow to High Art from which it has never recovered'. How wrong he was: ten years later Lawrence's body lay in state at the Royal Academy prior to his funeral in St Paul's Cathedral, a national event observed with more solemnity than George IV's funeral six months afterwards, while an immediate retrospective exhibition of his work was enthusiastically supported by George himself, who lent thirty-one pictures – twenty-one of them from the Waterloo Chamber at Windsor. Sir William Knighton's comment to the King after Lawrence's death – 'you have no substitute for him' – was incontrovertible.[15]

In his portraits of the Regent, Lawrence could scarcely avoid the royal penchant for uniforms. While George never actually took advantage of his Regency powers and freedoms to go anywhere near his serving armies abroad, his mania for militaria was undiminished, and his correspondence with his brothers was as full as ever of gossip about the latest styles and colours. The cavalry 'have *all* got shoulder straps as broad as my hand resembling the old French contre epaulettes', the Duke of Cumberland found time to inform him on the eve of the momentous Battle of Leipzig in 1813.[16] A few months later Cumberland wrote from Hanover:

> I send by messenger a Hannoverian sword knot which I am proud in being the first to offer you. I also send you the pattern of the sash which you directed me to get made after the pattern of the Prussian one. There was no time to get one completed but this is a sample of the web. When finished it will cost but 25 dollars or 5 £ English, that is to say to go twice round the body with crépines. Those for the General Officers should have bouillons to them and they will cost 5 dollars more which will make a General Officer's sash cost about 6 louis ... It is exactly as the Prussians wear them in black and silver, and the Russians in black orange and silver.[17]

George remained all his life transfixed by the smallest detail of military uniform, from epaulettes to buttons (a tongue-in-cheek cartoon of the summer of 1830 imagined the button-making trade 'plunged into distress by George IV's death'[18]). 'Let us bury in oblivion', Robert Huish pleaded in 1831, 'those numerous and important orders issuing from the Horse-Guards, to determine the position of a button, the adjustment of a sash, or the colour of a facing.' At the Regent's Court, he opined, 'the question of the superiority in point of elegance of the buckle over the shoe-tie was argued with greater gravity, than the expediency of the battle of Algiers, or the consequences of the Treaty of Vienna.'[19]

Even Princess Charlotte observed that her father was only in 'the most perfect good humour' in her presence when 'being fully occupied with discanting and discouraging upon the merits and demerits of such and such a uniform, the cut of such a coat, cape, sleeve, small clothes etc.'[20] In 1817 George announced that henceforth 'all his state and household officers' were 'to wear costly dresses of home fabrication ... to be made in three classes of uniforms, according to the respective ranks of these officers'.[21] Ostensibly the purpose of this measure was to promote the British textile industry at a time of economic downturn. In truth, however, George cared little for the long-term prospects of his country's manufacturers (as evidenced by his passion for French furniture and porcelain), and the order was almost certainly primarily designed so that he could exercise his talents as a military couturier.

As well as dressing himself and others in a variety of uniforms, George also loved to collect the insignia of military and chivalric orders. As Stephen Patterson has written, 'George IV probably received more foreign Orders than any other sovereign before him and he lavished much money on the stars and badges that he could wear.' The self-congratulatory aftermath of the Napoleonic Wars, in which every Allied ruler and government felt obliged to contribute to the bewildering merry-go-round of awards, was George's idea of heaven. In 1814, for example, Louis XVIII made him a member of the newly refounded Order of the Holy Spirit. The uniform of the Order, as detailed by the *Gentleman's Magazine* of February 1815, sounds to be just what he most liked:

> The mantle all around the border is embossed with gold, representing the emblems of war and the H surrounded by the Imperial crowns. It measures at the bottom of the mantle from one end to the other twenty-four feet. The tippet which goes underneath the mantle is of green sarcenet; the figures on it are exactly the same as on the mantle but on a much smaller scale. The collar that goes over the tippet is of beautiful French lace, valued at twelve hundred pounds. The collar or necklace is composed of diamonds, rubies, emeralds, etc and is very beautiful. The hat is made of black velvet, embossed with gold round it with a beautiful ostrich feather at the top. The breeches are of white sarcenet and made in the antique way, embroidered with silver, and a pair of hose of white silk. The shoes are made of silver tissue with roses of white satin, there are two swords, very beautiful, with golden hilts.[22]

The superb collar passed ignominiously to the royal jewellers Rundell, Bridge and Rundell in 1830 in settlement of the late King's enormous outstanding debts.

Louis XVIII was by no means the only Allied sovereign to bestow decorations like confetti. In 1815 George was appointed a member of Portugal's Order of the Tower and Sword, and in 1818 became only the twentieth recipient of the new Grand Cross of the Military Order of William, invested by William I of Halle. For himself, George revived Ireland's Most Illustrious Order of St Patrick, which had been terminated by his father in 1794. The sash badge and star he devised for his own use were made by Rundell, Bridge and Rundell from no fewer than 394 stones, most of which had formerly belonged to Queen Charlotte. The sash badge alone comprised a double order of diamonds, surmounted by a diamond scroll and a diamond crown with a ruby cushion.[23]

George's lust for new Orders and their insignia never dimmed. As late as 1828, when he was somewhat inexplicably appointed to the Danish Order of the Elephant (he was the first non-Danish monarch to be so honoured), he immediately commissioned an expensive version of the badge from his jewellers. On his death, he possessed no fewer than fifty-five bejewelled badges for the Order of the Garter. And while the statutes of the Order laid down that the Garter collar should remain unadorned, this did not prevent him loading his already heavily-weighted costume with other items of insignia – the garter itself, a sash badge (the 'Lesser George'), a pendant badge (the 'Greater George'), a star, and sundry other jewels.[24]

His Regency also allowed George to satisfy his long-frustrated yearning for high military rank. Possibly his first act as Regent was to promote himself Field Marshal: a delicious revenge for all the years during which, at his father's insistence, he had remained a mere Honorary Colonel. (His second act in this vein was to reinstate his brother as Commander-in-Chief – a rehabilitation which, *The Examiner* candidly claimed on 2 June 1811, was widely 'felt as a blow given to all the better reason and feeling of the nation'.) As the new Regent made his entrance, the three thousand guests at the fête held on 19 June 1811 were able to enjoy his brand-new Field Marshal's uniform, every inch of which was encrusted with gold embroidery. He wore another version of this peacock's plumage to visit Louis XVIII at Stanmore in Middlesex in April 1814, following which these two overdressed whales made one of the most laughable State Entrances London has ever seen. As Peter Pindar wrote, the crowds who turned out to welcome 'France's hope and Britain's heir' saw only 'Two round, tunbellied, thriving rakes,/Like oxen fed on linseed cakes.'[25]

Rather insensitively, George wore yet another sumptuous Field Marshal's uniform at the fête he held on 21 July 1814, supposedly in honour of a genuine Field Marshal, the Duke of Wellington. But such lapses of taste were habitual. His conduct at this party would have convinced an ignorant onlooker than he, not the Duke, had defeated the French in battle, while a cynical observer might have supposed that he had stage-managed the entire visit of the Allied sovereigns and leaders as a spectacle designed to provide him with an excuse to parade himself in one outrageously bizarre uniform after another. He who had never heard a shot fired in anger was apparently oblivious of the irony inherent in arraying himself in splendid regimentals of blue and gold to greet Tsar Alexander I, who had led his Russians into battle. The sight of the Regent's military finery seems to have momentarily robbed the Tsar of his sang-froid: introduced to Lady Hertford, he murmured merely that she looked 'mighty old', and moved swiftly on.

George's boyish love of opulent uniforms in no way diminished as his girth increased. When he visited Scotland in 1822, David Wilkie was surprised to see him alighting at Leith clad in yet another largely imaginary Field Marshal's uniform, complete with the green ribbon of the Order of the Thistle. Seven years later, George sat to Wilkie for what was to be the last full-length oil of him, dressed in the costume of newly-devised Royal Stewart tartan worn for his Edinburgh levée. As late as 1829, John Lockhart wrote to Walter Scott that 'The King is mad enough to be dreaming of dressing the guards now and afterwards all the Infantry in blue' – charitably attributing this quirk to 'the Duke of Cumberland's nonsense'.[26] Such interference in matters of dress did not go down too well with the army. In April 1813 Sir George Beaumont complained to Joseph Farington 'of the great expense Officers were subject to for dress &c which was changed as their whims varied. The Officers and Men also were made ridiculous by it, and on service could scarcely be distinguished from the French troops.' Even Wellington, he added ominously, 'had objected to it'. Huish later suggested that 'The different uniforms of the army' and the 'trappings and fopperies of the German soldiery' having become 'the peculiar objects of the gracious attention of the Prince Regent and our brothers of York and Cumberland', the new dress the princes had devised – 'setting aside the expense to the nation' – had made the British army 'the laughing-stock of the public'.[27]

Nor did the Prince Regent ever lose his love of staging mock battles. A 'sea battle' arranged at Portsmouth on 25 June 1814 for the entertainment of his Allied guests disgusted William Cobbett, who despised the 'shows of the most expensive decoration' and 'all the parade capable of being furnished by [the Regent's] extravagant government'.[28] This grand set-piece was followed by a 'Battle of Trafalgar' conducted in miniature on Hyde Park's Serpentine Lake on 1 August. Such events were manna to the caricaturists, of course. As the drama of Napoleon's final defeat was being played out in France and the Low Countries, the cartoonists depicted George playing in his Serpentine 'washing tub'.[29]

Weaponry was yet another object of George's collecting mania. By 1814 the Carlton House Armoury, tantalisingly depicted in a water-colour of that year by A.C. Pugin, contained hundreds of daggers, arrows and swords, many of which had formerly been owned by celebrated monarchs; Chinese ceremonial staves brought back in 1804; whole suits of Indian and Persian armour; a Japanese helmet; a Turkish shield; an oriental cannon; the armour of a seventeenth-century English pikeman; 'gold-embroidered horse furniture' presented by the Dey of Algiers to the Prince Regent on 25 February 1811; armour and clothes worn by the legendary Tipu Sultan, killed when Seringapatam was taken by forces under Sir Arthur Wellesley in 1799; and a Congreve fire rocket of 1808.[30] The noted antiquary Samuel Rush Meyrick looked after this wonderful hodge-podge, and was later called upon to arrange the Royal Collection at Windsor. His *A Critical Inquiry into ancient Armour ...,* published in 1824 and dedicated to the King, was almost the first book on the subject, and long remained the classic work.[31]

No blood was drawn with these fearsome weapons, of course: George preferred his battles executed in paint or plaster. In the state rooms of Carlton House were hung two pairs of portraits of great naval heroes, one pair from the century just past – Admiral Keppel and Admiral Rodney – and one from the present – Admiral Nelson and Admiral St Vincent. (Despite this professed enthusiasm, he was singularly uninterested in his brother William's much less heroic naval career.) George also acquired numerous portraits and busts of British military heroes. By 1814 the Marquess of Granby, hero of the Seven Years' War, was represented at Carlton House by two portraits (by Joshua Reynolds and David Morier), and one specially-commissioned bust (by Joseph Nollekens).[32] To further indulge his military fantasies, George even had Walsh Porter erect a 'Military Tent Room' at Carlton House. Devised to give the illusion of a tent on the battlefield, this room was not of course hung with plain tent canvas, but fitted up with pale blue-and-white striped sarsenet and quilted chintz. George, always a schoolboy at heart, even had a bed made in the shape of a tent.[33]

The colourful image of himself and his Regency which George tried so hard to create was far removed from the reality. In 1811 he was no arbiter of Europe's destiny, as he fantasised, but presented a ludicrous public spectacle as a fat middle-aged roué. A twisted ankle ignominiously incurred while teaching Princess Charlotte to do the Highland fling in November 1811 was a gift to the satirists[34] (some slyly suggested the injury was actually the result of an assault by Lord Yarmouth, the Regent having been over-attentive to his wife – an all-too-believable calumny). The Grand Duchess Catherine of Oldenburg, visiting London in March 1814 in advance of her brother the Tsar, felt constrained to warn Alexander that the Prince was 'a man visibly used up by dissipation and rather disgusting', that 'His much boasted affability is the most licentious, I may say obscene, strain I have ever listened to', and that he had 'a brazen way of looking where eyes should not go'.[35]

The journalist Leigh Hunt dared to put into words what many thought of the Prince at the beginning of his Regency. Writing in *The Examiner* of 22 March 1812, he described him as a 'corpulent man of fifty', and accused him unambiguously of being

a violator of his word, a libertine over head and ears in debt and disgrace, a despiser of domestic ties, the companion of gamblers and demireps, a man who has just closed half a century without one single claim on the gratitude of his country or the respect of posterity.

Hunt was charged with 'intent to traduce and vilify' the Regent, tried and found guilty, imprisoned for two years, and fined £500. He quickly became a popular martyr, and was visited in prison by a succession of celebrities, led by the poets Moore, Byron and Shelley. Thomas Moore, once enchanted by George's warmth and familiarity (and the prospect of a snug sinecure), had by 1813 turned sharply against him.[36] To Percy Shelley, the Regent was 'that infernal wretch' and 'crowned coward', and Leigh Hunt had been indicted merely 'for not thinking [him] slender and laudable'. Carlton House was, he declaimed, an Augean stable – 'with filth which no second Hercules could cleanse'. If murderers, he daringly suggested, ended on the gallows, 'how much more does a Prince whose conduct destroys millions deserve it?'[37] In similar vein, John Keats noted that he could 'pass a summer very quietly without caring about Fat Louis, fat Regent or the Duke of Wellington'.[38] By this time Byron, too, was disgusted with the Prince Regent. His famous lines on Princess Charlotte, printed anonymously in 1812 (when George attributed them to Moore), were republished under his name two years later:

> Weep, daughter of a royal line,
> A sire's disgrace, a realm's decay;
> Ah, happy! if each tear of thine
> Could wash a father's fault away!
>
> Weep – for thy tears are virtue's tears –
> Auspicious to these suffering isles;
> And be each drop in future years
> Repaid thee by thy people's smiles.

Byron later listed the symbols of historic excess with whom the Regent had been compared: 'Nero, Apicius, Epicurus, Caligula, Heliogabulus, Henry the VIII' – plus, rather unfairly, King George III.[39]

Some of the great literary figures of the Regency previously assumed to have been grateful recipients of George's patronage were, in truth, more in sympathy with Byron and Moore. Jane Austen, for example, is frequently cited by apologists who depict the Regent as her principal patron. His support was enlisted only as a matter of form, however, and the prospect of meeting him in person was viewed by Miss Austen with horror. In 1815 she was told by one of the royal doctors, then treating her brother Henry, that the Prince was 'a great admirer of her novels' and that 'he read them often, and kept a set of them in every one of his residences'. She was subsequently invited for a private tour of Carlton House, during which George's librarian, the Revd James Stanier Clarke, told her he had been directed 'to pay her every possible attention', and commissioned by the Prince to say that she was 'at liberty to dedicate' any forthcoming novel to him. Miss Austen was shrewd enough to appreciate the possible commercial value of this compliment, and to secure confirmation of it in writing. In doing do, Mr Clarke made a point of reiterating that 'The Regent has read and admired all your publications'. Miss Austen duly provided a dedication for her new three-volume novel *Emma*, then printing, and instructed her publisher, John Murray, to send a bound set to the Prince, under cover to Clarke, 'three days before the work is generally public'. However, Murray embellished his author's terse 'Dedicated by permission to HRH The Prince Regent' with 'most respectfully', and cast her as the Prince's 'dutiful and obedient humble servant'. Whether or not the Regent indeed read *Emma*, and whether or not the dedication had any direct effect on sales, the novel was a commercial success and its print run – 2,000 copies – was the largest yet for an Austen novel.[40]

So far, everyone had played his or her expected part. But Mr Clarke could not resist the role of literary advisor, and made helpful suggestions as to characters Miss Austen might 'delineate' in future works. First it was 'an English clergyman ... of the present day, fond of and entirely engaged in literature', then an English clergyman at sea (possibly 'the friend of some distinguished Naval character about the Court'); and then, at the time of Princess Charlotte's marriage to Prince Leopold (Clarke had been appointed the Prince's chaplain and private English secretary), he suggested that 'an historical romance illustrative of the august House of Cobourg would just now be very interesting', to be dedicated to Prince Leopold. Miss Austen firmly rebuffed Mr Clarke: she could 'no more write a romance than an epic poem', she told him, and 'if it were indispensable ... never to relax into laughing', whether at herself or other people, she was sure she would be hung before she had completed the first chapter. Instead, she privately satirised Mr Clarke's presumptuous plots in her sketch, 'Plan of a Novel'.[41]

In truth, although Jane Austen was happy enough if the Prince Regent's name sold more of her books, she had no interest in him as a person. In June 1811 she had bought mourning clothes in expectation of George III's imminent death rather than celebrate the new Regency, and two years later had written of her disgust at the way George was treating his wife:

> I suppose all the World is sitting in Judgement upon the Princess of Wales's Letter [published in the *Morning Chronicle*]. Poor woman, I shall support her as long as I can, because she is a Woman, and because I hate her Husband – but I can hardly forgive her for calling herself 'attached and affectionate' to a Man whom she must detest ... but if I must give up the Princess, I am resolved at least always to think that she would have been respectable, if the Prince had behaved tolerably by her at first.[42]

This leaves no doubt as to Jane Austen's low opinion of the Regent, and thus suggests that her dedication of *Emma* to him in 1816 was rather hypocritical. Roger Sales, however, interprets it as 'an ironic statement' given added substance by the fact that the novel 'celebrates as well as repudiates Regency values'. He also suggests that a pointed allegory of the Prince's behaviour is implicit in the plot of *Mansfield Park* (1814), in which the character Tom Bertram runs up huge debts, gambles, eats and drinks heavily, and is 'only interested in the ceremonial and theatrical aspects of government'.[43] It is worth nothing that Victorian editions of *Emma* were published without the dedication to the Prince: the author's reputation was clearly higher than that of her royal 'patron'.

For the numismatist, antiquary and arbiter of taste Richard Payne Knight, writing in 1814 in the *Edinburgh Review* – an influential periodical 'read by everyone of cultural pretensions' – the Regent's excesses and fitful patronage merely ensured that 'all the quiet elegance of liberal art, and intellectual gratification, sink neglected and expire' in a country in which 'Even the monster Nero, had he occupied a private station of middle rank ... would have been neither more nor less than a well-bred, well-drest, accomplished, and selfish voluptuary.'[44] Most famously, to man of letters Charles Lamb, George was little more than 'the Prince of Whales':

> Not a fatter fish than he
> Flounders round the polar sea.
> See his blubbers – at his gills
> What a world of drink he swills ...
> Every fish of generous kind
> Scuds aside or shrinks behind;
> But about his presence keep
> All the monsters of the deep ...
> Name or title what has he?
> Is he Regent of the sea?
> By his bulk and by his size,
> By his oily qualities,
> This (or else my eyesight fails),
> This should be the Prince of Whales.

Lamb's memorable lines formed the basis of many a Regency satire, most notably George Cruikshank's print *The Prince of Whales or the Fisherman at Anchor*, in which the whale–Regent spouts the Dew of Favour upon the Tory ministry of one of Lamb's principal 'monsters of the deep', the Prime Minister, Spencer Perceval.[45]

Literary figures were not the only ones disseminating unfavourable opinions of the Prince Regent. In 1806 Joseph Farington had noted that 'The Prince is not popular' and that toasts were being given to 'the Prince of Wales *for ever*' (implying a wish that he should never succeed to the throne). The following year he noted that during an ill-tempered tour George made of Gloucestershire, 'wherever He went the people were dissatisfied with his behaviour'. As this dissatisfaction spread to all levels of society, even those close to Carlton House beginning to believe the most outrageous rumours. In June 1816 Lady Holland confidently informed her friend Mrs Creevey that the Regent 'is to be summoned they say upon a charge of high treason, which if made out, is to pave the way to the Throne for Princess Sophia of Gloucester'.[46] Three years later Lord Folkestone told Creevey of a rumour that the crown jewels were being taken by the Prince to Brighton, so that 'they might find their way out of the Pavilion by some back stairs, to France for instance'. Moreover, Lord Folkestone confided,

> There is a report that your old friend Prinny is gone mad, that he is so haunted by the apparition of seeing his Wife that he is under the constant delusion of supposing her by his side; the only thing that gives him pleasure and satisfaction is tumbling over (not Lady Hertford or Lady Conyngham) but jewels and trinkets.[47]

Rumour begat protest. On 15 November 1816 'Orator' Henry Hunt, followed by a large crowd who had gathered to hear him speak at Spa Fields, was rebuffed at the gates of Carlton House when he attempted to hand in a petition for reform. On 28 January 1817 George's carriage was pelted and its windows smashed while he was on his way to open Parliament; one eye-witness 'heard the Prince Regent say that He felt a bullet or stone pass before His face'. Even a sympathetic observer like John Croker was forced to admit that 'it could not be denied even by the Regent's best friends that he had seriously mismanaged his affairs', and in the aftermath of this 'assassination attempt' George was reported to be considering placatory gestures regarding his expenditure. As we have seen, however, nothing came of his vague promises to retrench,[48] and two years later his approving message to the magistrates responsible for the Peterloo Massacre merely enhanced his growing reputation as a reactionary.

Nor were George's brothers much of an asset. The Duke of York was still tainted by the sale of army commissions scandal of 1809 and the Duke of Kent had been publicly labelled an incompetent martinet. And in 1810 had occurred the incident involving the Duke of Cumberland and his valet. The subsequent enquiry cleared the duke, but the sitgma of the episode clung to him for the rest of his life.[49]

The notorious Carlton House fêtes provided ample evidence of George's extravagance. The fittings alone for the party of 19 June 1811 cost £2,585. The two-hundred-foot-long supper table was crammed with silver-gilt plate, much of it from the 'Grand Service' recently ordered from Rundell, Bridge and Rundell at a cost of £61,340 1s. 3d.[50] The very table decorations were outrageous and expensive. 'Along the centre of the table', reported the *Morning Chronicle*, 'a canal of pure water continued flowing from a silver fountain, beautifully constructed at the head of the table. Its faintly waving, artificial banks were covered with green moss and aquatic flowers' between which 'gold and silver fish ... were seen to swim and sport through the bubbling current, which ... formed a cascade at the outlet'. (Princess Charlotte, barred from attending the event, later commented that 'the goldfishes [had] acted the most conspicuous part at the great fête' – which, she added, had been put off so often because of her father's ill-health that 'all the poultry died and were sold off at half price', an action which constituted the sole public benefit of the occasion.) The cascade was fed by 'a circular lake surrounded with architectural decorations, and small vases, burning perfumes, which stood under the arches of the colonnade around the lake.' George himself, wearing 'a scarlet coat, most richly and elegantly ornamented in a very novel style with gold lace, with a brilliant star of the Order of the Garter', was seated 'on a throne of crimson velvet, trimmed with gold'. Behind his chair was 'a sideboard, covered with gold vases, urns, massy salvers &c; the whole surmounted by a Spanish urn, taken from on board the "Invincible Armada".'[51]

Unsurprisingly, Shelley's reaction to the party was not as adulatory as that of the *Morning Chronicle*. Reporting popular gossip 'that this entertainment will cost £120,000', he observed 'How admirably this growing spirit of ludicrous magnificence tallies with the disgusting splendours of the stage of the Roman Empire which preceded its destruction!'[52]

Small wonder that by August 1812 over £20,000, it was estimated, had been spent during the past fives years on royal parties alone. For the 1814 fête, supposedly honouring Wellington's campaign victories and the Bourbon restoration, Nash designed a special rotunda 120 feet in diameter. This was hung with muslin draperies and curtains supplied by Tatham, Bailey and Sanders, lit by twelve glass chandeliers and punctuated in the centre by a floral temple for the orchestra incorporating 1,448 yards of artificial flowers. For St James's Park, Nash also designed a bridge and pagoda, with its own internal firework display. This caught fire and fell into the water, killing two bystanders.[53]

As we have seen, most commentators followed Byron's example and turned for inspiration to the more appetising image of the Prince Regent's daughter. But her death in childbirth in 1817 necessitated a refocusing of expectation and a reconsideration of the slender merits of the Prince Regent and his brothers. By the time of George III's death, the sentiments expressed by the *Black Book* of 1820, which poured scorn on the discredited pomp of Carlton House as mere 'Pageantry and show, the parade of crowns and coronets, of gold keys, sticks, white wands and black rods; of ermine and lawn, maces and wigs', were those of many more than a mere handful of radicals.[54]

13

George and Napoleon

The dinner, you know, was in gay celebration
Of *my* brilliant triumph and H–nt's condemnation.
Thomas Moore, *The Twopenny Post-Bag*, Letter III

TWO GOVERNING PASSIONS of George's life, as we have seen, were his love of France, and of militaria. When combined with his own ebullient ego and Lawrence's carefully-crafted image of a heroic Patriot Prince bestriding the European stage like a Colossus, it was perhaps inevitable they should lead George to measure himself against the one man who, during his lifetime, really did dominate Europe: Napoleon Bonaparte.

From the earliest years of the century, when Napoleon became First Consul for Life, George was constantly trying to emulate if not surpass his example, and once he had the financial resources of full Regency powers behind him he announced that henceforth he and his Court would 'quite eclipse Napoleon'.[1] By the time of the Emperor's fall, this perhaps understandable aim had metamorphosed into blatant self-promotion. Napoleon's surrender in April 1814 prompted George to announce to his mother: 'I have fulfilled and done my duty at least' – a piece of breathtaking self-delusion offset by the pathetic suggestion that 'perhaps I may be vain enough to hope that you may feel a little proud of your son'.[2] For the rest of his life George persisted in the fiction that he alone had been Napoleon's nemesis, the happy illusion of his later years that he had actually played a key role at Waterloo fuelled by his consumption of laudanum and alcohol.

George's propensity for seeing himself as the nation's bulwark against Napoleon was not completely ridiculous. Britain had, after all, shouldered the financial burden of the alliance against the French, and had on more than one occasion found herself fighting alone. Nor, despite the obvious disparities in background and upbringing, were the two rulers wholly different in temperament. Both liked to build, and to impress with extravagance. Both were energetic and perceptive patrons of art. More significantly, both recognised the importance of art and architecture in the creation of a public image of sovereignty which did not necessarily mirror reality. Thomas Lawrence was to George what Jacques-Louis David was to Napoleon: both artists fashioned images of their patrons, explicitly designed for public consumption, in which actuality was suspended in favour of an enduring if fictional iconography. Interestingly, both sovereigns were also fascinated by the lure of myth. Napoleon, like George, was a great admirer of the 'poems of Ossian' – revered as a relic of a noble Celtic past when first published in the 1760s, doubted by Dr Johnson, and later exposed as a hoax. For both men, the appeal of 'heritage', whether real or invented, was compelling. Where Napoleon sought to legitimise his rule and erase the traditions of the Bourbons, George's aim was to recast the traditions of his forebears in the context of an imaginary pan-British pageant.

To George, what we now term the Napoleonic Wars were not really about nations or systems of government, but about great men – principally, about himself and Napoleon. Frustrated by his father's refusal to let him serve with the army in any real capacity, George's service was of a different kind. He celebrated Wellington's victory at Vitoria in 1813 by arranging a gourmand's breakfast with Lord Yarmouth. He ordered a 'brilliant Fête', as we have seen, to celebrate first the illusory victory of 1814 and then the final victory of Waterloo, while preferring to receive Joseph Bonaparte's dress sword from the Duke of Wellington rather than meet Napoleon or any of his relatives face to face.[3] To outshine Napoleon's Paris, Nash was directed to build the Regent's Park terraces. And rather than visit his troops abroad, George satisfied himself with brave speeches of defiance delivered from Carlton House.

'A new era has arrived', George declared to his brother York on his assumption of full Regency powers in February 1812:

> I cannot but reflect with satisfaction on the events which have distinguished the short period of my restricted Regency. Instead of suffering in the loss of her possessions by the gigantic force which has been

employed against them, Great Britain has added most important acquisitions to her Empire [and] the national faith has been preserved inviolate towards our allies ... I have no predilections to indulge, no resentments to gratify, no objects to attain but such as are common to the whole Empire. If such is the leading principle of my conduct, and I can appeal to the past as evidence of what the future will be, I flatter myself I shall meet with the support of Parliament and of a candid and enlightened nation.[4]

Genuine commanders such as Wellington and even the Duke of York must have been alarmed by George's proud prophesies that he would soon be directing the armies in the Peninsula. Thankfully, this vainglorious flight of fancy was soon forgotten by all concerned.

Although as already noted George did not, like so many of his countrymen, make his way to occupied Paris, but contented himself with accompanying Louis XVIII to Dover, in the aftermath of Napoleon's abdication in April 1814 he convinced himself that he had been the inspiration behind the victorious coalition, a conviction which reached its climax with his invitation to the Allied leaders to visit London. This gesture was a stroke of genius: whatever the Continental monarchs might think of her Regent, they were inescapably obliged to Britain both financially and militarily. However, this wily attempt to write himself into history backfired when the principal guest, Tsar Alexander I, proved more popular with the crowds than George himself.

George's reaction to either triumph or disaster was equally overwrought. Informed of Wellington's victory at Waterloo, he allegedly had a fit of hysterics and resorted to one of his accustomed props – a beaker of brandy. Nelson's victory at Trafalgar and subsequent death had prompted an even more melodramatic display: by all accounts, he was overwhelmed with grief. George III, presumably aware of the excesses his eldest son was capable of, refused to let him act as chief mourner at Nelson's funeral, but the Prince attended in a private capacity. His profound display of 'grief' did not, however, prevent him from persistently ignoring Nelson's wish that a government pension might be provided for Lady Hamilton, and he also became conveniently deaf to stories of the dead hero's real opinion of himself. (Nelson had unambiguously labelled him 'an unprincipled liar' and 'a false lying scoundrel' who consorted 'only [with] people of *notorious ill fame*'; he had especially warned Lady Hamilton not to let herself become 'a whore to the rascal'.[5])

By the time of the Regency George was probably, in truth, no longer eager to serve at the front. Instead, as we have seen, he fought battles on canvas. Denis Dighton's graphic interpretation of 1816 of *The Battle of Orthez*, however, he found too blood-curdling for his tender sensibilities, and only three weeks after its purchase it was sent to the new Marquess of Anglesey, who as Lord Uxbridge had lost a leg at Waterloo. George did, however, keep Dighton's two Waterloo pictures of 1816, *The Charge of the Second Brigade of Cavalry* and *The General Advance of the British Lines*, which the artist, newly-appointed Military Painter to the Prince Regent, had begun to plan on the battlefield itself only days after Wellington's victory.[6] More than twenty years after the event, David Wilkie's depiction of *The Defence of Saragossa* of 1827–8 provided George with a comfortable expression of his solidarity with Spain's struggle for independence against Napoleonic France, and in 1829 he also bought three more of Wilkie's depictions of the war in Spain: *The Spanish Posada* and the rather more cloyingly romantic sequence *The Guerrilla's Departure* and *The Guerrilla's Return*.

George's appropriation of British victories went beyond merely hanging his walls with heroic battle scenes. In the Throne Room at St James's Palace, George Jones's grand depictions of Vitoria and Waterloo were hung either side of a Lawrence full-length of George, not Wellington. The implication was unavoidable. In the ante-room hung Turner's *Battle of Trafalgar* (commissioned in 1823), balancing Philip de Loutherbourg's *Action of the First of June* of 1797. In 1828 George ordered busts of Wellington, victor of Waterloo, and Castlereagh, architect of the Congress of Vienna, from Francis Chantrey; both were destined for prominent positions at Windsor Castle, planned as the apotheosis of George the Great. Nor were ancient battles neglected: George was happy to associate himself with any British hero who had successfully resisted the French. The portraits of Peter Stroehling, appointed Historical Painter to the King in 1810, were particularly audacious in this respect. Stroehling's first full-length portrait of the Regent, painted in 1811 (and inexplicably lost after a general exodus of pictures to the Royal Lodge in 1823), cast him somewhat improbably as the Black Prince, victor of Crécy and Poitiers (his sitter had even provided Stroehling with a drawing of the Black Prince to help him along). Stroehling's second, delivered in 1813, depicted the Regent stuffed into a Hussar uniform, mounted on a grey. They were perfect expressions of George's wish-fulfilment.[7]

This identification with the Black Prince and his father Edward III grew in intensity as time went on. In George's febrile imagination, Waterloo was his Poitiers, and he pictured himself as the trim hero painted by Thomas Lawrence in 1815, leading his nation's army against the French. His preoccupation with the Order of the Garter, whose star bedecks almost every room at Windsor Castle, was a logical extension of this fantasy, since the Order had been founded by Edward III at Windsor in 1348. In this complicated conflation of imagery he had Wyatville design St George's Hall at Windsor Castle as the backdrop to a Plantagenet pageant, and at the same time add a 'Waterloo Chamber' filled with portraits of kings, statesmen and generals. In the iconography of Windsor, Napoleon simply became a more recent manifestation of Edward's French foes of the Hundred Years' War.

The contents of the Waterloo Chamber had in fact already been prefigured on a smaller scale. From 1801, when he was appointed Enamel Painter to the Prince of Wales, Henry Bone had been required to churn out numerous miniature copies in enamel of paintings of great military heroes, and these George kept in his Private Bedroom at Carlton House. Following the conclusion of peace in 1815, George resolved to replicate this collection on a far more heroic scale and to provide for it a setting the architectural equivalent of the Sun King's bedroom at Versailles: the actual and symbolic epicentre not just of the building but also of the kingdom.

As reported to Parliament, the excuse for the Waterloo Chamber was to house a series of portraits of the great and the good who, in George's opinion, had been instrumental in freeing Europe from Napoleon's tyranny. It was no particular surprise that the bulk of the planned series was entrusted to his favourite portraitist, Thomas Lawrence. Having been knighted for this purpose in 1815, between 1818 and 1820 Lawrence toured Europe sketching and painting kings, ministers and generals. In Vienna he was treated as the Regent's official envoy; in Rome, where he delighted in the nickname of 'Il Tiziano Inglese', he was received by the Pope and given a sumptuous suite of rooms in the Palazzo del Quirinale.[8]

The portraits Lawrence produced were undoubtedly impressive. While he successfully conveyed the inner strength and calm of military leaders such as General Blücher (whose portrait was one of those painted during the false peace of 1814 and exhibited at the Royal Academy in 1815), he was also able to endow even the most homely and uninspiring individuals with a heroic grace or inspiring majesty. As

Van Dyck had in painting Charles I's family and courtiers, Lawrence avoided where possible the depiction of physical blemishes and disfigurements. The nervous frigidity of Lord Castlereagh, British Foreign Secretary and architect of the Treaty of Vienna (who, the victim of overwork and a sexual scandal, committed suicide long before the Chamber's completion), was transformed by Lawrence into assurance and even warmth, while flatteringly slender proportions and a windswept background metamorphosed such ungainly figures as Archduke Charles of Austria and George's brother, the balding Duke of York, into Olympian figures. Curiously, the only protagonist whose likeness was not cast in a suitably heroic mould was the often-overlooked figure of the British Prime Minister at the time of Waterloo. In Lawrence's Windsor canvas, Lord Liverpool's rather frog-like face benefits little from artistic licence, while the Rembrandt-like sombreness of his background is in marked contrast to the vaulted interiors or ravaged landscapes of the other Chamber portraits. Liverpool's is thus the most lacklustre in the whole room. To suppose that George intervened in any way to ensure that his Prime Minister should not catch the eye in any favourable way at all, however, may be to surmise a little too much.

While the downplaying of Lord Liverpool may have been coincidental, it was not by accident that the military heroes of the field of Waterloo itself were notably under-represented in the 'Waterloo' Chamber. In 1830 the portraits in the room were preponderantly those of George IV's family and of European royalty, not of British generals. (By 1835 even the old Duke of Cumberland had been promoted to the Chamber. As early as 1810 his portrait by Reynolds had been sent for restoration; on its long-delayed return, William IV insisted that his rakish uncle, dead more than a quarter of a century by the time of Waterloo, be admitted into the hall of fame.[9]) Relatively few serving soldiers, other than commanders-in-chief of royal blood such as the Duke of Brunswick and the Duke of York, were originally hung in the Chamber. Apart from Wellington himself, no British general officers were commemorated in George IV's lifetime, yet George commissioned Lawrence to paint his former drinking friend Charles X of France, who had contributed little to the war effort (and was soon to be ejected from his throne by his subjects). The portraits currently hanging in the Chamber of Wellington's generals Anglesey, Picton, Hill and Kempt were all painted in the 1830s (the first two by Sir Martin Archer Shee in 1836). Neither was James

Lonsdale's portrait of Sir William Congreve, completed about 1810, part of George's original programme. For a prince whose own Waterloo glory was the product of his imagination, it was more comfortable to be surrounded with images of European royalty and aristocracy than with those of men who had actually fought in battle. George naturally had no choice but to place the imperious if awkwardly-composed portrait of Wellington over the head of the Chamber's dining table; but he was able to balance the account in nearby St George's Hall, where the sequence of portraits on the north wall culminated in a Lawrence full-length of himself. The site of the new Hall was that formerly intended by Benjamin West for his 'Chapel of the Revealed Religion', and in a sense a religion *was* being celebrated here: the cult of the hero-king.

Neither George nor Lawrence lived to see the Waterloo Chamber finished. George did not even see the completion of Wyatville's Guard Chamber, devised as a prelude to the Chamber and to prepare visitors for the martial glory to come. Originally its centre-piece was a bust of Nelson, standing on a plinth carved from a section of the *Victory*'s mast. The romantic antecedents of the plinth did not, however, prevent it from crumbling away during Victoria's reign; and in 1901 Edward VII gave the bust to the Royal Naval College at Greenwich.

Reactions to the Waterloo Chamber were mixed. The artist James Northcote declared of Lawrence's series that 'there has been nothing like it except in the instances of Rubens and Vandyck', and that 'It would raise the credit of English art abroad and make it more respected at home.' To Benjamin Haydon the Chamber was a travesty, 'a disjointed failure'. Lawrence, he commented (in the words of one who had failed to win George's consistent patronage), was nothing more than 'Perfumer to His Majesty'.[10]

George also wanted to commemorate 'his' victory in sculpture, and in 1819 commissioned Richard Westmacott to create a 'Waterloo Vase' for the Waterloo Chamber. Appropriately, it was fashioned from an object with a solid Napoleonic pedigree. In 1815 the Duke of Tuscany had presented the Regent with a half-completed vase which had been carved for Napoleon in Tuscany from a fifteen-foot-high block of marble; George now asked Westmacott to adorn it with representations of Napoleon's defeat. The finished article, showing George on his throne watching Napoleon dismount from his horse, was the very epitome of George's ambitious thinking. The completed vase weighed forty tons, however, and was far too heavy for the Chamber's raised floor, supposing it could ever have been carried safely up the stairs. In 1836 William IV donated it to the new National Gallery, and after 1906 it was positioned in the gardens at Buckingham Palace, where it remains, cruelly exposed to the elements.[11]

Westmacott's weighty vase was not the only sculptural memorial to Napoleon's supposed defeat by George. From Matthew Cotes Wyatt, who in 1820 had carved Princess Charlotte's Cenotaph, was commissioned a giant group of 'St George and the Dragon', to be sited prominently in St George's Hall at Windsor. Again, there was little doubt as to the allegorical symbolism: George clearly intended to be seen as the eponymous saint, slaying the dragon of Napoleonic tyranny. By the time of his death, only the horse and dragon had been completed, however, and the unfinished group languished for years in Wyatt's studio. As a desperate measure Wyatt had the group cast in bronze and exhibited at the Great Exhibition of 1851, but even this well-patronised event turned up no buyer for a piece whose symbolism was now distasteful as well as unfashionable. Fifteen years later Wyatt's son sold the group, appropriately enough, to the second Duke of Wellington. Initially exhibited at Apsley House, in 1950 it was moved to Stratfield Saye, the country house given by a grateful nation to the first duke.[12]

The fantasy of George's personal triumph over Napoleon was not just to be projected in paintings and sculpture. The Prince and John Nash envisaged for London a broad triumphal processional route to Carlton House that would rival the grand boulevards of Imperial Paris. Nash was already the architect to the Office of Woods and Forests when the lease of Marylebone Park, to the north of London's West End, reverted to the Crown in 1811. He was asked to prepare a scheme for the development of the park as a fashionable residential area, and a new processional way, centred on what was to become Regent Street, was planned to link Carlton House with a grand Summer Pavilion for the Regent in the middle of the park.

Not everyone shared George's enthusiasm for Nash's scheme. Perceval, the Prime Minister, who lived nearby, would have preferred to see the park improved and the semi-rural character of the neighbourhood preserved. He was thus among those who objected to Nash's first plans for the site, which as well as the Prince's pavilion included more than fifty tree-girt villas set in a landscaped park and a dense urban grain of terraces on the periphery. To defuse the protests,

Nash reduced the number of terraces and dropped some of the more grandiose elements of his plan, such as the double circus proposed for the park's centre and the church-filled circus at the head of Portland Place (which instead became Park Crescent and Park Square). The villas – which Nash stoutly maintained 'should be considered as Town residences and not Country Houses' – were also reduced in number, and hidden away from the principal public areas, and from each other. Keen to ensure their sale to the respectable upper-middle classes, Nash was adamant that 'no Villa should see any other, but each should appear to possess the whole of the Park'.[13]

The element of rivalry with Napoleon's capital was plain. Nash had visited Paris in October 1814 and again in November 1815 to investigate the work of Napoleon's architects at first hand. So impressed was he that the house he built for himself in Regent Street (1822) was a homage to Percier and Fontaine. One contemporary declared of it that:

> The café de mille colonnes, or Napoleon's Salle des Maréchales, are nothing to it, for flutter, multiplicity of mouldings, filigrain and leaf gold. Mr Nash seems to have emulated in these apartments the laboured elaborateness of finish that characterizes the works of M Percier.[14]

He later boasted that Chester Terrace, on the eastern edge of the new Regent's Park, was 'nearly as long as the Tuileries', while Carlton House Terrace was explicitly designed as a setting for Carlton House to rival Napoleon's Place de la Concorde.

Revealingly, Nash's grand terraces bear names associated with the Regent and his unpopular family. George had summarily squashed a proposal that the park be named after Wellington, in honour of his Waterloo victory, and also vetoed Nash's idea of a circular Grecian temple at Piccadilly Circus to commemorate William Shakespeare. Only the Prince and his dismal relatives were to be perpetuated in this new development.

Splendour and reflected glory were the object of the exercise, but cost was also a consideration. Nash thus did what he could to ensure that his terraces, though built of bricks and stucco, were as grand as possible. The Crown leases for these new buildings therefore specified that the stucco be painted 'in imitation of Bath stone', the window joinery 'in imitation of oak'. Not all the blocks were designed in detail by Nash himself; some were the work of the young Decimus Burton (whose first scheme for Cornwall Terrace was condemned as 'too dull' – it resembled, Nash declared, 'a hospital, alms-house, work-house or some such building'[15]). Park Village East and Park Village West, of 1824–8, were erected under the direction of Nash's pupil James Pennethorne. These two collections of detached and semi-detached houses, designed to look like villas, had their origins in Nash's arcadian thatched community of Blaise Hamlet of 1810–11. By the mid 1820s, however, they had evolved into something far more exciting: the prototypes of London's Italianate suburbs of the 1840s and 50s.

The design for Regent Street itself was influenced not only by the linear boulevards of Napoleon's Paris but by a model closer to hand: Oxford's medieval high street. Like the High, Regent Street curved subtly in a most un-Napoleonic way, allowing its visitors an ever-changing prospect. The eastward bend at the lower end ensured that the street reached Carlton House without passing through the disreputable quarters of Soho or St Giles, thus enabling Nash to sell the sites along the route at a premium price. It was his intention that this new road form a boundary between the fashionable 'first rate' houses of Mayfair, immediately to the west, and the 'fourth rate' slums of Soho ('the narrow streets and meaner Houses occupied by the mechanics and the trading parts of the community'). The new thoroughfare thus constituted an unabashed exercise in social demarcation. Henry Brougham had already protested in the House of Commons that the near-enclosure of Marylebone Park was 'trenching on the comfort of the poor for the accommodation of the rich'; now the sinuous path of Nash's Regent Street proved to be 'not Hogarth's Line of Beauty but the developer's line of maximum profit'.[16]

Regent Street was intended by Nash to be lined with civic monuments, squares and circuses. These, however, were either never built, or swiftly demolished. By the mid 1820s Regent Street was instead visually anchored at its north end by an audacious piece of sculpture: Nash's All Soul's church, with its daring circular porch and steeple – upon which caricatures of the day showed its architect impaled. The whole composition was judged by George's advisor Charles Long, Lord Farnborough, to constitute 'the finest street in Europe'. Yet by the time Farnborough uttered these words, Regent Street had been robbed of its *raison d'être*. Its intended culmination, Carlton House, was in the process of being demolished, and George, now growing ever more reclusive, contemplated any public procession through the streets of London with horror. The regal parade route thus found itself without a purpose. (As the final ignominy, many of Nash's graceful Regent Street colonnades were removed in 1848, and the street as a whole was thoughtlessly demolished early in the twentieth century to make way for Sir Reginald Blomfield's pallid Beaux-Arts canyon.)

Regent's Park and Regent Street were not enough to satisfy the Prince and his favourite architect. Even before Queen Charlotte's death in 1818 George had in mind a remodelling of her London residence, Buckingham House, although in the end the work did not proceed until 1825. One of the outstanding features of the new palace was to be a triumphal archway which would stand as a definitive expression of George's fantasy-victory over Napoleon. It would recall the great monuments of Ancient Rome erected by victorious Caesars; furthermore, triumphal arches had also been prominently used by Napoleon. There were thus two immediate sources for what became known as the Marble Arch. The first was fourth-century Roman: in 1829 Nash candidly admitted to the Duke of Wellington that his design 'was a plagiarism of the Arch of Constantine'. The second and more immediately relevant source was Imperial Paris: Napoleon's great monuments to conquest, the Arc du Triomphe, begun in 1810, and Percier's earlier Arc du Carrousel, built in the grounds of the Tuileries in 1806–8, both of which Nash would have noted during his visits in 1814 and 1815. Like the Arc du Carrousel, the arch planned by George and Nash was to fulfil the functions of both gateway and memorial, and announce 'the presence of a victorious sovereign in the palace behind'.[17]

Nash was not the only one to benefit from a first-hand examination of Parisian architecture. As Andrew Saint has pointed out, during 1825–6 Nash's assistant James Pennethorne was studying in Paris under Louis Lafitte, who had designed the sculptural programme for Napoleon's Arc du Carrousel. It is thus perhaps not surprising that the arches of the Carrousel framing the entrances to the Tuileries are of almost exactly the same dimensions as the openings in the triumphal arch which originally framed the entrances to Buckingham Palace.[18]

Nor was Nash's concept wholly original. The idea of a placing a triumphal arch at the western approaches to London, astride the route the sovereign would take in travelling from Windsor, was first suggested by Robert Adam in 1778. John Soane, too, envisaged triumphal arches as part of his grand scheme to provide London with a series of imperially-scaled royal buildings and monuments. (In 1827 Soane also proposed a chapel dedicated to Waterloo 'and the other splendid successes obtained by the exertions of British Valour by sea and land', to be sited in front of Horse Guards and dedicated to the recently-deceased Duke of York – who would be watching over 'both the statuary combat on the structure's podium and the real-life marshalling of the Horse Guard on the Parade below'.) Following the rejection of Soane's vision, architects William Wilkins and J. M. Gandy planned a Commemorative Tower at the north end of Portland Place, where today stands a statue of George IV's petulant and inept brother, the Duke of Kent.[19] It was Soane's colleague as 'Attached Architect' of the Royal Works, John Nash, who was chosen to build a triumphal arch, however. Nash's novel idea was not to isolate the monument astride the King's route from Windsor, as Soane had proposed, but to employ it as the entrance gateway to the new palace planned for the western end of St James's Park.

The design for the arch evolved by Nash in conjunction with Pennethorne and, until his death in December 1826, the sculptor John Flaxman, was far more a commemoration of George's supposedly personal triumph over Napoleon than of the realities of Waterloo or any of its predecessors. The planned relief of the Battle of Waterloo was relegated to the west (now the north) side of the arch; on the opposite side was to be one depicting the life of Nelson. Most significantly, on the plinth over the attic storey there was to be a giant equestrian statue of George himself, by Francis Chantrey. Below this, on either side of the plinth, were to be reliefs featuring Wellington and Britannia. From the evidence of the 1826 model now in the Victoria and Albert Museum, these would have been somewhat difficult to see from the ground.

The symbolism of the design was clear: Napoleon's defeat was principally George's achievement, rather than that of the military heroes who had fought in his father's name. Most revealingly, George later opposed Wellington's eminently sensible suggestion of 1829 that the names of officers who had served at Waterloo be inscribed on the arch. He preferred representations of classical gods and goddesses – beings whose mythic nature would not detract from his own allure, and with whom he might indeed be idly compared.[20] Central to the composition was a figure of Napoleon, deliberately carved by Westmacott to resemble that of Trajan on the Arch of Constantine, with the Emperor's cloak fluttering dramatically behind him.[21] Thus was George IV personally identified with Napoleon's ruination and implicitly elevated to the stature of the great Roman Emperors.

Estimates of 1825 mention that the projected arch was, like the new Buckingham Palace, to be faced in Bath stone, but subsequently it was decided instead to face it in grey 'ravaccione' marble from quarries near Carrara. In 1816 George had acquired marble-and-bronze models of the three great surviving triumphal arches of Ancient Rome, those of Titus, Septimius Severus and Constantine. These had been marble-clad, whereas Napoleon's arches were not sheathed in marble, but merely enriched with Carrara sculptures.[22]

Work finally began on the arch in January 1828. By this time Flaxman was dead, so Nash had to bring in other leading sculptors such as Richard Westmacott, Edward Baily and John Rossi to carve the reliefs from Flaxman's sketches. Problems immediately arose with the foundations, when a branch of the river Tyburn was found to run beneath the proposed site; then work on the whole palace was halted in the summer of 1828 while a parliamentary enquiry assessed its progress and expense. The archway was still far from complete when, following George's death, work on the palace was again stopped, by order of Parliament, in October 1830.

> Behind the scenes was a shambles – sheds and materials lying around in the park, and an increasingly frustrated and shrill [marble supplier] Joseph Browne pleading with the Office of Works and with Nash for money he was owed both for the original marble purchase and now for fixing marble.[23]

Nash's work was once more closely scrutinised by a Parliamentary Select Committee, and this time he was sacked. (He spent most of his remaining years, until his death in 1835, attempting to exact compensation from the Treasury.)[24] Both palace and arch were instead finished by Parliament's preferred architect, the unimaginative Edward Blore. Most of the sculptural programme was abandoned, including Chantrey's equestrian statue. The reliefs already completed by Westmacott and the others, of Trafalgar and Waterloo, were placed by Blore on the west and garden fronts of the new Buckingham Palace, with no thought for their symbolism. The attic of the Marble Arch was thus left bare and truncated, and the completed attic statues, designed to stand atop the framing columns, were 'lent' to William Wilkins for use on the façade of his National Gallery, then under construction. Other elements of the frieze were dispersed or stored; some resurfaced to be sold at London auction houses during the 1980s and 90s. One portion, by Edward Baily, somehow ended, rather appropriately, in the props department at the Shepperton film and television studios, and was sold at Sotheby's in May 1999.[25] As we have seen, Chantrey's statue of George IV eventually found a home in Trafalgar Square at the end of the 1830s.

What remained was widely ridiculed. A cartoon of June 1829 showed John Bull interrogating 'the Architect Wot Builds the Arches' and pointing out that 'the Bill is more than double the Estimate'; the figure of Nash replies that 'We never minds no estimates'. Another cartoon, of August 1829, depicted a penniless John Bull in clown's costume atop the arch, in lieu of the proposed equestrian statue of the King; on the summit of the pediment behind stood the jubilant and amply-proportioned figure of Lady Conyngham.[26]

The Marble Arch stood in the path of the new east wing of the Palace designed by Blore in 1846 – Nash's original having been speedily demolished – and critics were swift to declare that in any case it had always appeared undersized against the bulk of the Palace; its central opening, moreover, like that in Kent's Horse Guards, was rather too low and narrow for grander carriages to negotiate safely. Thus the decision was taken in 1850 to move the arch to a new site. Bereft of its intended sculpture and its equestrian statue of George IV, the Marble Arch was to be placed on Tyburn Hill – the notorious spot where, until as late as 1783, public hangings had taken place. There could scarcely have been a clearer expression of contempt for the late King. The arch, dismantled and re-erected in four months, was whole again by March 1851 – and further embellished, as *The Times* reported: 'The upper part of the arch has been constructed as a police station, and will contain a reserve of men.'[27]

The acquisition of personal belongings or significant items relating to a vanquished foe was a means by which successful generals had over the centuries emphasised the scale of their victories: the design and much of the contents of Blenheim, for example, were explicitly intended to underline the Duke of Marlborough's triumph over Louis XIV. The Duke of Wellington was perhaps unusual in being largely unconcerned to enhance his reputation through the medium of art or architecture; as a recent military historian has noted, he 'strongly disapproved of all attempts to turn the battle of Waterloo into either literature or history'. He was especially embarrassed by the Regent's gift of Canova's eleven-foot statue of Napoleon, and the only place he could find for it was in the staircase well of his London home.[28]

George, however, with no genuine reputation to gild, had scruples to match, and his amassing of items having a connection with Napoleon had begun long before Waterloo. To his collection of French clocks from the *Ancien Régime* George had added a large number in the 'Empire' style made by Napoleon's favourite clock-maker, Thomire, while the two Council Chairs delivered by Tatham and Company for the Throne Room at Clarence House in 1812, with their prominent sphinx supports, recalled the throne Percier and Fontaine had made for the coronation of the French Emperor in 1804. A piece with more personal associations eventually found its way into George's private bedroom at the Royal Pavilion, when he acquired a desk made for Napoleon himself by Jacob-Desmalter. George would doubtless have been gratified to know that by 1827 Jacob-Desmalter was in the London workshops of George Seddon, making furniture for Windsor Castle.

George's purchases of Napoleonic memorabilia did not stop with furniture. In 1808 he acquired from Colnaghi's an ink-and-wash battle scene depicting 'The Death of General Desaix at the Battle of Marengo', completed in 1801 by the artist J.-F.-J. Swebach-Desfontaines. Not only had Napoleon considered Marengo his finest victory and Desaix, in 1801, his favourite general – 'the man whom I loved and esteemed the most', as he wrote afterwards – but for an assiduous collector of Sèvres porcelain there was an added significance, in that Swebach-Desfontaines was one of the principal painters at the Sèvres factory. This combination of felicities must have delighted the picture's new owner.[29] George also bought Isabey's drawings of the Congress of Vienna and the same artist's painting of Napoleon's Review of 1799, plus numerous drawings of French officers' uniforms.[30] His enthusiastic appreciation of the works of Antonio Canova is likely to have been further enhanced by the knowledge that the Italian had been Napoleon and Josephine's favourite sculptor.

By far the most evocative of all George's Napoleonic acquisitions was the Table of the Grand Commanders, one of two similar tables made for Napoleon in 1806. Supported by Roman fasces and a plinth in the form of a shield and with gilt bronze mounts, the circular tops were of Sèvres porcelain painted by L.B. Pavant in a design featuring framed heads of great generals of antiquity, arranged round the profile of a celebrated military leader – Alexander the Great on one table, Napoleon in the other. They were an obvious embarrassment to Louis XVIII (whatever his failings, he at least had the sense not to attempt to pass himself off as Napoleon's equal), and in 1817 he gave the Alexander table to the Prince Regent, who had already eagerly offered to buy it. The table became one of George's most prized possessions, and was eventually placed at the centre of the State Dining Room at Buckingham Palace.[31] Before that, he had posed with it for Lawrence's full-length portrait of 1818, and it remained in the revised version painted for the Coronation in 1821. This opulently redolent portrait constituted one of George's most blatant attempts to transcend Napoleon's energetic self-promotion and, in particular, to eclipse the memory and iconography of Napoleon's Imperial Coronation of 2 December 1804. George's hand rests lightly upon the table in a gesture which manages to express both his artistic connoisseurship and a disdainful dismissiveness embodying his own imagined contribution to the subjugation of Napoleon. It entranced George so much that he had it repeatedly copied and sent to friends, foreign embassies and European courts: it was, as Oliver Millar has said, 'a perfect image of the hero of the alliance to be sent overseas'.[32]

Yet while George delighted in posturing as Napoleon's nemesis, he recoiled from any opportunity to meet his foe face-to-face – doubtless chary of the unfavourable physical impression he would make when compared to the Conqueror of Europe. When Napoleon, escaping after Waterloo, surrendered to the captain of a British warship, the *Bellerophon*, and penned an appeal to the Prince Regent as 'the most powerful, the most constant, and the most generous of my enemies', it was in the expectation that he would be allowed to retire to Britain. Both the Regent and his government, however, quailed at the thought. While the *Bellerophon* was still at sea, it was resolved that Napoleon should be exiled to the South Atlantic island of St Helena, where he would neither pose a threat to the stability of the British nation – nor disrupt George's martial fantasies.

Commentators like Farington were not alone in their indignation over the way such victories as Salamanca had been reinterpreted by the Regent as his personal triumphs,[33] and the crowds thronging the victory parades held in London to celebrate Napoleon's exile to Elba in 1814 rapturously acclaimed the visiting Tsar Alexander I of Russia and King Frederick William IV of Prussia, but greeted George in near-silence. Only in ultra-conservative Oxford, which he visited in June

1814, did he receive an animated reception.[34] He was sufficiently irritated by the Tsar's evident popularity to quarrel publicly with him, and indeed the only lasting friendships he formed as a result of the visit were with the Austrian ambassador Prince Esterhazy and with Princess Lieven, the notably attractive wife of the Russian ambassador.[35] Most of his subjects were well aware of George's irrelevance to the recent military victories, and found his subsequent attempts to assume a central role in the defeat of Napoleon ludicrously inappropriate.

After George's death, the anonymous commentator of *The Westminster Review* ensured that the King's fantasies were buried with him:

> ... during the reign of George IV, many proofs were given by the British army of extraordinary valour, and by some of our generals, of great military skill; but, as the king had no share in these achievements, they resound not to his credit, and personally no admiration is due to him on their account ... For the conduct of the campaigns, it is plain that no praise is due but to the general and his army. No admiration, for example, is due to George IV, from the circumstances that the Duke of Wellington, at Waterloo, was not completely out-manoeuvred by Napoleon, and that the soldiers of the British army, by their unconquerable courage, turned the fate of the day. This victory has no more connection with ... George IV, than has the discovery of the spinning-jenny by Arkwright; that of the safety-lamp by Davy; the principle of population by Malthus, or that of foreign trade by Ricardo. The king is as completely separated from the military as from the philosophic renown.[36]

The self-conscious 'Britishness' ascribed by Linda Colley and others to the late Georgian period, and in particular to the post-Waterloo era, was a national identity in which the monarch, in popular opinion, played a merely symbolic role. George IV was barely even a convenient figurehead; too often he was perceived as an embarrassment, to be glossed over as quickly as possible. Yet during his lifetime he persistently postured as a dominant figure at the centre of Europe's stage, at the expense of those military heroes he professed to admire. When in 1817 John Nash proposed a column celebrating the victory to finish his new Waterloo Place, George was markedly unenthusiastic and allowed the idea to be talked down on grounds of cost. In George's mind, he and his family had been the principal bulwark against Napoleon's tyranny, and he preferred to mark Waterloo Place not with any commemoration of Wellington's triumph but with a giant memorial to his brother, the unlamented Duke of York, sacked as army Commander-in-Chief in 1809. By the time of his death, surrounded with evocative Napoleonic memorabilia and images of the flatteringly heroic persona created for him by Thomas Lawrence, fact and fiction had for George IV become so inextricably confused that the image *was* the reality, but without its disappointments.

14

The Masquerade of Rooms

The same long Masquerade of Rooms,
Tricked in such different, quaint costumes ...
Thomas Moore, *The Twopenny Post-Bag*, Letter VIII

AT THE BEGINNING of the nineteenth century, those European rulers installed as part of the new Napoleonic system often strove to define and legitimise their rule through ostentatious patronage of the visual arts, aping the eighteenth-century dynasties they had so recently replaced. Whether as Prince of Wales, Regent or King, George clearly had no need to demonstrate his claim to the throne; nevertheless, images which emphasised the enduring character of the British monarchy, in contrast to the temporary nature of the dominion the Napoleonic *arrivistes* might expect to enjoy, were constantly implicit in the iconography of his Regency and reign. At the same time – particularly after 1815 – he sought to promote himself as Europe's leading figure. To this end he attempted to create sumptuous palaces more appropriate, he considered, for a ruler of his stature than the relatively modest residences preferred by his father.

Such building work could also be read as a realisation of the Masonic ideal of kingship with which he had been familiar since childhood. While his father was never a Freemason, his grandfather Frederick, Prince of Wales and his disreputable uncle Cumberland were both keen adherents of the Craft. It was possibly the latter who introduced the young Prince to the pleasures of the Lodge and, more pertinently, to the principles set down in James Anderson's masonic *Constitutions*. The dedication of the 1738 edition, to Prince Frederick, called on the royal family to inaugurate great architectural schemes, specifically labelling architecture the 'royal art':

Your ROYAL HIGHNESS well knows, that our *Fraternity* has been often patronized by *Royal* Persons in former Ages; whereby *Architecture* early obtain'd the Title of the Royal Art ... The *Fraternity* being All duly sensible of the very great Honour done them by your becoming their ROYAL *Brother* and *Patron* have commanded me thus to signify their Gratitude, their brotherly Love to your *Royal* Person and their humble Duty to Your Royal PRINCESS ... Whose Descendants shall also prove the Patrons of the *Fraternity* in all future Ages.[1]

Since freemasonry was at this stage very much a British phenomenon – and for much of the eighteenth century was effectively prohibited on the Continent – its creed was doubly attractive to a Prince who constantly sought to emphasise his patriotism. The masonic exhortation to become a great architectural patron evidently made a considerable impression on him; it was indeed one of the few pieces of advice he imbibed as a youth which he followed throughout his life.

As George's interest in politics evaporated (together with his Whig principles), so it appeared that his urge to impress the world with the energy and scale of his patronage increased, to become virtually all-consuming by the time of his accession to the throne in 1820. Yet since his vision remained always vague and malleable his building programme, like his collecting, depended heavily on the guidance of stronger personalities. By 1825 Charles Long, subsequently first Baron Farnborough, was not only acting as his principal advisor on fine art, but also shaping his architectural ambitions.

George's Regency gave him freer access to the money with which to indulge his architectural imagination, and over the next decades the public purse bore the brunt of the cost of his ambitious building schemes. Of these the Earl of Essex's waspish comment was, 'C'est magnifique, mais qui payera?'[2] In 1814 the Whig front-bench spokesman George Tierney demanded 'an effectual check to all those embryo palaces and villas that, as he understood, were about to start up',[3] but all attempts to supervise or curb the Regent's architectural aspirations proved largely ineffectual. Understandably, the three new 'Attached Architects' appointed to the Office of Works in 1813 sought to win rather than frustrate royal commissions, while their nominal superior, the Surveyor-General Colonel Stephenson, was an ineffectual person who easily capitulated to royal pressure, and was rarely helped by consistent support from the government. After an incident in 1823 in which the wretched colonel unwittingly countermanded a royal decree at Windsor, not only did the King demand that the Prime Minister 'should impress upon [Stephenson], humility and obedience' but Liverpool himself, in passing on this message, advised the Surveyor-General to observe 'the greatest caution and delicacy as to the Mode of Conducting the Business of your Department, particularly with respect to those palaces in which His Majesty actually resides'.[4] Clearly it was not Stephenson's brief to restrain his royal master.

In 1811 the new Regent had decided he could not live in Windsor Castle. The draughty rooms reminded him too much of his father the King – whose asylum it frequently was – and of unhappy, chastening visits to his parents as a child. Following his mother's death in 1818 and his father's two years later, however, he began to feel differently, and Windsor came to feature in his plans. From there in October 1823 Wellington wrote that the King 'talked to me a good deal about his Improvements here', that 'His Mind is full of them', and that 'He will not be satisfied with anything excepting the Grant at once of a large sum of Money for this purpose' – a matter which, the Duke predicted, would give him and his fellow ministers in the Liverpool government 'some trouble this Winter'.[5]

There had been a castle at Windsor since William the Conqueror's invasion of 1066, and apart from minor alterations commissioned by George III in 1776, little had been done in the way of modernisation since Hugh May's remodelling of the Hall, the Chapel and some of the state apartments for Charles II in the 1670s. As the historian W.H. St John Hope declared in 1913, regarding the alterations instigated by George IV, 'However much the antiquary may regret the destruction of ancient features and obliteration of much architectural history ... there can not be any doubt that the castle has become quite unfitted for use as the residence of the sovereign.'[6] The castle's gaunt chambers may have suited the stoic temperament of George III and his wife, but held little appeal for a man accustomed to the unambiguously ostentatious display of a Carlton House or a Brighton Pavilion.[7]

From the moment that George IV signalled his intention to rebuild the castle, effective control of the project passed from his own increasingly languid hands into those of Sir Charles Long. It was Long who invited the greatest architects of the day, including Robert Smirke and John Nash, to participate in a competition for the commission. It was Long who chose the eight commissioners who were to decide the winner and, crucially, it was Long who composed the brief for the competition. His guidelines were explicit, requiring that 'the period of Edward the 3rd ... should generally predominate', that the Keep should be heightened '20 or 30 feet' to give it more architectural authority, that a new gateway be formed to create a vista down the Long Walk across the Great Park, and that all the external façades of the Upper Ward – today largely classically fenestrated – be gothicised in the Decorated manner.[8] While the initial idea of transforming the gaunt fortress into a romantic medieval fantasy may have been George's, it was Long who ensured that the fantasy became reality.

The competition winner was not Smirke, or Nash. Long, the King and their fellow-commissioners chose the relatively lesser-known Jeffry Wyatt – later permitted to Frenchify his name to Wyatville, to distinguish himself from the other architects of the Wyatt tribe. Wyatville was a competent but uninspired country-house architect who had trained first under his uncle Samuel and then under his uncle James Wyatt. He had set up a building firm in Pimlico, an involvement in 'trade' which delayed his election to the Royal Academy for years, and designed dull neoclassical and eccentric 'Tudor Gothic' houses for the Whig gentry and aristocracy. His selection over more famous architects such as John Soane and Robert Smirke suggests that his main asset was his pliability – although the sixth Duke of Devonshire, for whom Wyatville worked at Chatsworth after 1820, persistently maintained that it was his personal recommendation that carried the day.[9] Once again, a malleable second-rate talent seems to have been preferred to the potential obstinacy of one more outstandingly gifted. Combined with Long's detailed brief, 'which Wyatville carried out in a workman-like but not over-sensitive manner',[10] the inevitable result was a charming and theatrical stage-set.

On 2 April 1824 Wyatville's estimate of £150,000 for the proposed new work at Windsor was approved by the House of Commons, and exactly two months later he unveiled his designs before thirty-two invited guests. However, almost as soon as work began his estimates were found to be as fictional as Nash's for Brighton. Parliament, emboldened by the unexpected repayment of Britain's wartime loan to Austria, was not slow to vote another £100,000, yet by February 1828 'repairs' and new work executed to date had cost £388,000. By the end of the year the total was £494,000, and by January 1830 expenditure had mounted to £622,000. The Parliamentary Select Committee appointed to enquire into the cost of completion estimated that an additional £277,000 would be needed to finish the job.[11]

At Windsor, as at Carlton House, both architect and decorator were theoretically answerable to the King, but how far the decisions made were actually George's is still uncertain.[12] Wyatville, ever the urbane diplomat, always took care to defer to him; it was Wyatville's idea to invite George to lay the foundation stone of the new work on his birthday, 12 August 1824 (when 'Wyatt' also became 'Wyatville'), and to have his workmen cheer the birthday boy from the newly-completed battlements two years later.[13] However, most of the planning decisions seem to have been left to Long and Wyatville, George involving himself, on the rare occasions he emerged from his Great Park fastness, with the more detailed aspects of the furnishings.

The 'new' castle was an assortment of allegories designed to associate George both with his illustrious medieval forbears and with the more recent defeat of Napoleon. Castellation of the rebuilt curtain wall gave May's classicised residence a far more ancient and military appearance. Inside, the rebuilt two-hundred-foot long St George's Hall was deliberately proportioned to enable George to celebrate that most resonant of chivalric ceremonies, the procession of the members of his favourite Order of the Garter, as impressively and medievally as possible. Previously, the procession had had to be marshalled partly in the open courtyard – not so amusing, nor, if it rained on the day, so picturesque. Wyatville created an impressive sequence of rooms leading from the Brick Court via a new staircase, a vestibule, and the Queen's Guard Chamber to a hall big enough to accommodate the whole procession. The original termination of this vista was a Gothic throne, designed by Wyatville, at the east end of the Hall.[14] To hammer home the link, statues of George IV's martial ancestors Edward III and the Black Prince, executed by Westmacott, were placed in niches inside the Upper Ward quadrangle, close to the entrance to the state apartments. Ironically, in the striving for a suitably fourteenth-century effect genuinely medieval elements of the castle's fabric such as the Horn Court were sacrificed in favour of Wyatville's wafer-thin Gothic – as were Hugh May's splendid Hall and Chapel of 1675–84, additions which John Britton in 1828 believed Wyatville 'had a duty to sweep away' but the obliteration of which has recently been designated by John Martin Robinson 'a major architectural tragedy'.

As with so many other expressions of George's historical imaginings, the details often did not bear close examination. Wyatville made successful use of the latest technology to create his enlarged spaces, employing iron beams, for example, to take the weight of his new

State Dining Room and the adjacent state apartments; but he also used numerous short-cuts and economies, so that the fabric appeared stronger and more durable than it actually was. After the fire at the castle in 1992, for example, English Heritage's historians found that the ceiling of St George's Hall had been 'jerrybuilt', and that 'in order to make up the beams and bosses, huge thicknesses of solid plaster had been cast onto armatures made of thin timber battens, nails and six-inch spikes, wound about with string'.[15] The ceiling of one of the most important new spaces in Wyatville's castle was made not of stone or of wood but of plaster, grained in imitation of wood. Similarly, the walls of the Hall were not of ashlar but, again, of plaster, brushed over with fine sand while still damp to suggest the texture of stone and then painted with trompe-l'oeil jointing. As built, Wyatville's mock-medieval plaster Hall was in itself, albeit unintentionally, a splendid allegory of George's flawed aspirations.

Other influences were at work in the new iconography of the castle. While St George's Hall was decked out in fake medieval imagery, as we saw in the last chapter the Waterloo Chamber – the second principal focus of the new state apartments – was created to epitomise George's self-identification with the great British triumphs of the Napoleonic Wars. Nor perhaps was the Chamber the only element designed with the vanquished French in mind. John Martin Robinson has suggested that the Grand Corridor, lined with bronze and marble busts on scagliola pedestals, was specifically intended to recall Napoleon's Grande Galerie at the Louvre.[16]

While he was clearly interested in the new spaces Wyatville was creating for him at Windsor, George became positively enthusiastic when it came to choosing the furnishings for the remodelled interiors. He himself appointed the castle's decorators and furniture suppliers, Morel and Seddon. (Nicolas Morel had previously worked at Carlton House with Holland and Daguerre – he was a witness to Daguerre's will – and after 1795 provided furniture for The Grange in Hampshire, for which he was only paid in 1800–1. In 1827 he abandoned his former partner Robert Hughes for George Seddon, but while the furniture was made at Seddon's workshop – the biggest in London – Morel appears to have made the firm's aesthetic decisions.[17]) Morel and Seddon's designs generally seem to have required the King's approval, and to this end miniature room sets were produced for his inspection. While he was apparently happy to defer to Charles Long over architectural matters, he did not always accept professional advice. In a letter to Knighton of 1 January 1827, for example, he insisted that the armorial glass from Thomas Hopper's now-demolished Gothic conservatory at Carlton House should be re-used at Windsor, and the drawing for the King's Bathroom at Windsor is annotated, in his own hand, 'colour of hangings to be changed'. According to Francis Chantrey, George also 'supervised personally the hanging of the pictures and the placing of the busts' in Wyatville's Grand Corridor, and subsequently returned some Bellangé tables Morel and Seddon had bought in Paris. Geoffrey de Bellaigue and Pat Kirkham concluded in 1972 not only that George 'did intervene personally in the design of the chairs and in the choice of colours' at Windsor, but that the castle's 'full-blooded gothic' was his own idea. Most of the important architectural decisions appear rather to have been made by Long, however. It has recently been suggested that the Grand Reception Room, for example, was largely Long's inspiration, and that he – not Wyatville, not George, not Morel and Seddon – was responsible for the extensive use throughout the castle of marbling and scagliola, finishes he had recently employed at his own home.[18]

Together Long and Wyatville and their royal master created not only one of the most romantically powerful silhouettes in Britain, but also some of the most eclectic interiors. Their predilection for diversity anticipated and possibly influenced that Victorian passion for mixing provenances and periods so prevalent in British middle-class homes by 1850. Some of the new furniture at Windsor, for example, was authentically medieval in inspiration. Morel and Seddon hired the young prodigy A.W.N. Pugin, only fifteen years old in 1827, to work alongside the firm's émigré French neoclassical experts, such as Boileau and Jacob-Desmalter, to produce 'Gothic' furniture ('juvenalia' later disowned by Pugin as 'employed with so little judgement of propriety, that although the parts were correct and exceedingly well executed, collectively they appeared a complete burlesque of pointed design'[19]). Yet, as de Bellaigue and Kirkham have noted, the castle furnishings also demonstrate George's enthusiasm for 'the French styles of his youth and middle-age [and] the Louis XVI and Empire styles', and reveal that 'he was among the first to experiment with the Louis XV revival style in the interior design of a room'.[20] In 1825 George directed his agents to acquire a number of Boulle pieces in Paris, the beginning of a buying spree which included four huge candelabra by Caffiéri and Desjardins and the Comtesse de Provence's Riesener jewel cabinet, and culminated in 1828 with his installation of a statue of Louis XIV in the dining room. Guided by Long, George insisted on the insertion of a Louis XIV-style plaster ceiling in the King's Guard Chamber, in which were hung the thirty-six Gobelins tapestries and the French boiseries bought by Long in Paris in 1825. George had the gall to inform Wellington that the newly-acquired French pieces were 'quite appropriate for Windsor Castle', maintaining that the mounting over-expenditure on the project had 'entirely arisen from the age of the Castle' – a blatant lie. 'God knows, at my time of life the nation has a much greater interest in this Royal edifice than I can have', he concluded, with more effrontery than plausibility.[21]

Occasionally, even his advisors felt moved to object to the prominence of *Ancien-Régime* taste in George's residences. At Windsor, Jeffry Wyatville protested against the 'introduction of old French boiserie of the age of Louis XV, which would never have appeared in the Castle had the architect been guided solely by his own judgement' (he had, however, apparently felt no qualms about obliterating most of Hugh May's splendid post-1675 additions). Prince Pückler-Muskau thought the French furniture and decoration at Windsor 'too gaudy' and 'enormously overloaded in parts', while the Whig leader Lord Grey considered such pieces 'unsuited to the character of the building'. The Louis-Quatorze character of the Grand Reception Room was entirely George's idea, and had little to do with Wyatville's own vision. The King firmly insisted that the rococo woodwork provided the best context for his picture collection – as it had for Louis XIV's own Dutch and Flemish pictures. Visiting Windsor in the 1840s Joseph Nash agreed, admitting to having been both impressed and overcome by the 'brilliant and highly-ornamented' Grand Reception Room, with its 'imperial magnificence of ... furniture and decorations':

> The walls are hung with the richest Gobelins tapestries in frames, carved in the taste, so styled, of Louis XIV. The candelabras, canopies, fauteuils, chairs, and other minor utensils are all designed after the same model; and the gorgeous gilding and beautiful silken covers and hangings afford an adequate idea of the effect of this, the prevailing taste of 'LE GRAND MONARQUE'.[22]

Winning the Windsor commission undoubtedly set the final seal on Wyatville's career. In 1822 he had at last been elected an Associate of the Royal Academy; in 1824 he became a full Academician. At the same time, George also authorised an augmentation to Wyatville's new coat-of-arms: a view of the proposed 'George IV Gate' and the use of the word 'Windsor' as a motto. On 8 December 1828, having taken formal possession of the completed royal apartments, George knighted his happy architect and bestowed on him a grace-and-favour apartment in the Winchester Tower. Although Wyatville's appearance was hardly prepossessing – he was described as being 'of low stature and inelegant personal form' – and although he retained a strong Midlands accent (no more fashionable then than now), his ability to charm and, where appropriate, to boast served him in good stead in dealing with Long, with his royal master and, after June 1830, with the MPs sent to investigate his work.

In marked contrast to the widespread derision with which Nash's Buckingham Palace was greeted, Wyatville's remodelled Windsor Castle was generally admired by his contemporaries. Sir Walter Scott judged the interiors 'a great national object', W.H. Pyne lauded Wyatville's 'magnificent Gothic staircase' (much of it executed in plaster), while Joseph Nash later praised 'the unity of design, of tone, of decoration, and of contour and general form'. Long, now Lord Farnborough, found much to applaud, and particularly congratulated the architect for sticking to his brief: 'What Mr Wyatville appears very successfully to have attempted has been to unite the ponderous grandeur of the earlier periods of architecture, with the lighter style adopted in the reign of Queen Elizabeth and James I.' Even the jaded Prince Pückler-Muskau declared that 'All the recent additions are ... so perfectly executed that they are hardly to be distinguished from the old part'.[23]

What was originally represented to Parliament as little more than a 'repair' job predictably turned out to be hideously expensive. John Martin Robinson has estimated that the whole cost was approximately £1 million at 1820s prices – upwards of £60 million today. At Windsor, as so many years before at Carlton House, George's suppliers were advised not to stint on the finery. Morel and Seddon exceeded their original estimate for the furnishings by almost fifty per cent, presenting a bill in 1830 that was more than sixty thousand pounds above their original quotation of £143,000. Additionally, thousands were spent on plate from Rundell, Bridge and Rundell – pieces such as Flaxman's 'National Cup' of 1824, featuring a medley of quasi-Tudor motifs which reflected the Elizabethan imagery of George IV's coronation and costing £870. Three years later Rundell delivered the 'Coronation Cup', designed by Pugin and almost a Gothic counterpart to Flaxman's stunning achievement.[24]

Such commissions led to costs spiralling out of control. In January 1829 Sir William Knighton went so far as to summon Mr Bridge to his office where, in an attempt to protect his own reputation as Keeper of the Privy Purse should Parliament again become inquisitive about royal expenditure, he formally notified him that he could not 'too strongly express his regret that H.M. should have become again so large a Debtor to the House of Messrs Rundell and Bridge'.[25] Probably the firm was not unduly worried about whether the King could pay on time: for years they had made money out of their reputation as George's favoured jewellers and goldsmiths – reselling plate and jewellery bought from French royalist refugees before 1815, for example – and so recently as 1827 Philip Rundell had been able to leave his great-nephew £900,000.[26]

Knighton's instincts had not misled him, and in 1830 a Parliamentary Select Committee was indeed appointed to enquire into the costs of the work. In the event, the Committee charitably judged 'the complete repair of this ancient and Royal Residence' to be 'an object of national concern, for which it is essential that Parliament should adequately provide'. Windsor thus fared better than other projects, where work was stopped at George's death and bills remained unpaid, and Wyatville better than Nash over Buckingham Palace. The Committee, 'entertaining a favourable opinion of the manner in which the work has been executed by Sir Jeffry Wyatville', ruled that 'for the sake of uniformity of character and design' the work should 'be completed under the same direction' – though with an annual budget of no more than £50,000.[27] Wyatville's charm, the fact that the building was almost complete, and the knowledge that William IV admired Windsor all no doubt helped to concentrate the MPs' minds wonderfully. Even Morel and Seddon were paid slightly more than half their additional costs, though the Treasury had initially refused to reimburse them beyond their original estimate – the Committee finding itself unable to establish criteria by which to judge the value of their work. Morel himself, however, notoriously extravagant, was a casualty: after 1831 his name disappears from the royal accounts, and subsequent furniture for Windsor was produced by George and Thomas Seddon alone.[28] Wyatville's success at Windsor was surely the envy of many more established practitioners such as John Soane, who no doubt found it galling to see Wyatville – whose talents were generally acknowledged to be inferior to his own – basking in the King's favour. Soane, a proud and bitter man strongly predisposed in favour of monarchy, had for years had in mind an idea which would 'present the restored Westminster Hall like a medieval jewel ... in a showcase of Neoclassical ranges', re-emphasising the heart of government as a centre of royal as well as parliamentary influence. An invitation in 1794 to suggest possible improvements to the House of Lords had burgeoned under his enthusiasm into an elaborate scheme for both Houses of Parliament. This was officially approved in 1794 but because of the wars with France never executed, and when the project was revived in 1800 it was phrased in a romantic Gothic by that style's arch-exponent, James Wyatt.[29] But Wyatt's work at Westminster did not meet with wide approval, and on his death in 1813 it was expected that Soane, by now regarded as one of the country's leading architects, would succeed him as Surveyor-General. As we have seen, however, Wyatt's financial incompetence prompted a reorganisation of the Office of Works, and Soane had to be content with appointment as one of the three 'Attached Architects'. He was inclined to blame the Regent's Private Secretary Sir Benjamin Bloomfield for this blow,[30] but the fact that his particular responsibilities included the royal properties in St James's, Whitehall and Westminster must have given him a sense that his ambitions were about to be realised. George's accession, however, appeared to bode well for Soane's career in general, and for his Westminster schemes in particular.

Having competently restored Westminster Hall in 1819–20, in 1821 Soane was entrusted with erecting the temporary iron galleries required for Queen Caroline's trial in the House of Lords, and in February of the following year he was commissioned to provide a new Royal Entrance. Two medieval chambers were demolished to make way for a new sequence of linear spaces linking a *porte-cochère* (designed by Soane, reluctantly, in a Gothic style) with the Throne in the House of Lords. At the heart of this scheme lay a daring piece of Renaissance-style braggadocio: a grandiloquent Scala Regia in the style of Bernini, up which the King would progress in the manner of a seventeenth-century pope. (It was, even more interestingly, also reminiscent of an equivalent feature designed by Percier and Fontaine for Napoleon at the Tuileries.) Thereafter he would pass through a new Royal Gallery, which was to contain paintings of Trafalgar, Waterloo and other great victories over Napoleon – appropriated, as later in Windsor's Waterloo Chamber, to enhance his own reputation.

Yet while Soane was devising an architectural context fit for a great sovereign, his King was beginning to withdraw from public life. After the débâcle of Queen Caroline's trial and the exhausting pomp of his coronation, George was rarely in London; he even avoided opening Parliament if he could. The Scala Regia was rushed to completion for the State Opening of February 1823, but George refused to appear; the new Royal Gallery was ready in time for the State Opening of February 1824, yet once again the King was not there. Soane's Royal Entrance was finally used when George opened Parliament in November 1826 – the loose informality of which occasion was so scathingly recorded by Prince Pückler-Muskau. Perhaps the design of Soane's entrance was in itself part of George's problem with opening Parliament. Soane's Scala Regia predicated a great Prince capable of processing up it on his way to sanction the meetings of the nation's assembled representatives; George needed help getting out of his carriage, let alone climbing the three short flights of the Scala Regia (Soane had originally envisaged a longer flight of steps, but was tactfully dissuaded by the King's courtiers). Sean Sawyer suggests that Soane's aim was 'to construct a symbolic mise en scène in which George IV could briefly transcend the realities of debility and ineptitude for the illusions of monarchical apotheosis'.[31] Alas for Soane, those stairs were too much. And not only could the King not physically play his part – as the years wore on, he lost all interest in doing so. To add injury to insult, in 1834, the year after Soane's retirement, the whole of the Palace of Westminster except Westminster Hall itself burnt to the ground, destined to be rebuilt in Tudor–Gothic. The ageing but still alert Soane no doubt regarded Barry's and Pugin's designs, despairingly, as a triumph of gimcrack Wyatvillian pseudo-medievalism over his own pure neoclassicism.[32]

Between 1816 and 1818 Soane had made five designs for a 'National Monument', none of which was executed. And when, in 1824, work was begun on an entrance screen at the corner of Hyde Park, it was designed not by Soane but by Nash's principal assistant at Regent's Park, Decimus Burton, a connection which must have recommended him. This triple screen was originally to be adorned with an equestrian figure of George III, carved by the young John Henning; however, only Henning's classical reliefs were completed by the time of George IV's death.[33]

In January 1828 the ever-persistent Soane dedicated to the King a revised version of his 'Designs for Public Improvements in London and Westminster'. As Sean Sawyer has put it, this 'explicitly cultivated royal favour by casting Soane's civic architecture as a framework for a Processional Route from Windsor to the House of Lords'. The scheme combined Soane's recent public works, such as the new Royal Entrance to the Lords, with projects he had long been maturing. His ambitious goal was to construct an approach to London, rivalling anything in Europe, which would enable George IV to open Parliament in the style befitting the sovereign of Europe's most powerful state – to 'delineate Westminster as a civic space symbolic of the Crown's historic legitimacy'.[34] George would arrive from Windsor at Kensington Gate and a 'Grand National Entrance into the Metropolis', a tripartite archway with elements of the 'National Monument' to Waterloo about it, then pass through Hyde Park along the King's Private Road and through a single triumphal arch at Hyde Park Corner. Here he would enter the forecourt of a royal palace Soane designed athwart Constitution Hill with an entrance portico-cum-*porte-cochère* which took account of George IV's increasing infirmity.[35] The route from the new Palace would take the King down The Mall to Horse Guards Parade past a 'Monopteral Temple' honouring the Duke of York, and a 'Sepulchral Church' dedicated to Waterloo 'and the other splendid successes obtained by the exertions of British Valour by sea and land', with a sanctuary above and catacombs below for war heroes.

The procession would then turn left into Downing Street. Work had recently finished on Soane's new Board of Trade and Privy Council offices there, and his vision for the Processional Route further embellished either end of Downing Street with triumphal arches, commemorating George III and the great naval victories of the Napoleonic Wars at the western end and, at the eastern end, George IV – 'as the Guardian and Protector of our Laws and Liberties' – and Waterloo. The symbolism was unambiguous: not only were the Hanoverians intimately linked with Britain's recent victories abroad, but their military and moral stature, as exemplified in stone and marble at either end of the street, dwarfed the nation's prime minister, living modestly at Number Ten.

From Downing Street the procession would turn south, past Soane's new Law Courts and into Old Palace Yard, to draw up beneath the *porte-cochère* leading to the new Royal Entrance to the House of Lords. In processing from there to his Throne in the House of Lords, 'George IV would be able to indulge his fondest monarchical reveries ... and for a moment transport the nation along with him.'[36] Soane's Processional Route would appear nicely calculated to appeal to a sovereign who saw himself as the genius behind Napoleon's defeat. Yet once again his plans were studiously ignored by Farnborough and the

King. Soane was not to know that by now George was more interested in rearranging his cosy, secluded nest at Royal Lodge in Windsor Great Park than in a processional route which would involve exposure to his subjects, whom he increasingly feared and despised. A commission to restore Inigo Jones's classical masterpiece, the Banqueting House in Whitehall, was all Soane's reward. Even a knighthood, hinted at by George in callously capricious vein, was not forthcoming until 1832 when Soane, nearly eighty, retired from the Office of Works.

We have seen how Nash's assistant Decimus Burton, rather than Soane, was commissioned to build an entrance archway to Hyde Park. In 1827 it was Burton again, rather than Soane, who provided designs for an imposing arched entranceway to the new palace arising on the site of Buckingham House. Based loosely on the ancient Arch of Titus in Rome, Burton's archway was erected (as Soane himself had suggested) to the north of the palace, astride the road to Windsor. Burton too suffered from George's increasing reclusiveness, however: the King rarely made use of his arch, and since neither William IV nor Victoria cared for ostentatious processions it swiftly became redundant. In 1883 it was moved to the top of Constitution Hill, across Piccadilly from Wellington's Apsley House and Burton's entrance screen into Hyde Park, where it was considered it would be less disruptive of traffic. In the meantime, the arch had become an object of national ridicule by virtue of Matthew Cotes Wyatt's ludicrously overscaled equestrian statue of Wellington which was placed atop the attic in 1846. '*Nous sommes vengés*', a French officer is reported, possibly apocryphally, to have exclaimed at the sight of it. Burton, whose original design featured a quadriga and statue of Britannia, was so distressed that for many years his will included the provision of £2,000 for the removal of the despised sculpture. However, only when the arch was moved in 1883 was Wyatt's statue finally banished to army training grounds near Aldershot.[37]

Since George was never notable for taste or tact in his dealings with his family, it is not surprising to find that he was making plans for a new palace to replace Buckingham House even before his mother Queen Charlotte, whose London residence it was, had died. Old Buckingham House was a plain, nine-bay brick box with two-storey wing pavilions, in character much like George III's Court – 'dull, dowdy and decent'.[38] Originally built by William Winde for the first Duke of Buckingham in 1702–5, it had been enlarged for George III and his Queen after 1762 and again in 1792–9. When the matter was first raised, following

Queen Charlotte's death in November 1818, Lord Liverpool warned that the voting of large sums of money even for alterations would be particularly unpopular at a time of economic recession and hardship. George was not to be put off, and raised the matter again in 1819. Yet it was not until 1825 that he managed to badger Liverpool into agreeing to an expenditure of £150,000 over three years. (Predictably, George complained of the paucity of the award, declaring it to be 'altogether inadequate' and suggesting it should be trebled.[39])

Following his father's death and his own accession in 1820, George's attentions were initially distracted by such matters as his wife's trial, his coronation, and his visits to Ireland and Scotland. Nevertheless, in July 1821, having advertised his intention to abandon Carlton House for a home at the other end of the Mall, he ordered the Surveyor-General, Colonel Stephenson, to provide Nash with all known plans of the building.[40] This was one more slap in the face for John Soane, who as the Attached Architect with responsibility for Buckingham House was actually directing repairs there when ordered by Stephenson to send plans to Nash. Soane was justifiably furious, and his temper was not improved by a letter from Nash:

> Brother Soane, You was in a miff when I saw you at the head of Your Masons. One of the Masonic rules, I am told, is to acquire a meek and humbled spirit. I fear therefore You are not qualified for Grand Master. Now, if You will but come here and copy me for a month, You will certainly be appointed to a higher niche in Your Lodge ...[41]

The fact that as early as December 1813 Soane had been installed as the Freemasons' Grand Superintendent of Works can only have added to his irritation at this sally. 'I am old,' Nash attempted to reassure his rival, 'but feeling my head on my shoulders I marched off to Buckingham House ...'[42] Nash was still involved in work at Brighton Pavilion and Regent's Park, so that between these commitments and Parliament's reluctance to sanction the work, it was not until 6 June 1825 that building actually began at Buckingham House. Here, as at Brighton, there was a tendency for both architect and patron to regard Nash as working for George in a private capacity, and since budgeting did not come naturally to either, this proved financially disastrous. A Treasury Order of August 1825 that all contracts entered into must be subject to Office of Works approval was not sufficient to regulate Nash's haphazard methods, and only four months into the work Colonel Stephenson was exclaiming that all Nash's contracts with suppliers were unsatisfactory: 'some are in writing, some merely verbal, but all are in my opinion more or less improvidently made, as compared with those ... for similar works by this department'. Such written contracts as Nash did issue were often fatally vague, and only caused confusion.[43]

Furthermore, the most rigorous cost-control is never proof against an interfering client. As Nash was very ready to inform the Select Committee appointed in 1831 to look into the work at Buckingham House, George himself had been much involved in the planning of the new palace. His own original thoughts, Nash declared, had been limited to adding a few rooms to the old house. Predictably, however, the King had wanted far more, hence Nash's subsequent proposal for a wholly new palace, on the same axis as Pall Mall. Then George surprisingly announced that he remained attached to the house in which he had been brought up – 'There are early associations that endear me to the spot', Nash recalled the late King as having said. Although acceptance of this novel interpretation of his childhood involved a suspension of disbelief of epic proportions, it was on this basis that George asked Nash to remodel the existing building rather than build anew.[44] Nash went on:

> The building being so enlarged, and additions daily suggested, I began to think the King might be induced to make use of it as the State Palace ... but he persisted in saying, he should continue to hold his Courts at St James's, and that he never would hold them at Buckingham House.

After a substantial amount of building work had already taken place, George changed his mind yet again, informing Nash that 'the State Rooms you have made me are so handsome that I think I shall hold my Courts there'. By his own account Nash, who had made little provision for rooms of the size required for state apartments, was far from pleased: 'I took the liberty,' he remembered in 1831, 'to submit to the King how unfair such a determination was to me as his Architect'.[45] As many other artists working for George had found, his whims were not conducive to any consistency in planning.

Nash's new palace design had come a long way from his original modest intentions:

> The wings of the house were to be taken down and rebuilt with a colonnade on either side of an enlarged courtyard. A portico forming a porte-cochère was to be added to the entrance front; the hall and great staircase

were to be reconstructed; galleries were planned on two floors; the library to the south, and the corresponding wing to the north were to be heightened, as was the old Prince of Wales's wing on the north front; and to the west was to be added a range of rooms flanked by pavilions or conservatories.[46]

As conceived, Nash's principal elevation had little in common with Winde's plain brick façade. Of Bath stone, and punctuated by a two-storey Corinthian portico, its colonnaded open courtyard and frequent subdivision appear to have been heavily influenced by what Nash had seen in Paris in 1814 and 1815.

There was also input from another quarter. George's artistic advisor Charles Long, Lord Farnborough, as francophile as his royal master, had during 1817 visited Paris a number of times specifically to glean ideas from the work of Percier and Fontaine, and Nash subsequently mimicked at Buckingham Palace much of their decorative work at the Tuileries. The extensive use of scagliola panels in the Palace interiors (as at Windsor) was also Long's idea. Cheap and light in weight compared with the marble it imitated, scagliola's use on walls had only previously been attempted in Russia. (George corresponded with Tsar Nicholas I on the subject in 1828–9.)[47]

By May 1829 the cost of rebuilding Buckingham House had risen to £496,169; on 16 February 1831 Nash estimated that the whole project had to date cost £640,010.[48] By October 1828, £19,420 had been spent on imported marble alone: Joseph Theakston's marble chimney-piece for the Grand Hall had cost £1,000; the Chinese chimney-piece in Nash's Yellow Drawing Room, executed by Jones and Parker, £922; and Joseph Brown's fireplace surrounds for the Picture Gallery and Drawing Rooms had earned him £6,000. Samuel Parker's splendid gilt-bronze balustrade for the grand staircase – which Nash, following Soane's example at the Palace of Westminster, had based loosely on the concept of Bernini's Scala Regia at the Vatican – cost a substantial £3,900. The circular Music Room, its shape and gilded ceiling based on the Saloon at Brighton Pavilion, was provided with a floor inlaid by George Seddon's craftsmen, complete with the King's monogram, at a cost of £2,400.[49]

Long before George's death, officials and satirists had begun to pull Nash's accounts and his reputation apart. In February 1828, barely a month after the shell of the new palace had been completed, the MP Henry Bankes demanded to know details of the Attached Architects' salaries, arguing that 'Very large sums were lavished upon works the most tasteless and the most inconveniently contrived, that it was possible to imagine, while there seemed to be no other control over the actions of the architect than his own whim or caprice.'[50] Bankes's assault led to the appointment of a Parliamentary Select Committee, which interrogated Nash concerning his supervision of the works at Regent Street, Carlton House Terrace and Buckingham Palace. His architects, George spluttered impotently, had been 'infamously used' by the Committee. Payments for work at Buckingham Palace were interrupted, and Wellington's government then restricted annual expenditure on the site to £10,000; Nash meanwhile blamed the Office of Works (which he had in practice barely consulted) for the fact that the estimates for the project had been so grossly exceeded.[51] The full details of his slender grasp of financial control surfaced during the deliberations of the Select Committee of 1831.

By that time, however, the man for whom the whole expensive exercise was undertaken had died, without ever living in his new palace. On 23 August 1829 the *Observer* had announced, with a whiff of sarcasm: 'We are credibly informed that Mr Nash has promised to have the new Palace ready for occupation by August 12th, 1830' – the date of George's sixty-eighth birthday. Not only was this hopelessly optimistic, but by August 1830 Nash's 'patron and protector' was dead.

George expired not only before his new palace was completed but also before he had rewarded his architect. In June 1829, belatedly, he indicated his wish to make Nash a baronet, to which Wellington objected on the not unreasonable but hardly conclusive grounds that the Report of the House of Commons' Select Committee into the building of Buckingham Palace had not yet been published.[52] George could have overriden his Prime Minister's opposition, but instead meekly abided by his judgement. His death a year later removed the safety-net on which Nash had over-confidently relied: his career, never mind any chance of a knighthood or more, was effectively at an end.

Even Nash acknowledged that his design for Buckingham Palace was flawed. 'I was not aware that the effect would have been so bad,' he later admitted, 'but now I think that any wings would take from the dignity of a palace.' Nor did all the new interiors work as well as had been expected. William Seguier, by now Conservator of the Royal Picture Galleries, pointed out that Nash's innovative gallery, top-lit by glass domes in a Soaneian manner, illuminated the floor nicely but not, alas, the pictures on the walls. Experts also later discovered that much of the splendid cast-iron work introduced inside the palace was insufficiently supported, and in danger of dropping through floors and ceilings below at any time. Few indeed could be found to say a good word about the palace as it stood in 1830. Caricaturists had a field day with its cost and its design; one print of January 1830 adapted the rhyme *This is the House That Jack Built* to lampoon Nash's 'Punches and pigmies cut out of plaster' and 'the pudding of state' dome which sat jauntily atop the 'Toad in the hole'. The satire's anonymous author commiserated with the British taxpayer, who, 'by Taxes all torn,/By Tithes, rates and Imposts is driven Forlorn/... to pay for the House that George built':

> These are the *Tasters* of tasteless renown,
> That have muddled the thing in a *manner their own*,
> That have piled up a mass of shapeless confusion
> In patch, pudding and peacemeal have sunk half a million.[53]

It seemed no one was willing to defend the late King's favourite architect, and disparagement of Buckingham Palace grew louder and more vehemently hostile. Robert Huish declared it an 'abomination' which created 'a blush even on the face of official hirelings':

> ... the extravagance, impolicy, and injustice, which attended this precious proceeding, utterly overwhelmed the long-tried impudence of Downing Street. The ministers, one and all, shrunk at the very mention of this scandalous attack on the pockets of the people.

Thomas Creevey thought that 'the costly ornaments of the State Rooms exceed all belief in their bad taste and every species of infirmity', citing in particular Farnborough's 'Raspberry-coloured [scagliola] pillars without end that quite turn you sick to look at.'[54] In 1838 W.H. Leeds lambasted what remained of Nash's design, at the time being remodelled by Blore and Pennethorne: 'Uglier structures of the kind there may be many,' he railed, 'yet scarcely any one that is more deficient in grandeur and nobleness of aspect', and proceeded to castigate the 'puniness' and 'pettiness that stamps every individual feature'. Unlike Huish, however, Leeds reserved his venom for the building's architect, rather than for that architect's patron. Suggesting (wrongly, as it now seems) that 'Mr Nash may be said to have thrust a design upon his royal patron, without affording him the opportunity of making any selection' of alternative designs, Leeds declared that 'Mr Nash appears to have sat down to his drawing board without previous grasp of the subject ... [and] without feeling in the slightest degree inspired to energy by the thought that the opportunity was then before him of achieving a worthy monument of architecture.' In Leeds's view Nash (who, having died three years previously, was unable to answer back) could do nothing right. The under-sized Doric order of the basement was judged 'poor and maimed' and 'insignificant in proportion to the whole'; the coupled columns of the portico were labelled 'decidedly improper' and the terminating pavilions 'petty'; the interiors were 'inadequately lit', 'over-gilded' (or, confusingly 'rather too sombre') and, in the case of the Yellow Drawing Room, executed 'in a style of ... *recherché* costliness'.[55]

Not all critics joined in the attack. *Fraser's Magazine* of 1830 found much to praise in Nash's heavily gilded coved ceilings:

> It is indeed, not easy to conceive anything more splendid than the designs for the ceilings which are to be finished in a style new in this country, partaking very much of the boldest style in the Italian taste of the fifteenth century ... They will present the effect of embossed gold ornaments, raised on a ground of colour suitable to the character and other decorations of the rooms.[56]

The Select Committee of 1831 condemned Nash as negligent, and immediately replaced him with Edward Blore, architect of Sir Walter Scott's Abbotsford. George Seddon, supplier of furniture and fittings to Buckingham Palace as well as to Windsor Castle, was lucky not to be dismissed also. Questioned by the Select Committee concerning a bill for £1,986 for supplying an inlaid floor of satinwood and white holly in the Bay Drawing Room, Seddon got away with the rather surprising explanation that he had had no previous experience of laying parquet.[57]

Nash lived to suffer the ignominy of knowing that William IV had offered the incomplete palace as a replacement for the Palace of Westminster when it burnt down in 1834, and that the offer had been declined. Blore's diplomatically over-complex and pessimistic rehearsal of the many practical reasons why such a relocation would be neither spatially nor financially feasible was scarcely consoling. Queen Victoria later labelled Buckingham Palace 'a *disgrace* to the country' and, typically pragmatic, found fault with its 'total want of accommodation for our little family, which is fast growing up'. Within fifteen years Edward Blore had closed in Nash's courtyard, and removed the undersized 'pudding' dome above the central portico – ridiculed by Peter Cunningham in 1849 as 'a common slop pail turned upside down'.[58] In 1851 the palace gateway, as we have seen, was removed and re-erected at the north-east entrance to Hyde Park. Today in the dull eastern façade of the palace (built by Blore and recast by Aston Webb in 1913) there is nothing of George IV or Nash. Only the garden front of Bath stone retains the rhythms of Nash's original work. Inside, it is necessary to look up at his elaborate coved ceilings for an inkling of the interiors of 1830. For all his grandiose aspirations, at Buckingham Palace the fruits of George IV's architectural patronage survive only as a dim echo.

15

The Coronation

A new era's arrived – though you'd hardly believe it –
And all things, of course, must be new to receive it.
                    Thomas Moore, *Parody of a Celebrated Letter*

THE CORONATION OF George IV in 1821 can be interpreted as the
first to celebrate nation before monarch. As Linda Colley has
pointed out, when George's great-grandfather was crowned in 1727,
'Whig and Tory activists in many provincial centres organised separate and competing festivities for the occasion. By contrast, most of the
local committees organising celebrations in 1821 (George IV's coronation), 1831 (William IV's coronation) and 1837 (Queen Victoria's coronation) were ostentatiously bipartisan, and controversial emblems,
mottoes or colours were banned from their arrangements.' Certainly
by the time of Victoria's accession coronations had become patriotic celebrations in which the sovereign was reduced to a ceremonial
figurehead. It was Prince Albert's assiduous efforts after 1840 to rein-
tegrate a working monarchy into the constitutional fabric of Westminster which restored the sovereign to a central place in both palace
and nation.

Yet post-Waterloo Britain was by no means a nation of republican
enthusiasts. All but the most radical fringe continued to revere the
monarch – in the abstract, if not in person – as the corner-stone of
Britain's avowedly successful constitution and thus the guarantor of
the nation's cohesion, strength and liberty. After 1815, as Linda Colley
observes, London's newly-enriched plutocrats 'lavished money on
royal banquets, bestowed their Freedom on as many members of the
Royal Family as would accept it and invested in special banners to be
used on all occasions of royal celebration, emblazoned with the letters

S.P.Q.L. Leading citizens of the new Rome, they wanted Caesar in their midst and were prepared to fête him.'[1] The Caesar they increasingly preferred, however, was an idealised representation of monarchy plucked from the rose-tinted mists of Britain's past, not the portly reminder of the unedifying history of the House of Hanover, a man whose way of life rendered him ever more embarrassingly irrelevant to the constitutional equation.

George himself saw his coronation not merely as an excuse for dressing up, or for a party – both in themselves sufficient reason, he would doubtless have thought, for spending large sums of public money. It also offered him an opportunity to eradicate the memory of his recent disastrous attempt to divorce his estranged wife; by casting himself as the embodiment and inspiration of a newly-confident and militarily-successful nation, he hoped to improve his public image.

George was uniquely equipped with the vision and the props to create this theatrical extravaganza. His coronation brought together several of the governing passions of his life: his own perennially robust ego, dressing up, a romanticised version of Britain's past, and his strong sense of rivalry with Napoleon, intermingled in a multi-layered jumble of allusion and illusion. Though Napoleon's sumptuous Court had collapsed in 1814, the lavish spectacle of 1821 was explicitly designed to outshine Napoleon's imperial coronation of 1804. A tailor was even sent to Paris to inspect and measure the Emperor's robes, to ensure that those being made for George would be finer, and the train longer. The permanency and legitimacy of Britain's hereditary monarchy, and its central position in the lives of Britons – as against the short-lived glories of the First Empire and its satellite puppet-rulers – was exemplified in the use of costume to evoke the fabled lives and military successes of George's Tudor ancestors, and to identify him with the iconic resonance of the English Renaissance and, specifically, the Court of Elizabeth I. George was to play the same role as the Virgin Queen: symbol of the nation's cultural richness and martial glory.[2]

Certainly George had been looking forward long enough to being King; equally certainly, his coronation was to far outdo in splendour the reputedly dowdy ceremonial which had marked his father's, in 1761. Such a humdrum precedent was to be ignored by the courtiers and officials charged with the planning, who instead were to use as their bible Francis Sandford's detailed description of James II's coronation, published in 1687 – an apposite choice, given George's well-documented fascination with the House of Stuart.

The work of preparing for the ceremony, planned for 1 August 1820, began as early as 29 March, but in the months that followed it became increasingly doubtful whether there would be any coronation at all. The new King was fifty-seven years old, his health was notoriously bad and, as we have seen, severe illness immediately following his accession caused many of his subjects to wonder whether he would live to be crowned. Farington expressed the general concern that, if he did, he would surely expire before the end of the long ceremony.[3] Eventually the decision was taken to postpone the coronation. There followed the fruitless attempt to divorce Queen Caroline, a proceeding so generally unpopular that a further postponement was deemed advisable. When the ceremony eventually took place, a year after the Queen's trial, the spectre of the popular unrest it had fomented hung over the event like a black cloud, and twenty-four regiments of soldiers were stationed in London to prevent any possible insurrection in favour of Caroline.

The postponement of George's coronation to 19 July 1821 at least had the merit of allowing more time for the practical arrangements. To accommodate guests, John Soane was directed to build tiers of timber seats in Westminster Hall, a raised floor and dais, boxes at the sides for the royal family, a triumphal arch, and stables for the Royal Champion's horse. The style required was perhaps not to Soane's impeccably neo-classical taste, but the Gothic theme of the panelling, chairs and other finishes helped to reinforce the sense of Tudor pageantry George was attempting to evoke, and was effective in blending Soane's temporary structures into the architectural context of the Hall. Across the road, Westminster Abbey's organ case was provided with a fake-Gothic façade, and everywhere there were British textiles – 'blue and gold brocade for the altar, garter-blue and gold Wilton carpet on the altar steps and sacrarium floor, crimson velvet and sarsenet for the royal box and a good deal of crimson cloth for the boxes and benches inside the western aisle'.[4] Between the Abbey and Westminster Hall, a raised platform-cum-walkway 1,500 feet long was constructed, ensuring that the crowds would be able to see the King and the coronation procession and, perhaps more importantly, that the stunningly expensive costumes to be worn would not become soiled.

Rather in the manner of a Hollywood film director marshalling his extras for a crowd scene, the College of Arms issued guidance on the style of dress to be adopted by those attending rather than actually taking part; as Aileen Ribeiro has noted, the choice of costume 'gave the processions and ceremonies the kind of visual unity that had been lacking at previous coronations'. To make the official costumes for the State Officers, the Lord Chamberlain's department hired twenty-eight tailors plus other tailoring experts, six gold-lace makers, two sword cutlers and two goldsmiths. The coronation was certainly a boon to those whose trade specialised in luxury items; Valerie Cumming cites one robemaker who earned £2,044 4s. from mantles and garments worn by royal officials on the day.[5]

Those who attended were not on the whole an impressive lot. Farington castigated the peers present as 'old and feeble', and repeated the rumour that more than a third of those invited had sent their excuses. He also noted that the 'Application for Seats to see the Procession were owing to the apprehension of tumult very slack.'[6] The high price of tickets may have deterred the more impecunious aristocrats. Certainly it was obvious to all who were there that 'many of the boxes and galleries, which were erected at an enormous expense, were altogether unoccupied'. Princess Lieven later declared that members of the crowd had been paid to cheer the King as he passed.[7]

George's coronation costume cost £24,704. 8s. 10d., and was so heavy that he almost fainted more than once.[8] The vivid reds, blues, whites and golds of his robes were set off by an enormous plumed hat in the style of Henry IV, the first Bourbon King, atop thick curls (George in his vanity had long been wearing false hair to perpetuate the impression of youth). He had ordered a new Crown of St Edward to be made, featuring many more jewels than his predecessors had considered necessary, and hired as many as 12,314 diamonds. Royal jewellers Rundell, Bridge and Rundell estimated that the new crown would cost at least £100,000 – approximately £5 million in today's values – and the jewelled circlet to adorn the King's Cap of State a further £8,000.[9] Altogether, the Treasury estimated in 1823, the coronation had cost the nation £238,238 0s. 2d. Of this, £100,000 was voted by Parliament; the balance was paid for out of war reparations imposed on the French in 1815. (Valerie Cumming has pointed out that 'The French nation therefore had, directly and indirectly, paid for the two most lavish coronations celebrated in the period 1800 to 1840: the Emperor Napoleon's on 2 December 1804 and King George IV's.'[10] In view of the rivalry with Napoleon which George had assumed, he would surely have been delighted with the delicious irony of this.)

Uniquely, the coronation of 1821 was a bespoke creation. As Mark Girouard has noted, neither before nor since has 'almost everyone who took part ... worn clothes designed especially for the occasion'.[11] Even the Privy Councillors were stuffed into 'white and blue satin, with trunk hose and mantles, after the fashion of Queen Elizabeth's time'.[12] To complete the pantomine effect, their white shoes were fixed with huge red rosettes. On the way back from the Abbey to Westminster Hall for the coronation banquet, the King wore a royal purple Cap of State surmounted by that eight-thousand-pound jewelled circlet and large white ostrich feathers, while the pages at the banquet were dressed in coats of scarlet trimmed with gold lace, with blue sashes and white silk stockings. The *Annual Register* for 1821 could not resist a barb or two, describing the participants' costumes as 'Splendid, and in some instances grotesque', and singling out those worn by 'the gentlemen pensioners [and] the attendants of the lords spiritual' ('fashioned after the model of the earliest times') as among the more outlandish confections.[13]

Sir Walter Scott, while in general loyal to a fault, had qualms about the cost, telling his daughter that 'The expense of the robes may amount to £400 a piece' and that 'All the ermine is bought up at the most extravagant prices'. He managed to convince himself, however, that what was spent on the event itself, 'so far as it is national, has gone directly and indirectly to the encouragement of the British manufacturer and mechanic', and criticised those who 'sneer coldly at this solemn festival, and are rather disposed to dwell on the expense which attends it, than on the generous feelings which it ought to awaken'.[14]

At 10 a.m. on 21 July George IV arrived in Westminster Hall, fresh from a night's sleep at the Speaker's House next door. This overnight stay – for which the Speaker, Charles Manners-Sutton, went to the considerable expense of commissioning a lavish State Bed – was a notable departure from precedent. Of George's Stuart ancestors, Charles I had arrived at Westminster Hall by water on the morning of his coronation, while James II had processed to Westminster from Whitehall. George III, with his typical parsimony, had arrived at the Hall doors by sedan chair.

George, however, in poor health and increasingly reliant upon quantities of laudanum and alcohol, had to face the prospect of remaining on his feet for much of the next day, and the risk of revealing his physical infirmities in public. He was also concerned about his personal security, not entirely without reason. In 1812 the Prime

Minister, Perceval, had been shot and killed in the very lobby of the House of Commons and, as we have seen, on 25 January 1817 George himself had perhaps been fired at, and his carriage attacked by the mob, as he was returning from opening Parliament.

Thus, to avoid the possibility of presenting a comical spectacle as he lumbered along the route chosen by James II, a target for any lurking assassin, George spent the night before his coronation in the Speaker's House. He would be relatively fresh for the events of the following day, and more malicious observers would be denied the enjoyment of his attempts to extricate himself from his carriage. (His arrival at the Speaker's Entrance the evening before the ceremony was timed for half-past eight, just as it was growing dark – presumably for similar reasons.) He would also be able to dine with his friend Charles Manners-Sutton. Elder son of the Archbishop of Canterbury, whom George knew well (and who was painted by Hoppner at his request), and Speaker of the House of Commons since 1817, Manners-Sutton was an anti-Catholic Tory lawyer who happened to be a kinsman and protégé of George's former drinking crony the Duke of Rutland. The family connections went even deeper: his uncle, Thomas Manners-Sutton, had briefly been George's Solicitor-General in 1800–2, and had recently led the prosecution of Queen Caroline.[15]

On the morning of his coronation, George was dressed in silver doublet and hose, crimson surcoat and ermine-lined, gold-embroidered crimson velvet mantle so long and heavy that it required eight peers' sons to carry it, rather than the usual six. He tottered to the Abbey beneath a gold canopy carried by the sixteen Barons of the Cinque Ports, preceded by the King's 'herbwoman', Miss Fellowes, and her six maids, who strewed the raised platform leading to the Abbey with fragrant herbs. (Miss Fellowes was the daughter of the Lord Great Chamberlain's secretary, who had also spent the preceding night at Speaker's House, next door to the King.)[16]

The weather was kind, and bright sunshine filtered through the Abbey windows, making the vividly-coloured fabrics glitter – and all but causing disaster. The King, too-tightly corseted beneath his weighty velvet and ermine robes, found its heat excessive and at one point 'appeared distressed, almost to fainting'. Happily, he soon recovered, and survived the five hours of ceremonial surprisingly well. Meanwhile, many of those who had gathered to watch the procession enter the Abbey subsequently rushed away to Green Park 'to witness the ascent of Mr Green in a magnificent air balloon', then to Hyde

Park to see William Congreve's marvellous firework display. Those inside the Abbey were equally restless, or perhaps merely ill-informed as to the sequence of events: at the point in the service when the King left the main body of the Abbey for St Edward's Shrine (where he stayed a mere ten minutes), most of them got up and left. *The Observer* of 22 July 1821 commented with undisguised relish that 'When the King returned, he had empty benches, covered with dirt and litter, on one hand, and the backs of his courtiers expediting their exits with a "sauve-qui-peut like" rapidity, presented themselves to his view on the other.' The result was, the paper noted, an 'unpicturesque arrangement' which had 'the appearance of a want of respect to the Sovereign'.[17]

Meanwhile, the figure at the centre of the ceremonial played his role of icon of the nation's cultural and martial supremacy rather less well than the Virgin Queen had. As Wellington's friend Mrs Arbuthnot later noted in her journal,

> The King behaved very indecently; he was continually nodding and winking at Lady Conyngham and sighing and making eyes at her. At one time in the Abbey he took a diamond brooch from his breast and, looking at her, kissed it, on which she took off her glove and kissed a ring she had on!!! Any body who could have seen his disgusting figure, with a wig the curls of which hung down his back, and quite bending beneath the weight of his robes and his 60 years would have been quite sick.[18]

Queen Caroline's attempt to gate crash the coronation threatened to turn it into a farce. Hearing of George III's death while she was still in Italy, she had made preparations to return to England immediately. Shortly after her arrival she wrote to Lord Sidmouth demanding that she be crowned at the same time as the King, disingenuously claiming that she merely sought 'not ... to impose any new expense upon the nation'. Resisting all attempts to deter her, she presented herself for admission to the Abbey, but was repeatedly refused entrance by the burly guards, among them some of the famous pugilists of the day, who had been primed for just such an attempt. William Cobbett was particularly affronted on her behalf: 'When she got to the door, and made an attempt to enter, she was actually thrusted back *by the hands of a common prize-fighter.*' Caroline then stormed across to Westminster Hall – where she was espied by Lord Hood, who 'thought she looked like a blowsy Landlady' – only to have the doors slammed in her face.

The widespread public support she had enjoyed at the time of her trial and acquittal had largely evaporated over the ensuing months, and by now there were apparently few at any level of society who sympathised with her plight. Farington declared that 'Her reception was generally unfavourable. "Shame, shame" and "Off, Off" was the general cry though a few cried "Queen".' Sir Walter Scott was of the opinion that her 'misguided' interruption was 'the only disagreeable event of the day', and that, 'not being in her proper place, to be present in any other must have been voluntary degradation'. (Brougham, on the other hand, later wrote that 'She was saluted by all the soldiery, and even the people in the seats, who had paid 10 and 15 guineas down, and might be expected to hiss most at the untimely interruption, hissed very little and applauded loudly in most places.') While the mob (dismissed by Scott as 'a small body-guard of ragamuffins') that followed Caroline back to her friend Alderman Wood's house in South Audley Street broke house windows in the fashionable districts of Piccadilly and St James's, among them those of Castlereagh, the Foreign Secretary, the serious violence and insurrection feared by the authorities did not materialise.[19]

Inside Westminster Hall, following the service in the Abbey, the scarlet-and-gold pages served the assembled guests food that had cost £25,000:

> Twenty-three kitchens, supervised by Jean-Baptiste Watier, produced 160 tureens of soup, a similar amount of fish dishes, roast joints of venison, beef, mutton and veal, vegetables and appropriate gravies etc. presented in 480 sauce boats. Cold dishes, including ham, pastries, seafood and jellies number 3,271. All this was washed down with 9,840 bottles of various wines and 100 gallons of iced punch.[20]

It must have been thought that the ritual of the King's Champion would emphasise George IV's ancient heritage and at the same time reinforce the image of him as Napoleon's conqueror. Yet somehow it failed – perhaps inevitably – to live up to expectations. The hereditary office of King's Champion, allegedly imported along with so much else by Duke William of Normandy in 1066, had since at least the beginning of the fifteenth century been vested in the manor of Scrivelsby in Lincolnshire, held by the Dymoke family. Armed *cap-à-pie* and with red, white and blue feathers in his helmet, supported on either side by the High Constable of England and the Earl Marshal of

England, the King's Champion rode into Westminster Hall during the first course of the banquet which immediately followed the Coronation service in the Abbey, and offered combat to any who disputed the sovereign's title. Three times the challenge was read out by a herald and the gauntlet was thrown down: at the entrance to the Hall, in the middle, and before the high table at which the King was seated. When the gauntlet had been taken up for the third time (there is no recorded instance of the challenge having been accepted, though there was some talk at the time of George III's coronation of a Jacobite doing so) the sovereign drank to his Champion from a silver-gilt cup; this was then handed to the Champion, who drank to his sovereign and kept the cup as his fee.

Unfortunately for George IV, the hereditary Champion of the day, John Dymoke, was also the rector of Scrivelsby, and had asserted that the nature of his calling prevented him from offering violence by throwing down his gauntlet in public (the picture of an Anglican cleric thus conjured up is compelling, and possibly played its part in Mr Dymoke's decision). Instead, John Dymoke sent his son Henry in his place. Henry, alas, who was only twenty, looked rather too young for his appointed task, and was too small for his inherited suit of Elizabethan armour. He was also unsteady on his horse – even though it was, appropriately enough, a trained animal, used to crowds, specially 'hired from Astley's circus for the occasion'.[21] Even Sir Walter Scott acknowledged that Dymoke had 'a little too much the appearance of a maiden-knight to be the challenger of the world in the King's behalf' (he also, somewhat pedantically, complained that Dymoke's shield was 'a round "roundache", or Highland target – a defensive weapon which it would have been impossible to use on horseback').[22] Nevertheless, to the sound of trumpets Dymoke entered the Hall (and the horse defecated dramatically) with the High Constable (Wellington) on his left and the Earl Marshal (Lord Howard of Effingham, deputising for the Catholic Duke of Norfolk) on his right, the challenge was read and the gauntlet thrown down three times, the toasts were drunk with the King, and he left with his cup.

It was like something from the pages of one of Sir Walter Scott's own novels – though Scott would clearly have been more meticulous as to detail – but nevertheless failed to add to the sense of occasion. All sense of decorum had already been largely destroyed, quite inadvertently, by Lord Anglesey. When the first course was brought in Anglesey, as Lord High Steward, had to ride down the length of the

Hall with the High Constable and the Earl Marshal, leading the procession carrying the dishes for the royal table; the three had then to back down the Hall and leave, still on horseback. Anglesey had, it will be recalled, lost a leg at Waterloo. In general he managed very well with various false ones, but had overlooked the fact that a part of his duties as High Steward was to return, dismounted, to remove the covers from the royal dishes: the King could not eat until he had done so.

> He had neglected to provide himself with one of his 'walking legs', which were of a different type from those which he wore for riding. [Summoned by a herald, he] at once returned, still on horseback, to explain in person to the King that he was 'unable to walk with *his riding leg on*'. This produced a great roar of laughter which echoed round the crowded hall ...[23]

Laughter turned to admiration, however, when instead of excusing himself he dismounted and carried out his task supported by his pages. More seriously, when George left the Hall, unseemly pandemonium broke out as guests rushed to seize the banqueting plate. The Lord Chamberlain managed to secure the most valuable items from plunder, but much was lost.

The recorded impressions of most spectators appear to correspond with their pre-existing prejudices. Those who deemed George IV a reckless spendthrift and a figure of fun saw exactly that. One cartoon depicted it as the coronation of 'King Punch', with George drunk on brandy. A Westminster schoolboy thought the King looked 'more like an Elephant than a man', Lady Cowper that, as he snuffled *sal volatile* from a lady's vinaigrette, he resembled 'more ... the victim that the hero of the fête'.[24]

However, those more kindly disposed to George, those who had expected to find the ceremonial uplifting, were less ready to find fault. Lord Denbigh told his mother that the coronation 'exceeded all imagination and conception' – although his subsequent comments suggest he was more interested in the value of the jewels his fellow-dignitaries were wearing than in the significance of the ceremony itself (Prince Esterhazy, he goggled, was 'said to have had jewels on his person estimated at *eighty thousand* pounds'). The poet Thomas Hood declared that the coronation had 'brought home to the observers the full dignity of kingly office'. Benjamin Haydon, cynic that he was, admitted that despite Dymoke's shaky challenge his imagination 'got so intoxicated that I came out with a great contempt for the plebs'.[25]

In contrast to the observations of Farington and others on the thinness of the crowd, Sir Walter Scott later claimed that the 'long galleries stretched among the aisles of that venerable and august pile' had been 'filled even to crowding with all that Britain has of beautiful and distinguished'. Scott's reinterpretation of historic British myth, *Ivanhoe*, had been published in 1819 and his *Kenilworth*, a celebration of the pageantry of Elizabeth I's court, only a few months before the coronation. His imagination was clearly in tune with the King's, and he was very ready to see in the coronation an illusion of his own novels made real, a pan-Britannic celebration which reincarnated George IV as the Father of the Nation. Accordingly he relished

> ... the rich spectacle of the aisles crowded with waving plumage, and coronets, and caps of honour, and the sun, which brightened and saddened as if on purpose, and now darting a solitary ray, which catched, as it passed, the glittering folds of a banner, or the edge of a group of battle-axes or partizans, and then rested full on some fair form, 'the cynosure of neighbouring eyes', whose circlet of diamonds glistened under its influence.[26]

Compare this with passages in *Ivanhoe*, in which medieval tournaments were held where 'the sun shone fierce and bright upon the polished arms of the knights of either side, who crowded the opposite extremities of the lists, and held eager conference together', and 'magnificent pavilions' were 'adorned with pennons of russet and black'. The parallels in *Kenilworth*, a tale of royal banquets and challenges centering on the progress of Elizabeth I to an ancient castle, are more obvious still. The entrance into Kenilworth involved 'a great display of expensive magnificence ... nought was to be seen but velvet and cloth of gold and silver, ribands, feathers, and golden chains', and the sovereign was 'arrayed in the most splendid manner, and blazing with jewels'. The pageantry of the evocation of the Lady of the Lake is reminiscent of the Champion's challenge; indeed, elements of it reappear in Scott's concocted ceremony of the Washing of the Royal Hands, staged at the Parliament House banquet in Edinburgh the following year.[27]

Quite apart from the episode of Anglesey's leg and the fact that Henry Dymoke was no Wilfred of Ivanhoe, the coronation pageantry, for all Scott's rosy-hued reportage, failed to transcend the reality of the teetering, corpulent figure of George IV at its heart. But what Scott looked for in the coronation – a reaffirmation of the values of kingship, and reassurance that George IV was uniquely fitted for the role – was what he, personally, found. 'Certainly', he wrote afterwards, 'never Monarch received a more general welcome from his assembled subjects' – subjects for whom, he optimistically asserted, the coronation was 'a happy holiday to the monotony of a life of labour'. Perhaps inevitably, his account of the coronation in the *Edinburgh Weekly Journal* of 20 July 1821 was over-indulgent. In particular, his story of the audience's reaction to 'the affectionate and sincere reverence in the embrace interchanged betwixt the Duke of York and his Majesty that approached almost to a caress' – 'I never heard plaudits given more from the heart than those that were thundered upon the royal brethren when they were thus pressed to each other's bosoms' – was a highly-coloured mixture of fact and wishful thinking. His brief postscript to this episode noting George's typically over-emotional reaction to his brother's effusive greeting (which caused 'some alarm among those who saw him as nearly as I did') is perhaps a little nearer the mark.[28] When he came to create the programme for George's visit to Edinburgh the following year, Scott was careful to plan every event himself.

Benjamin Haydon may have been 'intoxicated' enough to think that 'The way in which the King bowed was really royal' – the King looked, he said, 'like some gorgeous bird of the East' – but nevertheless brought a more jaundiced eye than Scott's to bear on the proceedings. He noted that 'Many of the doorkeepers were tipsy', and that loud and often violent quarrels took place over the seating arrangements. He observed, too, what he took for an eruption of the old rivalry between Wellington and Anglesey. 'Wellington in his coronet walked down the Hall, cheered by the officers of the Guards. He shortly returned mounted, with Lords Howard and Anglesey. They rode gracefully to the foot of the throne, and then backed out. Lord Anglesey's horse was restive. Wellington became impatient, and I am convinced, thought it a trick of Lord Anglesey's to attract attention. He never paused, but backed on, and the rest were obliged to follow him.' For Haydon, the climax of the day was evidently not George's glittering apparel, nor even the coronation itself, but the mouth-watering spectacle of Miss Fellowes' herb-girls in their dresses of ivory gauze and their 'Medici' ruffs:

> The grace of their action, their slow movement, their white dresses, were indescribably touching; their light milky colour contrasted with the dark shadow of the archway, which, though dark, was full of rich crimson dresses that gave the shadow a tone as of deep blood.[29]

The splendours of 19 July 1821 were never to be repeated. As Walter Scott's son-in-law and first biographer later noted, 'The coronation of George the Fourth's successor was conducted in a vastly inferior scale and splendour and expense.'[30] Never again would a royal coronation involve the medieval pageantry enacted by George IV. His brother William IV dispensed with the Hereditary Champion, the Hereditary Herbwoman, the coronation banquet, and indeed with the whole idea of a procession from Hall to Abbey, a concept which was only revived in 1952 for the coronation of Elizabeth II and the television age. As David Cannadine has remarked, 'George IV's flirtation with grandeur was so unsuccessful that it was not repeated.'[31]

16

The Visit to Edinburgh

He looks in the glass – but perfection is there,
Wig, whiskers, and chin-tufts all right to a hair ...
Thomas Moore, *The New Costume of the Ministers*

A S WE HAVE already seen, the strong romantic attachment to his
Stuart forbears and the long-exiled Catholic Jacobites cultivated
by George as Prince of Wales had ceased to be politically suspect with
the death in 1806 of the last direct Stuart claimant to the British
throne, Cardinal Henry of York, for with him perished the last vestige
of potential danger from a French-backed Jacobite claimant. His
death also encouraged George, great-grandson of the king whom
Charles Edward Stuart had sought to replace in 1745, to see himself
as heir to the royal heritage of both the Hanoverians and the Jacobite
Stuarts, a conceit made much of by his master of ceremonies, Sir
Walter Scott, when George, as King, visited Scotland in 1822. His biographer John Lockhart remembered Scott 'over and over again, alluding to George IV as acquiring a title, *de jure*, on the death of the poor
Cardinal of York'.[1] The *Edinburgh Observer*, swift to follow Scott's line,
announced at the time of the King's arrival that:

> We are now all Jacobites, thorough-bred Jacobites, in acknowledging
> George IV ... Our King is the heir of the Chevalier, in whose service the
> Scotch suffered so much, shone so much, and he will find many a Flora
> MacDonald amongst the 'Sisters of the Silver Cross', and many a faithful
> Highlander attending his throne with the forester's bugle and bow.[2]

George's visit to Ireland immediately following his coronation had
been a qualified success – even if he was more interested in staying

with Lady Conyngham at Slane Castle than in making himself popular with his Irish subjects. He was the first English sovereign to visit the island for peaceful reasons since Richard II more than four centuries earlier (although Richard II, in view of his deposition and murder, was perhaps not the best ancestor to invoke in these turbulent times). Reprehensibly heartened by the death of Caroline of Brunswick on 7 August, he appeared to be in good spirits, entering Dublin on 17 August with a broad smile on his face and a large bunch of shamrock stuffed into his Field Marshal's hat. Four days later, to his evident delight, more than a thousand women were presented to him, following which Dublin Corporation staged a lavish banquet, similarly enlivened by the presence of numerous female guests. The former Prime Minister Lord Sidmouth, senior government official accompanying the King, judged that 'the testimonies of dutiful and affectionate attachment, which His Majesty has received from all classes and descriptions of his Irish subjects, have made the deepest impression on his mind', and promised that 'he looks forward to the period when he shall revisit them with the strongest feelings of satisfaction'. Writing more informally to a friend on 8 June he noted: 'I can truly say, that I have not heard an unpleasant word nor seen a sullen look since I came into the country.' As Sidmouth's biographer has commented, the King, 'unused to such affection, in his turn revealed a warmth and charm which had all too rarely appeared in recent years'. More characteristic, however, was the occasion towards the end of his stay when George, eager as always to lay his troubled brow in Lady Conyngham's lap, abruptly abandoned a visit to the Royal Dublin Society without bothering to look at, let alone taste, the elaborate refreshments which had been prepared for him and escaped to the Slane Castle. Croker's diary noted the 'great disappointment and some criticism, which five minutes more would have prevented'. Furthermore, neither Sidmouth nor his sovereign was prepared to entertain any pleas for concessions to the Catholic population. Everpartisan, Huish was not far off the mark in declaring that, 'kept in a whirl of pleasure and dissipation, [George IV] left the Irish coast as ignorant of the internal discord and misery of the country, as when he landed on it'.

Within ten days of returning from Ireland George was off again, to make what was to prove his last visit to Hanover. He journeyed by way of Brussels and the battlefield of Waterloo, which he visited with Wellington in the pouring rain. Wellington was rather disgusted with

George's alternately sullen and melodramatic response to his personal tour, writing later that he 'never asked me a single question, nor said one word, until I showed him where Lord Anglesey's leg was buried, and then he burst into tears'. George left after directing that a tree which had been shattered by cannon-fire should be chopped down and its wood used to make a chair for Carlton House; the finished product was vaingloriously inscribed with the words 'GEORGIO AUGUSTO EUROPAE LIBERATORI'. Clearly, in George's own mind, if in no one else's, it was he and not Wellington or Blücher who was the liberator of Europe.[3]

Once in Hanover, George charmed his subjects by wearing only the newly-created Hanoverian Guelphic Order on his well-fleshed chest, and speaking to them in his accented German. His gout prevented him from travelling to Vienna, as he had planned, but the Austrian Chancellor, Prince Metternich, came to Hanover. George had first encountered Metternich in London in 1814, when the Chancellor presented him with three gifts of the sort in which he took most pleasure – a chivalric order, a regimental colonelcy, and a sumptuous uniform. Metternich now suggested that the King make a more extended visit to the Continent the following year, pressing on to the Prussian Court at Berlin and to Habsburg Vienna, where the Congress of Nations was due to convene to discuss the prospects for the new Europe being created under the Treaty of Vienna. The cost of George's Irish and Hanoverian expeditions had however been such that the government was reluctant to entertain the prospect of the further drain on the public purse an unnecessary and extended Continental jaunt represented. Instead, Liverpool recommended a less ambitious diversion, to Scotland. In this he was, unusually, supported by Lady Conyngham, who in one of her customary fits of petulance declared she would not go to Vienna. (She subsequently refused to go to Edinburgh, too – a blessing for the organisers, who were thereby spared George's embarrassing public displays of affection for her.)

George's visit to Scotland, a far more formal affair than his trip to Ireland, was imbued with considerable symbolic significance, both for him, as we have seen, and for the nation. It would be the first visit of a Hanoverian king to Edinburgh, and the first of any British monarch since Charles I's coronation there in 1633. And, while it was by no means intended to be taken as an apology for the brutal aftermath of Culloden – when the British army and London legislature spared no severity in suppressing all taints of Jacobitism – it was hoped that it would go some way towards healing the wounds caused by the repression of Scottish identity after the defeat of Bonnie Prince Charlie. The King and his advisors thought it preferable to stress the indissoluble links between the two nations, rather than recall ancient grudges. As Linda Colley has pointed out, the royal visit gave the people of Scotland a glimpse of the reality of monarchy – as Walter Scott enthused, 'they could compare the actual thing called Majesty, with all they had from childhood dreamed and fancied of it!' Thomas Carlyle, more cynically, saw it all as little more than 'an efflorescence of flunkeyisms'.[4]

Until the beginning of the Regency Scott was largely known as a poet and literary editor, far from negligible accomplishments the financial success of which enabled him to purchase his estate at Abbotsford in 1811. Two years later, and to his surprise, the Regent proposed that he should become Poet Laureate. Acknowledging that his verse was neither so popular nor so forceful as that of rivals such as Byron he wisely declined, however, recommending instead Robert Southey. Such evidence of George's support and admiration nevertheless appears to have encouraged him to broaden his horizons, and in 1814, anonymously, he published his first novel, *Waverley*. It was an instant success, introducing to novel-writing an historical perspective never before exploited. Eight years later, a similar inspiration was the background of the mock-medieval pageant he staged in Edinburgh. Scott was always fulsome in his praise of George, and never hesitated to defend him against his critics either before or after his death. In 1818 he was offered (and eventually accepted) a baronetcy.

Scott's vision of kingship was, as we have seen, remarkably similar to George's own. The foundation for the visit was laid with his rediscovery of the Royal Scottish Regalia, the ancient 'Honours of Scotland', in which George displayed great interest. The regalia had lain forgotten in Edinburgh Castle since the Act of Union of 1707 which obviated the need for these medieval symbols had caused them to be placed in a chest and tucked away for safekeeping. Scott's researches indicated where they might be found, and on 4 February 1818 he and his party duly discovered 'the Crown, Sceptre and Sword of State ... in perfect order and preservation' ('The Crown', noted one official, 'is said to be particularly fine).'[5] Scott also ensured that his close friend Adam Ferguson was appointed Keeper of the Regalia.

The Scottish Regalia subsequently became the centre-piece of Scott's plans for the King's visit. On 12 August 1822, three days before George came ashore at Leith (and also, as it happened, his birthday), Scott was to star in a ceremony of his own invention in which the Regalia was to be transferred with great solemnity from the Castle to the Palace of Holyroodhouse, escorted by a motley assemblage of members of the Celtic Society in elaborate tartan costume. (The Celtic Society, its principal objective to foster the wearing of Highland dress, had been founded in 1820: first President, Sir Walter Scott.) The event took a bizarre turn with the unheralded arrival of Alasdair Ranaldson MacDonell, 14th Hereditary Chief of Glengarry, self-appointed epitome of Highland traditions, who attempted to place himself at the head of the procession. Though Glengarry was a good friend, Scott was mortified to have his ceremonial upstaged by a figure whose idiosyncratic version of Highland dress made a mockery of his carefully-costumed event. (Glengarry had previously been excoriated by the Celtic Society for not wearing his tartan in the fashion they favoured, and for being unable to speak Gaelic, the language of the Highlander. As John Prebble has commented, 'He wore nothing but ... kilt, plaid and bonnet, strapped himself with barbaric arms at every opportunity, and went nowhere without a chief's tail of henchman, bard, piper and gillies.') General Stirling, leading the parade, was speechless at Glengarry's presumption; seemliness was only restored when Glengarry's horse was forcibly led away by a quick-thinking naval officer. The collapse of some seating being built for spectators, killing two and injuring many others, was a more serious omen.

Glengarry, a man of uncertain temper, was furious at the perceived slight and threatened to challenge the officer responsible to a duel. Three days later he gatecrashed another of Scott's neatly choreographed processions, galloping up to the King soon after his landing to cry out 'Your Majesty is welcome to Scotland'; he was only mollified by being allowed to escort George's empty carriage from Holyroodhouse two days later.[6] Ironically enough, Glengarry was widely held to have inspired the Highland chieftain Fergus Mac-Ivor in Scott's *Waverley* of 1814, described there as 'cautious of exhibiting external marks of dignity' and wearing Highland dress 'in the simplest mode'. It seems that Scott would have liked to be able to cast Glengarry as a contemporary hero with 'a martial air' approximating to his Romantic view of Highland history, for he wrote of him thus a year or so after George's Scottish visit:

This gentleman is a kind of Quixote in our age, having retained in its full extent the whole feelings of Clanship and Chieftainship elsewhere so long abandoned. He seems to have lived a century too late and to exist in a state of complete law and order like a Glengarry of old whose will was law ... Kindhearted, generous, friendly, he is beloved by those who know him and his efforts are unceasing to show kindness to those of his clan who are disposed fully to meet his pretensions ... To me he is a treasure as being full of information as to the history of his own clan and the manners and customs of the highlanders in general. Strong, active and muscular, he follows the chase of the deer for days and nights together sleeping in his plaid when darkness overtakes him in the forest.[7]

Those of Glengarry's tenants who remained in the Highlands would scarcely have recognised their landlord in Scott's encomium. Forced evictions meant that by 1820, only thirty-five tenants remained of the 1,500 original inhabitants of his farms.[8]

Henry Raeburn's skilfully flattering portrait of Glengarry, completed some time before 1812, when it was exhibited at the Royal Academy, and now in the National Gallery of Scotland, portrays him in full Highland dress; yet it involved as much fancy-dress posturing as Lawrence's later portraits of the Prince Regent. It has been suggested that from the outset both Raeburn and Glengarry had a London audience for the portrait in mind, the one for the 'impact of its exoticism' and the other for its 'element of reasserted triumphalism' (the proscription on the wearing of Highland dress had been lifted in 1782, and Celtic Revivalism was in full swing). The English were free to take the image at face value, as the portrait of a quintessential Highland chieftain and evidence of Scotland's renaissance.[9]

In reality, Glengarry's proud pose was little more than empty theatre. He had never fought in battle. In 1794 he had raised the Glengarry Fencibles, and they were to him much what the 10th Dragoons had been to George: he was their Colonel, and he dressed them in his favourite tartan. By 1802, deep in debt, Glengarry had begun to evict his tenants (many of them parents of the men he had recruited into the Fencibles) and replace them with sheep. Robert Burns had labelled him a tyrant – both for his evictions, and for his strenuous attempts to prevent his former tenants from emigrating. Glengarry, however, saw himself as encapsulating the martial ardour of the Highlands: 'naturally generous as well as brave, and an enemy to anything wearing the semblance of opposition'. In practice, rather than defending the rights of his own tenant families, this took the form of despatching his heavies to strong-arm Thomas Telford's engineers, engaged in the cutting of the Caledonian Canal to the south-west of Inverness.

In 1815 Glengarry found an outlet for his rich man's fantasies by helping to found the preposterous Society of True Highlanders. This had been ostensibly devised in support 'of the Dress, Language, Music and Characteristics of our illustrious and ancient race in the Highlands and Isles of Scotland, with their genuine descendants wherever they may be'. In truth, the Society was little more than a dining club for the Scots gentry and aristocracy. As Prebble has acutely observed:

> Membership of the Society would not have included the men and women of Kildonan who took ship for Canada that same month, nor the hundreds of common tenants who had been leaving Glengarry's lands since the days of his grandfather. This was an exclusive organization of the . . . Highland gentleman and lady, thoroughly anglicized now, but happy to play-act their ancestors while the summer sun lasted . . . With their glens emptied and their land under sheep, the lairds had time and money to spend on the Society's theatricals.

Glengarry was an unmistakable presence at the Society's dinners and balls, clad in what he interpreted as traditional Highland dress, acoompanied by his personal piper and bard. Crashing their dirks into the table in a puerile attempt to recreate the martial ardour of their ancestors, Glengarry and his wealthy friends made ostentatious Jacobite toasts and boasted of the feared reputation of Highland soldiery of old – many of whose descendants Glengarry and his fellows had more recently forced to emigrate to the New World.[10]

Glengarry was by no means the only Highland chieftain to involve himself in Scott's royal pageant who was at the same time engaged in destroying the social fabric of the Highland glens he professed to love. The fourth Earl of Breadalbane, a prominent figure in the processions and ceremonies of August 1822, had for some years past been filling the ancient lands of the clan Campbell with sheep while his former tenants queued for steerage passages to Canada or the United States. In a similar vein, the Marchioness of Stafford – Countess of Sutherland in her own right, whose estates covered much of northern Scotland – ensured herself a leading role in the royal visit. Her son, Lord Francis Leveson-Gower, was deputed by Scott to carry the rediscovered Sceptre of Scotland before the King

(Lady Stafford having vehemently asserted the hereditary right of the Earls of Sutherland to this honour), while she provided a contingent of 'two hundred well-dressed Highlanders of the clan in Edinburgh' for Scott's processions. Meanwhile, the Sutherland glens were being emptied and tenants' homes burned. James Loch, Commissioner for the estate and right-hand man to Lord and Lady Stafford, boasted following the clearances that 'the character of this whole population will be completely changed' and that 'the children of those who are removed from the hills will lose all recollection of the habits and customs of their fathers'.[11] Debt drove the MacDonells from Glengarry, Lord Stafford was created Duke of Sutherland by William IV, and within thirty years relatively few clansmen remained in a Highland landscape now largely populated by sheep. Instead the Highlands had become, in Prebble's felicitous phrase, 'Britain's Alps, a stage for romanticism and healthy sport' – the foundations of which were laid by Scott, in his 'Waverley' novels and in his preparations for George IV's visit in 1822.

The King's faltering health, however, meant that the proposed visit was constantly postponed, and even a month before it was due to begin there was still a chance that it might not take place at all. As late as 11 July 1822 Lord Montagu wrote to Sir Walter Scott that there was 'still no certainty whether the King will or will not go to Scotland':

> It now appears he will not go by land & his Doctors will not allow him to go by Sea. One would think in this case there would be no difficulty in deciding not to go, but I suppose he really does feel hampered with his engagement [to Hanover] & can not quite make up his mind to give it up. In the mean time the inconvenience is great to all concerned, & whether he goes or not this long hesitation must have a bad effect ...[12]

Only on 24 July was it confirmed that the King would indeed journey north, arriving in Edinburgh approximately three weeks later, and only a week before his arrival did it become clear that George did not, after all, intend to progress throughout Scotland, but was confining his visit to a short stay in Edinburgh.

The Lord Provost of Edinburgh asked Sir Walter Scott to arrange matters, and Scott's house at 39 Castle Street accordingly became the centre of frenetic activity: 'Local magistrates, bewildered and perplexed ... threw themselves on him for advice and direction about the merest trifles; and he had to arrange every thing, from the ordering of a procession to the cut of a button and the embroidery of a cross.'[13]

Buttons were one thing; the tartan kilt, as worn by Glengarry, which in Scott's pageantry became such a powerful symbol of Scottish identity, was quite another. Its very provenance was dubious. As Hugh Trevor-Roper has pointed out, at the time of Bonnie Prince Charlie's failed invasion of 1745 the shorter, tailored kilt (as distinguished from the *fealeadh mor*, the all-in-one, untailored, belted plaid and kilt) was generally acknowledged to be a relatively recent and English invention, while the idea of 'clan' tartans simply did not exist. The 1747 Act of Proscription forbidding the wearing of 'Highland Garb' included under this heading kilt, plaid, trews and tartans: by thus defining the Highlanders' wardrobe, it probably did as much as anything before George's visit and Scott's activities to imbue these garments with such legendary status and martial resonance that they were adopted by the new Scottish regiments enthusiastically recruited for the British Army after Culloden. After 1782, when the ban was lifted, the Highland peasantry generally eschewed the draughty and impractical 'belted plaid', while the upper and aspiring middle classes rapidly attached themselves to the shorter kilt:

> Anglicized Scottish peers, improving gentry, well-educated Edinburgh lawyers and prudent merchants of Aberdeen – men who were not constrained by poverty and who would never have to skip over rocks and bogs or lie all night in the hills – would exhibit themselves not in the historic trews, the traditional costume of their class, nor in the cumbrous belted plaid, but in a costly and fanciful version of that recent innovation, the philibeg or small kilt.[14]

While some now denounced the kilt as a recent and impractical innovation, when this argument was finally put to the kilt-wearing Scottish regiments in 1804, the proposal to substitute trews for kilts was met with derision and outrage. Already myth had become more powerful than truth: the regimental colonels insisted that the kilt had been the traditional dress of the Highlander, and the Highland regiments' prominent role in Wellington's victory at Waterloo helped to fix the concept in popular mythology. Indeed, it was perhaps this indirect evocation of the battlefield of Waterloo (which he had personally visited only the year before) that George was consciously promoting by his decision to wear a tartan kilt at the climax of his Edinburgh visit. As Trevor-Roper has noted, the 'Waverley' novels Scott published after 1814, full of romantic references to Scottish history and replete with kilt-wearing Highlanders, helped to spread this new orthodoxy still

further, to an international audience. Any protest in favour of historical accuracy was now met with stunned disbelief. Clan chiefs who
should have known better cheerfully acquiesced in the 'authentication'
of one of their many plaids as the officially-registered 'clan tartan' by
George Hunter or his rival weavers. Even Glengarry was appalled,
resigning from the Celtic Society with the parting comment that 'I
never saw so much tartan *before* in my life, *with so little Highland material*
... There may be some very good and respectable men amongst them,
but their general appearance is assumed and fictitious, and *they have no
right to burlesque the national character of dress of the Highlands.*' More importantly, as John Prebble has noted, for many Scots the kilt had by now
become 'the hated uniform of the young Highlandmen whom oppres-
sive land-owners had committed to endless wars'.[15]

George was never slow to seize the opportunity of acquiring a
splendid new costume, and as early as 1789 had purchased himself
some 'Scottish' clothes.[16] Predictably, the 'Highland' dress and accoutrements he ordered for himself in honour of his visit to Edinburgh
bore little relation to those of ordinary Scots. His effeminate white,
silk-lined goatskin sporran cost £105, and he spent £375 on a 'highland' bonnet badge made of gold 'set with Diamonds, Pearls, Rubies
and Emeralds' and £262 on a massive, almost unusable 'Highland
Dirk ... inlaid with gold'. Then there was £157 10s. for 'A fine basket
gilt Highland sword of polished Steele ... inlaid with gold' and £42
for a pair of matching 'Highland pistols'. Altogether, the cost of his
order for Highland dress from George Hunter of Edinburgh of
September 1822 was £1,354 18s. Even the most well-meaning
observer could not fail to note the contrast between the luxurious
trappings of the self-appointed heir to the Jacobite dynasty and 'the
simple belted plaid once worn by the Highlander'.[17]

Not only the fortunes of George Hunter, but also the propagation
of the myth of the tartan kilt was given an enormous boost by the
King's visit to Edinburgh. Celtic Society founder and Scott's advisor,
Colonel David Stewart of Garth, even devised a new tartan for the
King himself, appropriately entitled 'Royal Stewart'. To Stewart and
Scott, George IV's proposed visit was a godsend. The ceremonials and
dress codes they concocted for the royal occasion were all the products of their own enthusiasm and passion. Thus was the royal visit
transformed into a romantic Celtic fantasy in which the players
dressed in stage-clothes and led 'tails' of stage-clansmen. As one
observer later commented of Edinburgh, 'A tartan fit had come upon

the city, and putting a plumed bonnet on her brow, stepping to the sound of a pibroch, and calling on her tail to follow, she marched out, wondering at her own shadow.' Yet not all was romance. Hugh Trevor-Roper and John Prebble have documented the way in which, well before George's visit, Regency textile manufacturers took advantage of a burgeoning market first fuelled by the international popularity of Scott's kilt- and plaid-wearing heroes, by adapting or simply inventing a whole series of tartans, each supposedly appropriate to one particular clan. The young hereditary chief of one of the most prominent Highland clans, Ewen Macpherson of Cluny (known like all chiefs of that name as Cluny Macpherson), was dressed for George's visit by William Wilson and Son of Bannockburn in what was allegedly a 'Macpherson tartan' – but which had previously been sold as 'Kidd' tartan and, before that, merely as 'pattern number 155'. Business boomed so encouragingly that in 1822 Wilson and Son built forty new looms in Edinburgh for the production of 'clan' tartans alone. In Stirling the local newspaper noted that 'almost all the persons formerly engaged in the weaving of muslin in this quarter have commenced the weaving of tartan, in consequence of its affording a better return for their labour'.[18]

And as Edinburgh was 'tartanised' to receive her King, Scottish history was reinterpreted or glossed over. The ceremonials of August 1822 represented Scotland as a land not of the Clearances, of economic hardship or of Highland–Lowland enmities, but as one of happy clansmen and ancient traditions, their origins conveniently lost in the mists of time. Scott – a Lowlander by birth but nevertheless apparently happy to jettison his native region's own cultural and political identity – presented the King with a theatrical spectacle revolving around colourful or romantic figures and ideas, recognising that here in Edinburgh, as in Dublin the year before, George had no desire to concern himself with economic or political realities. What he wanted was entertainment – a brief, dazzling display of historical half-truths. 'Highlanders are what he will best like to see,' Scott advised one chief, suggesting that he 'bring half-a-dozen or half-a-score of clansmen, so as to look like an island chief, as you are'.[19]

The extravaganza which followed represented Scotland and the Scots as George expected them to be, as he had read of them in Scott's own novels. In the same way that the Westminster coronation had exploited Tudor imagery to counteract such disagreeable realities as the King's attempted divorce and poor personal reputation, by means of invented or exaggerated ceremonial surrounding George's Edinburgh visit Scott sought to eradicate memories of Culloden, the brutal pacification of the Highlands which followed and the subsequent Clearances. He conjured up an elaborate pageant which took as its inspiration a semi-mythical Jacobethan era of peace and harmony, in which convenient, harmless and picturesque images of Scottish identity and the Union with England were intermingled. At Scott's request, George had revived some of the Jacobite Highlanders' peerages, titles which had been suppressed in the wave of attainders that followed Culloden. Scott had stern words of guidance for the principal players in his charade, directing that 'those who wear the Highland dress must ... be careful to be armed in the proper Highland fashion – steel-wrought pistols, broad sword and dirk'. Yet the colourful Highlanders who made up the great chieftains' tails were no threat now to the nation's peace and security: rather than intimations of violence, their swords and pistols were more like quaint theatrical props for a Raeburn or Lawrence portrait.[20]

Scott's painstakingly-assembled tableaux were to some extent undermined by various pragmatic considerations, chief among them George's safety, in the light of the assassinations and assassination attempts of late years and the supposedly uncertain nature of the Edinburgh populace. The government's choice of the 13th Foot, ordered into the city to guard the person of the King, was however somewhat tactless: memories were long, and the 13th, having helped to win the battle of Culloden, had been closely involved in policing the country after the collapse of the Forty-five. Their employment now was highly provocative, and sat uneasily with Scott's quixotic attempts to heal old wounds. Rather more appealing to George's sense of personal destiny must have been the presence in Edinburgh of the 66th Foot, which until the previous year had been guarding Napoleon in his exile on St Helena. As at the coronation, however, in the event the troops were needed for nothing more serious than controlling over-zealous crowds (by the second week of August, more than 50,000 visitors had streamed into Edinburgh).

Not everyone was prepared to go along with Scott's romantic reinterpretation of Scottish history. Retired soldier Duncan Mac-Gregor of Learnan excused himself to his clan chief: he was so dissatisfied with 'the manner in which the Spurious Highlanders are to be disposed of during the Sovereign's visit to Dun Edin to the prejudice of those whose claims to distinction have been often inscribed in characters of blood' – the Clan Gregor had been active on the Jacobite side in 1715 and again in 1745 – that 'I trust you will excuse my not appearing as a clansman on the approaching occasion.' Sir Evan MacGregor himself, however, was enthusiastic enough to spend nearly £300 (double his retainers' wages bill for the event) on tartan outfits for his 'tail'. The Duke of Atholl, a fellow of the Royal Society, similarly expressed his unease at 'the madness or the Highland garb', and was both appalled and amused by 'the different persons dressed by Sir W. Scott in fantastic attire'.[21]

Scott, concerned that 'the whole goodly display' should not 'sink . . . into dis-organisation and confusion', was clearly determined to avoid some at least of the less decorous scenes which had marred the coronation. He stipulated that the *Royal George* should arrive at the port of Leith, where Scottish monarchs of the past had landed, and that the King should then progress to the Palace of Holyroodhouse by way of Leith Walk, a wide, recently-built and largely neoclassical avenue. The *Royal George* was preceded into port by the steam-packet *City of Edinburgh*, carrying a hundred huge cases of royal essentials for George's visit. These included not only a throne and quantities of plate but also a large consignment of live poultry, a commodity the Royal Household clearly believed would be unobtainable in Edinburgh.[22]

Directly he arrived, on 14 August, George demanded that Sir Walter, who as the chief orchestrator of the visit was 'the man in Scotland I most wish to see', come on board. Scott presented him with a silver St Andrew's Cross, which George wore prominently during his visit. Having drunk his sovereign's health in George's favourite Maraschino, Scott sentimentally asked if he might keep the glass as a memento, wrapped it up and placed it in his coat-tail pocket. Years afterward he admitted to Lockhart that, some hours later, he had absent-mindedly sat down in company 'and the glass was crushed to atoms'.[23]

Because of rough weather, George did not disembark until midday on 15 August – coincidentally (probably) Scott's birthday – dressed in the flamboyant uniform of a full admiral and rowed ashore by sixteen seamen impeccably turned out in blue coats and black velvet caps. As Gerald Finley has suggested, this arrival by sea cleverly side-stepped the awkward symbolism an overland 'entrance' might have been held to bear, avoiding memories of conquering English and, in particular, of the arrival of 'Butcher' Cumberland's avenging army in 1746.[24] The disembarkation on the quayside, like his overnight stay in the Speaker's House before his coronation, also meant that George, now increasingly stout and infirm, could arrive, fresh, at the heart of events, having denied the assembled crowds the spectacle of him clambering awkwardly in and out of carriages.

Although George did not stay there (preferring the Duke of Buccleuch's modernised Dalkeith House, just outside Edinburgh), the ancient royal palace of Holyroodhouse and its curtilage were newly fitted-up at the considerable cost of £4,859 under the direction of the Surveyor-General, Colonel Stephenson, and the 'King's Architect and Surveyor in Scotland', Robert Reid – a niggling man variously described by his less than admiring contemporaries as 'a dull, staid personage' and as 'Mr Trotter, His Majesty's Upholsterer in Scotland'. Gas lighting was installed in the palace and the surrounding streets, and three hundred gas lamps were erected between Holyroodhouse and Dalkeith House to light the sovereign's way.[25] With a sense of the theatre of history equal to Scott's, George had insisted that the apartments used by Mary, Queen of Scots and the scene of Rizzio's bloody murder remain untouched.

Scott's opening spectacle was the entry of the King, in his carriage, into the city (it was too risky, it was thought, for him to enter on horseback, in the manner of Charles I). Triumphal arches were erected at various points along the route, suggesting parallels with monarchs and generals of old and, more specifically, recalling the great triumphal arch under which Charles I had passed in 1633. One flattering banner went so far as to bid welcome to the 'Descendant of the immortal Bruce'. Everything passed off remarkably well, marred only by Glengarry's uncouth irruption and George's tendency to ogle the women along his route and ignore his male subjects. For Scott, the procession to Holyroodhouse was as satisfying as those of his imagination in *Ivanhoe* and *Kenilworth*:

> It was now visible, in all its gorgeous length of chariots and steeds, plumed heads and shining mantles, tabards and bannered trumpets, rich liveries, romantic tartan, military scarlet and naval blue … This dazzling train came onwards upon a broad pavement, holding a straight course [with] countless subjects … marshalled in steadfast and deep alignment on both sides of his route, compacted in gallery, balcony and scaffold, without end, stationed in every window, perched upon every house top, and more ambitious yet, crowded upon every height from which a view could be caught of this most unusual of spectacles. The whole way for three miles from the shore to the palace, was one mass of hope and joy, all engrossed with one object, and responding to one pulsation.[26]

The parade took its visual inspiration from the coronation procession from Westminster Abbey to Westminster Hall the previous year,
and Scott had ensured that everyone was sumptuously dressed for the
occasion. Sir Patrick Walker, Usher of the White Rod, wore a cap of
black velvet looped with gold and surmounted by a large feather, a
jacket of crimson and gold, a white satin cloak lined in crimson,
crimson breeches, and gold-tasselled boots. The Knight Marischal, Sir
Alexander Keith of Ravelston, wore a scarlet and gold frock-coat,
white waistcoat and breeches, and white silk hose; to complete the
picture, he rode a coal-black horse. Only the Earl of Erroll, the Lord
High Constable, let the organisers down. His costume, designed with
Scott's assistance, did not arrive in time; so, surrounded by attendants
in white and gold, with gold-edged purple cloaks, he wore only the
drab blue uniform of an English Lieutenant of Lancers.[27]

At the Holyroodhouse levée on the afternoon of Saturday,
17 August, when two thousand 'gentlemen of Scotland' were presented to him in little over an hour, George chose to wear his 'Royal
Stewart' tartan, devised for the occasion by Colonel David Stewart of
Garth, authentic hero of the Napoleonic Wars, historian of Scottish
regiments, co-founder of the Celtic Society, and 'clan tartan' enthusiast. The kilt and matching stockings were inherently unflattering to
a man of less than elfin proportions, but George ensured that the
overall effect was even more ludicrous by his adoption of flesh-
coloured leggings to hide the imperfections of the bloated royal
knees. Scots observers of the time were astounded, but George was
clearly delighted with the appearance he presented, convinced that it
underlined his claim to be the legitimate heir of the House of Stuart.
Painting the scene some years later, David Wilkie tactfully omitted the
leggings and endowed his tartan-swathed sovereign with bare and surprisingly well-formed knees.

The specially-concocted Royal Stewart tartan was also worn at the
levée by Sir William Curtis, son of a Wapping sea-biscuit manufacturer and former Lord Mayor of London, ageing and Falstaffian boon
companion of the King, who had accompanied him to Scotland.
Lockhart later remarked that Curtis's presence 'cast an air of ridicule
and caricature over the whole of Sir Walter's Celtified pageantry',[28]
and George Cruikshank and other satirists were quick to seize upon
his pantomime apparel in ridiculing the pretensions of the whole visit.

Even more outlandish than Curtis in Royal Stewart were the uniforms of the Royal Company of Archers, on Scott's recommendation

appointed The King's Body Guard for Scotland. Though not an ancient foundation, the Royal Company dated from the seventeenth century, thus boasting some links with Scotland's pre-Union past. If their loyalty had been suspect at the time of the Jacobite rebellions, its members were now largely harmless, ageing enthusiasts. The first version of the uniform Scott helped to design for them – to fit in with the overblown historicism of his theme – had to be scrapped when it was discovered that all the ruffs, pleats and toggles made it impossible for any of the Archers to actually draw his bow.

Scott himself wore Campbell tartan, 'in memory of his great-grandmother' but in truth as bogus as most of the costumes on show. He also ensured that his specially-composed 'national' ballads were sung at the royal banquet of 15 August, and later boasted to his son that the Highland clans were 'all put under my immediate command by their various chiefs, as they would not have liked to have received orders from each other'.[29]

On Tuesday, 20 August, 457 ladies were to be presented for royal inspection at a Drawing Room at Holyroodhouse, but even this treat prompted only a tantalisingly brief appearance by the King. Not all Scott's painstakingly arranged pageantry could wholly counteract George's ever-increasing indifference to his subjects, of either sex. He did not emerge from Dalkeith House at all on Wednesday the 21st; and that evening merely dined privately with Scott.

The following day Scott had arranged a procession for the conveyance of the Regalia from Holyroodhouse back to the Castle. For this George donned a splendid Field Marshal's uniform. But his ceremonial dress was outshone by the stage-Van Dyck 'cavalier' costume of the Duke of Hamilton, notoriously vain, who bore the Crown of Scotland. Not that it mattered; through the persistent drizzle few of those assembled caught more than a fleeting glimpse of George, comfortably propped up on cushions in his closed carriage. One disappointed observer summed up the day in two sentences: 'The King went up to the top of the Castle and bowed, rather absurd. It was, on the whole, a failure.' Interestingly, the replacement of the regalia in the Crown Room at the Castle on 24 August – a ceremony which, as Finley has pointed out, 'might have reminded Scotsmen of an aspect of the union that was most regretted: the loss of Scotland's parliament and thus of its political independence' – was by contrast a deliberately low-key affair, in which the sovereign was not involved.[30]

The review of 3,300 troops on Portobello Sands arranged for

Friday, 23 August appeared to be more to George's taste, allowing him to indulge himself once again in the fantasy of generalship. The presence of so many Highland soldiers who had seen service in the Napoleonic Wars – most memorable of all the dashing cavalrymen of the Royal Scots Greys – perhaps led his mind to wander again to the field of Waterloo, feeding the apparent conviction of his last years that he himself had led a crucial charge in Wellington's great victory.

That evening George put in a brief appearance at a great ball held in the Assembly Rooms, lit by chandeliers and girandoles costing £1,200. He was still wearing his riding boots – surprising absent-mindedness in one who was once so punctilious about his dress. The next day, properly attired (once more as a Field Marshal), he attended a great banquet at Parliament House. The parallels between this dinner and the coronation banquet are inescapable. Like Westminster Hall, the Great Hall of Edinburgh's Parliament House had a medieval hammerbeam roof, evoking rich historical associations, and there were similarities in scale – three hundred guests dining at six huge tables – and expense to the coronation banquet:

> These tables, covered with brilliant white cloths, were laden with rich foods, including meats of all sorts: venison, stewed carp, roast grouse and turkey; there were vegetables, grilled mushrooms, aspic and other tempting dishes in apparently endless array. Silver, fine crockery, richly cut glass and decanters all glistened under the flickering radiance of massive crystal chandeliers.[31]

It was all very reminiscent, too, of the great banqueting scene in the twentieth chapter of Scott's *Waverley*. Sir Walter had donated the 'Stuart goblets' from which the King was to drink, and ensured that traditional Scots dishes were provided (including haggis and sheep's-head), and that the bands played only traditional Scottish tunes. In place of the formal challenge of the King's Champion was a far more decorous ceremony involving the presentation to the King of a silver basin of rose-water, for him to wash his hands, by William Craufurd of Braehead and Craufurdland – like the unfortunate Dymoke of Scrivelsby, he had inherited his peculiar office. Craufurd's pages, dressed in scarlet and white satin, handed George 'a damask napkin of Scottish manufacture, and of the finest texture' on which to wipe his pudgy fingers. The curious royal toasts, to 'the land of Cakes' (even this had Glengarry and the other professional Celts thundering in response) and to his absent friend Sir William Curtis, failed to dim the lustre of the occasion. Glengarry's melodramatic toast 'To the health of His Majesty as King of the Isles' was received rapturously, and only a rambling, self-serving speech by the Duke of Hamilton threatened to unbalance the evening. Sir Walter Scott was repeatedly and deservedly thanked for his prodigious industry.[32]

On Sunday 25 August, looking tired and ill, George attended a service at the High Kirk of St Giles. Here a touching gesture planned by the Principal of Edinburgh University, in which the King would make a generous donation to the poor-plate by the door, was ruined when it was found at the last minute that someone had officiously removed the plate (bewildered, George thrust his little packet, inscribed 'One Hundred Pounds from the King', at the Principal). Two days later the King was present at the Theatre Royal for a dramatisation of Scott's own novel *Rob Roy*, an occasion Scott had intended as an opportunity for the 'middling classes ... who cannot pay their respects at Court or in the assemblies of the higher rank' to see their sovereign.[33]

During the last four days of his visit George was scarcely seen at all. He even failed to appear to lay the foundation stone of W.H. Playfair's National Monument on Calton Hill on Tuesday the 27th, an absence, for which no reason was given, taken by many as a calculated insult to Scotland. (In a gesture of faintly ridiculous loyalty, the ground for the monument had been broken on George's birthday.) On Wednesday he stayed only an hour at Newbattle Abbey, where his host, the Marquess of Lothian, had arranged a concert; Lothian, something of a sycophant, later boasted that he had taken an impression of the unwitting King's footstep as he entered the house. That evening, full of whisky-laden Atholl Brose, George tearfully assured his attendants he would return to Scotland as frequently as possible.[34] It was a vow that went the way of most of his promises.

The last event was a 'breakfast', a midday reception for the King at Hopetoun House on 29 August on which the Earl of Hopetoun spent more than a thousand pounds. It rained, and the Archers' intended display fell victim to 'the soggy weight of soaked tartan'.[35] Inside the house, George demonstrated once again that, while his manner with adults was frequently offhand, he could be charm itself with children. He also knighted Scott's Keeper of the Regalia, Adam Ferguson, and the painter Henry Raeburn, whom he asked to paint him 'in Highland dress', as he had Glengarry. The following year Raeburn was appointed the King's Limner and Painter for Scotland (the first professional painter for more than a hundred years to hold the office, which had become a sinecure), but died before he could undertake the commission. It was subsequently executed by his successor, David Wilkie, whose finished portrait was only finally presented to the King in 1829. Although Wilkie eschewed the overt flattery of Lawrence or Raeburn – George's tartan clothes, for example, are visibly straining at the seams, while his face is pouchy and florid – his depiction was still respectful enough to omit the hideous flesh-coloured leggings, as well as the gaudier bejewelled badges and swords and the ludicrous silk-lined sporran.[36]

The Hopetoun House party was the same mixture of political symbolism and pageantry as the rest of the visit. Lady Hopetoun was the granddaughter of an attainted Jacobite, found guilty of treason and executed on Kennington Common in 1746. Lord Hopetoun, not wishing to call attention to his wife's ancestry, wore 'Vandyke' dress, harking back once again to the last visit of a reigning monarch to Edinburgh in 1633 (as Captain-General of the Royal Company of Archers, he had come to terms with Scott's penchant for outlandish costumes). George greatly enjoyed himself flirting: Lady Margaret Maclean noted how, wearing a wig she generously characterised as 'contrived to add to his height', he 'graciously touched with his cheek the cheek of each Lady in a surprising manner as they passed by singly'. A few hours later he boarded the *Royal George* at Port Edgar and set sail for England, carrying with him a box of souvenirs from Sir Walter Scott. The contents encapsulated their shared, romantically-focused vision of the United Kingdom's heritage:

> There was a splinter of yew from Wallace [the Bruce]'s home at Elderslie, from the oak that protected him from his pursuers, a piece from another yew beloved by Mary Queen of Scots, a particle of the *Victory*'s anchor-stock, and another from the elm that sheltered Wellington at Waterloo. All were enclosed in a border of blackened oak from the Armada galleon sunk in Tobermory Bay.[37]

Scott was delighted with the success of his two-week programme. 'All ... has gone off most happily and the Edinburgh populace have behaved themselves like so many princes,' he wrote to his son in Berlin. 'The Celtic Society "all plaided and plumed in their tartan array" mounted guard over the Regalia while in the Abbey,' he boasted proudly, while outside stood 'two or three hundred highlanders ... brought down by highland Chiefs and armed cap à pie'.[38]

In general, Scott's journalistic contemporaries in Scotland were of his opinion. *Blackwood's Magazine* confidently declared that 'the people had now before them the unquestioned heir of the ancient line, the blood of the Bruce, the reconciler of all their feuds of sovereignty – the doubled right of Stuart and the Brunswick, was comprised and consummated all in their King'. *The Times* in London, however, was censorious of Scott's own role, accusing him of 'meddling in all the details of matters for which his habits and pursuits so ill fitted him'.[39]

Two weeks later, in a letter to Sir William Knighton, Scott was a little on the defensive:

> Grounds for congratulation on the King's visit to Scotland continue to increase daily. It is impossible for anyone to have forseen its extent and amongst a people who are tenacious to a proverb of the opinions which they adopt, I have no doubt its effects will be long felt perhaps after we are dead and gone. Everything around His Majesty's person was so admirably managed that there did [not] arise a single whisper or misrepresentation on which a sneer could be hung, and those who didn't join in the general congratulation (their number must have been very few) were fain to acquiesce and look on in silence. On returning to this country I found from my own people that a belief had been circulated amongst the commonality to an extent I could not have conceived, representing His Majesty's person as overgrown beyond all the usual exertions of action. So much for lying newspapers and caricatures. Their delight was extreme at seeing a portly handsome man looking and moving every inch a King, and they expressed the greatest possible indignation at the imposition which had been put on them and their delight with the personal appearance and manners of their Sovereign.[40]

In retrospect, even Scott's friend, son-in-law and biographer was far from easy in his mind as to the value and the ramifications of all the Celtification. 'It appeared to be very generally thought', he later recorded, 'that the Highlanders, their kilts, and their bagpipes were to occupy a great deal too much space in every scene of public ceremony.' He also made the point (one which Scott had purposely ignored) that the Celtic Highlanders had 'always constituted a small and almost always an unimportant part of the Scottish population'. Lockhart was one of few contemporary observers to draw attention to the dislocation between the picturesque tartan pageantry of the visit and the plight of genuine Highland tenants: 'when one reflected how miserably their numbers had of late years been reduced in consequence of the selfish and hard-hearted policy of their landlords, it almost seemed as if there was a cruel mockery in giving so much prominence to their pretensions'. His distaste for what he called the 'collective hallucination' of the King's visit was subsequently echoed by the historian Lord Macaulay who, although himself a Highlander in origin, denounced kilts as 'striped petticoats' and tartan in general as apparel 'considered by nine Scotchmen out of ten as the dress of a thief'.[41]

Recent commentators have with unquestionable accuracy castigated the whole charade as 'a bizarre travesty of Scottish history [and] Scottish reality'[42] – yet Scott's myth has proved more appealing, and thus more long-lasting, than the truth. Even as Lockhart and Macaulay were dismissing the inventions of 1822 as picturesque and even offensive fantasies, the textile manufacturers of the Lowlands and self-appointed cultural historians were perpetuating and extending the myth. The intricacies of clan and tartan lore were exploited (or invented) in works such as James Logan's *Clans of the Scottish Highlands* (1843) and the Allen brothers' ostensibly antiquarian *Vestiarium Scoticum* (1844), and the demand for tartan in London almost outstripped supply. Prince Albert's purchase and remodelling of the Balmoral estate in the Cairngorms and Queen Victoria's best-selling *Highland Journals*, published in the 1860s, set the seal of fashion on this interpretation of Scotland and Scottish history. Scott's fiction became accepted fact, historical truth a barely-remembered casualty.

The enterprising souvenir-seller who inserted mahogany planks into the landing-stage at Leith where the King would first step ashore, intending to make the timber thus hallowed into memorial snuff-boxes, was but the first of many to take pecuniary advantage of the Highland fantasy so successfully realised for George's benefit in 1822. Ever since, Edinburgh's shopkeepers have made money from credulous visitors eager to secure a souvenir of the 'ancient' traditions of Scotland. Today the Royal Mile, along which George's carriage was conducted in 1822 with as much pomp as Scott and his colleagues could muster, is crammed with retail outlets dripping in 'clan tartan'. Perhaps these shops offer one of the most telling legacies of George IV's reign.

PART V

The Image Askew

17

The King as Caricature

... all things fitting and expedient
To *Turkify* our gracious R–g–nt!
Thomas Moore, *The Twopenny Post-Bag*, Letter II

G EORGE IV WAS undoubtedly the most caricatured monarch in British history. Twentieth-century sovereigns were perhaps fortunate in the relative docility of their satirists, few of whom sought, or dared, to emulate the ferocity and cruelty of a Gillray or a Cruikshank. Not that George deserves pity on this score. He brought it upon himself: his irresponsible and undisciplined behaviour, his over-indulgence, his girth, his mistresses, his fantasies, his exotic palaces and his capacity for self-delusion and self-promotion practically invited artists to devise satires and print-sellers to make money at his expense.

By the late Georgian period prints were reaching broader middle- and lower-class audiences, sharing, as Diana Donald has noted, 'the general late eighteenth-century tendency toward diversification of products to cater to different tastes and social levels'. Caricatures, costing as little as a penny or even a half-penny – when the national average weekly wage for a labourer was around four shillings – were especially affordable, though not in the same way as today's down-market press. As Sheila O'Connell has pointed out, 'even the cheapest prints ... remained vastly more expensive in real terms than today's tabloid newspapers'. Works by such celebrated, professionally-trained artists as James Gillray invariably commanded premium prices, and hand-coloured prints by Gillray and the Cruikshanks and their like, often priced at two shillings or more, were thus pitched at the middle rather than the labouring classes. However, less scrupulous printers often sold pirated versions of the more expensive, quality images, poorly-executed but still recognisable.

The French Revolution in particular proved a boon, a rich seam of inspiration, and during the 1790s sales burgeoned in all sectors of the print trade. This led to the spread of caricatures not only throughout Britain – some firms actually began to target the 'country' market specifically – but also across Europe. Later, William Hone's wood-engraved pamphlets, less expensive to produce than etchings, which first appeared in 1819, were a deliberate attempt to exploit the possibilities of the cheaper end of the market.[1] Thus were all classes of British society, along with much of the Continent, made fully aware of Royalty's many failings.

George's illegal marriage to Maria Fitzherbert was the first public scandal involving him to be exhaustively exploited by the satirists. An anonymous caricature of March 1786 depicting Mrs Fitzherbert as *Fat, Fair and Forty* was followed a few days later by the slightly kinder *Tender, Trim and Only Thirty*, which was a little more accurate as to her age as well as more positive in its interpretation of the relationship. In the same month, James Gillray's *Wife and no Wife* showed Fox giving the bride away in the presence of Burke, robed as Jesuit priest, and George's drinking companions Hanger and Sheridan; the same cast of disreputable stock characters often featured in subsequent prints. William Hogarth's *Marriage à la Mode* of forty years earlier was a particularly fruitful source of inspiration. In an inverted allusion to the chained pair of hounds in Hogarth's first plate, a print of May 1786 compared the newlyweds to two panting dogs; Gillray cleverly reversed elements of the second plate for his *The Morning after Marriage* of 1788 – casting the Prince of Wales as the yawning wife.[2]

Gillray's most telling early satire of the Prince, referred to in an earlier chapter, dealt not with Maria Fitzherbert or with his rakish companions, but with his already notorious appetite for food, drink and (less obviously) illicit sex. In *A Voluptuary under the Horrors of Digestion* of 1792 George is depicted again in Hogarthian fashion, slumped in a sybaritically comfortable armchair, barely able to support his vast paunch and coarsely picking his teeth with a fork, surrounded by the accoutrements of debauchery and inevitable ruin – empty bottles, dice, unpaid bills, and medicines to combat venereal disease.[3] For perhaps the first but certainly not the last time, one of his main residences – in this case presumably Carlton House, the expenditure on which was rapidly becoming a national scandal – was recruited as an allegory of his wasteful life. Gillray's grotesque parody of a fashionable neoclassical interior has a grand girandole decorated with a coat-of-arms of a crossed knife and fork, topped by Prince of Wales's feathers; a decorous Pembroke table supporting a grotesquely overflowing chamberpot; and unnecessarily lavish curtains framing a view of Holland's new Grecian portico – a conceit again borrowed from Hogarth (Plate III of *Marriage à la Mode* depicts the new Palladian mansion visible through Lord Squanderfield's window, indicating the social pretensions and consequent over-extended finances which ultimately spelt the ruin of his family). Gillray expanded on this theme in two other prints of 1792: in *Vices overlook'd . . .*, George III and Queen Charlotte are represented as 'Avarice' with George cast as 'Drunkenness', while in *Modern Hospitality* the Prince is depicted merely as a conniving card-sharper. In William Dent's panoramic print *Road to Ruin*, also of 1792, the three royal brothers are again the principal target, shown at the head of a queue waiting to cross the River Styx to everlasting perdition.[4]

Throughout the 1790s George continued to provide the satirists with plenty of material. His liaison with Lady Jersey (and the resulting promotion of Lord Jersey) and his enforced and patently disastrous marriage proved especially inspiring. Some of the satires on his marriage were remarkable for their venom. The anonymous artist of *Future Prospects, or Symptoms of Love in High Life*, published on 31 May 1796, depicted the Prince as a brutal bully, kicking over a laid table behind which cowered a demure Princess of Wales and their cradled baby. While George cries out that 'Marriage has no restraints on me! no Legal tie can bind the will – Tis free and shall be so', Lord Jersey, aptly provided with a cuckold's horns, is opening the door to reveal his wife lying on the bed in the next room, ready to receive the Prince's embrace. Gillray's *Fashionable Jockeyship*, issued a day later, expanded on the theme – a portly Prince rides her cuckolded husband (he had recently been appointed George's Master of the Horse) to Lady Jersey's bed. While these prints were certainly merciless, they were not unduly unfair, and reflected little more than the unsavoury truth, yet it is small wonder that June of 1796 found George wailing to his father about 'the studied and cruel calumnies I have been branded with of late.'[5]

In the view of both William Pitt and George III, the ever more radical and anti-monarchical tenor of the French Revolution rendered

such unrestrained ridiculing of the royal family increasingly dangerous. Accordingly, in 1796 Pitt came to a secret accommodation with
Gillray, the most prominent offender: the artist would receive an
annual pension of £200 in return for eliminating the royal family, and
in particular the Prince of Wales, from his work. (Ironically, one of
Gillray's most vicious earlier prints, *Presages of the Millennium* of 1795,
shows George as a satanic imp, clinging to Pitt while holding a
demand for an annual grant of £125,000.) This compact lasted until
after the fall of Pitt's government in 1801, when payments to Gillray
ceased. Gillray resumed his attacks, but his criticisms of the Prince
were generally more muted and more piously moral – though
sufficiently biting to prompt George to pay distributors to suppress
his *L'Assemblée Nationale – Grand Cooperative Meeting at St Anne's Hill* of
1804, in which Gillray linked George III's recent illness with a notional
resurrection by Fox and the Prince of schemes for a Regency. In 1806
George appeared in Gillray's *A Tub for the Whale* (possibly the first
instance in which he was publicly cast as the 'Prince of Whales') as a
broad-bottomed ship whose destination was Despotism.[6]

George seems to have done less than usual to inspire the satirists
during the early years of the nineteenth century, even if the conduct
of the war with France had not provided targets to spare. Gillray in
any case lapsed into imbecility after 1811, and Isaac Cruikshank died
about this time – but George III's deteriorating condition after 1810
inevitably propelled his eldest son back to centre-stage and the attentions of their successors. George Cruikshank's *Regency à la Mode* of
1812 was just one of many prints of this time to express outrage at
the surge of spending which followed George's access to Crown
funds on his assumption of full Regency powers. Cruikshank's print
was directed in particular against George's expenditure on clothes.
Again there was a backward glance to *Marriage à la Mode*: the 'Bills'
file on the shelf is stuffed with unpaid tradesmen's accounts –
'hatters Bill', 'Taylors Bill', 'Hair Dresser', 'Silversmiths Bill' and so
on – while the file marked 'Recetts' is gapingly empty.[7] And so it
went on.

Among the avalanche of satires which poured forth, Peter Stuart's
lame pamphlet of December 1812, *Thoughts on the State of the Country*,
was almost the only one expressing active support for the Regent.
Stuart was clearly well aware of his rarity value, and subsequently
wrote to George's Private Secretary in a manner which suggests that
some sort of reward had been his real aim:

Allow me, Sir, to request, that after offering my most humble duties to His Royal Highness the Prince Regent, you would represent, that four months ago I had the satisfaction of being the author of a pamphlet intituled *Thoughts on the State of the Country*, &c &c that this pamphlet has had the singular good fortune of being the *first* and *only one* in vindication of the PRINCE REGENT and HIS GOVERNMENT; that its author, like most authors, is at this time far from being rich; that he is still considerably more than two hundred pounds minus by paper, print &c &c; ... and that as literary men have often been rewarded by *permanent* situations under Government, a hint to that effect from the Prince Regent, would ... be construed into a Royal Command.[8]

Meanwhile, George went on feeding the cartoonists red meat. His attempts to assume the King's place as Father of the Nation met with derision, while his assumptions of statesmanlike gravity proved unintentionally comical rather than awesomely inspiring. Every time he tried to promote himself as the Allies' inspiration he was let down by his own thoughtless or foolish actions, encouraging the satirists to parade the foibles and vices of his past and current life for public inspection. Even the ankle injury innocently sustained while teaching his daughter the Highland fling in November 1811 was seized upon as an opportunity for ridicule and innuendo. There were suggestions that the injury had occurred during sexual dalliance with either the wife or the mother – Lady Hertford – of his confidant, Lord Yarmouth. A George Cruikshank print of January 1812 went so far as to imply that his manic behaviour, as exemplified by this accident, betrayed symptoms of the mental instability that was clouding his father's last years. Another Cruikshank cartoon of three months later, *Princely Predilections*, implied that he was having an affair with the wife of his Private Secretary, Colonel MacMahon.[9]

For the British public at large, by the middle years of his Regency the lives of George and his family had become little more than *The Grand Entertainment*, the title of a Cruikshank engraving of August 1814 depicting George, as the star of the 'Royal Raree-Show', dancing with Lady Hertford and her husband in front of Carlton House (the 'Temple of Folly': a 'puerile taste,/And ridiculous waste/Contended in this Entertainment'). Cruikshank's satire must be interpreted in the context of the momentous events which had been taking place abroad: while the Allied armies fought the French to a standstill, and Napoleon was taken prisoner and exiled to Elba, George, as far as the print-makers and their public were concerned, had been of negligible importance in the struggle against tyranny. He was fit to drink with Marshal Blücher, but little else – a point which Cruikshank's 1814 satire, *The Two Veterans*, made very forcefully. A battlefield from which a desperate Napoleon flees before him floats over Blücher's head; above George's are Punch and his wife, fighting. Yarmouth fills the drunken Regent's glass (he is, once again, surrounded by countless empty bottles), while Marshal Blücher is sober and alert; the verse below declares the difference between the two to be 'in the modes of their strife: *One* had fought with the *French* – t'other with his —'.[10]

Even the blind, mad and increasingly Lear-like old King was in popular estimation a more suitable figurehead for the victorious British than his preposterous eldest son – who, as the Allied armies dealt with Napoleon, merely orchestrated miniature naval battles in the Serpentine. Numerous prints of 1814 and 1815 show George playing with toy soldiers or make-believe fleets. In one he constructs tiny ships out of walnut-shells to 'sail' on his dining table – a most appropriate choice of battlefield; in another, he sets toy ships afloat in the 'Regency Washing Tub'.[11] At the time of Napoleon's escape from Elba, George was depicted not at the head of his army, his government or his nation, but ordering yet another fête, or languishing at Brighton in the company of his mistress – such was the gulf between real events and the surreal fantasy environment inhabited by the Regent.

The victory of Waterloo did little to alter this general perception of the Prince Regent. He may have been eager to cast himself as Napoleon's mortal enemy, but nowhere in the popular or official art of the time – only in the canvases he himself commissioned from Lawrence or others – was he portrayed either as the cornerstone of the Alliance or as the embodiment of a victorious nation. Even a pro-government print of April 1816 devised by John Williams showed him in a desperately unheroic pose, with a gouty leg and a crutch – fitting substitute for a field sword. Instead, he remained the butt of low humour. He was execrated by George Cruikshank in July 1815 as the 'poor man's woe' and 'the nation's mourning', and his reputation meant he could never be taken seriously as the inspiration of his country in her hour of victory, nor reap the advantage he hoped from the brief post-Waterloo period of euphoria. To most observers Wellington rather than the Prince Regent was the epitome of Britain's military success and national self-confidence. In the months following Waterloo George was instead variously depicted as a drunk clutching a wine-bottle sceptre in a sordid tavern, and as the languid and grossly fat couch-companion of the unedifying Lady Hertford. Cruikshank deliberately contrasted this last image of oriental indolence and civilian debauchery with the martial promise once implied by images of the young Prince in the uniform of the 10th Dragoons. The anonymous author of *A New way of mounting your horse in spite of the GOUT* of March 1816 pointed up the gulf which separated George from his victorious generals, showing a fat, gout-ridden and bemedalled Regent in an invalid chair being propelled up a wooden ramp onto his horse. This farcical scene had, *The Times* averred, actually taken place:

> An inclined plane was constructed, rising to about the height of two feet and a half, at the upper end of which was a platform. His Royal Highness was placed in a chair on rollers, and so moved up the ascent, and placed on the platform, which was then raised by screws, high enough to pass the horse under: and finally, his Royal Highness was let gently down into the saddle.[12]

In similar vein, three years later Cruikshank depicted George as an elderly, corpulent invalid, sarcastically named 'Britannia's Hope', being carried to the Royal Barge from a Brighton bathing-machine staffed by two smiling naked women. When he was reported as having expressed an interest in the newly invented velocipede or dandy-horse, an early form of bicycle, the thought of the bulky Regent and his mistress in connection with such a device was too delicious to resist. Cruikshank showed the portly pair riding (in both senses of the word) to the 'Horn's Inn, Hertford'.[13]

After his accession George became even more unpopular through his attempts to divorce his wife, and payments were made to artists and publishers in a renewed effort to stem the flood of satires. Cruikshank was in financial difficulties at this time, so in June 1820 George's agents were able to persuade him to accept £100 'in consideration of a pledge not to caricature His Majesty in any immoral situation'.[14] The previous month his brother Isaac Robert had accepted £60 not to print a caricature of the King unambiguously entitled *The Dandy at Sixty*. Cruikshank apparently kept to the letter of this agreement. His *Manchester Heroes* of 1819 had explicitly sided with the victims of Peterloo: the Regent, balance-scales on which 'Peculators' outweigh 'Reformers' issuing from his head, exhorts the Yeomanry to strike at the crowd – 'cut them down, don't be afraid, they are not armed'. In 1820, however, *Coriolanus addressing the plebians* shows a decidedly idealised new King confronting a rabble of Jacobins, among them the Cato Street conspirators[15] and (perhaps to reaffirm his own radical politics) Cruikshank himself. His print of 1821, the *Royal Extinguisher*, took this theme further, showing George snuffing out radicals, to the evident delight of Lord Liverpool's cabinet. It was all reassuringly loyal. Yet at the same time Cruikshank, against the spirit of the agreement, was providing illustrations for the robustly opprobrious pamphlets published by William Hone, merciless lampoons such as *The Queen's Matrimonial Ladder* (with its famous depiction of the 'first gentleman in Europe' recovering from a debauch) and *Non mi Ricordo*, both of 1820 and both supporting Queen Caroline's cause. Nor could Cruikshank resist the fertile theme of the royal visit to Edinburgh, and in September 1822 depicted George and his ancient crony Sir William Curtis ludicrously arrayed in tartan – the King sporting an unsubtly over-sized and drooping sporran.

George was a gift to the caricaturists, with his bloated size, his excessive drinking, his vain attempt to divorce his wife and the extravagance of his coronation, in addition to the eccentricity of Brighton Pavilion and Carlton ('Harloton') House. Since poor-quality prints could now be produced so cheaply, efforts to stem the satirical tide were doomed. George was cast as 'King Naughty', as Henry VIII, as 'Sultan Sham' with a harem full of obese women, or as Nero. He was given a fool's cap and bells or Chinese garb, and generally surrounded with broken or empty bottles – long since a visual shorthand for his excesses.[16] For obvious reasons he was never able to shake off the charge of over-indulgence, particularly in regard to alcohol and women, and by 1820 the image of him as an inebriated Lothario was common currency. Satires of his coronation, in particular, depicted him as a slouching drunk accompanied by a large bottle of brandy, curaçao, or other preferred tipple.[17]

The caricaturists were not alone in having fun with the image of George IV as an oriental despot. Byron's play *Sardanapalus* of 1821 invited comparisons between Britain's sovereign and the last Assyrian king, notorious for his love of luxury, who 'wrong'd his queen' and 'wrong'd his people'. The parallels leap from the page:

> ... even yet he may redeem
> His sloth and shame, by only being that
> Which he should be, as easily as the thing
> He should not be and is. Were it less toll

To sway his nations than consume his life?
To head an army than to rule a harem?
He sweats in palling pleasures, dulls his soul,
And saps his goodly strength, in toils which yield not
Health like the chase, nor glory like the war –
He must be roused …

There was also an unmistakable reference to Brighton Pavilion and George's predilection for grandiose fêtes and other costly entertainments in the tyrant's order that 'the pavilion over the Euphrates/Be garlanded, and lit, and furnish'd forth/For an especial banquet'. More clear-sighted than George, Sardanapalus admits that 'here in this goblet is [my] title/To immortality – the immortal grape'. The device of a goblet becomes the symbol for the Assyrian's drunken misrule, as empty bottles were one of the cartoonists' most frequent indicators of George's excesses. Byron's Sardanapalus redeems himself, however, fights bravely leading his troops into battle, and dies an heroic death.[18]

In the early years of George's reign satirists seized on Cruikshank's earlier conception of the royal family as theatrical diversion, *The Grand Entertainment*. In 1821 he was being depicted as the star of the 'New Farce' – As Performed at the Royalty Theatre'; two years later William Heath used biting vignettes from his life to create a theatrical spectacular in his print *All the World's a Stage*.[19] As we have seen, the melodramatic staging of the coronation and the visits to Dublin and Edinburgh also provided a ready contrast between the spectacular, surreal pageantry of the King's immediate context and the concerns of the real world outside.

The few royal duties George undertook as his reign wore on scarcely needed elaboration from the satirists to provoke laughter. At the opening of Parliament on 1 December 1826, Prince Pückler-Muskau observed that the King 'looked pale and bloated, and was obliged to sit on the throne for a considerable time before he could get breath enough to read his speech'. Any semblance of majesty was dissipated by his notorious tendency to cast 'friendly glances and condescending bows towards some favoured ladies' and to read his speech 'with that royal "nonchalance" which does not much concern itself what His Majesty promises'. Pückler-Muskau was bitterly disappointed that 'the most powerful monarch of the earth' felt 'obliged to present himself as the chief actor in a pantomine'. His damning conclusion was that 'the whole pageant, including the King's costume, reminded me strikingly of one of those historical plays which are here got up so well'. This impression of the Court as pantomine was confirmed at a dubbing ceremony Prince Pückler-Muskau attended a few days later: the King, 'on account of the feeble state of his health, remained seated', while the Duke of Wellington could not at first extract the royal sword from its scabbard. At last it was placed in the pudgy royal hands, and George summoned the effort to raise the sword; however, 'instead of alighting on a new knight, [it] fell on an old wig, which for a moment enveloped King and subject in a cloud of powder'.[20]

Prince Pückler-Muskau's distressing observations are but one indication that George was becoming little more than a caricature of himself. During his reign the majority of satires at his expense tended to focus on George in one of three principal guises. The intriguing idea of George as The Great Baby – a figure of ludicrous whim and excessive indulgence, bent to the will of his mistress-mother or of the last politician to address him – had originated long before his coronation. Thomas Rowlandson was perhaps the first to depict the adult Prince as a child, in a cartoon of January 1789 which showed him as a toddler being restrained by Pitt.[21] In 1811 Percy Shelley referred to him as an 'overgrown bantling' in his celebrated and prescient letter attacking the expense of the new Regent's fête ('Nor will [the fête] be the last bauble which the nation must buy to amuse this overgrown bantling of Regency. How admirably this growing spirit of ludicrous magnificence tallies with the disgusting splendours of the stage of the Roman Empire which preceded its destruction!'). In 1812, and again in 1820, he appeared in Cruikshank prints as 'The Great Babe' – a bewhiskered infant 'feverish and fractious' in his cot, attended in the first instance by Lady Hertford and in the second by Lady Conyngham. In the latter version, Canning carries away a steaming chamber-pot (representative of the evidence the King's ministers were being asked to collect against the Queen) and Castlereagh dries nappies by the fire, while the ever-loyal Henry Addington, now Lord Sidmouth, rocks the cradle and sings a lullaby:

Hush! GREAT BABE! lie still and slumber,
Troopers of Lancers guard thy bed,
Chinese gimcracks, without number,
Nicely dangle o'er head ...

Paris Dolls will much amuse you
When fatigued with forms of state,
Should the living fair refuse you,
They might yield no common treat ...

Hold the Press in close submission,
Keep the radicals in awe;
Call Reform the worst Sedition,
Yet, observe the FORMS of Law!

Thus you'll pass your time securely,
And your baubles all retain;
I shall aspire demurely
Heavens! what a GLORIOUS *Reign!*[22]

In January 1821 J.L. Marks imagined the 'low life above stairs' of the 'Great baby in B***ht*n'. By the last years of his reign the 'Great Babe' was a familiar image, pictured asleep in his cradle, rocked by Lady Conyngham or, alternatively, coddled by Wellington in the guise of an old nurse – a reference to Wellington's success in persuading him to sign the Catholic Emancipation Act of 1829. In one print Wellington tries on the crown while the monarch–baby sleeps; on the floor lie the baby's toys, among them a model of Buckingham Palace. In an amusing reconstruction of a meeting in 1828 between George and Maria, the nine-year-old Queen of Portugal, he is shown as much of an age with her: 'Master George'. Henry Brougham allegedly reacted to a rumour that George would marry Lady Conyngham by announcing that her son, Lord Albert (popularly rumoured to have been fathered by the King), would doubtless be created 'Great Infant of England'.[23]

Another favourite symbol in the caricaturists' lexicon was Brighton Pavilion. Its exotic architecture and Chinese interiors – so expensively created by Nash, Jones and Crace, and so out of step with the decorative fashions of their time – epitomised George's extravagance and excess as well as his remoteness from his subjects. The politician John Croker was by no means the only contemporary commentator to castigate the Pavilion as 'an absurd waste of money' – and, he added, it would 'be a ruin in half a century or sooner'.[24] Almost from its inception it was both an object of ridicule and a physical confirmation of George's withdrawal from his subjects. As early as 1816, a year after Nash's transformation of Holland's chaste neoclassical retreat into gaudy Indo-Chinese Pavilion had begun, George Cruikshank depicted the Regent as a grossly fat Emperor of China attended by a sycophantic and complaisant Chinese court, among them Lady Hertford *en décolletée* with her complaisant, cuckolded husband and George's miserly mother. Behind the Emperor looms a grotesque representation of George in contemporary dress, labelled with heavy irony 'the British Adonis'. In most of the prints employing the device of the Pavilion or other Chinese elements, however, he is pictured clad in appropriately Oriental costume. Shortly after Waterloo, George Cruikshank featured him as Nebuchadnezzar, bursting out of vaguely eastern robes. The following year another Cruikshank print showed the Prince, enormously fat and with crutches, beneath one of the Pavilion's fabulous Chinese dragons, wearing a vainglorious display of medals, a Chinese head-dress topped with a conical cap, itself adorned with Chinese bells, and Chinese slippers. Carême's appointment in 1816 to preside over the kitchens at Brighton gave the satirists a chance to combine the bizarre and expensive interiors of the Pavilion with the familiar themes of over-eating and drunkenness. In one print George, comprehensively drunk, eats in the Pavilion kitchen itself, attended by Bloomfield, equally intoxicated, and a sycophantic Carême, and watched gravely and suspiciously by the servants. In others the Regent is shown attempting to seduce the kitchen-maids and embracing 'a very fat and florid cook' or, more daringly, actually astride the Pavilion 'cook', now transformed into a hideously fat Lady Hertford. At the time of Peterloo and of serious economic depression, George was cast by the Cruikshanks in their print *Blockheads* as a 'Grand-Lama', drunk and almost asleep while Lady Hertford proffers wine and, ominously, a demon throws a noose at his head.[25]

During the proceedings against Caroline of Brunswick George was pictured in the company of Lady Hertford (or alternatively, from the summer of 1820 onwards, Lady Conyngham), generally at or on his way to Brighton Pavilion. In one print he was represented, dressed in Chinese costume, waiting in terror at the Pavilion for the arrival of the Queen; his allies in Liverpool's government – Sidmouth, Castlereagh and Eldon – were also, unusually, shown in Chinese dress. Later the same year he was again illustrated wearing Chinese garb, this time cast as a fat mandarin, 'Kouli Khan', who spent his time sprawling on a sofa, incarcerating his daughter in a Chinese prison, playing dice and drinking and, finally, fainting on the return of the Queen (Caroline, significantly, was shown dressed in contemporary English fashions). I. R. Cruikshank's 'Great Babe' of July 1820 lay in a Chinese cot, and in the celebrated but anonymous cartoon of October 1820 in which the sun of George's face is eclipsed by Caroline's moon, the scene is clearly set in the sky above Brighton Pavilion.[26]

Hypersensitive though he could be, George initially shrugged off all ridicule levelled at his fantasy-palace in Brighton, and remained inordinately proud of his achievement. In 1826 he asked John Nash to commission a series of water-colour views of the Pavilion; these were published in one volume in spring 1827, at a cost of £3,628 18s. 6d., eighty-six copies in special bindings embossed with the royal arms, to be given as presents to the favoured few.[27] But the building in general, and its outrageous Chinoiserie in particular, were not to everyone's taste. The poet Thomas Moore had dedicated his 'amatory and convivial' metrical translation of Anacreon to the Prince of Wales and was graciously received by him in 1800; as a Roman Catholic, however, he was dismayed by the reactionary turn taken by George as Regent after 1811, and vented his disappointment in the series of lampoons which furnish the chapter openings for this book. In the early 1820s he wrote a thinly-veiled satire on 'Fum and Hum, The Two Birds of Royalty' which questioned whether the Pavilion was 'Palace or China-Shop'. 'Fum' and 'Hum' referred to the mythical Chinese birds adorning the Pavilion's Banqueting Room, and originated with Byron's *Don Juan* of 1816 which, asking 'where is "Fum" the Fourth, our "royal bird"', thereby established 'Fum' as one of George's numerous nicknames.[28] A print of October 1821 which showed the King canoodling with Mrs Quentin, wife of the colonel of the 10th Hussars, was not only set in a Chinese context but included two references to him as 'Fum'.

A year later Henry Cockburn likened the royal visit to Edinburgh to a pageant featuring a 'Chinese Emperor with his gongs, elephants and mandarins'. And in a William Williams cartoon of November 1822 George is once more shown in the guise of a Chinese mandarin. Even the royal arms have metamorphosed into a Chinese design, with dragons for supporters, which would seem to indicate a perception of the whole royal family (not just George, but his brothers too) as divorced from the popular definition of British nationhood. In a print by the same artist of February 1823 the Chinese motif is applied to a screen, an intriguing metaphor for George's growing reclusiveness which was used again a few years later.[29]

By 1828 cartoonist William Heath was borrowing the exoticism of the Pavilion and the separation from national life this exemplified for

Nash's new work at Buckingham Palace, mischievously shown flanked by Chinese pavilions and dressed with Chinese bells. But the apogee of the satirists' identification of George IV with his own Chinese Pavilion was reached with Robert Seymour's splendid cartoon of early 1829: *The Great Joss and his Playthings*. The King, yet again represented as a hugely fat Chinese mandarin, is shown sitting in a Chinese room, attended by Chinamen, and surrounded by his toys. The latter include a giraffe (for which see below); models of Nash's Buckingham Palace and Burton's Hyde Park screen and Constitution Hill screen and arch; toy soldiers in the uniform of the King's Life Guards; plans for Windsor Castle and for various churches, including Nash's All Souls, Langham Place (on whose suspiciously Gothic spire the architect is again seen impaled); and a glass case of fish, 'Caught in Virginia Water'. Behind his head, inevitably, is a model of the Pavilion.[30] Ironically, by the time Seymour's print appeared George had not visited Brighton for two years, finding the Pavilion now too public.

If cartoonists tired of the Pavilion as oriental metaphor, they could always turn to the fantastical 'Chinese' landscape being developed at Virginia Water during those years. Prints portrayed George visiting Virginia Water as a baby or a child, generally led about by one or more of the triumvirate of Lady Conyngham, the Duke of Wellington and Sir William Knighton. In 1826 he was more than once depicted as the 'King Fisher', in one instance specifically fishing for additional revenue; a year later he was the 'Fat Gentleman who Bobs for Eels' at the same location, standing in a fishing-smack while giving Lady Conyngham a smacking kiss.[31]

The third popular metaphor used as shorthand for George's character was a pair of boots – generally jack-boots, above-the-knee cavalry boots. The symbolism here was deliberately double-edged, targeting his notorious predilection for extravagant military dress and his reactionary views – echoing the famous cry of 1768, 'Wilkes and Liberty and no Jack-boot'. Whether he was portrayed by George Cruikshank as Henry VIII in February 1821 or, in subsequent months, with cumbersome prop sword or merely as 'Great Boots', those boots were always military in style and invariably over-scaled.[32] In the last years of his reign this communicative construct was still being used.[33] Moreover, the boots depicted were by then often of a German type, suggesting the absolutist regimes of Prussia and the smaller German states so admired by George and his brothers – including, of course,

Hanover, to which he had more than once petulantly threatened to retire. Never did the satirists forget the royal brothers' frequently-expressed preference for a system of government which dispensed with a troublesome representative assembly and relied on the threat of military force to extort money and enact policies. *A King Fisher*, of 1826, graphically enumerating the sources of quasi-official revenue plundered to pay for the Royal Lodge, seen under construction in the background – 'Stamps, Grants of Places, Privy Purse, Duchy of Lancaster, Civil List, Excise, Customs, Duchy of Cornwall, Post Office Revenues' – dressed George in enormous thigh-length boots; and a swaggering King illustrated in May 1827 wears ominous-looking Hessian cavalry boots, as do his fellow conservatives.[34]

Few cartoons depicted George in anything other than a ludicrous light. Even when he won temporary popularity following his appointment of the liberal Tory Lord Canning as Prime Minister in 1827, many prints ascribed this slight change in political direction to the influence of Knighton.[35] The preferred image was of a man remote from reality, a baby to be lulled to sleep with brightly-coloured toys. The more bizarre and eccentric George's enthusiasms, the more the caricaturists seized on his apparent remoteness and self-obsession. The gift of a giraffe from the Pasha of Egypt in August 1827 was manna: tall and slender and exotic, this animal was perfect for empha-sising not only the comical corpulence of George and his mistress – both invariably placed astride it – but also, by inference, the gulf between his outlandish tastes and the harsh economic realities endured by his subjects. The symbolism could also be extended to international politics and George's political conservatism, since giraffes were used as a decorative device by the unpopular absolutist French king Charles X – who had also received one as a present.[36] George's giraffe thus became a singularly redolent trope during his twilight years. His profound grief and that of Lady Conyngham over the animal's death in the summer of 1829, which was widely reported, became in the cartoonists' hands the ultimate example of his indifference to his subjects and his obsession with exotic trivia.[37]

In his *Memoirs of George IV*, written shortly after the King's death, Robert Huish recalled glimpsing his late sovereign at Sandpit Gate Lodge in Windsor Great Park. About to set off to visit his giraffe in the Royal Menagerie, George was 'seated in his pony-chaise with his favourite cockatoo on his arm', enjoying 'his glass of cherry-gin which was always kept in preparation for him' – a bitter-sweet scene which neatly encapsulates all the elements that made George the inevitable butt of caricaturists. The innate absurdity identified by Huish ensured that, in death as in life, George IV remained a target for ridicule rather than, as he had always seen himself, the nation's inspiration.[38]

18

Recluse

So, let your list of *she*-promotions
Include those only, plump and sage,
Who've reached the *regulation*-age ...
Thomas Moore, *The Twopenny Post-Bag*, Letter II

THE PITILESS CARICATURES which assailed George IV even in the last months of his life merely encouraged him to withdraw even further from the public's critical gaze. By 1830 the rakish young Prince who fifty years before had been an habitué of most of the disreputable clubs and gaming-houses of London was a confused and disappointed wreck who rarely strayed far from the seclusion of Windsor Great Park. His mutation into a senile and drink-addled recluse is one of the saddest aspects of a colourful yet ultimately unfulfilled life.

This tendency to seclusion exhibited itself as early as the first months of George's Regency. A series of murders in the East End of London in December 1811 was said 'to have so much alarmed the Prince Regent as to cause him to give orders to Colonel Bloomfield not to allow any stranger to be admitted to Carlton House after 8 o'clock', and a few months later Lord Rivers declared to Joseph Farington that the Regent was 'so nervous that the appearance of a strange face almost oversets him'.[1] After the assassination of Spencer Perceval in 1812, George ordered all London arms depots to be secured and, more significantly, in October 1813, that the public road which ran from the Sandpit Gate to Bishopsgate in Windsor Great Park be diverted, to ensure that the Royal Lodge was hidden from the sight of passers-by.[2] Such measures could not, however, wholly shield him from the violent times in which he lived. The apparent assassination attempt at the beginning of 1817 and the death of Princess Charlotte towards the end of that year caused him to withdraw even further into his shell. John Croker reported that 'He sees nobody but his own attendants, the Royal Family' and necessary ministers; 'he never stirs out of his room, and goes to bed sometimes at eight or nine o'clock'. By 1818 Maria Fitzherbert in Brighton was observing that, while 'The Regent and all his household are here, as he never stirs out of his parlour and no one sees him, it makes no alteration in our proceedings.'[3] The Regent was later reported by a captain in the Guards as unwilling to be seen even by his own servants, and in 1819 is alleged to have exclaimed: 'I will not allow these maid-servants to look at me when I go in and out; and if I find they do so again, I will have them discharged.'[4]

George's growing passion for privacy was only exacerbated by the vehemence of the public reaction to his attempted divorce, and especially by the noisily partisan mobs which supported his wife. In September 1820 Lady Granville wrote to Lady Morpeth: 'Mr Montagu told us at dinner that his two brothers met the King as they were riding through the park at Windsor' and that 'the next day an order was issued forbidding any one to enter it.' Two months later she reported that the King 'shuts himself up, will see nobody, and is having new keys made to all the gates, to prevent the neighbourhood having access to the park and *alentours*.' New guard-rooms and entrance lodges were also added to the Royal Lodge.[5]

Perceived threats to his life were not the only cause of George's increasingly evident passion for seclusion from his subjects. He was often ill, and reluctant to be seen so in public. More importantly, his increasing bulk meant that even when corseted, and whatever the inventive artifice of Thomas Lawrence might suggest to the contrary, he no longer resembled the Prince Florizel of his youth.

Since George had always displayed all the signs of an ardent hypochondriac, it is difficult to know just how genuine his apparent agonies were, or how much their aim was to win sympathy. If they were not exchanging information concerning the latest military uniforms, he and his brother York liked nothing better than to swap accounts of their respective ailments; writing on 7 October 1820, for example, George began:

> I have only just receiv'd your kind letter, and it gives me much pain to learn that you have been indispos'd ... You talk of an attack of bile; I also have had my share of it, for although not absolutely confin'd to the House, I have had bile, and my old enemy the gout flying about me, for a couple [of] days past, which has incommoded me a good deal ...[6]

Whatever the nature of George's sufferings, however, they certainly discouraged him from making unnecessary public appearances. A month before his visit to Edinburgh in 1822 he was all but confined to his rooms at the Pavilion: 'He never, since he has been at Brighton, has left his own room, except to walk *across* at half-past three or four to Lady C[onyngham]'s house, and at six to walk back, he then dresses and comes down to dinner, and that is the whole of his air and exercise.' This lethargy, and his detachment from his guests, combined to make life at the Pavilion unwontedly sombre. In 1818 Princess Lieven compared its tedium to the notorious dreariness of the Kremlin, and a visitor to the Pavilion after George's coronation found still further deterioration: 'The dinner was cold and the evening dull beyond all dulness', the rooms were 'not furnished for society' – and '[I] only hope that I may never go there again'.[7]

On his return from Edinburgh in 1822 – his last major visit – George appears to have become more and more secretive and reclusive. He went to London as seldom as possible, and was reported to be seeing 'fewer strangers than ever'; in May 1824 he himself admitted his 'determination... to withdraw himself to the very utmost from every eye'. In 1827 Thomas Creevey caught a glimpse of 'the King Fisher himself' at Virginia Water, 'in a little phaeton with Lady Conyngham', but reported that he was mostly 'hiding himself' in his Great Park refuges. On his visit to Windsor of August 1827 Prince Pückler-Muskau noted that the King had 'had several roads cut, for his own special and peculiar use, thro' the most interesting parts' of the park, and that his 'favourite spots are, for further security, thickly surrounded with screens of wood, and plantations are daily laid out to add to the privacy and concealment'. He concluded from these observations that 'It is unpleasant for [him] to see a strange face, or indeed a human being of any kind whatsoever, within his domain', and that the Park was deliberately and 'hermetically sealed to everyone without exception who does not belong to his own company'. George apparently preferred to amuse himself in private with his seven phaetons, 'all with very low wheels, almost as light as children's carriages, and drawn by little poneys'.[8]

Increasingly, George was coming to regard the proximity to the public thoroughfare of the ground-floor State Rooms at both Carlton House and Brighton Pavilion as insupportable. 'I do not like Carlton House standing in a street', he is reported to have said to Lord Farnborough shortly before deciding on its demolition. And despite the town's best efforts to keep him entertained, on 7 March 1827 he left Brighton, never to return. It had effectively been his second home for the better part of forty years, and it was only five years since work on the Pavilion had been completed. The Duke of Wellington glee-fully repeated the rumour that a quasi-Biblical admonition etched by a disapproving local on one of its too-easily-accessible windows had finally prompted his decision to leave.[9]

George now sought a more secluded residence. Both Windsor Castle and Buckingham Palace were currently being rebuilt, at vast expense. In June 1826 Wellington dismissed the idea of 'obtaining for the King's use the apartment in St James's hitherto allotted to HRH the Duke of Cumberland', since 'It is a single house in the centre of the town, not closed from the street, overlooked on all sides to such a degree as that every movement in the apartments can be seen by the opposite neighbours; and the avenues to it are through the most fre-quented parts of the town and park.' As an alternative, Wellington suggested Kensington Palace – close to the seat of government, where the King 'could see whom he pleased without being overlooked or [suffering] the comments of observers'.[10] In the event, this sensible proposal was not acted upon, and George retreated instead to the thickets of Windsor Great Park, thirty miles from Parliament.

In the Great Park, George was able to create yet another, and indeed his last, fantasy environment. The park was big enough to accommodate his various architectural whims and empty enough for him to deny the public access without incurring their wrath; it was also far enough from Westminster and the London mob to ensure him a tranquil seclusion, but close enough for him to return quickly in the event of an emergency. And it was handy for short carriage-drives to examine Wyatville's work at the castle.

In December 1823 the Treasury approved George's request to remodel the Royal Lodge in the middle of Windsor Great Park (at the same time, the King ordered the closure of the public footpath which, passing through Home Park, linked Windsor with Datchet).[11] The Lodge had already been extensively rebuilt: in November 1812 Treasury approval was given to John Nash's estimate of £2,750 to provide a small 'cottage ornée'. A year later Nash, who had since been asked to rebuild nearby Cumberland Lodge to provide extra accom-modation for the Royal Lodge, requested an additional £13,250. The conservatory added in 1814 cost £2,429, and the chimney-pieces of the same date £1,471; by 1816 the costs had exceeded £30,000, with a further £17,000 for furniture. Castlereagh was guilty of a certain casuistry in telling the House of Commons in May 1815 that the Royal Lodge 'might be called a cottage, because it was thatched', and merely represented 'a very comfortable residence for a family, and the only one the Prince could make use of when he went to Windsor'. Few of the Prince's subjects, of course, were able to challenge this opinion with first-hand evidence, since the Lodge was increasingly well-hidden from prying eyes.[12]

Between 1820 and 1828 what had been a small, rustic retreat was extended, rebuilt and reclad beyond all recognition. By the time of George IV's death it had become one of the largest 'cottages' ever seen, virtually a Gothic counterpart to the Brighton Pavilion. In 1821 a suite was added for the King's Private Secretary – scarcely necessary if George not been planning to spend a good deal of time there. In 1823 Wyatville replaced Nash, and the extravagance and the vagueness of the costings continued: in January 1825, for example, the expenditure of £8,000 on further alterations ('for continued residence during the repairs of Windsor Castle') was sanctioned; unsurprisingly, perhaps, the total was more than double that amount.[13] The Lodge as it stood in 1829 was an irregular, asymmetrically picturesque composition with Tudor chimneys, late-Gothic ogee-arched windows, stuccoed walls and prominent bargeboards – exactly the sort of charming but hopelessly inauthentic confection that A.W.N. Pugin was to condemn so vehemently seven years later. Intrinsically it was a palatial version of the delightful thatched cottages John Nash had built at his fantasy-village of Blaise Hamlet to the west of Bristol in 1810 (Nash had even included at Royal Lodge a 'rustic columned Viranda ... covered with a thatched roof'; as the building expanded after 1823, however, tiled roofs were introduced). This was no 'cottage ornée' on the model of Walsh Porter's modest Craven Cottage at Fulham. The Royal Lodge even boasted a chapel, a hundred yards from the main building but linked to it by a covered walkway, which was added despite the fact that nearby Cumberland Lodge already had its own chapel and St George's Chapel at the Castle was barely a mile away.[14] George was evidently determined to travel no further than was absolutely necessary.

The revamped Royal Lodge attracted mixed reviews. A visitor of November 1825 praised its interiors as 'low but light' and was particularly impressed with Nash's conservatory: 'a lovely Greenhouse in which the King's private band plays when he has his parties'. Princess

Lieven hailed the rooms as 'the rarest reunion of comfort, elegance, and unspoiled magnificence'. Others were not so generous, however. Sir Walter Scott was summoned to the Lodge in October 1826, and afterwards felt constrained to admit that the building was 'too large perhaps for the style [of] cottage ornée'; he further observed that the plantings of 'immense trees' round its perimeter meant that 'you only see parts of it at once'. He was also evidently a little dismayed to find that there 'was no company beside the royal retinue – Lady C[onyngham], her daughter, and two or three other ladies' – a defect also noted by Charles Greville, who found the miniature Court stultifying. Greville reported that Lady Conyngham 'looks bored to death, and she never speaks, never appears to have one word to say to the King, who however talks himself without ceasing'. Scott loyally judged, however, that 'A sort of reserve, which creeps upon [the King] daily, and prevents his going to places of public resort, is a disadvantage, and prevents his being so generally popular as is earnestly to be desired.' He blamed this 'reserve' on 'the behaviour of the rabble in the brutal insanity of the Queen's trial, when John Bull, meaning the best in the world, made such a beastly figure'.[15]

Some critics took particular exception to the aspersions the King's withdrawal seemed to cast on his subjects: 'Enshrined within the precincts of his cottage,' thundered Robert Huish in 1830, 'the King appeared to take little or no interest in the public or political affairs of the nation', employing 'his favourite outrider Hudson [to] cast ... his eyes into every brake or thicket, to ascertain if some prying, inquisitive intruder' lurked there, while 'the park keepers were abroad in all directions, invested with the royal mandate to let no human being be seen within the range of the vision of royalty.' Like Nero, the King clearly 'expected to see an assassin in every bush'. In Sir Owen Morshead's neat synopsis, George IV 'withdrew because he was unpopular, and was unpopular because he withdrew'.[16]

Proposals for further building works at the Great Park lodges after 1828 – notably the addition of stables at Cumberland Lodge, which Wyatville estimated would cost £12,000 – were frustrated by the government. They may have shut the stable door, but the horse had already bolted: in February 1830 George authorised Wyatville to make yet further changes to the Lodge (estimate, £8,500). By the time of the King's death, when work was abruptly halted, a new dining room and an octagonal tent room had been added – and the dining room, as we have seen, was one of the few elements to survive the wholesale demolition of the Lodge which followed William IV's accession.

Elsewhere in the Great Park, George had been indulging himself in the erection of sham ruins, and a fishing temple in the 'Chinese' manner. He was a keen angler, and indeed fishing was one of the few sports his ever-increasing girth did not rule out. In 1824 a Mrs Ustonson received the Royal Warrant for supplying the King's fishing tackle, to the tune of nearly £200 in the first year. In 1825 a Treasury official minuted laconically: 'We are informed that His Majesty frequently enjoys the recreation of Fishing upon the Virginia Water', and authorised the construction of a Chinese fishing temple there to the designs of Jeffry Wyatville. The rooms of the temple were carefully decorated by the firm of Crace and Company, whose work at the Pavilion had been so impressive. As at Brighton, their initial calculations were rapidly and grossly exceeded: Crace's estimate of £500 for additional works to the temple, dated December 1827, had 'one week later risen to about £1,600'. The reaction to the finished temple was generally favourable, however. In June 1826 Lady Holland admired the 'gilt dragons for ornaments', while Princess Augusta praised the 'pretty Chinese building' of 'three rooms and a Veranda', the interiors of which were 'papered with the grey ground and bamboo panels, the same as the Pavilion at Brighton'. Even Prince Pückler-Muskau conceded that the buildings at Virginia Water were 'executed with taste and not caricatured'.[17]

While the fishing temple was going up, George used various colourful tents erected on the lake's eastern shore. Some of these had been found in old Queen Charlotte's garden at Frogmore, and were believed to have belonged originally to Tipu Sultan in India; others were newly-made, out of canvas taken from Ordnance stores for which George had no intention of paying (the Treasury had later to reimburse the Treasurer of the Ordnance, Thomas Creevey, £3,170). A fleet of boats was also kept at Virginia Water for the King's 'enjoyment on the lake', and in 1827 a fountain in which 'Ten Dozen of Gold and Silver Fish' swam was added to the garden.

A few months later a picturesque classical ruin, grandly named the Temple of Augustus, rose on the lakeside. The ruin was concocted by Wyatville out of antique columns from Leptis Magna in Libya, a gift from the Bashaw of Tripoli which had lain neglected in the courtyard of the British Museum for eight years until rescued by George. Once again a Bourbon connection can be traced: Leptis Magna was the source from which George's exemplar Louis XIV had obtained marble for building the Tuileries and Versailles. In August 1828 this resonant, re-erected ruin was embellished by the addition of the 12- and 24-pounder guns captured by 'Butcher' Cumberland during the War of the Austrian Succession in the 1740s, assembled on the lake-side specifically to fire a Birthday Salute – another instance of George happily appropriating other people's martial triumphs.[18]

George's embellishment of Windsor Great Park did not stop with the work at Virginia Water. In 1828 he authorised Wyatville to enlarge Henry Flitcroft's Belvedere Tower, the small rococo 'castle' atop a rise in the Great Park known as Shrub Hill – originally built by 'Butcher' Cumberland and a favourite haunt of that later Duke of Cumberland who had introduced George to the sybaritic pleasures of Brighton. The result was a castle for toy soldiers, rechristened Fort Belvedere, which typified the fantasy-world in which George pre-ferred to live. From its Gothic battlements he could imagine himself as Edward III or the Black Prince, gazing over his domain or watch-ing his knights parade before him. Inside its quasi-medieval walls, he could retreat from the world within Gothic-papered rooms.

So proud of his new sham-castle was George that he not only cele-brated his birthday there in 1829 but stayed for most of the summer. As might have been expected, the cost of the remodelling was exces-sive: £3,300 in one year. Though the rebuilding work had scarcely been completed when George died, this was one of the few of his additions to the Great Park which William IV actually enjoyed visit-ing, and it was thus spared the immediate destruction which was the fate of much else.[19]

Building activity continued all over the park up to the very day of George's death; only shortly before it, indeed, a back-bench MP had complained of the annual grant of £20,000 paid by the Treasury to furnish Windsor Great Park with 'the silly gewgaws resulting from the bad taste of a High Personage'. Late in 1829 George, either to increase the seclusion of the Great Park or because he never felt he had enough houses, bought Holly Grove (which he renamed Forest Lodge) and its fifty-acre estate from a Mrs Broadhead for a handsome £21,000; and almost the last decision he made was to add 'a New Piggery' at the Home Farm. On what was to prove his last birthday, 12 August 1829, he drove out from Fort Belvedere to lay the foundation stone of the rustic base Wyatville had designed to support a giant bronze statue of George III. The statue had already been commissioned from Richard

Westmacott, and when it was installed on its plinth – more than a year after George's death, in October 1831 – the *Windsor and Eton Express* commented that it was large enough for twelve workmen to eat their dinner inside. However, the memorial was something of a disappointment. George had declared that he did not want his father depicted as 'a private gentleman with tight, coiffed hair, pigtail and high boots' – although this was how most of his subjects remembered Farmer George – and opted instead for a portrayal which reflected how he had reinvented himself. The result was comical and wholly inappropriate, with George III as a Roman Emperor on horseback, in a pose borrowed – equally unsuitably – from Zauner's monument to King James II in Vienna.[20] Wyatville's rusticated base (costing £16,000) was even more ludicrous, resembling a grotto turned inside out.

So busy was George with the playground he was creating in the Great Park that he became increasingly indifferent to the work going on at the nearby Castle. It was perhaps not with great surprise that the nation learned in 1829 that the King intended after all to stay permanently at the Royal Lodge. On 20 September 1829 Creevey reported that George's mind was 'quite made up *never to live in the Castle*, which considering the hundreds of thousands which have been expended upon it inside and out is amiss. He says it is too *public*, so I take for granted the new Palace at Pimlico [Buckingham Palace] will share the same fate.'[21] Reluctant to carry out official engagements in London, or even at Windsor (though happy enough to travel to nearby Ascot for the racing), George preferred to remain at the Royal Lodge or one of the other newly-fabricated *pieds-à-terre* in the Great Park, where he could entertain Lady Conyngham, drink Maraschino, dose himself with laudanum, sleep and eat to his heart's content, and occasionally bestir himself to censure the Office of Works for all their delays.

As George became increasingly reclusive, so prospects receded of any scheme for a triumphal processional route into London ever being realised. At the beginning of his reign he seems to have had the intention – or the hope – of countering his unpopularity by means of royal spectacle and ceremonial; an instance was his alteration of the route to be taken by his procession to open Parliament on 27 April 1820, to include Whitehall and Parliament Street (rather than cutting across St James's Park). 'His choice of this markedly more urban route', Sean Sawyer has suggested, 'clearly demonstrated his intention of utilising the State Opening and Closing to reform his public image.' His commission to John Soane to remake the Royal

Entrance to the House of Lords was part of this plan. However, the public reaction to Caroline of Brunswick's trial that year increased his fears for his own safety, as we have seen; this, combined with the exhausting physical demands of the coronation in 1821 and the Edinburgh pageantry of 1822, seem to have determined him to avoid similarly ambitious public appearances thereafter. Huish was exaggerating a little in stating that 'The last time the King exhibited himself in public, with the exception of the prorogation of Parliament, was in a visit to ... two theatres in 1823', but it is true that he became increasingly reluctant even to open Parliament. Perhaps he had reason: the State Opening of February 1822 almost ended in farce. Stepping from his coach at the Royal Entrance to the House of Lords, George 'seemed to collapse under the weight of his robes, his crown slipped forward to his nose, and the drag of his train pulled at his fat neck'[22] – exactly the sort of embarrassment he had sought to avoid at his coronation the previous July by spending the preceding night at the Speaker's House. Once George had recovered his poise, the rest of the ceremony, like so many others, was memorable only for his incessant winking and smiling at the female members of the audience.

After this débâcle George came to London to open Parliament only once more before his death, in 1826, when the only other engagements to winkle him from the confines of the Royal Lodge were eight meetings of his Privy Council, three of which he held at Windsor, and three trips to London to see his ailing brother York. In 1828 Croker noted the precautions surrounding one of the King's infrequent visits to St James's Park: 'they have in the last two days substituted a close gate to prevent people's seeing the operation of moving His Majesty in and out of his carriage'. Although he so rarely graced the Park with his presence, George's obsessive need to instigate new building projects prompted him as late as 1829 to commission Nash to enclose and wholly re-landscape the area.[23]

Charles Greville observed in 1828 that, seemingly, George preferred to languish in the stiflingly hot rooms of the Royal Lodge, 'getting every day more averse to exercise and more prone to retirement' and keeping 'everybody at a great distance from him'. Even his visits to Windsor Castle usually took place on a Sunday, to avoid the crowds. One of his servants later wrote that 'the Monarch seldom rode in the Long Walk from the Castle because he feared to meet the Windsor people on his way to Frogmore', while when he went to Virginia Water 'there were always servants stationed ... to prevent the intrusion of strangers upon the King's privacy'.[24]

George's reluctance to attend to his official duties caused adverse comment in many quarters. In 1826 the Prussian envoy, Prince Pückler-Muskau, noted 'as proof of the extraordinary voluntary seclusion of the present sovereign' that, despite having been *en poste* for two years, 'our Secretary of Legation was presented with me *for the first time*' to the King on 5 December. In January 1829 Charles Greville reported Lord Mount Charles's comments that 'The King's indolence is so great that it is next to impossible to get him to do even the most ordinary business', the sovereign preferring to 'talk ... of horses or any trivial matter'.[25] George's outbursts of irrational temper were also becoming more pronounced, as was his tendency to become tired and emotional at the least provocation and over the most trivial issues.

In February 1826 the *World of Fashion* expressed disapproval of such patent dereliction of duty, albeit in wondrously toadying style:

His Majesty is passing so very retired a life at Windsor that the inhabitants of every other part of the United Kingdom seldom hear or know of our beloved King being in existence. To speak plainly, we do not approve of such retirement; we think so great a Monarch, and one so universally cherished, should be more frequently in his capital.[26]

Robert Huish was more forthright in 1831 about what he saw as the late King's greatest failing, a desertion of his subjects which wholly unbalanced the British constitution. 'There was something in that seclusion so anti-national, so openly at variance with what the English people have a right to expect from their sovereign', he declared bitterly in his *Memoirs*, arguing that, in failing to appear beyond the confines of Windsor Great Park – and particularly in failing to open Parliament – George had sundered the contract between monarch and nation created at the time of the Glorious Revolution. 'A patriot King should', he suggested, 'be himself consistent'; George IV, however, was capable of 'the grossest inconsistency', and of letting his 'love of show' dictate 'plans of organised dissoluteness and haughty seclusion'.[27]

Huish possibly attributed to George more positive resolution than he was actually capable of in his last years. No one had ever been sure whether his fantasies about his involvement in the Napoleonic Wars – in which his role tended to become ever more active and heroic over

the years – were just that, trotted out on the assumption that his audi-
tors would not dare to contradict him, or the product of a disordered
mind, the truth of which he actually believed. In his latter years
George's public reveries were not confined to the Napoleonic Wars:
in November 1829 Creevey noted that the King

> tells almost daily how he won the Cup at Goodwood by his *own riding*. 'I
> kept the old Mare back till I was within fifty yards from home, and then,
> by God! I made such a rush with her, &c &c.' He tells likewise, in the pres-
> ence of Wellington, how *he* gained the battle of Salamanca by bringing up
> a Regiment of heavy German Cavalry ... *when things were looking very ill
> indeed.*[28]

Nearly thirty years later William Thackeray delighted in asserting that
George 'had heard so much of the war, knighted so many people, and
worn such a prodigious quantity of marshal's uniforms, cocked hats,
cock's feathers, scarlet and bullion in general, that he actually fancied
he had been present in some campaigns, and, under the name of
General Bock, led a tremendous charge of the German legion at
Waterloo'.[29] George had indeed been known to tell stories like this,
confusing himself perhaps with the real General Eberhardt von Bock,
who had led the King's German Legion at Salamanca – *not* Waterloo,
for he was lost at sea in 1814. After being called on to corroborate one
such anecdote, Wellington had been heard to mutter that he believed
insanity ran in the family; but in general he was tactful enough merely
to murmur 'So you have often told me, Sir' – or, in the case of a story
about the King leading a charge down a particularly precipitous slope,
nodding 'Very steep, Sir.'[30]

At other times George's fabrications rewrote his chequered past
rather than inventing its incidents; in 1825, for example, he publicly
denounced the 'absurd story' of his 'supposed marriage' to Maria
Fitzherbert. Perhaps he came to believe that it had never taken place.
Christopher Hibbert relates the story of how he solemnly assured
Lady Cowper 'that he had visited her mother, Lady Melbourne, every
day as she lay dying and that she had expired in his arms, when Lady
Cowper knew perfectly well that he had never been near the house'.[31]

There are indications that by the spring of 1827 George's mind was
becoming decidedly confused. For example, a letter of 26 March he
wrote to Knighton on the subject of Canning's suitability for the
premiership (following the paralytic stroke suffered by Liverpool the

previous month) is notably incoherent and circumlocutory, and even fuller of emphatic underlinings and more orotund and self-justificatory than usual. Determined to have a Tory government but distracted by the thought of a Prime Minister known to favour Catholic Emancipation, George was having to come to an accommo-dation with Canning on this point, and the strain told on him:

All that good temper, all that conciliation, all that *the strictest sense of honor & liberality* can dictate, *I am ready & prepar'd to act upon & to meet* with even the very essence of that spirit. But, let the stake be *what it may*, & the risk be *however great, I must not, I can not, & more I will not tolerate, even the possibil-ity of the most trivial breath of inconsistency, or of duplicity* being affix'd *upon me, or my character.*[32]

By this time George was in fact writing very little, either because of his recurrent illnesses or inherent sloth or because his mind was failing. 'Clearly his thoughts went faster than his pen' was the charitable expla-nation of Sir Arthur Aspinall, cataloguer of his letters, for George's preference for conversation over correspondence. Increasingly he spent much of the day in bed, when he was not sitting placidly with Lady Conyngham. In March 1826 Princess Lieven had commented that the incessant bleeding he requested 'gives him an excuse for staying in bed a little longer, which he likes better than anything'.[33]

George, once so very particular, was also becoming neglectful of his personal appearance. Wellington once found him discussing the progress of Windsor with Wyatville and Chantrey while still in bed, dressed only 'in a dirty flannel waistcoat'. On another occasion George received the Duke 'in bed, dressed in a dirty silk jacket and a turban nightcap, one as greasy as the other'; Wellington subsequently wrote disgustedly that 'notwithstanding his coquetry in public he was extremely dirty and slovenly in private'. Sir Walter Scott had heard it rumoured that a Privy Council meeting had been held with the King dressed only 'in a white cotton nightcap and a rather dirty flannel jacket, propped up with pillows, and sipping his chocolate'.[34]

Though his dress became ever more slovenly, George grew increas-ingly obsessed with jewellery. From 1820, unable to resist the idea of a new Order with his own image at its centre, he began to distribute 'Family Orders', portrait miniatures of himself, set in diamonds and suspended from a ribbon. Among the many recipients was Princess Victoria, daughter of George's late and unlamented brother the Duke of Kent. In a much-quoted letter, Victoria recalls being given the Order:

> When we arrived at the Royal Lodge the King took me by the hand saying, 'Give me your little paw'. He was large and gouty but with a wonderful dignity and charm of manner ... Then he said he would give me something for me to wear, and that was his picture set in diamonds, which was worn by the Princesses as an order to a blue ribbon on the left shoulder. I was very proud of this, – and Lady Conyngham pinned it on my shoulder.[35]

It is to Victoria's credit that she should have ignored the notoriously damp, over-heated and stifling atmosphere of George's retreat and glossed over the ubiquitous presence of Lady Conyngham, highlighting instead one of the declining King's better qualities: in the years before his death, indeed, George was attentive not just to his niece but to all the children who visited him. As if to make up for his appalling treatment of his own daughter, or perhaps as some sort of compensation for his own lost and not entirely happy youth, he showered presents upon Lady Conyngham's young relatives and any other children who were brought to see him, and was happy to play with them as far as his bulk allowed. Years after his death, Lord Melbourne famously remarked to Queen Victoria that the late King 'always was fond of children', a sentiment with which the Queen readily agreed. Christopher Hibbert has noted that 'he bought an enormous amount of playthings to give away as presents ... dolls and lead soldiers, boxes of ninepins, miniature farm yards, play houses, mechanical animals, rocking-horses, games and toys of every description'.[36]

Even in his latter years, George remained the target of allegations of sexual impropriety. In 1821 he hired a twenty-two-year-old actress, Eliza Chester, as his 'Reader', at a remarkably generous annual salary of £600. His eyesight was certainly failing, but it did not escape notice that Miss Chester was both young and pretty. Creevey related their first meeting with relish: 'It is said Prinney fell over head and ears in love with Miss Chester, the actress, the two nights he was at the play, and that Lady Conyngham has been made very uneasy.' In truth, however, ageing and constantly ill, George was probably beyond sexual cavorting, and there appears to have been an unwritten agreement with Miss Chester that he could look but not touch. The satirical prints still contained references to alleged affairs – one cartoon of 1826 had him gazing with, in Dorothy George's words, 'senile amorousness' at the *décolletée* of the Duchess of Marlborough – but his body was simply not up to it.[37]

Eliza Chester was not hired to read George the Classics. He preferred 'the lighter literature of the day', having never greatly cared for serious reading-matter. Indeed, the monarch who has on occasion been lauded as one of literature's greatest royal patrons was the man who tried in 1823 to sell to the highest bidder the magnificent Royal Library George III had built up over the years. It was only the vehement opposition of his brothers York and Clarence to the sale, in support of the British Museum's trustees, that persuaded him to donate the library intact to the museum. He was, however, an avid fan of more salacious productions, and several drawers full of pictorial and printed pornography (euphemistically labelled 'Free Prints and Drawings') were tactfully destroyed by his executor Sir William Knighton after his death.[38]

By 1828 many regarded Knighton, abetted by Lady Conyngham, as the real power at Court. When *The Times* suggested that Lansdowne's moderate Whigs should be asked to form a government in place of Goderich's administration, the leading Tory William Huskisson had Knighton in mind when he opined that these proposals arose in 'a quarter which warranted them as much as if they came from the King himself'.[39] In June 1827 Charles Greville recounted a typical instance of Knighton's influence over the King:

> While the Tyrolese were dancing and singing, and there was a sort of a gay uproar going on with which [George IV] was greatly delighted, he said 'I would give ten guineas to see Knighton walk into the room now!' as if it were some Master who was absent, and who should suddenly return and find his family and his servants merrymaking in his absence; it indicates a strange sort of power possessed by him.

One consequence of George's increasing reclusiveness was that Knighton achieved an altogether improper stranglehold on government business ('Nothing can be done but by [Knighton and Lady Conyngham's] permission', spluttered Greville in May 1829). The lady had apparently no fault to find with the arrangement, for although by this time she only saw the King for about an hour in the late afternoons, he continued 'to heap all kinds of presents upon her'. Greville's calculation was that she 'lives at his expense', and 'The wealth she has accumulated by savings and presents must be enormous.'[40]

Years earlier, George had told Knighton 'how uncomfortable and how miserable I always feel when I have not you immediately at my elbow', even when he travelled overseas.[41] Now that dependence became even more marked. Originally, Knighton had secured his position by secretly conducting Lady Conyngham to George's Carlton House apartments and retrieving royal correspondence from MacMahon's house, as much as by his medical services; he now cultivated an aura of secrecy which appealed to George's jaded passion for intrigue and privacy and was helpful in keeping potential rivals at bay. After the enforced retirement of Sir Benjamin Bloomfield as the King's Private Secretary in March 1822, Lord Liverpool had protested that 'the introduction of Sir William Knighton into your Majesty's family even in no other character, than that of domestick physician, would very much augment all the difficulties attendant upon the removal of Sir B. Bloomfield'; but with the support of Lady Conyngham Knighton had secured the post of Keeper of the Privy Purse (the Private Secretaryship in all but name) and, having given up his medical practice in order to concentrate on the King's service, felt in a strong enough position to force George to double the proposed salary of £25,000.[42] Thereafter his relationship with his master was a peculiar one, increasingly based on George's indolent acquiescence in his judgement, and on the consternation aroused in him by the demands of the outside world. 'There is no personal attention, there is no sacrifice, there is no pain or penalty that I am not ready to undergo', he wrote obsequiously to the King in April 1822, 'to shew my sincere devotion, my affection and the real purity of all my motives in what relates to your Majesty's happiness.'[43] Early fruit of this ostensible subservience was membership of the Privy Council in 1823, opposed by Liverpool and his cabinet but insisted upon by George. Yet the civil servant Charles Arbuthnot declared that the King hated Knighton 'as a madman hates his keeper', while Charles Greville reported that on one occasion George had cried out in public 'I wish to God somebody would assassinate Knighton!' Certainly Knighton's efficiency and skill were invaluable to an old man steadily losing interest in reality. He had long been reading confidential papers and despatches with far more attention than his royal master; now, in George's last years, Greville remarked that Knighton was 'the only man who could prevail upon the King to sign papers'.[44]

Certainly it would have been easy for Knighton, aided by Lady Conyngham, to abuse the power of his position had he so wished. In the last year of his life George paid almost no attention to government business, and was content that Knighton should handle all official matters. Greville described the King in March 1829:

> He breakfasts in bed, does whatever business he can be brought to trans-act in bed too, then reads every newspaper quite thro', dozes three or four hours, gets up in time for dinner, and goes to bed between ten and eleven. He sleeps very ill, and rings his bell forty times in the night; if he wants to know the hour, though a watch hangs close to him, he will have his valet de chambre down rather than turn his head to look at it. The same thing if he wants a glass of water; he won't stretch out his hand to get it.[45]

Knighton's service did not end with George's death. As his principal executor, he was in an excellent position to sift through the King's papers and belongings and to extricate – and if necessary destroy, as in the case of the 'Free Prints and Drawings' – any potentially incriminating evidence pertaining to himself or to his master. The refashioning of George's tattered reputation into the image of a munificent Patriot King was, however, a task beyond even the most indefatigable Private Secretary.

George's death, anticipated as it had been from the very beginning of his reign, came as no surprise. In May 1829 it was observed that he 'talked constantly of his brother, the Duke of York, and the similarity of their symptoms and was always comparing them'. From 1827 onward George's health had steadily deteriorated, and his death was constantly expected. On 19 January 1828 he told Knighton that 'I have delayed writing to you till I had tried how far my strength would allow me to sit up, and to be moved to the next room', adding that a disappointment 'has entirely knock'd me up and destroy'd almost all the little amount of strength I had', and asking that the Privy Council meeting due to be held be postponed once more. Two months later a household official announced that the King suffered 'dropsy to the most dreadful degree' and surmised that he 'most probably would not live six months'.[46]

In his last years, George III had been blind as well as mad. Recalling this, his son must have wondered, as his own sight began to fail, whether insanity too was impending. On 23 September 1829 Wellington reported, regarding a forthcoming eye operation, that the King was 'always perfectly cool, and neither feared operations nor their possible consequences'. By May 1830, however, George could not see even to sign Acts of Parliament, and a stamp bearing his signature was applied to documents in the presence of three witnesses. Greville noted in February 1830 that he was 'very blind – did not know the Lord Chancellor, who was standing close to him, and took him for Peel.' As the darkness closed in, so a bewildering variety of ailments beset that faltering body. In February 1829 Mr Arbuthnot told his wife that, having seen the King at Windsor, 'he thought him dreadfully altered since last year and grown excessively old and infirm'.[47] George IV's subjects watched, and waited for him to die.

19

Conclusion

I am proud to declare I have no predilections,
My heart is a sieve, where some scatter'd affections
Are just danced about for a moment or two,
And the *finer* they are, the more sure to run through ...
Thomas Moore, *Parody of a Celebrated Letter*

GEORGE IV DIED at a time of renewed unrest in northern Europe. During the summer of 1830 the Belgians were revolting against their Dutch overlords, and opposition to the reactionary and insensitive Charles X of France was erupting into a revolution which was to end with his abdication. In Britain, however, even the assassination attempts of the Regency years and the agitation at the time of Caroline of Brunswick's trial were a distant memory. The reform movement which reawakened the late 1820s was not a matter of Parliament against monarchy – which since the Revolution of 1688 had been a constitutional monarchy, of circumscribed powers, whose current representative was a distant and eccentric figure more than usually irrelevant to the political process. Instead it was a conflict of party against party, reformers against reactionaries, within the Houses of Parliament themselves.

William IV was generally less troublesome to his ministers than his brother – Wellington famously declared to Greville that 'he had done more business with him in ten minutes than with George IV in as many days' – but when in November 1834 he apparently attempted to interfere in government by dismissing Lord Melbourne from the premiership, the reaction of those who had grown accustomed to dealing with a remote figure who took little active interest in politics was one of horror. Melbourne told the King that he was doubtful of his ability to carry on his ministry, and William's formal letter of dismissal was leaked to *The Times*. Condemning the King for his precipitate and foolish action, the paper ascribed it to the pernicious influence of his wife – 'the Queen has done it all' – and William was so incensed that he demanded the immediate resignation of Melbourne's cabinet.[1] Lord Holland ominously warned that William had made a 'fatal' mistake, while the Whig *Morning Chronicle* demanded that 'Englishmen must be up and doing'. Had Melbourne not calmly expressed 'sorrow rather than anger' at the turn of events, it might have proved a damaging time for the monarchy. As Philip Ziegler has noted, 'William's actions betrayed an alarming misconception of his position, and of his influence in parliament and in the country'.[2]

William IV's cheerful amateurism, bluff and careless familiarity and constitutional tactlessness earned him a wide measure of popularity, but did little to repair the damage done by his brother to the image of the monarchy. George's scandalous life and notorious extravagance, combined with the obsessive reclusiveness of his last years, had largely destroyed public respect for the person of the monarch, while the perceived capriciousness of his contributions to government had engendered a widespread feeling that the day-to-day business of politics could be carried on very well – perhaps better – without him.

Three grandchildren were born to George III in 1819, but it was the middle child who succeeded William IV in 1837: Victoria, daughter of William's brother the Duke of Kent, rather than the sons of Kent's younger brothers Cumberland and Cambridge. Her youth and gender dispelled some of the pessimism with which the House of Hanover was regarded, kindling memories of Princess Charlotte of Wales, of whom so much had been hoped. However, her initial reliance on Lord Melbourne, her first Prime Minister, suggested an inability to form clear opinions independent of stronger (and older) characters, and that she was not, after all, dissimilar to George IV, while the satirical print-makers began to circulate lascivious hints about the nature of the relationship between the Queen and her Prime Minister.

Victoria's marriage to Prince Albert changed all that. While Victoria and Albert delighted in pseudo-medieval pageantry borrowing directly or indirectly from George IV's coronation and the novels of Sir Walter Scott, theirs was no mere escapist Gothic Revivalism: Albert's dedication to the applied arts, science and manufactures ensured a distinctly contemporary reinterpretation of medieval forms and concepts, inextricably fused with the latest technological achievements and the manufacturing genius of Industrial Britain. He also introduced a socially concerned, benevolently paternal component into the constitutional equation, without which it is conceivable that the British monarchy might have gone the way of so many of those on the Continent during the nineteeth century. Albert's constitutional legacy was so strong that the memory of its benefits even survived Victoria's retreat into seclusion after his death in 1861.

The new Queen was more thorough than William IV had been in distancing the monarchy from the symbols of George IV's excessive expenditure. She disposed of Brighton Pavilion to the local corporation (having quietly spirited most of the interior fittings away to Buckingham Palace), and evinced no more public interest in George's art collections than in his palaces, agreeing with Melbourne that his much-loved Dutch and Flemish pictures were examples of 'a low style'.[3] Faced with the opulent, gilded interiors of Nash's Buckingham Palace and the cold Gothic corridors of Windsor, Victoria eagerly supported her husband's proposals to create two new royal residences, at Osborne and Balmoral, far more suited to the demands of a growing family.

Nor were Victoria and Albert alone in their prejudices. The topographer and antiquary John Britton told the Queen that, 'excepting Windsor Castle', George IV's royal palaces were 'a reproach to the monarchy, and to the nation'. In refusing William IV's offer of Buckingham Palace after the Houses of Parliament burned down in 1834, Melbourne had been relieved to have the support of Nash's successor Edward Blore, who considered the proposal 'so thoroughly inexpedient and ... attended with so many disadvantages and inconveniences that a worse selection could not well be made'. Melbourne himself had observed to the King that it would be 'very difficult to avoid providing much larger accommodation for Spectators as well as for Members', and, in a veiled allusion to the events of the French Revolution, asked him 'to recall ... the fatal effects which large Galleries filled with the Multitude have had upon the deliberations of public Assemblies'.[4] Even had it been a practical proposition, there was an understandable reluctance to use a building so redolent of royal irresponsibility and fiscal excess as the seat of Government.

Instead, the new Palace of Westminster that slowly arose from the ashes after 1840 encapsulated Parliament's vision of the benefits of a mixed constitution. It celebrated the enduring benefits of monarchy as much as the historic sovereignty of the Commons (the statue of Oliver

Cromwell waving his sword threateningly at the Abbey was added only decades later). Yet the concept of monarchy evoked in stone, paint and plaster drew heavily on long-distant, almost abstract martial glories in a clever synthesis of national aspiration and carefully-chosen tradition. There was no room in this vision for the tawdry reputations of Victoria's Hanoverian predecessors, none of whom – not even George III – featured in the principal iconography. The great Waterloo and Trafalgar frescos of Daniel Maclise dominate the walls, but the figure of George IV is nowhere to be seen in the adjacent celebration of warring monarchs; indeed, the most recent former sovereign to be depicted was William III. The new Palace of Westminster was a celebration of the ideal of constitutional monarchy, not of its most recent physical manifestations.

The influence of Sir Walter Scott's medieval romances was as evident in the Gothic pageantry of Barry and Pugin's Palace of Westminster as it had been in George IV's coronation and in the spectacles devised for George's visit to Edinburgh. Scott had bravely attempted to present George as a figure worthy of his Tudor and Plantagenet ancestors: he was, as Scott loyally protested in 1826, 'in many respects the model of a British Monarch', possessing 'little inclination to try experiments on government otherwise than through his Ministers' – a generous gloss on George's propensity to agree with his most recent strong-willed interlocutor and his readiness to abandon his professed political principles if adherence to them would prove awkward for him personally. Scott's other encomiums were similarly rosy-hued and defensive, most notably his assertion that George was a fitter monarch 'than one who would long to lead armies, or be perpetually intermeddling with *la grande politique*.'[5] Scott was apparently blind and deaf to George's long-running bluster about his desire to serve in battle and his consistent attempts after 1815 to present himself as the arbiter of European affairs.

Robert Huish, as we might expect, took a very different view. Having begun his account of his subject with the promising statement that 'there is scarcely a monarch ... whose private and public life abounds with more extraordinary and interesting incidents than that of George IV', his subsequent judgement was that George's Regency and reign represented a tragically missed opportunity. For Huish he was a man who might have 'exhibit[ed] himself at one time a Colossus of virtue, standing upon an eminence which few would essay to reach', at another as 'sovereign of the greatest and most civilised nation of the world', but who was more generally perceived as having been happy to 'sink into an abyss of profligacy characteristic of the most degenerate reprobate'. His palaces, Huish insisted, had been erected 'at the expense of a people already overwhelmed by a severe, unjust and unequal taxation', the public purse constantly raided 'to satisfy the insatiable appetite of royalty for ... terraces and towers' which by the time of his death in 1830 appeared as no more than 'lasting monuments of the vanity and folly of their projector'. Huish had a stinging rebuke for any who dared hail as a remarkable architectural achievement the eclectic array of royal residences George had created:

> The reign of George IV has been called a splendid reign – and justly so, if the Pimlico Palace, the [castle] of Windsor, the nicknacks of the Pavilion, the fleet on Virginia Water, the elegant jumble of the royal cottage, and the *soi-disant* great public improvements, had either been promoted or encouraged by the King for the happiness of the people.

He was equally dismayed by George's admiration, in his maturity, for the absolutism of 'continental systems' (a trait many Whigs were quick to discern in his brother in 1834). Huish's grim conclusion was that the late King was never in a position to 'demand honour from mankind ... neither as a public nor private individual', and that 'If posterity award approbation to his memory, the task of discovering the grounds on which it is to rest may be well left to their labour and ingenuity.'[6]

Huish's great contemporary William Cobbett was of much the same opinion. Rushing into print with a biography of the late King, as had Huish, he sternly warned future Parliaments against sanctioning such self-centered and wanton excesses as had been permitted George IV:

> When we behold such mighty and fatal effects, arising ... from the mortification, the caprice, or the antipathy, from the mere selfish passions, and, almost, from the animal feelings and propensities of *one single man* ... must we not be senseless indeed, must we not be something approaching to brutes, if we do not seek for some means of protecting ourselves against the like in future?

Cobbett's proto-republicanism reached its climax in the magisterial conclusion to his biography: 'England never appeared little in the eyes of the world', he declaimed, 'till the time of this Big sovereign.'[7]

Although not so damning as Cobbett, Princess Lieven found George's character similarly wanting. 'Full of vanity' and open to being 'flattered at will', the late King was, in her opinion, 'Weary of all the joys of life, having only taste, not one true sentiment'; in consequence he was 'hardly susceptible to attachment, and I believe never inspired anyone with it'.[8] The Princess was not the only observer of the Court and government to detect serious flaws. Junior minister (and future Prime Minister) Lord Aberdeen acknowledged sadly in 1829 that his sovereign had 'no idea of what a King of England ought to do'. Charles Greville was far more vehement in his appraisal of George's 'littleness of ... character'. His vices and weaknesses were, he adjudged after close inspection, 'of the lowest and most contemptible order'; his Court was fuelled by 'every base, low and unmanly propensity, with selfishness, avarice, and a life of petty intrigue and mystery'; and he himself 'was more than anybody the slave of habit and open to impressions'. Greville's conclusions pulled no punches:

> A more contemptible, cowardly, selfish, unfeeling dog does not exist than this King... He has a sort of capricious good-nature, arising however out of no good principle or good feeling, but which is of use to him, as it cancels in a moment.[9]

Others preferred to eschew the open criticism of Huish, Cobbett and Greville. Robert Peel, studiously avoiding any comment on the late King's character, declared rather that he was 'universally admitted to be the greatest patron the arts had ever had in this country'. *The Times*, however, refused to equivocate, and after his death castigated George's 'most reckless, unceasing and unbounded prodigality', and in particular 'the tawdry childishness of Carlton House and the mountebank Pavilion'.[10]

Sterner mid-Victorian critics like William Thackeray tended to reflect Huish's sentiments, shuddering as they recalled the royal profligacy of the 'Regency' era. To Thackeray himself, George IV was a complete irrelevance: 'nothing but a coat and a wig and a mask smiling below it – nothing but a great simulacrum' and 'but a bow and a grin'.[11] After 1918, however, royal apologists – in particular those who were or had been professionally or personally intimate with the contemporary royal family – preferred to follow Peel's example, commending George's aesthetic sensibilities while glossing over his unsavoury personal habits and inexcusable excesses. Between 1918 and

1939 George IV's reputation was rebuilt along these lines by a series of historians well-connected with the Court of George V. In the teeth of all the evidence for the outrageous expense and failed vision of Nash's Buckingham Palace, courtier-historian Clifford Smith felt impelled nevertheless to rush to Prinney's defence, declaring: 'Despite the conventional view of King George IV's reign, there can be no doubt that he considerably enhanced the dignity of the Crown.' Smith saw George as the creator of Regency London rather than as the shabby recluse or neglectful friend: 'Possessed of much taste, a fine intelligence, practical abilities and immense energy, he proceeded with a despotic determination to provide the English capital with a harmonious and beautiful appearance.' In common with many historians of architecture and the decorative arts before and since, Clifford Smith believed George IV's innate good taste had been undermined and betrayed by the new values of the industrial age:

> It was his misfortune to reign at an epoch when the middle class was emerging into power, so that his activities were immediately misrepresented by a class to which 'taste' and 'art' were apt to be synonymous with waste and licentiousness.[12]

Historian Sir Shane Leslie, biographer of Maria Fitzherbert, similarly blamed George's subjects for the failure of his over-inflated vision. 'The middle classes', he boldly asserted in the General Strike year of 1926, 'hated the artist in him as they hated Shelley and Byron.'[13] Royal biographer Roger Fulford (knighted in 1980, three years before his death) also excused George many of his worst excesses by pointing the finger at his blameless subjects, contrasting their necessarily more pragmatic priorities unfavourably with the vision of their connoisseur-King. Fulford's 1935 biography of George IV deprecated his orgy of expenditure, but judged: 'We can feel thankful that the money was spent by a Prince who, from our point of view, used it far more generously and effectively than if it had been left to fructify in the pockets of the middle classes, and swallowed up in the great maw of commercial England.' Smith, Leslie and Fulford all displayed a horror of the middle classes possibly more expressive of their own patrician backgrounds and aspirations than of the relationships between the social strata of Regency England. Fulford at least did not overstate his case – 'No reign can ever have begun more dismally than George IV's', he admitted – but he was careful to preface his account by dissociating the current sovereign from his namesake: 'the reader will almost feel that the Monarchy of George IV is a different institution from the Monarchy of George V', he suggested.[14] Since George V's Court and private life were noted for their dull and dreary respectability, Fulford's readers perhaps occasionally sighed for the days of his profligate predecessor.[15]

The image of George IV as First Gentleman of England – if not of Europe – and unsurpassed royal patron of the arts has been particularly enduring. Until the 1960s, most twentieth-century writers seemed to concur with Canova's estimation of him as a 'Sovereign in whose address were ... combined, the suavity of the amiable man, and the dignity of the great Monarch'.[16] Max Beerbohm saw him as 'a splendid patron [who] ... inspired society with a love of something more than mere pleasures, a love of the "humaner delights".' He was, Beerbohm concluded, 'a giver of tone'.[17] Peter Ustinov played him in this vein, with remarkable restraint, in Curtis Bernhardt's 1954 film *Beau Brummell*, and he was similarly described in Joanna Richardson's biography of 1966 ('George IV', she subsequently declared, consciously or unconsciously echoing Clifford Smith and Roger Fulford, 'has always suffered from the philistines').[18] In 1969 Sir Oliver Millar, then Surveyor of the Queen's Pictures, not only lauded George IV, quite justifiably, as a collector – 'No other Prince or King in the history of the royal collection has ever assembled such a distinguished portrait-gallery' – but also depicted him 'at the heart of ... a galaxy of talent, charm and high spirits'.[19]

It was Christopher Hibbert who first attacked the concept of George IV as a latter-day Sun King, the inspiration and epicentre of a glittering Court, motivated by taste and instinctive discernment, in his masterly two-volume biography published in 1971–2. In the course of the preceding three decades, Sir Arthur Aspinall had examined and catalogued such late Georgian royal papers as survived Sir William Knighton's bonfire of 1830, and had published successive instalments of George IV's correspondence as Prince and King. (Aspinall was himself not unaware of George's failings; nor did he hesitate to express his distaste for the less attractive elements of his character. In 1970, for example, Aspinall remarked on George's 'characteristic irresolution, manifested whenever unpleasant decisions had to be made'.[20]) Hibbert used Aspinall's invaluable work to produce the first properly balanced study of George IV, setting his undoubted eye for art and talent for patronage against his numerous personal failings.

His was the first biography in which George did not escape criticism simply because of his talent for collecting and building, and the first to castigate him for his costly whims and damaging delusions.[21]

Clifford Smith's positive interpretation of George IV's legacy has recently been revived by the late E.A. Smith who, while acknowledging many of his personal failings, saw George's reign as a milestone in the development of Britain's constitutional monarchy, 'midway between the "personal rule" of George III and the monarchy of Queen Victoria as defined by Walter Bagehot in the 1860s as a consultative and not executive body'; however, it requires a considerable leap of faith to relate the machinations of the 'cottage coterie' at the Royal Lodge with the Liverpool government's direction of policy. Most of George's attempts to intervene in politics during the 1820s ended in ignominious failure. Pressed by Lady Conyngham to obstruct Canning's desire to recognise the new South American republics, for example, he got nowhere; as Smith himself admits, 'Faced by a unanimous Cabinet, he backed down.'[22] E.A. Smith was eager not to characterise George's subsequent friendship with Canning as an instance of 'the surrender of a weak man to a stronger personality' – though the ageing King appeared increasingly reliant during his last years on the opinions of his mistress and his advisors. Smith's attempts to portray George as a skilful politician may seem equally unconvincing. Interpreting what Arthur Aspinall called his 'masterly inactivity' as evidence of George IV's political wisdom rather than of his accustomed indolence, Smith bravely tried to decipher a consistent plan in his laudanum-and-Maraschino-fuelled protestations, seeing in his fluctuating opinions a conscious policy of playing off one side against the other. Yet having announced in March 1827 that he would not appoint 'a Roman Catholic premier', the following month George asked the pro-Emancipation Canning to form an administration, and on 13 April 1829 he signed Wellington's Catholic Relief Act. Smith attempts to put a favourable gloss on this last betrayal of High Tory principles, declaring that it showed George was sensible enough to 'accept the limits beyond which he could not safely go' and concluding that his 'willingness to bow to what was politically inevitable saved the country from a confrontation between monarchy and what might be called democracy'. This is surely crediting the King with far too much political concern and adroitness, however. We have repeatedly seen that George's principles were barely even skin-deep, while his political will was a straw which bent to the promptings of his most recent advisor. He himself may not have been 'a bigoted anti-Catholic on principle'; yet in the aftermath of consultation with staunch 'Protestants' like the Duke of Cumberland, he certainly sounded remarkably like one.[23] Smith quotes Lord Binning as saying 'that the King has "immense power" when he chose to exert himself', but over the Catholic question – the issue which dominated politics in the late 1820s and on which the sovereign was said to have 'strong opinions' – George's machinations, strangely interpreted by Smith as proof of surviving liberal instincts, had little effect. Even his attempt to have his own nominee, J.C. Herries, appointed to the Exchequer in 1828 in order (it was thought) to secure a more kindly official view of his expenditure at Windsor Castle and Buckingham Palace, failed abjectly; Herries's nomination merely had the effect of helping to bring down Goderich's short-lived ministry.

In truth, George cared little for anything except his building projects and his collections, and possibly his current paramour. E.A. Smith confidently concludes that 'It was George IV, rather than his niece Victoria, who took the decisive role in creating the constitutional monarchy of the age of Gladstone and Asquith.'[24] Yet it is difficult to see how George was ever 'decisive', except in the purchase of furniture, works of art or new uniforms, or in his determination to build yet another residence. Rather than representing a crucial link in the evolution of the constitution, George merely succeeded in rendering the monarchy increasingly superfluous to the process of government and the life of the nation.

E.A. Smith's bravely revisionist stance is not without its supporters. Blaming Victoria's Court for blackening the names of George III's sons, Frank Prochaska has recently attempted to recast George IV and his brothers in the rather unexpected guise of exemplars of charity. Even the Duke of Cumberland and the Duke of Kent are depicted as active in the support of several charities, while George IV's charitable impulses in Dublin in 1821 and in Edinburgh the following year are cited as prime examples of his royal benevolence, gestures which 'added to the magical effect of the monarchy on the public'.[25] Here Dr Prochaska is perhaps confusing the image George wished to create with the reality that lay behind the pageant.

George IV may have been, as E.A. Smith suggested, 'unfortunate in his times'.[26] However, every monarch, and every subject, is afflicted with the same misfortune. It is up to each individual to make something of his or her life, however unwise their upbringing. George IV certainly left a glittering legacy of stunning – though at times highly eccentric – royal residences and collections. He also bequeathed to future generations, and particularly to the sovereigns who were to follow him, an object lesson in how, and how not, to conduct oneself. In many ways he was a strikingly modern monarch – not in the constitutional sense, but in the way in which he seems to have known instinctively that an attractive manufactured image could be used to hide or divert attention from the more dubious aspects of the life of a public figure. In this context, his obsessive desire to be taken for something he plainly was not can be seen as anticipating the 'celebrity' culture of contemporary Britain and, more pertinently, as foreshadowing the attempts during the last four decades to repackage and market the British monarchy. George IV's crucial mistake was to believe in the image he had created.

Notes

PREFACE

1. See Smith, *George IV*, 19.
2. Lacey Baldwin Smith, *Henry VIII, The Mask of Royalty*.
3. E.A. Smith, viii–x.
4. Ibid, xi.
5. BM 12305 and George, *Catalogue of ... Satires*, IX, 431.

CHAPTER I: THE FACE OF DEATH

1. Sir William Knighton's Diary, entries for 8 February and 20 February 1830, quoted in Aspinall, *Letters of George IV*, III, 471; Huish, *Memoirs of George IV*, II, 405.
2. George IV to Sir William Knighton, 26 December 1829, quoted in *Letters of George IV*, III, 467; Wellington, *Wellington Letters*, 90; Hibbert, *George IV*, 763.
3. Halford MSS, DG24/849/3, 849/6, 885/2, 879/9; J.G. Lockhart to Sir Walter Scott, 17 May 1830, quoted in Partington, *Private Letter-Books of Scott*, 159; Southey, *Life of Southey*, 102.
4. Fulford, *Autobiography of Miss Knight*, 145.
5. Nisbet, *The Royal College of Physicians* (1817), 1–6; Halford MSS, DG24/822/4. As to Halford's professionalism, there is the tale that soon after Charles I had been reburied 'it emerged that Sir Henry had abstracted a bone from the Martyr King's coffin which he, the President of the Royal College of Physicians, liked to show to his guests at the dinner table': Röhl et al., *Purple Secret*, xi.
6. Halford MSS, 795/14; *Dictionary of National Biography*.
7. Halford MSS, DG24/879/13, 1056/2; *The Lancet*, June 1830, quoted in George, *Catalogue of ... Satires*, XI, 288.
8. Jennings, *Croker Correspondence*, II, 57.
9. Wilkins, *Mrs Fitzherbert and George IV*, II, 213–14, 215–16.
10. Halford MSS, DG24/849/37 and 879/7, 879/16, 19, 21; Lockhart, *Memoirs of Scott*, 706.
11. Halford MSS, 879/20; BM 200691, 200667 (see George, op. cit., XI, 318 and Barlow, *The Prince and his Pleasures*, 58–9).

12. At least according to Halford. Huish cites the very precise time of 8.13 a.m. but gives no source for his exactitude.
13. Taylor, *Autobiography of Haydon*, II, 490; *Croker Correspondence*, 65; Halford MSS, 879/23.
14. Halford MSS, 879/24.
15. Huish, op. cit., 410; Röhl et al., op. cit., xi.
16. Halford MSS, 879/23; Macalpine and Hunter, *George III and the Mad-Business*, 240; *Parliamentary Debates*, second series, XXV/707–9, 29 June 1830.
17. Quoted in Taylor (ed.), op. cit., II,489.
18. Quoted in Miles and Brown, *Wilkie of Scotland*, 36; Sir Walter Scott to Sir William Knighton, 14 July 1830, in Grierson (ed.), *Letters of Scott*, 374.
19. See Prochaska, *Royal Bounty and the Making of a Welfare Monarchy*, 46–7. While *The Westminster Review* Vol. 14, Jan. 1831 acknowledged George IV's 'charitable wishes', it sought to place his benevolence in the context of his customary behaviour. 'He sends a thousand pounds to the poor weavers at Spitalfields', the anonymous obituarist wrote, 'but does any one believe that the King sacrificed ought by this act of ostentatious charity? Did one wish go ungratified in consequence? Did one bauble go unpurchased? Was one idle whim unsatisfied? Was there a statue less on Buckingham-house?' (loc. cit., 112–13).
20. Huish, op. cit., 411, 413; Cannadine, 'The Context, Performance and Meaning of Ritual: The British Monarchy and the Invention of Tradition', in Hobsbawm and Ranger, *Invention of Tradition*, 116, 118; Joseph Jekyll, quoted in Hibbert, *George IV*, 778; *The Times*, 16 July 1830.
21. Huish, 412, 415–16.
22. Cobbett, *History of George IV*, 493.
23. PRO WORK 5/6.
24. Colvin and Port, *King's Works*, VI, 651.
25. Robinson, *Letters of Princess Lieven*, 225.
26. Southey, op. cit., 102.
27. *Windsor and Eton Express*, 7 April 1832, quoted in Morshead, *George IV and the Royal Lodge*, 40; Greville, *Greville Memoirs*, II, 150; BM 16189, published July 1830 (see George, op. cit., IX, 317–18).
28. Robinson, *Letters of ... Princess Lieven*, 224.
29. Geoffrey de Bellaigue and Pat Kirkham, 'George IV and the Furnishings of Windsor Castle', in *Journal of the Furniture History Society*, Vol. VIII (1972), 9, 24.
30. *Greville Memoirs*, II, 26; *Windsor and Eton Express*, 7 April 1832 (quoted in Morshead, op. cit., 4).
31. Harris et al., *Buckingham Palace*, 15; Ziegler, *William IV*, 250–1.
32. PRO, WORK 19/5–6. See also Andrew Saint, 'The Marble Arch', in *The Georgian Group Journal*, Vol. VII (1997), 83–5.
33. *Windsor and Eton Express*, 10 July and 2 October 1830 (quoted in Roberts, *Royal Landscape*, 319).
34. Roberts, op. cit., 421.

35. Morshead, op. cit., 42–3.
36. Valerie Cumming, 'Pantomime and Pageantry: The Coronation of George IV', in Fox, *London – World City*, 49–50; Robinson, *Letters of Princess Lieven*, 224.
37. *The Times*, 16 July 1830.
38. Huish, op. cit., II, 53; I, 526; Trotter, *Memoirs of Fox*, 417; Smith, *George IV*, 287; David Cannadine, 'The Context, Performance and Meaning of Ritual: The British Monarchy and the "Invention of Tradition" *c.* 1820–1977', in Hobsbawm and Ranger, *Invention of Tradition*, 118.

CHAPTER 2: FAMILY AND FRIENDS

1. See Jane Roberts, 'Sir William Chambers and George III', in John Harris and Michael Snodin (eds), *Sir William Chambers* (Yale, 1996), 49.
2. Kew Gardens had been laid out for George III's mother, Princess Augusta, from the late 1750s. See Colvin, *Dictionary*, 240 and 584, and Colvin and Port, *King's Works*, V, 227.
3. See Willis, *Ernest Augustus*, 12n.
4. Quoted in Joanna Richardson, 'George IV: Patron of Literature', in *Essays by Diverse Hands*, Vol. xxxv (1969), 129.
5. See David, *Prince of Pleasure*, 14–15.
6. Hibbert, *George IV*, 27; Leslie, *George the Fourth*, 19.
7. Rush, *A Residence at the Court of London*, 67. George III's architectural sketches and drawings after his tutor Chambers remain in the Royal Collection, and were exhibited in 1996 on the bicentenary of the architect's death; for the catalogue, see note 1 above.
8. Huish, *Memoirs of George*, I, 21–5.
9. Wilkins, *Mrs Fitzherbert and George IV*, I, 165, 261.
10. Aspinall *Prince of Wales Correspondence*, I, 5; Hibbert, *George III*, 100–1.
11. Farington, IX, 3433; X, 3669; Princess Charlotte to Miss Mercer Elphinstone, 10 January 1812, in Aspinall, *Princess Charlotte Letters*, 23.
12. Brooke, *George III*, 544; *Creevey Papers*, 52; Gray, *Perceval*, 442.
13. Hibbert, *George IV*, 31; Thomas Grenville to Lord Cornwallis, 20 December 1787, quoted in George, *Catalogue of . . . Satires*, VI, 428; Hibbert, *George IV*, 107.
14. Hibbert, *George IV*, lxviii.
15. See *Prince of Wales Correspondence*, II, 295–6; Farington, I, 340.
16. Quoted in Hibbert, *George IV*, 299, 301.
17. *Greville Memoirs*, 91.
18. Fulford, *Royal Dukes*, 95; Lady Anne Culling-Smith, quoted in David, *Prince of Pleasure*, 304; *Royal Dukes*, 275–7; Princess Charlotte to Miss Mercer Elphinstone, 9 November 1811, in *Princess Charlotte Letters*, 11.
19. Farington, I, 480.
20. Hibbert, *George IV*, 506.
21. *Royal Dukes*, 208.
22. Aspinall, *Letters of George IV*, I, 255.

23. Princess Charlotte to Miss Mercer Elphinstone, 9 December 1811, in *Princess Charlotte Letters*, 16.
24. Queen Charlotte to the Prince Regent, 27 May 1815, quoted in *Letters of George IV*, II, 64, *Prince of Wales Correspondence*, II 177; Farington, VII, 2605; *Letters of George IV*, II, 91, 110; I, lxix.
25. Fulford, *Royal Dukes*, 239, 244; Huish, II, 387.
26. Quoted in *Royal Dukes*, 125–6; Willis, *Ernest Augustus*, 183. It is worth remembering that, until the birth of Queen Victoria's first child in 1842, the Duke of Cumberland (King of Hanover after William IV's death in 1837, since Hanoverian law proscribed a woman inheriting the title) was the heir to the throne.
27. Quoted in Hibbert, *George IV*, 257.
28. *Royal Dukes*, 302; Farington, VII, 2698; Hibbert, *George IV*, 741.
29. Brooke, *George III*, 570. The Prince of Württemberg was so fat 'that Bonaparte said that God had created him merely to demonstrate how far the human skin could be stretched without bursting' (Hibbert, *George IV*, 340–1).
30. Farington, XI, 4130–1; *Letters of George IV*, III, 468; *Prince of Wales Correspondence*, VII, 49.
31. Brooke, op. cit., 567.
32. See Mitchell, *Charles James Fox*, 60.
33. *Prince of Wales Correspondence*, II, 501.
34. Prince of Wales to George III, 11 November 1793, quoted in Sichel, *Glenbervie Journals*, 57.
35. *Prince of Wales Correspondence*, I, 86.
36. Huish, I, 31.
37. Simon, *Buckingham Palace*, 55; *Prince of Wales Correspondence*, III, 79.
38. Taylor, *Autobiography of Haydon*, II, 490.
39. Francis, *Last Journals Walpole*, II, 384, 404–5; Parry, *Queen Caroline*, 73.
40. Barrett, *Cosways*, 64.
41. Farington, VI, 2253. Lake held the Receivership for only a few months before his death, after which it reverted to Sheridan for the rest of his life.
42. Barman, *Divorce of Queen Caroline*, 7; Lloyd, *Quest for Albion*, 64.
43. Huish, I, 141–2.
44. Farington, V, 1920; Hibbert, *George III*, 265; *DNB*; George, *Catalogue of ... Satires*, VI, 131, 220.
45. George, op. cit., VI, 223.
46. See for example George, op. cit., VI, 528–9, 583; Foreman, *Georgiana*, 211.
47. George, op. cit., VI, 517; Bessborough, *Georgiana*, 163; *Prince of Wales Correspondence*, II, 96. Similarly generous loans were simultaneously made by Orléans to the dukes of York and Clarence.
48. See David, *Prince of Pleasure*, 132–3.
49. Parry, op. cit., 65; see Anon [Charles Pigott], *The Jockey Club, or Sketch of the Manners of the Age* (1792); Farington, VI, 2112.
50. Thackeray, *Four Georges*, 97.

51. Farington, II, 345; *Westminster Review*, Vol. 14 (1831), 111.
52. See O'Toole, *Traitor's Kiss*, 236, 238, 245, 248.
53. Biltmore Archive, box 7, VIII, 76, Prince of Wales to Richard Sheridan, 19 September 1792. I am grateful to Leslie Mitchell for bringing this to my attention.
54. *Prince of Wales Correspondence*, III, 221, 217–18.
55. Quoted in Macalpine and Hunter, *George III and the Mad-Business*, 126.
56. O'Toole, op. cit., 378; see *Prince of Wales Correspondence*, VI, 262.
57. Quoted in O'Toole, 442.
58. Sichel, *Sheridan*, II, 177; Mitchell, *Charles James Fox*, 86. O'Toole (op. cit., 447) supports Sheridan's story that his solicitor 'simply decided on his own behalf to seize the money as payment for Sheridan's debts to himself'.
59. O'Toole, 448, 465, 460.
60. Price, *Letters of Sheridan*, III, 248; *Letters of George IV*, I, 365; Farington, VI, 2253; *Letters of George IV*, III, 194; Jennings, *Croker Correspondence*, I, 312; *Westminster Review* (loc. cit.), 112.
61. *Prince of Wales Correspondence*, I, 269; Hibbert, *George IV*, 203, 213.
62. Wilkins, *Mrs Fitzherbert and George IV*, I, 96, 103, 105.
63. *Prince of Wales Correspondence*, VIII, 73.
64. Farington, XI, 4031; quoted in David, op. cit., 129.
65. Reeve, *Greville Memoirs*, I, 144; see for example George, op. cit., VI, 56, 292, 295, 298, 299, 309, 313, 314, 317.
66. Thackeray, op. cit., 106.
67. Roberts, *Royal Landscape*, 62; Huish, II, 288, 291.
68. Huish, II, 337.
69. See Sales, *Jane Austen and Regency England*, 65.
70. Crook and Port, *King's Works*, VI, 337; Huish, I, 114; David, *Prince of Pleasure*, 287–8.
71. Huish, I, 164.
72. *Prince of Wales Correspondence*, I, 164.
73. *Prince of Wales Correspondence*, I, 179–81.
74. Cobbett, op. cit., 35; *Prince of Wales Correspondence*, I, 294, 302.
75. *Prince of Wales Correspondence*, II, 96; George, op. cit., VI, 783; *Prince of Wales Correspondence*, I, 340–1n.
76. *Prince of Wales Correspondence*, II, 352; Aspinall, *Correspondence of George III*, II, 256.
77. Farington, IV, 1269; see *Prince of Wales Correspondence*, IV, 347.
78. George, op. cit., VI, 417; VII, 186, 173.
79. *Prince of Wales Correspondence*, IV, 269; Jefferys, *Review of the Conduct . . .*, 13, 19–20, 25, 29; Farington, III, 696.

CHAPTER 3: THE 'AMOROUS AND INCONSTANT SEXAGENARIAN'

1. 'George III himself, when Prince of Wales, appears to have secretly married Hannah Lightfoot, the daughter of a Quaker tradesman. A witness statement to their marriage in Kew Chapel on 17 April 1759,

signed by J.Wilmot, a clergyman and confidant of the Prince, was recently found in the Court of Chancery files by Kenneth Griffith … It states that the marriage was "solemnised this day according to the rites and ceremonies of the Church of England" … Lightfoot died in 1768, describing herself in her will as Hannah Regina.' (David, *Prince of Pleasure*, 33.)

2. Aspinall, *Prince of Wales Correspondence*, I, 48; Farington, II, 569; quoted in Fulford, *George IV*, 21.
3. Bessborough, *Georgiana* 76.
4. George III to the Prince of Wales, 14 August 1780, quoted in *Prince of Wales Correspondence*, I, 33–5.
5. Huish, *Memoirs of George IV*, I, 80; Campbell, *Most Polished Gentleman*, 19; Foreman, *Georgiana*, 475.
6. Campbell, 30–2; *Westminster Review*, Vol. 14 (1831), 106.
7. See Parry, *Queen Caroline*, 56–9; *Carlton House*, (exhibition catalogue), 236.
8. George, *Catalogue of … Satires*, VI, 167, 501; VII, 152; VI, 98–9, 158, 264; Foreman, 80; *Prince of Wales Correspondence*, I, 266; II, 31. The payment to the Duchess of Devonshire in August 1789 merely encouraged her to approach the Prince again in November 1789, twice during the summer of 1790, and again during 1791 (*Prince of Wales Correspondence*, II, 44, 46, 102, 125, 181).
9. George, op. cit., VI, 242, 249, 319; W.H. Pyne in *Fraser's Magazine*, Vol. xxii (1840); Barnett, *Cosways*, 71, 114. If all the rumours were true, Maria Cosway was a busy girl; the 1995 Merchant Ivory film *Jefferson in Paris* even indicated an affair with the American Minister in Paris, Thomas Jefferson (US President 1801–9), a suggestion borne out by recent scholarship.
10. Farington, IV, 1341; Hibbert, *George IV*, 174; Huish, I, 112. Lady Melbourne's son George Lamb was widely believed to be the illegitimate son of the Prince of Wales.
11. Huish, I, 262–3; Levy, *Mistresses of George IV*, 194.
12. Huish, I, 402; Cobbett, *History of George IV*, 30.
13. Huish, I, 124; see Wilkins, *Mrs Fitzherbert and George IV*, I, 37–8.
14. Chatsworth MSS, 675, quoted in Leslie, *Mrs Fitzherbert*, I, 22; Aspinall; *Prince of Wales Correspondence*, III, 189–201; Wilkins, *Mrs Fitzherbert and George IV*, I, 57.
15. Quoted in Levy, op. cit., 47, 53.
16. Wilkins, op. cit., II, 41–2.
17. Jennings, *Croker Correspondence*, 125.
18. BM 201166, 201426; George, *Catalogue of … Satires*, VI, 294, 319, 400.
19. Leslie, *Letters of Mrs Fitzherbert* II, 9.
20. '… in every word that Fox uttered, tending to deny the marriage, he was making a dupe of the English nation' (Huish, I, 159).
21. See BM 201438: *The — Nursery, or Nine Months After*, 9 May 1786; BM 205791, 207978.
22. Leslie, *Letters of Mrs Fitzherbert*, II, 75; Hibbert, *George IV*, 92n; Campbell, *Most Polished Gentleman*, 135–8; ex. inf. the late Juliet Barnard; *Prince of Wales*

Correspondence, VI, 377n. See also Foord-Kelcey, *Mrs Fitzherbert and Sons*. James Ord was later told by a Catholic priest of his putative father; he thereupon wrote to Mrs Fitzherbert, who did not reply.

23. *Prince of Wales Correspondence*, VIII, 483. Saul David has recently suggested that Henry Hervey was actually the son of Lady Anne Lindsay, not Mrs Fitzherbert (see David, *Prince of Pleasure*, 78); he does not explain, however, whether he believes the father to have been the Prince of Wales, the 4th Earl of Bristol (after whom he was named, and a decidedly suspicious character) or Lady Anne's subsequent husband, Andrew Barnard.

24. Leslie Grout, 'George Payne of Sulby Hall', in *Friends of Kensal Green Cemetery Newsletter*, Summer 1995, 8. The last of these alleged children, George Payne, was born in April 1803 at Sulby Hall.

25. Quoted in Mitchell, *Lord Melbourne*, 5.

26. See Levy, *Mistresses of George IV*, 193–4.

27. RA 29974–97, 30370; *Prince of Wales Correspondence*, VIII, 483. George Crole died in 1863 and is buried in Highgate Cemetery: see Lydia Collins, 'George Seymour Crole – A Son of George IV', in *The Genealogist's Magazine*, Vol. xxi (September 1984), 228–35. E.A. Smith points out the interesting coincidence that Crole's half-sister married one of the Duke of Clarence's illegitimate children by Dorothea Jordan (Smith, *George IV*, 291).

28. RA 29957–73, 39524–6; David, *Prince of Pleasure*, 80.

29. Wilkins, *Mrs Fitzherbert and George IV*, I, 149; Huish, I, 291; Farington, II, 293; George, *Catalogue of ... Satires*, VI, 898; Philip Withers, *Alfred, or A Narrative of the daring and illegal measures to suppress a pamphlet intituled Strictures of the Declaration of Horne Tooke Esq respecting HRH the Princess of Wales commonly called Mrs Fitzherbert* (London, 1789), 25.

30. Farington, I, 232; Hawes, *Brougham*, 116; Langdale, *Memoirs of Mrs Fitzherbert*, 125.

31. Fraser, *Unruly Queen*, 81, 86–7.

32. Huish, I, 489, 51, 54; II, 53.

33. See Wilkins, op. cit., II, 21–2.

34. Bessborough, *Georgiana*, 219; Leslie, *Letters of Mrs Fitzherbert*, II, 30–1.

35. Fraser, *Unruly Queen*, 41; Farington, XIV, 4912; BM 8811; Huish, I, 263; Wilkins, II, 16; Fulford, *George IV*, 71.

36. Quoted in Wilkins, I, 63; *Prince of Wales Correspondence*, II, 493; Huish, I, 328.

37. Fraser, *Unruly Queen*, 43; Farington, II, 627; *Prince of Wales Correspondence*, III, 3n.

38. Malmesbury's Diary, 28 November 1794, quoted in Smith, *Queen on Trial*, 2; *Westminster Review*, Vol. 14 (1831), 108; Malmesbury's Diary, loc. cit., 9 December 1794.

39. Malmesbury's Diary, 16 December 1794, 6 March 1795.

40. Malmesbury's Diary, 5 April 1795.

41. *Westminster Review*, Vol. 14 (1831), 102; Huish, I, 400.

42. Thackeray, *Four Georges*, 111; Fraser, *Unruly Queen*, 62; Lady Charlotte Bury, quoted in David, *Prince of Pleasure*, 168.

43. Jesse, *Life of Brummell*, I, 31; quoted in Levy, 47; Lady Rose Weigall, *Memoir of Princess Charlotte*, 6.

44. BM 8806–7, 24–5 May 1796, in George, op. cit., VII, 253–4; Fraser, *Unruly Queen*, 90; Malmesbury Papers, diary entry for 18 March 1796, quoted in David, op. cit., 169; Fraser, 66, 62.

45. See Joanna Richardson, 'The Princess Charlotte', in *History Today*, Vol. 22, no. 2 (1972), 87; Malmesbury Papers, quoted in David, 170; Farington, III, 920.

46. Bury, *The Court Under George IV*, I, 143; quoted in Fraser, *Unruly Queen*, 70.

47. See Fraser, 79–80. For the Prince of Wales's histrionic epistolary exchanges with his wife, see *Prince of Wales Correspondence*, III, 168–74.

48. *Prince of Wales Correspondence*, III 188, 190–2, 197–8.

49. 'Humphry was a considerable time with the Margravine of Anspach (Lady Craven) yesterday at Brandenburgh House. – She spoke of Lady Jersey, and allowed her beauty, but said she had thick legs. – The Margravine added that the Prince had denied the Child being his ...' (Farington, II, 627: 1 August 1796). Interestingly, it was at Brandenburg House that Caroline expired in 1821.

50. Millar, *Later Georgian Pictures*, 33; Farington, III, 671.

51. Farington, II, 553, 559.

52. *The Times*, 25 July 1796, in *Prince of Wales Correspondence*, III, 246n.

53. Farington, III, 696.

54. Farington, II, 589; quoted in Fraser, *Unruly Queen*, 91.

55. BM 9373 (J. Macerius) & 9382 (Isaac Cruikshank) in George, *Catalogue of ... Satires*, VII, 548, 551; quoted in *Mistresses of George IV*, 102.

56. *Prince of Wales Correspondence*, III, 138.

57. Farington, VII, 2785; Hibbert, *George IV*, 210n.

58. Hibbert, *George IV*, 227–8.

59. *Prince of Wales Correspondence*, IV, 2.

60. The 'Egyptian' house that William Porden built for her was, rather alarmingly, blown down in a gale in 1805. Porden replaced it by an Italianate villa with a small Catholic chapel at the side.

61. Leslie, *Life of Mrs Fitzherbert*, I, 212. In April 1820, in a fit of remorse, George IV raised this to £10,000 a year.

62. Leslie, op. cit., I 183; Fraser, *Unruly Queen*, 200; Langdale, *Memoirs of Mrs Fitzherbert*, 133.

63. Quoted in Hibbert, *George IV*, 332–3.

64. *Prince of Wales Correspondence*, VI 501n.

65. Leslie, op. cit., I, 201. Leslie alleges that William IV, having been assured of the validity of the 1785 marriage, offered Maria a ducal coronet, but that she declined it, asking only to dress her servants in royal livery.

66. *Prince of Wales Correspondence*, VIII, 347–8; quoted in Parry, *Queen Caroline*, 83; John Croker diary entry for 7 December 1818, quoted in Leslie, *Letters of Mrs Fitzherbert*, II 203; Butler, *Regency Visitor*, 173.

67. Possibly as a result of this, the King's last Private Secretary, Sir William Knighton, clearly formed a very bad impression of her. Mrs Fitzherbert, he alleged in 1830, had a violent temper and was 'artful, cunning, designing, ... very selfish ..., and entirely under the influence of Popish superstition' (Aspinall, *Letters of George IV*, III, 482). His subsequent declaration that the King 'had a horror of her' is, however, somewhat undermined by George's determination to be buried with her likeness around his neck.

68. Leslie, op. cit., I, 22; *Letters of George IV*, I, 281, 344, 513; Fulford, *Autobiography of Miss Knight*, 120.

69. Wheatley, *Wraxall Memoirs*, V, 357–8.

70. Quoted in David, *Prince of Pleasure*, 277.

71. Sichel, *Sheridan*, II, 373; Farington, XI, 3896 (18 March 1811).

72. Levy, *Mistresses of George IV*, 133–4.

73. Quoted in Hibbert, *George IV*, 324.

74. Farington, XI, 3896; BM 8634; *A Meeting of Creditors*, published 3 April 1795 (George, *Catalogue of ... Satires*, VII, 166); Barlow, *Prince of Pleasures*, 12–13; BM 11888–9, 11893, 11897, 12800, 13220, 13232 (George, op. cit., X, 114, 117, 121, 124, 696, 893, 900).

75. BM 13234 (May 1819) in George, op. cit., X, 901–2.

76. In October 1820 an anonymous satirist, possibly William Heath, showed the King in a Chinese interior kissing Mrs Quentin, wife of the Colonel of the 10th Hussars, on his lap (BM 207992). It had been widely alleged that the Colonel was only saved from a court martial by his wife's intimacy with the King.

77. Levy, op. cit., 153; David, op. cit., 390; BM 13770: *How to get un-married ...* (n.d.: ?July 1820); Reeve, *Greville Memoirs*, 9 June 1820.

78. Mrs Arbuthnot's Journal, quoted in Smith, *Queen on Trial*, 182; quoted in Prebble, *King's Jaunt*, 48, 51, 53.

79. Leveson-Gower, *Letters of Countess Granville*, I, 207, 214.

80. Wilkins, *Mrs Fitzherbert and George IV*, II, 165; George, op. cit., X, 586; BM 15848 (George, op. cit., XI, 180); Hibbert, *George IV*, 628–9n.

81. Jennings, *Croker Correspondence*, I, 173; see Hibbert, *George IV*, 633–4.

82. The Earl of Liverpool to George IV, 22 January 1822, in *Letters of George IV*, II, 999.

83. *Letters of George IV*, II, 490–2, 498, 505, 512, 522; III, 4, 16, 78, 91, 101; Robinson *Letters of Princess Lieven*, 161.

84. Wilkins, II, 194. George IV never returned to Brighton after March 1827; Maria Fitzherbert was back there the following November.

85. See for example George, op. cit., XI, 182 (BM 15844), 191 (BM 15864), etc.

86. Robinson, *Letters of Princess Lieven*, 32, 383; BM 200694 (William Heath); Barlow, *Prince of Pleasures*, 56.

87. Lord Francis was initially sent in September 1822 on a diplomatic mission to Stockholm, which he ungratefully bemoaned as 'a terrible destiny'. See George, op. cit., X, 311.

88. Prebble, *King's Jaunt*, 58.
89. 1st Duke of Wellington to Charles Arbuthnot, 17 November 1821, quoted in Wellington, *Wellington Letters*, 17; Robinson, *Letters of Princess Lieven*, 145, 161.
90. Robinson, op. cit., 223; RA 32696, 26161.
91. Wilkins, II, 163; Gore, *Creevey Papers*, 187; Robinson, op. cit., 178.
92. *Wellington Letters*, 70; Barlow, 19; Robinson, 36.

CHAPTER 4: DRESS AND MILITARIA

1. Diary of Lady Charlotte Finch, quoted in Smith, *George IV*, 6.
2. Stephen Lloyd, 'Fashioning the Image of the Prince: Richard Cosway and George IV', in Arnold, *Squanderous and Lavish Profusion*, 6, 8.
3. Bessborough, *Georgiana*, 289.
4. Farington, IV, 1326; Thackeray, *Four Georges*, 92.
5. Hibbert, *George III*, 193.
6. RA 29210, 29230–1.
7. Ribeiro, *Art of Dress*, 230–1; Farington, V, 1932.
8. RA 29331–29347; Hibbert, *George IV*, 234.
9. RA 29315, 29408, 29320, 29414.
10. Valerie Cumming, 'Pantomime and Pageantry: The Coronation of George IV', in Fox, *London – World City*, 40.
11. Aspinall, *Prince of Wales Correspondence*, I, 55–6.
12. *Prince of Wales Correspondence*, I, 57, 62.
13. David, *Prince of Pleasure*, 48.
14. Farington, II, 621.
15. Farington, I, 232 (13 December 1794).
16. Mollo, *Prince's Dolls*, 9.
17. *Prince of Wales Correspondence*, IV, 298.
18. Ibid., IV, 423.
19. Mollo, 2; Evans, *Princes as Patrons*, 17.
20. *The Times*, 24 July 1792.
21. Mollo, 8–9, 15.
22. *Prince of Wales Correspondence*, III, 34.
23. *Prince of Wales Correspondence*, III, 19; Mollo, 14; The Prince of Wales to King George III, 9 March 1795, in Aspinall, *Correspondence of George III*, II, 313; *Prince of Wales Correspondence*, III, 41, 45, 46.
24. King George III to the Prince of Wales, 8 April 1795, in *Correspondence of George III*, 329.
25. Hibbert, *George III*, 222.
26. *Prince of Wales Correspondence*, III, 313–16, 428.
27. Ibid., IV, 387, 391–2, 395–6; quoted in Fulford, *George IV*, 85.
28. *Prince of Wales Correspondence*, IV, 422, 425, 427–34.
29. See Hibbert, *George III*, 336–43; *Prince of Wales Correspondence*, IV, 493; V, 8–9.
30. RA 29250, 29253, 29273, 29364, 29370, 29384–8, 29424.

31. The picture was subsequently bought by the Rothschilds and now hangs at Waddesdon Manor – appropriately, adjacent to Reynolds's 1778 full-length of the Prince's drinking and racing friend Colonel St Leger.
32. Millar, *Later Georgian Pictures*, I, xxiv, xxvi, xxx; Evans, *Princes as Patrons*, 70, 94, 96, 99. Today the Royal Collection includes two pictures of Cumberland by Morier.
33. BM 8811; Mollo, 25.
34. Mollo, 33.
35. *Carlton House* (exhibition catalogue), 144.
36. Mollo, 99, 104.
37. Quoted in Mollo, 191–2; *Wellington Letters*, 6.
38. Mollo, 15.
39. Jesse, *Life of Brummel*, I, 30–1, 35; Ribeiro, 234.
40. David, 283–4. David cites his popularity with men, his failure to marry and his flirtatiousness with both sexes.
41. Thomas Raikes, *A Portion of the Journal Kept by Thomas Raikes Esq, 1831–47* (1856–7), II, 206; Jesse, I, 64.
42. David, 283; Ribeiro, 48, 64, 214–17; Jesse, II, 7; Hibbert, *George IV* (1976), 645–6.
43. See Ribeiro, 105, 107.
44. Ribeiro, 99, 100.
45. RA 29583.
46. In the tumult over Caroline's 'trial' in the summer of 1820, regular soldiers publicly cheered her as she passed. In June, the mutiny of a battalion of The Guards, partly in protest at George's treatment of his wife, shocked the government as well as the king, and had ministers speculating on the prospect of using poorly-trained local militia to subdue regular troops. See Chapter 10.
47. RA 29603, 29635, 29642–3.

CHAPTER 5: ARCHITECTURAL PATRONAGE

1. William Chambers, *Treatise on Civil Architecture* (3rd edn, 1791), quoted in Harris and Snodin, *Sir William Chambers*, 45; Hibbert, *George III*, 179. See Roberts, art. cit. note 1 Chapter 2, 41–54.
2. See Parissien, *Regency Style*.
3. Kimerly Rorschach, 'Frederick, Prince of Wales (1707–51) as Collector and Patron', in *Journal of the Walpole Society*, lv (1989–90), 22–3.
4. Evans, *Princes as Patrons*, 104.
5. See *Carlton House* (exhibition catalogue), 210, 226.
6. *Ibid.*, 214.
7. See Parissien, *Regency Style*, 14.
8. See *Prince of Wales Correspondence*, IV, 256–7.
9. Quoted in Stroud, *Henry Holland*, 84.
10. Farington, X, 3614. By the time Farington related this exchange, on 12 March 1810, both Porter and Bourgeois were dead; Farington, VII, 2745; Jefferys, *Review of the Conduct*..., 61.

11. Aspinall, *Prince of Wales Correspondence*, V, 252–3.
12. *Carlton House* (exhibition catalogue), 21, 219; Farington, XIII, 4525.
13. See Hugh Roberts in Evans, *Princes as Patrons*, 99–100, entry 93.
14. Farington, XI, 3884–5.
15. Oliver Millar, 'Introduction', in Evans, *Princes as Patrons*, 15; Summerson, *Microcosm of London*, 24.
16. The Prince of Wales to the Earl of Southampton, 1 September 1784, in *Prince of Wales Correspondence*, I, 159.
17. RA 25075, 35048, 35085–35090; Crook and Port, *King's Works*, 308.
18. Geoffrey de Bellaigue, 'George IV and French Furniture', in *Connoisseur*, Vol. 195 (June 1997), 121; de Bellaigue, 'The Furniture of the Chinese Drawing Room, Carlton House', in *Burlington Magazine*, Vol. cix (1967), 519. Sir Geoffrey comments that both these estimates 'are clearly suspect ... because they were drafted with a view not of presenting a faithful picture of the Prince's future requirements, but as part of a device for securing more money'.
19. *Prince of Wales Correspondence*, II, 302.
20. Jane Geddes, 'The Grange, Northington', in *Architectural History*, Vol. 26 (1983), 36–48; RA 35342; Geddes, 'The Prince of Wales at the Grange, Northington: An Inventory of 1795', in *Furniture History*, Vol. xxii (1986). After 1809 The Grange was wholly rebuilt by William Wilkins as a Greek temple.
21. *King's Works*, VI, 359; *Carlton House* catalogue, 15; *King's Works*, VI, 357; John Harris, 'Bicentenary of Kew Gardens', in *Country Life*, Vol. cxxv (1959), 1182–4; Aspinall, *Letters of George IV*, III, 191; *King's Works*, VI, 369; RA 35217–18. Even floors were re-used – not just those of stone or marble, but also 'oak floors of Four Rooms on the principal Story, South front' and five other wood floors.
22. *King's Works*, VI, 85, 313, 315.
23. Farington, XII, 4424; *King's Works*, VI, 99.
24. Colvin, *Dictionary*, 687; Summerson, *Life of Nash*, 90, 93–5. Summerson subsequently dryly observed of Nash: 'With some difficulty we remind ourselves that his actual status in the hierarchy of government at this time was still the exceedingly obscure one of joint architect in the Office of Woods ...'. To his credit, Romilly repeatedly refused Nash's offer of a lucrative, improved office in a new administration.
25. RA 25341; see Geoffrey de Bellaigue, 'The Furnishings of the Chinese Drawing Room, Carlton House', loc. cit., 518–28 (the new seat upholstery lasted eight years, until the room itself was dismantled in 1819); *King's Works*, VI, 315; *Carlton House* catalogue, 217. Tatham's furniture was supplied by Morel and Hughes.
26. RA 33498; Musgrave, *Royal Pavilion*, 17; RA 33507, 33519; Musgrave, 39.
27. See E.W. Brayley's commentary to the 1838 edition of A.C. Pugin's watercolours of the building, originally commissioned by Nash and first published in 1826; quoted in Gervase Jackson-Stops's Preface to the 1991

reprint of Nash's *Views of the Royal Pavilion*. Musgrave (p. 28) points out that this gift was not made until 1802, a year after Holland's first Chinese scheme.

28. RA 33542, 33578–9. A drawing of 1801 from Holland's office shows the Pavilion recased in a Chinoiserie jacket.

29. Farington, VIII, 2868.

30. RA 33586.

31. RA 33591, 33662, 33593–4: William Porden to Robert Gray, 22 January 1807.

32 RA 33677, 33943, 33975, 33984, 33963–4, 33973, 33991.

33. *King's Works*, VI, 125; Cookson, *Liverpool's Administration*, 86–7; Aspinall, *Letters of George IV*, II, 158–161; RA 34223–4; *Letters of George IV*, II, 289; quoted in Hibbert, 521.

34. Pugin's *Contrasts* of 1836 revealingly used the example of Nash's richly-gilded Chapel Royal, adjacent to the Pavilion, to illustrate the depths religious architecture had plumbed during the Regency era. The chapel, not actually within the Pavilion's walls, was reached by a connecting passageway from the south wing into the top floor of what had formerly been the Castle Inn. There is something particularly appropriate about George, who expressed little interest in organised religion, having a chapel constructed inside a former pub.

35. Most of this southern wing, facing onto North Street, was demolished after 1850; however, though the servants' rooms and the 'steaming kitchen' have gone, the King's Kitchen remains. Appropriately, the Pavilion shop now occupies the area formerly devoted to visitors' apartments.

36. Rutherford, *Brighton Pavilion*, 38. See also the same author's 'Lighting in the Royal Pavilion, 1815–1980', in *Country House Lighting* (Temple Newsam, Leeds, 1992).

CHAPTER 6: CONNOISSEUR OF FINE ART

1. Farington, XIV, 4871; XII, 4162.

2. Quoted in White, *Dutch Pictures ...*, liv.

3. Kimerly Rorschach, 'Frederick, Prince of Wales (1707–51) as Collector and Patron', in *Journal of the Walpole Society*, lv (1989–90), 51–76; Hibbert, *George III*, 10.

4. See Aspinall, *Prince of Wales Correspondence*, V, 417–18; VII, 23.

5. Farington, XV, 5312; J.M. Robinson, *Windsor Castle*, 89.

6. Haydon, *Haydon: Correspondence*, 151–2. Haydon subsequently displayed a more realistic attitude, admitting to his diary that 'The King thought there was too much in *Punch*. He admired the apple-girl excessively, but thought the capering chimney-sweeper too much like an opera dancer' (Elwin, *Autobiography of Haydon*, 463). Haydon's fiscal desperation may have caused him to exaggerate Seguier's role; by May 1830 Haydon was again in prison for debt.

7. See Barnett, *Cosways*, 136–7, 170.

8. Combe MSS, quoted in Stephen Lloyd, 'Fashioning the Image of the Prince: Richard Cosway and George IV', in Arnold, *Squanderous and Lavish Profusion*, 12–13. For the description of Cosway, see Millar, *Later Georgian Pictures*, I, xxiv.

9. Quoted in White, *Dutch Pictures*, lx.

10. Ibid., lvii.

11. Ingamells, *Hertford as Collector*, 9, 20; Farington, XI, 3948; Harris, de Bellaigue and Millar, *Buckingham Palace*, 269 and passim.

12. Ingamells, 24, 31. The architect Decimus Burton had built the villa, which the Marquess named 'St Dunstan's', in 1825.

13. D'Oench, *'Copper into Gold'*, 85–7. Smith's print *Albina* of 1791 may be a portrait of Mrs Fitzherbert (D'Oench, 138–9).

14. Farington, IV, 1130, 1147; Millar, *Later Georgian Pictures*, I, xxvi.

15. See Oliver Millar's Introduction to Evans, *Princes as Patrons*, 15; Millar, *Later Georgian Pictures*, I, 40.

16. Pressly, *Revealed Religion*, 19–20. For details of West's commissions from George III see *George III, Collector and Patron* (exhibition catalogue), 19. The Chapel commission was cancelled by George III in 1804.

17. In 1812 Farington (XI, 4075) tried to avoid direct criticism of the Prince Regent by suggesting, wrongly as it turned out, that George was trying to prevent his mother from ending the pension.

18. Lloyd, *Quest for Albion*, 13 ('The decorations on the ceiling of the principal room were executed by a German artist called Haas in the rare medium of coloured marble dust ... based on sketches dating from 1787–8 provided by West'); Pressly, op. cit., 52.

19. Ex. inf. Dr Martin Postle; Farington, IV, 2469. I am indebted to Martin Postle for his suggestions and advice on this subject.

20. Postle in Simon, *Buckingham Palace*, 199, 122; Farington, VII, 2581.

21. George's prized Reynolds portrait of the duc d'Orléans was ruined in the Carlton House fire of 8 June 1824.

22. Millar, *Later Georgian Pictures*, I, xxv; *Carlton House* (exhibition catalogue), 70.

23. Farington, VII, 2049; X, 3831. See Richard Walker, 'Henry Bone's Pencil Drawings in the National Portrait Gallery', in *Walpole Society*, Vol. lxi (1999), 305–67. Bone's son later became Enamel Painter to both Queen Adelaide and Prince Albert.

24. Millar, op. cit., I, 82.

25. Ibid., 122–4, 127.

26. Ibid., xxix; Lloyd, *Quest for Albion*, 78. The *Waterloo Allegory* has since been lost.

27. Farington, VI, 2307; RA 32221, 42950; Millar, op. cit., I, 5.

28. *George III, Collector and Patron* (exhibition catalogue), 20, 79; Millar, op. cit., I, 50.

29. Farington, VII, 2571; VIII, 3036.

30. Farington, XII, 4227; Jones, *Chantrey*, 114. Owen was offered a knight-

hood by the Prince, but refused. From 1820 he was crippled by illness, and died of an overdose of opium in 1825.

31. Farington, XI, 3919; Aspinall, *George IV Letters*, I, 262; Beckett, *Life of Ward*, 115. Copley's picture is now in the Museum of Fine Arts in Boston.

32. Vigée-Le Brun, *Souvenirs* (1984), II, 126, 130, quoted in Goodden, *Sweetness of Life*, 241; Goodden, 258–9.

33. Farington, XIV, 4930; XII, 3947, 4165; XI 4083. The architecture of Hampton Court was not it seems to George's taste; he evidently preferred the sham Tudor Gothic of Hopper's Carlton House Conservatory and Wyatville's Windsor Castle to the real thing.

34. Farington, X, 3691; XI 3919. In September 1813 Wilkie still had not been paid for *Blind Man's Buff*.

35. Farington, XV, 5314, 5385.

36. Farington, XVI, 5595; see Whitley, *Art in England 1821–37*, 35, 92, 109.

37. *Carlton House* (catalogue), 43–4; Simon, *Buckingham Palace*, 233. In 1790 George III had recoiled from Lawrence's astonishing bravura portrait of Queen Charlotte seated by a window at Windsor. Happily, the picture is now exhibited for all to see at the National Gallery, rather than squirrelled away at Buckingham Palace.

38. Taylor, *Autobiography of Haydon*, I, 353; II, 477; J.G. Lockhart to Sir Walter Scott, 28 November 1828, in Partington, *Letter-Books of Scott*, 157; Cunningham, *Life of Wilkie*, II, 11, 13.

39. Taylor, II, 478; Haydon, *Haydon: Correspondence*, I, 153.

40. Evans, *Princes as Patrons*, 72.

41. Farington, XIII, 4689, 4746; XIV, 4805, 4908, 4913, 4920; Memes, *Memoirs of Canova*, 475–6; *Canova* (exhibition catalogue), 19.

42. Malcolm Baker, Alison Yarrington et al., 'The Chantrey Ledger', in *Journal of the Walpole Society*, lvi (1991–2), 188, 165.

43. Jones, *Chantrey*, 113, 116.

44. 'The Chantrey Ledger', loc. cit., 166.

45. PRO WORK 19/3.

46. Gunnis, *Dictionary of British Sculptors*, 326–7.

47. Flaxman's silver-gilt Shield of Achilles, bought by George IV for the substantial sum of 2,000 guineas in 1821, occupied a prominent position at the King's coronation banquet. Three years later he bought Flaxman's National Cup, a Gothic work studded with diamonds, emeralds, rubies, amethysts and turquoises – an extravagant display much to his taste. See Irwin, *Flaxman*, 196, 202.

48. Colvin, *Dictionary*, 688.

CHAPTER 7: CONSPICUOUS CONSUMPTION

1. BM 8095, 8112: see George, *Catalogue of ... Satires*, VI, 909, 920.

2. Farington, X, 3589; XII, 4162; XIV, 5073.

3. *The Brighton Ambulator*, quoted in Rutherford, *Royal Pavilion*, 35.

4. Sara Paston Williams, *The Art of Dining* (1993), 231; Anne Willan, *Great Cooks and their Recipes* (1992), 143–4.
5. Farington, III, 814.
6. Farington, VII, 2791; quoted in Evans, *Princes as Patrons*, 89.
7. Farington, IV, 1324.
8. Macalpine and Hunter, *George III and the Mad-Business*, 229, 240.
9. Farington, VIII, 3036.
10. Farington, X, 3545, 3716; Valerie Cumming, 'Pantomime and Pageantry: The Coronation of George IV', in Fox, *London – World City*, 41; Prebble, *King's Jaunt*, 44; Fulford, *George IV*, 292; quoted in Smith, *George IV*, 269.
11. Quoted in Macalpine and Hunter, op. cit., 231–2, 234.
12. Aspinall, *Letters of George IV*, I, 232, 240; Farington, XI, 4036; XII, 4152; XII, 4255; Hibbert, *George IV* (1976), 326.
13. Farington, XI, 4034; Macalpine and Hunter, op. cit., 229; Buckingham, *Memoirs of the Court 1811–20*, I, 145.
14. Countess Granville, *Granville Correspondence*, II, 429.
15. Farington, XII, 4321; Aspinall, *Letters of George IV*, I, 478.
16. Macalpine and Hunter, 235; *Letters of George IV*, I, 193; Gore, *Creevey Papers*, 150; Macalpine and Hunter, 244.
17. Quennell, ed, *Private Letters of Princess Lieven*, 11; (ed. Reeve) *Greville Memoirs*, I, 23; Farington, XVI, 5566, 5686.
18. In Macalpine and Hunter's judgement, Caroline was also porphyric: 'this metabolic disorder may well have been the only thing which, unbeknown to themselves, George IV and his Queen had in common' (Macalpine and Hunter, 250). Had George suspected this, a relapse must surely have been guaranteed.
19. Gore, *Creevey Papers*, 144–5; Prebble, *King's Jaunt*, 249.
20. Quennell, *Private Letters of Princess Lieven*, 150, 252, Gore, *Creevey Papers*, 217; Macalpine and Hunter, 238; *Carlton House* (exhibition catalogue), 28.

CHAPTER 8: POLITICAL POSTURING

1. *Westminster Review*, Vol. 14 (1831), 106, 132.
2. *Greville Memoirs* (ed. Reeve), 155.
3. Farington, X, 3837.
4. Huish, *Memoirs of George IV*, II, 53; *Westminster Review*, loc. cit., 109.
5. Robinson, *Letters of Princess Lieven*, 55.
6. Sichel, *Sheridan*, II, 62; Smith, *George IV*, 23.
7. Quoted in Foreman, *Georgiana*, 156.
8. Quoted in Mitchell, *Charles James Fox*, 89.
9. Dropmore MSS, quoted in Mitchell, op. cit., 90.
10. Mitchell, op. cit., 62, 88, 90.
11. Edmund Burke to William Pitt, 12 December 1788, in Aspinall, *Prince of Wales Correspondence*, I, 414; Mitchell, op. cit., 85.
12. See Mitchell, op. cit., 90–1.

13. Moore, *Memoirs of Sheridan*, I, 470; Aspinall, *Correspondence of George III*, I, 149–51.
14. Farington, VIII, 2873; Mitchell, op. cit., 132.
15. George, *Catalogue of ... Satires*, VII, 17, 203; Farington, III, 807; Fraser, *Unruly Queen*, 108.
16. *Prince of Wales Correspondence*, IV, 249; Mitchell, op. cit., 211; Wilkins, *Mrs Fitzherbert and George IV*, I, 82.
17. See the Prince of Wales to Charles James Fox, 26 November 1804, in *Prince of Wales Correspondence*, V, 140–1.
18. Charles James Fox to Lord Grenville, 6 February 1806, in BL Add MS 58953, f 14; Mitchell, op. cit., 225–6.
19. Hibbert, *George IV* (1976), 328.
20. The Prince of Wales to Lord Holland, 10 and 12 September 1806, in *Prince of Wales Correspondence*, V, 426–7.
21. *Prince of Wales Correspondence*, V, 499; BL, Add MS 51520.
22. Lord Holland, *Memoirs of the Whig Party*, II, 69.
23. For an excellent summary of this reaction, see *Prince of Wales Correspondence*, VI, 145–8.
24. *Prince of Wales Correspondence*, VI, 146–8, 247; Busco, *Westmacott*, 72.
25. *Prince of Wales Correspondence*, VII, 114.
26. Ibid., VIII, 9.
27. Macalpine and Hunter, *George III and the Mad-Business*, 155; *Prince of Wales Correspondence*, VIII, 313; Aspinall, *Letters of George IV*, I, 104n; Grey and Grenville to the Duke of York, 15 February 1812, quoted in Cobbett, *History of ... George IV*, 108; Sales, *Jane Austen and ... Regency England*, 59–60.
28. Huish, *Memoirs of George IV*, II, 56; Farington, XI, 4068, 4143.
29. *Westminster Review*, loc. cit., 130; Brougham, *Statesmen*, II, 63; Gray, *Perceval*, 89–90.
30. See, for example, George, *Catalogue of ... Satires*, IX, 121.
31. Hinde, *Canning*, 393.
32. Recently, Frank Prochaska has attempted to recruit George to the anti-slave trade campaign. However, while his support for this cause in 1814 appears to have been genuine, it was, like most of his expressions of social concern, fleeting, and he soon moved on to more pressing matters, such as the great summer fêtes and the remodelling of Brighton Pavilion. See Prochaska, *Royal Bounty*, 35.
33. *Letters of George IV*, III, 99.
34. Mitchell, op. cit., 206.
35. Gore, *Creevey Papers*, 39; Farington, VIII, 2998; XII, 4291; Trotter, *Memoirs of Fox*, 377.
36. *Prince of Wales Correspondence*, VIII, 313, 316; quoted in Smith, *George IV*, 141–2.
37. *Letters of George IV*, III, 97.
38. Ibid., III, 180–1; II, 424–5; Gore, *Creevey's Life and Times*, 237.
39. *Greville Memoirs*, 92–3; George, *Catalogue of ... Satires*, X, 583.

40. *Letters of George IV*, III, 275, 194, 276–7.
41. Ibid., III, 429, 438; Quennell, *Private Letters of Princess Lieven*, 150.
42. Ibid., 182, 185; Willis, *Ernest Augustus*, 178; Willis, 179.
43. *Prince of Wales Correspondence*, 246–7; *Greville Memoirs*, 153–4; George IV to the Duke of Wellington, 4 March 1829, quoted in Fulford, *George IV*, 285.
44. See George, *Catalogue of . . . Satires*, XI, 128–33, 135–6, and passim.

CHAPTER 9 : THE ANCIEN RÉGIME

1. Barnett, *Cosways*, 95, 114.
2. Colley, *Britons*, 215.
3. See Robinson, *Windsor Castle*, 88.
4. See Ribeiro, *The Art of Dress*, 234.
5. Quoted in J.M. Robinson, op. cit., 88.
6. *Carlton House* (exhibition catalogue), 39: Geoffrey de Bellaigue, 'George IV and French Furniture', in *The Connoisseur*, Vol. 195 (1977), 116.
7. *Carlton House*, 204–5.
8. *George IV and the Arts of France* (exhibition catalogue), 4, 7, 30, 51.
9. Millar, *The Queen's Pictures*, 130, 150.
10. *Carlton House*, 72.
11. Colley, op. cit., 215.
12. de Bellaigue, art. cit., 124.
13. *Carlton House*, 65.
14. Clifford Smith, *Buckingham Palace*, 258.
15. *Carlton House*, 88.
16. See Ake Setterwall, 'Some Louis XVI Furniture decorated with *pietra dura* reliefs', in *Burlington Magazine*, Vol. ci (December 1959), 425–35.
17. *Carlton House*, 202–3; Robert Wenley, 'French Royal Bronzes in Great Britain', in *Apollo*, Vol. cl (September 1999), 3–7.
18. *Carlton House*, 62; de Bellaigue, art. cit., 122.
19. John Whitehead, 'George IV: furnishing in the French taste', in Simon, *Buckingham Palace*, 90.
20. White, *Dutch Pictures*, lix.
21. Evans, *Princes as Patrons*, 71.
22. *Carlton House*, 138–40.
23. Parry, *Queen Caroline*, 62.
24. Harris, de Bellaigue and Millar, *Buckingham Palace...*, 203; de Bellaigue, art. cit., 125.
25. *Carlton House*, 201.
26. Aspinall, *Letters of George IV*, lxxxi.
27. Malcolm Baker et al, 'The Chantrey Ledger', in *Walpole Society*, Vol. lvi (1991–2), 245, 171.
28. Linstrum, *Wyatville*, 193.
29. Valerie Cumming, 'Pantomine and Pageantry: The Coronation of George IV', in Fox, *London – World City*, 39; Huish, *Memoirs of George IV*, 53, 385.

30. *Carlton House*, 83, 175; *George IV and the Arts of France*, 39.
31. Faringon, XIII, 4520 (22 May 1814); Millar, *Queen's Pictures*, 156; *Carlton House*, 48.
32. Stephen Lloyd, 'Fashioning the Image of the Prince: Richard Cosway and George IV', in Arnold, *Squanderous and Lavish Profusion*, 6–7.
33. George, *Catalogue of ... Satires*, IX, 248.
34. Garratt, *Lord Brougham*, 87.
35. Prebble, *King's Jaunt*, 54; Lees-Milne, *Last Stuarts*, 172.
36. Patterson, *Royal Insignia*, 108.
37. In his *The Last Stuarts*, James Lees-Milne suggested that the bodies of the Young Pretender and Cardinal Henry of York were re-interred in the *grotte vaticane* beside that of the Old Pretender, their father, rather than beneath the new memorial. Canova himself stated in a letter of 22 June 1820 that George IV 'had voluntarily and spontaneously offered to contribute towards the expense' of the memorial's erection.
38. In 1701 James II's embalmed body was taken to a Benedictine monastery in the Faubourg St-Jacques in Paris, his heart to the home of the order of the Réligieuses in Chaillot, also in Paris. The rest of his entrails, apart from his heart, were placed in an urn, which was buried at St-Germain-en-Laye, where he had spent his years of exile. The two resting-places in Paris were obliterated during the French Revolution, and only the St-Germain memorial remains. George's new monument, installed the church in 1824, is a simple affair, probably designed by a local sculptor rather than any of his British favourites. In 1855 Queen Victoria, partly from curiosity and partly from contrition, visited the mausoleum her uncle had funded. I am indebted to Andrew Holt for his thorough investigation of this affair.
39. *Carlton House*, 48.
40. Aspinall, *Letters of George IV*, I, 199.

CHAPTER 10: SEPARATION AND DIVORCE

1. Aspinall, *Prince of Wales Correspondence*, III, 190–3.
2. Aspinall, *Correspondence of George III*, II 536.
3. Faringon, II, 560; Fraser, *Unruly Queen*, 97.
4. Cobbett, *History of ... George IV*, 67; Fraser, 109.
5. Fraser, 121; *Prince of Wales Correspondence*, IV, 283.
6. The traditional home of the Ranger, the Queen's House, was so dilapidated that Caroline lived at nearby Montague House: see Julius Bryant, 'Ranger and "Royal Wanderer"', in Arnold, *Squanderous and Lavish Profusion*, 31–6.
7. Gray, *Perceval*, 78–83.
8. See Robert Hammer's incomparable Ealing Studios film of 1949, *Kind Hearts and Coronets*; RA Geo IV, P219.
9. In the spring of 1803 the Princess sent personal letters to Manby in care of a mutual friend, Admiral Nugent. By design or accident, Nugent left

the letters in his carriage, and they were subsequently bought by George for £2,000. Obviously, however, they were as embarrassing to the Prince as to his wife, and he never revealed their contents. See Bickley, *The Diaries of ... Lord Glenbervie*, II, 133–4. On 6 June 1806 Caroline's former page, Robert Bidgood, testified to the Prince's commission that he had on one occasion seen Manby and the Princess 'kissing each other's lips', and often seen them retiring alone together.

10. Farington, VII, 2793; Jefferys, *Review of the Conduct...*; Harroby MSS, IV, f 43: Richard Ryder to Lord Harrowby, quoted in Gray, op. cit., 82.
11. Gray, op. cit., 82–3.
12. BL Add MS 38564, f 91: King George III to Lord Hawkesbury, 23 April 1807; *The Times*, 29 June 1807.
13. Cobbett, *History of ... George IV*, I, 215.
14. *DNB*; Aspinall, *Politics and the Press*, 407–8; Farington, X, 3824; Gray, op. cit., 88–9; *The Morning Post*, 8 March 1813.
15. See for example *Prince of Wales Correspondence*, VI, 169, 171–80.
16. Farington, VIII, 3108.
17. Gore, *Creevey's Life and Times*, 65; Farington, VIII, 3000; XIV, 4894, 5105, 5126.
18. Bury, *The Court Under George IV*, I, 16; Fraser, *Unruly Queen*, 211; Farington, XII, 4300.
19. Aspinall, *Politics and the Press*, 91.
20. Fraser, 250.
21. Hibbert, *George IV* (1976), 530.
22. Yonge, *Life of Banks*, II, 11.
23. Bury, I, 4; Parry, *Queen Caroline*, 214; RA Geo 8/6: Ompteda's report of 1 March 1815.
24. See Levy, *Mistresses of George IV*, 387–8. For a detailed account of the Milan Commission, see Fraser, *Unruly Queen*, 304–21.
25. Cookson, *Liverpool's Administration*, 205–6; Reeve, *Greville Memoirs*, 24.
26. Aspinall, *Letters of George IV*, II, 400. On 3 March 1821 the Queen, her customary ragged spelling in evidence, begged of Liverpool that 'the same sentimens of Justice which has prevailed in her favour will also effect upon the Heart of the King, by plaicing her name in the Liturgi as Queen, as such having been the Rights and custum of Her Predecessors' (Smith, *Queen on Trial*, 172).
27. Henry Brougham to Queen Caroline, St Omer, 4 June 1820, from the *Life and Times of Henry, Lord Brougham*, quoted in Smith, op. cit., 21–2.
28. Cobbett, *History of ... George IV*, 425. See Fraser, *Unruly Queen*, 363 and passim.
29. *The Republican*, 25 February 1820.
30. Colley, *Britons*, 265; *The Times*, 20 September 1820.
31. BM 200869 and Barlow, *Prince of Pleasures*, 64.
32. Reeves, *Greville Memoirs*, I, 100.
33. *The Times*, 4 August 1820; Somes Layard, *Lawrence's Letter-Bag*, 159;

Princess Lieven to Prince Metternich, 19 August 1820, quoted in Smith, op. cit., 72; Fraser, op. cit., 396.

34. Quoted in Levy, op. cit., 403.
35. See Fraser, 422–42, and also the useful selection of contemporary documents relating to the proceedings in Smith, *Queen on Trial.*
36. Robinson, *Letters of Princess Lieven,* 66.
37. BM 200966, 205790 (see Barlow, op. cit., 66–7).
38. See for example David, *Prince of Pleasure,* 410, 413; *Greville Memoirs,* I, 105.
39. BM 13974: William Heath, *The Triumph of Innocence over Perjury, Persecution and Ministerial Oppression,* published 6 November 1820; Smith, op. cit., 142.
40. *The Times,* 30 November 1820.
41. Lady Erne to Lady Caroline Stuart Wortley, 6 December 1820, quoted in Smith, op. cit., 164; *The Times,* 26 December 1820; Cobbett, op. cit., 447.
42. Gore, *Creevey's Life and Times* 135; Farington, XVI, 5660–1.
43. *The Life and Times of Henry, Lord Brougham,* quoted in Smith, op. cit., 179, 190; Fraser, *Unruly Queen,* 459.
44. Ilchester, *H.E. Fox Journal,* 81; Fraser, 454, 461; Hibbert, *George IV,* 453.
45. Fraser, 459; *Letters of George IV,* II, 454.
46. Gore, 135.
47. See *Letters of George IV,* II, 455–7 and Fraser, 463–5.
48. Hibbert, *George IV,* 620n.

CHAPTER 11: THE IMMENSE GIRL

1. Aspinall, *Prince of Wales Correspondence,* III, 126–7; Aspinall, *Correspondence of George III,* II, 352.
2. See *Prince of Wales Correspondence,* II, 132–9.
3. See ibid., II, 146–8; ibid., III, 188–93; Weigall, *Memoir of Princess Charlotte,* 14.
4. *Prince of Wales Correspondence,* V, 73, 89.
5. Ibid., III, 384; IV, 27, 43; VIII, 29–30.
6. Aspinall, *Letters of George IV,* II, 64.
7. Aspinall, *Letters of Princess Charlotte,* x–xi; Fraser, *Unruly Queen,* 206.
8. Quoted in Fraser, 220.
9. Fulford, *Autobiography of Miss Knight,* 131–2; *Letters of Princess Charlotte,* x, xii. Technically, Dr Nott was dismissed on the (spurious) grounds that he had encouraged Charlotte to make a bogus will, and to read books not previously approved by her 'educational supervisor', the Bishop of Exeter.
10. Quoted in Fraser, 205, 223 and Hibbert, *George IV,* 318; *Autobiography of Miss Knight,* 115, 136.
11. Farington, XIV, 5097–8, 5102; Fraser, 229; BM 200832: *A DUTCH TOY! – or, a pretty Play-thing for a Young Princess!!!*
12. See Thackeray, *Yellowplush Memoirs,* first published as 'The Yellowplush Papers' in *Fraser's Magazine,* 1837–8.
13. Quoted in Prochaska, *Royal Bounty,* 22.

14. Prochaska, 31; *Letters of Princess Charlotte*, 37, xiv–xv; Fraser, 221; Fulford, *Autobiography of Miss Knight*, 144; Wilkins, *Mrs Fitzherbert and George IV*, II, 117; Weigall, op. cit., 51.

15. Margaret Mercer Elphinstone subsequently won George's admiration, for in 1817 she married Napoleon's former aide-de-camp, the comte de Flahault.

16. Huish, *Memoirs of George IV*, I, 564; Albemarle, *Fifty Years of my Life*, I, 331.

17. *Letters of Princess Charlotte*, 53; Fulford, *Autobiography of Miss Knight*, 105, 114, 120, 140, 157, 160.

18. Quoted in Fraser, 228; *Autobiography of Miss Knight*, 111–12, 129–30.

19. Roger Fulford described William as 'One of those extraordinarily unattractive Princes of Orange who have periodically cast a calculating, matrimonial eye on the English throne' (*Royal Dukes*, 273).

20. *Letters of Princess Charlotte*, xix; Fraser, 237, 242; Bury, *The Court ... Under George IV*, I, 169.

21. *Autobiography of Miss Knight*, 306.

22. *The Morning Chronicle*, 14 July 1814; Princess Caroline to the Prince Regent, 14 January 1813, quoted in Stewart, *Diary of ... Lady Charlotte Bury*, 117.

23. *Diary of ... Lady Charlotte Bury*, 323–4; BM 206250.

24. *Autobiography of Miss Knight*, 166; quoted in *Letters of Princess Charlotte*, 139.

25. *Letters of Princess Charlotte*, 233.

26. Princess Charlotte to the Prince Regent, 7 February 1816, in *Letters of George IV*, II, 146; op. cit., II, 142; Princess Charlotte to the Princess of Wales, 10 October 1817, in op. cit., II, 203; see for example *Autobiography of Miss Knight*, 152 (November 1813).

27. Colvin, *Dictionary*, 732; The summer-house was subsequently remodelled as a memorial to Charlotte – an approach taken again at Althorp House in Northamptonshire 180 years later, for Diana, Princess of Wales. Farington, XIV, 5097–8.

28. See Macalpine and Hunter, *George III and the Mad-Business*, 241–6; Farington, XIV, 5105–6.

29. Berendt, *Royal Mourning*, 23–4.

30. BM 200563; quoted in Behrendt, 25–6.

31. Fraser, *Unruly Queen*, 300.

32. Farington, XIV, 5124, 5101–2; II, 223.

33. *Letters of George IV*, II, 218n.

34. Huish, II, 251. Papworth and Hiort's work at the Claremont mausoleum had been relatively inexpensive.

35. *Letters of George IV*, III, 468. After George's death Leopold (having declined the throne of Greece) was in 1831 elevated to the newly-created Belgian throne.

36. For a discussion of the 'merchandising of mourning' after Charlotte's death, see Behrendt, op. cit.

37. *The Gentleman's Magazine*, Vol. 89 (1819), 176; *The Literary Chronicle and Weekly Review*, 28 February 1823, 141. Sixty years later, Queen Victoria

attempted to make amends for her uncle's disappointing behaviour by personally commissioning a triptych in honour of Princess Charlotte from the sculptor F.J. Williamson. Destined originally for Claremont House, but now in the nearby Church of St George, Esher: see Behrendt, 210, and Nicholas Penny, *Church Monuments in Romantic England* (1977), 59 and plate 125.

38. Percy Shelley, *An Address ...* (1818), 233, 239, quoted in Behrendt, 230–5.

CHAPTER 12: IMAGE AND REALITY

1. Quoted in Macalpine and Hunter, *George III and the Mad-Business*, 143, 150–1.
2. Mollo, *The Prince's Dolls*, 89.
3. Macalpine and Hunter, 165, 167–8, 170; Aspinall, *Prince of Wales Correspondence*, VIII, 2.
4. Wilfred Dowden, ed., *The Letters of Thomas Moore* (1964), 152–3.
5. See Hibbert, *George IV*, 375.
6. See David Cannadine, 'The Context, Performance and Meaning of Ritual: The British Monarchy and the "Invention of Tradition", *c.* 1820–1977', in Hobsbawm and Ranger, *Invention of Tradition*, 109 and passim; quoted in George, *Hogarth to Cruikshank*, 166.
7. See Goldring, *Regency Portrait Painter*, 213–14.
8. Whitley, *Art in England*, 246, 290.
9. When she saw the replica of his 1818 Garter portrait commissioned by the Papal States, Dorothea Schlegel remarked, apropos Lawrence's notoriously lavish use of his medium, that 'even the mice will find no little comfort in it as there is at least ten pounds of oil paint smeared upon it' (Garlick, *Lawrence*, 23).
10. RA 23362.
11. Farington, XVI, 5697. Benjamin West had told Farington that Lawrence 'would not have the least chance of being elected President' (Farington, XI, 4132).
12. Farington, XIV, 4877.
13. RA 27083.
14. Farington, IV, 1524–5.
15. Taylor, *Autobiography of Haydon* (1926 edn), 473–4; Garlick, op. cit., 29.
16. Aspinall, *Letters of George IV*, I, 271.
17. Ibid., 325.
18. George, *Catalogue of ... Satires*, XI, 270.
19. Huish, *Memoirs of George IV*, II, 243, 393.
20. Aspinall, *Letters of Princess Charlotte*, 242.
21. *Annual Register* (1817), 100, quoted in Valerie Cumming, 'Pantomine and Pageantry: The Coronation of George IV', in Fox, *London – World City*, 42.
22. Patterson, *Royal Insignia*, 10, 16.
23. Ibid., 110.

24. RA 26326; Patterson, 89.
25. Quoted in Fulford, *George IV,* 134.
26. Partington, *Private Letter-Books of Scott,* 158.
27. Farington, XII, 4332; Huish, II, 52.
28. Cobbett, *History of ... George IV,* I, 281.
29. George, *Catalogue of ... Satires,* IX, 430–1.
30. *Carlton House* (exhibition catalogue), 227.
31. Girouard, *Return to Camelot,* 52.
32. *Carlton House,* 54.
33. Morley, *Regency Design,* 269.
34. *Carlton House,* 37, 80.
35. Quoted in David, *Prince of Pleasure,* 349.
36. Following George's relatively successful visit there in 1821, Moore reversed his earlier judgement, assuring John Croker that he would henceforth 'praise him with all my heart for his wise and liberal conduct in Ireland'. In his *Life of Sheridan* of 1825, however, Moore once again depicted the King as a fair-weather friend.
37. Shelley to Elizabeth Hitchener, 16 April 1812, and to Catherine Nugent, 7 May 1812, in Ingpen, *Letters of Shelley,* I, 292, 308.
38. Quoted in Joanna Richardson, 'George IV: Patron of Literature', in *Essays by Diverse Hands,* Vol. xxxv (1969), 134.
39. Lovell, *Conversations of Byron,* 48.
40. Austen-Leigh, *Memoir of Jane Austen,* 118–121; Chapman, *Austen Letters,* 184; Tomalin, *Jane Austen,* 248.
41. Austen-Leigh, 124; Tomalin, 249. 'Plan of a Novel' in facsimile, with Miss Austen's key to which of her advisors was responsible for which idea, is to be found in R.W. Chapman's 'Oxford Illustrated Jane Austen', Vol. VI, *Minor Works* (revised edn, 1963).
42. 'I had just left off writing and put on my Things for walking to Alton, when Anna and her friend Harriot called in their way tither, so we went together. Their business was to provide mourning, against the King's death; and my Mother has had a Bombasin bought for her' (Chapman, 291); Chapman, 504.
43. Sales, *Jane Austen and ... Regency England,* 72.
44. Quoted in Morley, *Regency Design,* 347.
45. BM I 1877. See Barlow, *The Prince and his Pleasures,* 12–13.
46. Farington, VIII, 2926, 3147; Gore, *Creevey's Life and Times,* 102.
47. Gore, op. cit., 126.
48. Farington, XIV, 4968; Jennings, *Croker Correspondence,* I, 102; Farington, XIV, 4971.
49. For details see Hibbert, *George IV,* 351–3. Hibbert also mentions (353n) the existence of a document – a memoir of another of Cumberland's servants, written in 1827, after the Duke's death – which may imply that the Duke was indeed the murderer. Cumberland was subsequently accommodated at Carlton House while, ghoulishly, his rooms at St

James's Palace, the scene of the crime, were opened to the public. The Duke appears to have tried to bury the event, as his brother buried unpleasantnesses, by dosing himself with large quantities of laudanum. At the enquiry which followed Cumberland was cleared of any wrongdoing by a jury who, led by the radical Francis Place, judged that Sellis had become insane.

50. Evans, *Princes as Patrons*, 109.
51. *Morning Chronicle*, 21 June 1811; Fraser, *Unruly Queen*, 222; Huish, *Memoirs of George IV*, 46.
52. Shelley to Elizabeth Hitchener, 20 June 1811, in Ingpen, *Letters of Shelley*, I, 100.
53. PRO WORK 4/21/247; *Carlton House* (exhibition catalogue), 30; Smith, *George IV*, 152.
54. Quoted in D. Sutherland, *The Landowners* (1968), 158.

CHAPTER 13: GEORGE AND NAPOLEON

1. Thomas Moore to James Corry, 24 October 1811, quoted in J. Mordaunt Crook, 'Metropolitan Improvements ...' in Fox, *London – World City*, 78.
2. The Prince Regent to Queen Charlotte, 9 April 1814, quoted in Aspinall, *Letters of George IV*, I, 419.
3. Sichel, *Glenbervie Journals* (1910), II, 176; *Carlton House* (exhibition catalogue), 164.
4. Aspinall, *Prince of Wales Correspondence*, VIII, 371.
5. Wilkins, *Mrs Fitzherbert and George IV*, II, 57; Hibbert, *George IV*, 327–8.
6. Millar, *Later Georgian Pictures*, I, xxxi, 31–2, 139–40.
7. Millar, op. cit., I, 119. The 'Hussar' painting was given by George to Lady Conyngham in June 1822. He also commissioned from Stroehling portraits of Alexander I of Russia and Frederick William III of Prussia, both on horseback; of the Duchess of York, with four of her dogs; of Prince Louis Ferdinand of Prussia, who had been killed at the Battle of Saalfeld in 1806; and of Allied generals Uxbridge, Blücher and Platov. His attachment to these military heroes is demonstrated by the fact that he took their pictures with him to the Royal Lodge in 1823.
8. Garlick, *Lawrence*, 21.
9. Millar, 99.
10. Quoted in Lloyd, *Quest for Albion*, 22; Taylor, *Autobiography of Haydon* (1926 edn), 480.
11. Harris, de Bellaigue and Millar, *Buckingham Palace ...*, 96.
12. Gunnis, *British Sculptors*, 447.
13. Summerson, *Life of Nash*, 66–9; J. Mordaunt Crook, 'Metropolitan Improvements: John Nash and the Picturesque', in Fox, *London – World City*, 81. Nevertheless, by 1819 only 3 sets of villas had been let, and in 1823 the decision was taken to reduce their number still further, to 26; by 1826 there were only 8 left.

14. Quoted in Summerson, *Life of Nash*, 133.
15. Saunders, *Regent's Park*, 135, 208n.
16. 1828 Select Committee report, 74, quoted in Arnold, 'George IV and Metropolitan Improvements', in Arnold, *Squanderous and Lavish Profusion*, 52; Crook, art.cit., 81, 90.
17. *Wellington Despatches*, VI, 3–4; PRO, CRES 2/1737; Andrew Sanders, 'A Place in History', in Simon, *Buckingham Palace*, 74.
18. Saint, 'The Marble Arch', in *Georgian Group Journal*, 77.
19. Crook and Port, *King's Works*, VI, 295; Sawyer, 'Soane's Symbolic Westminster', in *Architectural History*, 55–8; Crook, 92.
20. Busco, *Westmacott*, 61. The figure of Trajan on the Arch of Constantine is one of the many sculptural elements 'borrowed' from Trajan's Column of two centuries earlier.
21. Saint, art. cit., 76.
22. See Saint, 78.
23. Saint, 83.
24. PRO WORK 19/4/640.
25. Saint, 85; *The Guardian,* 14 May 1999.
26. Quoted by Andrew Sanders in Simon, *Buckingham Palace* (where both cartoons are reproduced), 74–5.
27. Quoted in Saint, 86.
28. Keegan, *Face of Battle*, 117. Canova's statue, commissioned in 1802, was inspected by Napoleon in 1811, but he found it 'too athletic' and declared that the sculptor had 'failed to express his calm dignity'. The piece was accordingly hidden away in the Louvre until 1816, when it was bought by the British government at George's behest and given to Wellington. (Jervis, Tomlin and Voak, *Apsley House*, 30.) At Apsley House the statue is, ironically, now looked down upon by Charles X, as painted by Gérard.
29. See Evans, *Princes as Patrons*, 94.
30. *George IV and the Arts of France* (exhibition catalogue), 46–50; Farington, XIV, 4969.
31. A second version of the table, with Napoleon's own profile in the centre, is currently at the Malmaison. I am grateful to Christine Riding for her help in this matter. See Geoffrey de Bellaigue in *Furniture History*, Vol. 35 (1999).
32. Valerie Cumming (in Fox, *London – World City*, 45) has noted that 'it is impossible to understand the 1821 coronation without briefly considering the magnificent pageantry of Napoleon's coronation in 1804' (see chapter 15, below); Millar, *Later Georgian Pictures*, I xxxiii.
33. For example, Farington, XII, 4197.
34. Ziegler, *Addington*, 334. This did not, however, prevent the cartoonists from caricaturing George's visit to Oxford as a farce, and the Regent himself as a deluded fool. See George, *Catalogue of ... Satires*, IX, 411.
35. Farington, XIII, 4540.
36. *The Westminster Review*, 134–5.

CHAPTER 14: THE MASQUERADE OF ROOMS

1. James Anderson, *The New Book of Constitutions of the Antient and Honourable Fraternity of Free and Accepted Masons* (1738), Dedication, v-vi. I am indebted to Jacqueline Riding for bringing this source to my attention.
2. Aspinall, *Prince of Wales Correspondence*, V, 161.
3. *Parliamentary Debates*, xxviii, 421.
4. BM Add MS 38564, f 120; Crook and Port, *King's Works*, VI, 106–7. E.A. Smith (*George IV*, 244) interprets this episode as evidence of George's practical interest in architectural matters, but no other evidence is offered in support of this thesis – which presupposes rather more in the way of strenuous and directed activity than George customarily expended.
5. Duke of Wellington to Mrs Arbuthnot, 9 October 1823, quoted in *Letters of Wellington*, 39.
6. St John Hope, *Windsor Castle*, I, 354.
7. J.M. Robinson, *Windsor Castle*, 86.
8. Robinson, 90.
9. In May 1824 the Duke was invited by George IV to be on the rubber-stamp commission overseeing the rebuilding of the castle and boasted that it was the result of the King 'having taken my recommendation of Jeffry Wyatt'; he later suggested that his showing of a single sketch to the King had made up the royal mind. See Linstrum, *Wyatville*, 39. Smirke had to wait until the reign of William IV to receive his knighthood, bestowed in 1832.
10. Colvin, *Dictionary*, 1130.
11. St John Hope, 355.
12. Hugh Roberts' forthcoming study, *The Decoration and Furnishing of the Private Apartments at Windsor Castle 1827-30*, will presumably help to clarify this situation.
13. See Linstrum, op. cit., 175.
14. Ex. inf. Dr J.M. Robinson. The removal of the Gothic throne was instigated by the Duke of Edinburgh.
15. Brindle and Kerr, *Windsor Revealed* (1997), 58–9.
16. Robinson, op. cit., 110, 106–7. Dr Robinson also remarks on the strong resemblance between Wyatville's St George's Hall and Sir Walter Scott's home, Abbotsford.
17. Beard and Gilbert, *English Furniture Makers*, 623–4, 795.
18. Geoffrey de Bellaigue and Pat Kirkham, 'George IV and the Furnishings of Windsor Castle', in *Furniture History*, Vol. viii (1972), 2–4; John Martin Robinson, 'The Nash state rooms', in Simon, *Buckingham Palace*, 57.
19. Beard and Gilbert, op. cit., 796.
20. de Bellaigue and Kirkham, art. cit., 6.
21. Robinson, *Windsor Castle*, 105, 108–9.
22. Linstrum, *Wyatville*, 193.
23. Sir Walter Scott to David Wilkie, 21 December 1828, quoted in Cunningham, *Life of Wilkie*, II, 18; quoted in Linstrum, op. cit., 187; Farnborough, *Short Remarks*, 34; quoted in Robinson, op. cit., 92.

24. de Bellaigue and Kirkham, art. cit., 7; see Timothy Schroder, 'Royal Opulence Displayed in Silver', in *Country Life*, Vol. cxcii, 6 August 1998; Alexandra Wedgwood, 'The Early Years', in Paul Atterbury and Clive Wainwright (eds), *Pugin* (1994), 26.
25. Robinson, op. cit., 89; de Bellaigue and Kirkham, art. cit., 15; Beard and Gilbert, op. cit., 624; quoted in *Carlton House* (exhibition catalogue), 45.
26. J. Mordaunt Crook, *The Rise of the Nouveaux Riches* (John Murray, 1999), 53.
27. Quoted in St John Hope, op. cit., 359.
28. Beard and Gilbert, op. cit., 796.
29. On 5 July 1799 James Wyatt had told Joseph Farington that 'it is now in agitation to have all the new buildings including the House of Lords of Gothic Architecture, so as to make a whole mass of that kind of building. The King and others approve the idea.' (Farington, IV, 1249.)
30. Summerson, *Life of Nash*, 158. Soane's perceived relationship with William Pitt possibly did nothing to advance his cause when he was soliciting George's patronage in the mid 1790s. In 1796 he prepared a scheme for remodelling Holwood House, the Prime Minister's country home; but by 1799, when he was submitting designs for a new House of Lords, he had, according to Farington, 'lost all footing with Pitt'. Even George III commented on Soane's 'peculiarities'. Nevertheless, he was tipped by many to follow Wyatt as Surveyor-General prior to the reorganisation of the Office of Works.
31. Sawyer, 'Soane's Symbolic Westminster', in *Architectural History*, 55–60, 72.
32. See C. & J. Riding, *Houses of Parliament*.
33. Dana Arnold, 'George IV and the Metropolitan Improvements: The Creation of a Royal Image', in Arnold, *Squanderous and Lavish Profusion*, 55.
34. Sean Sawyer, 'The Processional Route', in *John Soane, Architect* (RA Exhibition catalogue, 1999), 254; Sawyer, art. cit., in *Architectural History*, 54.
35. Sawyer, ibid., 55–8.
36. Sawyer, art. cit., in *John Soane, Architect*, 254–5.
37. Gunnis, *British Sculptors*, 447–8. In 1912 a bronze quadriga and figure of Peace by Adrian Jones finally completed Burton's design; on 5 October 1999 the government announced that the arch was to be restored, and its interiors reopened to the public, at a cost of £1.5 million.
38. W.H. Leeds, *Illustrations of the Public Building of London – Supplement* (1838), 103.
39. *King's Works*, VI 263.
40. On 27 October 1821 John Nash reported to Farington that the King 'had felt a dislike to Carlton House and wished to remove to Buckingham Palace' (Farington, XVI 5741).
41. Crook and Port, *King's Works*, VI 112.
42. See David Watkins, 'Freemasons' Hall', in *John Soane, Architect*, 264; between 1826 and 1828 Soane was working on plans for a new Freemasons' Hall.

43. See Crook and Port, *King's Works*, VI, 134, 136–7.
44. Mrs Arbuthnot, writing in 1825, believed the government had obstructed the building of a wholly new palace, fearing the vast costs it would involve (*King's Works*, VI, 264).
45. *Report of the Select Committee...* (1831), Appendix, 270.
46. *King's Works*, 264.
47. See *King's Works*, 266 and n4; also J.M. Robinson, 'Nash State Rooms', in Simon, *Buckingham Palace*, 57.
48. PRO WORK 19/3, f 77.
49. PRO WORK 19/3, ff 26–7; Harris, de Bellaigue and Millar, *Buckingham Palace*, 44, 61; J.M. Robinson, art. cit., in Simon, *Buckingham Palace*, 60.
50. *King's Works*, VI, 158.
51. See Clifford Smith, *Buckingham Palace*, 42.
52. Clifford Smith, op. cit., 38.
53. Summerson, *Life of Nash*, 164, 166; PRO WORK 19/4, f 19: Joseph Bramah, *Report on the Cast Iron Work Used in Buckingham Palace*, 7; BM 16005 (see George, *Catalogue of ... Satires*, XI, 252).
54. *Westminster Review*, 136; Huish, *Memoirs of George IV*, II, 133; John Harris, 'From Buckingham House to Palace' in Simon, *Buckingham Palace*, 31; Harris, de Bellaigue and Millar, *Buckingham Palace*, 15.
55. Leeds, *Buildings of London*, 105, 107n, 106, 115–22.
56. Quoted in Simon, *Buckingham Palace*, 59.
57. Morley, *Regency Design*, 261; the Bay Drawing Room is the present-day Music Room.
58. Andrew Sanders, 'A place in history', in *Buckingham Palace* (1993), 76.

CHAPTER 15: THE CORONATION

1. Colley, *Britons*, 231–2.
2. Girouard, *Return to Camelot*, 26.
3. PRO WORK 21/14; Farington, XVI, 5509.
4. Valerie Cumming, 'Pantomime and Pageantry: The Coronation of George IV', in Fox, *London – World City*, 43–4.
5. Ribeiro, *Art of Dress*, 231–2; Cumming, art. cit., 46.
6. Farington, XVI, 5962, 5635, 5703.
7. PRO WORK 36/68, *The Observer*, 22 July 1821; Prebble, *King's Jaunt*, 44.
8. RA 29592 and passim; Fraser, *Unruly Queen*, 456.
9. Memorandum from Rundell, Bridge and Rundell dated 18 April 1820, in Aspinall, *Letters of George IV*, 323.
10. Cumming, loc. cit., 42. Valerie Cumming has recalculated the expense of the coronation as amounting to £211,428 17s. 5d.
11. Girouard, op. cit., 26.
12. Lockhart, *Memoirs of Scott* (1845), 455.
13. *Annual Register* (1821), 346.
14. Walter Scott in *The Edinburgh Weekly Journal*, 20 July 1821.
15. 'His Majesty was conducted to the suite of rooms prepared for his recep-

tion, and subsequently supped with the Speaker' (Huish, *Authentic History of the Coronation*, 188). Thomas Manners-Sutton became Solicitor-General in 1802, and was created Baron Manners in 1807; in 1835, on his retirement as Speaker, Charles Manners-Sutton was created Viscount Canterbury (*DNB*).

16. Michael Stenton, *Who's Who of British Members of Parliament* (Harvester Press, Hassocks, 1976), I, 370; *DNB*.
17. PRO WORK 36/68.
18. Mrs Arbuthnot's Journal, quoted in Smith, *Queen on Trial*, 182.
19. Cobbett, *History of George IV*, 456; Farington, XVI, 5703; *Life of Brougham*, quoted in Smith, *Queen on Trial*, 180; Walter Scott to James Ballantyne, 20 July 1821, in Grierson, *Letters of Scott*, VII, 495.
20. *Annual Register*, 111–12, 381; Cumming, loc. cit., 44.
21. Cumming, 43; this was the last coronation at which the Champion appeared, and the Scrivelsby armour was sold at Christie's in 1877, when it was bought for the Royal Collection at Windsor.
22. Lockhart, *Memoirs of Scott* (1845) 495, 499.
23. See Anglesey, *One-Leg*, 164–5.
24. BM 14204 (see George, *Catalogue of . . . Satires*, X, 232; Cumming, loc. cit., 47.
25. Quoted in Hibbert, *George IV*, 192–3; quoted in Fulford, *George IV*, 232; Taylor, *Life of Haydon*, I, 314.
26. Grierson, *Letters of Scott*, VII, 495.
27. Walter Scott, *Ivanhoe* (1819; new edn 1933), 111, 96; Scott, *Kenilworth* (1821; new edn 1999), 284, 286, 290.
28. See Finley, *Turner and George IV* (exhibition catalogue), 5–7.
29. Taylor, *Life of Haydon*, I, 314.
30. Lockhart, *Memoirs of Scott* (1845), 454.
31. David Cannadine, 'The Context, Performance and Meaning of Ritual: The British Monarchy and the "Invention of Tradition" *c.* 1820–1977', in Hobsbawm and Ranger, *Invention of Tradition*, 118.

CHAPTER 16: THE VISIT TO EDINBURGH

1. Lockhart, *Memoirs of Scott* (1845), 755.
2. Quoted in Prebble, *King's Jaunt*, 206.
3. Ziegler, *Addington*, 396–7; Huish, *Memoirs of George IV*, II, 322; Jennings, *Croker Correspondence*, I, 206; Hibbert, *George IV*, 646–7.
4. Colley, *Britons*, 235; Maclean and Skinner, *Royal Visit*, 2.
5. John Wilson Croker to Sir Benjamin Bloomfield, 7 February 1818, quoted in Aspinall, *Letters of George IV*, II, 245.
6. Prebble, *Highland Clearances*, 139; *King's Jaunt*, 218, 220, 241, 247.
7. Walter Scott, *Waverley* (1814, new edn 1972), 153–4; Anderson, *Scott Journal*, 88–9.
8. Colonel David Stewart of Garth, *Sketches of the Character, Manners, and Present State of the Highlanders of Scotland* (1820), quoted in Hibbert, *King's Jaunt*, 40.

9. Thomson, *Raeburn*, 152.
10. Quoted in Prebble, *Highland Clearances*, 142–3.
11. Quoted in *King's Jaunt*, 33.
12. NLS MS 3895, f 7.
13. Lockhart, *Memoirs of Scott*, V, 192.
14. Hugh Trevor-Roper, 'The Invention of Tradition: The Highland Tradition of Scotland', in Hobsbawm and Ranger, *Invention of Tradition*, 23–5.
15. Prebble, *King's Jaunt*, 106.
16. Ribeiro, *Art of Dress*, 231.
17. RA 29600; *King's Jaunt*, 76.
18. Trevor-Roper, loc. cit., 28, 30; *King's Jaunt*, 131; Finley, *Turner and George IV*, 5; Cunningham, *Life of Wilkie*, II, 83.
19. Grierson, *Letters of Scott*, VII, 213.
20. Prebble, *King's Jaunt*, 250. In 1820 Scott, a newly-created baronet, had been delighted to be painted, at the King's request, by the creator of George's official image, Sir Thomas Lawrence.
21. *King's Jaunt*, 192–3, 133.
22. Ibid., 101–2, 185.
23. Lockhart, *Memoirs of Scott* (1845), 482.
24. Finley, *Turner and George IV*, 8.
25. Colvin, *Dictionary*, 796; Prebble, *King's Jaunt*, 174, 179.
26. Simpson, *Letters to Scott*, 46–7.
27. See Prebble, *King's Jaunt*, 242–3.
28. *DNB*; quoted in Maclean and Skinner, *Royal Visit*, 5.
29. Lockhart, *Memoirs of Scott* (1845), 482–3, 486.
30. *King's Jaunt*, 293; Finley, *Turner and George IV*, 10.
31. Mudie, *Historical Account*, 231.
32. Finley, op. cit., 13; Prebble, *King's Jaunt*, 318.
33. BM, Add MS 40317, ff 3–4: Sir Walter Scott to Lord Melville, 25 August 1822.
34. See Prebble, *King's Jaunt*, 339–40.
35. 'An attempt to bring Locksley and the outlaws of *Ivanhoe* to further life by a display of archery ended almost before it was begun, with wet bow-strings, drooping bonnets, and the soggy weight of soaked tartan' (*King's Jaunt*, 350).
36. Thomson, *Raeburn*, 28. John Prebble's judgement on Wilkie's canvas is predictably severe: 'closer though it is to a truth the tailors and jewellers distorted, the portrait is still a sad lie' (*King's Jaunt*, 76). At the Royal Academy exhibition of 1830 critics poured scorn on Wilkie's companion piece *Entry of George IV at Holyrood House*, abandoned in 1825 and only recently finished. The *Court Journal*, for example, found the canvas 'meagre, mean and altogether unsatisfactory' (Miles and Brown, *Wilkie of Scotland*, 35, 225).
37. Maclean and Skinner, *Royal Visit*, 20; *King's Jaunt*, 353.

38. Sir Walter Scott to Walter Scott the Younger, 28 August 1822, quoted in Grierson, *Letters of Scott*, VII, 240.
39. *Blackwood's Edinburgh Magazine*, xii (September 1822), 272, quoted in Finley, *Turner and George IV*, 67; *The Times*, quoted in *King's Jaunt*, 360.
40. Sir Walter Scott to Sir William Knighton, 12 September 1822, in Aspinall, *Letters of George IV*, II, 539.
41. Lockhart, *Memoirs of Scott*, VII, 49; Lockhart, *Memoirs of Scott* (1845), 481; quoted in Trevor-Roper, loc. cit., 70.
42. Trevor-Roper, loc. cit., 71.

CHAPTER 17: THE KING AS CARICATURE

1. Donald, *Age of Caricature*, 2, 20–1; O'Connell, *The Popular Print*, 181–2.
2. See Barlow, *The Prince and his Pleasures*, 32–6.
3. See Donald, op. cit., 100–1.
4. Donald, 105; BM 8073, 8075; 8095: see George, *Catalogue of . . . Satires*, VI, 895, 896–7, 909–10.
5. BM 8810–1 (George, op. cit., VII, 256); Donald, 101–2; Prince of Wales to King George III, 22 June 1796, in Aspinall, *Prince of Wales Correspondence*, III, 237.
6. See Frances Homan, '"Enchantments Lately Seen": Caricatures of the Prince of Wales 1782–1806', in Arnold, *Squanderous and Lavish Profusion*, 20–1; Donald, op. cit., 26, 165.
7. BM 11847 (George, op. cit., IX, 85); Hill, *Mr Gillray*, 122.
8. Aspinall, *Letters of George IV*, I, 187.
9. BM 11746, 11841 (George, op. cit., IX 37, 80); Wardroper, *Caricatures of Cruikshank*, 31.
10. BM 12303, 12296 (George, op. cit., IX, 429, 422).
11. Cartoons by George Cruikshank and J.L. Marks, both published in August 1814 (BM 12305–6).
12. BM 12578, 12791 (George, op. cit., IX 563, 687); *The Times*, 25 March 1816.
13. BM 13259, 13733 and Barlow, op. cit., 14–15; BM 13213, 13220–3 (George, op. cit., IX, 889, 893–5).
14. Quoted in Anne L. Helmreich, 'Re-forming London: George Cruikshank and the Victorian Age', in Debra Mancoff and D.J. Trela, eds, *Victorian Urban Settings* (University of Chicago Press, 1996). See also Donald, op. cit., 26–7. Marc Baer (in *Print Quarterly*, Vol. 10, September 1993) has argued rather unconvincingly that Cruikshank's retreat from castigating the Prince Regent occurred because the artist was 'terrorized by the possibilities of democracy', rather than simply strapped for cash.
15. Donald, op. cit., 192–3, 27.
16. Wardroper, op. cit., 16, 107; BM 14008, 14024–5, 14030, 14049, 14108 (George, op. cit., X. 142, 150, 152, 158, 182).
17. BM 14203, 14238.
18. Lord Byron, *Sardanapalus*, 11. 1, 4, 18–27, 47–9, 173–4 (Frederick Page and John Jump, eds, *Byron, Poetical Works* (John Murray, 1970), 453 and passim).

19. BM 14118, 14637 (George, op. cit., X, 188–9, 409-10).
20. Butler, *Regency Visitor*, 89, 95–6.
21. George, op. cit., VI, 583.
22. Percy Shelley to Elizabeth Hitchener, 20 June 1811, quoted in Ingpen, *Letters of Shelley*, I, 100.
23. BM 11904, 13847 and George, op. cit., X, 91; BM 14111, 15521–2, 15565, 15772 (George, op. cit., XI, 16–17, 43, 147); Gore, *Creevey's Life and Times*, 187.
24. Jennings, *Croker Correspondence*, I, 125; BM 200641 and Barlow, op. cit., 17–18. The Pavilion might, indeed, have fallen into ruin but for the attention and commitment of Brighton Corporation after 1850.
25. BM 12578, 12791, 13208, 13211, 13215, 13346 (George, op. cit., IX, 687–8, 886, 888, 890, 956–7).
26. BM 13847, 13831–40, 13733 (George, op. cit., X, 93, 89–90, 52); BM 205790.
27. Summerson, *Life of Nash*, 109.
28. *DNB; The Poetical Works of Thomas Moore* (n.d.), 587, 591. Moore's *Dialogue Between a Sovereign and a One Pound Note*, of about the same time, had George IV acknowledging that 'Fair Pound, we can never live together.'
29. BM 207992; quoted in Maclean and Skinner, *Royal Visit*, 2; BM 14400, 14500 (George, op. cit., X, 314, 354–5); and see, for example, Robert Cruikshank's *The King at Home* of 1825 (BM 14940).
30. BM 15545, 15667 (George, op. cit., XI, 33, 95–6).
31. BM 15126, 15147, 15410, 15413 (George, op. cit., X, 585, 599, 686, 688).
32. BM 14118, 14125, 14168, 14207, 14221, 14241.
33. For example, BM 15126 and 15147, published in 1826 and featuring George IV fishing at Virginia Water.
34. BM 15400 (George, op. cit., X, 679); BM 200965 and Barlow, op. cit., 16.
35. For example, BM 15373 (21 April 1827).
36. BM 11019, 15425.
37. For example, BM 15845, published on 11 August 1829 and entitled *Le Mort* (George, op. cit., XI, 182).
38. Huish, *Memoirs of George IV*, II, 360.

CHAPTER 18: RECLUSE

1. Farington, XI, 4053, 4102.
2. Gray, *Perceval*, 459; Roberts, *Royal Landscape*, 315.
3. John Croker to Lord Whitworth, 14 November 1817, quoted in Jennings, *Croker Correspondence*, I, 105; Maria Fitzherbert to Thomas Creevey, 28 December 1818, quoted in Gore, *Creevey's Life and Times*, 115.
4. Gronow, *Reminiscences*, II, 256. In this the Prince Regent was following the example set by the 5th Duke of Portland at Welbeck Abbey; see Girouard, *Life in the English Country House*, 285.
5. Leveson Gower, *Letters of Countess Granville*, I, 172, 191; Roberts, *Royal Landscape*, 315.

6. Aspinall, *Letters of George IV*, II, 370–1.
7. *Croker Correspondence*, I, 249; Musgrave, *Royal Pavilion*, 90, 92; Reeve, *Greville Memoirs*, I, 49.
8. *Croker Correspondence*, I, 264; George, *Catalogue of ... Satires*, X, 411; Gore, *Creevey's Life and Times*, 229; Butler, *Regency Visitor*, 256.
9. Quoted in Simon, *Buckingham Palace*, 39, see Musgrave, *Royal Pavilion*, 97.
10. *Letters of George IV*, III, 153–4.
11. Roberts, op. cit., 80; Morshead, *George IV and the Royal Lodge*, 11.
12. Roberts, op. cit., 201, 313–15; Morshead, op. cit., 12–13.
13. The cost of all the new work in the Great Park, largely borne by the Office of Woods and Forests, was approximately £85,000. See Crook and Port, *King's Works*, VI, 151.
14. Roberts, 77; Morshead, 23.
15. Letter from the Chaplain to the Duke of Devonshire, quoted in Morshead, op. cit., 24–5; Morley, *Regency Design*, 218; *Journal of Scott*, 20 October 1826, 279; Morshead, op. cit., 32.
16. Huish, *Memoirs of George IV*, II, 359–60; Morshead, 25.
17. Roberts, op. cit., 79, 413, 417–18; Butler, *Regency Visitor*, 256.
18. Roberts, 413–14, 459; Morshead, 33.
19. Roberts, 453–5.
20. Roberts, 201; PRO WORK 19/44, f 17; Morshead, 34; Busco, *Westmacott*, 68–9.
21. Gore, *Creevey's Life and Times*, 307.
22. See Sean Sawyer, 'Sir John Soane and the Origins of the Royal Entrance', in C. & J. Riding, *Houses of Parliament*; Prebble, *King's Jaunt*, 59–60.
23. Nash was asked to redesign the lake, to replant the park and to lay new gravel paths. The result was, unusually, praised by Pückler-Muskau, who admired 'the judicious division and series of the work, the ingenious modes of transport, the movable iron railings ...' (Mavis Batey and David Lambert, *The English Garden: A View Into the Past* (1990), 255–6).
24. Huish, *Memoirs of George IV*, II 352; Jennings, *Croker Correspondence*, I, 408; Morshead, op. cit., 26; Reeve, *Greville Memoirs*, I, 143–4; Morshead, 25.
25. Butler, *Regency Visitor*, 95; Reeve, *Greville Memoirs*, I, 154–5.
26. Quoted in Morshead, 26, 31.
27. Huish, *Memoirs of George IV*, II, 360, 362, 48.
28. Gore, *Creevey's Life and Times*, 313.
29. Thackeray, *The Four Georges*, 98.
30. Leslie, *Mrs Fitzherbert*, I, 150; Hibbert, *George IV*, 463.
31. Parry, *Queen Caroline*, 83; Hibbert, op. cit., 463.
32. Aspinall, *Letters of George IV*, III, 211; Canning in any event died in August 1827.
33. Aspinall, *Prince of Wales Correspondence*, VIII, lxiv; Robinson, *Letters of Princess Lieven*, 363.
34. Linstrum, *Wyatville*, 42; Morshead, op. cit., 33; Partington, *Private Letter-Books of Scott*, 159.

35. *Letters of Queen Victoria*, 1st Series, I, 16, quoted in Pattison, *Royal Insignia*, 134–5.
36. Hibbert, *George IV*, 632n.
37. Gore, *Creevey's Life and Times*, 234; George, op. cit., X, 213; BM 151540 (George, X, 593).
38. Huish, *Memoirs of George IV*, II, 399; RA Vic Add MS, T/73. For details of the proposed sale of the King's Library, see Hibbert, *George IV*, 690.
39. BL Add MS 38753, f 122.
40. Reeve, *Greville Memoirs*, I, 207; Morshead, op. cit., 32.
41. Hibbert, *George IV*, 643.
42. *Letters of George IV*, II, 503; Smith, *George IV*, 217.
43. Quoted in Smith, *George IV*, 220.
44. Hibbert, *George IV*, 664, 666. For an excellent account of Knighton's role and influence, see Smith, *George IV*, 216–25.
45. *Greville Memoirs*, I, 189.
46. *Greville Memoirs*, I, 231; quoted in Macalpine and Hunter, *George III and the Mad-Business* 238, 240; Thomas Creevey's report of 8 March 1828 of Henry Stephenson's comments, quoted in *Creevey's Life and Times*, 262.
47. Lady Granville, 12 November 1828, quoted in *Letters of Countess Granville*, II, 35; Bamford and Wellington, *Journal of Mrs Arbuthnot*, II, 241.

CHAPTER 19: CONCLUSION
1. Mitchell, *Melbourne*, 147; Ziegler, *William IV*, 256.
2. Mitchell, op. cit., 148; Ziegler, op. cit., 257.
3. White, *Dutch Pictures*, lxxi.
4. Leeds, *Buildings of London*, 113; Ziegler, op. cit., 251.
5. Lockhart, *Memoirs of Scott* (1845), 640.
6. Huish, *Memoirs of George IV*, I, 4, 483; II, 54, 55, 133, 383, 418; *Westminster Review*, 136–7.
7. Cobbett, *History of George IV*, 54, 497.
8. Quoted in Morshead, *George IV and the Royal Lodge*, 31.
9. Reeve, *Greville Memoirs*, 155.
10. Quoted in Evans *Princes as Patrons*, 13; Hibbert, *George IV*, 782–3.
11. Thackeray, *Four Georges*, 90.
12. Clifford Smith, *Buckingham Palace*, 34.
13. Quoted in Clifford Smith, 35. Leslie inherited the family baronetcy in 1944.
14. Fulford, *George IV*, 9, 170, 215.
15. It is interesting to see that George V's eldest son, who reigned briefly the year after the publication of Fulford's biography, seemed to inherit more of George IV's character than any other member of the royal family. Both Edward VIII and George toyed in their youth with the idea of radical politics, and both turned increasingly reactionary in middle age. Both worked hard to create a dashing public image; both were undeniably vain, exemplars of fashion in their earlier years. Both were products of a

stultifyingly dull and 'respectable' Court, presided over by dour and humourless parents. And both consistently preferred older women (though Wallis Simpson was not quite in the image of Lady Conyngham – she was far too thin, and Edward married her: but both were passionately acquisitive where jewellery was concerned). Edward VIII was fortunate in not having to suffer the bitter satires of a Gillray or a Cruikshank. The public evisceration in print of George's conduct is in striking contrast to the self-imposed silence on the subject of Edward VIII's relationship with Mrs Simpson more than a century later.

16. Butler, *Regency Visitor*, 319; Memes, *Memoirs of Canova*, 476. In May 1828 Prince Pückler-Muskau commented in his diary that 'the monarch himself is, as is well known, prouder of nothing than of the title of "the first gentleman in England".'

17. Quoted in Joanna Richardson, 'George IV: Patron of Literature', in *Essays by Diverse Hands*, Vol. xxxv (1969), 128.

18. Richardson, art. cit., 146.

19. Millar, *Later Georgian Pictures*, I, xxviii.

20. Aspinall, *Prince of Wales Correspondence*, VII, 137.

21. See for example Hibbert, *George IV*, 783, 787.

22. Smith, *George IV*, 206, 228.

23. See ibid., 240, 231, 236.

24. Ibid., 240.

25. Prochaska, *Royal Bounty*, 29–30, 43.

26. Smith, *George IV*, 286.

Bibliography

I LIFE & POLITICS

1.1 MSS

British Library:
–Add MSS 47559–62/65/67–71/79–80/82–3/85/89–91
–Add MSS 13741 and passim
–Add MSS 38190 and passim
–Add MSS 515550/592/799/731–8
–Forth MSS/Add MSS 65146
–Add MSS 38760 and passim
Royal Archives, Windsor
Public Record Office, Kew; Office of Works papers
Leicestershire Record Office; Halford MSS

1.2 Principal Printed Sources

Anglesey, The Marquess of, *One-Leg* (Cape, 1961)
Annual Register, 1821
Annual Register, 1831
Sir Arthur Aspinall (ed.), *The Letters of George IV, 1812–30* (3 vols, Cambridge University Press, Cambridge, 1938)
——*Politics and the Press, 1780–1850* (Home & Van Thal, 1949)
——*Letters of Princess Charlotte, 1811–1817* (Home and Van Thal, 1949)
——*Mrs Jordan and her Family* (Arthur Barker, 1951)
——*The Later Correspondence of George III* (5 vols, Cambridge University Press, Cambridge, 1963–70)
——*The Correspondence of George, Prince of Wales, 1770–1812* (8 vols, Cassell, 1963–71)
J.E. Austen-Leigh, *Memoir of Jane Austen* (Oxford University Press, Oxford, 1926)
F. Bamford and the 7th Duke of Wellington (eds), *The Journal of Mrs Arbuthnot, 1830–2* (2 vols, Macmillan, 1950)

William Dodgson Barman, *The Divorce Case of Queen Caroline* (George Routledge, 1930)

C.J. Bartlett, *Castlereagh* (Macmillan, 1966)

Stephen C. Berendt, *Royal Mourning and Regency Culture* (Macmillan, 1997)

Bessborough, 9th Earl of, *Georgiana* (John Murray, 1955)

Francis Bickley (ed.), *The Glenbervie Journals* (Constable, 1928)

John Brooke, *George III* (Constable, 1972)

Henry Brougham, *The Life and Times of Henry, Lord Brougham* (3 vols, William Blackwood, Edinburgh, 1871)

——*Statesmen of the Reign of George III* (2 vols, Blackwood, Edinburgh, 1853)

Buckingham and Chandos, 2nd Duke of, *Memoirs of the Courts and Cabinets of George III* (4 vols, Hurst & Blackett, 1853–55)

——*Memoirs of the Court, 1811–20* (2 vols, Collins, 1856)

——*Memoirs of the Court of George IV* (2 vols, Collins, 1859)

Anon [Lady Charlotte Bury], *The Court of England Under George IV: The Diary of a Lady-in-Waiting* (first published 1828; 2 vols, John MacQueen, 1896); *see also* Stewart

E.M. Butler (ed.), *A Regency Visitor: The English Tour of Prince Pückler-Muskau Described in his Letters, 1826–1828* (Collins, 1957)

Patrick Cadell, *Royal Visits to Scotland* (National Libary of Scotland, Edinburgh, 1977)

Kathleen Campbell, *Beau Brummel* (Hammond Hammond, 1948)

Cynthia Campbell, *The Most Polished Gentleman* (Kudos, 1995)

R.W. Chapman (ed.), *Jane Austen: Selected Letters, 1796–1871* (Oxford University Press, Oxford, 1985)

William Cobbett, *A History of the Regency and Reign of George IV* (Mills, Jowett & Mills, 1830)

Linda Colley, 'The Apotheosis of George III: Loyalty, Royalty and the British Nation 1760–1820', in *Past and Present*, Vol. 102 (1984)

——*Britons* (Yale University Press, New Haven and London, 1992)

J.E. Cookson, *Lord Liverpool's Administration* (Scottish Academic Press, Edinburgh, 1975)

The Creevey Papers (B.T. Batsford, 1963); *see also* Jennings, Maxwell

Croker Correspondence: see Jennings

Revd George Croly, *Life and Times of George IV* (James Duncan, 1830)

Valerie Cumming, 'Pantomime and Pageantry: The Coronation of George IV', in Celina Fox (ed.), *London – World City* (Yale, London and New Haven, 1992)

Saul David, *Prince of Pleasure* (Little, Brown, 1998)

Harry Edgington, *Prince Regent: The Scandalous Private Life of George IV* (Hamlyn, Feltham, 1979)

Joseph Farington: *see* Garlick et al.

Gerald Finley, *Landscapes of Memory: Turner as Illustrator to Scott* (Scholar Press, 1980)

——*Turner and George the Fourth in Edinburgh, 1822* (Tate Gallery exhibition catalogue, 1981)

Jim and Philippa Foord-Kelcey, *Mrs Fitzherbert and Sons* (The Book Guild, 1991)

Amanda Foreman, *Georgiana, Duchess of Devonshire* (Harper Collins, 1998)

Charles James Fox, *Speeches during the French Revolution* (Dent, London, 1924); *see also* Trotter

Henry Richard Fox, 3rd Baron Holland, *Memoirs of the Whig Party During my Time* (ed. 4th Baron Holland, 2 vols, Longman, Brown, Green & Longman, 1852–4)

——*Further Memoirs* (ed. 4th Earl of Ilchester, Longmans, 1905)

Flora Fraser, *The Unruly Queen* (Macmillan, 1996)

Roger Fulford, *The Royal Dukes* (Duckworth, 1933)

——*George IV* (Duckworth, 1935)

——(ed.), *The Autobiography of Miss Knight* (William Kimber, 1960)

——*The Trial of Queen Caroline* (Batsford, 1967)

Kenneth Garlick, Angus Macintyre and Kathryn Cave (eds), *The Diary of Joseph Farington* (16 vols, Yale University Press, New Haven and London, 1978–84); *see also* Newby

G.T. Garratt, *Lord Brougham* (Macmillan, 1935)

Mark Girouard, *The Return to Camelot* (Yale University Press, New Haven and London, 1981)

——*Life in the English Country House* (Yale University Press, New Haven and London, 1978)

The Glenbervie Journals: *see* Bickley, Sichel

John Gore (ed.), *Creevey's Life and Times* (John Murray, 1934)

Hon. F. Leveson-Gower (ed.), *The Letters of Harriet, Countess Granville, 1810–45* (Longman, Green & Co., 1894)

Countess Granville (ed.), *Lord Granville Leveson-Gower (First Earl Granville): Private Correspondence 1781–1821* (2 vols, John Murray, 1916)

Denis Gray, *Spencer Perceval* (Manchester University Press, Manchester, 1963)

Greville Memoirs: *see* Reeve

H.C. Grierson (ed.), *Letters of Sir Walter Scott* (12 vols, Constable, 1932–7)

R.H. Gronow, *The Reminiscences and Recollections of Captain Gronow, 1810–1860* (2 vols, 1892)

Christopher Hibbert, *George IV* (Penguin, Harmondsworth, 1976)

——*Wellington, A Personal History* (HarperCollins, 1997)

——*George III, A Personal History* (Viking, 1998)

Wendy Hinde, *Canning* (Collins, 1973)

Eric Hobsbawm and Terence Ranger (eds), *The Invention of Tradition* (Cambridge University Press, Cambridge, 1983)

Lord Holland: *see* Henry Richard Fox, 3rd Baron Holland

Robert Huish, *Memoirs of Charlotte Augusta* (Thomas Kelly, 1818)

——*An Authentic History of the Coronation of His Majesty, King George the Fourth* (Thomas Kelly, 1821)

——*Memoirs of George the Fourth* (2 vols, Thomas Kelly, 1830–1)

Ilchester, Earl of (ed.), *Journal of Henry Edward Fox, 1818–30* (Constable, 1923)

R. Ingpen (ed.), *The Letters of Percy Bysshe Shelley* (2 vols, Isaac Pitman & Sons, 1912)

Nathaniel Jefferys, *A Review of the Conduct of HRH The Prince of Wales in his various transactions with Mr Jefferys during a period of more than twenty years* (London, 1806)

Louis J. Jennings (ed.), *The Correspondence and Diaries of the late Rt. Hon. John Wilson Croker* (3 vols, John Murray, 1884)

W. Jesse, *Beau Brummel* (first published 1844; reprinted by The Navarre Society, 1927)

Charles Langdale, *Memoirs of Mrs Fitzherbert* (Richard Bentley, 1856)

Lees-Milne, James, *The Last Stuarts* (Chatto & Windus, 1983)

Lady Sarah Lennox (ed. Countess of Ilchester and Lord Stavordale), *The Life and Letters of Lady Sarah Lennox* (2 vols, John Murray, 1901)

J.R. Shane Leslie, *George the Fourth* (Ernest Benn, 1926)

——*Life and Letters of Mrs Fitzherbert* (2 vols, Burns Oates, 1939–44)

M.J. Levy, *The Mistresses of King George IV* (Peter Owen, 1996)

Princess Lieven: *see* Quennell, Robinson, Temperley

H.E. Lloyd, *George IV: Memoirs of His Life and Reign* (Treuttel and Würtz, Treuttel and Richter, 1830)

J.G. Lockhart, *Memoirs of the Life of Sir Walter Scott* (7 vols, Robet Cadell, Edinburgh, 1837–8; one-volume edition, Cadell, 1845)

Ida Macalpine and Richard Hunter, *George III and the Mad-Business* (Allen Lane, 1969)

James Maclean and Basil Skinner, *The Royal Visit of 1822* (University of Edinburgh, Edinburgh, 1972)

Sir Herbert Maxwell (ed.), *The Creevey Papers: A Selection from the Correspondence and Diaries of the late Thomas Creevey MP* (London, 1905)

Lewis Melville, *Life and Letters of Beau Brummel* (Hutchinson, 1924)

Leslie Mitchell, *Charles James Fox* (Oxford University Press, Oxford, 1992)

——*Lord Melbourne* (Oxford University Press, Oxford, 1997)

John Mollo, *The Prince's Dolls* (Leo Cooper, 1997)

Thomas Moore, *Memoirs of R.B. Sheridan* (2 vols, John Murray, 2nd edn 1825); *see also* Price

Robert Mudie, *An Historical Account of His Majesty's Visit to Scotland* (Edinburgh, 1822)

Evelyn Newby, *The Farington Index* (Yale University Press for the Paul Mellon Centre, New Haven and London, 1998)

Fintan O'Toole, *A Traitor's Kiss* (Granta, 1997)

Sir Edward Parry, *Queen Caroline* (Ernest Benn, 1930)

Wilfred Partington (ed.), *The Private Letter-Books of Sir Walter Scott* (Hodder & Stoughton, 1930)

Stephen Patterson, *Royal Insignia* (Merrell Holberton, 1996)

John Prebble, *The Highland Clearances* (Penguin, Harmondsworth, 1969)

——*The King's Jaunt* (Collins, 1988)

Cecil Price (ed.), *The Letters of Richard Brinsley Sheridan* (3 vols, Oxford University Press, Oxford, 1966)

J.B. Priestley, *The Prince of Pleasure and his Regency, 1811–20* (William Heinemann Ltd, 1969)

Frank Prochaska, *Royal Bounty and the Making of a Welfare Monarchy* (Yale University Press, New Haven and London, 1995)

Peter Quennell (ed.), *The Private Letters of the Princess Lieven to Prince Metternich, 1820–26* (John Murray, 1937)

Henry Reeve (ed.), *The Greville Memoirs* (Longman, Green & Co., 1875)

Loren D. Reid, 'Sheridan's Speech on Mrs Fitzherbert', in *Quarterly Journal of Speech*, Vol. xxxiii, February 1947

Aileen Ribeiro, *The Art of Dress* (Yale University Press, New Haven and London, 1995)

Joanna Richardson, *The Disastrous Marriage* (Jonathan Cape, 1960)

——*George IV, A Portrait* (Sidgwick & Jackson, 1966)

——'George IV, Patron of Literature', in *Essays by Divers Hands*, Vol. xxxv, 1969

——'The Princess Charlotte', in *History Today*, Vol. 22, No. 2 (1987)

Christine & Jacqueline Riding (eds), *The Houses of Parliament* (Merrill, 2000)

Lionel G. Robinson (ed.), *Letters of Dorothea, Princess Lieven, during her Residence in London 1812–34* (Longman, Green, 1902)

John C.G. Röhl, Martin Warren & David Hunt, *Purple Secret – Genes, 'Madness' and the Royal Houses of Europe* (Bantam, 1998)

P.J.V. Rolo, *Canning* (Macmillan, 1965)

Richard Rush, *A Residence at the Court of London* (3 vols, 1833; reprinted Century, 1987)

Lord Russell of Liverpool, *Caroline the Unhappy Queen* (Robert Hale, 1967)

Roger Sales, *Jane Austen and the Representation of Regency England* (Routledge, 1996)

Sir Walter Scott: *see* Anderson, Grierson, Lockhart, Partington, Simpson

——*The Journal of Sir Walter Scott, 1825–32* (David Douglas, Edinburgh, 1891 edn)

Philip W. Sergeant, *George, Prince and Regent* (Hutchinson, London, n.d.)

R.B. Sheridan, *Letters: see* Price

Walter Sichel, *Sheridan* (2 vols, Constable, 1909)

——(ed.), *The Glenbervie Journals* (2 vols, Constable, 1910)

James Simpson (ed.), *Letters to Sir Walter Scott ...* (Waugh and Innes, Edinburgh, 1822)

Henry Singleton, *George IV and Mrs Fitzherbert* (London, n.d.)

E.A. Smith, *A Queen on Trial* (Alan Sutton, Stroud, 1993)

——*George IV* (Yale University Press, New Haven and London, 1999)

Robert Southey (ed. Revd C.C. Southey), *The Life and Correspondence of the Late Robert Southey* (Longman, Brown, Green and Longman, 1850)

Francis Stewart (ed.), *The Diary of Lady Charlotte Bury* (Longman, Green, 1908)

D. M. Stuart, *Daughter of England* (Macmillan, 1951)

——*Portrait of the Prince Regent* (Methuen, 1953)

Harold Temperley, 'Canning, Wellington and George IV', in *English Historical Review* 38, April 1923

——(ed.), *The Unpublished Diary and Political Sketches of Princess Lieven* (Jonathan Cape, 1925)

W.M. Thackeray, *The Four Georges* (lectures of 1855–7, first publ. 1860; Smith, Elder & Co., 1879)

——*The Memoirs of Mr C.J. Yellowplush* (Smith, Elder & Co., 1879)

Claire Tomalin, *Jane Austen – A Life* (Penguin, 1998)

——*Mrs Jordan's Profession* (Viking, 1994)

J.B. Trotter, *Memoirs of the Later Years of the Right Honourable Charles James Fox* (3 vols, Sherwood, Neely & Jones, 1811)

Lady Rose Weigall, *A Brief Memoir of Princess Charlotte of Wales* (John Murray, 1874)

The Duke of Wellington (ed. 7th Duke of Wellington), *Wellington and his Friends: Letters of the First Duke of Wellington* (Macmillan, 1965)

——*Despatches, Correspondence and Memorials of Field Marshal Arthur, Duke of Wellington, KG* (1877)

The Westminster Review, Vol. 14 (January 1831)

Henry Wheatley (ed.), *Memoirs of Sir Nathaniel William Wraxall, 1722–1784* (5 vols, London, 1884)

John Whittaker and George Nayler, *The Coronation of His Most Sacred Majesty, King George the Fourth* (2 vols, H.G. Bohn, 2nd edn, 1837)

W.H. Wilkins, *Mrs Fitzherbert and George IV* (Longman, Green & Co., 1905)

John Wilks, *Memoirs of Her Majesty Queen Caroline Amelia Elizabeth* (Sherwood, Neely & Jones, 1822)

G.M. Willis, *Ernest Augustus* (Arthur Baker, 1954)

Philip Withers, *Alfred* (London, 1789)

Wraxall Memoirs: see Wheatley

Charles D. Yonge, *The Life and Administration of Robert Banks, Second Earl of Liverpool, KG* (3 vols, Macmillan, 1868)

Philip Ziegler, *Addington* (Collins, 1965)

——*King William IV* (Cassell, 1989)

——*Melbourne* (Collins, 1976)

2 ARCHITECTURE

2.1 General

Dana Arnold (ed.), *Squanderous and Lavish Profusion* (The Georgian Group, 1995)

H.M. Colvin, *Biographical Dictionary of British Architects 1600–1840* (Yale, London and New Haven, 3rd edn, 1995)

John Cornforth, *W.H. Pyne's Royal Residences* (Joseph, 1976)

J. Mordaunt Crook and M.H. Port, *The History of the King's Works*, Vol. VI (HMSO, 1973)

John Morley, *Regency Design* (Zwemmer, 1993)

Steven Parissien, *Regency Style* (Phaidon, 1992)

John Steegman, *The Rule of Taste* (Macmillan, 1968)

Dorothy Stroud, *Henry Holland* (Country Life, 1966)

John Summerson, *The Life and Work of John Nash, Architect* (George Allen & Unwin, 1980)

David Watkin, *The Royal Interiors of Regency England* (Dent, 1984)

2.2 London

The Microcosm of London (3 vols, Rudolf Ackermann, London, 1808–10; plates by Thomas Rowlandson, A.C. Pugin, et al.; ed. John Summerson, Penguin, Harmondsworth, 1943)

Wilfred Blunt, *The Ark in the Park* (Hamish Hamilton, 1976)

John Britton and A.C. Pugin, *Illustrations of the Public Buildings of London* (2 vols, John Neale, 1825–8)

Lord Farnborough, *Short Remarks and Suggestions* (J. Hatchard, 1826)

Celina Fox (ed.), *London – World City, 1800–1840* (Yale University Press, London and New Haven, 1992)

John Harris, Geoffrey de Bellaigue and Oliver Millar, *Buckingham Palace and its Treasures* (Thomas Nelson, 1968)

Simon Jervis, Maurice Tomlin and Jonathan Voak, *Apsley House* (V. & A. Publications, 1995)

W.H. Leeds, *Illustration of the Public Buildings of London – Supplement* (John Neale, 1838)

Andrew Saint, 'The Marble Arch', in *The Georgian Group Journal*, Vol. vii (1997)

Ann Saunders, *Regent's Park* (David & Charles, Newton Abbot, 1969)

Sean Sawyer, 'Sir John Sloane's Symbolic Westminster: The Apotheosis of George IV', in *Architectural History* 39, 1996.

——'The Processional Route', in *John Soane, Architect* (Royal Academy exhibition catalogue, 1999)

Second Report from the Select Committee on Windsor Castle and Buckingham Palace, 14 October 1831 (and Appendix)

Select Committee on the Office of Works and Public Buildings, 19 June 1828

Robin Simon (ed.), *Buckingham Palace* (Apollo, 1993)

H. Clifford Smith, *Buckingham Palace* (Country Life, 1931)

John Soane, *Designs for Public Improvements in London and Westminster* (London, 1828)

David Watkin, *Sir John Soane* (Cambridge University Press, Cambridge, 1996)

Andrew Saint, 'The Marble Arch', in *The Georgian Group Journal*, Vol. vii (1997)

2.3 Brighton

John Dinkel, *The Royal Pavilion Brighton* (Philip Wilson, 1983)

Gervase Jackson-Stops, *Views of the Royal Pavilion* (Pavilion, 1991)

John Morley, *The Making of Brighton Pavilion* (Philip Wilson, 1984)
Clifford Musgrave, *Royal Pavilion* (Leonard Hill, 1959)
John Nash, *The Pavilion at Brighton* (London, 1826)
Jessica M.F. Rutherford, *The Royal Pavilion, Brighton* (Brighton Borough Council, Brighton, n.d. [1995])

2.4 Windsor

Henry Ashton, *Illustrations of Windsor Castle by the late Sir Jeffry Wyatville* (London, 1841)
W.H. St John Hope, *Windsor Castle* (2 vols, Country Life, 1913)
Derek Linstrum, *Sir Jeffry Wyatville* (Clarendon Press, Oxford, 1972)
Owen Morshead, *George IV and the Royal Lodge* (Regency Society of Brighton and Hove, Brighton, 1965)
——*Windsor Castle* (Phaidon, Oxford, 1971)
Jane Roberts, *Royal Landscape* (Yale University Press, New Haven and London, 1997)
John Martin Robinson, *Windsor Castle* (Michael Joseph, 1998)

3 ART

3.1 General

Mark Evans (ed.), *Princes as Patrons* (Merrell Holberton, 1998)
George III, Collector and Patron (Queen's Gallery exhibition catalogue, 1974)
George IV and the Arts of France (Queen's Gallery exhibition catalogue, 1966)
John Ingamells, *The 3rd Marquess of Hertford as a Collector* (Trustees of the Wallace Collection, 1983)
Christopher Lloyd, *The Quest for Albion: Monarchy and the Patronage of British Painting* (Queen's Gallery exhibition catalogue, 1998)
Oliver Millar, *The Later Georgian Pictures in the Collection of Her Majesty the Queen* (2 vols, Phaidon, 1969)
——*The Queen's Pictures* (Weidenfeld & Nicolson, 1977)
Christopher White, *The Dutch Pictures in the Collection of Her Majesty the Queen* (Cambridge University Press, Cambridge, 1982)
William T. Whitley, *Art in England, 1800–20* (Cambridge University Press, Cambridge, 1928)
——*Art in England, 1821–37* (Cambridge University Press, Cambridge, 1930)

3.2 Artists

Cosway
Gerald Barnett, *Richard and Maria Cosway* (Westcountry Books, Tiverton, 1995)
Stephen Lloyd, *Richard and Maria Cosway* (National Portrait Gallery of Scotland exhibition catalogue, Edinburgh, 1995)
George Williamson, *Richard Cosway, RA* (George Bell, 1905)

Bibliography

Haydon

Malcolm Elwin (ed.), *The Autobiography and Journals of Benjamin Robert Haydon* (Macdonald, 1950)

Eric George, *The Life and Death of Benjamin Robert Haydon* (Oxford University Press, 1967)

B.R. Haydon: Correspondence and Table-Talk (2 vols, ed. F.W. Haydon, R. Worthington, New York, 1878)

John Jolliffe, *Neglected Genius* (Hutchinson, 1990)

Tom Taylor (ed.), *The Autobiography and Memoirs of Benjamin Robert Haydon* (3 vols, Longman, 1853)

Lawrence

Walter Armstrong, *Sir Thomas Lawrence* (Methuen, 1913)

Kenneth Garlick, *Sir Thomas Lawrence* (Routledge and Kegan Paul, 1954)

——*Sir Thomas Lawrence* (Phaidon, Oxford, 1989)

——*Sir Thomas Lawrence: Portrait of an Age, 1790–1830* (Art Services International, Alexandria VA, 1993)

Douglas Goldring, *Regency Portrait Painter* (Macdonald, 1951)

George Somes Layard (ed.), *Sir Thomas Lawrence's Letter-Bag* (George Allen, 1906)

D.E. Williams (ed.), *The Life and Correspondence of Sir Thomas Lawrence* (Henry Colburn and Richard Bentley, 1831)

Raeburn

Duncan Thomson, *Raeburn: The Art of Sir Henry Raeburn, 1756–1823* (Scottish National Portrait Gallery exhibition catalogue, Edinburgh, 1997)

Reynolds

David Mannings & Martin Postle, *Sir Joshua Reynolds – A Complete Catalogue of his Paintings* (Yale University Press, New Haven and London, 2000)

Nicholas Penny (ed.), *Reynolds* (Royal Academy exhibition catalogue, Weidenfeld & Nicolson, 1986)

Martin Postle, *Sir Joshua Reynolds: The Subject Pictures* (Cambridge University Press, Cambridge, 1995)

Ellis Waterhouse, *Reynolds* (Kegan Paul, 1941)

Vigée-Le Brun

Angelica Goodden, *The Sweetness of Life* (Andre Deutsch, 1997)

Élisabeth Vigée-Le Brun, *Memoirs* (1869; translated by Camden Press, 1989)

Ward

Oliver Beckett, *The Life and Work of James Ward, RA* (The Book Guild, Lewes, 1995)

West

John Dillenberger, *Benjamin West, The Context of his Life's Work* (Trinity University Press, San Antonio, 1977)

Nancy L. Pressly, *Revealed Religion: Benjamin West's Commissions for Windsor Castle and Fonthill Abbey* (San Antonio Museum of Art exhibition catalogue, San Antonio, 1983)

Helmut Von Erffa and Allen Staley, *The Pictures of Benjamin West* (Yale University Press, New Haven and London, 1986)

Wilkie

William Bayne, *Sir David Wilkie, RA* (Walter Scott Publishing Co., 1903)

Allan Cunningham, *The Life of Sir David Wilkie* (3 vols, John Murray, 1843)

H.A.D. Miles and D.B. Brown (eds), *Sir David Wilkie of Scotland* (North Carolina Museum of Art exhibition catalogue, Raleigh, 1987)

4 PRINTS

David Alexander, *Richard Newton and English Caricature in the 1790s* (Yale University Press for the Paul Mellon Centre, New Haven and London, 1998)

Marc Baer, 'Cruikshank', in *Print Quarterly*, Vol. 10, September 1993

Andrew Barlow, *The Prince and his Pleasures* (Brighton Borough Council, Brighton, 1998)

Ellen G. D'Oench, *'Copper into Gold', Prints by John Raphael Smith 1751–1812* (Yale University Press for the Paul Mellon Centre, New Haven and London, 1999)

Diana Donald, *The Age of Caricature: Satirical Prints in the Reign of George III* (Yale University Press for the Paul Mellon Centre, New Haven and London, 1996)

M. Dorothy George, *Catalogue of Political and Personal Satires Preserved in the Department of Prints and Drawings in the British Museum*, VI–VIII (British Museum, London, 1938–54)

——*English Political Caricature* (2 vols, Clarendon Press, Oxford, 1959)

——*Hogarth to Cruikshank: Social Change in Graphic Satire* (Allen Lane, 1967)

Draper Hill, *Mr Gillray the Caricaturist* (Phaidon, Oxford, 1965)

Sheila O'Connell, *The Popular Print in England, 1550–1850* (British Museum Press, 1999)

Robert Patten (ed.), *George Cruikshank's Life and Times* (Rutgers University Press, New Brunswick, 1992)

John Wardroper, *The Caricatures of George Cruikshank* (Gordon Fraser, 1977)

5 SCULPTURE

Malcolm Baker et al. (eds), 'An Edition of the Ledger of Sir Francis Chantrey, RA, at the Royal Academy, 1809–41', in *Walpole Society*, Vol. lvi, 191–2

David Bindman (ed.), *John Flaxman* (Royal Academy exhibition catalogue, Thames & Hudson, 1979)

Marie Busco, *Sir Richard Westmacott* (Cambridge University Press, Cambridge, 1994)

Canova (Correr Gallery exhibition catalogue, Marsilio, Venice, n.d. [1992])

Rupert Gunnis, *Dictionary of British Sculptors 1660–1851* (Abbey, 2nd edn, 1965)

John Holland, *Memorials of Sir Francis Chantrey, RA* (Longman, Brown, Green & Longman, 1851)

David Irwin, *John Flaxman, 1755–1826* (Studio Vista, 1979)

George Jones, *Sir Francis Chantrey, RA* (Edward Moxon, 1849)

John S. Memes, *Memoirs of Antonio Canova* (Constable, Edinburgh, 1825)

6 FURNITURE

Paul Atterbury and Clive Wainwright (eds), *Pugin* (Yale University Press, London and New Haven, 1994)

Geoffrey Beard and Christopher Gilbert, *Dictionary of English Furniture Makers 1660–1840* (W.S. Maney, 1986)

Geoffery de Bellaigue, 'The Furnishings of the Chinese Drawing Room, Carlton House', in *Burlington Magazine*, Vol. cix, September 1967

——'The Vulliamys and France', in *Furniture History*, Vol. iii, 1967

——'George IV and French Furniture', in *The Connoisseur*, Vol. 195, June 1977

——'The Vulliamys' Chimney-Pieces', in *Furniture History*, Vol. xxxiii, 1997

——and Pat Kirkham, 'George IV and the Furnishings of Windsor Castle', in *Furniture History*, Vol. viii, 1972

Carlton House (Queen's Gallery exhibition catalogue, 1991)

Jane Geddes, 'The Prince of Wales at The Grange, Northington: An Inventory of 1795', in *Furniture History*, Vol. xxii, 1986

Nicholas Goodison, 'The Vulliamys' "Great Lamp" for the Royal Academy', in *Furniture History*, Vol. xxxiii, 1997

F.J.B. Watson, 'Holland and Daguerre', in *Apollo*, Vol. 96, October 1972

Index

432

Index

Index

Index